THE STATE IN NEW ZEALAND
1840–1984

THE STATE
IN
NEW ZEALAND
1840–1984

Socialism Without Doctrines?

Michael Bassett

Auckland University Press

First published 1998
Auckland University Press
University of Auckland
Private Bag 92019
Auckland, New Zealand

ISBN 1 86940 193 X

Publication is assisted by the New Zealand Business Roundtable.

Typeset by Pages Literary Pursuits
Printed by Publishing Press Ltd, Auckland

CONTENTS

Abbreviations   6

Introduction   9

1. Establishing Order in Colonial New Zealand   26

2. Settlers Search for Prosperity   43

3. The Search for Security   66

4. The Essential Goodness of State Action   93

5. World War Winds Up the State   123

6. The State Under Challenge: The 1920s
   and the Depression   150

7. Labour, Social Security and 'Insulation'   179

8. War and the Omnipotent State   215

9. Freedom or Controls? National Deals with
   Labour's Legacy   253

10. Labour and National Struggle with the
    Economy, 1957–72   291

11. Big Government Begins to Overreach Itself, 1972–79   324

12. Big Government's Last Hurrah, 1979–84   352

    Notes   376

    Index   441

Abbreviations

AALR	Recent Treasury files, National Archives
AANY	Recent Internal Affairs files, National Archives
AATJ	Recent Trade and Industry files, National Archives
ACC	Accident Compensation Corporation
AG	Department of Agriculture files, National Archives
AIM	Auckland Institute and Museum
AJHR	*Appendices to the Journals of the House of Representatives*
AS	*Auckland Star*
ASB	Auckland Savings Bank
ATL	Alexander Turnbull Library
CA	Department of Civil Aviation files
CEC	Cabinet Economic Committee
CER	Closer Economic Relations (with Australia)
CM	Cabinet Minutes
CP	Cabinet Papers
CPI	Consumer Price Index
CSIC	Colonial Secretary's Inwards Correspondence
CSOC	Colonial Secretary's Outwards Correspondence
DNZB	*The Dictionary of New Zealand Biography*
DSIR	Department of Scientific and Industrial Research
DOM	*Dominion* (Wellington)
ED	Electricity Department files, National Archives
EEC	European Economic Community
EP	*Evening Post* (Wellington)
GATT	General Agreement on Tariffs and Trade
GDP	Gross Domestic Product
HD	Housing Department files, National Archives
IA	Department of Internal Affairs files, National Archives
IC&A	Industrial Conciliation and Arbitration
I&C	Department of Industries and Commerce
IC	Department of Industries and Commerce files, National Archives

LT	*Lyttelton Times*
MDIC	Mines Department files, National Archives
MHR	Member of the House of Representatives (until 1907)
MP	Member of Parliament (after 1907)
MRP	Maximum Retail Price
NA	National Archives
NBR	*National Business Review*
NAFTA	New Zealand–Australia Free Trade Agreement
NZG	*New Zealand Gazette*
NZH	*New Zealand Herald* (Auckland)
NZJH	*New Zealand Journal of History*
NZJPA	*New Zealand Journal of Public Administration*
NZLP	New Zealand Labour Party
NZOYB	*New Zealand Official Year Book*
NZPD	*New Zealand Parliamentary Debates*
NZT	*New Zealand Times* (Wellington)
ODT	*Otago Daily Times* (Dunedin)
OECD	Organisation for Economic Cooperation and Development (Paris)
ONS	Organisation for National Security
PM	Prime Ministers' files, National Archives
Press	*Press* (Christchurch)
SDN	*Southland Daily News* (Invercargill)
SFS	State Forest Service
ST	*Southland Times* (Invercargill)
T	Treasury files, National Archives
TLS	*Times Literary Supplement*
TO	Tourist and Publicity Department files, National Archives
WA	War Archives, National Archives
WEA	Workers' Educational Association

Introduction

The British Fabian socialists loved New Zealand. After a visit in 1898 Beatrice Webb declared that if she had to bring up a family outside of Great Britain she would choose New Zealand. She had seen a commendable degree of comfort and independence among the working population, liked the country's new Arbitration Court, approved of New Zealanders' 'free and easy tone' and endorsed what she believed to be a search for equality. While she found a lack of originality in the country's educational system and New Zealand's politicians were 'vulgar', the acidulous Webb was delighted to find 'no millionaires and hardly any slums, among a people characterised by homely refinement, and by a large measure of vigorous public spirit'.[1] Webb's faith in the capacity of politicians to build a new world had been enhanced by her trip down under. Thirty-six years later, her fellow Fabian, George Bernard Shaw, was nearly as fulsome. Calling New Zealand's pioneering welfare state 'communism', he told audiences that the Government should extend bread subsidies to cover milk as well, thus keeping the necessities of life within everyone's reach. Shaw sailed from the country declaring: 'If I were beginning life, I am not sure that I would not start in New Zealand.'[2]

Enthusiasm for New Zealand's state activity was not confined to a handful of British social reformers. Towards the end of the nineteenth century there was a steady stream of visitors from other parts of the world. Many liked what they saw. In 1899 the American reformer, Henry Demarest Lloyd, was most impressed by the lack of strikes in New Zealand. He, too, noticed an egalitarian streak and pronounced New Zealand to be an '"experiment station" of advanced legislation. Reforms that others have been only talking about, New Zealand has done . . . .' One newspaper observed that Lloyd seemed intent on 'New Zealandising the rest of the world'.[3] Frank Parsons, a friend of Lloyd's, wrote about 'the Aurora Socialis of New Zealand', describing the antipodean country as 'the birth place of the 20th Century'. Parsons liked New Zealand because of its progressive taxation, its labour legislation and its old age pensions.[4] The American Socialist Party, which reached its zenith in the American presidential election of 1912, often ran articles about New Zealand in its newspaper, *Appeal to*

Reason.[5] One leading American socialist, Charles Edward Russell, thought he detected in New Zealand a commendable determination to have 'less wealth and more health'.[6] To outside reformers, New Zealand was a social engineer's dream.

Explaining why this remote colony had embarked on so much more state activity than other countries also intrigued observers. The British lawyer and historian, James Bryce, noted that from the earliest days of colonisation New Zealanders had developed a very direct form of democracy designed to wring maximum benefits from the Government.[7] In 1904 a French political scientist, André Siegfried, observed a 'perfect mania for appealing to the State'. First the New Zealand Company and then provincial and central Government were expected to help colonists. Governments were able to involve themselves in so many aspects of life because New Zealand enjoyed a simple democracy, lacked 'reactionary influences' and experienced only the feeblest conservative tendencies. According to Siegfried, New Zealand's 'simple' society lacked the 'inextricable tangle of interests, traditions and prejudices' that complicated the political process in older societies. He concluded: 'When a colonial finds himself face to face with some difficulty it is almost always to the State that he first appeals. The Government is thus brought to perform functions which in the old countries would lie within the province of private initiative.'[8]

These early observers from Europe occasionally used the word 'socialism' to describe New Zealand's state intervention, yet they detected no consistent ideology. Siegfried found the absence of revolutionary ideas 'striking': 'As for the idea of revolution, the New Zealander has little sympathy with it. The word does not seem to be part of his political vocabulary.'[9] Siegfried's fellow countryman, André Métin, concluded that both Australia and New Zealand practised 'socialism without doctrines'.[10] He was, of course, comparing the antipodean lack of interest in theory with the ferment of ideas sweeping Europe at the time, neglecting to note, perhaps, that pragmatic interventionism was itself in the process of becoming something akin to a South Seas ideology. A willingness to experiment with the State's powers underpinned colonial socialism in Australia and New Zealand, just as it did in several other new societies.[11]

New Zealand scholars have also examined the country's passion for state activity, concluding that it was based on little more than a popular feeling that government intervention seemed likely to produce worthwhile results. An early and influential scholar, J. B. Condliffe, was inclined to feel it was 'colonial opportunism' that drove governments.[12] Keith Sinclair, in his influential *History of New Zealand* (1959), argued that state

10

intervention was more deeply based and referred to the settlers' 'idealisation of the State'. He noted that state activity began early and had bipartisan acceptance: 'The Conservatives were at one with the local radicals in the alacrity with which they founded state enterprises and extended state control.' Sinclair attributes to some (but by no means all) politicians an egalitarian purpose behind their use of the State.[13] He dedicated his book to J. C. Beaglehole, among others. However, Beaglehole was nearer to Condliffe in his assessment and doubted whether New Zealanders were moved at all by theory. Somewhat cynically he observed that they were 'on the average . . . fifty years behind the Old World in social thought'. He added that 'of few [New Zealand] ministers can it be said that they have brooded over any coherent body of principle'.[14]

Sinclair's view has tended to dominate more recent scholarship. Others have noted that there was at least some social imperative behind aspects of Edward Gibbon Wakefield's plans for 'scientifically controlled' colonisation. In the 1840s Wakefield sought to ensure that the evils of English society were not reproduced, although he expected – over-optimistically as it turned out – that there would be a reasonable number of wealthy people among his first settlers.[15] Fifty years later, both Richard John Seddon and his successor as Prime Minister, Sir Joseph Ward, were even more convinced that New Zealand must not become a class-based society. 'God's Own Country', as Seddon often described the young nation, was to be democratically based; politicians should ensure that no interest group got the upper hand. The historian David Hamer notes that most Liberals in the era 1891–1912 saw the State as the embodiment of the people. Few felt any need to justify state intervention, regarding it as 'a distinctively New Zealand way of dealing with social problems'.[16] One Liberal reformer, William Pember Reeves, went further and labelled himself a 'socialist', referring to influences that he drew on from abroad. But he was quick to concede that his socialism was 'experimental, not theoretical'.[17]

Another historian, Erik Olssen, has written about the later 'political discourse' that developed after World War I in working-class Dunedin, concluding that while most wanted a 'just social order', few workers would have called themselves Marxists, let alone Bolsheviks.[18] In the 1920s and 1930s a handful of supporters of the New Zealand Labour Party read some of the works of Karl Marx. Ormond Wilson, who was MP for Rangitikei 1935–38, had been a student of G. D. H. Cole at Oxford and observed that consciously or unconsciously, Marxist dogma influenced some of Labour's thinking in the 1930s.[19] However, there was nothing revolutionary about the Labour Party; during the Great Depression its leaders were constantly at war with Communist Party ideologues who preached class revolution.[20] The Labour Party retained the word 'socialisation' among its policy objectives until 1951 but the historian, Bruce Brown, notes that by then it had been 'forgotten in practice'.[21] The party now stated that its goal was to 'educate the public in the principles of co-operation and socialism'. The Federation of Labour occasionally talked about socialism. Significantly, however, unionists in the 1940s and 1950s nicknamed K. M. Baxter, the Federation's secretary, 'Karl Marx' because they found his frequent references to the socialist theoretician amusing.[22]

In the early years of the twentieth century many intellectual influences were brought to bear on New Zealand's political reformers. None dominated. In his earlier days H. E. Holland, the leader of the Labour Party from 1919 to 1933, referred to himself occasionally as a 'militant' or a 'revolutionary socialist'. Yet his reading, writing and speeches reveal an eclectic mind that was equally intrigued by the works of Edward Bellamy, Sidney Webb, J. A. Hobson or treatises on Chinese history, Canadian workers' compensation, or currency reform.[23] It could never be said of Holland's successor, M. J. Savage, that he was an ideologue; if his mind fastened on the works of any theorists they were those who wrote glibly about what Savage quaintly labelled 'the money system'. Immediately after Labour won its first election in November 1935, Savage stated that his goal was simply to 'begin where Seddon left off'.[24] To an interviewer he said that the chief problem of the time was one of fair distribution rather than production. He aimed to 'make security a reality' for people.[25] Savage's biographer, Barry Gustafson, notes that he was 'not interested in abstract theories but in practical measures'.[26] Keith Sinclair concluded that Savage 'smelt of the church bazaar and not at all of the barricades'.[27]

Close observers of Labour governments between 1935 and 1975 cannot help but notice that few if any of their interventions were ideologically driven. Peter Fraser was the most widely read member of Savage's Cabinet. By this time he used the word 'socialism' only occasionally; there seems to be no mention of it in his election pamphlets. When he did talk of socialism, Fraser defined it loosely. He is said to have referred to the introduction of 'free' milk in schools in 1937 as 'one of the most progressive instalments of socialism New Zealand had ever had'. In fact, there was no ideological imperative for 'free milk'; it owed more to the growing local enthusiasm for better childhood nutrition at the time than to any left-wing philosophy.[28] Sinclair described Walter Nash's concept of socialism as being 'applied Christianity', a term that was also used occasionally in the late 1930s by Savage.[29] W. B. Sutch noted the non-ideological approach to decisions taken by the Labour Government in 1936, its first year in office.[30] He served in the offices of two Ministers of Finance during the 1930s and confessed that as far as he could see there was no theory at all guiding Labour's housing policy in the late 1930s.[31] Soon after the Labour Party came to power in 1935, one influential MP, E. J. Howard, declared that the new Government's intention was simply 'to make New Zealand a place where the underdog could enjoy comfort and happiness'.[32] By the 1970s early socialist dogma in Britain had dissipated into a vague egalitarianism: the ideas that drove New Zealand's reformers had never been much more than that.

By the time he became Prime Minister in 1972, Norman Kirk's capacious but untrained mind was filled with inspirations gleaned from many sources. As he and his growing family shifted about the country in search of work in the 1940s, Kirk spent his spare time at public libraries reading everything he could lay his hands on. His nationally delivered pamphlet for the 1969 election was entitled *This Man Kirk*. It noted that he was 'impatient with "isms" and political doctrines', and had only one overriding belief: 'that people matter most'.[33] Members of the Third Labour Government that Kirk led for twenty months shared a common belief that governments could usefully intervene on behalf of those sections of the population that were less able to look after themselves. This was little different from the attitudes of Seddon and Ward at the turn of the century, or Savage and Fraser, who followed them in the 1930s and 1940s.

However, from time to time some politicians argued that Labour's policies should be more clearly underpinned by a set of philosophical principles. At the same time as the Australian Labor Party was debating its 'socialist objective' in 1977, delegates to the New Zealand Labour Party conference that year – against the better judgement of their leader Bill Rowling – grappled with the meaning of the term 'democratic socialism', which some thought should be affixed to the party. There was no resolution to the debate. Subsequent discussion scarcely developed beyond a series of speeches to party branches by a senior member who was subsequently a minister, F. D. O'Flynn QC. He conceded that the term 'socialism' was now seldom debated within the party and was usually avoided by Labour MPs.[34]

Meanwhile, most conservative politicians talked free enterprise on the campaign stump. However, they were no less prepared to use the State on behalf of those they deemed deserving. Farmers and businessmen received help from the governments of W. F. Massey, Gordon Coates, Sidney Holland, Keith Holyoake and Robert Muldoon, and each of those ministries continued with the state ownership and management of the many trading enterprises they inherited. The early use of price controls during World War I, the establishment of producer marketing boards in the 1920s, the introduction of Family Allowances in 1927, restraints on mortgagees' rights during the Great Depression, continuing use of controls and subsidies to restrain consumer prices after 1949 and use of tariff protection and import controls to further the goal of full employment were examples of the State being used by so-called conservative administrations to ensure 'fairness' for all classes and 'the well-being of the country as a whole'.[35] The National Party's general objectives in 1936 made no mention of 'conservatism', speaking instead about the new party's desire to 'pursue a policy of progressive and humanitarian legislation'.[36] Robert Muldoon proudly declared in the 1970s: 'The National Party has never been a bunch of bloody-minded right wing Tories! Never!'[37] The doctrines of Adam Smith, Friedrich Hayek or even Quintin Hogg were as foreign to the National Party as those of Marx and Engels were to Labour. By 1984 the term 'socialist' was as likely to be used of Muldoon as of any Labour politician.[38]

The pragmatic economic and social interventions of successive New Zealand governments in the 144 years after the signing of the Treaty of Waitangi became part of New Zealand's historical folklore. State spending as a proportion of GDP grew slowly at first. In 1924 it constituted 14 per cent of GDP. After another world war and a raft of interventions by the First Labour Government (1935–49) this had doubled to 28 per cent. Further bursts of activity during the next 35 years raised the Government's share of economic activity to 41 per cent of GDP in 1983–84.[39] By the 1950s and 1960s election campaigns had become auctions where parties tried to outdo each other with competing promises to spend the taxpayers' money.

History books have tended to concentrate on health and welfare interventions and on those pieces of legislation that influenced the labour market, such as compulsory arbitration. A nostalgic hankering after those earlier days of big government permeates much modern academic writing about New Zealand's welfare state. Academics still write enthusiastically about the incrementalism of state activity, as well as its increasing cost to the taxpayer. The more daring concede that by 1984 some changes to methods of benefit delivery were needed.[40] No one, however, has examined whether incremental interventionism, whatever its short term benefits to particular groups, was a reliable basis for long-term prosperity. There is no study of the myriad of reasons behind the many acts of government intervention during our history. Nor has anyone attempted to analyse whether the social engineering goals pursued by politicians at the point of intervention were achieved – or could have been – over the medium or longer term.

One or two writers have argued that there were occasional doctrinal influences on New Zealand's interventionist past. Concentrating on the land reforms of Jock McKenzie in the 1890s, particularly his generous leasehold legislation, historian Tom Brooking argues that some of New Zealand's settlers were subject, consciously or otherwise, to nineteenth-century European discourse about land tenure and the evils of monopoly.[41] Given the speed with which McKenzie's goals faded as pound signs flashed before the eyes of the beneficiaries of his legislation, one can only conclude that few of them shared his ideological passion.

A careful study of most state activity fails to reveal any consistent philosophical input from any source. This certainly became an underlying problem with the interventionist state. Structures erected of bricks that vary in size and shape are often called 'jerry built': made to sell, but not to last. They are seldom elegant and have difficulty standing up to stress. Constant improvisation became a problem with New Zealand's state edifice. Endless tinkering eventually produced diminishing returns and brought statism into disrepute with many New Zealanders. This book concludes that by the 1980s some layers of well-intended intervention conflicted with others and that an over-regulated, over-legislated society had become virtually ungovernable. Which is not to say that New Zealand would necessarily have fared better had its haphazard state activity been more philosophically consistent. Nowhere in the world has socialism, with or without doctrines, proved a panacea for modern times.

The State in New Zealand makes no claim to be a study of all state activity since 1840; so extensive has been the scope of intervention that such could not be contemplated within one volume. An early account entitled *State Socialism in New Zealand*, published in 1910 when state spending approximated 10 per cent of GDP, ran to more than 300 pages.[42] This book analyses the rationale for much state activity and attempts to discuss the effects over time of the public's early belief in government omnipotence. The book further notes the mounting unsustainability of the structure as successive governments added to it. Difficulties first became noticeable during the fiscal crisis of the 1880s, when politicians found it hard to borrow abroad to sustain the works programmes on which many settlers had come to depend. During the Great Depression of the 1930s it was clear that New Zealand's cost structure and heavy debt level were seriously out of kilter with its income.

After 1945 there followed another two decades of good export receipts accompanied by more and more state spending. They were years of boundless optimism about social progress; there was faith in the benign power of the State to improve people's lives.[43] Politics was dominated by great expectations. Both major political parties made 'full employment' rather than international economic competitiveness their first priority, and used up much of New Zealand's seed corn in the process. In practice, full employment resulted in a high level of job vacancies. By now a centralised labour market existed; wages were set between 1940 and 1968 by General Wage Orders and national awards and then in later years by regulations and budget pronouncements. One commentator has noted that after 1968 'the economy [was] exposed to a leapfrogging of prices, wages and markups' and that it was soon locked into a wage–price spiral. In earlier times, Arbitration Court awards took into account the overall state of the economy, but did not reflect regionally differing cost structures. After 1968 politicians frequently intervened in the wage-settlement process without any of the previous restraints that had governed wage-setting. The profitability of New Zealand's exports was further imperilled.[44] Labour legislation that had been put in place in earlier times to assist unions in their time of weakness was now making workplace flexibility difficult. Employers found themselves locked into patterns of production that they might otherwise have shucked off in the hope of retaining a competitive edge.

What gave a critical edge to these developments was that after 1965 New Zealand's commodity exports sold on a generally declining world market and the country's relative export income began a long, downward trajectory. A crisis of some kind could not long be averted. Successive ministries spent time devising incentives and plans in frantic attempts to speed manufacturing growth and to diversify New Zealand's traditionally limited range of exports and market destinations.[45] Success proved elusive.

In 1950 New Zealand was cutting with the grain of world opinion; other developed countries were now doing more of what New Zealanders had been engaged in for half a century. But some of New Zealand's politicians began to experience doubts. Keith Holyoake's National Government (1960–72) concluded that several aspects of the State's apparatus needed reform. Ministers embarked on piecemeal change, but only with the greatest trepidation, fearing a political backlash. There were tentative moves to open New Zealand to the wider world when the country joined the International Monetary Fund in 1961 and began a substantial review of tariffs. But changes that ensued were generally too little and too late; some conflicted with those protective devices that governments retained. Moreover, the country's overseas earnings and its domestic growth rate were seldom enough to sustain more generous social policies. Every time ministers of finance sought to accelerate growth, the highly centralised system – like a clapped-out car – overheated, leaving balance-of-payments crises behind at most elections between 1949 and 1984.[46] In 1979 the Department of Trade and Industry frankly described New Zealand's basic economic problem as 'the inability of the economy to grow without creating balance of payments difficulties and inflation'.[47]

By the late 1970s, constant intervention and mounting government expenditure were retarding, rather than stimulating economic growth.[48] In too many cases for comfort, the long-term economic and social consequences of the State's activity had come to outweigh the benefits once so confidently anticipated. The earlier public perception of politicians' omnipotence, of their capacity to fulfil the contract between citizen and government, flagged. Betrayal was in the air. In 1975 politicians' standing with the public, once so great that people would travel hundreds of kilometres to hear them, was not much higher than that of used-car salesmen. It got worse.[49]

The rest of the world had slowly joined New Zealand's movement towards state activity; in many cases others edged back from it somewhat earlier. However, state involvement in the New Zealand economy intensified in the late 1970s. Under the government of Robert Muldoon (1975–84), interventionism reached the stage where many aspects of the New Zealand economy were out of touch with the world marketplace. Four hundred Acts of Parliament and approximately 1000 sets of Regulations, plus an array of subsidies and tax breaks, tariff protection and exchange controls, as well as restrictions on the exporting of meat, wool and dairy products, were coupled with a high level of government investment in social policy. Each was an integral part of a very complex yet vulnerable political economy; every new intervention seemed to necessitate another.[50] Any moves in a more liberal direction – and there were several during Muldoon's years – usually placed extra stress on those control mechanisms that remained.

Beginning in the late 1940s and intensifying over subsequent years was a trend towards more and more key decisions being made by politicians and bureaucrats in Wellington, rather than by private individuals. In the 1950s New Zealand's economy was labelled a 'mixed economy', part private, part state.[51] By the early 1980s under Muldoon it more closely resembled a 'command economy', one in which the State was the all powerful player. As Malcolm Fraser, Prime Minister of Australia at the time, later observed, 'a fabric of intervention was established [by Muldoon] which was bound to fail'.[52] By the time of the 1984 election effective economic power rested in the hands of the Prime Minister, who was his own Minister of Finance. One of his close colleagues has observed that by this time Muldoon seemed to be suffering from 'arteriosclerosis in thought and action'.[53] So did the system he constantly endeavoured to fine tune. Donald Brash, who became Governor of New Zealand's Reserve Bank in 1988, describes New Zealand as having reached a bureaucratic 'sort of serfdom' by 1984.[54] Another economist has observed that New Zealand's vulnerable economy had 'fallen only just short of the whole Soviet "hog"'.[55] Jim Sutton, a backbencher in the Labour Government elected in July that year, claimed that the economy was being run like a Polish shipyard, where most incentives for economic activity pointed in the wrong direction.[56]

Looking back over New Zealand's history, it is clear that during the early days of colonisation when the State's activity accounted for approximately 10 per cent of the economy, the results were largely beneficial. Prior to World War I much of the business of government centred on what today would be called the provision of 'public goods' – education, law and order and public works. State enticements to migrate were an essential part of the settlement process. They built up expectations among migrants. So far was New Zealand removed from the sources of private capital investment that governments took a direct part in creating the transport and telecommunications infrastructure; they produced electricity, built schools and funded hospitals. Without these, economic development and rising living standards would have moved at a slower pace. Economists agree that by 1900 New Zealand was 'one of the most prosperous nations on earth'.[57] It had a healthy private sector, a highly literate population by world standards, and its health statistics were among the best in the world. State activity which was still on a relatively small scale had played a major part in bringing this about. Moreover, various rudimentary forms of assistance to agriculture – help with settling and developing the land, a variety of advisory services, and livestock inspection at freezing works and on farms – enabled New Zealand to perform very profitably as 'Britain's outlying farm' during two world wars and beyond.[58]

However, the developing culture of state activity encouraged governments to go further than was prudent. They entered the insurance industry, encouraged or established trading enterprises such as flax and timber milling, bought and operated bus services and involved themselves in coal mining, tree nurseries, salt making and the management of tourist and health resorts. Eventually they set up airlines and a shipping corporation as well. Some state ventures enjoyed a modicum of financial success. The telecommunication section of the New Zealand Post Office made money, despite the fact that for political reasons it usually carried more staff than was needed to perform effectively. But the Post Office was always short of development capital. For more than half a century customers put up with waiting lists for telephone connections. Electricity generation and the two airlines, National Airways Corporation and Tasman Empire Airways Limited, also constantly requested more state investment, but managed to post profits, as did both Government Life Insurance and State Insurance.

With railways it was a different story. Having invested more than £60 million by 1935 in tracks and rolling stock, a government department continued to run the service except for three brief periods of board or commission control in 1889–94, 1931–36 and 1953–56. For most of the time after the early 1920s Railways was a financial sump hole. Services declined despite governments giving monopoly status to rail for long-distance haulage. Rolling stock became antique and by 1981 the service was grossly over-staffed because successive governments had also been using Railways as an employment agency.[59] The Government's investment in tourism was a constant drain on the taxpayer too and the New Zealand Shipping Corporation, after its formation in 1973, was never more than a financial embarrassment. The state-owned coolstore which opened in Bahrain in 1979 to help penetrate Middle Eastern markets turned into a $30-million white elephant. It was built in the wrong place and suffered from poor management. It made losses for each year of its operation, and they totalled more than $10 million by the end of 1984.[60]

Adding to successive governments' accumulated losses were the large sums of money lent over more than half a century to a wide range of private companies for specific purposes at concessionary interest rates. Where the companies survived, much was written off by the State and the residual owners, rather than the wider public, usually became the beneficiaries of the Government's historical largesse. No section of the community failed to tap into New Zealand's benevolent state.

So active had the State become by the late 1940s, that a leap-frogging process had begun with interest rates; such a great deal of money was being sucked up to pay for government projects that the private sector was obliged to pay higher rates to attract investment.[61] When the Holland Government in 1950 sought to attract private investors to buy the National Airways Corporation and endeavoured to lure international capital to build what became the Tasman Pulp and Paper Company, it discovered there was some hesitation about investing in a country where the State bulked so large in the economy. An agency that had stimulated private endeavour in the 1860s was by now its control agent as well, something that now deterred, rather than encouraged, private initiative.

However, in a world where state activity was still viewed as effective, New Zealand governments vigorously pressed ahead. They became planners, funders and controllers of more and more economic activity. 'Fine tuning' the economy was a term often used by later ministers of finance. This further discouraged private endeavour. Even in agriculture, from which the overwhelming bulk of New Zealand's export income still flowed, much state effort eventually became self-defeating. By the early 1980s government payments to farmers encouraged them to keep doing what they had always done, rather than to adapt to the rapidly changing signals from the world's marketplace.

After 1935 huge intellectual and financial investment was put into diversifying the New Zealand economy through industrial development. It produced jobs, although they were often at the expense of employment in other sectors. In spite of frequent declarations from ministers that local manufacturing industries must be competitive, a large proportion of them survived only because of their high degree of protection. By 1980, after decades of government stimulation, New Zealand's manufactured exports provided only a relatively small portion of the country's overseas earnings. And since high interest rates, ratcheting labour costs, tariffs and import controls and a variety of regulations made manufactured goods for local consumption much more costly to produce than alternatives available on the world market, they contributed to New Zealand's high and growing domestic cost structure. Farmers complained that government policy had made motor vehicles among the dearest in the world.[62] The same was true of consumer durables. A country with an economy that was historically vulnerable to the slightest ripple in international trade had saddled itself with costs that were significantly in excess of its customers'.

State provision of social services, particularly in education and health, grew tentatively after the abolition of provincial government in 1876. David Thomson has shown that in a relatively young society there was a reluctance by governments to become involved with help to indigents, and a desire to make individuals and communities pay a significant share of the costs of their hospitals and charitable aid. Initially, politicians preferred to encourage friendly societies rather than embark on state provision of welfare.[63] After 1891 government policy lurched erratically between schemes designed to coerce, or encourage people to save for their old age, and an increasing level of dependence on the State. Friendly societies, public service superannuation schemes that were established between 1893 and 1908, the National Provident Fund (1911) and Labour's New Zealand Superannuation Corporation of 1974 were designed to encourage personal thrift. Old Age Pensions (1898), Widows' Benefits (1911), Universal Superannuation (1938), the Domestic Purposes Benefit (1973) and National Superannuation (1976) were all posited on a belief that the taxpayer, not the individual, should provide for particular categories of people in need. For more than a century there was no ideological consistency to policy governing welfare, although state provision gradually gained the upper hand. By 1980 retirement benefits alone had become one of the biggest items in the nation's rapidly expanding annual budget.

Some politicians and bureaucrats began to realise in the 1920s that the State was unable adequately to control its social expenditure. Rising hospital costs were a particular concern. In 1949 the First Labour Government which did so much to raise popular expectations of a 'free' health service, contemplated drastic centralisation of hospital services to control runaway expenditure.[64] A heavily bureaucratic ministry and sizeable provider workforces were emerging and they overwhelmed the Third Labour Government's efforts to control expenditure when it issued a White Paper on hospital reform in 1974. Providers, press and politicians conspired to let the expenditure juggernaut roll on. Efforts to apply the brakes or reassess policy goals were usually too little and too late. After 1960 New Zealand's place as a leader in health and educational statistics began a steady downwards trajectory. The original purpose of the State's involvement got lost in a maelstrom of provider disputes, some territorial, others about levels of remuneration and conditions of service. The basic problem was that the economy was not growing at a sufficient rate to sustain the expanding expectations of so many.

As the economy slowed, new experiments in state welfare after 1970 added an extra budgetary burden. They produced social consequences that were unintended by the politicians.[65] Middle-class capture of much social spending became a feature of New Zealand's ageing welfare state, as it did in other countries. Successive governments found their desire to reform was circumscribed by middle-class expectations, provider capture of decision-making and media manipulation by people within the delivery 'industries' that had been suckled by the State for many years.

This escalating level of government activity in an economy that was very dependent on world commodity prices and unfettered access to European markets eventually depressed living standards. After 1960 governments tried to arrest, but in practice contributed to, New Zealand's relative economic decline. Politicians were torn between taking hard decisions that could build for the future and enticing voters at pending elections. The latter option always commended itself. The result was predictable. Still rated in the top few countries in terms of per capita income in the middle 1950s, New Zealand began to experience a prolonged period where growth was below the OECD average. Between 1960 and 1984 other OECD countries grew their economies 2 per cent per year more rapidly than New Zealand. By 1985 the country's per capita income was less than 65 per cent of the OECD average and had sunk to twenty-first in the world. The British political economist, Edmund Dell, has pointed out that after 1945, Britain saw its standard of living trail countries that had lagged behind it for at least two centuries.[66] New Zealand experienced an even faster relative decline.

New Zealand had become one of the developed world's economic laggards. Pressure groups that expected much of the omnipotent State found themselves squabbling over a diminishing cake. In the 1970s the Government tried to maintain big spending by borrowing but it pushed the country's underlying rate of inflation to a point that was significantly above the average of the OECD nations. A draconian wage-price freeze in June 1982 failed to suppress inflation.[67] It has been estimated that when rising tax burdens and inflation are factored into the equation, workers' take home pay had been declining for many years before 1984.[68] The growing budget deficit and overseas debt caused pressure on the country's exchange rate, despite efforts to peg it. Major international agencies lowered New Zealand's credit ratings. During the election campaign in 1984 the Reserve Bank was obliged to borrow $1.7 billion in four weeks to prop up the currency because capital was flowing out of the country.[69]

Within 24 hours of the election result on the night of 14 July 1984 the Governor of the New Zealand Reserve Bank closed the foreign exchange market. It remained closed for four days, by which time the new Labour administration, not yet sworn into office, had prevailed upon the outgoing regime to devalue the currency by 20 per cent and remove various currency controls. A crisis had enveloped a century and a half of state experimentation in New Zealand, just a few years before more rigid socialist economies in Eastern Europe collapsed for similar reasons. The turn-of-century fairyland of the British Fabians and American radicals had long since lost its tinsel. New Zealand was soon being heralded as a leader in market reforms that are everywhere expected to dominate the twenty-first century.

In 1984 the Fourth Labour Government began a zero-based exercise that questioned the State's involvement in many aspects of New Zealand life. It scrutinised the various beneficiaries of state activity, concluding that all too often they were no longer the people whom the original intervention was designed to assist. Changes that ensued meant that New Zealand was unlikely ever to be the same again. One hundred and forty-four years of interventionism had run its course. What Robert Skidelsky has called 'shock therapy' brought to an end many of the seemingly inevitable results of the 'age of collectivism'.[70]

Having said that, this book is not intended as a defence for the changes that occurred after July 1984. The incoming government was faced with tough choices and the jury is still out on whether it chose correctly. What this book does argue, however, is that escalating state expenditure could not be met by constant fiddling with an antiquated, jerry-built economic structure such as existed in the middle of 1984. Any government wishing to pursue the goals of economic growth and better living standards for ordinary people had to make radical changes. Critics may well argue that this conclusion gains from hindsight. Good history, of course, always does. More to the point, as Edmund Dell has pointed out in his study of British economic management after 1945, a great deal that can be seen today could also be seen yesterday. 'Fear of exploiting the benefit of hindsight', he says, 'is a great, but often unjustified, protector of reputations. Experience can be shattering and educative but many of the lessons that can be learnt from experience should have been learnt before.'[71] New Zealand is no exception. As early as 1951, T. N. Gibbs sounded a number of warnings about risky spending policies in his Ministerial Inquiry on Taxation. No one listened. Given New Zealand's constant degree of vulnerability to overseas fluctuations from most of which we have proved unable to shield ourselves, we need to be alert to economic trends, domestic as well as foreign, and be able to calculate the cumulative effects over time of policy decisions that may seem attractive at the point they are taken. The real question before us now is whether we collectively have enough sense to ensure that we do not have to learn these lessons all over again.

This book originated in a chance conversation I had in 1993 with Roger Kerr, Executive Director of the New Zealand Business Roundtable. In response to a question about my writing, I told him that I intended to recount the story of the Fourth Labour Government after 1984, but that I first had to understand how it was that New Zealand had come to the stage where drastic restructuring had become a matter of urgency. Roger Kerr suggested that I might undertake that initial study; the Business Roundtable would pay some of the expenses involved in researching such a big project. I agreed to the proposition, although it was understood that the book would be mine and would not be subject to editorial direction from the Business Roundtable. Roger Kerr probably disagrees with some of the conclusions I have reached and if it were his book, he might well draw different inferences from the material I unearthed. While he has read the manuscript and has proved to be a most careful proofreader, at no point has he, or any other member of the Business Roundtable, sought to interfere or to change the text. This, of course, is in the spirit of the original agreement and I am grateful for their forbearance.

As always when preparing a book of this scope, one incurs many debts. Simon Sheppard worked with me in a research capacity for several months. Paul Goldsmith read and commented on the full text and helped at a couple of points with some intricate pieces of archival research. Professor Gary Hawke of Victoria University of Wellington also read the manuscript and made many helpful suggestions. Both Professor Barry Gustafson of the University of Auckland and Brian Easton also read it and volunteered suggestions, many of which I accepted. Dr Bryce Wilkinson read much of the manuscript and made some penetrating comments about its overall shape. Dr John Martin of the Historical Branch of Internal Affairs perused several early chapters and gave helpful advice. David Bold, a Ph.D student at the University of Auckland, was a mine of information about the development of New Zealand's steel industry and located some photographs for me. Joan McCracken and her staff at the Alexander Turnbull Library assisted with many other photographs. My wife Judith read and discussed drafts of the book, and, as always, made shrewd observations about its structure.

In the course of my research I interviewed many participants in the events I was describing. Of special assistance was Professor Geoffrey Schmitt who, besides having an early career in the bureaucracy, was later an academic and served for some years as CEO of Tasman Pulp and Paper Ltd. The son of an influential Secretary of the Department of Industries and Commerce, he was able to provide much valuable information about the public service in the 1940s and 1950s. Sir James Fletcher, Sir Frank Holmes, Sir Roger Douglas, Rt Hons R. J. Tizard, Jonathan Hunt and Frank O'Flynn, Hon. J. K. McLay, Alan Gibbs, Brian Chamberlin and Ian Lythgoe generously agreed to be interviewed. I had earlier been able to question Sir Arnold Normeyer, Sir Tom Skinner, Sir Terence McCombs, Norman Douglas, Samuel Leathem and Henry May, all of whom willingly shared their judgements on events during their careers. Access to interviews conducted by Michael King twenty years ago with several politicians and bureaucrats proved helpful. Hon. Simon Upton has often discussed some of the issues dealt with in this book, as has Hon. Derek Quigley, as well as many of my former colleagues in the Labour Party. My own voluminous notes and jottings during a political career that spanned the years 1966 to 1990 occasionally proved helpful.

While preparing the book I spent hundreds of hours in the National Archives with the papers of various government departments, especially those of Prime Minister, Treasury, Industries and Commerce, Internal Affairs, Agriculture, Foreign Affairs, Housing, Electricity, Civil Aviation, Mines and Tourism. Alison Neville of Treasury helped me to access several of that department's more recent files. Many archivists at National Archives assisted my efforts to penetrate the inadequate finding aids. Trade magazines and union publications were also perused, as well as some private papers of individuals who played a role in political activities. I can claim to be the first person to have attempted to relate the contents of such a large number of untouched bureaucratic files about business and financial matters to New Zealand's wider historical picture. Whatever mistakes there are in the book – and there are bound to be many – are mine. The book is dedicated to those hardy souls who have been big enough to question whether big government can produce the best outcomes for ordinary New Zealanders. Tony Blair recently observed that the only true defenders of the welfare state are those who are prepared to reform it. To those who have put countless hours into trying to devise better ways of ensuring a fairer society for ordinary people, this book has special relevance.

MICHAEL BASSETT
Auckland, June 1998

Chapter 1

Establishing Order in Colonial New Zealand

Captain William Hobson stepped ashore at Kororareka on the afternoon of 30 January 1840. He proceeded to a small church. There he read Queen Victoria's commissions that annexed New Zealand to the British Crown and appointed him Lieutenant Governor of New Zealand.[1] He had brought with him several officials from Sydney who were to form a rudimentary civil service. Their combined authority depended on the outcome of negotiations with Maori for the cession of sovereignty of New Zealand to the British Crown. After discussions with local Maori, the Treaty of Waitangi was signed by Hobson and many Maori chiefs on the afternoon of 6 February 1840. Other chiefs signed the Treaty during the next few months. In theory the country now possessed a fledgling form of European authority by consent of the indigenous people. As Ranginui Walker puts it, 'the British Crown [had] a tenuous beachhead on New Zealand soil'.[2]

According to the historian Harrison Wright, 'almost everybody in New Zealand, both Maori and white, welcomed the British annexation when it came'.[3] Within their tribal structures, Maori had usually respected leadership and acknowledged the authority of their chiefs. Since the 1820s Maori society had been devastated by inter-tribal warfare which was made more lethal by European muskets. Maori leaders expressed their unease at the threat settlers posed to their social cohesion in their 1831 petition to King William IV and the Declaration of Independence in 1835.[4] In 1840 Maori saw advantages to be gained from the arrival of British sovereignty. A Kaitaia chief is said to have welcomed Hobson's arrival in New Zealand with the words 'Now we have a helmsman'.[5] Most Pakeha settlers also greeted the arrival of an authority figure in the north. Putting an end to chaos was the first justification for Hobson's new government. Kororareka had become a 'vile hole' in the opinion of one of his officials. It seemed full of 'half-drunken, impudent devil-may-care' European inhabitants. The historian J. C. Beaglehole called it 'an al fresco thieves' kitchen'. Previous efforts to bring order to the area had largely failed.[6]

In the weeks after the signing of the Treaty Hobson also became a repository for people's ambitions. There were approximately 100,000 Maori in the whole country in 1840. They were more densely concentrated in the north. For five years now they had been seeking ways among themselves to regulate trade and land dealings with the steadily increasing number of European settlers, who totalled approximately 2000 at the time of the Treaty.[7] Europeans with access to the Lieutenant Governor and his officials soon sought to use his authority for their own purposes. The residents of Kororareka who signed a memorandum on 3 February 1840 welcoming Hobson's arrival craved the introduction of enforceable rules and regulations. Some wanted to buy more land, others to sell land or services to the new administration, often at inflated prices. Others were beginning to think about the desirability of assistance with transport and communications. The very first settlers envisaged a role for government that went far beyond law and order.

Hobson's deputy, Willoughby Shortland, who was confirmed as Colonial Secretary on 7 March, received a similar welcome to Hobson's when he went south, arriving in Wellington on 2 June 1840. The Lieutenant Governor's authority was much in demand despite the pitifully small budget at his disposal. Governor Gipps of New South Wales had transferred only £3,000 to New Zealand's account in the Bank of Australasia before Hobson left Sydney in January 1840,[8] and Hobson had barely 100 troops to back his authority throughout the country.

Settlements were springing up in other parts of New Zealand. While Auckland advanced in an ad hoc, unplanned manner, there was little that was laissez faire about those in the middle of the country. To use J. D. Salmond's expression, they were 'essentially regulative' in origin.[9] Planning was in their woof and warp. Edward Gibbon Wakefield, whose hand lay behind Wellington and Wanganui (1840), Nelson (1841), New Plymouth (1842), Otago (1848) and Canterbury (1850), wanted the process of colonisation to be 'scientifically controlled'. Wakefield set out his views in *A Letter from Sydney* and later in *A View of the Art of Colonisation*. The words 'plan' and 'systematic colonisation' were often used as he wrestled with what was needed to produce his 'best society' in the South Seas. If land was sold to settlers at a uniform and 'sufficient' price then there would be money for public works and some left over to pay for the fares from the British Isles of a labouring class. In this way a vertical slice of English life would be transferred to the new settlements.[10] This was New Zealand's first experiment in social engineering.

The fact that many of the early settlers received assistance with their

Edward Gibbon Wakefield: promised steady employment and opportunities in the new land.
ATL F-131790 1/2

fares led them to claim something akin to a contractual relationship with authorities in the new land. They expected much after being enticed half way round the world. Once in New Zealand they became conscious of being in the most remote place on earth. New Zealand's rugged terrain made many parts of it difficult to penetrate. 'The hills and dense forest by which we are enclosed . . . will cause it to be some time before we shall know much about our whereabouts', wrote one of the first Wellington immigrants.[11] Felling trees and planting grass was arduous work. Labour was in short supply. In the various encampments there was little fencing; animals roamed about, sometimes destroying newly planted gardens. All settlements initially consisted of tents, makeshift housing and a grog shop or two. Roads were no more than bridle paths. It was not until the middle of the 1850s that any of New Zealand's settlements could be said to resemble a small British market town.

Assistance with communications and with opening up the land became early settler priorities. However, some expectations went beyond this. As John Martin shows, the New Zealand Company led the first workers in Nelson and Wellington to expect assistance in finding employment. Systematic colonisation hinted at a new social order, where labourers could reasonably expect to improve their lot by jobs, fair wages and access to land. What Martin calls 'a long term relationship between politics, public works and the pattern of protest' soon developed, and it carried on into the twentieth century.[12]

The first area where Hobson sought to establish his authority was the pivotal issue of land sales. For reasons paternal, as well as the Government's financial needs, Hobson took for the Crown the sole right to purchase land from Maori. He soon promised to investigate deals struck between individuals and Maori before the signing of the Treaty. This worried many in the Wakefield settlements. A lot of migrants had signed up for land before leaving England. It transpired that in some cases the land had not been purchased at the point it was onsold to them. While the Wakefield settlers enjoyed a special relationship with the New Zealand Company, they always felt that the Governor was the ultimate guarantor that their expectations would be fulfilled. Like the northern settlers, they wanted his authority to back the land they had bought in good faith. They were kept in suspense. It was not until 1845, during Governor FitzRoy's term of office, that the Land Claims Commissioner, William Spain, recommended confirmation of several land purchases made by the New Zealand Company. In the end the New Zealand Company was required to pay more money to local Maori. This only reduced the company's available resources for infrastructural projects demanded by the settlers. Once more settlers turned to the Governor. The reality was that while the bulk of Wakefield immigrants had received some assistance with their passages, organised settlement fell short of Wakefield's ideal.[13] Ultimately government intervention became necessary, as it would on many future occasions, to ensure that the blandishments waved before emigrants before they left the 'Old Country' turned into something approaching reality in the new.

In all settlements the newcomers were impatient for the Crown to purchase further land, and for it then to be onsold. In Taranaki where New Zealand Company claims were largely disallowed after Spain's investigations, settlers became obsessed with the desire for more space. Everywhere the settlers also wanted an active immigration policy. A rapid inflow of people was likely to provide more labour in the new country and it would push up the value of land already in settler hands. Nowhere is there evidence that any settlers wanted an inactive government, or believed that they were in the best position to control their environments. Constructive use of authority was essential to success in early colonial life.

Maori, on the other hand, were ambivalent about land sales. While the concept of selling land was alien to their customs, many liked the trade that settlers brought with them. Before 1840 many Maori had readily provided access to land. Others, however, were more cautious, soon realising that settlers regarded access to Maori land as something permanent. In the years immediately after the Treaty, Maori hoped that Hobson's Government would ensure that articles two and three of the Treaty spelling out their rights would be enforced. Since Maori were numerically so much stronger than the settlers, a fact that made all the settlements 'mere encampments on the fringe of Polynesia',[14] the governors had of necessity to be mindful of Maori rights. Governor FitzRoy, who became governor at the end of 1843, was regarded by settlers as too pro-Maori. In fact he lacked the force to be otherwise. However, as Alan Ward points out, the first governors made little effort to 'engage the Maori leadership in the formal machinery of state'. Maori did not become part of the Governors' travelling police detachments, nor was there much effort made to incorporate their customs into British law as it was gradually enforced throughout the country. These failures contributed to a sense of subordination that led to resentment among Maori.[15]

Governor Sir George Grey (1845–53) made a better attempt both to understand and consult Maori. And he contrived to give the impression that his government was fair. But it was mutual economic advantage that maintained a degree of racial harmony in the early years of Pakeha settlement. According to Ranginui Walker, 'the first fifteen years after the Treaty saw a period of economic expansion and prosperity for many tribes, especially those close to Pakeha markets'.[16] De facto authority at the local level lay with Maori. So long as governments did nothing to disturb the status quo both races were, by and large, prepared to accept the Governor's authority.

Among the settlers, expectations of the new Government were high. When officials first arrived at Kororareka, commercial activity was rudimentary. Hobson found it necessary to appoint a Colonial Storekeeper before he left Sydney. His job was to purchase goods on the Government's behalf. The handful of Kororareka retailers soon sought government assistance with the importing of supplies. The irregularity of shipping meant retailing was a chancy business. Dr William Davies, who took office later in 1840 as Colonial Surgeon, expected the Colonial Secretary to purchase, among other things, supplies of aqua rosa, nitric acid, potassium sulphate and sarsaparilla on his behalf. The local harbourmaster wanted the Colonial Secretary to procure him a boat. A postal official sought a canoe to reach outlying places. It was soon clear that no service worked unless Hobson's officials gave it a helping hand.[17]

Settlers' demands grew exponentially. Besides order, they soon wanted employment opportunities and an array of services. On 11 April 1840 a group of 37 inhabitants of Kororareka sought to have Hobson introduce a form of town planning to ensure that the narrow streets with their sea of tents did not 'prevent altogether the rise of the township'. There was a steady stream of place-seekers, too, who looked to the new administration to provide paid employment. And those accustomed to access to hospitals in the 'Old Country' expected such amenities in the new, and were not too fussy about who took the initiative. On 28 May 1840 Hobson chaired a meeting of between 30 and 40 residents of Kororareka to discuss the setting up of a local hospital. There was talk of private subscription, but there seems to have been an underlying assumption that the Crown would take a role in financing the hospital's construction. The State was being drawn into activities by force of circumstance.

Education quickly became an issue in Kororareka, since several of Hobson's officials had children. The Colonial Secretary was soon involved in efforts to establish a school. In August 1840 he was asked to purchase 8 Bibles, 24 spelling books, 24 slates and 100 pencils to help with the children's instruction. The provision of education elsewhere in the colony was not yet regarded as a government responsibility, although the Colonial Secretary's files in the 1840s reveal many requests for government help from missions providing education.[18] Settlers were possessed of what might be called pragmatic pioneer experimentalism. From earliest days the line between what was their own responsibility and what could reasonably be expected of the Government was blurred. If authority was close at hand, settlers did their best to take advantage of it.

While the settlers were for the most part able-bodied and young, a few fell by the wayside. In 1841 the Governor refused to entertain making money available for an indigent brought to his notice, arguing that it was 'a case for private charity'. Such arguments soon became hollow; whatever virtues the settlers possessed, private charity, which was premised on some people having surplus resources, was not their strong suit. A few well-positioned women donated their time to charitable concerns. However, most of those with spare money preferred to speculate; the pickings could be lucrative. Even as late as 1900 relatively few people who had succeeded in accumulating wealth left charitable bequests.[19]

Governors were slow to find a way of dealing with those who seemed unable to look after themselves. In the Destitute Persons Ordinance 1846 responsibility for the poor and elderly, of whom there were as yet very few, was placed firmly on 'near relatives'. If there were none, then the Government would help so long as a Justice of the Peace or a Magistrate first reviewed the case. By 1850 there were 28 such indigents in Auckland receiving daily rations from the Government. The Colonial Surgeon

Auckland Colonial Hospital about 1859. AIM

recommended charity admission to the Colonial Hospital for those in need of attention but unable to pay. The number of people receiving what was known as 'indoor relief' rose. Maori, too, soon availed themselves of hospital services in Auckland. In January 1852 Dr Davies reported to the Governor that 'their frequent applications for admission, and the difficulty I experience in inducing them to leave the hospital when perfectly reestablished in health affords conclusive proof of [Maori's] estimation of the value of such an establishment'. In the same year Auckland's first psychiatric hospital was built – also with government funds.[20]

Given the importance in New Zealand that eventually attached to state-provided pensions, it is worth noting that by 1850 money was being paid from the account labelled the 'Commissariat Chest' to soldiers injured on military duties. Many hundreds of pounds had already been paid out. However, there was a means test. In 1852 the Governor decided that if a military pensioner needed to go to hospital, the pension would cease unless his family was destitute.[21] During and after the wars of the early 1860s pensions became a more significant public issue.

In the Wakefield settlements the New Zealand Company's resources were slim and government authority seemed distant. Margaret Tennant notes that there were reports of near starvation in Nelson in 1843. More people were affected the following year when an economic downturn forced the company to cut its budget. It resented being expected to provide the sort of relief which in England would have come from the parish. However, religious affiliations did not always survive the journey to New Zealand, and the early churches had little cash.[22] They were struggling to buy land, erect buildings and promote missionary activity. Besides, religiosity was often shaken off by colonists, many of whom were young and socially independent individuals. It slowly became clear to settlers in the Wakefield settlements that security and advancement were more likely to come from the hands of the Government than their own impoverished company officials. No other institution seemed to have the capacity to provide services.

As the New Zealand Company's financial fortunes waned, and confidence in it subsided, the Wakefield settlers came to resent the Governor's distant authority, and his inability to perform the miracles so many felt they needed. Nelsonians were irritated to discover how few resources FitzRoy possessed. Some tried to play off the beleaguered company against the Government, but by 1850 the company was heavily indebted. It teetered on until 1854, at which point central government had no option but to take over its debts. By this act, central government assumed some responsibility for the failed Wakefield exercise in social engineering. Assistance with access to land, help with hospitals, education and jobs could come from nowhere else. Charity, too, stopped at the Government's door. By 1860 most provinces had some provision for charitable aid on their books.[23]

Otago and Canterbury varied only slightly from the earlier Wakefield settlements. Otago was established in 1848 with limited help from the New Zealand Company. Captain William Cargill and the Rev. Thomas Burns arrived with two boatloads of young Scottish families intent on establishing what historian Erik Olssen calls a 'godly experiment'. They were the advance guard for 12,000 largely Presbyterian immigrants who followed over the next twelve years. But even before Cargill arrived the company's finances were sorely stretched. The new Otago settlers were so distant from central government, or indeed from the other settlements, that they were effectively on their own. What has sometimes been called a canny Scottish self-reliance in the far south of New Zealand probably had as much to do with the isolation settlers faced for many years after their arrival as any inherent character traits. The Otago Association reported to the Governor in April 1851 that the locals had nearly completed their own hospital. Cargill was trying to devise ways around appointing a Colonial Surgeon by requesting that the handful of medical practitioners in his community provide free services on a roster basis. Public works seemed to have a higher call on his funds than social services. Cargill sought money to improve a bridle path to Port Chalmers and to improve a bridge in the centre of the town. His appeal to the Government for funds was necessary, he said, on account of the 'retirement of the Company' from funding. It had 'thrown upon our little community a burden which is really beyond their means'.[24] During the first few years settlers were finding they had to prioritise their expenditure. It is difficult to generalise, but in Otago an expectation developed that settlers would attend to their own social needs. Public authorities would assist where possible with infrastructural developments. The boundaries, however, were never rigidly fixed.

Formed in 1850, Canterbury experienced the same financial difficulties as Otago. Wakefield made special efforts to ensure that his 'slice of English life' reached Christchurch. For some months the settlement even had a bishop. W. J. Gardner asserts that the 3500 initial settlers were 'the nearest approximation to a "Wakefield" colonial nucleus in both homogeneity and numbers'. But by 1852 the Canterbury Association was in financial straits and unable to pay its debts, let alone find money for public works. The association's members were most willing to hand over their responsibilities to the new provincial government established as part of the new constitution granted to the then governor, Sir George Grey in 1852. But the provincial assembly, too, had little ready money.[25]

The search for order in the new colony was a fumbling affair. In the north the Governor's agents occasionally overstepped the mark. On 19 June 1840 Henry Williams complained from Paihia that several policemen were helping themselves to firewood by 'cutting anything, anywhere'. He didn't want them cutting down peach trees or 'disturbing the pigs'.[26] For a time no one seemed clear about who owned what, nor where, precisely, authority ended, and individual responsibility began.

The concept of personal responsibility was still strong in Victorian England at the time when New Zealand was established.[27] It did not have an easy passage to New Zealand, nor for that matter, to any other British colony. Since most settlers were young and able-bodied, the need for charitable aid was initially small. But in every other respect the settlers' needs were large. Wakefield and non-Wakefield settlers tried to extract as much help as they could from established authority wherever it existed. New arrivals hoped for quick results from their endeavours but found the necessary infrastructure such as roads, bridges and transport nonexistent. But provincial and central government seldom lived up to expectations. Gardner notes that between 1840 and 1845 New Zealand was 'usually in debt and at times insolvent'.[28] Government revenue was short, and labour was hard to come by. Government officials initially hoped that land sales would provide a reasonable source of revenue. Encouraged by Ngati Whatua and Ngati Paoa Maori who wanted a closer association with the Government to ensure better trading opportunities on the Auckland isthmus, Hobson shifted his capital to Auckland in February 1841. A brief building boom followed as the Governor and his staff constructed new houses. In April 1841 a public auction of land recently purchased from Maori was held. It produced £21,499 9s for the Government's coffers. But prices subsided thereafter, and throughout the 1840s revenue from land sales failed to cover the cost of government services. Moreover, in order to encourage enough settlers to come to New Zealand it soon became necessary to sell land on a system of deferred payment. This did little to revive the Governor's cash flow.[29]

If governors were to provide rudimentary services and satisfy settler expectations, they had to raise revenue by other means if they were to use their authority creatively. By the end of 1840 Hobson had decided to introduce a general tariff. The Customs Department quickly became the biggest agency of State. There were officers in almost every port. For the rest of the century governments relied largely on customs levies for their revenues. While Governor FitzRoy briefly experimented in 1844 with a form of income tax, there was no legislative provision for income tax until 1891. Under the system of provincial government after 1852, money from land sales went to the provinces while customs dues were the principal form of central income. One commentator, Marion McEwing, has argued that while the first tariffs were introduced solely for revenue purposes, they did have a mildly protectionist economic impact and helped industries to develop by affording a small degree of preference against competing imports. However, it was not until the late 1880s that there was a conscious shift towards using tariffs for the social end of protecting New Zealand industries and producing jobs.[30]

Money was also raised from a rudimentary licensing regime which emerged during the first days of settlement. In effect the Governor charged for granting permission to pursue various activities. The sale of liquor was one of the first areas affected. In December 1840 several licences to sell 'wholesale fermented and spirituous liquors' were granted for a fee. In 1852 a publican's licence cost £40 pa. By this time so many licences were being issued that the power was delegated to magistrates.[31] The Government also charged for a timber cutting licence.

This licensing regime was extended and fees increased whenever the Government was particularly short of revenue.[32] During the 1840s permission was required to take sand from beaches and to set up brickworks or erect saw mills. By 1852 gold prospecting fees were also being charged. In November 1852, when a trader sought permission to operate a schooner between Coromandel and Auckland bringing wood and fresh water to the capital, he was given permission by the Colonial Secretary on condition that he pay 2 guineas per day. Auctioneers paid licence fees, as did those operating slaughterhouses, or running cattle markets or pounds. By the middle of the 1850s central government was charging a fee for permission to sell ammunition.[33] Revenue needs drove all these early licensing regimes, many of which, over time, were deemed to serve social goals as well. From earliest times licensing played an important role in the commercial life of New Zealand.

Both settlers and Maori expected that the Government would assist commerce. There was much trade between Maori and Pakeha. In the Colonial Secretary's papers there are occasional inventories from the early 1840s listing the produce sold by Maori from their canoes drawn up on the Auckland waterfront. Settlers often sought favours from Government for whatever was their chosen field of endeavour. Government, too, extracted quid pro quos from entrepreneurs so as to achieve social goals. In January 1853 a Waiuku applicant to the Colonial Secretary for a hotel licence was promised it at a reduced price so long as he kept 'a commodious canoe' that could be used to assist the comings and goings of traders from the south.[34] This decision reveals an early propensity for administrations to make ad hoc decisions, and to mix together social, revenue, and general economic goals at the same time. In the interests of serving 'the public good' a complex web of relationships was being woven between private enterprise and public authority.

Settlers' wish lists flashed with pound signs. Yet, few settlers, and even fewer Maori, possessed much money. Russell Stone notes that Aucklanders came 'with more hope than capital'.[35] Few had any lines of credit to 'the Old Country'. Immigrants were for the most part young English, Scots, or Irish in search of a better life. Edward Gibbon Wakefield might have hoped that he could transfer propertied people as well as labourers, but his goal proved illusory. Adequate land was never available in sufficient quantities to attract the wealthy from Britain; emigration to a country which, for many years, enjoyed little more than a subsistence economy and few social amenities, held little attraction for British men and women of substance. Nor was there much spare labour. Among the middle and lower middle classes who made the journey, there were many more men than women; what was regarded in England as normal social life was hard to find.[36] Nearly all of those who made the journey to New Zealand possessed barely enough money for their share of the fare and, at best, a few pounds extra with which to purchase some land. Legal tender was scarce; many early transactions in the new colony were conducted on the basis of barter.

Banking enjoyed a head start in Auckland over other parts, since it was the seat of government until 1865. Yet even there, bank deposits came in slowly.[37] In Wellington the Union Bank of Australia found the services that it provided in the early 1840s unprofitable.[38] In Dunedin it took the gold rushes of the early 1860s to stimulate a group of businessmen to establish the Bank of Otago.[39] In general, a shortage of money in early New Zealand meant that loans were hard to come by. If money was available for lending, the law of supply and demand meant that interest rates were much higher than settlers had been accustomed to in Britain. As Jim McAloon comments, 'prosperity in nineteenth century New Zealand was particularly dependent upon the inflow of money, that is, upon exports, external public borrowings, private capital imports, and bank credit'.[40].

Settler expectations of government kept coming back to infrastructural needs. As Sir Keith Hancock has noted of Australia, 'collective action is indispensible if an obstinate environment is to be mastered'.[41] By the middle of the nineteenth century migrants to both countries were leaving a country that was engrossed in the industrial revolution. Britain's share of the world's manufacturing production was increasing at a rate that far outstripped any other country's. George Stephenson had long since invented a steam locomotive, and demands for rail transport were sweeping the British Isles in the 1840s.[42] It was axiomatic to impatient settlers that before they could utilise their skills or the meagre resources available to them, they needed a capacity to move freely. A Government that was regulating so many areas of commercial activity was expected to be a key player in any major construction project.

Roads and bridges were the first infrastructural requirements. Even before Hobson's administration had shifted to Auckland, public servants were drawn into roading decisions in Kororareka.[43] The administration struggled to keep control of initiatives that some officials purported to take in the Governor's name. In October 1842 Willoughby Shortland, who became Administrator after Hobson's untimely death, was obliged to advise Colonel William Wakefield in Wellington that his plans to build roads at central government's expense did not have his approval.[44] The absence of roads constantly frustrated residents in Auckland. However, when race relations in the northern areas deteriorated in the middle of the 1840s, the administration was obliged for military reasons to pay for the draining of swamps along Manukau Rd and to let contracts for roads and bridges further south at Otahuhu. By 1846 the Colonial Secretary was also taking an interest in the possible construction of a road between Auckland and Wellington that could be ridden within ten days.[45] No matter how urgent the need, any money spent in Auckland caused envy in other parts of the colony.

While all settlements wanted a better transport infrastructure, progress was invariably slow. Construction of the road over the Rimutaka Ranges to the Wairarapa took longer than expected, and was over budget.[46] By the early 1850s the economy had produced few riches. Raising crops and animals was mostly for local consumption. It was not until the discovery of gold in Australia in 1851 that significant trade developed with the colony of Victoria. An air of impatience suffused settler dialogue, and dominated political gatherings. Edward Stafford early developed a skill at arguing aggressively for more development money for Nelson, a skill that provincialists used in later years against the central governments that he headed.[47]

Overseas communication was vital to settlers who experienced a profound sense of isolation from the rest of the world. One of the first actions of the House of Representatives in 1855 was to authorise the Government to subsidise a shipping line that would agree to deliver the mails from Europe in an expeditious manner. The following year Stafford's Government despatched two ministers, Henry Sewell and John Logan Campbell, to Australia to negotiate a shipping deal. They were unable to do so. It was not until 1866 that an agreement for a service between Panama and the various provinces of New Zealand came into operation. After the completion of the trans-American rail line in 1869 a subsidised service operated to and from San Francisco.[48] Contract arrangements failed from time to time in the 1870s and 1880s, but by the 1890s a reasonably reliable service operated between San Francisco, Vancouver and New Zealand. By then the steamers carried passengers as well as mail.[49]

Given the level of settler impatience about progress it was inevitable that government borrowing would become a vital political issue. A factor, as Gary Hawke notes, was that governments could usually borrow more cheaply than individuals; banks allow a premium for the surety that governments can offer because of their unique ability to levy taxes.[50] Hobson and Shortland borrowed from the British Treasury to the point where the administration's total debt in 1843 exceeded its estimated annual revenue. FitzRoy endeavoured to survive with a variety of new taxes and by resorting to the issue of debentures, a back-door form of borrowing. It took a trebling of the British Treasury grant and other initiatives after 1845 to improve the Government's financial position.[51] But overseas borrowing on a large scale was not undertaken until the late 1850s. It became a regular feature of infrastructural financing after 1861.

*

From 1841 till 1865 government authority emanated from Auckland. Until 1853 governors ruled with the assistance of an Executive Council that consisted of three senior officials. There was also a Legislative Council. It was made up of the Executive Council augmented by three nominated representatives. Theoretically they represented the settlements. Circumstances conspired to give the Governor wide powers. When Sir George Grey became Governor in 1845 the more generous grant of money he received from the Colonial Office enabled him to employ a more effective security force. When he purchased bigger blocks of land from the Maori, stepped up the influx of immigrants, thus stimulating land prices, and was able to calm tensions that had developed in the north, many settlers forgave his autocratic style. Inhabitants in the centre of the country endorsed Grey's imprisonment of Te Rauparaha, who had been at the centre of a violent land dispute at Wairau in 1843. There were few complaints in 1848 when he failed to meet his Executive Council for seven months. Early New Zealand settlers, no less than later generations, tolerated arbitrary government if it could deliver the order and progress they sought. Demands for consultation then, as now, were cries from the excluded.

At first Grey experimented with limited devolution of power, although he was careful always to retain overall authority in his own hands. Between 1848 and 1852 there were two provinces for administrative purposes, New Ulster in the north, and New Munster from Wellington southwards. Grey also allowed limited local government in Auckland and Wellington. His constitution in 1852 abolished New Ulster and New Munster. Reflecting the fact that New Zealand was still a collection of settlements, often with few links between them, he set up six provincial governments (eventually nine). They had mini-legislatures. At the centre the 'general' government consisted of the Governor, a Legislative Council and a House of Representatives.[52]

When the House of Representatives first met in 1854 ministers immediately requested responsible government. After several tense scenes with Lt. Col. Wynyard, Acting-Governor after Grey's departure, the British Government acceded to the request on 8 December 1854. On 18 April 1856 the first Cabinet took office under the brief premiership of Henry Sewell. Members of the old Executive Council were pensioned off. A few constitutional limitations still applied to the powers of the new General Assembly. The Governor, now Colonel Thomas Gore-Browne, remained an important constitutional figure. In practice, however, limitations on the power of the Government were few. A capacity for decisive administration was circumscribed only by the mental abilities of legislators and governors, a shortage of funds at their disposal, and the fact that for the next twenty years considerable power still resided with the superintendents of the provincial councils in the far-flung settlements.

By 1856 a fairly sizeable bureaucracy was in place throughout the country – 191 central government officials, and several hundred more in the employ of the provinces.[53] In their search for order and progress in the South Seas, settlers were giving birth to big government. By now many of the institutions and attitudes to government of a century later were falling into place. They were carried over into the era of Cabinet Government and further developed over time. Powerful executives existed both provincially and centrally. They were expected to regulate, assist, police and finance many aspects of the colonial economy. Taxation precedents had been established, and governments – provincial as well as central – soon embarked on substantial borrowing programmes.

The introduction of responsible government was a milestone in New Zealand's development. But it did not by itself improve New Zealand's economy or its creditworthiness. Ministers rather than governors were now in charge of promoting New Zealand abroad, while the new provincial governments had the right to dispose of waste lands purchased by Grey. He and his chief purchasing officer, Donald McLean, bought 32 million acres, including much of the South Island, for £50,000. This bountiful supply of land made it easier for Grey to promote his dearly held aim of a country composed of 'small landed proprietors'. His decision to reduce the price of land to settlers in 1853 was intended to assist those with few resources to get on to the land. But it had the effect in practice of helping a number of Australian runholders with capital to buy up large tracts for pasturing sheep, especially in Canterbury and the Wairarapa.[54] This was an early example of social engineering intended for one purpose which had a different outcome in practice – a phenomenon that many later governments were to experience.

Not surprisingly, irritation grew among many small settlers. They resented the number of large runholders and absentee owners who were benefiting from policies intended to help them. The notion that governments had a responsibility to help the small man while restricting opportunities for the large was developing. As yet, however, few settlers saw any conflict between the growing interventionism of governments on the one hand, and the expectation that a considerable degree of self-help and self-reliance would be required on the other. The two moved uneasily side by side, with settlers trying to work out where the boundaries between each should be, or indeed whether there should be any boundaries at all.

*

40

Many people have tried to construct theories about the enthusiasm for government shown by settlers in what Alexander Brady called 'the socio-political laboratory of Australasia'.[55] Geoffrey Blainey argues that in Australia, at least, the migrants before 1850 came more from cities, and were slightly less willing to stand on their own feet than many settlers from rural backgrounds who went to the United States. Australian settlers were therefore more inclined to welcome the paternalistic State.[56] Leaving aside Blainey's arguable assumption about the preferences of urban workers, there is not enough evidence about New Zealand's settler mix to enable us to arrive at a similar judgement.[57] New Zealand historians have acknowledged that theories shaped some ideas about settlement. Believing as he did in the need for 'ample government', Wakefield's 'experimental mind', according to Erik Olssen, tried valiantly to make New Zealand a 'new and civilised society'. In the long run his 'scientific experiment' enjoyed little immediate success, although Wakefield's belief that societies could be scientifically planned outlived him.[58] At the time, however, Wakefield may have been 'zealous for a theory, [but] many of his backers were keener on cash'. No one, says Oliver, could be credited with having planned the kind of country that ultimately emerged.[59]

Others also downplay the role of theory. Practical necessity, not ideology, drove settler behaviour. In an extreme view, Miles Fairburn doubts that New Zealand's immigrants idealised the State, or even gave it much thought. He notes that settlers perceived New Zealand to be a country of 'natural abundance', with 'ample opportunities for labouring people to win an "independency"'. However, in Fairburn's view, few gave any credit to the Government for any special characteristics of New Zealand society. The inference seems to be that New Zealand just grew.[60] If this were the case, there is a great deal of special pleading by settlers to explain away. Hancock observed that Australian settlers soon came to see the State as 'a vast public utility, whose duty it [was] to provide the greatest happiness for the greatest number'.[61] The same can be argued for New Zealand.

New Zealand's active government matured the way it did because of the unique mix of circumstances in the new country. The sizeable number of indigenous people in the north, and the nature of the treaty arrangements made with them, required a sense of security if settlement was to proceed. Some form of authority was vital. The physical conditions of the new country meant that infrastructural developments were bound to be expensive if settlers were to turn their land to good use, to 'get ahead', as many of them described it. Having found in Hobson a governor who was willing to accept some responsibility to assist in their enterprises, settlers

41

sought similar help from his successors. Interventionism was incremental; tariffs, licences, controls, ordinances and spending on public works, all introduced for a melange of reasons, contributed towards a political culture that was distinctly interventionist by the time responsible government was introduced.

The novelist Anthony Trollope visited New Zealand in 1872. He had been one of Gladstone's Liberal candidates in 1868 and was disposed towards mildly interventionist government. But in his view New Zealand had already gone too far. It was 'over-governed, over-legislated for, over-provided with officials, and over-burdened with national debt'.[62] A settler in the Kaipara area in the middle of the 1880s observed that New Zealand had become 'altogether over-governed, and that is one of the reasons why so many of our enterprises turn out commercially unsuccessful . . . .' The number of ministers and the size of New Zealand's bureaucracy forced up costs, which militated against successful commerce. 'The colony', wrote P. W. Barlow, 'may at present . . . be likened to a goodly fruit tree full of bud and promise, but suffering from the ravages of a host of caterpillars, which are destroying its blossoms, and with them the chance of fruit.'[63] Yet the Government's share of economic activity at the time was still barely 10 per cent of national income.

The French academic, André Siegfried, visited New Zealand in 1904 to study its social and political attitudes. He remarked on the large size of the state apparatus that had been constructed and suggested that it was typical of colonial societies. Immigrants to a new country usually cooperated little, and found that government was the only bond that united them. 'The Government is thus brought by the force of circumstances to perform functions, which in the old countries would lie within the province of private initiative.' New Zealanders, Siegfried suggested, were not 'State Socialists', just 'cynical and practical opportunists'.[64]

This is a view which the economic historian, Gary Hawke, expresses more simply. 'European observers', he says, 'thought that New Zealanders practised socialism without doctrines, but they thought in European terms. New Zealanders simply found new roles for government in a pioneering society.'[65] In their search for order in the new land, settlers had come upon a helpmate. In time, it developed into a control agent as well.

Chapter 2

Settlers Search for Prosperity

If the main concern of the first settlers was the creation of an orderly, secure society, where they could gain access to land, and the finance and infrastructure to service it, the goals of the first wave of politicians who met in Auckland in May 1856 centred on the creation of prosperity and a more widely based economy. This required a steady flow of immigrants and a faster rate of land settlement. Inevitably this led to confrontation with Maori. The New Zealand Wars of the 1860s produced a decade of insecurity as settlers and Maori fought over whose authority was to be paramount. Maori eventually lost this struggle because rapidly increasing settler numbers tipped the balance of power against them.

Provincial governments wielded local power and built roads and bridges. They also contributed in varying degrees to educational and health needs. But the over-arching importance of central government grew at the expense of provincialism, largely as a result of the war. The financial basis of the provinces, which had never been strong, declined further once central government took decisive steps to expand the economy as well as its infrastructure in the 1860s and 1870s. The abolition of the provinces in 1876 led on to further extensions of central authority. This meant that local government in post-provincial New Zealand never became more than a junior partner. The paternalistic power of central government was the dominant feature of New Zealand life by 1890.

In the seven years between the censuses of December 1851 and December 1858 the European population in New Zealand more than doubled, reaching almost 60,000. Settlers now equalled the total number of Maori, whose ranks had been thinned by war and disease.[1] Considerably more than half the settlers were young men; in 1851 there was only one person in Auckland over the age of 60.[2] While all the settlements grew, the easier terrain and smaller numbers of Maori in the South Island meant that the new districts of Canterbury and Otago expanded quickly. Altogether 15,612 Wakefield settlers had been brought to New Zealand by 1854.[3]

Auckland was the largest of the unplanned settlements. According to Russell Stone there were about 10,000 people living on the Auckland isthmus by 1856.[4]

As settlers poured into New Zealand they pressured the Crown to speed the rate of land purchase from Maori. Those who had already acquired land were engaged almost entirely in agricultural production for local and Australian consumption. New Zealand's overseas earnings derived from official salaries paid by the British Government, from the export of foodstuffs to the Australian goldfields,[5] especially during the years 1851–55, and from wool, kauri gum and flax. Together this income funded the imports necessary for New Zealand's expanding population. Milling timber, fencing land, cultivating grain crops, planting grass, cutting flax, husbanding sheep and building houses were the occupations of settlers in all provinces, while those in the north also gathered kauri gum. The nearest thing to a staple money-earning export was wool. By 1861 there were approximately 2 million sheep in the country, a figure that grew to 10 million a decade later.[6]

The first wave of politicians that gathered in Auckland in 1856 was a varied group. They shared youth, some claims to be educated and a fair propensity for vituperation. When they arrived the capital was in recession. This was due largely to a fall-off in Australian demand as the steam went out of the Victorian gold rushes after 1855. Auckland's commercial leaders who dominated provincial politics tried to break out of stagnation by encouraging rapid immigration to their province. New settlers were offered 40-acre farms.[7] Further south, several of Taranaki's early politicians prospered from providing services to troops stationed in the area. They championed faster land purchasing, immigration and public works.[8] Edward Stafford was Nelson's leading politician and became New Zealand's longest-serving nineteenth-century premier. He came from an area where, to quote Jim McAloon, 'if the settlers were aware of the [Government's] budgetary problems they gave no sign of it'. Stafford was a devout advocate of roads and bridges as well as an active immigration policy. These he saw as vital to small farmer prosperity.[9] In Scottish Dunedin where the small settlement of 600 people had as recently as 1852 gone eight months without news of its nearest neighbour Canterbury, a desire for more immigrants, better shipping connections with other settlements, public works and railway construction enlivened public debate for the rest of the decade.[10] Development was on everyone's lips.

In spite of sections 18 and 19 of the 1852 Constitution specifying the functions reserved to central government, there was always confusion over

Edward Stafford, the longest-serving nineteenth-century premier, struggled to expand New Zealand's economic base. ATL F-12439-1/2

which jurisdiction was responsible for providing some services.[11] In return for a portion of the customs dues and the revenue from the disposal of lands that had been bought by the Crown, the provincial governments were expected to deal with local matters, especially those affecting the general health, education and welfare of their people. Central government, on the other hand, had responsibility for the courts. It administered the criminal law, ran the Post Office, maintained coinage and currency and, under the Treaty, was expected to guarantee the ownership of land to which Maori had not yet surrendered title. The General Assembly was made up, for the most part, of provincial leaders who regarded themselves as delegates from their provinces. Most sang variations on a common tune: they lacked the finance to provide adequate services and expected central government to assist. Virtually all their complaints can be traced back to money.

Stafford's Ministry held office from June 1856 till July 1861 and again in 1865 till 1869. The secret to his longevity in an era marked by fierce debate and ever-changing political coalitions was his optimism about the future of New Zealand, a commonsense approach to government, and his willingness to use central government pragmatically. Henry Sewell's Ministry lasted only one month in 1856 but he served as Colonial Treasurer in Stafford's Government before going to Australia and then London later that year. While still a Member of the Executive Council he acted in Britain as 'a sort of proto high commissioner'.[12] Stafford wrote to Sewell at length, outlining various proposals to strengthen the colony's economic base, and asking for his assistance, particularly in securing British Treasury backing for a half-million pound loan. If Sewell could secure Treasury support it would mean a lower interest rate from London financiers. Stafford sought to restructure the Government's existing debts and to purchase more land from Maori. He also wanted to establish efficient shipping links both within New Zealand and abroad. Chambers of Commerce, which were developing in the main centres, and several MHRs expressed their 'utmost' support for any moves by Government to contribute towards the cost of shipping services. Sewell enjoyed some success; by October 1857 a general restructuring of New Zealand's debt was under way. The development of a reliable shipping link to London, however, took another 30 years, despite the Government's offer of generous subsidies.[13]

Stafford also sought to widen the country's economic base by fostering industries deemed to have economic possibilities. The potential of flax had been discussed for a decade. On 20 December 1856 Stafford's Government gazetted an offer of a reward of £4,000 for the 'discovery of efficient means for rendering the flax and other fibrous plants of New Zealand, available as articles of export'.[14] Government thinking had been amplified a few weeks earlier by the Colonial Secretary's chief officer. William Gisborne wrote to Baron de Thierry: 'The Government are aware of the difficulties which attend the establishment of a new branch of trade. . . . These difficulties it will be their anxious desire to remove as far as possible. . . . The House of Representatives . . . are now considering the question of offering to assist by a limited advance of capital a company or companies, should such be found to consist of responsible mercantile men of established character on terms which may secure the Government from loss. If mercantile men of this class cannot with such offer of assistance be found to embark in this undertaking, that will be evidence that as yet the matter is not ripe for serious consideration by Government.' In effect, if such endeavour was successful, then at that point the reward would be paid out. When de Thierry sought the reward up front to enable him to expand his flax works, Gisborne informed him: 'it is not thought advisable to appropriate public money to the prosecution of a private undertaking'.[15] Clearly there were limits to the Government's interventionist inclinations.

An industry employing mostly Maori in its early days, flax became the subject of much government attention as inventors constantly sought to uplift the reward by claiming to have invented machinery that would scrape from the leaf its glutinous substance and then wash it.[16] But the Government's 'mercantile men of established character' were slow to materialise. The reward lapsed. Flax exports were averaging only £56,000 pa by the end of the 1860s. A desire to stimulate the flax industry took on renewed urgency when the economy turned down in the late 1860s. In a lengthy debate in August 1869 parliamentarians from all parts of the country lent their support. John Hall from Canterbury, who later became a rather crusty, conservative premier, urged the establishment of a Flax Commission to collate information. In his opinion it was 'imperative' that Government 'do its best to foster any native industry which would help to relieve the Colony from its present depression, by furnishing a valuable article of export, and thus affording employment to a considerable number of persons'. The newly appointed Colonial Treasurer, Julius Vogel, endorsed these sentiments. Other MHRs saw the role of government to be one of stimulating, rather than usurping market development of the industry. However, the then Premier, William Fox, had doubts about government stimulation of trade, arguing that if an industry was viable, the marketplace would soon make that fact clear. It was left to the recently defeated Stafford to explain the majority sentiment in favour of a commission; in the process he tried to define a boundary line to public assistance: 'Where any particular manufacture had been long established,

Baling flax fibre in Northland about the turn of the century. ATL G-10555-1/1

Government interference would be pernicious; but where it was sought to create a new article of commerce, and make known in what way it could best be brought to market, the isolated knowledge of a few individuals might with advantage be collated. . . .'[17]

The Flax Commission was gazetted on 15 September 1869. Gisborne told the newly appointed commissioners: 'The Government anticipate that the result of the labours of the Commissioners, whose knowledge of, and interest in the subject . . . are well known, will be productive of important benefit to the industry and commerce of New Zealand'.[18] Hearings were held, but the Commission never produced a booming industry. Years later in 1893 the House of Representatives established a select committee to investigate the potential of the flax industry. It strongly urged Seddon's Government to 'encourage' the industry with an offer of further bonuses. These were made available once more, but proved hard to uplift. Few men of substance were prepared to risk much capital. At its peak around 1906 there were 240 small mills in operation, employing approximately 4000 people. They were to be found mostly in Northland, Manawatu, Canterbury and Otago and produced flax worth £557,000. The industry then declined even though the Government was now paying bonuses on processing machines. A yellow leaf disease hit crops. During World War I overseas demand surged briefly, and 32,000 tons were exported in 1916. Prices subsided after the war, but politicians nursed hopes that government subsidies would revive the industry during the Great Depression. Assistance for the production of linen flax was forthcoming after 1935, and an industry was producing linen flax on a commercial basis by 1940. More than 20,000 acres of flax was being cultivated for processing and export by 1942. Demand fell off after World War II. Only two factories, one at Geraldine, the other at Fairlie, remained in operation by 1957. They were under the jurisdiction of the publicly owned Linen Flax Corporation.[19] This early government experiment in picking an export winner clearly failed, although in the interim many people had been employed in a subsidised industry.

Stafford's hope for a timber industry had better long-term prospects, although there was to be little progress in his lifetime. In the middle of the 1850s some concern was expressed at the speed with which New Zealand's native forests were being milled or burned. In 1856 Stafford's Government despatched samples of many kinds of native timber to Sydney for analysis of their properties and relative strengths.[20] The premier hoped for wider usage of native timbers, and better management as well as replanting of popular species. These goals gained some currency after the visit of the Austrian geologist, Ferdinand von Hochstetter in 1858. A few years later the House paid for a translation of his book, which criticised forest management in New Zealand. By the end of the 1860s parliamentarians were convinced that better use should be made of New Zealand's forests, many of which were being wasted in the rush to produce pasture. Central government began subsidising replanting in the provinces of Canterbury and Otago in 1871. A study by Dr James Hector of the Colonial Museum in 1873 argued, however, that milling of timber was best left to private enterprise.

Central government continued to take the lead in urging better forest management techniques. The first Forests Bill was introduced in 1874. However, after complaints from provincial councils about the setting aside of forest land as security for railway loans, the Bill was amended before passage. The truncated Act provided for an annual sum of £10,000 for 30 years to be paid out of the Consolidated Fund for state employees to manage and develop forests. By 1906 this had risen to £20,188 pa.

The first Conservator of Forests, Captain J. Campbell Walker, was appointed in 1876. His job was to collect information on New Zealand's forests, and to make submissions about the creation of a State Forests Department. Over the next decade it was established within the Lands and Survey Department. Counties, especially in the South Island, were granted parcels of Crown land for afforestation purposes. Research was undertaken that involved plantings of indigenous and exotic trees at Whangarei and Te Kauwhata. Under the State Forest Act 1885 authority was given for reserving state forests, establishing a school of forestry and the hiring of more state employees. The depression of the 1880s limited government endeavours and some workers were laid off. However, forest activity revived in the 1890s under the Liberal Ministry. State nurseries sprang up in Whangarei, Rotorua, Seddon, Hanmer, Ranfurly and Tapanui. Between 1896 and 1912 a total of £96,593 was spent on nurturing 44 million young trees and planting them on nearly 19,000 acres. Government efforts rather than private vision drove early forestry policy. Private enterprise confined its efforts to milling and marketing. These were areas where the Government was soon showing an interest as well.[21]

In July 1896 a conference of timber merchants met in Wellington. The Premier, Richard John Seddon, addressed them. He invited suggestions about how the Government could further assist the industry. In a rambling speech that was a mixture of tub-thump and homespun theory, Seddon declared: 'It has often been said in the past that governments should not interfere in matters that should be dealt with by commercial men. . . . We have been told time after time [that the timber industry] is not a matter for Government concern, but that those engaged in commerce and industries will settle it for themselves. Well, my experience through life has been this: that what is everybody's concern is no one's concern, and if you trust to everybody, you will find . . . that no one is doing anything. . . .' He cited various actions that his Government had taken such as sending a trial shipment of timber to London to test the market. After admitting that this experiment had been a costly failure due to an accident with leaking tallow en route, Seddon concluded with the words: 'If the Government and all engaged cooperate together, and work together, then all will have a corresponding advantage'.[22] This was a philosophy much repeated in later years as New Zealand developed what came to be called a 'mixed economy'.

As a result of the conference a Timber Industry Board was established. The board urged the Government to undertake further trial shipments to London, which it did. None produced a profit. However, milling from Crown land and state forests produced a small but steady revenue for the Government. It totalled £146,000 for the decade 1894–1904.[23] By 1907 the Government owned and operated a small mill at Kakahi in the King Country, the acquisition of which went beyond Hector's advice of 1873. The mill made a good profit from its small operation. A Royal Commission made up mostly of parliamentarians examined the timber industry in 1909. It advocated afforestation programmes on Crown land deemed unfit for pasture. The report suggested that the State's nurseries should provide all settlers with tree plants at a small charge.[24] During World War I the powers of the Commissioner of State Forests were extended to enable a wider range of activities. Eventually a forestry branch was separated off from Lands and Survey in 1919. In the Forests Act 1921–22, the State Forest Service had its functions more clearly defined. By this time the area of state forests and provisionally designated land under SFS control amounted to 5 million acres, of which approximately 37,000 acres had been planted, some of it in exotic trees. A major expansion of the State's interest in forestry was still to come.

The State's early interest in stimulating industry was not confined to flax and timber. In July 1870 a parliamentary committee considered what steps were necessary to develop manufacturing industries. Over the next few years it concluded that simply encouraging immigration and building better communications were not sufficient to stimulate prosperity; parliamentarians 'should do all in our power to promote the development of those industries which can be worked to the greatest advantage to the labouring classes, and thereby promote a constant flow of immigration'.[25] The committee believed that the Government should accept responsibility for ensuring an adequate flow of water to potential goldfields so as to assist with sluicing, and should take over from provincial governments all regulations relating to the discovery and working of minerals. MHRs argued that a 'suitable reward' should be provided for discovery of tin that could be mined profitably, and that central government should lend for the construction of tramways or railroads to 'any responsible company' prepared to work New Zealand's coal mines. The boundaries of state investment were being steadily expanded.

Import substitution industries with the potential to save overseas exchange and employ settlers were also promised assistance by provincial and central governments. In 1865 the Otago Provincial Council resolved to pay a 'bonus' to encourage paper-making in the province. The sums promised grew more enticing over the next decade and were payable on the erection of buildings and the installation of machinery. As John Angus shows, the Mataura Paper Mill Company received its initial stimulus from these subsidies.[26] Central politicians, meantime, wanted the Government to pay £50 per acre for the first five acres of mulberry trees planted and cultivated for a minimum of two years, believing there might be a rosy future for a silk industry in New Zealand. If a mulberry grower could get a minimum of one hundredweight of silk cocoons with a market value of £50, then he should be paid a premium for this production not exceeding £500 per annum. The Colonial Industries Committee observed: 'Where private assistance is afforded by the State in the manner now proposed, it is of the utmost importance to confine it to those who have taken up a subject enthusiastically, and made it, as it were, their specialty'.[27]

There is no evidence of strong opposition to the development of an activist State. The caution shown by Stafford's Government in the 1850s had been thrown to the winds by the 1870s. Economic adversity led politicians to contemplate monetary assistance to many private enterprises. On 19 February 1874 the Government introduced a bonus of sixpence per gallon for the local production of kerosene. It had to be marketed 'at a fair price, the quality being approved by the Government'. Any bonus claims had to be filed with the Colonial Secretary by the end of the year.[28] The Colonial Industries Committee also recommended that any glass industry willing to produce bottles should also be paid one shilling per dozen bottles up to the first 10,000 dozen produced locally.

The prospect that the country's west coast iron ore deposits could be used for manufacturing had occurred to several entrepreneurs as early as 1858. Inquiries were made to the Colonial Secretary about renting parts of beaches around New Plymouth. In the early 1860s authority to remove sand for experimentation was given.[29] The Colonial Industries Committee after 1870 went further, arguing that development of the country's iron ore deposits was worthy of a bonus of up to 25 per cent of the cost of any plant, and 25 per cent towards machinery. The Government remained cautious. When there were renewed calls in 1887 for steel subsidies for a private Taranaki company, the deepening depression caused ministers to decline the request 'at present'.[30]

Not all recommendations from the Colonial Industries Committee were accepted by ministers. However, while he was in the United States in 1871, Julius Vogel, the Colonial Treasurer, gave instructions for the purchase of 4000 young mulberry trees. Limited funds were made available to assist experimental plantings. Yet, after more than a decade of effort, no substantial silk industry had developed, although some optimists still nurtured hopes for it in the late 1880s. The Auckland *Evening Bell* believed that silk, more than other industries, could perform a useful social and moral purpose because it could be worked on in people's homes. The silk industry 'leads people away from the crowded haunts of men and brings them face to face with nature, with all her healthful, moral and physical influences'.[31] Throughout New Zealand history a wider moral purpose has often been ascribed to government intervention in the economy.

Provincial governments played their part in the economy. Several experimented with afforestation; both Canterbury and Otago imported a variety of seeds from California in 1871.[32] Rewards were offered for the discovery of gold, and Southland set up a coach service to access the goldfields in the 1860s. However, assistance to industry was not seen by early politicians as aid-in-perpetuity. Many bonuses and other support mechanisms had time limits. The Colonial Industries Committee noted approvingly in 1870 that earlier tariff protection given to the domestic brewing industry could soon be dispensed with because local brewing and malting 'has become so efficient'. MHRs did not favour 'an indiscriminate system of protective duties'.[33] In those days government assistance was of the 'kick start' variety; it was not to keep the engine running.

While governments sought to widen New Zealand's economic base they realised that the pastoral industry was likely to remain the principal revenue earner in the foreseeable future. Assistance to agriculture dates from earliest times. Government agencies involved themselves in expanding the area of land under cultivation. The Crown purchased land from Maori but during the provincial period the provinces received the revenue from its sale to settlers. After 1876 the General Crown Lands Office with its eleven branches spread across the colony took over sales. They were made through Land Boards, although at first the rules varied within the former provincial districts. A Crown Lands Guide was made available to prospective settlers; it listed the quantity and quality of land available for sale or leasing. Revenue from sales went to central government's Consolidated Fund.

Ministers encouraged clearing, felling and planting and regulated where necessary to safeguard the expanding pastoral industry. By 1882 more than 5.1 million acres of land was in production and had been broken up into 17,732 freehold holdings.[34] In the 1860s and 1870s regulations were issued to protect New Zealand livestock from any imports of diseased cattle and sheep. In December 1877 in response to the plague of rabbits developing in the South Island the Government announced bonus payments for the export of rabbit skins under the Rabbit Nuisance Act 1876. Customs officers were required to verify the passage of the skins across the waterfront before money was paid out.

Two events during Stafford's first premiership had a huge impact on the country's economy. The first was the war in Taranaki that began in March 1860. Both the lead-up to it, and the war itself, became a bonding exercise between settlers and what they now regarded as exclusively their Government. The second was Gabriel Read's fortuitous discovery of gold at Tuapeka on 25 May 1861, six weeks before the fall of Stafford's first ministry.

The rapidly deteriorating position in Taranaki in early 1860 stemmed from the pressure which settlers placed on the Government to acquire more land, and the increasing reluctance of Maori to part with it. When war broke out the Governor and settlers called it 'native rebellion'. Over the next five years fighting raged, simmered then ignited once more. After 1865 smouldering discontent erupted occasionally and continued to do so for the better part of the next two decades. By this time the rift between Pakeha and a majority of Maori ran deep. Maori faith in the protection afforded them by the Treaty of Waitangi had largely evaporated. Central government seemed to have given up on power sharing or any solicitude for Maori interests; for Maori, resort to arms seemed to be their only option.

When war broke out settlers rallied round their government. Messages of encouragement were sent to Stafford's ministers from Wanganui, Wellington, the Hutt Valley and Hawkes Bay. Residents of New Plymouth wanted 'prosecution of the present war until a permanent and honourable peace has been ensured'. Far removed from the hot spot, Charles Bowen of Canterbury declared that local people 'feel their provincial prosperity depends in a great measure upon the maintenance of good order in the Colony at large'.[35]

The Government borrowed and spent, and the 20,000 British troops who served in New Zealand during the decade stimulated demand.[36] The public service grew rapidly and gave New Zealanders an early taste of emergency government. There were four ministries between July 1861 and October 1865 before Stafford returned to office. Each rose and fell over its conduct of the war. Each sought to wrap its fortunes around settler security, welfare for soldiers or their widows, post-war prospects for those who had served, and the well-being of refugees from the front. War, as it has been in so many countries, became the engine of state intervention. Pensions to widows, medical care for those involved in the fighting, settlement schemes for ex-soldiers in the Waikato, and compensation to farmers, especially those in Taranaki whose land or possessions had been damaged as a result of the fighting, preoccupied the ballooning public service.[37] By the time the fighting died down, most North Island settlements, and even Nelson, where many Taranaki women and children had taken refuge during the emergency, felt their lives to have been directly touched by the war, and by the Government's attitude towards their welfare.

During the early years of responsible government MHRs surrendered considerable powers to the Cabinet. Files of the *New Zealand Gazette* show that ministries had gained powers to issue regulations on a wide variety of subjects. In the lead-up to the outbreak of hostilities with Maori in March 1860 the Government regulated the importation or sale of arms, gunpowder or 'other warlike stores'.[38] Orders in Council proliferated. Customs and quarantine regulations, new rules governing naturalisation, and alterations to land registry procedures were all spelled out in *Gazette* notices rather than in statutes. Businessmen soon found it prudent to consult the *Gazette*. Chambers of commerce sought and gained a place on central government's 'free list' of recipients of the journal.[39] Instruments allowing executive government to rule during a war are seldom surrendered in their entirety when peace returns. In this instance the lingering unease after fighting died down and the demands of the Government's bold expansionary programme in the early 1870s required their retention. Parliamentarians occasionally complained about too much power being vested in the Governor-in-Council.[40] However, like their constituents, most liked strong, authoritative government so long as it produced results.

By the later stages of the war, the Government was determined to increase immigration, principally to strengthen settler numbers against Maori. Ministers accepted the advice of the *Lyttelton Times*, which argued in April 1861 that it was the Government's duty to ensure that employment existed before people were induced to immigrate.[41] In April 1864 Gisborne set out in detail the rules that should govern the promises given to would-be immigrants from Great Britain. In cases of 'actual necessity', agents were to be instructed that 'assistance' could be given to emigrants before their departure. Intending settlers should be told that allotments of land would be ready for them on arrival, and that they would receive accommodation for up to two months after disembarkation. The Government would fund employment for at least six months after they arrived in New Zealand.[42]

Varying assurances were given to migrants over the next fifteen years. The promise of employment which was specifically set out in 1864, but implied more vaguely in later years, meant that encouraging industries with the potential to provide jobs became equally important. The need to bolster settlers' sense of security was seen as necessitating some government involvement in the marketplace. The difficulty which ministers encountered was that most people who were ambitious to prosper had little capital. Governments were obliged to stimulate in the hope of providing a thriving economy and employment. For the overwhelming majority of settlers and their political representatives, questions of ideology seem never to have arisen. Pragmatism ruled.

Read's modest gold discovery in Otago in 1861 provided an upturn in the economy during the war. The immediate effect was that 2000 pro-spectors per week, mainly from Victoria, poured into Otago. They doubled the population of Dunedin within six months. This rush continued until the winter of 1862 by which time the population of the whole Otago province topped 60,000. It dropped only slightly when some prospectors made their way across the Southern Alps to Hokitika's brief rush.[43] The fillip to Dunedin in particular meant that its urban population became the biggest of the four main cities.[44] By August 1867 numbers at Thames in the North Island were on the increase and for the next three years there was a modest gold rush on the Coromandel peninsula. After 1873 the number of active miners in New Zealand fell away. Only in the late 1880s, with the aid of British capital, did gold exports rise again, this time much of it coming from the Waihi mine where the cyanide process of extraction was used. Overall the gold rushes in New Zealand were a pale shadow of those in Australia. New Zealand's £46 million worth of gold produced constituted about 13.5 per cent of the Australasian total in the years 1851–90.[45]

Nevertheless, the sudden net gain of 46,000 people between 1861 and 1865, with another 20,000 arriving over the next four years,[46] answered many prayers. There was a brief air of recklessness. In Auckland alone, imported goods quadrupled between 1860 and 1864.[47] Predominantly

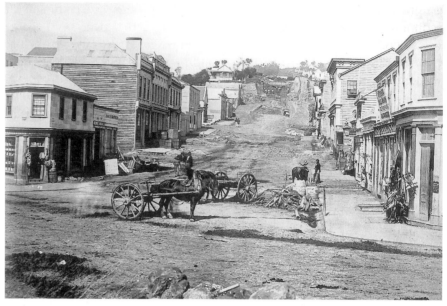

Dunedin's High Street, 1862. ATL G-17877-1/1

younger men, more Irish and Catholic than the earlier settlers, and none with much capital when stepping ashore, augmented the earlier settlers in such numbers that they finished off Wakefield's earlier fond hopes of carefully controlled settlement.[48] However, people alone did not spell riches. After 1864, with the war spluttering out in the north, and receipts from gold declining, the provincial economies subsided once more, causing central government to adopt a more cautious demeanour. Only Auckland retained a precarious prosperity into the next decade, buoyed for a time by proceeds from the Thames rush. When Stafford returned to office in 1865 he was staring at a deficit of £136,500. He had little option but to retrench.[49]

Stafford and his principal adviser, William Gisborne, turned their attention to the country's bloated bureaucracy. During the war central government's employees had blown out to 1602, with many hundreds more working for the provincial governments. The colony's total population stood at 202,000 at the time when the capital shifted to Wellington, holding its first meeting there on 26 July 1865. The shift provided the opportunity to prune central government's payroll. A Royal Commission in 1866 examined all departments of State. New office management techniques were introduced, as well as a more orderly system for recruitment, promotion and dismissal. However, it proved hard to reverse the momentum of the last few years; staff lay-offs were few; central

56

government's employees still numbered 1476 in July 1869.[50] By this time economic conditions had worsened. When wool prices dropped in 1867 several provincial governments had difficulty repaying their loans. Central government was in no position to assist. It faced the prospect of the British withdrawing their troops which would inevitably mean more spending from local coffers on domestic security. Central government put a stop to provincial borrowing. Public activity at the local level wound down, and provincial governments never revived.

In a burst of recession-inspired activity, central government now attempted to stimulate local investment. Stafford's Government legislated to enable a public savings bank to be opened at every post office in 1867. Two years later, on Vogel's initiative, a State Life Insurance Office was established. In 1873 a Public Trust Office opened its doors, its principal novelty being the creation of a Public Trustee to administer estates, particularly those of people who died intestate. There was a common thread to each of these moves. A government guarantee was extended to funds invested in each. In an era of some spectacular bank and insurance company collapses abroad, this reassured domestic investors. Moreover, the returns on life insurance and trust monies invested in New Zealand were potentially higher because the local rate of interest hovered round 5 per cent instead of 3 per cent paid by London-based institutions. While there were advantages for local investors, the Government also stood to gain. Money invested in New Zealand by settlers could be tapped by the State for its purposes. By the end of the 1870s, the Post Office Savings Bank, the State Life Insurance Office and the Public Trust Office had many of their assets tied up in government securities.[51] The notion that New Zealand's capital should be used for the advantage of New Zealanders was catching on, thus helping to edge forward the growth of a separate, independent colonial economy.

At first the concept of a Public Trust Office was controversial. A Public Trustee Bill was introduced in 1870. It passed the House of Representatives but was defeated in the Legislative Council. Throughout debates politicians grappled with the appropriate boundaries between public and private enterprise. Ministers stressed that there would be no compulsion to lodge private trust properties with the Public Trust Office. Critics argued that the State had no role at all in the investment of private funds. One parliamentarian declared that he was opposed to bills which 'would have the effect of placing the private business of the country . . . in the hands of the Government'; another declared that 'self-reliance was a habit that they ought to cherish in their fellow countrymen'.[52] In 1873 a majority endorsed a modified Bill. Once more they were happy to use the powers of the State for wider purposes. The Public Trust Office became a respected, if small agency of State. A century after its introduction it administered more than 20,000 estates and funds with a value of nearly $220 million. By this time the Public Trust Office was investing only 20 per cent of its funds in government or local body stock.[53]

The defeat of Stafford's Government on 24 June 1869 opened the way for a new burst of state activity. William Fox became Premier four days later with Julius Vogel as his Colonial Treasurer. A mercurial London Jew, who had made and lost money on the goldfields of Australia before becoming editor of the *Otago Daily Times*, Vogel was the most influential political figure in New Zealand for the next decade. In his view economic stagnation called for innovation. He produced it in his budget on 28 June 1870. It was a bold expansionary document based on the faster purchase of Maori land, assisted immigration, and active railways and public works programmes that would open up the land, thereby increasing production. The new policy, like the later 'Think Big' strategy of the 1980s, was to be financed by borrowed money.

The debate on the Immigration and Public Works Bill 1870 reveals little ideological division between MHRs. Fox told Parliament that 'the time has come when we should again recommence the great work of colonising New Zealand, and the object of the Government proposals is, if possible, to re-illumine that sacred fire'. William Gisborne, who had stepped up from being departmental head to Colonial Secretary, declared that by colonising the country 'the political distinctions which now divide district from district will melt away and disappear as morning mists before the light and warmth of the sun'.[54] All this was heady stuff. Politicians, for the most part, were simply dazzled by the optimism and daring of Vogel's artificial gold rush. The *Otago Daily Times* enthused that ministers had 'caught the popular tone, and have pitched their proposals in unison with it'.[55] When the policy was announced the usually cautious *New Zealand Herald* observed:

> The policy of borrowing, and that largely, for public works in a young and undeveloped country like New Zealand is undoubtedly a wise one. Without these public works the known but hidden, and as yet unproductive wealth of the colony cannot be made available, and as the benefit accruing from works such as are proposed . . . namely main trunk roads and railways, will be permanent and lasting – it is perfectly equitable to the present and the future to spend the cost over a considerable period.[56]

William Fox, Premier 1869–72; and Sir Julius Vogel, Colonial Treasurer as well as Premier in the 1870s: Vogel was a man with bold expansionary views about the role of the State. ATL G-1322-1/1; F-928981/2

Some settlers sensed that Vogelism would be the final *coup de grâce* for Maori insurrection.

The only resistance to borrowing came from a handful of politicians who feared that Vogel's 'largesse . . . may be mismanaged' and from the Wellington *Evening Post*. It was certain that the 'ignorant and deluded' would be sure to waste the money.[57] Former premier Frederick Weld, now Governor of Western Australia, was also sceptical. He sniffily described Vogelism as 'the gambler's stake played by one who personally has nothing to lose, on behalf of others who have'.[58] The wider public, however, had no such qualms. Having seen the Government fight a war, provide for veterans or their widows, sponsor immigrants and promise to find them employment, they expected the Government to be able to conjure up prosperity as well.

Borrowing on the London market was an essential aspect of Vogelism. By 1870 the country's public debt amounted to £8 million, of which £3 million had been borrowed by the provinces. Vogel proposed to raise another £10 million over ten years in the belief, as Keith Sinclair puts it, that 'money, men and public works' would develop the country 'at an unprecedented pace'.[59] The Treasurer was soon back and forth to Australia, and twice travelled to London in search of loans. Two commissioners, F. D. Bell and Dr Isaac Featherston were despatched to London for the specific purpose of promoting rapid immigration to New Zealand.[60] In 1871 Featherston became Agent-General in London. He was given wide discretion to offer assisted passages to an initial 8000 immigrants. Urgency governed his activities; central government was in no mood to indulge the provinces' quibbling about their traditional role in the migration process. When Featherston's quota was unfilled by the end of 1872 he was empowered to offer free passages as an inducement.

On 11 October 1873 Premier Vogel took over as Minister of Immigration. Using the cable facilities already in place from Melbourne to London, he told Featherston not only to pay for passages but to contribute towards migrants' travel to the port of embarkation. Should it be necessary, Featherston could provide clothing for the voyage as well. Vogel wrote to the National Agricultural Labourers' Union: 'the position of a prosperous farmer is open to the immigrant who lands on the shores of New Zealand, no matter how poor he may be, if he is only gifted with temperate habits, frugality and industry'.[61] It was scarcely surprising that many immigrants took these promises from the premier and his agents as a guarantee of success in the new land. The concept of a 'social contract' was gathering momentum.

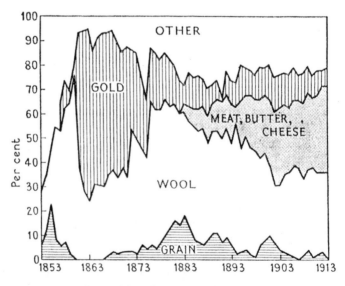

Composition of Exports, 1853–1913.
From Simkin's Instability of a Dependent Economy

The peak period for immigration was 1874–75, when 31,000 people arrived in New Zealand over a twelve-month period. Of the 490,000 in New Zealand at the census of 1881, about 100,000 had come during the 1870s with various forms of assistance, most of it provided by the Government. Many immigrants were agricultural labourers, shepherds, navvies for the railroads, mechanics and domestic servants of good character. Others had more dubious backgrounds, leading Vogel's former paper, the *Otago Daily Times*, to denounce one shipload as 'certificated scum'.[62] This verdict was strongly refuted in later years by the historian Rollo Arnold. But there can be no denying that many immigrants expected that the Government which had assisted them to come to New Zealand would help them adapt to it. Vogel himself became worried about the lavish promises made to would-be immigrants by English agents, and in a series of letters to the Agent-General from September 1874 advised him to be more cautious, especially with promises of easy access to land. But by that time many inducements had already been offered and taken up.[63]

Central government's sponsorship of colonial development was the central feature of the first half of the 1870s. Railway construction progressed apace. A few years later an Australian observer noted: 'As if by enchantment, an eruption of . . . railways broke out all over the two islands. They cut their way through the densest scrub, they ran up steep hills, they spanned roaring torrents, and lept over gullies. Sir Julius Vogel had said the word, and nothing could stop them.'[64] At first the Government hoped not to have to undertake all railway construction. Interest in building some of New Zealand's railways was expressed by a Dunedin company, Ross, Hotson, Peyman and Walker, and by a Nelson individual, James Sims. The Government was cool to the Dunedin consortium and only slightly warmer to Sims, probably because it feared that neither possessed the resources to construct at the speed which ministers required.[65] When he was in London in 1871 Vogel talked to John Brogden who had built the Auckland–Drury line in the 1860s. Six contracts were entered into. But Brogden's base was 12,000 miles from New Zealand. He moved cautiously. Moreover, the provinces became querulous over their construction rights, which threatened further delays. Other considerations worried Vogel too. The realisation that some essential lines would not necessarily pay their way quickly, and that construction, if left to private enterprise, could result in a variety of gauges as in Australia, helped convince him that the State should take total control of the whole railway programme from design through to the operation of services.[66]

In the end, the need for speed was probably the biggest factor in determining the State's paramount role. With so much money being borrowed, ministers could not afford to dally. Immigrants were soon pouring into the country in search of promised jobs. The Government was nervous. There was no time to waste on lengthy negotiations with distant contractors. Political considerations simply removed from the equation any serious prospect that New Zealand's railway building could be undertaken by private enterprise. In 1886 when the Stout–Vogel Government was short of money, a contract was entered into with a private London-based company called Midland Railway. It was a land grant project whereby, in return for construction of a line from Springfield in Canterbury to Brunnerton on the West Coast and thence to Nelson, six million acres of land would be granted to the company. Each time a section of the line was opened for traffic, blocks of land could be subdivided and sold to offset construction costs. Like Brogden, Midland's London directors were cautious. On 27 May 1895 building of the Midland line was taken over by the Government. A lengthy process of arbitration then took place over compensation. This experience simply confirmed politicians in the wisdom of their earlier decision to have the Crown build and operate lines. By 1900 only 88 miles of private line still existed, and in 1908 the last private line (between Wellington and the Manawatu) was taken over by the Government.[67] An observation by a

Railways creeping across difficult terrain: a trip to the Wairarapa about 1905.
ATL G-341-1/2-APG

Government Railway Commissioner in 1894 summed up some of the issues facing the Government:

> Had the building of railways been left to private enterprise, there is little doubt that the colony would not at this date have been so well supplied with the means of communication which have proved so large a factor in its advancement. The construction and working of the lines by the State seem in new communities to be a necessary preliminary to the development of [their] resources, for private undertakings are to a great extent controlled by the expectation of immediate returns, which in the case of the State can well be deferred so long as collateral advantages are being obtained in other directions.[68]

Instead of private enterprise, the Public Works Department, formed in 1870, designed and built most of the lines. Ministers specified the track to be laid – which occasionally led to accusations of political favouritism – then commissioned their construction. Gauges were standardised at 3 feet 6 inches, which made investment go further although the trains were slower.[69] The Government's construction costs in the early stages were deemed reasonable; the average cost per mile at £7,703 was more than the £3,531 per mile of the very first lines constructed, but below the cost of some private lines such as the Wellington–Manawatu line at £9,187. Reasonable construction costs enabled fares and freight rates to be kept down. A later Minister of Railways, Sir Joseph Ward, was able to crow in 1905 that the Government's railways were returning 3 per cent on the capital cost of construction,[70] although it should be added that after 1896 the Government did not oblige them to include interest on the money borrowed for construction. It was argued that railways existed not to earn profits but 'to assist the development of the country'.[71] This exemption gave the railway accounts a rosier glow than they deserved, and was not corrected until 1925. Nevertheless, in the early days of state construction, the public sector could often post results that seemed satisfactory, something which, over time, led to complacency and ultimately to a fall-off in performance.

To the 65 miles of line open for traffic in 1872 was added another 1107 miles by 1879–80. By then nearly three million passengers and more than one million tons of freight were being carried each year. Twenty years later there were 2235 miles of line in operation, carrying 6.2 million passengers and 3.4 million tons of freight.[72] By the end of the century railways had long since replaced coastal shipping as the principal communication artery of the country. They provided the first links that drew the struggling provincial economies into a wider national entity.

Roading construction also sped up after 1870. Initially a sum of £50,000 pa was earmarked for distribution to provincial roads boards for constructing roads to outlying districts. At least £8.3 million was spent by the Government on roads and bridges between 1870 and 1900, with many of the early construction workers being Vogel's immigrants.[73] There were flow-on results from all this activity. Migration itself created jobs. Carpentry skills were much in demand to house the new arrivals. By use of legislation and orders-in-council issued mostly under the Immigration and Public Works Act and the Native Lands Act 1873, central government drove infrastructural development at a speed that sidelined critics and private competitors.

By the late 1870s most ports enjoyed regular shipping links and were tied to their hinterlands by rail. Telegraph, too, soon demonstrated its usefulness in bringing the provinces together. It was used to pass military information in the later stages of the war. Parliamentarians became regular users of the new service. As with railways, early provincial erection of telegraph wires was in the hands of private contractors, some of whom continued briefly to own the lines.[74] But central government's needs, especially during the war, seem to have provided the impetus for establishing a Telegraph Department. A. C. Wilson notes that 'by the middle of the 1860s the Department had become the major player in the country's [telegraph] network'.[75] When the provinces backed out of public works because of a shortage of funds after 1867, private interests sold their completed lines to central government and ceased further construction. Publicly built lines were swaying across the country by the late 1860s. Communication was established between Auckland, Wellington and the South Island in 1872. In 1874, steps were taken by the congenitally optimistic Vogel to lay a telegraph line over the ocean floor to New South Wales. It began transmission in 1876 and had the direct benefit of connecting New Zealand with Great Britain. Two years later the first internal telephone demonstration was staged between Nelson and Blenheim. By 1900 connections were proceeding apace and there were nearly 8000 telephones in the country.[76] Political considerations simply pushed private enterprise aside.

Many economists and historians have endorsed Vogel's centrally driven economic extravaganza. Most have called it right for the times, and noted beneficial effects from Vogel's actions. Gary Hawke claims that real income probably grew in the 1870s as a result of Vogel.[77] In 1986 when reviewing a biography of Vogel, the then Minister of Finance, Roger Douglas, remarked that Vogel was correct to stress the development of New Zealand's infrastructure in the 1870s: 'without basic transport and communications and without large-scale immigration, the potential wealth locked up in New Zealand's hinterland would have remained locked up a lot longer'. Douglas noted, however, that Vogel's propensity for large-scale borrowing was to live on in New Zealand's political folklore, and be applied in later circumstances that were not so likely to produce beneficial outcomes.[78]

Provincialism was sidelined by central government's public works programmes. It became the major casualty of Vogelism. Since it was now possible to talk of a growing national entity rather than a group of scattered, unconnected settlements, the now nine provinces had outlived their usefulness. Harry Atkinson, who was Premier by the time they vanished, expressed the view that 'a very large saving [would] ultimately be made by the amalgamation of the general and provincial services'. The Abolition of the Provinces Act 1875 came into force on 1 November 1876. It vested the powers and property of the provinces, described by Atkinson as 'nine sturdy mendicants', in the central government.[79]

Chapter 3

The Search for Security

Historians have underestimated the significance of the abolition of the provinces. By that act the developing colony abandoned the possibility of a decentralised structure; the administrative changes of the next two years vested in central government many of the functions formerly performed by the provinces. The transfer occurred at a time when the New Zealand economy was beginning to subside after several hectic years of Vogelism. A mounting fiscal crisis reinforced the trend to centralism as a procession of Colonial Treasurers grappled with declining revenue and high interest payments on Vogel's borrowed money. It was another twenty years before economic recovery looked permanent. In the intervening years politicians were obliged to consider the rights and responsibilities of individuals, and the roles of local authorities and the State. For the first time there were sustained debates among New Zealand's leaders about British theories and practices, and their application to New Zealand conditions. As a result the State's activities were intensified rather than wound back.

In 1876 it seemed as though some savings could be made by abolishing provincial bureaucracies. Atkinson's Government pensioned off 102 provincial officials. However, new constitutional structures had to be created. They were municipalities, counties, road and river boards. No guidelines were provided about size. Small, parochial units mushroomed, encouraged by the fact that in the Financial Arrangements Amendment Act 1877 the Government agreed to pay a £1 subsidy for every £1 collected in property rates by local authorities. Further subsidies were added over the next three decades. Local authorities were receiving nearly £120,000 directly from the Consolidated Fund by 1906, much of it intended for roading. Elected special purpose boards were gradually added to the initially simple local structure in the years after abolition. Eventually the Premier, R. J. Seddon, complained that every second man he met seemed to be a member of an elected public authority. The first substantial effort at local government reform began in 1895, but the multiplicity of authorities defied a century of reformers. Substantial changes did not occur until October 1989.[1]

A major logistical exercise was involved in centralising education and health after 1876. Substantial government funding was at stake, so careful thought was required. Demands for assistance with education were common after 1840. Missionaries lacked the resources to educate all Maori and Pakeha. Subscriptions to private schools were not numerous since most of the wealth possessed by settlers was tied up in their land, and not easily accessible for social purposes. Grants were made from both central and, later, provincial governments. Money was short in Canterbury because of the New Zealand Company's financial woes. Provincial politicians soon reconciled themselves to taxing to finance education.[2] In Wellington private and church organisations had rather more success running schools, but by the end of the 1860s their systems were breaking down from lack of funds. In 1871 the Wellington Provincial Council took over the organisation of primary education in that province.[3] In Dunedin in the early 1860s, when citizens banded together to form benevolent societies to assist the poor to educate their children, they too asked for help from public authorities. In 1864 Otago's provincial government began a 'Ragged School' in Stafford Street. Within a short time it had a roll of 80 youngsters from deprived backgrounds. Five years later cooperation between provincial and central governments was necessary before New Zealand's first university opened its doors in Dunedin.[4]

By 1876 some parts of the country such as Canterbury and Otago possessed reasonably efficient educational systems. In others, as the new minister, C. C. Bowen lamented, there was nothing at all.[5] A majority of parliamentarians favoured the State establishing a universal system of primary schooling, and this was incorporated in the Education Act 1877. Government money on a per capita basis was channelled to these schools through regional education boards. Two years later, 1773 teachers were on the State's payroll. They were teaching 75,666 students in more than 800 schools. State support dropped away once a child left primary school. There were only ten high schools receiving state supplements. This money was paid on top of fees, which approximated £10 each year for a child. A handful of talented children got into high schools because they won scholarships. These entitled them to free tuition. A separate system of Native Schools was also set up and subsidies were paid to 'industrial' and other schools catering for special needs, or problem children. Inspectors became an integral part of the system. They reported directly to boards and to the

Foxton School in the Manawatu County, March 1878. ATL G-344-1/1

minister.[6] The University of New Zealand, which was established by an act of Parliament in 1870, also received a grant from central government. By 1876 the University of New Zealand had two campuses, Otago (1869) and Canterbury (1873). Auckland (1883) and Victoria (1897) joined the national network in later years. As with high schools, it was expected that fees would supplement the Government's grant.[7]

Education soon became a major item in the Government's budget. In Bowen's view, he who paid the piper called the tune: 'It is absolutely necessary . . . that, where this Parliament supplies the larger part of the funds, it should retain the ultimate regulation and control', he told Parliament.[8] Not surprisingly, schools, private as well as public, always wanted more assistance. The annual reports of the Minister of Education contain special pleading from anxious boards and hungry educationalists. Lobbying by public service providers came early to New Zealand.

Health care provided a similar challenge in the post-provincial era. Hygienic conditions were nonexistent in many early towns. This contributed to sanitary problems that public authorities, local as well as national, dealt with in an ad hoc manner. Hobson allowed prisoners to be used to clean up Auckland's filthy Ligar Canal in the early 1840s, yet by 1847 Auckland 'ha[d] enough filthy lanes and dirty drains to keep up a perpetual plague'.[9] Public health was one of the first concerns of the local council elected in

1851. Anxiety about typhoid and other diseases among Maori in the Wellington region influenced Grey to approve the construction of a Colonial Hospital. It opened its doors in Pipitea Street in September 1847.[10] Central government often felt obliged to fill vacuums that existed in provincial services. Round the swamps of North Dunedin, where prospectors camped on the way to the goldfields, the squalor, disease and misery cried out for intervention from those in public authority. Erik Olssen observes that the mortality rate among Dunedin children exceeded that in England. The Otago Provincial Council felt it had no option but to act; in 1864 the council appointed a Sanitation Commission. The commissioners reported an urgent need for clean water. The Council decided to subsidise private efforts to supply clean water. For a time commissioners tried to run what was in reality a private company. Providing water did not prove profitable and in 1875 private interests surrendered their involvement to the Dunedin City Council. It also began supplying gas when a private company failed in 1871.[11] Long before the abolition of the provinces, public authorities were being obliged to intervene in areas where private or even charitable institutions would probably have shouldered the burden in the 'Old Country'. No one else had enough resources to do what was needed on so many fronts at once.

Between 1852 and 1876 the provinces were responsible for general and mental hospitals, and provided charitable aid as well. After 1872 local boards of health met occasionally within each of the provinces. Central government was responsible for the appointment of port officers of health and public vaccinators. In 1876 a Central Board of Health was established. It met when an emergency arose. Funding of hospitals was provided on the same basis as had applied under the provinces. In the Financial Arrangements Act 1878, the Government formalised a subsidy regime for maintaining hospitals. Some hospitals deemed of special importance received two thirds of their monthly expenditure, others only half.[12] Areas with an existing hospital board were obliged to raise their own money if they wished to expand facilities. Hospitals were told that they must collect money from those patients who could afford to pay. The money should preferably be gathered in advance of treatment. 'Pauper patients', the Colonial Secretary informed the Timaru Hospital Committee, 'will of course only be admitted on proper proof of their poverty.' The Colonial Secretary's office became a claims centre. Each year it handled hundreds of inquiries from boards and issued cheques to them. It handled requests for new buildings, and agreed to salary increases for staff. In January 1878 the Colonial Secretary was even invited to intervene when attempts were made to commandeer the surgeon's sitting room for medical training at Christchurch Hospital.[13]

One factor in the Government's desire to share hospital costs with local authorities was a belief that they were better placed than any centralised authority to monitor expenditure. The Under-Secretary to the Colonial Secretary, G. S. Cooper, told the Mayor of Christchurch in 1878: 'It needs no argument to show that local supervision at the hands of those who have a direct interest in seeing to the efficiency and economy of the management of [hospitals] can alone effectively ensure the attainment of these ends.' Cooper suggested that councils might care to take over the management of hospitals.[14]

However, when the economy began contracting in the late 1870s, calls on local authority revenue increased rapidly. On 1 April 1881 many councils ceased providing money for local hospital maintenance. The Government felt an obligation to fill the gap. But its own revenue was also under strain. Ultimately, passage of the Hospitals and Charitable Institutions Act 1885 gave the Government authority to devolve revenue-raising on to 28 hospital boards. Government subsidies payable on locally collected funds were reduced to ten shillings for every pound raised. Local authorities were obliged to play a larger role in maintaining their hospitals.

After the abolition of the provinces health special pleading became commonplace. A careful reading of official correspondence reveals that parliamentarians were soon putting pressure on ministers to provide more for their areas. In 1883 Wellington Hospital was asked to expand its number of days for treating outpatients. A few years earlier, the Colonial Secretary's office had been astonished to discover that the Government was obliged to pay a £2 for £1 subsidy as a result of promises rashly made in Tuapeka by the Colonial Treasurer during the 1879 election campaign.[15] 'Politically driven' hospitals were an early feature of New Zealand life. The rules governing funding could always be bent under pressure, something that continued until the principle of 'equitable funding' of hospitals was introduced in 1983.[16]

A mix between central and local funding of hospitals lasted until 1957, when the Government assumed responsibility for all public hospital costs. During the intervening years an increasingly centralised system developed, with governments paying a growing proportion of total costs. When the Board of Health proved itself ineffective in combating the arrival of bubonic plague in New Zealand in 1900, the Colonial Secretary, Joseph Ward, created the Department of Health. It was the first such centralised health authority in the then British Empire. Initially the department concentrated on ensuring better sanitation, clean water and sewage disposal, and dealt with quarantine matters. Some local authorities resented central intrusion, but their objections were brushed aside. In the Hospital and Charitable Institutions Act 1909, 36 hospital districts were established, each with an elected hospital board. Psychiatric institutions continued to be administered centrally, first by the Department of Education until 1911 and then by the Department of Health. In 1972 they, too, were transferred to hospital boards' jurisdiction, and were funded out of the Government's block grants.[17]

The early insistence that locals should shoulder some responsibility for services lay behind the post-provincial approach to the destitute. Expecting families to support them worked only where there were families and they agreed to cooperate. Parliamentary debates about indigence in the 1870s turned around three options for the future: sharing the costs of poor relief between central and local government, having the State pay all the costs, or introducing a 'poor rate' at the local level. In the end a majority favoured sharing costs.[18] Complex negotiations took place between the Colonial Secretary and the Mayor of Wellington in early 1877; the resulting agreement became the funding basis for the rest of the country. Benevolent societies were soon receiving grants on a pound for pound basis. A 'Female Refuge' in Christchurch, a 'Home for Friendless Women' in Wellington, an orphanage in Christchurch and an 'Old Men's Refuge' in Auckland received assistance from the Government.[19]

These administrative changes at the end of the 1870s greatly enhanced the power of central government which, by now, was taking a close interest in most developments within the colony. Private endeavour also came under its scrutiny. The Colonial Secretary's incoming mail reveals that entrepreneurs interested in activities as diverse as the development of inter-provincial coach links, coal and oil exploration or the staging of a local exhibition first sought financial assistance from the Government. There were requests for help from people wishing to attend, or display goods at international exhibitions. The notion that private enterprise had an entitlement to socialise their early development costs, the better to capitalise later gains, was a philosophy that inspired New Zealand entrepreneurs for another century.[20]

Vogel's economic pump-priming produced its best results in 1873. Thereafter the economy subsided. Meantime, immigrants were pouring into the country. The capacity for both the public and private sectors to provide employment soon flagged. In the lead-up to the general election

*Early charitable aid: two Yugoslav lads
soliciting help for their father on the West
Coast, late 1880s.* ATL, Steffano Webb
Collection, G-49635-1/2

of January 1876 politicians found themselves under heavy pressure to prime
the pump.[21] Much of the next decade was spent coming to terms with the
flow-on effects of Vogel's hubris. Political coalitions came and went; those
of Harry Atkinson (1876–77) and John Hall (1879–82) tended to be
more cautious borrowers. Sir George Grey's (1877–79) purported to be a
reform administration and borrowed another £5 million. But with these
loans came a condition: since its net public debt stood at £21 million,
New Zealand must stay clear of the London market for a further three
years. Grey's Government spent much of its time tending to the brittle
fortunes of urban speculators in its midst, rather than dealing with rising
concern about unemployment.[22] A land tax on larger estates was introduced,
angering most farmers who now liked to picture the premier as a tool of
urban moneylenders heading a government of 'sound and fury'.[23] New
Zealand politics was entering the stagnant, vituperative 1880s.

Atkinson became Colonial Treasurer in Hall's Government in October
1879. He endeavoured to reorganise the country's finances by reducing
waste and lowering colonists' expectations. A Royal Commission into the
public service was appointed in March 1880. It was chaired by Alfred
Saunders, a journalist, farmer and politician, with some pretensions to being
a historian.[24] The report's sweeping assertions shocked many. The
commission described 'an aristocracy of Government officials' who enjoyed

substantially better conditions than those in the private sector. One adult male in every thirteen in the colony (a total of 10,853) was directly or indirectly on the Government's payroll. The Saunders Commission called for 'heroic sacrifices'. Asserting that governments had 'fostered unreasonable and unattainable expectations', had inflated wage rates and had artificially influenced the development of resources in the country by a decade of activism and 'reckless spending', it recommended that the cost of government be reduced 'without impairing or lessening its efficiency'. So startling was the report that the Government seemed unwilling to believe aspects of it, and little was done to implement its recommendations.[25]

Another royal commission was appointed in March 1880 under the chairmanship of J. W. Bain, a conservative Southland identity. He also favoured less government intervention in the economy. The Royal Commission on Local Industries sought to tackle head on the arguments being advanced for higher tariffs by those who believed they would stimulate job creation. It recommended great caution when making changes to customs dues except when they were revenue measures and applied across the board. The Government should be careful 'lest, for the sake of hastening the prosperity of a particular industry, or affording special advantages to a particular section of the community, a blow should be unintentionally but none the less effectually struck at other industries in the prosperity of which all sections alike are interested'. The report favoured no tariffs on raw materials, and only sparing use of them on finished products.

Echoing comments that were being made in Australia at the time, Bain's Commission expressed the opinion that high wages in New Zealand were a big factor militating against the successful promotion of local industries. However, while the commission opposed tariffs, it was not against direct government support to selected industries. It built on the recommendations of the parliamentary committees of the 1870s, recommending monetary incentives for home-grown tobacco, sugar, linseed oil, silk and starch, and active encouragement of honey production. While commissioners doubted whether the iron industry had yet reached a stage where bonuses were warranted, maximum effort should be made to ensure that locally produced coal was used as a fuel 'because it enters more or less into the economy of every local industry in the country'. The report drew attention to the dominant role of the State in public works construction, noting that inflated wages were luring skilled workmen away from private firms. In effect the Bain report argued for a level playing field for wages. It was a perceptive contribution to a debate that would rage for another century.[26]

The Government's fiscal crisis stimulated political thought and the propensity for further state experimentation. Atkinson's efforts in 1880 did reduce expectations. But the notion that governments had something approaching a solemn contract with colonists to use resources for their direct benefit did not wither so easily. From the earliest days of colonisation central government felt a degree of responsibility for the welfare of the waves of settlers that came to New Zealand. Migration was the result of both carrot and stick. It was not just the privations of industrial Britain that drove people to travel half way round the world. They needed incentives as well, such as the prospect of land and opportunity. Most liked the thought of a fresh start in life. A sense of adventure could propel young men, especially if much, or all of the passage was paid by the Government. When El Dorado failed to materialise, and people found themselves out of work, they grumbled. John Martin observes: 'The unemployed considered that they had a social contract with the government, who by bringing in immigrants should also provide them with work in times of need'.[27] Grievance politics was an early part of New Zealand life. It thrived during the long depression, helping ultimately to drive further state expansion.

Settlers had some cause for dissatisfaction. The New Zealand Company had been careless with its purchases; 'land jobbers' and absentee owners bought up large tracts, forcing up prices; often short-term employment was all that was on offer when many settlers expected something more permanent.[28] Disease and accident did their part to make settler life far from ideal. Fires or floods could destroy livelihoods in a few minutes. Many had no family to turn to in distress.[29] Desertion of wives and children was not uncommon, and alcoholism plagued frontier societies in all parts of the world.

Debate over public provision of welfare was probably less intense in colonial societies than in Great Britain. Traditional lines between state and private responsibility ran deeper in Britain and charities were more numerous because there was more private wealth to tap. Most of New Zealand's early politicians had brought their British attitudes with them. Hobson granted aid to indigents with reluctance. Margaret Tennant reports that several 'self help' institutions in the form of lodges and friendly societies had been set up in New Zealand as early as 1841. Yet they were of benefit only to those in permanent employment who could pay regular premiums. A crisis was averted for many years because the early settlers were so uniformly young that problems of sickness and age did not show up on the same scale as in the British Isles.[30]

However, by the late 1870s the mounting costs of social services began to worry governments. The ageing process was catching up with many of the original settlers at the time of economic downturn and there was unease in political circles. During the parliamentary session of 1875 members debated the need to encourage more thrift. Much on their minds was the need to raise the numbers of workers investing in friendly societies so that they could benefit from sickness and retirement entitlements. In June 1876 the Colonial Secretary, Dr Daniel Pollen, introduced a bill to require friendly societies to submit annual returns of their accounts to a registrar. Supporters of the Government enthused about the work done by friendly societies and the need to protect those who joined them. The Bill failed to pass; MHRs wanted more time to study the issue. A few complained about 'government interference' in private contractual arrangements.[31] In July 1877 the Friendly Societies Bill was back in Parliament with modifications after ministers had studied similar British legislation. This time there was little debate; the Bill passed without a division. Ministers hoped that by ensuring a greater degree of friendly society accountability to their members, confidence in them would rise, more people would join, and requests to Government to help those in need would be reduced.[32]

Within eighteen months of the passage of the Friendly Societies Act, 123 societies had complied with its requirements. But membership of friendly societies did not keep pace with the population growth. Moreover, as David Thomson has shown, many of the societies were actuarially unsound, promising more than they could possibly deliver from the premiums paid.[33] Atkinson began casting about for further detail on overseas self-help schemes. He concluded that the Government could not afford to pay for the growing incidence of poverty and that it was necessary to compel people to insure themselves against possible misfortune. On 10 July 1882 he introduced a National Insurance Bill. The Bill turned the concept of voluntary insurance into a compulsory system. According to Atkinson it was impossible to rely entirely on benevolent institutions, hospitals and charitable aid. They were 'temporary palliatives'. Friendly societies, while admirable, reached too few people. Individuality and independence could best be maintained if all employees were levied £8 per year and the money paid into a general national insurance fund. 'The only effectual remedy against pauperism seems to me to be not private thrift or saving, but co-operative thrift or insurance, and that, to be thoroughly successful . . . must be national and compulsory,' he said. The State would use rents from the Government's leasehold land to support widows and orphans who could not afford to pay their premiums. As a safeguard against those who might 'rip off' the system, lists of recipients of sickness benefits would be posted outside each local authority. People would be invited to inspect them and report 'malingerers'.[34]

Atkinson in later years had the reputation of being a conservative. He regarded himself as a 'liberal', while others painted him as 'an ardent socialist'.[35] Atkinson made it clear that he was not opposed to an activist State:

> In this country the Government has already done many things which fifty years ago the greatest Radical would probably have declared beyond the functions of Government. We have State railways, State telegraph, State post office savings-banks, and . . . State education, all of which in their turn have been declared entirely beyond the proper functions of Government, and ruinous to the independence of the people who adopt them. But I will point out this fact: that nothing can be done nowadays without combination . . . if we can promote the well-being of the people, – if we can really strike a fatal blow at pauperism, – then this matter is clearly within the proper functions of Government.[36]

There were two interesting aspects to the debates of 1882. The first was a general unease about the lack of settler frugality. Many seemed to expect help in times of need, but were not prepared to insure against hard times. Atkinson, at one point commented: 'We know, unfortunately, that the majority of men are either unthrifty, careless, or of such a happy-go-lucky disposition that they do not make proper provision for the morrow.'[37] He and his supporters believed that the State must be paternalistic, and do for settlers what they appeared unwilling to do for themselves. The second interesting aspect to the debate is the difference of opinion about how, precisely, the State should intervene. Atkinson wished to maintain the principle of people contributing equally towards their own ultimate benefit. As he described it, he would 'saddle the cost of the system upon the men who will use it hereafter', adding that if that was 'an interference with the liberty of the subject which a civilised man can complain of, then I do not understand the meaning of civilisation'.[38] In today's parlance, Atkinson believed in a rough and ready form of 'user pays'.

Sir George Grey, on the other hand, worked himself into a lather over Atkinson's proposals. It is far from clear whether Grey was completely opposed to national insurance. As his speech progressed he made several interesting comments. 'A man will not watch his neighbour when he is getting Government money in the same way as he would watch him if he were an independent member of society. The payment [from] the Treasury is so distant from the man . . . that it does not produce the same effect on his mind. . . . [Atkinson's] plan will have the same effect of sapping all the finer elements of our nature.' It can be inferred from this observation that Grey favoured a personalised scheme of national insurance more akin to the New Zealand Superannuation system adopted briefly in 1974. But having made his observation, Grey veered away, saying that if there were to be any form of national insurance, then he favoured it being funded through general taxation – where the benefits, of course, were even further removed from the contributors! Grey insisted that the propertied should pay most towards helping those in need. Grey's speech was an early version of the 'soak the rich' approach to funding New Zealand's welfare policy. It helps explain why some of the more advanced Liberals of the 1890s regarded Grey as their elder statesman, and why in 1900 the Government willingly contributed £1,000 towards a statue of him in Auckland.[39] The arguments that were canvassed in 1882 contained many of the ingredients of a debate over the welfare state that would rage for a century to come.

Atkinson's Bill was ahead of its time. Many MHRs did not take it seriously. There was no vote, and no system of national insurance was established. The State carried on contributing towards the growing incidence of 'pauperism' out of the Consolidated Fund. Assistance was extended to several thousand people in the mid-1880s through what was called 'outdoor relief' provided by public hospitals that doubled as charitable-aid boards.[40] There was no mood to increase taxation as envisaged in Atkinson's scheme.

The depression of the 1880s deepened. Borrowing in London was possible only intermittently. By 1888 the country's net indebtedness stood at £35.4 million for a population that numbered only 600,000.[41] A frozen meat market in London opened up after refrigeration was first used in 1882 for shipping meat. However, meat prices collapsed in 1887. Immigration tailed off. Circumstances now forced severe retrenchment on to reluctant governments. Unemployment steadily increased. More work camps were set up on the edges of towns where men were paid four shillings a day. A total of £22,246 was paid out in government grants to unemployment schemes between 1884 and 1887.[42] William Rolleston, who was Minister of Lands 1879–84, promoted what came to be known as 'village settlements' for immigrants. His scheme allotted sections ranging between one half and two acres that were near railway lines. Without village settlements, Rolleston declared, there would be 'a floating population wandering about the country, having no interest in the Colony and never becoming good citizens'.[43] Both John Ballance during the Stout–Vogel Ministry 1884–87 and Atkinson later in the decade promoted variations of Rolleston's scheme. Nothing, however, could stop a net outflow of settlers from New Zealand which was under way by 1888. The implied contract between immigrants and a now impecunious State, was fracturing badly.

As desperation set in, the Government reflected the popular mood. Saddled with office in 1887 for what was to be his last term, Atkinson and his ministers in the 'Scarecrow Ministry' were battered about by an increasingly articulate group of opponents. They were beginning to call themselves 'Liberals' and seemed intent on using the powers of the State to increase job opportunities. Some of those who gathered around John Ballance in 1888 appeared to acknowledge a degree of responsibility for immigrants to whom earlier promises of employment had been made. Others knew that expressions of concern were good politics. Preserving jobs for settlers was a strong theme underlying the debates in 1887–88 on restricting Chinese immigration. Pushed along somewhat against his will, Atkinson agreed to a poll tax of £100 to be paid by all Chinese immigrants. Further restrictions were imposed in the 1890s and early 1900s.[44]

When Atkinson felt obliged in 1888 to increase government revenue by taxing items such as tea, his Customs and Excise Bill became the plaything of those with more radical inclinations. Tariff protection for New Zealand industries had been advocated by several protection leagues for many years and was proposed by the Stout–Vogel Ministry before its defeat in 1887. Proponents believed that protection would increase the number of jobs.[45] Atkinson scorned tariffs intended for purposes other than revenue. Faced with a depression, however, MHRs with urban constituencies where the unemployed tended to congregate, willingly embraced protection. Increases of from 5 per cent to 25 per cent were imposed, with an average duty of about 20 per cent on all imports. They effectively doubled existing customs duties on many items.

Despite MHRs' intentions, there is doubt about how much these tariffs assisted the gradual increase in manufacturing output that took place after 1888.[46] However, a precedent had been set: New Zealand was now committed to moderate protection against the better judgement of farmers, who saw tariffs as favouring urban workers at a cost of raising import prices. Social engineers were cock-a-hoop, seeing tariffs as a cure-all for the economic ills of the day. The new Christchurch parliamentarian, William Pember Reeves, expressed their views succinctly: 'Holding as I do that a protective tariff is the greatest benefit that a Government can possibly offer to the people of New Zealand just now, I accept this measure with gratitude. . . . We want outlets for capital; this tariff will provide them. We want employment for our working people: this will give it. We want something to check the exodus of population; this will check it.'

Some outside observers such as André Siegfried thought the tariff was high enough 'to allow the New Zealanders to settle for themselves the conditions of production without paying much attention to outsiders'. He was convinced that New Zealand's pioneering labour legislation of the 1890s would not have been possible without the degree of economic insulation that the tariff provided. In effect New Zealand was passing another milestone in the growth of state intervention in the economy. But tariffs remained controversial, as disliked by the farming community as they were popular with manufacturers and trade unions. In the hope of placating the rural sector, the Liberal Government in 1900 exempted a large list of agricultural implements and machinery from the tariff, but other goods remained on the tariff schedule, defying intermittent efforts to remove them.[47]

John Ballance's Liberal Party came to office on 24 January 1891 after Atkinson's defeat at the polls the previous December. At the time neither party appeared to have a radical set of policies. A majority of adherents to the new Liberal Government had voted for protection in 1888, and for the abolition of multiple voting as well as the introduction of universal manhood suffrage the following year. This last measure increased the number of voters, and allowed men without property to vote. Many Liberal MHRs went further, supporting Ballance's arguments in July 1890 that the abolition of the property tax, and substitution of it with land and income taxes, would be more equitable, and likely to increase land settlement which had slowed during the 1880s.[48] Most Liberals accepted the evidence of 'sweating' of women and children in factories. They adopted a more moderate attitude towards the strikes of 1890 that were the first nationwide example of trade unionists flexing their muscles in industrial confrontation. Yet it was not support for the strikers so much as a wish to devise a way in which disputes between capital and labour could be amicably resolved that motivated Ballance's supporters. If anything bound the Liberals together it was the fact that they were younger, newer immigrants with several first generation New Zealand-born politicians in their midst. They were all hungry for office and willing to use the power of the State to administer affairs in a manner that enhanced individual opportunities. They wanted no special privileges for any segment of the community. 'Fairness' became a word much in vogue.[49]

Caution reigned under Ballance's two-year premiership; the Premier

Liberal spending on roads helped open up remote areas; carting a kauri log out of the Northland bush at the turn of the century. National Archives

exhorted ministers to watch spending until revenue improved. However, there were signs that a new broom was sweeping in Wellington. Mindful of the urban dwellers, many of them Vogel's immigrants who supported Ballance at the election, his ministry took steps to increase employment opportunities within the public service. Postmaster General, Joseph Ward, a dapper, entrepreneurial Irish Catholic from Southland, sensed that a reduction in postal rates would produce more work for the Post Office at little cost in lost revenue. He proved to be right. The posting of newspapers and parcels increased by 85 per cent in the first year of the new rates. Ward soon took the same gamble with telegram and telephone rates, again with the same result. Post Office work expanded rapidly, the Government's revenue rose and staff numbers increased. As the economy slowly improved, the construction of roads, railways and bridges stepped up. When he became Minister of Railways in 1900, Ward tried his old trick yet again. He reduced rail charges. Patronage increased and extra revenue flowed into the Government's coffers.[50] The number of Railways staff rose steadily. After years of controversy over the route to be followed, the North Island Main Trunk line opened in 1908. By this time ministers had convinced themselves that state ownership of utilities was central to economic expansion. In his dual capacities as Postmaster General and Minister of Railways, Ward saw himself as the facilitator of private endeavour. In 1906 he wrote:

> The duty of the State is to foster the industries of the country, cheapen the cost of transport, and by so doing to assist in funding profitable employment for the people and remunerative markets for the fruits of their labour, and there is no more efficient means to these ends than State ownership of railways.[51]

Public service numbers rose gradually during the 1890s, stepping up as new departments and services were added to existing ones. Many jobs were in remote parts of the country. However, for more than a decade Wellington enjoyed the fastest rate of population increase of any city.[52] The Post Office employed 2225 people in 1890 and 7258 by 1912.[53] Railways had 4116 people on its books in 1890. Numbers stood at 13,523 by 1912.[54] There were 788 employees of the Public Works Department in 1891. These had risen to 5828 by the end of the Liberal era. The Charitable Aid Boards had been eyeing these three departments as a potential source of jobs since the early 1880s.[55] They easily filled that role under Liberal patronage. Police numbers also nearly doubled from 492 in 1891 to 835 in 1912. Such raw figures tell only part of the story. The public service employed roughly 10,000 in 1890. The total number of people on the State's payroll rose to approximately 30,000 in 1904 and stood at more than 40,000 by 1912. Housing the Government's mushrooming public service provided construction jobs, particularly in the capital. While the public service rose fourfold, the population moved only from 634,000 in 1891 to 1.1 million by the time the Liberals left office.[56]

A job in New Zealand's public service became synonymous with security. Ward introduced a variety of superannuation schemes for government workers, arguing always that the State had a duty to be a good employer. Beginning in 1893 with the Civil Service Insurance Act, there followed special schemes for post office and railway workers, and then teachers. Finally, beginning on 1 January 1908, a comprehensive retirement scheme for all remaining state employees came into force.[57] Elementary schemes for top civil servants dated back to 1858 but the Liberals legislated for the ranks. Increasingly generous contributions towards superannuation entitlements were paid out of the Consolidated Fund by the Government. Employees contributed a fixed percentage of their wages to an increasingly complex pay-as-you-go scheme. It was small wonder that big departments requiring minimal skills such as Railways, Public Works and the Post Office always had waiting lists of people wanting employment.[58] The Liberal

Government made a valiant effort to fulfil the implied contracts that so many earlier immigrants believed they had with the Government that had brought them half way round the world.

It suited the Liberal Government's electoral purposes to label their political opponents as conservatives and themselves as the architects of a new world of social responsibility.[59] Ballance and his successor, Richard John Seddon, were good publicists for their cause. No occasion was too unimportant for a tub-thump from Seddon. With the extension of the franchise first to the unpropertied, then to women in 1893, politics became more folksy. Seddon's inclusive style of politics was appropriate to the widening electorate. As in Great Britain, meetings and rallies became a form of mass entertainment.

The extent to which 1890 marked a watershed in the development of relationships between the people and the State will always be debated. As has been shown, successive governments with few genuflections at overseas experience or ideology had been pushing out the frontiers of government involvement in the New Zealand economy since the early days. The process began long before John Ballance came to office. However, under Seddon's premiership (1893–1906) the Government's role in the economy and in the provision of public welfare expanded rapidly. Some of the changes were forced upon the Government, others were the product of shrewd calculations by Seddon and Ward. Many came as the result of perceived political advantage. 'Liberalism', New Zealand style, came to mean pragmatic use of the State on behalf of any section of society deemed worthy of assistance by the ministry.

Occasionally the Government's actions were pushed along by strongly held theories or attitudes imported from Great Britain. Jock McKenzie, who was Minister of Lands and Agriculture 1891–1900, was described by one of his critics as 'a large, bovine, honest wrong-headed man'.[60] Others worshipped him. Of Highlands origin, he hated the evils of land monopoly in Scotland and held passionately to a belief in small farming. He stepped up the rate of purchase of Maori land, acquiring several large estates. They were then subdivided into smaller units and let out to new farmers on Crown leases. In his reluctance to encourage the freehold, McKenzie echoed the views of Ballance and a former premier, Robert Stout.

The concept of leasing Crown land had been incorporated in legislation since 1882, but prior to McKenzie there had always been periodic revaluations. Many leaseholders also had the right to purchase their leases. However, McKenzie regarded land as an exhaustible resource which ought to remain as much as possible within the Crown's estate. In a series of

Openings of public buildings were gala occasions: the new Government Building at Bluff,
21 November 1900.

enactments he changed the rules. First he set about 'busting up' the big
privately owned estates using new tax provisions. Besides introducing New
Zealand's first income tax for those with incomes exceeding £300 pa, the
Land and Income Tax Act 1891 enacted a graduated land tax on estates
worth more than £5,000.[61] McKenzie pursued his goal more vigorously in
the 1892 Land for Settlement Act. It empowered the Government to
purchase suitable properties for leasehold purposes. In the more radical Land
Act of 1892, the emboldened minister set out the terms under which settlers
could gain access to new land that the Government was purchasing from
Maori. No one could buy more than 640 acres of prime land or 2000 acres
of 'second class' land. These sections could either be purchased for cash,
leased at 5 per cent of the current value with a purchase clause to be exercised
later, or leased in perpetuity for 999 years. Leases-in-perpetuity were to be
at 4 per cent of Government valuation per annum, with no periodic
revaluation or recalculation of the rent. Criticised by some as tantamount to
the State providing what amounted to freehold land at cheap prices, they
were popular with those who had little money but wanted to get on to the
land. In the first two years of operation, nearly twice as much land was
leased in perpetuity as was sold under the other two options combined.[62]

In 1893 McKenzie purchased the 84,755-acre Cheviot Estate in North Canterbury for £260,220. Much of it was divided up for Crown leases. In 1894 a further Lands for Settlement Act consolidated the lease-in-perpetuity although there was some criticism from within the Liberal caucus. The Act also introduced the power of compulsory purchase of land. This move led a few to fear that the Liberals intended to expropriate private property altogether. Whatever McKenzie's initial intentions, a shortage of money hampered his use of the Act. The compulsory powers were seldom used. This was principally because, as Jim McAloon has shown, most large landowners sold willingly. They realised that divesting themselves of their large estates and investing the money in rural mortgages made better economic sense. 'There was a broad consensus [among the wealthy] on the need to encourage and facilitate closer settlement and some of the richer... even professed to support compulsory repurchase of land by the state.'[63] In the end, more than one hundred estates were purchased without compulsion. By 1909, 5174 tenants had taken up leases-in-perpetuity on smaller parcels of land that totalled 2.4 million acres.[64]

By the turn of the century colonists were competing vigorously to gain access to the rapidly dwindling supply of land. In addition to farming for wool, meat was regaining its earlier price level and dairy farming was proving increasingly profitable, particularly in the North Island. But there were many Liberals who thought McKenzie too generous. They believed that the rent paid for leasehold land should reflect its true value. A later Liberal government felt obliged to alter the legislation governing Crown leases. In 1907 the lease-in-perpetuity option was abolished for someone newly taking up Crown land. In its place came a 66-year lease with an option for revaluation, recalculation of the rental, and renewal of the lease at its expiry. Some argued that the term of the lease should be even shorter. As uncertainty reigned in Liberal ranks about the rules that should govern Crown leases, pressure from leaseholders themselves to be able to freehold their land at generous valuations mounted.

After the fall of the Liberal Government in July 1912 the new Reform ministry extended the freehold option to those leaseholders who had previously been denied it. The amount of land held under the Liberals' leases slowly declined. McKenzie's social engineering faded as pound signs flashed before farmers' eyes; they were understandably keen to be able to capitalise the improvements they had made, and to access the 'unearned increment' that population growth and the laws of supply and demand had added to the land's value. Farmers proved much less interested in Scottish theory than in the profits to which they convinced themselves they were entitled. Social experiments have usually been defeated by self-interest.

Between 1893 and 1896 the Liberal Government became involved in banking matters. It was not for any theoretical reason, but because without State intervention the major North Island bank, the Bank of New Zealand, would probably have collapsed. In similar vein, the Bank of New Zealand's takeover of the South Island's Colonial Bank in 1895 was to stave off calamity. Public confidence in banks began to slide in the state of Victoria in 1891. The unease spread to New Zealand. Trading bank depositors started transferring their money to the state-guaranteed Post Office Savings Bank during the early months of 1893. On 1 September there was a run on the Auckland Savings Bank. Other banks offered 'assistance' to the ASB, and Seddon also promised unspecified aid.[65] Confidence quickly returned. However, in June 1894 a more serious crisis developed within the Bank of New Zealand. Since the late 1880s the bank had been endeavouring to restructure because of bad debts stemming from years of injudicious land speculation.[66] But the bank's share price continued to slide, and on 25 June 1894 its directors approached Seddon and Ward for help. On the afternoon of 29 June the Premier saw the Governor, Lord Glasgow, and told him that unless the bank received immediate assistance it would have to close its doors.[67] Three bills were rushed through Parliament that evening before the anxious eyes of merchants, bankers and other commercial men.[68] In the main piece of legislation, the Bank of New Zealand Share Guarantee Act, the Government guaranteed an additional issue of shares to the amount of £2 million. It also appointed a president of the bank with veto powers, as well as an auditor.

These moves saved the bank, and won considerable applause for Ward, now Colonial Treasurer. Ironically, when the Colonial Bank began to collapse the following year and the restructured Bank of New Zealand was obliged to take it over, Ward became the biggest casualty of the merger. In June 1896 he had to resign from the ministry because of his heavy indebtedness to the Colonial Bank and the reluctance of the Bank of New Zealand to take up his debts. In July 1897 Ward became a bankrupt. He repaid his debts and emerged with renewed political vigour at the end of the decade to become Seddon's principal lieutenant once more.[69]

While there had been a state bank of issue briefly in the 1850s and during the 1880s many farmers pushed for the creation of a state bank that would lend at lower interest rates than commercial competitors, Seddon's banking bills were the first occasion on which the State became financially involved in a private bank.[70] It was a precedent that was referred to in 1933, when the Reserve Bank of New Zealand was established in the depths of the Great Depression and was quoted again in 1945, when the Bank of New Zealand was fully nationalised by Peter Fraser's Labour Government.

The developing relationship between farmers and the State moved closer after the election of November 1893. A friendship grew between McKenzie and Ward as the latter struggled to procure funds to help settlers on to the land. As Neil Quigley has shown, by then the Liberals' taxation and land policies had produced an unintended result. Investors began withdrawing from farm lending after 1891.[71] This pushed private interest rates upwards. In 1893 Ward briefly considered counteracting this movement by establishing a state bank to undercut the trading banks' rates of interest. After a resounding election victory followed by the banking difficulties of 1894 he decided instead that the State should take direct control of McKenzie's settlement programme. He decided to borrow abroad, then on-lend to farmers at a cheaper rate than was being offered by the private sector. High interest rates had made Ward's own financial position tottery and his interests, and those of the rural community as a whole, looked as though they would be more quickly served by an infusion of money to farming through a state department.

Ward's Advances to Settlers Act of October 1894 was posited on the assumption that the Government could borrow on the London market at 3.5 per cent and on-lend to farmers at no more than 4.5 per cent, at a time when the trading banks were charging between 6 and 8 per cent. In the event, Ward excelled himself. In 1895 he borrowed £1.5 million at 3 per cent, and was given a hero's welcome on his return to New Zealand.[72] An Advances to Settlers Office was established, and with McKenzie's encouragement loans were extended not only against the freehold, but leasehold properties as well. Peter Coleman observes: 'Cheap money was no guarantee that the Liberals' small farmers would turn a profit, but it gave them the kind of fighting chance settlers had never previously had.'[73]

In the Liberals' later years, the same principles lay behind their decision to on-lend money for urban housing under a branch called the Advances to Workers. Local authorities were brought into the system too, using their state loans for public works. In time the department became known as the State Advances Corporation. By March 1913, nearly £17 million had been lent to 48,000 farmers and workers.[74] These credit subsidies had their desired effect, and for a time the trading banks experienced stiff competition from the State. They were obliged to keep their interest rates as low as possible. While Ward denied that he was establishing any kind of state

Telephones and telegrams were labour-intensive, as this 1903 photograph at the Auckland telegraph office demonstrates. Operators knew all the gossip. AIM

bank, conservative critics warned that the Government was 'marching towards a condition of State Socialism'.[75]

With so much effort being directed towards the countryside, buoyant conditions returned quickly as soon as commodity prices rose in the middle of the 1890s. But ministers also wished to assist wage workers who were a growing part of the Government's electoral coalition. Speaking in support of the Wages Protection Bill in 1898, Ward summarised the Government's attitude to workers with the words:

> Almost every class in this country – the commercial class to a very large extent – is protected by legislation; the shipowners, the merchants, the landowners, the professional classes, all classes, in fact, are more or less protected by legislation and I say, therefore, it is very desirable to have the wage earners protected, and by so doing give effect to that which is the desire of the majority of the people of this colony.[76]

The Bill designed to protect workers' wage packets from arbitrary deductions by employers was about 'fairness'. Other ministers such as William Pember Reeves, who was Minister of Labour from 1892 until 1896, also used the word 'fair' a great deal. A small man with a quick, occasionally acid tongue (critics said that his sole idea of politics was that they were 'a war of tongues, and that he who can say the nastiest thing in the nastiest manner must inevitably win'), Reeves was a widely read journalist who dabbled in poetry.[77] Alone among Liberal ministers he often liked to use the language of class warfare. He was opposed to 'squatters', 'runholders', banks and 'monopolists' and could paint graphic word pictures about their 'inequitable' behaviour. Reeves went further. As he nestled into his reformer's role he sought to cast a nationalist cloak over his legislation, calling it an expression of New Zealand's growing sense of national identity. On this point he was right.

While Reeves could be aggressive, he could be equally conciliatory. He believed that the struggle between capital and labour evidenced in strikes such as the great maritime upheaval of 1890 was unnecessary; it could be calmed by conciliation and arbitration of the points at issue.[78] In 1892, when commenting on an early draft that he was circulating of his proposed Conciliation and Arbitration Bill, Reeves wrote: 'it is not a bill which attempt[s] to give an advantage to any one class: it [is] designed to fairly hold the scale between employer and the employed and [is] prompted as much in the interests of one class as the other'.[79] Underlying other legislation was his belief that organised labour, which had been badly beaten in 1890, should be helped to the point where unions could become equal partners at the negotiating table with employers. Reeves was nothing if not idealistic; his legislation was another early example of social engineering.[80]

One of Reeves's first moves on taking office was to establish a Labour Bureau to assist the unemployed find work. Information was distributed and workers were given free railway passes to travel to areas where there were vacancies. In 1892 the bureau, headed by a fellow idealist, Edward Tregear, became the Department of Labour. Over the next decade the department assisted more than 90,000 men and their dependents find a family income. Some were put on to a brief experiment in state farms near Levin.[81] For others in employment there was a series of acts including the Truck Act which obliged employers to pay their workers in money rather than kind. Two Factory Acts followed. The first, in 1891, gave legal definition to a factory, the second, in 1894, required registration and inspection of factories, specified maximum hours of work for women and young persons, and prevented those under fourteen being employed in factories. A Shop-assistants Act in 1892 also dealt with sanitation and inspection, and instituted a requirement for half holidays. By 1896 4600 factories with 32,000 workers and a further 7000 shop assistants were registered with the Department of Labour. The department employed 163 factory inspectors.[82] The Shipping and Seamen's Act 1894 specified minimum crews and other safety conditions for shipping. New Zealand's developing State could be every bit as paternalistic as a policeman.

The Industrial Conciliation and Arbitration Act 1894 is regarded by some commentators as the legislation that did most to influence thinking about social policy and the structure of twentieth-century New Zealand society. Reeves's biographer, Keith Sinclair, notes that without Reeves's personal effort, particularly his constant drafting and amending of the initial proposal, 'it is improbable that compulsory arbitration would have been introduced'. Certainly there was no widespread public demand for the legislation nor were other parliamentarians pining to see Reeves's scheme enacted. Some years later Reeves wrote of the scene when his bill passed: 'Mildly interested, rather amused, very doubtful, Parliament allowed [the I.C.&A. Act] to become law, and turned to more engrossing and less visionary matters'.[83]

The Act passed on 31 August 1894. The preamble described the new law as 'An Act to encourage the Formation of Industrial Unions and Associations, and to facilitate the Settlement of Industrial Disputes by Conciliation and Arbitration'. It made it easy for a group of seven or more workers to form a union, to seek registration and then enter by law into industrial agreements or awards with their employer over wages and conditions for terms of up to three years.[84] A breach of an agreement by either party could result in a fine. Disputes were to be brought before conciliation boards representing both parties. If the issue remained unsettled then either party could take it to the Court of Arbitration which was presided over by a Supreme Court judge. Strikes and lockouts were forbidden during this process. Between 1905 and 1908 the laws regarding strikes were tightened so that it became illegal for a union to strike while an award was in force.[85]

The I.C.&A. Act remained a cornerstone of New Zealand's industrial legislation for more than 70 years. Its origins were not pure theory. Reeves had read widely on the subject of labour relations. He carefully considered an unsuccessful bill providing for voluntary arbitration that had been introduced into Parliament in 1890. But as James Holt has pointed out, it was the political environment that Reeves operated in that enabled him to succeed. In the early 1890s the Liberals were still fashioning their electoral coalition. They were determined to draw wage workers into their fold. Given this political imperative, the opposition of employers to compulsory arbitration could be swept aside. Holt comments: 'The essence of the political situation which allowed compulsory arbitration to become law in

Bales of wool being loaded on to a train in the Rangitikei area, 1911. Wagener Museum

New Zealand . . . was that the unions, being industrially weak, lacked the will to oppose it, while the employers, being politically weak, lacked the power to prevent it.'[86]

More significant to the longer-term relationship between the people and the State were developments following the passage of the I.C.&A. Act. The culture of industrial relations that developed over the next two decades owed more to decisions by the Arbitration Court on workaday problems than to any legislative provision by Reeves. An elaborate balancing act between employers and unions that had little to do with realities within the wider industrial market place took place; governments in their capacity as legislators became the ultimate enforcement agency if one side or the other – it was usually perceived to be the unions – overstepped the mark. Within this framework the tussle between unions and employers continued. Unions were quick to organise, using the seven member rule; trade union members reached nearly 67,000 by 1912. Wages rose steadily, but prices tended to move slightly faster. In a 1919 study that is still regarded as definitive, G. W. Clinkard pointed out that between 1901 and 1919 food prices rose by 63 per cent while minimum wage rates rose only 52 per cent. During the same period the average hours worked dropped from 48 per week to 46, to put them amongst the shortest in the world. As the working hours decreased there was no marked increase in productivity as

90

envisaged by the most optimistic of the social engineers.[87]

Arbitration conferred more power on trade unions by increasing their bargaining capacity, and this in turn advanced the relative position of wage-earners as a class. But the changes came at a cost. Unskilled labour in New Zealand did better out of the years after the I.C.&A. Act was passed than skilled labour, with the result that there were seldom enough young men taking up apprenticeships. Moreover, as the Royal Commission on the Cost of Living in New Zealand pointed out in 1912, trends in prices and wages could not continue indefinitely without having a harmful impact on New Zealand's trading position.[88]

For nearly two decades employers constantly grizzled about the I.C.&A. Act, claiming that it had disrupted 'the natural and proper relation beween master and workman', and that the arrangements were 'too obviously artificial to be permanent'. In 1904 one employers' spokesman complained that the Liberals' labour legislation was 'sapping our energies and clogging our enterprise'. While many continued to rail against 'the baneful influence of ultra-Socialistic legislation',[89] most eventually came to value the Government's stiffer anti-strike measures, and applauded their use during later industrial upheavals. In the meantime, however, the power balance had clearly tipped by 1907 in favour of unionists. Having grown under state patronage, some began to regard the law as a 'straitjacket' that hindered their capacity to exploit their growing strength.[90] The Liberals were discovering what many others did in later years: the more governments do to help interest groups, the more those groups expect.

Of particular significance was the argument that went back and forth between unions, the court and employers over whether a company's profits were a relevant factor for the court to consider when arbitrating on wages. For many years the court knocked back such suggestions. As James Holt observes, there was also much discussion about whether a 'fair' standard of wages could be fixed, something envisaged by Alfred Deakin's Australian Liberals and by the Australian President of the Arbitration Court, Mr Justice Higgins. Important too was whether a minimum wage in some industries should apply for all parts of the country. In later years these issues widened as the concept of a national 'living wage' emerged; unions pushed for, then achieved, national contracts.[91]

In the 1890s New Zealand began to embark on a social concept of remuneration that in time divorced wages from many international marketplace realities. Sheltering behind protective tariff barriers, and operating within an increasingly regulated labour market, New Zealand wage workers, like public servants, eventually came to enjoy remuneration

The philosophers: 'Jock' McKenzie, with his ideas on land reform; and William Pember Reeves, the experimental socialist. ATL F-1054161/2; F-31783-1/2

that was high by world standards. The country was well on the way to becoming what Michael Joseph Savage later called an 'insulated economy'. In 1905 the benefits of such an economy were becoming apparent to many. Sir Joseph Ward declared on the stump during that year's election campaign that at £381 per annum, New Zealanders had the highest average per capita income in the world. His assertion, as Margaret Galt has shown, was probably correct.[92] Seddon had recently called New Zealand 'God's Own Country'. A supreme confidence in the paternalistic power of the State to bring about 'fairness' and social harmony seemed not out of place.

Not surprisingly, New Zealand's emerging welfare state enjoyed considerable public support. By any standards it seemed to be working. And a sense of national pride developed as overseas social reformers visited, often departing with a missionary zeal to introduce 'the New Zealand Way' to their own countries.

Chapter 4

The Essential Goodness of State Action

On 6 December 1905 Richard John Seddon enjoyed his last and biggest victory at the polls. He now commanded 60 MHRs in a Parliament of 80 members. Most urban workers, many small farmers (particularly those in remote areas), public servants and a considerable number of employers subscribed to the Liberals' interventionist vision.[1] 'God's Own Country' attracted visitors with an interest in politics and theory. After studying antipodean reforms, André Métin argued that there seemed to be no predetermined pattern to state intervention and that Australia and New Zealand were simply practising 'socialism without doctrines'.[2] Increasingly, however, foreign observers thought that the Liberal Government was going further and pioneering a new world order where 'the spirit of brotherhood' would 'supplant . . . the spirit of individualism'. Frank Parsons, a reformer from Boston, wrote in 1904 that he believed New Zealand was 'the birthplace of the 20th Century'.

For several decades to come, American, British and French commentators came, looked and wrote about New Zealand's state activity. Many argued that the antipodean approach to government ought to be emulated elsewhere. The English Fabian Society was developing an enthusiasm for the collectivist State. It argued that philosophers, engineers and scientists working through agencies of government could produce answers to social problems. Beatrice and Sidney Webb visited New Zealand in 1898. Although they found Seddon 'abominably vulgar', they were impressed with his Government's work. Beatrice concluded her diary with the words: 'Taken all in all if I had to bring up a family outside of Great Britain I would choose New Zealand'. Sidney noted there was less individualism in New Zealand and liked Seddon's quest for 'social and economic equality'.[3] Some visitors saw religious significance in the Liberals' reforms; the American journalist, Henry Demarest Lloyd pronounced New Zealand 'the most truly Christian country of the earth'.[4] André Siegfried admired many of the State's interventions when he wrote about New

Zealand in 1904. However, he was less inclined to think them exportable, arguing that the reforms were unique to New Zealand, a combination, as David Hamer has noted, 'of time, place and heredity'.[5]

In Australia and New Zealand there was a steady flow of literature from abroad that encouraged the emerging colonial intelligentsia to discuss ideas. Some American books glorified the State as an engine of progress. Henry George's earlier writing reached New Zealand, especially his *Progress and Poverty* (1879). It promoted a 'single tax' on land exclusive of improvements. The American Edward Bellamy's utopian romance, *Looking Backward* (1888), sold 200,000 copies around the world in less than two years. Situated in the year 2000AD, it told of a paternalistic state, something akin to heaven, that ensured employment for everyone, allowed people to retire at 45, ensured independence for women, cooked meals in public kitchens, maintained public laundries and educated everyone.[6] Herbert Croly's writing, particularly *The Promise of American Life* (1909), argued that in an ideal society the public, not the private sector, must dominate; the State, rather than the individual, 'would define the common good, and see to its fulfillment'.[7]

It would be an exaggeration to suggest that there was a substantial intellectual climate developing in New Zealand that favoured state intervention. While there were influential university teachers, such as the free spirits Alexander Bickerton and John Macmillan Brown at Canterbury University College, and younger men like J. G. Findlay and H. D. Bedford at Otago University, there were no homegrown philosophers of the standing of the Americans Croly or John Dewey to inspire a generation of reformers. Nor had there been a William Graham Sumner or a Samuel Smiles preaching the conservative gospel of self-help for people to react against, although, as Miles Fairburn has shown, Smilesian values had some following in New Zealand.[8] However, there was a growing confidence in governments as agents of progress. This was backed by books imported from abroad. John Stuart Mill was quoted in Parliament during the debates on charitable aid in 1877. In 1881 Atkinson bought eight books by American political economists; they were mainly publications from Harvard University Press. Ballance read Henry George and J. S. Mill; Pember Reeves developed a detestation of the English land system from reading *Williams on Real Property*; while Edward Tregear seems to have been steeped in the works of George, Mill and Bellamy.[9] In 1883 a Land Nationalisation Society was established in Dunedin and according to Timothy McIvor freethought associations were formed that year in several parts of New Zealand. Ballance and Sir Robert Stout took an interest in their activities.[10]

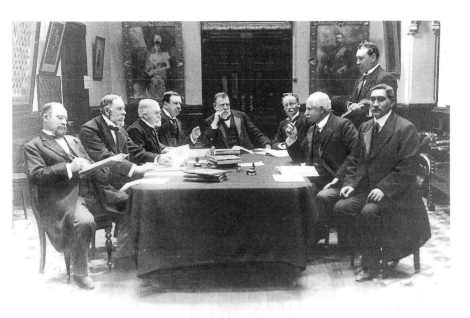

Prime Minister Seddon presides over one of his last Cabinets early in 1906. To his immediate left is William Hall Jones, who briefly succeeded him, while Sir Joseph Ward (immediately to Seddon's right) was overseas. ATL F-20806-1/2

Some of the discussion groups set up in the Antipodes took an interest in Britain's middle-class Fabian Society established in 1883.[11] In Australia there were reformers who glorified Alfred Deakin's tariff policies that he dubbed 'the New Protectionism'. They raised wages and protected them with a high tariff. Dr Harold Jensen's *The Rising Tide: An Exposition of Australian Socialism* (1909) was widely read. It defined socialism as 'science applied to life'. Like Bellamy, Jensen hoped for a utopian future where no one would need to work more than four hours a day. Deakin and Ward knew each other well.[12] New Zealand's best known reformers were Reeves and Tregear. They shared George Bernard Shaw's belief that 'science' – a word first used in the New Zealand social context by Wakefield – could be applied to society, and that it was possible to 'cultivate perfection of individual character' by 'scientific class warfare'.[13]

Where state help was required, however, no one thought people should be paid for doing nothing. Tregear, in particular, had no time for malingerers.[14] This strain ran through the Fabian discussion groups of the 1890s and was an underlying tenet of the Fabian Club that was established in Auckland in 1928. Long before then, however, a distinctive working-class culture to the left of the Liberal Party had taken root in New Zealand.

Arguing for an avowedly collectivist solution to workers' needs, it was fuelled by radical doctrines from Europe, often via Australia. However, in its heyday this new movement, too, laid stress on work, as well as the need for it to be justly rewarded.

It is hard to detect any very consistent ideology underlying New Zealand's Liberal reformers except an implicit faith in the 'goodness' of state action. Some of their eagerness to use the State stemmed from their belief that settlers who had been led to expect assistance in their quest for survival had a right to contract fulfilment. On other occasions the Liberals' actions were motivated more by a desire – as Gary Hawke puts it – 'to balance competing interests within New Zealand', to 'moderate conflict within society, as well as protect it from outsiders'. Ward, in particular, often described the State as an arbiter between interest groups, with a responsibility to help everyone.[15] A small minority wanted to press ahead in a paternalistic manner, using the State to develop a new society. McKenzie and some of the more enthusiastic leaseholders in the Liberal caucus clearly came into this category, and Reeves's views on arbitration put him among the more paternal social engineers of his day. This last group, which was sometimes labelled the 'progressives' or derided in later years as 'faddists', was distinctly middle class. They read widely and were more attuned to European and American thinking. For these people it was not enough to push ahead in a piecemeal, pragmatic manner helping people to 'get ahead'. Their eyes were on the future shape of society, one where, unless action was taken, land would all have been alienated into private hands, and European class war would become the dominant feature of life. During Ward's leadership of the party after 1906 the 'progressives' were a constant irritant. The Liberal MP, T. E. Taylor, and many of his fellow temperance workers, wanted the State to banish the trade in alcohol. Two MPs, A. W. Hogg and George Fowlds, had other ideas and struck off into uncharted territory, in Fowlds's case behind a banner labelled the 'New Evangel'. At their extreme the 'progressives' had more in common with the developing Labour political groupings whose *dirigiste* attitudes to the economy frightened the elderly, and many middle-class people.[16]

Echoing the comments of André Métin in 1901 and Pember Reeves the following year, Keith Sinclair observed that the Liberals on the whole possessed doctrines, but were not doctrinaires. They were experimental, not theoretical – a point made by Siegfried in 1904. In his unpublished memoirs Reeves denied any suggestion that he was 'an original thinker' and suggested that he, like his contemporaries, got his ideas on labour relations from English, American, German and Australian sources:

The air was thick with schemes and suggestions; there were even suggestions in New Zealand. What one had to do was to form a view of what was wanted and desirable in New Zealand. Then one looked round to see whether there were any schemes or suggestions that would be useful. From these you selected what seemed likely to be of service, taking one, rejecting many. What you took you pieced together, modified and endeavoured to improve upon. The result was something added to a bill, sometimes one clause, sometimes several. The work was interesting but extremely laborious. The amount of adapting, revising, adding and taking away was very great; over and over again one changed one's mind.[17]

This was the statement of a pragmatist, not an ideologue. J. C. Beaglehole observed many years later: 'of few ministers can it be said that they have brooded over any coherent body of principle'. Métin's quip about 'socialism without doctrines' applied to most Liberal parliamentarians. His view has been taken up by one of New Zealand's recent political theoreticians, Simon Upton, when comparing earlier politicians with those who were engaged in downsizing the State after 1984.[18]

Nor was there much sign that doctrine drove New Zealand's conservative thinkers at the time. In Upton's view, political conservatives in New Zealand, more than in older societies, were 'conservatives of interest' rather than 'conservatives of instinct'. Without any adherence to any conservative philosophy they simply went along with policies they deemed good for 'men of property'.[19] While they were usually more cautious, their principles were no less flexible than their Liberal counterparts'. As Jim McAloon has shown, they were easily led if their best interests were served by change. Atkinson's scheme for national insurance appealed to some, but by no means all conservatives; while it might be authoritarian, it obliged people to save for themselves. Another so-called conservative, William Rolleston, who was briefly Leader of the Opposition during the early years of Liberal hegemony, has been described by his biographer as 'a keen social reformer'. Francis Dillon Bell, who came to be regarded in the 1920s as the archetypal conservative of his generation, was a vigorous proponent of municipal works, libraries, bath houses, abattoirs and waterworks while Mayor of Wellington in the 1890s. He could complain about the 'dictatorship' of the Liberals but then support most of Reeves's labour bills in the House of Representatives between 1893 and 1896, believing them to be as helpful to employers as they were to unions. In middle life he keenly embraced the temperance movement, believing, paternalistically, that it would be good for the working classes, even though he was known, himself, to like whisky. McAloon points out that the Liberal Government's opponents seldom presented a consistently conservative alternative; the wealthy, he says, often simply 'kept their heads down in face of the [Liberals'] populist onslaught'.[20] More often than not the political divide in New Zealand has been between the winners and losers from a particular piece of state action, rather than over any disagreement on the principle of whether the State should have been involved in the first place.

Some historians have argued that the reformist zeal of the Liberals departed when Reeves left for London in 1896 to assume the High Commissionership.[21] In fact, the Liberal Government still had ahead of it sixteen years of energetic, pragmatic intervention. Some energy was spent on social policy. By the turn of the century the age and sex profiles of New Zealanders were becoming those of a mature society. The census of 1901 showed that women, who had been no more than 60 per cent of the male population in 1861, now nearly equalled them in numbers. Moreover, by this time there were many older people, a disproportionate number of them men. Most of the original settlers were nearing the end of their lives; a great many from the gold rush and Vogel years needed to retire. By the 1890s old age and poverty were more serious problems than when Atkinson had considered them a decade earlier. While many old people had families to rely on, lots of men had never married because of the shortage of women in early colonial society. A downside of the Arbitration Act's award wages was that some factories could no longer afford to employ old workers on a retainer basis. While the State had become involved in various social activities because there were so few charities in the new country, its busy experimentation sometimes deterred individual acts of charity.

By this time the earlier opportunity to provide a system of national insurance similar to Atkinson's proposal had been lost. During the worst years of the depression at the end of the 1880s the need to increase taxation to fund a compulsory contributory scheme deterred politicians from revisiting the issue. Nor did friendly societies enjoy a boom. In 1893 they had fewer than 30,000 members. While many workers had life insurance, the policies were for relatively small sums which, if cashed up, would not provide annuities.[22] In June 1894 when a parliamentary committee was established to consider making provision for the elderly, old age and poverty were catching up with New Zealand. Even if a decision had been made in the mid-1890s to revive Atkinson's proposals for future generations, there was an immediate problem that required a solution.[23]

In the event, because the economy was picking up and the Government's revenue was now rising steadily, the ministry decided to take the easy way out, despite some opposition within the Liberal caucus. The Government pushed aside arguments for a contributory system and introduced a taxation-based scheme. In July 1896, when Seddon introduced his first Old-age Pension Bill, an election was due in the spring and it was no time to raise taxes. The bill lapsed, was much discussed during the campaign, then introduced again in 1897. It passed the House but was defeated in the Legislative Council. In 1898 a new Old-age Pensions Bill was finally enacted. It was said to be the first such enactment in the British Empire. One leading backbencher summed up what many thought: 'it is the duty of the State to make proper provision for the aged'. The Act provided for a payment from the Consolidated Fund of a pension of £18 per annum to someone of 65 or more. The pension was increased to £26 in 1905 in time for another election. Asiatics and unnaturalised immigrants were not covered, and in 1901 Maori rights to the pension were reduced because, it was argued, too many recipients were handing their pensions over to their younger kin.[24]

Applicants for the pension were required to be of 'good moral character' and to be leading 'sober and reputable' lives. Applications had to be made in person before a magistrate and were not entertained from people who had been convicted of serious crimes during the preceding twelve years. Some said that a man had to be a saint to earn a pension in New Zealand. A means test cut the pension for anyone with an annual total income, including the pension, that exceeded £52 per annum. This was changed a few years later to £78 for a married couple and was to be altered again many times over the next 78 years. David Thomson has described the early payouts as 'decidedly mean by comparison with those enacted elsewhere around the turn of the century'. That deterred few from collecting; by 1912 a total of 16,649 people were receiving old-age pensions.[25]

In October 1911, on the eve of another election, a Widows' Pensions Act was passed by Sir Joseph Ward's Liberal Government. The Act consolidated the law relating to old-age and military pensions at the same time. The term 'widow' was defined sufficiently widely to include a woman whose husband was in what was then called a 'mental hospital'. However, payment of a pension was made only where there were children. Ward estimated there were 3000 likely beneficiaries.[26] A widow with one child under fourteen received £12 per annum, with a further £6 paid for each subsequent child. Again there was a means test. In the same year a Military Pensions Act was passed, although in 1912 payments were confined to veterans of the wars of the 1860s. In 1911 miners suffering from pneumoconiosis also began receiving payments from a small relief fund set up by the Government the previous year. Electoral considerations seem to have been the principal driving force behind the State's complex maze of state-funded, rather than contributory, pensions. So long as the Crown's income was rising steadily as a result of the buoyant economy, ministers felt emboldened to embark on spending programmes for those who had difficulty helping themselves.

Side by side with pensions paid from the Consolidated Fund, the Liberals also tried to encourage self-help among those who were fit and able. There were income tax exemptions for life insurance premiums. Friendly societies, which were increasing in number and reached 609 by 1910 with a combined membership of 68,000, were referred to by the Prime Minister as 'well-organised and deserving bodies'. Ward hoped that voluntary efforts to insure against sickness and bad health would mean there was no need to introduce the British system (or Atkinson's) of compulsory insurance. The Government hoped that friendly societies would expand their array of benefits to include unemployment, although Ward stopped short of legislation requiring them to do so.[27]

Prime Minister Ward took comfort from the rising numbers paying into Public Service Superannuation. In 1911 his government expanded the superannuation principle to the wider public. The National Provident Fund was sometimes referred to as a 'Government friendly society'. In return for contributions into the fund, any private citizens between the ages of 16 and 45 could have their accounts topped up by a state contribution. The scheme provided maternity medical expenses, sickness and death benefits, as well as a weekly pension at 60 which varied according to the level of contributions.[28] Despite the fact that its fund was guaranteed by the Government and its benefits were more generous than those offered by the average friendly society, the National Provident Fund enjoyed limited success. Only 29,441 members belonged to it in 1926.[29] The bulk of New Zealanders were demonstrating that they were not particularly provident, believing by this time that the State, in times of need, would probably provide at least minimal support.

The public's growing confidence in the State was not misplaced. When Ward became Minister of Public Health in November 1900 he appointed an energetic Scotsman, Dr James Mason, as his Chief Health Officer. Mason was a trained bacteriologist. Using the Public Health Act 1900 he oversaw a campaign among local authorities to improve sanitary standards and introduce cleaner drinking water.[30] Vaccination against several diseases was also promoted, but as late as 1912 only 5 per cent of children were being

Early dentistry in the Ureweras in the 1890s; Maori getting their own back? NZH

inoculated against smallpox. In that year the Liberal Government, a few weeks before it lost office, decided to initiate a system of medical inspections of children before they passed out of primary school.[31] In later years routine vaccinations of children against measles and whooping cough were administered by school doctors at no direct expense to the parents.

The last year of the Liberals' regime saw other significant health moves. The Pharmacy Board was working on a set of regulations governing the labelling of food and drugs, and the protection of meat and milk products. They were gazetted in March 1913 under the Sale of Food and Drugs Act 1907. In addition, Maori medical services, which had previously been provided in a haphazard way by several government departments, were coordinated under the aegis of the Department of Public Health. A rudimentary district nursing system was established in areas where Maori were numerous. The Inspector-General of Hospitals made it clear that the same principle underlining the provision of hospital services to Pakeha should apply to Maori. 'There is nothing in Act or treaty to show that the country is under any obligation to render free medical assistance to the

101

Early ambulance services; on the way to Rawene Hospital in the north, about 1900.
ATL F-34914-1/2

well-to-do Native; but for the indigent Native there is no doubt as to our obligations, and it is to be hoped that Hospital Boards, who sometimes resent the admission of these patients to their hospitals, will bear this in mind.'[32]

There is little doubt that plummeting infant mortality figures in the first decade of the twentieth century owed much to all this government activity on many fronts. Subsidies on a pound for pound basis were made available to local authorities for sanitation and water purification. In the Auckland region, Devonport was held to be the model local authority. It completed its drainage scheme in 1902 and cases of enteritis soon vanished from the borough's schools. Following an impassioned plea from dentists to the Government in 1905, steps were also taken to teach oral hygiene in schools.[33]

Contributing to infants' survival rates was the construction of St Helen's state maternity hospitals. They were provided for in the Midwives Act of 1904. Between June 1905 and April 1907 St Helen's hospitals opened their doors in all four main centres.[34] While they catered for women whose husbands earned less than £4 per week, they were not charitable institutions. They charged fees, although these were kept low by state subsidies. St Helen's hospitals also provided training experience for women who eventually became state-registered midwives. An increasing number of women chose to use the hospitals, availing themselves of the midwives' skills. As Charlotte Parkes has observed, the hospitals 'became institutions in New Zealand's tradition of liberal reform, providing a high standard of professional care for working-class women and setting the standard for midwifery practice throughout the country'. However, Philippa Mein Smith shows that by 1920 approximately 65 per cent of all births still occurred in homes.[35]

Despite intervention on so many fronts, the Liberal Government's health policies did not extend to subsidising visits to general practitioners. To have done so would have cut across the self-help message that ministers were trying to pass to people to join friendly societies. But some Liberal politicians were worried. Walter Carncross of Dunedin, an old friend of Ward's, who served almost continuously in the House and the Legislative Council between 1890 and 1940, commented in 1893:

> I know this is a big question, and that it is socialism to suggest that the Government should take part in a matter of this kind. But I believe it is one of the things which the Government will yet have to face. I know personally of poor people who have died for fear of incurring debt by calling in a medical man. I have known people who had children lying on what turned out to be their death beds; they put off until the last moment the calling in of a medical practitioner because they feared the bill they would have to pay afterward and those people have died. I believe . . . that attendance on poor people will yet become one of the offices of the State.[36]

Carncross lived long enough to assist in the passage of the Social Security Act in 1938, but died before the system of subsidies for visits to general practitioners went into effect.

The Liberal Government also expanded education at a fast rate. Many new schools were built each year, and the number of teachers in public primary schools grew more rapidly than students, enabling class sizes to be reduced.[37] By 1910 most teachers were fully certificated. In 1912 nearly 10,000 students went on to secondary schools. The number of 'free places' at these schools rose by 180 per cent in the period 1903–12 and by the end of the Liberals' term in office fewer than 20 per cent of all secondary students paid any fees.[38] Technical education expanded too, and in 1912, 13,500 students were attending classes at eight institutions around the country. Each technical school received a pound-for-pound subsidy on fees collected. Evening classes became more popular each year. By now more Maori children were attending public schools than native schools, indicating their increasing fluency in English. It was estimated that in 1911 almost 84 per cent of the entire New Zealand population could read and write, which was a high percentage by world standards of the time.[39]

A host of related benefits accompanied public education. After 1895 children could receive assistance with rail transport to and from schools, and over the next few years small boarding allowances were paid as well. Industrial schools that were really reformatories also received government subsidies,[40] as did schools for the blind and deaf. The Government paid for a school for intellectually handicapped children in North Otago. School libraries received pound for pound subsidies on funds collected locally, and the sum of £3,000 was set aside annually in the budget for the purchase of new public library books. Four university campuses were in operation by 1912. They taught 2114 students, a number that had risen rapidly in recent years. Since 1869 when a campus first opened in Dunedin, New Zealand's universities had produced a total of 1661 graduates.[41] Each year, as the economy improved, the governments of Seddon and Ward spent more and more on education, trimming the sums required of parents and their communities. The Government was well on the way to providing what later generations called 'free' education.

For the first time the Government became involved directly in permanent housing for families. As cities grew, jobs in manufacturing and servicing increased. The Liberal Party cultivated the growing urban work force, eager to ensure that workers saw the Liberal Party as their electoral vehicle, rather than the various labour political groups that were beginning to compete for their affections, and which had elected David McLaren as the first independent Labour MP in 1908.[42] This threat from the left led Seddon to promise during the 1905 election campaign that he would extend the Advances to Settlers scheme to loans for workers' housing. On 29 October 1906, nearly five months after Seddon had died on board ship while returning from an Australian trip, the Government Advances to Workers Act passed through Parliament. Applications for housing loans at an interest rate of 4.5 per cent were considered from January 1907. Loans were available to manual or clerical workers whose income did not exceed £200 pa, and whose sole land holding was the allotment on which it was proposed to erect a dwelling. Advances from the Government were secured by a mortgage over the whole property. By 1913 nearly 9,000 loans had been extended by the Government.[43] A government body that eventually became the State Advances Corporation, then the Housing Corporation of New Zealand, was beginning to take shape.

With the Workers' Dwelling Act 1905, the Government began to build rental accommodation for those whose incomes did not exceed £156 pa. Seddon's inspiration seems to have come from a visit to rental housing areas in London and Glasgow at the time of Queen Victoria's Diamond Jubilee in 1897. Tregear, as Secretary for Labour, convinced the Prime

Minister in 1904 that rental houses had the virtue of replacing private landlords with the more benevolent State, a move that could help cap the rising cost of living. When built, the houses were let for a fixed period at 5 per cent of the capital cost, plus insurance and rates, with a right of renewal after 50 years.[44] Seddon envisaged building 5000 workers' cottages. In the event only 646 were built, in Ellerslie, Otahuhu, Petone, Coromandel, Seddon Terrace (Wellington), Sydenham and Windle (Dunedin). Sir Joseph Ward, who became Liberal Prime Minister in August 1906, visited the first completed Worker's Dwelling at 25 Patrick Street, Petone, soon after taking office.

Efforts were made to 'talk up' Workers' Dwellings. But the concept never took off; many of the houses were two-storeyed and regarded as 'too swell'. Their rents were always too high for many low-paid workers, and most were not close enough to railway stations. Ward's decision to alter the rules in 1910 and to allow the houses to be purchased by their inhabitants failed to make the scheme more attractive, and few were sold.

After the influenza epidemic at the end of 1918 much official concern was expressed about substandard inner-city housing. A Housing Branch of the Labour Department was established, and in 1923 it became an integral part of the State Advances Office. However, the Reform Government placed its emphasis on home ownership rather than rental housing, with the result that poorest paid workers found housing a problem until the late 1930s when the Labour Government embarked on a huge state rental house building programme. While designed with flair, these dwellings were smaller; their subsidised rentals made them cheaper, too, than Seddon's workers' dwellings.[45]

Motives for the Liberals' state experiments varied. Electoral considerations and humanitarian concerns coincided occasionally with a belief that government money could be saved if the State involved itself in some activity. In 1901 the Government passed the Coal Mines Act, which established state mines in direct competition with privately owned mines. Coal was the major source of energy at the turn of the century. Ministers were worried about its rising cost for railways and heating government offices. A Royal Commission was established in 1900 to look at aspects of the coal industry. The commission's report in May 1901 suggested that if the State bought a Westport mine, retailed coal from it and established a 'fair price', then coal prices overall would probably fall.[46] Since the Government's agencies were consuming 12.5 per cent of all coal produced in the country, the idea of the State running a mine or mines had attractions. A Manager of State Mines, A. B. Lindop, was appointed. At the end of

Christchurch's State Coal Depot, 1905. Canterbury Museum

1902 100 miners were engaged to work a mine at Rununga. Within eighteen months coal was being marketed from it. The numbers of employees rose to nearly 400 by 1912. By this time the Government had invested £254,947 in State Mines.[47] There was a bonus inasmuch as any surplus coal could be sold through state depots in cities, thus ensuring competitive prices for urban consumers. Ministers adamantly denied any intention of engaging in 'ruinous competition' with the private sector, asserting that their object was simply to maintain a 'fair and reasonable average' price. Both the taxpayer and the consumer, so it was argued, would benefit from such state commercial activity.[48] It was an early example of government efforts to create a competitive market where it suspected that private producers were in collusion.

The demand for coal increased rapidly; between 1909 and 1912 it was necessary to import extra supplies. The shortages meant that the retail cost was higher in 1909 than when State Mines was initially set up. Prices continued to rise and in 1916 became the subject of a Board of Trade inquiry. Whether the experiment in state mining and supply kept prices below what they otherwise would have been, as ministers constantly argued, cannot be established with certainty. The State issued loan debentures to facilitate expansion. According to official figures State Mines was returning 5.28 per cent on gross capital expenditure in 1917. The mines, however, were always greedy for further investment. In 1913 a revaluation of the assets resulted in £45,000 having to be written off. Furthermore, State Mines was prone to industrial stoppages. Miners were beginning to realise that threats of political action would be taken seriously.[49]

By the middle of the 1920s State Mines was chronically short of working capital. It was unable to operate like an ordinary commercial concern. Treasury provided new investment money and was responsible for the interest and redemption of State Mines' debts. It creamed off any surpluses as it saw fit. On 31 March 1924 State Mines had liabilities totalling nearly £382,000 and assets worth £194,000. The operating account showed a net profit after paying interest of £15,742. In a time of high unemployment during the Great Depression a small level of profitability saved State Mines from the close scrutiny given to other government departments. By 1938 the two State Mines employed the same number of miners as in 1912. However, the total amount of coal being produced was 36 per cent below 1912. Profits had slumped badly and there was no longer any significant return shown on the State's investment in the mines.[50] Introduced initially to save money, State Mines were well on the way to becoming a dead weight on the exchequer.

Seddon's Cabinet extended Vogel's insurance scheme of 1869 in the belief that the public could benefit from lower insurance charges if the Government entered the marketplace. Following amendments to the Employers' Liability Act in the early 1890s many employers sought insurance coverage at a more competitive rate than was provided by private companies. Ward first advanced the idea of a state insurance scheme in 1896. In the New Zealand Accident Insurance Act 1899 the Commissioner of Life Insurance was given powers to insure people against accidents; he could also insure employers from liability for accidents to any of their employees.[51] At the same time other pressure groups were pushing for cheaper fire insurance coverage than was on offer from private companies. Eventually, after several trial bills, an act was passed in 1903 setting up a State Fire Insurance Office. A board consisting of the general manager, the Colonial Treasurer, the Government Insurance Commissioner and two other government appointees was appointed. Early in 1905 the office opened its doors for business.

State Fire's initial premiums were 10 per cent less than those charged by private companies. Agents drumming up business were specifically advised to inform customers that State Fire 'is a Government institution and consequently the insured are guaranteed by the State'.[52] When the private companies immediately retaliated and endeavoured to drive State Fire out of business by refusing to accept any reinsurance from it, Seddon labelled their conduct 'monstrous and immoral'. While in London in 1902 he had ascertained that it would be possible to get reinsurance abroad and through the Agent General in London he now negotiated with Lloyds of London. The private companies eventually learned to live with their state competitor. Despite the fact that State Fire enjoyed the advantage of not paying income tax until 1916, its early years were not easy. There were several when the office made a loss. Conservative ideologues were angered by the State's entry into a market where private enterprise was already well established. The idea that the Government was using public money to compete against private enterprise riled a later Minister of Finance, Downie Stewart, who wrote in 1910: 'The State ought not to sell services or goods to one portion of the community at less than the cost price and make up the deficit by taxes upon the whole community.'[53]

Until 1990, when Norwich Union purchased it, State Insurance, as it eventually became known, continued to trade as a government-owned organisation. It provided a wide range of insurance at competitive prices to clients who tended to be more numerous among middle and lower income groups. Alan Henderson, the historian of the Insurance Council, believes that State Fire's presence in the market place did keep other premiums lower than they might otherwise have been. Of particular note is the fact that State Fire was one of the first to introduce no-claims rebates. With all its backing it is not surprising that by 1920 State Fire carried a greater value of fire risks than any other company in New Zealand. Liberal, conservative and Labour governments retained it in public hands, all believing State Fire's position in the marketplace ensured genuine competition. Of particular significance is the fact that State Insurance traded profitably for most of its time in government hands. Its net profit in 1979 from underwriting and investments was nearly $11 million, on assets valued at $127.6 million.[54]

One further Liberal initiative deserves mention. During the late nineteenth century there was mounting international interest in tourism, and also in the supposedly healthy properties of mineral water. Seddon's ministers, most particularly Ward, decided that there was money to be made from attracting tourists to New Zealand's many mineral springs. In his 1897 budget the Prime Minister announced the Government's intention to appoint overseas 'agents' to publicise New Zealand. The Department of Tourist and Health Resorts was established early in 1901 as an adjunct to Railways. In April it became an independent department. It liaised with Industries and Commerce, sharing for a time the same Superintendent, T. E. Donne. Already various forms of government assistance had been

---

New Zealand Government

Scenic and Health Resorts.

Remember

❧ THAT a holiday once a year is a good investment.

○ ○

❧ THAT after a holiday you think better, work better, and live better.

○ ○

❧ THAT New Zealand has the grandest and most healthful holiday resorts in the world

○ ○

❧ THAT if thousands come from oversea to visit New Zealand resorts, it must be worth while to visit them.

○ ○

❧ THAT a short holiday and small amount of cash only is required.

Some North Island Resorts

ROTORUA, the World's Sanatorium and centre of New Zealand's Wonderland.

WAITOMO, ARANUI, and RUAKURI CAVES.

TE AROHA HOT SPRINGS; North Auckland, including HELENSVILLE, KAMO, WAIWERA, and other Hot Springs; LAKE WAIKAREMOANA.

WAIRAKEI, TAUPO; WANGANUI RIVER; TONGARIRO National Park; MT. EGMONT, Etc.

Some South Island Resorts

MOUNT COOK; SOUTHERN ALPS.
MILFORD SOUND (via overland route).
LAKES WAKATIPU, TE ANAU, MANAPOURI, and WANAKA.
HANMER HOT SPRINGS; MARLBOROUGH SOUNDS, Nelson District
WESTLAND, including BULLER and OTIRA GORGES; FRANZ JOSEF GLACIER and overland routes via Copland and FitzGerald Passes to Mount Cook.
STEWART ISLAND.

☞ **When you travel, book your tour at the GOVERNMENT TOURIST BUREAU.**

No extra charge for booking services. Itineraries prepared; travelling made easy. SAVE TIME, AVOID WORRY, TRAVEL IN COMFORT.

-- BOOKING BUREAUX at --

AUCKLAND (Custom Street); ROTORUA (Fenton Street). WANGANUI (Taupo Quay); NAPIER (Shakespeare Road). WELLINGTON (G.P.O. Building, opposite Queen's Wharf). CHRISTCHURCH (91 Hereford Street); DUNEDIN (Rattray St.) INVERCARGILL (Esk Street); SYDNEY (339 George Street). MELBOURNE (Union S.S. Co.'s Building, William Street).

All Tickets made up in handy booklet, which go in your waistcoat pocket. The motto of this system is "Travelling made Easy."

THE CHEAPEST AND BEST ROUTES SELECTED.

Call or write the Bureau in your district for full particulars of tours and booking; or drop a postcard to the General Manager, Government Tourist and Health Resorts, Wellington.

He will tell you WHERE to go; HOW to go; and WHEN to go.

Government Tourist Bureau advertisement, Christmas 1914.

given to develop thermal springs, such as a subsidy of £150 to help ensure a steady flow of water to the popular Te Aroha Springs. In the 1880s the Government allocated sole rights to a private contractor to draw and distribute the supposedly efficacious Te Aroha mineral water. At Hanmer in the South Island by the turn of the century there was a Government Sanatorium with 22 bedrooms, as well as a lodge and a licensed hotel. They had originally been built by the Government for travellers crossing the pass nearby. More than 2300 people visited Hanmer during the 1901–2 season.[55] A rudimentary tourist industry with the State as a major player was emerging.

At first sight it seems strange that a country which today entertains nearly 1.5 million tourists a year with big, privately owned tourist facilities, should need so much government involvement. Yet at the turn of the century there were fewer than 4000 overseas visitors a year, and only a handful of New Zealanders like Ward who had 'taken the waters' in Europe appreciated the fascination that Bath, Baden Baden and Aix les Bains held for those with money. Internal travel in New Zealand was arduous and expensive and the domestic tourist market was small. Few private individuals perceived any potential in tourism. To the entrepreneurial Ward, the opportunity to involve the visiting Duke and Duchess of Cornwall and

Government sanatorium, Rotorua, 1920s. ATL F-90815-1/2

York in the opening of the 'Duchess Pool' in Rotorua in June 1901, with the British press in attendance, was too good to miss.

Ward certainly convinced himself of Rotorua's curative powers; he and his wife became devotees, never missing an opportunity to visit. From minor village status in 1901 Rotorua expanded quickly, becoming in effect a government town with its own municipal legislation. Dr Arthur Wohlmann had been appointed Government Balneologist in 1898. He spent much of his time in Rotorua reporting on the state of the baths. In 1902 he prepared plans for what came to be known as the Aix Baths. They were necessary, he argued, because some of the public pools were 'more like pig sties than places for Christians to bathe in'. Construction progressed apace; requests to the minister for authorisation to spend money were answered immediately, sometimes even on the same day. There seems to have been no careful budgeting. Receipts for agricultural exports were moving upwards at a steady rate, state revenue was flowing, and senior ministers often felt free to authorise expenditure of money 'on the hoof'. The Aix Baths were functioning by the early part of 1903 but there were constant closures due to breakdowns in the water pumping system. Repairs proved expensive. In 1908 a new bathing complex was being planned. When finished it contained mud baths, massage facilities, electrical treatment, vapour and inhalation facilities. Wisely, perhaps, a doctor receiving a state subsidy was located nearby![56]

Under Ward, the Department of Tourist and Health Resorts became a publicity office for New Zealand, and incidentally, its increasingly self-important minister. Agencies opened in Sydney and Melbourne and in 1905 an advertising campaign was launched in Europe. A pamphlet entitled 'The Mineral Waters and Health Resorts of New Zealand' was produced and widely distributed. A sanatorium, several pools, spacious parks and launch trips on the lakes lured nearly 18,000 tourists to Rotorua in 1906. In time, a Tudor-style post office to match the architecture of the bathhouse complex appeared. Tourism certainly helped to 'kick start' Rotorua; from 1907 until 1923 it was administered directly by the Tourist Department.[57]

By this time the department had also built accommodation at Waikaremoana and there was a guest house at Waitomo Caves. Steamer services on the Whanganui River were part of an expanding network of North Island tourist attractions. Hanmer Springs, the Hermitage at Mt Cook, steamers on Lakes Wakatipu and Te Anau, and tramping on the Milford Track rounded out the South Island's attractions. Salmon and trout fishing in several lakes, as well as pheasant and deer shooting, enthused more than the handful of acclimatisation societies who were promoting leisure sports for New Zealanders. Overseas tourist numbers doubled every six or seven years. In 1906 more came from the United Kingdom than from Australia or from the United States.[58] New Zealand's Tourist and Publicity Department of later years enjoyed an early reputation as New Zealand's pre-eminent tourist agency. For a time it ran the country's native bird sanctuaries as well.

What is particularly interesting about the early Department of Tourist and Health Resorts is that it did not post profits. In spite of regular adjustments to its fees, most of its services usually operated at a loss. So did the booking services. At a time of adequate government revenue ministers seem never to have regarded the costs of the department as a cause for concern; even the cautious James Allen, who was Minister of Finance in 1912–15 and again in 1919–20, did no more than crow about the rising numbers of tourists, and the 'thoroughly up-to-date medical apparatus' recently purchased by the Balneologist. By 1918 the government-owned resorts were losing £20,000 and by 1924, nearly £30,000 pa. This figure continued to rise, the department losing £112,000 in 1930–31. Even with considerable redundancies and adjustments to fees during the depression, losses amounted to £41,000 in 1932–33. During the depression the Government went ahead with an earlier promise by Ward to construct what came to be known as the Blue Baths in Rotorua. They seem never to have made profits and were finally closed in 1982. By

1960 the department needed a subsidy from the taxpayer of £1.2 million to function.[59] Successive ministries always believed there was something sufficiently magical about tourism to warrant a departure from Ward's earlier insistence on an adequate return from state investment.

By the time of Seddon's death in June 1906 the New Zealand Government had become educator, banker, insurer, facilitator, promoter, provider, guarantor and helpmate of last resort. Cabinet was the all-powerful centre of the country's activities. Seddon was widely known as 'King Dick'. His question times in Parliament could range over an array of topics about which he, and his colleagues, were expected to have detailed knowledge. Seddon used such occasions shrewdly; he was never too shy to promote himself or his government. J. C. Beaglehole says that the Premier 'united within himself a whole orchestra, or, rather, brass band of achievement; and as a performer on the big drum he was without peer'.[60] The public admired him; some even loved the portly pugilist. The ministry now bulked large in colonists' lives. Many begged politicians to do even more. Dr Guy Scholefield wrote about this time:

> Scarcely a month passes without some convention passing a cheerful resolution demanding that the Government should step in and operate some new industry for the benefit of the public. Now it is banking: tomorrow bakeries: over and over again some moderate reformers have called upon the Government to become the controllers of the liquor traffic: once upon a time it was importuned to become a wholesale tobacco seller: more than once to purchase steamers to fight the supposed monopoly of existing lines.[61]

Because it could be both optimistic and cautious, the Liberal Government retained its appeal to the business community, as well as to farmers. As David Hamer observes, Liberal leaders insisted that reform should proceed only as fast and as far as public opinion would allow. While there were faddists in their midst, the ministry kept them under control until its last few years in office.[62] Seddon and Ward happily assisted industry, so long as employers and employees agreed that it was in their joint interest. Businessmen enjoyed dealing with Ward; he was credited with safe hands, despite his own bankruptcy in 1897.[63] Throughout his life he saw the State as the handmaiden of private enterprise, not its enemy. In a speech to friends in his home town in 1893 he said that by fostering the interests of Southland he was furthering his own interests. That, he said, was what they were all doing. 'If there was one thing wanted it was that the people of Southland should pull more together than they had ever done in the

The veteran government steamer, Earnslaw, *still plying its trade on Lake Wakatipu, 1951.*
ATL C-23148

past. One man might go on faster than another, but that was no reason why he should be tripped; tripping him reacted and retarded the progress of those who tried to trip him.'[64] Having the courage of his connections was second nature to Ward. Few pioneers understood what was meant by conflict of interest. In most new countries public and private enterprise strode boldly, hand in hand.

In January 1894 Ward became the first Minister of Industries and Commerce. His job was to promote New Zealand's trade and to find new markets for produce. The first report of the Industries and Commerce Department was published in 1902.[65] Three years later the department was still only small, with three officials operating out of Head Office. But they saw themselves as peripatetic trade facilitators. They helped with shipping and marketing of agricultural produce such as tinned meat, hay and oats to South Africa during the war, and kept a close eye on exports of frozen meat to the United Kingdom. The Secretary of Industries and Commerce explained his role in 1905 as 'keeping the products of the colony prominently before the consuming markets of the world'. To this end officers were despatched to the St Louis Exposition in 1904–5 with a variety of woollen goods for display. With the assistance of the Agent-General's office in London, which undertook a great deal of purchasing as well as promotional work on behalf of the Government, exhibits of New Zealand produce were displayed at the Crystal Palace in 1905. So good were the Government's exhibits that they won several trophies. Industries and Commerce played a major part in organising the New Zealand International Exhibition in Christchurch over the summer of 1906–7.[66] The accent was on products from the soil. In 1909 as part of several regroupings of departments, Industries and Commerce was tied to the Department of Agriculture and to Tourist and Health Resorts but its functions were undiminished.

The Liberals maintained their predecessors' interest in subsidising promising areas of industrial development. Bonuses for the export of canned and cured fish remained in place, the Government paying out a total of £10,981 between 1885 and 1901. In 1894 the Collector of Customs was given the task of assessing whether W. Gregg & Co. of Dunedin had qualified for the bonus offered for the production of 100 tons of starch.[67] In 1899 samples of Taranaki iron sand were sent for testing in London – at government expense. During 1905 there were trial shipments of poultry to London to ascertain whether there was a promising export market.[68]

The Liberal Government also agreed to assist recreation. In 1899 it offered to match on a pound-for-pound basis the outlay by acclimatisation societies to procure supplies of game birds, especially Virginian quail, ruffled grouse and prairie chicken. Such activities led on to the creation of state fish hatcheries and game farms and ultimately, in the hope of recouping the outlay, the issuing of fishing and shooting licences by the Department of Internal Affairs.[69] By 1906 the Government was operating experimental farms which researched animal breeding techniques and trained young farmers in up-to-date methods of agriculture. Farmers could have their soil analysed, their milk tested or plants identified free of charge. Over a 20-year period sums totalling £275,393 were spent on experimental farms.[70]

From 1895 until 1907–8 New Zealand's exports rose steadily; a slip in the price of one commodity was usually more than compensated for by a rise in another. A recession with its genesis in the United States impacted more broadly on the British market in 1907 and New Zealand's exports to London declined in total value in 1908. Ward's Government was obliged to tighten the belt early in 1909, although buoyant trading conditions quickly returned. The recession served only to increase demand for the Government's promotional efforts. The ministry ensured that a New Zealander was present at the Chambers of Commerce Conference in Paris in 1908, thus encouraging a practice that grew over the years whereby the Government paid for various sector groups to attend overseas conferences that dealt with matters of interest to New Zealand.

Considerable effort was made by Industries and Commerce to negotiate direct shipping with several new markets in Asia. However, the subsidies required for such a service were so heavy that they would have made the trade uneconomic. The Government retreated.[71] At the Colonial and Imperial Conferences of 1907, 1909 and 1911 Ward vigorously promoted Imperial trade and shipping, as well as his pet project of Imperial Federation. All his life he hoped that a mutually advantageous common market could be arranged among the British Dominions.[72] In those days there seemed no such thing as a cost-benefit analysis; what ministers believed to be good ideas were acted upon. Governments learned by trial and error.

While many wanted the State to promote their interests, others expected it to protect them from danger, especially civil emergencies. Local authorities had been pleading with central government for many years to help with flood relief; the ravages around Motueka in the later 1870s led to some pointed requests for aid which governments rejected at the time.[73] Seddon and Ward, however, adopted a different approach when unforeseen tragedies occurred. The ministry established a national appeal to help the families of 65 miners killed in an explosion at the Brunner mine on 26 March 1896. By 1910 the Department of Internal Affairs was dealing with requests for assistance whenever major civil emergencies occurred. On a Cabinet recommendation, pound for pound subsidies were paid to local authorities through the Department of Public Works.

From as early as 1878 the Government contemplated subsidies for volunteer fire brigades.[74] The Fire Brigades Act 1906 was the first serious effort to coordinate services variously funded by local authorities, insurance companies and the Government. The Act established an Inspector of Fire Services. Fire boards emerged in mostly urban areas of the country. Once recognised, a board became eligible for limited state assistance. While there was a strongly centralist streak to the Liberals, on some issues they insisted that communities shoulder their own burdens. Fire-fighting was one. The Government stuck determinedly to the principle that communities should provide and support their own fire-fighters. Most brigades got no more than limited funding for equipment, and transport costs to the biennial meetings of volunteer members of the United Fire Brigades Association. However, the number of fire boards increased steadily over the years, with a corresponding rise in the State's limited outlay.[75]

The benevolent climate generated by the Liberals led some interest

The pragmatists, Seddon and Ward: supreme confidence in a time of Liberal prosperity.
ATL F-109511-1/2; F-164121-1/2

groups to seek forms of legislative protection for their industries. When a conference of fruitgrowers gathered in Wellington in May 1896 they spent much of their time discussing the collegial obligations of growers to each other, and how government should ensure fair play within their industry. Of particular concern to them was the fact that while some growers were taking steps to protect their fruit against pests, others were not. The conference wanted legislation that would guarantee careful growers against the damage that could be inflicted on their produce by the less provident. The request was supported by the press.[76] Even staunch individualists saw the State's use of its regulatory powers as an aid to private endeavour. Several professional groups had already taken steps to license themselves – doctors in 1869, dentists and pharmacists in 1880, and lawyers in 1885. Since 1883 efforts had also been made to license auctioneers and restrict their practices; eventually land agents were also brought under legislative control. Agricultural producers, too, were beginning to discuss the commercial advantages of collective action and regulation, although it was some years before action was taken.

As the years went by, the wider New Zealand public welcomed the Liberals' active, paternalistic State, believing it to be in their general interests. However, the world of Liberal social engineering did not include all its citizens. Policies were Eurocentric. Asians and Maori were not afforded the same solicitude as Pakeha settlers and the Liberal Government maintained rigid, increasingly old-fashioned attitudes towards women. Chinese who had come to New Zealand during the gold rushes numbered 5000 in 1881. Ten years earlier a parliamentary select committee on Chinese immigration had dismissed the more hostile accusations about lack of cleanliness and the supposed threat which Chinese men were to European women and children. Nevertheless, successive governments legislated against Asian immigration. Hostility to Chinese reached its peak during the Liberal years when, ironically, the number of Asians was steadily declining. In 1906 there were only 2570 in New Zealand. The previous year New Zealand's first racial murder of an Asian had occurred: a madman, Lionel Terry, killed a Wellington Chinese outside his fruit shop.

Asians were excluded from eligibility for the old-age pension until 1936. Progressively higher barriers were erected to stop their migration to New Zealand, including poll taxes and reading tests. Once here, their citizenship status remained in doubt. At first, some gained naturalisation, but by the late 1890s delaying devices were used by the Colonial Secretary's Office to stall most Chinese applications. The Government became more blunt when Ward became Colonial Secretary in December 1899. He directed his officials to advise Chinese applicants that it was not his intention to recommend naturalisation 'to persons of the Chinese race'. This remained government policy until the minister went overseas for several months in 1906, whereupon a batch of Chinese applicants received their naturalisation from the acting minister. However, such was the hostility to Chinese by 1908 when the Immigration Restriction Act was passed that the Department of Internal Affairs began telling Chinese applicants for New Zealand citizenship: 'I am directed by the Minister of Internal Affairs to inform you that it is not considered expedient at present to grant letters of Naturalisation to persons of the Chinese race . . . '.[77] New Zealand's political leaders adopted an approach that was only slightly less paranoid about the 'Yellow Peril' than their Australian counterparts'. While occasional legislative tinkering was necessary because of British sensibilities, official policy remained unwelcoming to Asians until the 1950s.[78]

While Asians were very much in the Liberals' line of fire, Maori were largely beyond their vision. Concentrated in many of the more remote parts of the country, the Maori population declined after the wars to the

point where by 1890 settlers outnumbered them by fourteen to one. Maori
land holdings reduced to about 16 per cent of the total country and nearly
one quarter of Maori land was leased to Pakeha.[79] It was widely believed
that Maori were a dying race. Declining numbers, intermarriage and policies
of cultural assimilation led policymakers to expect ultimate amalgamation
of the races. Native education was promoted, but it was to be in English.
Employment opportunities were ephemeral, depending often on the whim
of Pakeha. Living conditions were usually substantially worse than those
enjoyed by settlers, and Maori rights to old-age pensions were reduced in
1901. The assumption was that Maori would be be looked after within
their traditional extended families. Keith Sorrenson notes that those Maori
who shut themselves away from European contact tended to be better off
than those who involved themselves. Sometimes a Pakeha 'Good Samaritan'
would take up their cause,[80] but most relied on the support of their iwi.

After 1896, when the Maori population began rising once more, some
social agencies started to adopt a more inclusive policy. Maori health came
under the aegis of the Department of Public Health, and two distinguished
Maori medical officers, Peter Buck (Te Rangihiroa) and Maui Pomare,
pushed ahead with campaigns to improve hygiene and sanitation. The
incidence of infant mortality and tuberculosis, however, remained
significantly worse for Maori than European.[81] While the Liberals embarked
on a large purchasing programme of Maori land, particularly in the North
Island, ministers began to show greater willingness to listen to Maori land
grievances. In 1905 under the Maori Land Settlement Act, state loans
were made available to Maori to develop their lands. Ten-year loans of one
third of the assessed value were lent at 5 per cent interest.[82] However, the
Crown's resumption of Maori land purchase in the same year gave rise to
varying forms of opposition among tribes, some of which endeavoured to
reopen compensation claims for land confiscated at the end of the wars of
the 1860s. With the election of 1911 on the horizon, Taranaki Maori in
particular began searching for alternatives to the Liberals. Dr Maui Pomare
had developed close ties with the Reform opposition and emerged as their
torch bearer.[83] Ultimately, he and his colleague, Gordon Coates, worked
with the young Liberal lawyer and parliamentarian, Apirana Ngata, to gain
some measure of recognition of Maori claims. The Liberals passed out of
power in 1912, largely unlamented by Maoridom except in Ngata's
electorate, where significant numbers had benefited from the State's
assistance to agriculture and tourist promotion.

Nor was the Liberal era one of empowerment for women. By the early
years of the twentieth century women were beginning to enter the

Farming always depended on women's work; a Waikato milking shed in 1911.
Wagener Museum

professions. They formed approximately 50 per cent of the teaching profession, and several women doctors were on the Department of Health's payroll in its early years. After passage of the Female Law Practitioners' Act in 1896 women lawyers slowly entered practice.[84] But progress within the public service was slow. The first woman had been appointed to the public service in 1876. Increasing use of typing within the public service opened up some career opportunities for women. However, until 1962 women received less pay for the same work than men. Some men opposed them having the right to join the Public Service Superannuation scheme where they enjoyed the option of earlier retirement. The advent of award wages in the private sector made employers wary of employing women. Their percentage of the work force dipped for a time. Edward Tregear, one of the high priests of Liberal reform, saluted this trend. In 1908 he wrote: 'In my opinion, the less the future wives and mothers of the nation have to encounter industrial toil and enter into industrial competition with men the better.'[85] Having said this, however, Tregear bemoaned the falling birth rate and what he believed would be an inevitable future shortage of men for the workforce – a conundrum that he and others of like mind seem never to have worked out to their satisfaction. While many Liberals supported women's suffrage in 1893, they did so not out of a belief in the rights of women but rather in the vague hope that women might restrain, even reform, colonial men.[86] Votes were one thing; it would be many years before governments espoused the cause of equal rights.

By 1912 Ballance, Seddon, Ward and his short-lived successor, Thomas Mackenzie, had built a complex additional structure on top of the substantial state edifice they inherited in 1891. By a variety of pragmatic interventions the Liberals hoped they had produced a more protective, congenial society in which New Zealanders could thrive. The results seemed heartening. While the country's total population grew by approximately 64 per cent during their years in office, the GNP rose 126 per cent over the same period. Buoyant export markets meant that for all but eight of their 21 years in office the Liberals witnessed real economic growth; in nearly half of those years growth exceeded 3 per cent pa.[87] However, it was not a cheap exercise. Both Seddon and Ward borrowed vigorously to support their experiments. In 1890 the country's net indebtedness was £37.28 million. By 1912 it had reached £82.24 million, of which £16.8 million represented money that had been on-lent by State Advances. Debt repayment was a constant political issue, especially during Ward's prime-ministership between 1906 and 1912.[88]

The economy was booming when the Liberals left office, but so too was inflation. Ward's Government decided to explore uncharted waters in 1910 when it passed the Commercial Trusts Act, which made it an offence to charge prices for flour, meat, fish, coal, sugar, oils and tobacco that were 'unreasonably high'. What constituted a 'reasonable' price was not defined, nor was there any mechanism established to police prices.[89] In some desperation during its last weeks in office the Liberal Government appointed a Royal Commission on the Cost of Living. Its members were strong believers in an active State; besides Tregear, two new Labour MPs were among the commissioners. They believed that by tinkering with rules, regulations and legislation, social outcomes could be improved. They concluded that there had been an increase in the cost of living of at least 16 per cent since the middle of the 1890s, but that it was approximately the same increase that had occurred in Great Britain, New Zealand's main trading partner. The commissioners suggested a host of interventions in the economy that could reduce workers' living costs, including an end to tariffs on foodstuffs, the creation of municipal markets and an extension of the Workers' Dwellings scheme. But there was uncertainty on one point: could prices continue to be pushed up by rising wages, and if so would they not make New Zealand's exports uncompetitive in the longer term?[90] Delivered to ministers in August 1912, a few weeks after the Liberals left office, the report contributed to a growing debate among social reformers. However, there is little evidence that the new Government took much notice of it.

In 1911 Ward budgeted for a small surplus. The Liberals never believed in setting aside much money, even in prosperous non-election years. A

David Low captures Sir Joseph Ward in election mode, 1911.

Public Debt Extinction Act was passed in 1910 which created what was called a Sinking Fund from which money was invested domestically with a view to earning a higher rate of interest than could be got overseas. The goal was to extinguish the public debt over 75 years.[91] New Zealanders had fallen into a pattern of living right up to, and beyond, their income. Yet, few thought government spending excessive. The Reform Party opposition promised to spend more.

Although the State was beginning to encounter problems, overseas commentators continued to visit New Zealand. Most still liked what they saw. Peter Coleman notes that what made Northern Hemisphere reformers sit up and take note was the fact that New Zealand's state involvement in the economy 'was so comprehensive in scope and so rapid in implementation'. A Scotsman, Hugh Lusk, who had briefly been a New Zealand MP in the 1870s before taking to the American lecturing circuit, became a publicist for the antipodean reforms. In 1913 he published a book called *Social Welfare in New Zealand*. He pointed to the country's 'great social and political experiment at once unique in character and remarkable in its effects'. After surveying the Government's efforts at 'State Socialism' he concluded that New Zealand was an 'object lesson' for other countries, especially the United States.[92] Peter Coleman mentions others who came in later years, who returned to the Northern Hemisphere as propagandists for the 'New Zealand Way'.

However, some observers found flaws in the system of State Socialism. Writing in 1910, the Dunedin lawyer, William Downie Stewart, and an American academic, J. E. Le Rossignol, observed that on the available evidence, governments were seldom as efficient as private enterprise when it came to managing enterprises. They drew attention to the criticisms that were now being levelled at Australia's state employees, whose easy-going pace of work was often referred to as 'the Government stroke'. And they warned against sloppy accounting by government businesses.[93]

This was a point taken up in 1916 by an American, Robert Hutchinson. He had spent eight months in the country the previous year. Echoing Frank Parsons's comments of a decade earlier, Hutchinson noted: 'The value of a glimpse into a country like New Zealand is that we can see a little of what it is likely to be further down the road than we ourselves are at present.'[94] He was worried about New Zealand's level of indebtedness, and the large repayments required on loans. Moreover, despite Ward's earlier claims that the Government was getting a return of 3 per cent on its investment in railways, Hutchinson questioned whether those returns were accurate.[95] It was a perceptive observation. While State Mines were still making a profit, the Department of Tourist and Health Resorts continually lost money. State trading organisations had many worse times ahead of them. But for the moment, New Zealanders were enjoying one of the highest living standards in the world and many envied this. Could these living standards survive a serious downturn in commodity prices? It was some years before it became clear that while the State could achieve some things, it was not omnipotent.

Chapter 5

World War Winds Up the State

The British historian A. J. P. Taylor began his history of early twentieth-century England with the words, 'Until August 1914 a sensible, law abiding Englishman could pass through life and hardly notice the existence of the state, beyond the post office and the policeman.'[1] As we have seen, this could not be said of New Zealanders who, since the 1840s, had witnessed one piece of state intervention after another. However, nothing that had occurred so far in either country could have prepared people for the hold which the State was to establish over them as a result of World War I. While that grasp relaxed a little when peace returned, it was not to slacken substantially until the 1980s. 'The rise of collectivism', as Robert Skidelsky has called it, took on an inexorable quality everywhere after 1914.[2]

On 10 July 1912 the New Zealand Liberal Party finally surrendered office after more than 21 years in power. A bluff Orangeman, William Ferguson Massey, a South Auckland farmer, replaced Thomas Mackenzie as Prime Minister; the austere Cambridge-educated Anglican businessman, James Allen, became Minister of Finance. He believed passionately in the doctrine of individual initiative. A lawyer and freemason, Alexander Herdman, a crusader for public service reform, became Minister of Justice; and Francis Dillon Bell, New Zealand's first King's Counsel,who had been Crown Solicitor in Wellington, was the new Government Leader in the Legislative Council. Sir Joseph Ward, who had played a major role in nudging government into many corners of the economy, retired to the Liberal Party's back benches for twelve months before becoming Leader of the Opposition.[3]

Both in ideology and experience the new Government presaged change. Yet surprisingly little altered. The only noticeable differences were inexperienced faces at the Cabinet table, a new system of public service classification introduced soon after Massey came to power, and two gestures towards Reform's faith in individualism – the freehold option for farmers holding leases-in-perpetuity, and a tougher approach to striking trade unions

123

W. F. Massey, Prime Minister 1912–25.
ATL G-1540-1/1

at Waihi and on the waterfront during 1912–13. In other respects, during its sixteen and a half years in office, the Reform Government wound the ratchet of state interventionism a little tighter.

It is not hard to explain why the State did not retreat after 1912. First, the Reform Party had not promised revolution. There was no mood within the party to undo the relationships that had grown up between the State and interest groups, only to adjust them. In opposition Reform had concentrated on the overtly political nature of the Liberal Government's public service and had exploited growing concern among farmers about the increasingly rigid approach to land tenure taken by the Liberal Government. Massey was not opposed to big spending by government; he sought only to redirect Public Works construction towards farming districts and to help the rapidly expanding North Island economy.

But even had there been a desire fundamentally to alter New Zealand's economic direction, the Reform Government was seldom in a position to contemplate it. From the middle of 1912 until the election of 1914 Massey had a constant struggle to survive and most of his Government's internal politicking was directed at firmly attaching to Reform those independent Liberals whose votes helped him to office in July 1912. Important to achieving this end was another state experiment. Three northern independents were instrumental in having a Royal Commission into the Kauri Gum Industry established in March 1914. The Kauri Gum Industry

Regulations governing economic activity were growing in number by 1900;
a gum digger's licence. Wagener Museum

Amendment Act 1914 resulted. It authorised the Ministry of Lands to advance up to 50 per cent of the assessed likely export receipts from gum to diggers. The department would take possession of the gum and sell it on the diggers' behalf, in much the same way that producer boards were to operate in the 1920s. A departmental spokesman later asserted that this new policy 'has had a beneficial effect on the industry, and this fact is generally recognised by the producers – the gum diggers and the small farmers'. He could have added the local politicans as well, for Vernon Reed, Gordon Coates and T. W. Rhodes had, by this time, become warm supporters of the Reform Government.[4]

The formation of a National Ministry on 12 August 1915 to assist with the war effort removed any prospect that anything controversial could be advanced until the bi-partisanship collapsed on 12 August 1919. During the intervening four years the Liberals once more held several key portfolios. Ward and his colleague, the Auckland brewer Arthur Myers, ran the war economy. It was not until the election on 17 December 1919 that Massey won his first substantial victory. However, a serious recession quickly set in. Over the next five years the simple act of survival proved, in Massey's own words, to be 'hell all the time'.[5]

In any event, no matter what hopes a few conservatives might have nursed, Massey's Cabinet showed the same incremental approach to state

125

activity as its predecessor. Reform backbenchers supported him. Parliamentary debates reveal that most Reform MPs wanted simply to redirect the attention of the State towards their areas of concern. One announced that 'there is no such thing . . . as Conservatism or Toryism in this Dominion'; another argued that the real liberals were sitting on the Reform benches.[6] Allen's first budget, on 23 August 1912, was cautious. While the new government would borrow less, it would maintain an active railway construction programme, pursue closer settlement of the land, and expand the country's state-funded health services, especially to rural areas. The Government would spend more on irrigation schemes, provide better educational opportunities for young farmers, and restructure, rather than sell, the Government's experimental farms.[7] A Board of Agriculture was soon empanelled consisting of a number of friends of the Reform Party. Its function was to make recommendations to Government on issues of vital importance to the rural sector. As its reports show, it was soon struggling to justify its existence.[8] The Board of Agriculture was a forerunner of many such quangos that were appointed for political purposes during the rest of the century.

A subsidy was introduced in 1913 to help the emerging fruit preserving industry, while ministers boasted about their big spending on draining 39,000 acres of the Hauraki and Rangitaiki Plains. In November 1914 an Iron and Steel Industries Act was passed. Its intention was to encourage the manufacture of iron and steel by the payment of bounties on pig iron and 'puddled bar iron'. In the same year the Government offered grants to assist private companies prepared to drill for oil. Several companies quickly lodged applications. These moves were simply extensions of the now traditional policies built up since Stafford's day.

The Reform Government's health policies were built on Liberal foundations. A substantial public hospital rebuilding programme was soon under way. More St Helen's hospitals were constructed, and authority to engage in slum clearance was taken under the Public Health Amendment Act 1915.[9] All this state activity suggests that a degree of consensus was emerging that governments were expected to play a dominant role in the country's life. Reform's Liberal opponents often gave the impression of opposing for the sake of it.

The outbreak of war in 1914 lifted Reform's *dirigiste* tendencies to a new plane. A huge public outpouring of imperial sentiment led politicians in all parts of the British Empire to sanction full use of the State's powers to win the war. An expansion of central authority was not unique to the British

The Governor, Lord Liverpool, flanked on his right by Sir Francis Bell and W. F. Massey and on his left by Sir Joseph Ward, declaring New Zealand to be at war, 5 August 1914.
ATL G-48457-1/2

Empire. Robert Higgs in his classic *Crisis and Leviathan* argues that in the United States there was 'an enormous and wholly unprecedented intervention of the federal government in the nation's economic affairs' between 1916 and 1918. He claims that the growth of centralist tendencies during those years far outstripped those of the Progressive era over the previous twenty years.[10] This was also the case in the United Kingdom and in New Zealand.

On 5 August 1914 the Governor, Lord Liverpool, read the proclamation of war from the steps of Parliament Buildings to a crowd of 15,000 cheering enthusiasts. Five days later Parliament passed the Regulation of Trade and Commerce Act. It was designed to give ministers the power to fix maximum prices by orders-in-council for the duration of the war. Selling goods in excess of maximum prices became an offence punishable by a fine of £500. On 23 October 1914, without any debate, Parliament passed the War Regulations Bill. Along with further amendments in 1915 and 1916, this measure gave the Government wide powers to gazette regulations affecting virtually every area relevant to the conduct of the war. Under the guidance

Ward and Massey meet the Pioneer Maori Battalion in France, 1918. ATL G-13283-1/2

of Solicitor-General, J. W. Salmond, who was a pronounced centralist, the Government took the powers to regulate on any matters deemed 'injurious to the public safety'. The Ministry could require companies to manufacture military supplies, and could involve itself in social areas such as the suppression of prostitution, the sale of liquor, and the prevention of venereal disease.[11] In Part 1 of the War Legislation Act 1916 Parliament armed itself with a complex piece of legislation to control rents at their level on the day before the outbreak of war. Parliamentarians were voting powers to the Government never contemplated in peacetime. Once gained, such powers were seldom abandoned.

About 14,000 men volunteered in the first week of war. On 16 October 1914 after a brief stint in camp, 8000 New Zealanders, jocularly known as 'Bill Massey's Tourists', sailed for the Middle East.[12] It was not until the middle of 1919 that those who remained of the 124,211 men who served in World War I were back in New Zealand. The official estimate of the monetary cost of participation was £79,289,454 for a country of 1.2 million people.[13]

There were no precedents for handling the sudden switch in economic priorities that war demanded. Massey's Government felt its way, believing that hostilities would soon be over. When this likelihood faded, and the Government's majority remained precarious, especially after the General Election on 10 December 1914, there was talk of the need for a coalition with the Liberals. In August 1915, Sir Joseph Ward finally agreed.[14] By this time the Government had already taken the power to raise extraordinary loans for the prosecution of the war. They were secured against reserves in London. In all £68.5 million was borrowed, much of it domestically. This brought the Government's total indebtedness to £201 million by 1920.[15] The rest of the cost of the war was raised by taxes levied after Ward became Minister of Finance on 12 August 1915. A graduated income tax was introduced in his first budget; the lowest paid were levied 3 per cent of gross wages, while the highest paid (those above £5,600 pa) were levied 10 per cent plus a temporary super tax that amounted to another 3 per cent. Many other taxes were levied in the same budget. They included an additional tax on profits made from farming because farmers were now earning big returns from the British commandeer of farm produce that came into effect in March 1915. Railway and Post and Telegraph charges were also raised, and duties were imposed on new cars, motor spirits and alcohol. Death duties, stamp duties and totalisator levies all increased. Ward set in place most of the taxes that were to be a feature of budget nights for the next 70 years. Interestingly, they were levied purely for revenue and were unrelated to the cost or use made of the goods or services.[16]

Much interest centred on Ward's promise to tackle rising inflation which began to emerge as a problem within days of the outbreak of war.[17] Soon after taking office, he assured Parliament that the Government would legislate 'to ensure that the cost of food, clothing, and shelter of the people [is] in no way unduly or artificially increased'. He was signalling an extension to his own Commercial Trusts Act 1910 and to Massey's Regulation of Trade and Commerce Act of 1914, neither of which had so far succeeded in holding down prices. Ward told his colleagues:

> Our desire should be that no part of the field of business opportunity may be restricted by monopoly or combination, and that the right of every man to acquire commodities, and particularly the necessaries of life, in an open market, uninfluenced by the manipulation of trust or combination, may be preserved, and the people not exploited.[18]

Ward's view reflected concerns felt in New Zealand and overseas that private monopolies were interfering with the market place, and that the State needed to stop the exploitation of ordinary people. The National Government's involvement in price control became wide-ranging. Ward signalled his intention to give traders some competition by increasing the powers of local bodies in line with the recommendations of the 1912 Royal Commission on the Cost of Living. By regulation boroughs could be granted the powers to inspect, sell and control local supplies of milk, to establish and maintain city markets, refrigerate meat, set up bakeries and equip fishing trawlers. With the prior permission of the Minister of Internal Affairs, local authorities could fix charges for services as they thought fit. In adopting these measures Ward was responding to the views of some of the trade unions and Labour MPs. Confidence that public intervention in the marketplace could ensure good outcomes had become axiomatic.

The Cost of Living Act became law on 12 October 1915. It established a Board of Trade which, unlike its predecessors, had powers of investigation. The wartime Board of Trade could inquire into 'every article of food for human consumption and every ingredient used in the manufacture of such articles'. However, it was made clear that costs beyond the producer's control were outside the scope of an inquiry. While some ministers such as Bell were less than enthusiastic about the Bill, feeling that it was unlikely to achieve what Ward hoped of it, the sole unionist in the Legislative Council felt the Government was on the right track and should have gone further. J. T. Paul regarded the Board of Trade as a first step towards civilising society. There was, in his view, a philosophical principle at stake. It was

> whether any man has an absolute right to do what he likes with his own. So far as his own affects the material and social interests of the community, his property and his business have to be subordinated to the interests of the community. After all, anarchy is only individualism carried to its logical conclusion. . . . If this Bill does nothing else, it says to certain sections of the community, 'You shall not do what you like with your own'.

The defect of the Bill in Paul's view was that it stopped short of examining the true costs of production, and was a compromise with his socialist objective, which was the 'scientific control of industry': 'Either we must follow our present system of production and distribution or we must, as far as possible, introduce scientific methods. . .'.[19] This was a well-articulated expression of views that were gaining currency amongst some unionists, many of whom became important figures in later social engineering.

As the war moved into its second and third years both Bell and Paul – viewing the issue from different ends of the political spectrum – had reason to be cynical about the Board of Trade. A three-member board, which Prime Minister Massey occasionally chaired, took office on 16 March 1916. For some weeks the Government's Assistant Law Draftsman struggled to devise regulations to define the Board's powers. He finally admitted that his draft regulations were 'so elaborate and technical that they will if adopted tend to hinder rather than promote' the Board's objectives. Massey accepted the argument that the Board could be considered to be a 'permanent commission of inquiry' and it proceeded for a time without regulations. However, having had costs beyond a producer's control eliminated from its scrutiny, the Board found itself powerless to control the steady upward trend in prices. Establishing what might be a 'fair profit', something which Ward had described as 'an exceedingly difficult matter', was also beyond it.[20] A world shortage of shipping pushed up freight rates, adding hugely to the cost of New Zealand's imports, and consequently to all manufacturers' costs. Coupled with the fact that high farming returns from exports were also fuelling inflation, the Board's task of controlling prices became virtually impossible. Ward conceded in June 1916 that there was little chance the Board would be lowering prices in present circumstances.

Instead, during the next two years the Board of Trade narrowed its focus. It tried, rather ineffectually, to prevent speculation in food and clothing. In 1917 and 1918 the Board imposed maximum prices on flour, bread and bran. The most enduring of these controls were those relating to bread prices which began on 19 March 1918.[21] An arrangement was also made with wholesale grocery merchants to control the prices of 57 basic food items. These were allowed to increase in price only with the Board's permission. The Board turned its attention to clothing in 1918 and investigated the possibility of producing a cheaper 'standard cloth'. A strong suspicion developed in official quarters that some lines of clothing were being hoarded, and that drapers were making exorbitant profits.[22] However, it was soon clear that inflation was sufficiently rampant that the Board had no option but to approve clothing price increases. And with each approval, union anger grew. The last year of the war was marked by industrial unrest in many parts of the country as wages slid further behind prices.[23]

Once committed to a line of action both politicians and the public found it difficult to resile. After the collapse of the National Ministry in 1919 Massey struggled valiantly to make good on his earlier promise to deliver effective price control. Faced with rocketing inflation and a difficult election, the Government passed a new Board of Trade Act. Now in opposition, Ward's Liberals had no option but to support it. Subtitled 'An Act to make better provision for the Maintenance and Control of the Industries, Trade, and Commerce of New Zealand', it gave formal recognition to a separate Department of Industries and Commerce which had previously been linked with Agriculture and Tourism.[24] The new Act retained the Board of Trade and expanded its membership to four. Once more the Prime Minister, or in his absence another minister, presided over its deliberations, again in the hope that tough decisions could be taken immediately.

The restructured board was given wide regulatory powers. It could prevent or suppress methods of competition considered prejudicial to an industry, and could fix maximum or minimum prices for goods and services. It became an offence for anyone 'who, either as principal or agent, sells or supplies, or offers for sale or supply any goods at a price which is unreasonably high. For the purposes of this section the price of any goods shall be deemed to be unreasonably high if it produces, or is calculated to produce, more than a fair and reasonable rate of commercial profit. . . .' Hoarding goods was banned.[25]

For many years now unionists had been arguing that the level of wages set by the Arbitration Court should take account of an employer's ability to pay. Now a government-appointed board had the power to decide what were 'reasonable' or 'unreasonable' profit margins. Marketplace considerations were being squeezed out in favour of social and political priorities.

The Board of Trade Act 1919 moved further across uncharted territory and provoked considerable public debate. The *Dominion* told its readers that the legislation 'is a measure of considerable promise', an opinion supported by the *Evening Post*. The paper from the biggest commercial centre, the *New Zealand Herald*, also cautiously endorsed the new Board of Trade. However, the Christchurch *Press* vigorously opposed the legislation, bemoaning what it argued had been a wholesale surrender of power by parliamentarians to the executive during the course of the war. Worse still, in the eyes of the *Press*, was the prospect that commerce and industry were being brought under 'bureaucratic control'. The *Otago Daily Times* was just as vociferous in opposing the new legislation. At best, the commercial world was divided, many observers suspecting that this could be a turning point in the relationships between business and government.[26]

Armed with very wide powers, members of the new Board tentatively took up their battle stations. Massey informed them in a memo on 24 November 1919 that he expected action to control prices 'at once'. With the election only weeks away, the Prime Minister announced that he was looking forward to a 'downward revision in wholesale and retail prices'.[27] However, the reforms to the Public Service that his own government had made in 1912 reduced the capacity of politicians to control appointments. The Public Service Commission eventually appointed two investigating accountants to undertake the Board's work, but they were unable to start for several weeks. By January 1920 ministers were becoming agitated at the slow progress. Massey was convinced that extensive profiteering was occurring, yet the Board was still not up to speed; further staff appointments were still pending.

After some weeks of intensive investigation the Board reported to an impatient Prime Minister that controlling prices was very difficult. They told him that 'no satisfactory price control can be established or maintained without the controlling authority also having control of the supplies'. While this was a view held by many, it was finally forced upon the department by several court rulings in cases where aggrieved businessmen accused of profiteering had sought rulings from magistrates. Moreover, by the middle of 1920 efforts to control the prices of sugar, timber, coal and cement were running up against world shortages in these commodities. Even harder to combat was the fact that some suppliers stockpiled or redirected stock to foreign markets where profit margins were not so tightly regulated.[28] The international marketplace seemed always able to find ways to circumnavigate Massey and his social engineers.

Efforts to control the price of coal were no more successful. On 26 May 1916 the Board of Trade established an inquiry into soaring prices in Auckland. It soon concluded that coal price movements since 1914 were 'wholly warranted'. Before long, however, industrial action in the mines held up supplies, thus compounding difficulties. Since coal was a major item in domestic heating, it was not surprising that the new Board returned to coal prices in the inflationary months of 1920. Once more the Board carefully scrutinised price movements, and in several cases requested balance sheets from coal merchants to see whether 'unreasonable' profits were being made. No evidence was uncovered.[29]

In his reports to the Prime Minister, the senior commissioner of the Board of Trade, W. G. McDonald, remained optimistic that if he only had more staff he could produce an effective system of price controls. In June 1920 Cabinet, which had been struggling to reduce public service numbers, broke its ban on new positions and approved extra staff. Bureaucrats at Industries and Commerce vigorously promoted price control. The Secretary wrote:

> In some quarters the Department is faced with an appeal for the relaxation of all State control, so that business competition may be unrestricted. Among the majority of businessmen there is a genuine conviction that . . . competition is the best remedy for our post-war difficulties. What these people frequently overlook is the fact that competition seldom, if ever, works freely, and Government interference is one of the minor conditions limiting it. In fact, businessmen themselves are showing a very prevalent tendency to combine

and agree for the purpose of eliminating many of the important features of competition. The Department has considered this matter from time to time, and it cannot agree that the total removal of Government restrictions will be either welcome or beneficial. The experiences of war have shown many opportunities for cooperative effort, especially in relation to the organisation and development of the secondary industries in the Dominion.[30]

However, despite bureaucratic encouragement, McDonald was soon obliged to abandon price setting except for bread, which remained controlled for many more years. The Board resorted instead to publicity about prices in the hope that consumers would use the information to shop about.

The crisis soon passed. Towards the end of 1920 world prices subsided and there was a sharp recession. Falling prices applied a regulatory regime more effective and hurtful for many than anything the Government could have devised. However, for 60 years to come politicians and bureaucrats strove to develop a workable system of price control. In part this was due to the prolonged influence of Dr W. B. Sutch, whose Ph.D. thesis at Columbia University in 1932 was about the experience of price control in New Zealand. Throughout his life Sutch favoured social control and had a deep distrust of the capacity of market forces to advance human welfare. He argued that the Board of Trade had been successful in some areas during World War I, especially with sugar and wheat where there had not been too many 'middlemen'. As experiments in price control failed in later years, he constantly sought refinements to the system. Many governments accepted his advice, and a wide variety of measures were tried after 1935.[31]

Meantime, both the Board of Trade and the Department of Industries and Commerce were engaged in other activities that affected the shape of the New Zealand economy. Concerned about the numbers of returned servicemen requiring employment, Massey asked the Board to report on the state of industry, to publish information that might be of assistance to them, and to procure 'by means of regulations . . . the due control, maintenance, and development of such industries'.[32] An Industries Committee had already been set up by Parliament in November 1918 to foster industry. In a lengthy submission to it dated 31 January 1919, Dr C. J. Reakes, principal officer of Industries and Commerce, presented a number of suggestions for future action. His list consisted of import substitution industries and exporting ventures where value added to goods in New Zealand could provide local jobs. One of his suggestions, the establishment of a cotton mill, was to be discussed for another 40 years, leading to an aborted effort to set up a mill at Nelson in the early 1960s with government assistance. Another of Reakes's suggestions was that the Government should attempt to push beyond earlier research ('not encouraging') into the establishment of a sugar beet industry. He also had hopes for a vegetable oil industry and a chemicals industry to supply local needs.

Ultimately of more significance was Reakes's suggestion that efforts be made to promote fruit-canning and tobacco-growing. Some small plantings of tobacco in Hawkes Bay had 'given good results', he claimed, and the earlier small subsidies to fruit preservers were proving successful. Reakes also pushed for more research into the use of forestry by-products. He was adamant that paper and stationery products could be made locally, and believed there was a future for furniture-making that used New Zealand's native timbers. He made a similar case for leather.[33]

Reakes's suggestions came at a time when interest was mounting in scientific and industrial research. This was being promoted from abroad as well as by the New Zealand Institute, which was a group of scientists that had enjoyed a government grant of £500 pa since 1869 enabling it to publish its findings. The Industries Committee strongly recommended that a Board of Science and Industry be established to coordinate research throughout the country. However, much of the wartime hype that drove state experimentation waned in the early 1920s with the onset of recession and a fall in government revenue. Establishment of the Department of Scientific and Industrial Research was delayed until 1926.[34] The political will to drive industrialisation flared only spasmodically during the 1920s.

In the face of falling overseas prices, ministers were trimming budgets by the middle of 1921. Serious consideration was given to abolishing the Board of Trade. The Department of Industries and Commerce also came under fire. There was consternation in the manufacturing world as news of these possibilities spread. On 1 December 1921 the Industrial Association of Canterbury wrote to the Minister of Industries and Commerce, E. P. Lee, telling him that the manufacturers of Canterbury viewed such talk 'with considerable alarm'; the work of Industries and Commerce was 'highly valued'. Lee responded that nothing more than amalgamation with another department was being considered. But that possibility, too, brought opposition from manufacturers, who were beginning to see in the department a guardian of their special interests. Ministers backed off. However, the work of the Board of Trade, particularly its price surveillance activities, scaled down at the end of 1922 with McDonald's retirement. A senior officer, J. W. Collins, told the new Minister of Industries and

Commerce, William Downie Stewart, that the department simply lacked the personnel to handle complaints, and that some businesses – he cited Northern Roller Mills – were not cooperating with the Board, and were refusing access to their books. The Cabinet agreed to amend the Act, believing that the return of a more stable economic environment no longer required a standing Board. The Board of Trade Amendment Act 1923 transferred its price surveillance powers to the Minister of Industries and Commerce. The minister could establish a Board if need be; once one had been set up it could conduct what amounted to a judicial inquiry into prices.[35] Price controls, principally covering bread, were occasionally gazetted, but others were repealed. By 1933 only seven sets of regulations under the Act continued in force.

However, the experience of the wartime Board of Trade was instructive. In a recent study of the World War I economy, A. J. Everton concludes with the words: 'In most cases the interventions were . . . unnecessary, unsuccessful in that they did not attain the desired end, or counter productive, in that they aggravated the problem they were intended to remedy, or all three. . . .'[36] It took many years for politicians to learn these lessons. There was greater success with price control during World War II but it came about in the context of a massive economic stabilisation exercise, something that was tolerable only in emergency circumstances. The history of price controls in peacetime has never been reassuring.

The wider role of Industries and Commerce was another matter. Reakes's submissions to the Industries Committee in 1919 reflected the growing public belief that governments had a responsibility to promote conditions where industries could flourish. The provision of jobs, and the saving of precious foreign exchange were matters much discussed. While many manufacturers resented what they saw as busybodying by the Board of Trade, most liked the access to ministers and officials which the bureaucratic structure afforded them. Regional manufacturers' associations and ultimately a national federation emerged during the 1920s. The practice of inviting ministers to industry functions developed. At conferences and dinners regular refrains were sung: protection was essential, and the public should be encouraged to buy 'Our own first, British second, foreign last'.[37]

The Department of Industries and Commerce reflected these views. Drawing on their wartime experience, officers were developing and promoting an economically interventionist culture, with a distinctly nationalistic bias. Long before Sutch joined the department it was a strong advocate of protection, state funding and any other form of assistance that might broaden the base of the New Zealand economy, or save foreign exchange. Public servants, many of them inexperienced in the world of factories, commerce, domestic or export trade, promoted views acceptable to politicians, producers, the public, and ultimately their own advancement. In the process they had a major impact on the direction taken by New Zealand manufacturing. The country was beginning to enter a cosy, some felt smug, era where the respective roles of the players became blurred. Bureaucrats and businessmen talked with each other, and then to the politicians; all of them then consulted the Minister of Finance. After arriving at a conclusion – one that would usually cost the taxpayer – they jointly informed the public of what had been decided, supposedly for the greater good. This relationship lasted another 60 years until subsidies and controls were largely abolished. Soon after, the department which was then known as Trade and Industry, was abolished as well.

The impact of World War I on New Zealand extended well beyond manpower and prices. Issues more personal to people could not be avoided. When the troops departed to the front they dislocated lives, families and financial commitments. Servicemen's mortgage payments were in danger of falling behind. The Government stepped in. In the Mortgages Extension Act passed on 14 August 1914 the rights and powers of mortgagees were limited for the duration of the war. Mortgages could not be called up, nor actions commenced; the sale of a mortgage was prohibited, as was entering into possession. Only interest on a mortgage needed to be paid. As the war dragged on, the life of the Act, intended initially to be one year, was extended until it was finally repealed in 1919.[38] The Act was a legislative intervention between mortgagor and mortgagee that riled some, and was recalled when similar interventions were undertaken by the Coalition Government during the Depression.

Contributions to the National Provident Fund and to friendly societies were equally vulnerable to wartime dislocations. By the end of 1915 more than 1500 contributors to the National Provident Fund had left for the front. Having preached the gospel of self-help, the Government found it had no option but to assist. Massey's Government decided to pay into the fund a sum equal to half the servicemen's contributions during their absence.[39] Friendly societies were already pressured by competition from the NPF and the more generous array of benefits it paid. By March 1917 the absence of 5488 friendly society contributors was causing them serious cash problems. Already in November 1914 the Government had decided to subsidise the reinsurance of death benefits that the societies offered – a promise that during the first three years of war cost the Government nearly

£12,000, and led to the establishment of the Departmental Reinsurance Fund.[40]

By 1917 many friendly societies were struggling to keep their soldiers in 'good standing' with their sickness funds. The crisis in liquidity necessitated the Government paying £10,000 into friendly societies' sickness and funeral funds in 1918.[41] Servicemen contributing to the Government Superannuation Fund had their status within the fund protected in the War Legislation Amendment Act 1916. The Government was not the only public agency helping to provide for servicemen and their families. Many local authorities also chose to make provision for dependent relatives. Legislative authorisation for this was provided in the War Contributions Validation Act 1914.

Since the 1840s governments had provided pensions for servicemen who had seen active duty, or their widows and dependants. Before the outbreak of war in 1914 there were already 568 pensions being paid for service in the New Zealand wars of the 1860s and the South African war of 1899–1902. The War Pensions Act 1915 provided pensions to World War I veterans or their families, even those who had not seen active service overseas.[42] In 1921 pensions were being paid to 31,764 soldiers, widows or dependants, the average annual pension amounting to £55 per recipient. This sum was nearly as much as the average widow's benefit at the time, and substantially more than the £37 being paid to old-age pensioners.

Miners incapacitated by phthisis, to whom Massey's Government extended pensions in 1915, received higher payments, at an average of more than £62 pa. These pensions, however, stood apart from others being paid. A fund set up in 1911 into which mine owners contributed collapsed with the virtual cessation of gold-mining at the outbreak of war. Unless the Government took over responsibility for the pensioners their benefits would cease. With an ill grace, Massey's Government took charge of the pensions. It was, as J. T. Paul noted during debates on the issue, the first occasion when the taxpayer assumed responsibility for compensation for an occupational disease.[43]

The notion that the State owed much to its servicemen had some similarities to the earlier obligations felt towards settlers. It underlay other efforts on behalf of returned soldiers. The aim of the Repatriation Boards established in 1918 was 'to secure for [every discharged soldier] a position in the community at least as good as that relinquished by him when he joined the colours'.[44] Such goals for returned men were not new. In 1903 Seddon's Government settled 36 Boer War veterans on farms around Te Kuiti.[45] In the Discharged Soldiers Settlement Act passed in October 1915 the Crown took the power to set aside Crown land for soldiers. A sum of £50,000 was provided to help soldiers settle. Terms of occupancy of the land were more generous to servicemen than what was currently available from the State Advances Office. The Act was extended in 1917; the Crown could now purchase private land on the open market and appropriate money to help with housing. Eventually 10,500 men took the opportunity to settle on farm land; another 12,000 were helped to purchase urban sections and to build, or purchase existing homes. Inevitably there were some servicemen who found employment hard to come by. Small 'Unemployment Sustenance Allowances' were paid to 188 men during the recession of 1921–22, and several training schemes for disabled soldiers were also set up. An average payment of £55 per trainee was spent on training and sustenance.[46]

Many returned soldiers gained access to land that might otherwise have been beyond their means. However, the Crown's active purchasing policy helped inflate land prices in the later stages of the war. Some soldiers who bought privately with government assistance paid high prices and suffered the highest failure rates when commodity and land prices collapsed in the early 1920s. As Ashley Gould has shown, all soldier settlers 'became dependent upon the financial assistance of the government'. When soldiers got into financial trouble the Crown foreclosed only as a matter of last resort. The number of failures compares well with those of farmers in general during the years to 1935. Yet, the soldier settlement scheme suffered a poor reputation. This had more to do, it seems, with soldiers' unreal expectations than any intrinsic fault in Massey's scheme, or the way it was administered. The political promise of 'a home fit for heroes' had been over-sold, and was impossible to deliver.[47]

The influenza epidemic in the last months of 1918 has been described as 'New Zealand's worst recorded natural disaster'. A total of 8500 people lost their lives. The death rates were at their highest among Maori, especially in the King Country, where there was as yet no hospital, and in the crowded inner-city suburbs of Auckland and Wellington. Massey later estimated the monetary cost of the epidemic in extra health services at £194,000.[48] Coming at the tail end of the war and affecting many servicemen returning from the front, this domestic emergency called for a government response in keeping with the efforts made on behalf of soldiers. Since many parents with dependants were swept away by the 'plague', the Cabinet, without statutory authority, decided to build on to its existing pension structure what came to be known as Epidemic Allowances. Paid out initially by local hospital boards but passed back to the Pensions Department for administrative purposes in 1920, a total of 939 were paid that year. Most recipients were widows, although 89 widowers also qualified. The average pension was a comparatively generous £83 pa. The number of Epidemic Allowances fell quickly in the 1920s as children reached an age where they were expected to fend for themselves. The last allowance was paid in 1938.[49] Nonetheless, a precedent had been established that would be recalled in later years.

The epidemic placed a strain on health services. This gave rise to an interesting public debate about the extent to which local or central authorities should be responsible for health care. The expanding role of the Department of Public Health and its powers in relation to local government were specially controversial. Departmental officers had been pushing for a more centralised health service before war broke out, and in 1915 they persuaded the Government to take the legislative power to declare some housing unfit for human habitation.[50] Departmental officers believed they needed even more powers at the expense of local authorities. They used the epidemic to advance such arguments. Some local authorities fed the move to centralise health services by arguing that the department should be doing more and asserting that it had been 'caught napping' with the epidemic.[51] When a Royal Commission sat early in 1919 to examine the causes of the plague and the steps necessary to prevent a recurrence, an opinionated departmental officer, Dr Robert Makgill, criticised the legislative status of the department and of existing hospital boards, arguing that this had limited the department's effectiveness during the epidemic. He recommended passage of new health legislation to strengthen the department's role.

Such statements provoked an angry retort from the Minister of Public Health, G. W. Russell. In a detailed statement to the commission Russell outlined the more traditional government concept of the relationship between central and local government in matters pertaining to health.

> It is not the policy of this or any Government to take away from the functions of city councils and other local bodies, but rather to enlarge those functions and to employ the Public Health Department as far as possible as an advisory and supervising authority. . . . The idea of the Public Health Department assuming anything more than supervising authority and powers of direction regarding sanitation, drainage etc., would be too ridiculous for words. . . . The people of New Zealand would never for one moment tolerate the establishment of a bureaucratic system as regards health or any other subject.[52]

Russell's was a minimalist approach to government. By this time it commanded less public support than in the Liberals' heyday. An MP of seventeen years' standing, Russell lost his seat at the election in December 1919.

Makgill's centralist philosophy continued to be heard. It strongly influenced the Health Act of 1920, which, in Geoffrey Rice's words, 'radically restructured New Zealand's public health administration'. The Act created seven separate divisions within the department with responsibility for public hygiene, hospitals, nursing, school hygiene, dental hygiene, child welfare and Maori hygiene. While local authorities were still expected to contribute to the cost of their hospitals, central control advanced substantially. The Chief Health Officer was henceforth designated the Director-General of Health, ruling over a department which grew steadily more powerful over the years ahead.[53]

Financing public hospitals bedevilled governments for the rest of the century. Under the Hospitals and Charitable Institutions Act 1909 local boards were expected to raise 50 per cent of the running costs of the hospitals in their districts. Local authorities were obliged to contribute. However, raising the local component of hospital costs by way of rates, especially in low income areas, was always difficult. Successive amendments to the legislation gave the Government the power to advance money to hospitals in anticipation of rating income, and the formula for calculating subsidies was constantly rejigged, usually at the urging of harassed chairmen of local boards. Boards resorted to some ingenious methods to milk government subsidies, especially those that had traditionally been paid on gifts and bequests. In December 1920 an Audit Office inspector perused the books of the West Coast boards. He reported: 'I am as a child in the hands of the West Coast Boards when it comes to claiming subsidies. Recently the Grey Board received a donation of a truck of coal and they point out to me that by drawing a cheque on it and receiving it back they are able to get 24/- in the £ on its presumable value, and I do not see that I can stop them.'[54] Eighteen months later the West Coast boards, which were always on the lookout for gifts that might qualify for subsidies, received a donation of money from the Kumara Racing Club. It seems clear that it was money that ought to have been paid to the club's creditors.[55]

Hospital boards with uncertain income flows from local authorities had difficulty budgeting. The Government experienced the same problem, especially since the amount of money required to subsidise gifts and bequests could never be accurately predicted. The more that central government insisted on localities paying their hospital dues and enforced penalties on those that fell behind, the angrier local boards became. A testy bunch of chairmen complained to Massey in July 1923 that government subsidies which purported to be 50 per cent of the total running costs had fallen to 42 per cent. The Government responded by amending the Act and providing relief for boards such as those in the Far North where it was proving difficult to collect rates levied on Maori-owned land. At the same time, other boards in wealthier areas such as Tauranga received substantial bequests that qualified for subsidies, resulting in the construction of facilities not enjoyed elsewhere, and for which further government maintenance subsidies now became payable.

During the 1920s subsidies to hospital boards rose at a much faster rate than inflation. In September 1927 Treasury's Chief Inspector, Bernard Ashwin, had some trenchant comments to make about the system:

> The Hospital Boards have at present not much inducement to exercise economy. Their rates are collected for them by the City Councils and other Local Bodies, and these Bodies receive all the odium that accrues from the collection of rates, although they merely act as agent in the matter. In the second place, subsidies from the Consolidated Fund are paid practically automatically. Further, it seems likely that in many cases the receipt of voluntary contributions and bequests (and particularly the latter) instead of relieving the charge on the ratepayer and the taxpayer merely increase their burdens. For instance, large bequests plus the State subsidy thereon are often used to erect additional buildings that are really not needed and would not otherwise have been erected. The State bears half the cost of the capital extravagance, and thereafter the State and the ratepayers have to share the cost of maintenance.[56]

Regional disparities in hospital facilities that remain a problem today began showing up in the 1920s. The Government had not set out to help more affluent areas, but this was an unintended consequence of their incremental subsidy system.

The rigours of World War I impacted in other ways on the relationship between the New Zealand people and their government. The popular demand for 'equality of sacrifice' was one factor in the introduction of conscription in 1916. More important, as Paul Baker has shown, was an urge for social control that was at its most fierce among the growing Protestant middle class. Industrial unrest, a perceptible rise in the number of Irish immigrants, working class 'idleness', drunkenness, prostitution and declining church attendance created the urge for more social discipline and efficiency.[57] In the years between 1909 and 1914 compulsory military training for young men became the norm. Dr Truby King enlisted political support – and in 1921, financial help as well – for his Plunket system of baby care which aimed at improving 'the health of the family, the nation, and the Empire'.[58]

The temperance movement, which had been growing for many years, came into its own during the war. Richard Newman has shown that the drive behind demands for prohibition that won the support of 55.8 per cent of the voters in a poll on 7 December 1911 was strongest in prosperous middle-class areas. The same people urged Massey to reduce drinking hours in two large parliamentary petitions presented in 1915 and 1916. Eventually on the recommendation of a self-important group of businessmen whom Massey appointed to a National Efficiency Board, the Government banned 'shouting' or 'treating' in hotels. In 1917 hotels were obliged to close at 6 pm. Consuming liquor in restaurants at any time when hotel bars were closed became an offence, while serving alcohol with meals in hotels after 8 pm was also outlawed.[59] Jock Phillips observes that by these actions, 'barricades had been erected to contain the drinking culture, and an uneasy peace prevailed virtually unchanged for the next 50 years'. Many of these prohibitions, some of them unenforceable, lasted until the liquor laws were partially relaxed in 1960. A Special Licensing Poll on liquor took place on 10 April 1919. Only a huge majority for continuance from returning servicemen saved New Zealand from prohibition.[60]

Other areas of personal life were the subject of legislative intrusion. In the Prisoners' Detention Act 1915 and the Social Hygiene Act 1917 the Government armed itself with greater powers to prevent the spread of sexually transmitted diseases,[61] while the Cinematograph-film Censorship Act 1916 made it unlawful to exhibit any film unless it had been approved by a censor. The Act stipulated that 'Such approval shall not be given in the case of any film which, in the opinion of the censor, depicts any matter that is against public order and decency, or the exhibition of which for any reason is, in the opinion of the censor, undesirable in the public interest'. In the War Legislation Amendment Act 1916 it became an offence punishable by a fine to use any word with reference to the war that 'may be offensive to public sentiment'.[62]

Massey's National Efficiency Board established in February 1917 was given a wide brief to review the economy in general, to inquire into industrial efficiency, and to recommend such measures as it thought necessary to reduce the cost of living, promote thrift and deter luxury. Chaired by William Ferguson, this unpaid group of Government supporters produced a lengthy report with a distinctly Calvinist bias. They recommended that the number of race days should be reduced, that there should be no new permits for picture theatres, and there should be less 'waste' on imported

Peace celebrations in Nelson, 19 July 1919. Nelson Provincial Museum

luxuries such as cars. With a zeal that would have inspired today's anti-smoking lobbyists, they recommended that bread should be at least twelve hours old before it was sold because stale bread was 'healthier' than fresh bread. Moreover, bakers would not need to begin work so early in the morning. The Board went too far for Massey's Liberal colleagues; in his 1917 budget Ward specifically knocked back those suggestions that might reduce the Government's Customs revenue.[63] But there could be no denying that there was an appetite for a socially active state among many of the country's more affluent citizens, especially those who were too old to fight, but who wanted to use the occasion of war to circumscribe the pleasures of the young.

By the end of the war there were two new forces pushing inter-ventionism. The first was the Returned Servicemen's Association. Its initial conference in Christchurch in May 1919 was alive with demands for more government action on behalf of returned soldiers. Higher allowances, better hospital facilities, and more 'courageous' treatment of venereal disease were just some of the topics discussed.[64] Ministers quickly learned the wisdom of attending annual conferences and listening intently to the R.S.A.'s pleadings.

An even more effective advocate of centralisation – since it involved itself directly in the political process – was the New Zealand Labour Party. Throughout the 1920s the Liberal and Reform parties manoeuvred carefully around this rising political force. Products of rapid urbanisation and a flourishing trade union culture that was partly encouraged by the I.C.&A. Act,[65] several political labour leagues emerged after 1905. They were determined to gain parliamentary representation for working men and women. David McLaren, secretary of the Wellington Waterside Workers' Union, was their first success when he won the seat of Wellington East in the election of 1908, courtesy of the short-lived second-ballot procedure.[66] The second ballot helped four Labour MPs into Parliament in 1911, and two more followed in by-elections in 1913. During the war six Labour or Social Democratic MPs under the leadership of Australian-born Wellington lawyer, Alfred Hindmarsh, constituted an unofficial opposition to the National Government. In July 1916 the various labour groupings united to form the New Zealand Labour Party. In 1918 three by-election victories added further strength to Labour's team.[67]

The ideological ingredients that went into the Labour Party's emerging philosophy were many and varied.[68] Harry Holland, who succeeded Hindmarsh as leader, was an eclectic reader whose background as a journalist kept him with pen in hand for most of his life. He produced many pamphlets. Steeped in unionist theory and socialist thought, he had edited the *International Socialist Review* in Sydney before coming in 1912 to New Zealand, where he soon became editor of Labour's *Maoriland Worker*. He held the position for five years before entering Parliament in May 1918 as MP for Grey.[69] Holland's chief strategic goal was to force the Liberal and Reform parties to merge, thus clearing the way for the Labour Party to establish a constituency with working people. Along with several other Australians such as Michael Joseph Savage, Robert Semple and Bill Parry, a Scotsman, Peter Fraser, and an Irishman, James McCombs, Holland helped to further the cause of socialism that had been developing under the wing of the 'Red Feds' since 1908.[70]

Central to Labour's philosophy was a belief in the essential benevolence of public activity and the need for government controls over private enterprise. Hindmarsh declared in his maiden speech that he favoured an extension of the functions of the State, and that they should be administered in a 'just, honest and straightforward' manner.[71] In one of his early speeches Peter Fraser, who won the Wellington Central by-election in October 1918, denounced private ownership of rental housing as 'a complete failure'. He urged the Government to use the labour of returning soldiers to build houses.[72] Holland wanted a more active Department of Health and an end to all profiteering. He disliked the War Regulations, labelling them both ineffective and 'the autocracy of mediocrity'. In a bold declaration of Labour's philosophy, Holland told Parliament:

> We do not come merely to attempt to make a change to individuals on the Government benches. We of the Labour Party come to endeavour to effect a change of classes at the fountain of power. We come proclaiming boldly and fearlessly the Socialist objective of the Labour movement throughout New Zealand; and we make no secret of the fact that we seek to rebuild society on a basis in which work and not wealth will be the measure of a man's worth. . . . We shall often shock the unthinking members of this House, and . . . often infuriate the intolerant members. But one thing is certain: we shall in the end succeed in converting the intelligent section.[73]

After he entered Parliament in 1919 Savage interested himself in finance, and argued for a state bank. In his maiden speech he attacked overseas borrowing, declaring that he did not wish to borrow anywhere. 'I do not want to give the Bank of New Zealand, the National Bank, or any other bank the right to use the public credit for private gain. I would sooner have a State bank, and use the public credit for the public good.'[74] These were the early days of a movement that succeeded after a lengthy apprenticeship during the 1920s, and considerable refinement of theory, in establishing hegemony over New Zealand's workers. Labour was to preach a philosophy of state intervention for the rest of the century.

By 1919 both the Liberal and Reform parties feared Labour. Before the election Massey conducted a scare campaign against it, portraying Labour's leading figures as Bolsheviks; his deputy, Sir James Allen, claimed that Holland was 'vindictive, disloyal, and a reveller in filth'.[75] Ward's Liberals adopted a radical manifesto for the election in the hope of outbidding Labour's appeal to workers.[76] It did them no good. Their seats fell from 33 to 19, and Ward lost Awarua, which he had held for 33 years. On 17 December 1919 Labour benefited from working-class hostility to rising prices and perceived profiteering, and nearly trebled the votes received by Labour groups in 1914. With almost 24 per cent of the national vote and a total of eight seats it was now a force to be reckoned with.

Over the longer term, Massey's Government tried countering Labour's growing appeal with further state intervention. In March 1920 the Prime Minister restructured his ministry, promoting to Minister of Public Works the war hero, Gordon Coates, who was known for his activist approach to government. Coates soon pushed ahead with road and rail construction and with electricity production.[77] Massey's budget of 27 July 1920 hinted at further government activity on many other fronts. Yet, at the end of an activist statement he ended with the words: 'The happiness and prosperity of the people . . . can best be secured by furthering the spirit of self-reliance, industry, and thrift which has been characteristic of our people . . .'.[78] Massey was revealing the degree of philosophical schizophrenia that lay behind his Government's policies. Claiming always to believe in private enterprise, his administration had become the most interventionist in New Zealand's history. In later years while the gospel of self-help marched hand in hand with state initiatives, it was invariably half a step behind.

Whatever Massey's intentions in the middle of 1920, the collapse of export prices towards the end of the year forced his Government to retrench. On 17 December he instructed his ministers to tell their departments to reduce spending 'as much as possible, having due regard to efficiency'. Any new expenditure had to be checked first with Treasury. In April 1921 a Government Service Commission was established to review public expenditure.[79] Top of its list of items for review was the now bloated public service. The number of employees had grown during the war and, after the introduction of minimum salaries for civil servants in June 1914, the cost of the bureaucracy rose steadily.[80] Sloppy work habits in the public service became a topic of adverse press comment in 1918.[81] In 1921 every department was requested to present the commission with a list of economies. Most suggestions minimised staff layoffs, relying instead on what came to be known in later years as 'the sinking lid'; employees who died or retired would not be replaced. Wages and salaries were cut back by between 7 and 10 per cent, and the bulk of employees in the Public Works Department were reclassified as relief workers. Railways made 105 men redundant. The total number of public servants declined until 1924 when they began inexorably to rise again. The Arbitration Court also reduced the basic wage by five shillings per week. Despite these moves the Government was obliged to use some of its accumulated wartime surpluses to balance its budgets.[82]

Farmers and stock and station agents became gravely apprehensive about the unprecedentedly steep drop in New Zealand's earnings overseas in 1920.[83] In the financial year 1920–21 New Zealand's imports cost £67.4 million, while exports brought in only £48.2 million. It was the largest deficit in overseas trade in New Zealand's history to date. While Massey was overseas for some months in 1921 the Government moved slowly. However, the emergence of a Country Party in rural areas galvanised the

Prime Minister into action on his return. The new party was arguing for credit reform, mortgage interest reductions, a state shipping line and state marketing of exports. The limitations on mortgagees' rights were revived, and on 19 December 1921 Massey announced that he was beginning discussions with producers' organisations with a view to taking over the export of all meat.[84] Despite criticism from exporting firms with a stake in the status quo, the Meat-export Control Act passed through Parliament on 11 February 1922. It was described as 'an Act to make provision for the appointment of a meat producers' board with power to control the meat-export trade'. A lengthy preamble described the current crisis and concluded that there was a need for a board 'with power to act as the agent of the producers in respect of the preparation, storage and shipment of meat and its disposal beyond New Zealand'. To a point, the legislation was permissive; a board consisting of two government nominees plus five elected by producers was given the discretion to adopt absolute or limited control over meat exports. But whichever option was chosen, meat producers could be levied in order to pay for the board's costs. In the meantime, the Minister of Finance was empowered to advance money to the board for operating costs. The board was deemed to be the agent of the owners of the meat.[85]

This was the first of what became a raft of export boards with their own acts of Parliament. The activities of the Meat Board bore some resemblance to the recent war-time commandeer; farmers were paid for their produce while a more distant authority, albeit theoretically under their control, accepted the responsibility for shipping and on-selling, principally in London.

Massey gave a rambling speech in justification of the Bill when he moved its second reading in February 1922. He argued that 'the setting-up and bringing into operation of a pool, controlled partly by the Government, partly by the producers' representatives and partly, probably, by commercial men, will be the best safeguard we could possibly have, because it will be their business to prevent any wrong doing in connection with the export of our produce'. The Labour Party declared itself in favour of 'State marketing' but felt the legislation fell short of the ideal. According to Holland, the Bill 'reads something like a species of high-brow syndicalism. It certainly does amount to a private profiteering department of industry having the whole credit of the State behind it.' Yet while the State accepted responsibility for the marketing of meat, in his opinion it lacked effective control.[86] This line of criticism from the left would be repeated in future as further planks of the welfare state were put in place and the roles of producers, workers, 'middlemen' and the State became entwined.

Not to be outdone by meat producers, many dairymen lobbied for the same system. For many years the National Dairy Association had been discussing what it saw as the need for cooperative marketing of dairy produce. Leaders of the dairy industry watched the work of producer boards in the United States and Scandinavia. In the six years before 1914 there were discussions between North Island butter factories about the advantages of careful control over the shipping to, and selling of produce on the London market.[87] In October 1921 the Government began experimenting with drip-feeding supplies of butter on to the London market in the hope that prices would improve. They did not. Instead, the British Government contemplated releasing the last of its war time stockpiles of New Zealand butter to satisfy local demand. Massey had an uncomfortable Christmas while cables flew back and forth to London. New Zealand's High Commission struggled to avert a catastrophe.[88]

In March 1922 a Dairy-produce Export Control Bill was introduced. Dairymen quickly revealed what became their identifying characteristic: they were more disputatious than their meat and wool brethren. While a majority always supported the legislation, there were many who regarded the Bill, in the words of one of Massey's correspondents, as 'drastic, arbitrary and unjust'.[89] Debate raged, fuelled by the propaganda of proprietary companies with an interest in the export of butter. They portrayed Massey's legislation as state socialism. With an election coming up, Massey decided not to force the issue. The Bill was held over and was not passed until 28 August 1923.[90] It was to be brought into force by proclamation only if it received majority support in a referendum of dairy producers – which it eventually got. There were 56,000 dairy producers entitled to vote. Some 24,233 (43.2 per cent) chose not to vote; of those who did vote, 22,284 (39.7 per cent of the total) supported compulsory pooling and selling of butter, while 9255 (16.5 per cent) opposed.[91]

Further producer boards followed. A Fruit-export Control Act and a Honey-export Control Act were passed in 1924. Together the boards can be seen as a milestone in the development of relations between the Government and private entrepreneurs. With the experience of wartime controls behind them, both had come to the view that better financial outcomes for individuals could be achieved through collective action rather than individual effort. It was a conclusion that other farmers and manufacturers arrived at in the years to come.

Chapter 6

The State Under Challenge: The 1920s and the Depression

The years of almost continuous prosperity from 1895 to 1920 ill prepared New Zealanders for the uncertainties of the 1920s. Export prices fell in 1920, rose again later in the decade, slid, then skyrocketed briefly before plunging to earth after 1929. Nerves rubbed raw by the bitterness of war were soothed in the first half of 1920 when prosperity and progress were on everyone's lips; they began trembling again during the recession that dominated the next two years. Unease crept back towards the end of 1925 and lingered as unemployment slowly gathered pace in the winter of 1926. Few private companies were now contemplating expansion. Yearning for pre-war certainties intensified, as average wealth, after rising steadily at the end of the war and peaking in 1924, fell away over the following decade.[1]

The 1920s were the first occasion when government intervention in the economy was seriously questioned. State trading enterprises such as Railways and State Coal Mines began losing money. Some businessmen said that the Government had overreached itself, that it was not capable of being a competent business manager, and that taxes were therefore higher than they needed to be – a point that was disputed by a Royal Commission into taxation in 1924.[2] Stronger forces weighed in to support further state activity. The era of government-led expansion, in which railways had played such a key role, was far from exhausted. Considerable faith in the magic of rail remained, especially in the more remote parts of the country that were yet to be linked into the national grid. Governments realised that the appearance of a railways gang in a marginal electorate during the run up to an election was good politics.[3] State unions agitated for better working conditions. When depression came and unemployment rose rapidly, workers expected the State to provide jobs, and when services were cut back, they rioted in 1932 with demands for more publicly provided relief. As prosperity eluded many, the New Zealand public valiantly held on to an article of faith: governments could do anything. Having won the war, politicians could easily win the peace and conquer depression. Confidence in what some called 'scientific' planning encouraged governments to intervene further. Coming after a long period of uninterrupted prosperity, the 1920s bore similarities to the 1970s and early 1980s. However, by then the State's apparatus had become top-heavy and was difficult to sustain; confidence in the omnipotent State was declining rapidly.

In December 1922 Massey's Reform Government faced its toughest election to date. It was finally saved on a parliamentary confidence motion in March 1923 because its opponents could not cooperate. The Government kept a tight rein on expenditure that year and efforts were made to improve the effectiveness of governmental activity. Talk of the need for more 'business efficiency' was common; on the eve of the 1925 election Reform borrowed the slogan 'more business in government; less government in business' that the Republican Party had nearly pummelled to death in the American presidential election the previous year. Sloganeering disguised a reality of the 1920s; there was more government in business by the end of the decade. Moreover, the rate of intervention stepped up during the depression that followed.

As Minister of Public Works, Gordon Coates played a major role in promoting state activity. In its early days the Reform Government had hoped to involve locals and private companies in railway construction, believing that if communities seriously wanted a new rail line then they would put their money where their mouths were. A Local Railways Act was passed in 1914 which set out the procedures which communities were required to follow. Little happened. Several small company lines were constructed, most of them between three and five miles in length.[4] The war intervened, and by the early 1920s state construction predominated. Despite an assertion in 1923 that he would test the efficiency of the PWD's contracting gangs by letting private contractors build branch railway lines, at no point does Coates seem seriously to have considered contracting out all construction work. On taking office in 1920 he was faced with a huge backlog of projects. Most public works had been suspended for the duration of the war, with only the Otira tunnel continuing at normal speed. Many of the stalled projects were rail links that had been promised at earlier elections. As Vogel had discovered half a century earlier, only the State seemed to be in a position to achieve quick results.[5]

Coates found himself subject to conflicting pressures. In the early 1920s it was impossible to ignore demands for more and better roads. By then there were more than 20,000 cars in New Zealand, and the number increased rapidly during the 1920s. Railways, the State's biggest trading

The activist Gordon Coates, Minister of Public Works 1920–25, Prime Minister 1925–28 and Minister of Finance during the depression's darkest days, 1933–35. Evening Post

department, earned the most revenue ever in 1920–21, but from then on passenger numbers slid because of competition from cars and buses. Work on roads was beginning to cancel out profits from rail.[6]

The story of how Coates slowed some railway lines, purchased new equipment, and concentrated on completing three main trunk lines, has been told elsewhere. Likewise, his moves to centralise main roads construction.[7] However, despite the Government's efforts to cut back on wasteful duplication and a peremptory knockback to the railway unions when they went on strike in April 1924, the construction and running costs of Railways continued to escalate. When Massey added the Railways portfolio to Coates's Public Works responsibilities in 1923, the minister was faced with a conundrum. On the one hand, Railway profits were sliding; on the other, the Government increasingly used Railways to mop up pockets of unemployment. The unions pushed for shorter hours, better superannuation, and more Railway houses. The minister tightened administrative procedures and searched for ways other than staff layoffs to reduce costs. He tried to avoid constructing lines likely to prove uneconomic.[8] But the intractable financial problem was the steady rise in staff; wages constituted 70 per cent of total expenditure. In 1918–19 Railways employed 12,391; in 1924–25 this number had risen to 16,353 and by 1929–30 there were 19,410 on the payroll. By this time nearly 5000 were casual workers. The key factor in keeping work contracts mostly 'in house' was almost certainly the Government's desire to retain an employment agency close at hand at difficult moments. It proved to be an expensive exercise. The average cost of constructing lines in 1930 was £35,000 per mile; estimates for new work were nearly always exceeded. The State was unable to prevent cost overruns.[9]

Ward's assurances in 1906 that Railways would return 3 per cent on capital did not take into account the interest on the money that was constantly being borrowed to develop new lines. On the one hand, Coates boldly asserted in 1923 that Railways 'have never been regarded . . . as a profit-making concern', and he doubted whether the public would approve of them being 'guided solely by considerations of financial return'; on the other hand, he was also pledged to 'business-like' methods, and it had never been envisaged that publicly owned transport services would become a burden on the taxpayer. Comments from journals such as the *New Zealand National Review* to the effect that Railways lacked business acumen stung Coates.[10] He agreed to the restructuring of Railways' accounts from 1 April 1925. Interest charges of 4.125 per cent (subsequently 5 per cent) were included on accumulated borrowings which then totalled £50 million. Operating returns immediately sank below target. Notwithstanding this, the department continued to take on more staff in 1926 and kept scheduling services that were poorly patronised. In 1926–27 Railways' gross revenue fell while costs continued to rise. The Government had no option but to pay a subsidy of £445,000 to keep branch lines operational; a further £193,000 went into various Railway superannuation arrangements.[11] The following year ministers agreed to reduce freight rates as part of a programme to encourage New Zealand production. This move further reduced Railways' income.[12] Not only was the State now openly in breach of its guidelines for operating public utilities; it seemed also to be losing control of its accounts. The Minister of Finance, William Downie Stewart, kept preaching the virtues of balanced budgets. Yet, if more and more subsidies had to be paid, balancing the budget could be achieved only by higher taxation. Moreover, continued borrowing was needed to maintain progress on an assortment of government construction schemes in order to justify keeping so many people on the State's payroll. All this was required at a time when earnings from exports were trending downwards and the Government's revenue was far from buoyant.

In 1928 a number of senior public servants as well as the press began grappling with Railways' dilemma. Coates, who was both Prime Minister and Minister of Railways by this time, sought the advice of his most trusted adviser, F. W. Furkert, who was Under-Secretary of the Public Works Department and Chairman of the Main Highways Board. Much of Furkert's professional career had been devoted to railway construction dating back to the days of the Midland Railway. He wrestled with Railways' predicament and reported in May 1928 that due to competition from roads, railways might no longer be worth the money invested in them. Instead of questioning the indisputable fact that Railways had become an employment agency as much as a transport service, Furkert suggested that road users, who were regarded as responsible for the problems of rail, ought to bear the cost. In effect he was arguing for a tax on motor fuel to support a mode of transport that the public was deserting. And since Railways were being used for the social purpose of minimising unemployment, their accounts should be topped up from the Consolidated Fund.[13]

A few weeks later a *Dominion* editorial supported Furkert's suggestions; it hoped, naively, that state subsidies would not distort the transport market or impact unfairly on private enterprise. Treasury endorsed Furkert's suggestion of a motor fuel tax, but opposed government subsidies.[14] Yet, in 1930 Railways required a government subsidy of approximately £1.2 million a year to keep functioning. Accumulated losses during the previous five years totalled £2 million.[15]

Furkert's ideas led in time to a raft of measures designed to protect Railways, ostensibly to safeguard the public's investment in their construction, but in reality to hide the fact that the department's core business had become as much concerned with welfare as transport. Large operational subsidies became a recurring feature of Railways' accounts in later years, and this trend was interrupted only briefly by the efforts of the Government Railways Board that managed Railways between 1931 and 1936.[16] Given the increasing competition that railways were encountering, the 1930 Royal Commission on Railways argued that they deserved protection. The Transport Licensing Act in November 1931 gave the Government wide powers to issue orders-in-council establishing licensing districts and to control the means by which goods were transported within these districts. A limit of 30 miles was soon imposed beyond which road transport was prohibited from carrying goods. When this monopoly provision proved to be no cure-all, the limit was extended in 1961 and again in 1977, when it was fixed at 150 kilometres. This monopoly for Railways was not lifted until passage of the Transport Amendment Bill (No.5) 1983, by which time restrictions on the cartage of goods by road were vigorously opposed by private enterprise and had long been flouted by trucking firms, with the connivance of producers.[17]

A wish to protect the Government's investment in Railways was the reason given for moves in the late 1920s to have Railways enter into direct competition with private bus transport. In November 1926 Railways bought an old bus fleet that was providing a service from Napier to Hastings. Over the next two years there were further purchases in the Hutt Valley, in Christchurch and in Oamaru. But these services, too, lost money, adding to the overall Railways debt.[18] Yet Railway Road Services expanded over the years, continuing into the 1980s. It rarely declared a profit.

In 1929 the Government hoped to ease Railways' burden in another way: it wrote off £8.1 million from the sum on which Railways had to pay interest. In 1931 a further £10.4 million was written off.[19] But there were still no operating surpluses when remaining debts were included in the accounts. Treasury pushed for a variety of fare rises, arguing that rail journeys 'belong to a class of State activity in which the principle of user pays should apply'.[20] This argument was vigorously supported by Professor B. E. Murphy of Victoria University College.[21] In reality, competition with road and the obligations on Railways to operate as an employment agency and provide subsidised housing for employees working outside the main centres were putting impossible burdens on operating costs.

Electricity generation was similarly brought under the State's wing after World War I.[22] Electricity was first produced in New Zealand for public use in 1887. By 1898 local authorities were producing it. Following advice from American experts in 1902, central government took the exclusive right under the Water Power Act 1903 to generate electricity using water, although this right could be – and sometimes was – delegated to a local authority, and after 1908 to private companies as well.[23] The process of government involvement was taken a step further in the Water Power Works Act 1910, when the Government gained authorisation to raise money to construct hydro-electric stations.[24] Work soon began at Lake Coleridge, where construction was completed in 1915. By this time electricity was also being produced in the Hutt Valley and at Waipori.

As with early railway construction, the State had taken the lead because there was insufficient interest being shown by private enterprise in developing a vital utility. Again there was debate in Parliament over whether the State should be encouraging private enterprise, or whether it ought to take the dominant role itself. The consensus that emerged was that in a small country like New Zealand, the desirability of preventing a private monopoly required an active State. Parliamentarians warmly endorsed government involvement. In the Legislative Council C. M. Luke declared:

In the absence of significant private interest, the State became involved in power production; Massey officially opens the Mangahao Power Station, November 1924.
ATL G-8607-1/1

'I believe the success of many of the enterprises the Government has undertaken in the past in the direction of encouraging the production of this country speaks eloquently for the administration of the country'. John Rigg hoped that electricity would be a major money-spinner for the Government: 'It should . . . be the duty of the State on entering upon a great enterprise of this kind to see that it returns a fair profit to the State on the investment, and that the whole benefit to be derived from it should not go to those who are consuming the power which is supplied by the Government.'[25] Rigg was reflecting a view that was gaining currency – the Government's role was both to generate and to redistribute wealth.

While the Government granted occasional licences to private companies to develop power, such licences were controlled carefully. In addition to local authority plants, many of them using coal, there was a small network of private producers in existence by the end of the war.[26] However, it was soon clear that only the Government could command the finance necessary to proceed with the grand plans produced in 1918 by Evan Parry, the Government's Chief Electrical Engineer. Parry envisaged a rapid increase in production as well as reticulation of the whole North Island.[27] Coates pointedly stated in July 1921 when announcing plans to construct three major hydro stations in the north: 'The Government's margin of credit and security is immeasurably greater than that of any local effort'. He added that in his view local authorities were most unlikely to be able to provide electricity as cheaply as the State.[28]

A few private entrepreneurs continued with thermal explorations in the hope of finding an economically viable alternative source of electricity but there were so many regulations to comply with after 1934 that most gave up. Private companies wishing to compete with the State's hydro network had effectively been squeezed out by the 1940s.[29] Electricity production became a huge state activity. Construction workers numbered 3993 in 1920. They topped 10,800 a decade later when the pressure was on to complete the difficult Arapuni dam on the Waikato River. Numbers fell back during World War II but rose again as new stations were completed in the late 1940s and 1950s.[30]

Once Coates had headed off the State's competitors in electricity production, efforts were soon underway to construct a national distribution grid. Getting details from local authorities and companies about existing grids was not easy.[31] However, by 1926 38 publicly elected power boards were using the Electric Power Boards Act 1925 to borrow, and were hard at work reticulating electricity to the nation's homes. In 1985 it was estimated that $5.6 billion had been spent generating, transmitting and distributing electricity throughout the country. Of that amount, more than 71 per cent had been raised and spent by central government; the rest was the responsibility of power boards.[32] As with the construction of railways, public authority once more triumphed over private intitiative. However, in the case of electricity, public demand never flagged. It was only the introduction of politically driven pricing policies in the middle of the century that ever adversely affected the profitability and social usefulness of this public utility.[33]

By the early 1920s State Mines was twenty years old. Like Railways, it still produced surpluses although it no longer paid interest on all money borrowed because some had been written off in 1913. Trading surpluses were not always invested profitably. On 19 December 1919 the Treasury's accountant checking the books of State Mines noted that the surpluses were 'idle': 'As this is a commercial department it should be run on practical business lines, and where there is an opening for investing advantage should be taken of the opportunity.'[34] Treasury, it seems, had been pocketing the interest on the trading surplus rather than crediting it to the Mines

Department. Burnt in earlier years by the over-capitalisation of State Mines, Treasury was keeping the department on short pay and rations.

State Mines always needed capital for expansion but was powerless to raise loans without permission from Cabinet. It was expected to operate commercially, yet it never enjoyed the autonomy of private enterprise. There is no indication that either Treasury officials or ministers ever questioned whether there was still a need – if indeed there ever had been – for the State to be owning and operating mines. In the uncertain 1920s the Government was beginning to reap the consequences of its huge capital investment in railways and mines, and the unbusinesslike management of these enterprises. The situation at State Mines deteriorated during the depression when demand for coal subsided. By then all state trading agencies had become employment agencies. Trading surpluses declined. Several city coal depots showed trading losses and were eventually closed. State Forests, too, operated at a loss throughout the depression, largely because it was expected to carry up to 848 relief workers planting exotic trees.[35]

While central government increased its infrastructural investments during Massey's later years, the State also edged forward in social policy areas. Although the Board of Trade went into hibernation in 1924 the power to regulate prices remained in force under the 1919 legislation. Bread was still controlled. Other regulations were gazetted from time to time. The 1924 Gas Regulations required that supplies be made available at specific calorific levels and at reasonable prices. The Tailoring Trade Regulations stipulated that all articles of clothing that claimed to be handmade had to contain a specified amount of hand work.[36]

Massey's Government accepted more responsibility for housing. Lending under the Advances to Workers scheme continued, and there was a steady rise in the number of government loans to local authorities for rental house construction as ministers strove to persuade councils to accept social responsibilities. Railway workers and State Coal miners were housed at subsidised rents. In the hope of controlling urban house rents the Government retained its wartime rent controls. Each year the legislation fixing rents at the level of 3 August 1914 was extended in a series of Rent Restriction Acts. Unions and the Labour Party set store by controlling rents, many arguing for controls in other areas as well.[37] But as the years went by Massey had cause to doubt the wisdom of government involvement in rent controls. In his budget of 1923 he claimed that the Government was doing a lot to help house families, but declared testily: 'It should not . . . be expected of the State alone to provide the means of meeting the [shortage of housing], and the housing problem will not be solved until private capital is more extensively employed than has been the case in the immediate past.'[38]

Two problems were becoming apparent with rent controls. In the first place, many private investors who owned rental accommodation in 1914 and who found their rents frozen, despite several years of steep inflation, were disposing of houses and investing elsewhere. This reduced the stock of rental housing.[39] By 1924 only a relatively small number of rental houses with controlled rents still existed. Secondly, landlords who built or bought untenanted houses after 1914 were not covered by the controls. Some workers who were lucky enough still to rent a house with a controlled rent were paying as little as £1 per week in rent; others with non-controlled rentals were paying as much as £4 per week. The Act was amended in 1924 to bring more houses under the umbrella of the controls. A 'standard rent' could be defined as 8 per cent of the capital value of a house, and could be fixed by a magistrate.[40]

This move did not solve the problem. Investors again edged away from rental properties. In August 1926 when the Rent Restriction Act was extended once more (the ritual continued until Labour passed the Fair Rents Act in 1936), Legislative Councillors roundly criticised the move, pointing out that rent restrictions had played a major part in creating a housing shortage rather than solving it. Rents were high because the legislation had resulted in a reduction of stock, thus pushing up rents for those houses remaining in the rental pool. A. S. Malcolm, a teacher, sportsman and land agent from Balclutha, commented, 'I can understand how difficult it is to get out of a bog such as this once we have entered into it. I do not think any country can venture to interfere with the law of supply and demand as we have done and keep it up continuously without great injury to the public.' Malcolm concluded that the Government's desire to help tenants 'ran in front of their judgement'.[41] Advocates of rent control refused to heed such judgements for another half century, hoping always that further refinements to the control mechanisms would result in an adequate supply of houses at low rents. Rent controls remained in force with diminishing effectiveness until 1985.

Meantime, Massey's Government was also putting more money into education. The number of teacher trainees rose steadily after the war, and more than kept pace with the primary school children who received the 'free, compulsory and secular' education provided by Education Boards. Attendance at the 130 Native Schools also rose and in 1923 the Education Department established a new category of schools known as Junior High

A state-provided school bus – with a puncture, 1924. Wagener Museum

Schools, later called Intermediates. Free places at secondary schools increased, as did the number of national scholarships.[42] In the Education Amendment Act 1924 all teachers were required to register, and the following year Education Boards were given wider powers to prevent overcrowding in schools.[43] In 1925 a Child Welfare Act was passed. It created a special branch of the Education Department known as the Child Welfare Branch, which was to look after children who were under the protection of the State and to provide for the education of indigent, neglected or delinquent children.[44]

There were changes, too, to the rules governing pensions. The restrictions limiting their availability were relaxed in 1924; widows could earn more before their benefits were abated. A new class of benefit, Blind Pensions, was also introduced. In this area as in so many others the Reform Government was carrying on the policies of its predecessor.[45]

It was noticeable that the same urge for social control that had come to the fore during the war continued into peacetime. In the Education Amendment Act 1921–22, all teachers, whether they were in public or private schools, were required to take an oath of allegiance. In 1924 an amendment to the Police Offences Act prohibited retailing on Sundays, although an exemption was provided for bookstalls at railway stations. The rules regarding rogues and vagabonds were tightened and it became

160

mandatory for there to be supervision of wrestling contests. The publication of unauthorised programmes for these contests was also outlawed.[46] In the same year a Masseurs Registration Amendment Act passed Parliament because legislators professed to be worried about the lax definition of what constituted a massage, and the extent to which sexual services were provided by some masseurs. Clause 2 of the Act tortuously defined a massage as:

> use by external application to the human body of manipulation, remedial exercises, electricity, heat, or light, for the purpose of alleviating any abnormal condition of the body, or the use for such purpose of any other method of treatment that may be recognised by the Governor General in Council as an approved method of performing massage, but does not include the internal use of any drug or medicine or the application of such appliance except so far as the application . . . is necessary in the use as aforesaid of manipulation, remedial exercises, electricity, heat, light, or other approved method.[47]

Two years later in an amendment to the Cinematograph-Film Censorship Act, the censor was given wider powers to prohibit the display of advertisements for films that contained 'objectionable' material.[48] In 1928 efforts were made to enforce a weekly block of time for religious study in state schools and another attempt was made to destabilise the delicate equilibrium that now existed over liquor licensing laws. The era of what the American historian William Leuchtenburg has called 'political fundamentalism' was bearing down upon New Zealand; sex, alcohol, disloyalty and greater freedom for women all passed under the scrutiny of legislators. Many were fighting to stave off modern times, growing affluence for some and temptations to many. Similar concerns underlay parliamentary debates on the Chattels Transfer Act 1924 and an amendment to it in 1931. Some MPs felt that credit was too easy to get, and that hire-purchase would open the floodgates to hedonism; the *Southland Daily News* bemoaned the fact that 'the unthinking' members of society were already able to buy goods too easily.[49] As the State intervened on behalf of those seen as deserving, there was a corresponding need to regulate the lives of those who were suspected of being improvident. As with the Liberals, state help was for the respectable.

Massey died of cancer on 10 May 1925. Gordon Coates soon succeeded him and was confirmed in office with a substantial victory at the polls on 4 November 1925. Coates was described by one opponent as possessing a 'radical temperament'.[50] He brought to the prime-ministership the same activist inclinations that had been at work in his ministerial portfolios.

During the election campaign he promised to introduce what became known as Family Allowances and talked vaguely of a national contributory insurance scheme that sounded not unlike Atkinson's. The idea was quietly dropped before the 1928 election. However, against the better judgement of some of his colleagues, Coates pushed through the Family Allowances Act during the parliamentary session of 1926. Extolling family values as he went, the Prime Minister established a small, means-tested mothers' allowance for the third and subsequent children in a family, paid from the Consolidated Fund. Reflecting the same sort of views on social control that had been current at the time of the Old-age Pensions Act in 1898, the benefit excluded mothers of illegitimate children, aliens and Asians.[51]

Further interventionist measures were taken by Coates's Government, despite the fact that his caucus was full of people whom John A. Lee colourfully described as 'elderly men of Victorian sentiment . . . washed out of their armchairs into the House, where they . . . busied themselves in trying to turn the clock back'.[52] Soon after the House assembled for the 1926 session a Town Planning Bill was introduced, and it became law on 9 September 1926. The need for town planning had been debated since before the war.[53] It had been the subject of a special conference in 1919. In the end it was left to Coates's ministry to legislate. The Act required every local authority with a population of 1000 or more to produce a town plan 'for . . . the development of the city or borough . . . in such a way as will most effectively tend to promote its heathfulness, amenity, convenience, and advancement'. 'Extra urban' schemes were also required from rural local authorities. The Act established a Town Planning Director and a Town Planning Board. Initially it was chaired by the Minister of Internal Affairs. Local plans were to be drafted, submitted for public comment then adopted by local authorities before 1 January 1930 – a date that was subsequently stretched until 1932. On 12 March 1927 the Government further promulgated a set of regulations outlining matters to be incorporated in a town plan.[54] For the first time, elected local authority members had been given powers to prescribe rules governing private developments in their areas, but the overall parameters were set by central government. A centralising process whereby the Government established its dominance over many aspects of life was gathering pace in the 1920s.

The Motor Omnibus Act 1926 was another piece of legislation increasing the powers of public authorities over private enterprise. For many years it had been permissible for local authorities to establish public transport (usually tramcars) for their citizens. Like railways, their economic viability was now being threatened by motor cars and privately owned bus

Coates's campaign leaflet for the Kaipara electorate, 1928.

companies. As with Railways, concern about public investment caused the Government to legislate to protect it. Foreshadowing some features of the Transport Licensing Act 1931, the Motor Omnibus Act divided the country into motor omnibus districts, made local authorities the licensing authorities, and required bus operators to hold a licence to operate. In effect, local authorities could license their own tramcars to the detriment of the private sector. There was a storm of protest from private bus operators, and some sharp criticism of the Government from within its own ranks. Several supporters called the legislation 'socialist', somewhat to the dismay of Coates's ministers.[55]

The rural sector also came in for its share of government activism. The crisis over the London marketing of dairy products in 1926–27 stemmed from over-confidence by the Dairy Board, the leaders of which invoked the full powers of the 1923 marketing legislation to fix butter prices in London and control its marketing. They hoped that British consumers could be forced to pay more for New Zealand butter than current market prices. The debacle has been written about elsewhere. It is a story of bull-headed ignorance by the Board's chairman, a Hokianga farmer called William Grounds, and lack of decisiveness by the Prime Minister, who dithered long after the perils of what the Board was trying to do became abundantly clear. British consumers boycotted New Zealand butter, which had never commanded more than 25 per cent of the market. Belatedly, at a meeting of the Board on 15 March 1927, the Government forced the Board to back down. Price fixing on the London market ended in a hail of recriminations.[56] The incident showed the dangers that could flow from delegating government powers to headstrong producers.

Behind the butter fiasco lay the sorry story of declining prices for New Zealand produce on the London market, largely because of the depressed state of the British economy. Declining commodity prices hurt New Zealand's farmers, many of whom were finding that their overheads outstripped their income. This was specially true for those who had paid high land prices, and borrowed heavily in the years 1917–21. Ever since the war there had been advocates of cheap credit to farmers. Some wanted a farmers' state bank – something to which the Secretary to the Treasury, G. F. C. Campbell, was not averse when it was first raised in 1919.[57] In 1925 a commission was set up to inquire into the need for financial assistance to farmers. This commission recommended the provision of 'intermediate rural credits' in addition to existing long-term advances.[58] Coates's Government accepted the advice. A Rural Advances Act 1926 established a separate branch within the State Advances Office to deal with farmers. In the 1970s this became a separate entity, the Rural Bank. Advances of up to £5,000 in certain circumstances could be made to farmers in need. In the first two years of operation, £2.6 million was authorised.[59] In 1927 further legislation was passed. The Rural Intermediate Credit Act provided for assistance to members of co-operative credit associations; further money was lent to farmers through Intermediate Credit Boards. In the first fourteen months of their operation £268,310 was advanced at between 6 per cent and 6.5 per cent. By this time the Government was also paying shipping subsidies (£22,500 pa), subsidies for grading and storing dairy products (£140,000 pa), subsidies to wheat growers (£400,000), and subsidies to Railways for the carriage of lime and fertilisers (£155,000 pa).[60]

Many years before Pember Reeves had written: 'In the colonies Governments are, rightly or wrongly, expected to be of use in a public emergency, and under the head of public emergency dull times are included.'[61] Coates was proving, yet again, the truth of that comment. As Gary Hawke notes, 'the close-knit homogeneous [New Zealand] settler community had evolved its own doctrine of what the state apparatus should do'.[62] But such subsidies meant that Downie Stewart could not seriously

The United Government tried to cure unemployment by expanding the State's payroll; postal delivery boys in Wanganui, 1930. ATL F-17061-1/1

contemplate tax reductions at a time when they might well have helped the ailing economy. A later Minister of Finance faced the same problem at the end of the 1970s.

During 1927 and 1928 Coates's Government had difficulty balancing the interests of farmers, manufacturers and workers. It ended up by satisfying no one. Ministers set out to exempt farmers and dairy factories from coverage by the Arbitration Court but staged a partial retreat before an onslaught from workers' and employers' representatives. There was tinkering with the tariff in 1927 when the Government sought to reduce duties on some foodstuffs, while providing further protection to industry as well as reducing duties on raw materials. But the changes won little support from sectional forces promoting their own agendas. An Industrial Conference met between March and May 1928 but was unable to arrive at substantial agreement on further tariff reform or changes to the I.C.& A. Act.[63] However, assisted immigration which brought into New Zealand more than 11,000 people in 1926 was trimmed back to fewer than 2000 in 1928 and fell further during the depression. The only thing that attracted anything approaching unanimity among the parties was more government expenditure. All parties to the conference supported railway freight concessions, which involved further subsidies.

Presiding over a bearpit of sectional forces, each trying to use the State for its own ends, Coates's Government achieved little during the 1928

165

*Prime Minister Ward, ailing like the economy, on his seventy-fourth birthday,
26 April 1930.*

session of Parliament. The Reform Government went down to defeat in
the election on 14 November at the hands of a resurgent Liberal Party,
now calling itself United. This new party's origin was largely ideological;
its organiser, A. E. Davy, warned in 1927 of the 'great impetus to the Red
Movement' taking place under Coates's Government. In March 1928 a
gathering of businessmen calling themselves the 1928 Committee identified
several areas from which they believed the State should withdraw. They
fastened their gaze on state trading organisations such as State Fire and
Government Life Insurance, State Coal, the Post Office Savings Bank and
the Public Trust Office. Forestry and Railways were both said to have
gone beyond 'legitimate' (but undefined) boundaries for state activity.
However, the anti-state party which businessmen wished to create was
snatched from its cradle. The United Party went into the election with the
aged Sir Joseph Ward as its leader. A diabetic with a dicky heart and poor
eyesight, Ward misread his speech notes at the opening of the campaign in
Auckland and promised to borrow £70 million overseas to stimulate New
Zealand's ailing economy. A wave of popular enthusiasm for a further round
of state activity engulfed the 1928 Committee and carried Ward into the
prime minister's office, where he led a weak minority ministry dependent
on other parties.[64] Like Stafford's Government in 1857, Fox's in 1869–70

and Grey's in 1877–79, New Zealanders again thought they saw salvation in borrowed money and state intervention.

His family and colleagues eased Ward from office in May 1930, a few weeks before his death. He had solved nothing. On 1 October 1929, which had been his last day in Parliament, he promised to banish all unemployment within five weeks. Throughout his career Ward had pushed the State into many areas of the economy. But this was the boldest declaration of government omnipotence to date. A few days after his promise – fortuitously perhaps – Ward was in hospital, fighting for his life. In his absence ministers tried valiantly to put the unemployed to work. While they managed to rustle up 4889 additional relief jobs within government departments, they were overwhelmed by a flood of new applications for work.[65]

None of Ward's £70 million was borrowed. Worse, export prices which were New Zealand's international lifeline were tumbling. Unemployment leapt in an alarming fashion between 1930 and 1933, leading to riots in Dunedin, Auckland and Wellington in the early months of 1932. Decades of heavy borrowing, inflated land prices and a high level of wages by world standards made New Zealand specially vulnerable to the catastrophic worldwide collapse in prices and economic confidence. Ramsay MacDonald, Prime Minister of the United Kingdom, labelled it an 'economic blizzard'.[66]

Those who remember the crisis of the 1980s may see some parallels in the 1920s: dubious state investments; a mixture of social and business objectives in government ventures that turned them into users of tax revenue rather than contributors to it; a heavy reliance by many on government funding and an over-optimistic confidence that governments could protect New Zealand's living standards in a volatile world. However, whereas the later crisis called into question the efficacy of government intervention in the economy, the crisis that struck New Zealand in 1929 did nothing to dim public faith in the all-powerful State. Everywhere in the world, the Great Depression ratcheted up the level of government intervention in everyday affairs. Robert Higgs observes that the people who lived through the depression were never the same again: 'the anxieties and convictions it fostered entered deeply into their attitudes and opinions. The political economy emerged from this wrenching experience altered to its core.' Higgs notes that in the United States there was a huge increase in the number of believers in the efficacy of state intervention.[67] It was certainly the case in New Zealand.

George Forbes has been described by Keith Sinclair as 'New Zealand's most improbable Premier'.[68] He succeeded Ward on 28 May 1930, heading a minority government. It was supported in the House alternately by the

The Coalition Cabinet, 1932: Prime Minister George Forbes in front with bowler hat; Coates, his deputy, far left; and then Minister of Finance, Downie Stewart, in the wheelchair. ATL C-21064

Labour and Reform parties. Neither was keen on the idea of an early election. On 22 September 1931 Forbes persuaded the reluctant Coates to join a coalition ministry and the two together ultimately shared the odium attaching to tough decisions. Re-elected on 2 December 1931, the Forbes–Coates Coalition Government extended its term by one year and ruled until defeated at the polls on 27 November 1935 by the Labour Party.

Like the public at large, Forbes and his ministers were alarmed at the escalating disaster. As early as 1922 the Department of Industries and Commerce had been asked to accumulate information from abroad about schemes to reduce unemployment. Officers gathered details about Queensland's legislation where workers, employees and the State paid equally into an unemployment fund that could be tapped by workers in times of need. As details came to hand they were sent to Reform Party supporters.[69] In its dying stages the Coates Government set up a special committee to investigate unemployment under the chairmanship of W. D. Hunt, a Wellington businessman specialising in taxation. The committee's 22-page report concluded that unemployment resulted from a chronic 'failure of the consumption of certain goods to keep pace with the production, or the failure of the demand for certain services to equal the supply'.[70] It was silent on measures that might be taken to stimulate demand.[71]

Meantime, economists the world over were arriving at the conclusion that protecting local markets was the best way to encourage consumption, and hence the creation of jobs. Everywhere tariffs were used as barriers against competition from the rest of the world. These policies were gaining academic respectability; John Maynard Keynes argued vociferously for protection throughout 1930–31.[72] Reports arriving in New Zealand from the United Kingdom, Canada and Australia all indicated that a wave of economic nationalism was sweeping the world. The New Zealand Parliament established an Unemployment Committee to examine ways of assisting secondary industries to absorb more workers. Manufacturers large and small were happy to cooperate. Most relied on domestic markets and wanted more protection. 'The safeguarding of our home industries with the adoption of a scientific tariff [is] the only measure by which it will be possible to maintain our people in material comfort and prosperity,' declared the organiser of the Canterbury Manufacturers' Association in November 1928. In this context he meant that tariffs should be raised to a level sufficient to make higher cost local goods competitive with imports. Another manufacturer urged that 'town and country . . . stand side by side and realise that primary and secondary interests both have their place in the scheme of things, and are complementary – not antagonistic'.[73]

Smaller manufacturers sought government loans at reduced rates of interest.[74] The Christchurch *Sun* supported a higher tariff so long as it was 'on a rational, scientific basis'.[75] Some farmers, especially tobacco producers, dropped their traditional enthusiasm for free trade as they pushed either for greater protection for their crops, or stepped up their requests for more subsidies. Most farmers, however, wanted to keep and extend their subsidies while denying others a higher tariff.[76] The Chambers of Commerce, representing among others the nation's importers, were not enthusiastic about any tariff increase. Every sector group seemed to feel that salvation lay in accessing government assistance while denying the advantage to others.

During 1929 attention focused more narrowly on New Zealand manufacturing. Relatively few factories employed 100 or more workers in the 1920s, but there had been a mushroom-like growth of smaller establishments, nearly all of them employing ten or fewer workers.[77] Few of these had the capacity to expand without substantial assistance. The Manufacturers' Federation lobbied on behalf of smaller industries in 1929, arguing strenuously for a 'Development of Industries Board'. Appeals for assistance flooded into the Department of Industries and Commerce. But, as the editor of the *Otago Daily Times* was to note, industrial growth in New Zealand had been 'haphazard in the past', and 'the encouragement of a lot of small, struggling inefficient industries all clamouring for protection, is not at all what is wanted'.[78]

Wary of possible retaliation from the United Kingdom if New Zealand pushed its tariffs too high, and sceptical about the capacity of many of New Zealand's industries to employ many more people, government officials counselled caution.[79] A Development of Industries Board was finally set up at the end of 1931 but instead of investigating tariffs, it was to look at a raft of new industries that officials believed might be profitably established, such as the production of pig iron, boosting the iron and steel industry at Onekaka in Golden Bay, the making of Benzol, motor spirit and kerosene cases, the printing in New Zealand of cinematographic films from negatives and an old hardy annual, the flax industry.[80] The Board was made up of successful businessmen and officials who shared the views of the new Minister of Industries and Commerce, Robert Masters. Masters wanted to insulate New Zealand's manufacturing as much as possible. It should use locally produced raw materials wherever possible, or, if this was not possible, only British materials.[81]

The Board wrestled with the criteria that should determine industrial development, especially new, job-rich industries. From these discussions emerged a new approach to state assistance that seems to have been largely the brainchild of G. W. Clinkard. Born in 1893, Clinkard was a Wellington-trained economist with long experience in Statistics and Industries and Commerce, of which he became Secretary in 1930. He favoured licensing of industries. Once there had been a careful study by officials, 'something in the nature of exclusive rights to manufacture' would be granted to a licensed industry – in other words, a state-protected and assisted monopoly would be created. Clinkard amplified his views in a memo to Parliament's Industries and Commerce Select Committee on 23 November 1932:

> It has been represented to the Development of Industries Committee that unless these new industries can have the assurance that no other factory of the same type will commence in the Dominion within a reasonable period of time those interested will not be prepared to invest the necessary funds. To enable this suggestion to be carried out it would be necessary for the Government to prohibit the manufacture of goods in question save under licence to be issued by the Government on such terms and conditions as might be considered appropriate.

Clinkard claimed there were precedents for the granting of monopolies and exclusive rights. Gas and electricity were publicly delivered, while the State itself ran the monopolies of Railways and Post and Telegraph. It also licensed the sale of liquor. Clinkard argued that any granting of 'exclusive rights' must always be under 'proper safeguards'. He listed some tests that should be applied before 'exclusivity' was extended to any new industry.

The industry must be of national importance; it must be 'a substantial employer'; it ought to use locally produced raw materials where possible; it should be of 'economic value' when compared with overseas supplies; any patents ought to be able to become the 'exclusive right' of the New Zealand industry; and the extent to which a large investment was involved should first be the subject of careful bureaucratic study. In Clinkard's view the State should be able to prescribe a time limit for the commencement of an industry that was granted a licence. Clinkard clearly envisaged that tariff protection would be necessary for an industry that was granted 'exclusivity', 'unless the further step were taken of prohibiting not only competitive local manufacture but competitive importation'. He had every confidence that legislative restrictions and safeguards could curtail any monopolistic tendencies in the interests of the public. The whole submission was posited on the assumption that careful attention to detail by bureaucrats could greatly improve on the market.[82]

More than half a century on, Clinkard's ideas seem bizarre. A heavily restricted, state-supported, guaranteed monopoly, enjoying tariff protection, producing what the industry, bureaucrats and ministers thought was in the national interest! Yet, these were the years when many intelligent people were watching the State's massive involvement in the Soviet Union where the worst effects of the depression had been avoided. The notion that the market was an antiquated instrument which could be 'scientifically' manipulated in the public interest also had a growing number of adherents in the West. Franklin Roosevelt was shortly to assume office and the United States Congress would pass a series of acts that greatly enhanced the President's powers in industry, banking and agriculture. The United States National Recovery Administration soon had power to draw up codes for fair trade and a seal of approval could be given to American industries that were deemed to be cooperating with bureaucrats' schemes. Clinkard's views were no more than an antipodean effort to apply a regulatory framework to a vulnerable economy which seemed to have limited industrial potential and no great prospect of developing a full range of competing industries in a small market.

For the moment, however, the Coalition Government was listening more attentively to other advisers who were worried about the dangers of licensing and protecting uneconomic industries. As Coates very rationally stated in 1934: 'It is . . . not in general of advantage to this or any other country that an industry should be fostered by tariff protection where direct and indirect cost of that protection is greater than the benefits likely to be derived by the community.'[83] Clinkard's ideas appealed more to the

Labour Party. Since the tariff debates of 1927 Labour had unequivocally favoured tariff protection for industries, especially those using locally produced raw materials.[84] Labour eventually wove Clinkard's suggestions into the Industrial Efficiency Act 1936 and the Bureau of Industry that it created. From then on politicians and their advisers, rather than investors alone, would make the key decisions about New Zealand's industrial structure.

Further adjustments to the tariff occurred during the depression. By now it had become both complex and arbitrary.[85] The Ottawa Conference in July and August 1932 obliged participants to review their tariffs and to erect barriers against British products only if protection would give a local industry a reasonable chance of success. If protection was given to a local industry then a British producer must be able to compete on the basis of economical and efficient local production. These were restrictions around which the various dominions' policy makers manoeuvred gingerly for many years to come. A Tariff Commission was established in New Zealand in May 1933 under the chairmanship of Dr George Craig, Comptroller of Customs. Its report in March 1934 concentrated on the need for a 'simple' tariff that would preserve Imperial preference, yet stimulate domestic employment. The report stressed the need to avoid a recurrence of the riots of 1932 that necessitated passage of the Public Safety Conservation Act greatly expanding the emergency powers of central government. Craig noted some of the limitations imposed on policy flexibility by the Ottawa agreements and was most anxious to avoid a situation that could exacerbate domestic tensions.

The Tariff Commission's report was a cautious document that rode along the high wire at the centre of the debate about industrialisation:

> If a considerable proportion of the rising generation of young people in our towns are not absorbed into industrial employment it is difficult to see what economic occupation will be available for the great many of them. . . . This must not be taken to indicate our approval of the establishment under protective tariff of uneconomic industries.

Yet the Commission was also mindful of manufacturers' desires for more protection. It fingered one of the century's key dilemmas when it noted that in certain circumstances a protective tariff 'may prove less burdensome than a direct dole or allowance, and would certainly be less demoralizing'.[86] From this careful balancing exercise emerged a cautious bill that raised some, and lowered other tariffs. The Australians held on to a higher level of tariff protection. The two countries were making their individual judgements about what they could get away with if they wished to secure greater access for their commodities to the British market in the post-Ottawa environment.[87]

New Zealand's export prices had meanwhile gone from bad to worse. Between 1929 and 1932 they dropped 45 per cent. A significant increase in the volume of exports only partly cushioned the impact of the price fall.[88] Rural incomes in New Zealand contracted sharply and the impact soon spread to towns and cities. Building fell below population needs. Real incomes declined across the board by between 10 per cent and 20 per cent. Government revenue sagged and the trade deficit widened. First Forbes's Government and then its Coalition successor embarked on drastic economies. Immigration was cut back further in the Immigration Restriction Amendment Act 1931; in 1934 only four assisted migrants came to New Zealand.[89]

In spite of cautious longer-term efforts to stimulate industries, Forbes's Government was faced with the immediate problem of ensuring that the unemployed did not starve. In July 1930 an Unemployment Act was passed. It established an Unemployment Board under the chairmanship of the Minister of Labour. Its activities were financed by a tax of 30s per annum on every male over 20. Revenue from the tax was topped up by a government subsidy. Taxes were further raised in 1931, then again in 1932 and 1934, to give the Board sufficient money.[90] The Board set up twelve schemes to provide work for the unemployed.[91] In September 1933, when the depression was at its worst, more than 75,000 men were on work schemes, the overwhelming number of them on Scheme 5, which subsidised local authorities to provide jobs, principally on roads, reserves and other public areas. As local authorities found it more difficult to produce work, the Government gradually accepted that there could be subsidised work on private property, so long as those in ordinary employment were not displaced.

At first the Government determined that all applicants for relief from the Unemployment Fund would have to perform some kind of work in return for relief pay. Cabinet resolutely refused to pay a dole. However, it was finally forced to pay a dole in July 1934 because government departments and local authorities had run out of work. By election time in November 1935 more than 25 per cent of all unemployed men were receiving sustenance payments without work. To an extent that was unprecedented in peacetime, the depression involved public authorities, local and central, as well as private companies, in the direction of a sizeable

The 'Buy New Zealand' campaign, early 1930s. Nelson Provincial Museum

chunk of the nation's manpower. Few people objected to this expansion of the State's role.

The Unemployment Board kept hoping that the private sector could be stimulated to a higher level of activity. It argued that £10 million worth of goods were imported into the country each year that could be produced domestically.[92] Citing advertising schemes being run in Canada and Australia, branches of the Manufacturers' Federation eagerly took up this war cry. They wanted a subsidised campaign to encourage New Zealanders to 'Buy New Zealand'. Eventually manufacturers and the Board agreed to share the costs of a newspaper campaign. 'The Hand that Rocks the Cradle, Controls the Purse – Buy New Zealand' declared one advertisement in daily papers in September 1930. Another read 'You Can Help "Square Up" New Zealand by demanding and using the Products of the Dominion'.[93]

The campaign continued during 1931. Many newspapers picked up the 'Buy New Zealand' theme in their editorials. 'If a locally-made article is purchased, it provides a job for someone to replace it', the Christchurch *Sun* told its readers in May 1931. The *Dominion* even ran articles on its children's pages exhorting the young to request New Zealand-made goods.[94] Goldberg Advertising Agency was paid £1,200, two thirds of it from the Board and one third from manufacturers, for a national campaign. The agency sought and received the support of all party and church leaders for the appeal.[95] Follow-up inquiries through district offices of the Department of Industries and Commerce revealed, however, that the campaign had had no perceptible effect on purchasing and was a sorry flop. Meanwhile other nostrums for curing unemployment came in from the public, including the suggestion that leaders should declare New Zealand to be 'the only real Winter Sanatorium' to which rich invalids from the Northern Hemisphere should repair, post haste.[96]

The contraction in government income caused Forbes to establish an Economy Committee of Cabinet under the chairmanship of one of his handful of experienced colleagues, Sir Apirana Ngata.[97] The committee met regularly from 6 January 1931 and scrutinised all departmental budgets, looking for ways to reduce expenditure. Interestingly, neither the submissions from the Treasury nor the Public Service Commission raised the fundamental question as to whether departments such as Railways, State Coal-mines, Printing and Stationery, or State and Government Life Insurance should be retained in government ownership.

However, ministers did depoliticise Railways. The Government Railways Board between 1931 and 1936 consisted of ministerial appointees. They were expected to run the services commercially. This inevitably meant an end (temporary as it transpired) to the old practice of running them like an employment agency. By 1934 there were 4500 fewer railway workers than in 1930. Railways accounts soon looked much healthier. The Board was really a forerunner of the corporatisation programme begun by the Fourth Labour Government in 1987. But on this occasion the Railways Board lasted only five years until the First Labour Government in 1936 brought Railways back under ministerial control and returned to the former policy of using it to soak up unemployment. By 1940 there were 25,710 employed by Railways, an increase of 11,000 since 1934.[98]

Other departments had their budgets pared to the bone during the depression. Departmental giveaways such as annual reports and copies of the *Gazette* were reduced, as were the railway passes for many categories of public servants, including a very angry Clerk of the Legislative Council. On 14 February 1931 Forbes announced that Arbitration award wages would be cut back and that there would be a 10 per cent reduction in all state salaries. In April 1932 the I.C.&A. Act was amended so as to make arbitration voluntary, rather than compulsory, in the event of an industrial dispute. Award rates fell by an average of 5.5 per cent in the period between March 1932 and June 1934.[99] With domestic prices falling, the Government sought to level the remuneration playing field by removing the advantages enjoyed by those whose wages and salaries were still pegged at what now seemed to be high levels; everyone was reduced a notch or two so that no one gained a privileged position from the nation's misfortunes.

Other measures followed as the Government now tried to raise the entire playing field. Efforts began with farmers whose incomes in many cases had shrivelled to levels not experienced in a generation. In his capacity first as Minister of Public Works and Transport, and then after 28 January 1933 as Minister of Finance, Coates fought at Ottawa for better access to Imperial markets. Then he sought to inflate farmers' incomes with a 25 per cent devaluation of the New Zealand pound in January 1933, which had the side-effect of making imports more expensive. This byproduct gave an extra boost to New Zealand's manufacturers. After advice from a group of academics known as his Brains Trust, Coates trimmed farmers' costs with the establishment of a Mortgage Corporation. He reformed the Dairy Board's legislation, and in the Agriculture (Emergency Powers) Act 1934 gave power to a newly constituted Dairy Commission to license farmers, supervise dairy factories and determine where dairy products were marketed. Coates gave indebted farmers greater security of tenure of their land with the Mortgagors and Tenants Relief Act of December 1933 and the Rural Mortgagors Final Adjustment Act in April 1935.[100] Each measure involved a further extension of the State's authority. The mortgage legislation gave the State wider powers to scrutinise farmers' indebtedness and to protect them against lenders than had been enacted during World War I. The new policies undoubtedly protected many farmers faced with foreclosure, although they did little for Coates's general reputation with the rural sector. He experienced a large swing against him in his electorate of Kaipara, much of it among the very farmers he had helped to save.[101]

A significant change in the State's relationship with banking took place in 1934 when the Reserve Bank of New Zealand opened its doors. As Gary Hawke has shown, the idea of a state bank of issue had been around in New Zealand since the beginning of responsible government.[102] Whenever interest rates rose and primary producers felt the squeeze, advocates of a state bank emerged, as they had at the end of World War I. During the uncertain 1920s both farmers' organisations and the Labour Party argued for a central bank with full control of note issue. Sir Otto Niemeyer of the Bank of England recommended setting up a reserve bank in 1931. Downie Stewart, who was Minister of Finance again from September 1931 to January 1933, drew up the Reserve Bank of New Zealand Bill; with modifications it was introduced on 19 October 1933 by Coates and passed a few weeks later.[103] In Coates's words the Reserve Bank was designed to:

> Assist the trading banks by pooling their reserves, extending them credit in a crisis, relieving them of note-tax, and freeing them of dead gold reserves which earn no profit; it will assist the people by providing a conscious monetary policy in place of the competitive extension of credit which aims at providing

176

dividends for shareholders rather than at promoting the economic welfare of New Zealand; finally, it will make credit easier and cheaper in times of depression, and have a restraining influence to prevent speculation in boom times.[104]

The bank's primary duty was to act so that 'the economic welfare of the Dominion may be promoted and maintained'. This was a significant step in the State's paternalism towards its citizens, one that the Labour Government built on in years to come.

The Reserve Bank, which was part state-owned, part private, began operations on 1 August 1934 with Leslie Lefeaux, the Assistant Governor of the Bank of England, as its first Governor. In 1936 the Labour Government bought out the private shareholding and the bank came more firmly under ministerial control where it remained until passage of the Reserve Bank of New Zealand Act on 20 December 1989. That Act defined the bank's function more precisely, giving it the responsibility for formulating monetary policy that had previously been in political hands and entrusting it with the task of promoting price stability.[105]

There were many signs of economic recovery by 1935. Export prices for wool and meat were rising and dairy products which had been the last to fall had turned the corner at last. Coates's trip to London in 1935 to forestall a levy which British ministers threatened to place on all meat imports was successful. Moreover, with their efforts to assist farmers, and the reduction in wage rates in 1931 and 1932 which brought them more into line with lower domestic prices, the Government had succeeded in reducing New Zealand's cost structure. This gave exporters a more competitive edge in world markets for some years to come.

Many conservatives who had been unnerved by Coates's legislation between 1926 and 1928 reacted with horror at his marketplace interventions. Coates was vilified, particularly by those who lent money and were the victims of arbitrary reductions in the terms of their mortgage contracts. No matter how hard he argued that his reforms were in the wider interests of the country, many refused to listen. One critic accused the Government of practising 'national State socialism'. George Bernard Shaw's visit to New Zealand in March 1934 had the unintended effect of adding fuel to the growing right-wing campaign against the Government. From one end of the country to the other, the 'gangling, opinionated, bumptious' Fabian socialist praised New Zealand's active government, calling its reforms, on one occasion, 'communist'.[106] Eventually a third party, the Democrat Party, was set up to fight the election against the Coalition Government, thus assisting its demise.[107]

George Bernard Shaw meeting with Maori at Ohinemutu, 1934.

Several weeks in the United Kingdom in the middle of 1935 exposed Coates to the new wave of Keynesian thinking that some New Zealanders with an interest in monetary reform had already been talking about.[108] In the Finance Act 1935 public service wage cuts were partially restored. Coates was soon talking of resuming borrowing for public works as well. However, it was too late for any stimulation of the economy to affect voters' perceptions of the Forbes–Coates Government. Conservative opposition to state intervention was simply swept aside by the voters. Public hopes and aspirations now rested with an alternative political force that had woven state intervention into every one of its public pronouncements.

Chapter 7

Labour, Social Security and 'Insulation'

B y 10 pm on Wednesday 27 November 1935 it was clear that New Zealanders had elected a new government. Crowds outside newspaper offices in the four main centres enjoyed the fine weather as they watched billboards flashing results. The Labour Party swept to victory, winning 53 seats (soon to be 55) in a House of 80. In front of the *Press* building in Christchurch a boisterous group watched Coalition candidates topple, chanting as each one lost his seat: 'Off with his head!' It might have sounded like the French Revolution to the paper's editor, who was said to be in tears. Good-humoured Aucklanders greeted each other the next day with 'Hullo, Comrade'; some wore red.

One of the new MPs, a 'small, tough, bearded Welshman' called Morgan Williams, talked of the advent of 'that Socialist Utopia of which we have all dreamed'. However, after nearly twenty years of struggle to attain office, Labour's leaders had learned discipline. 'We have got to have time. We have got to be cautious,' the new Prime Minister told a Mangere meeting a few weeks later. The London *Economist* shrewdly observed of the new ministry that 'the temper of their constituents is too conservative to warrant apprehension'.[1] For the most part the Labour Government experimented with planning capitalism rather than building socialism. Nevertheless, Labour wrought huge changes and won the adulation of a wide cross-section of the New Zealand community. The party held tenaciously to office, not surrendering it until 13 December 1949. By then many had come to believe that Labour's interventionism was one of the fundamentals of the modern state.

While Labour's seats had grown from eight in 1919 to 24 in 1931, the party's share of the poll improved only slowly. It moved from 23.5 per cent in 1919 to 27 per cent in 1925 before dropping back to 25.8 per cent in 1928, rising then to nearly 34 per cent in the depression election of 1931. Led by the dour intellectual Harry Holland until he died suddenly in October 1933, Labour sought to entice urban workers with promises of better health, education and housing, while waving land tenure reforms and changes to marketing and credit policies before farmers. For a long time these strategies failed to work; New Zealand's growing working class, as Miles Fairburn notes, was 'relatively conservative'.[2]

During the depression Labour's leaders devoured books about planning and the public use of credit. For many years now, Peter Fraser and Walter Nash had been attending Workers' Educational Association summer schools. The books of G. D. H. Cole were much in vogue; they argued the case for a 'national plan of production', where 'the available resources of materials, machinery and man-power are definitely assigned to different branches of production, as they are [in] the Soviet Union'. Labour's weekly newspaper, the *Standard*, reviewed Cole's *Simple Case for Socialism*, finding it compelling reading.[3] Many among a small but growing New Zealand intelligentsia subscribed to Britain's Left Book Club, initially through the Hamilton bookseller, Blackwood Paul. *Tomorrow* magazine first appeared in Christchurch in 1934. It has been called 'the central organ of radical and left wing thought and writing in New Zealand' in those days. It carried literary work and published articles on a variety of political subjects, many of them critical of the 'upholders of the present order of society'.

The subtext of most utterances from the left was that state intervention was 'democratic' and could not help but benefit the masses. Labour's new leader, Michael Joseph Savage, declared himself in favour of 'national planning'. The *Standard* peppered its pages with talk of 'plans', the likely effectiveness of which was never questioned. Occasionally the *Standard* ran articles about labour experiments in Soviet Russia, such as the Stakhanovite movement, but there was no editorial approval for them, and in November 1936 the executive of the Labour Party rebuffed an application by the Communist Party of New Zealand to affiliate. Yet Ormond Wilson, MP for Rangitikei 1935–38, who had been a student of G. D. H. Cole's while at Oxford, observed many years later that consciously or unconsciously, Marxist dogma influenced Labour's policies in the 1930s.[4]

The unemployed had also spent time reading about political, social and economic problems, as Dr G. H. Scholefield, the Parliamentary Librarian, noted. Evoking memories of the sentimental idealism that underlay the legislation of the Liberals half a century earlier, the *Standard* serialised Edward Bellamy's *Looking Backward* during the early months of 1936. Within the public service the culture of interventionism was also gaining adherents; in April 1937 a committee of able young bureaucrats headed by the lawyer F. B. Stephens produced a report for the Minister of Industries and Commerce which acknowledged 'defects' within the capitalist system.

The 1935 Labour Cabinet: front row: W. E. Parry, P. Fraser (Deputy Prime Minister),
M. J. Savage (Prime Minister), W. Nash (Minister of Finance), M. Fagan, R. Semple;
back row: Lee Martin, P. C. Webb, F. Langstone, H. G. R. Mason, F. Jones,
D. G. Sullivan, H. T. Armstrong. National Archives

Noting the worldwide trend towards 'industrial planning', the report thought it was 'a desirable ultimate objective and, indeed, the only logical outcome of present tendencies'. If the Government wished to provide the highest possible standard of living for everyone then 'they will have to build up a balanced internal economy on as stable a foundation as the structure will allow'. The authors envisaged more central control of the economy than ever before, and clearly relished the challenges this would offer to public servants.[5] People in many walks of life now supported state paternalism and were confident about the capacity of a left-wing government to direct it.

On the international scene Robert Skidelsky has called the Great Depression a 'virtual knockout blow' to economic liberalism.[6] In New Zealand the same collapse in incomes that occurred elsewhere, and a precipitous decline in home ownership, gave focus to Labour's plans. Savage became a vital factor in lifting public confidence. A softer man than Holland, Labour's new leader has been described as 'a benign, political uncle, cosy, a good mixer, with a warmly emotional appeal', who 'smelt more of the church bazaar and not at all of the barricades'.[7] He had a penchant for monetary reform and gave lengthy, often confused speeches punctuated with the exclamation 'Now then . . .'. To a Gisborne audience in July

1935 Savage stated boldly that a Labour Government would not borrow abroad for development but instead use 'the public credit'.

> There is plenty of work to be done in this country. Why, New Zealand wants painting from end to end; yet we put painters to work at the end of long-handled shovels. Qualified engineers, bachelors and masters of science, teachers trained at the public expense – all we can find for these people to do is to use the shovel. Under the Labour Party's policy of using the public credit, there will be no continuance of this system. Every man and woman will be found a place in the economic structure of the Dominion.

Savage was reflecting a climate which now favoured active promotion of employment by the Government and an autarkic approach to the world.[8] Savage had a remarkable political gift for personalising his policies, so that people could find in them solutions to their individual problems. After years of relief work and hardship, he became New Zealand's most loved political leader. His death on 27 March 1940 was followed by an unparalleled outpouring of emotion.

The electoral coalition that brought Labour to power in 1935 was both rural and urban and reflected the depression's heavy impact on all sections of New Zealand's population. However, trade unionists dominated the party's structure. Unionists numbered only 24,000 in 1901, but numbers rose rapidly. According to Erik Olssen, New Zealand was the third most unionised society in the world by 1913, and union influence on the economy grew commensurately. There were 101,000 unionists in 1930 before membership fell away during the depression to 72,000 in 1933.[9] Clause 18 of the Industrial Conciliation and Arbitration Amendment Act 1936 obliged all workers subject to an Arbitration Court award to belong to a union. Membership rocketed to 255,000 in 1939. One old unionist in the Legislative Council warned that this sudden rush of membership was bound to lead to a 'powerful plutocracy of officialdom that may be tempted to put its own comfort and the emoluments of office before the interests of [union members]'.[10] At the time, few were listening.

Many trade unions took advantage of the Political Disabilities Removal Act 1936 and affiliated and paid levies to the Labour Party. The party's president from 1937 to 1950 was Jim Roberts. He had been an early leader of the Waterside Workers' Union and played a major role in Labour politics during the depression. Without providing any supporting evidence, Roberts argued that New Zealand's workers were entitled to a 'comparatively high standard of living' because they produced 'more value per head employed than any other country in the world'.[11] Union leaders

'Taking up where Seddon left off'; M. J. Savage alongside a bust of Seddon in Parliament Buildings, 1935. ATL, S. P. Andrew Collection, 18444-1/1

quickly took advantage of the improving employment situation that developed into 'over-full employment' in the 1940s.

Many union secretaries prospered during Labour's fourteen years in office. Most worked closely with the governments of Savage (1935–40) and Peter Fraser (1940–49). Fintan Patrick Walsh, who was general secretary of the Seamen's Union, formed a close relationship with Fraser in his days as Minister of Marine. Walsh passed bits of intelligence to the minister about the activities of some of his MPs.[12] The unions usually supported the Cabinet line at annual party conferences, and they dominated party branches in some areas, especially in Wellington. They expected concessions in return for loyalty. 'Most union members', writes Olssen, 'assumed that their . . . demands were synonymous with the national interest.'[13] Walsh lobbied Fraser for legislation that would place workers' representatives on harbour boards. He also wanted to restrict Railways' competition with privately owned shipping companies so that the companies could make bigger profits and therefore afford higher wages for seamen.[14] Sometimes the Seamen's Union's pressure for new manning arrangements for ships cost the Government dearly. Subsidies to the Bluff–Stewart Island ferry

183

*'Big Jim' Roberts, President of the New Zealand
Labour Party 1937–50.* ATL C-23146

escalated rapidly after 1936 and eventually the service proved uneconomic. Shipping to the Chatham Islands suffered the same fate. In retrospect it is clear that many unions secured gains for their members at the expense of the long-term interests of both the public and, ultimately, themselves. Labour MPs found the constant pressure from unionists who seemed to care little about the financial situation increasingly hard to handle.[15]

By the end of World War II trade unions found they had to exert much more pressure if they were to make headway with the Labour Government. Economic stabilisation provided less room for them to achieve sectoral advantage. The Public Service Association under its leader Jack Lewin exercised considerable muscle with some success. A restructured Public Service Commission took office at the end of 1946 with a PSA nominee as one of a troika now running it.[16] Trade and public sector unions remained a vitally important component in the advancement of the State's influence in the economy. Roberts was often derisively referred to by Labour's political opponents as 'the uncrowned King of New Zealand'; Walsh, who became president of the Federation of Labour (which was formed in 1937 from an alliance between the old Alliance of Labour and the Trades and Labour Councils' Federation) in 1953, was nicknamed 'the Prince', or 'Black

Fraser's confidant, F. P. Walsh (left), discusses transport issues with the Commissioner of Transport, G. L. Laurenson, Secretary of Federated Farmers, A. P. O'Shea and a departmental official. ATL F-34417-1/2

Prince', by his detractors. Lewin could be tough as well as rude. After Prime Minister Fraser's speech to the PSA conference in 1947 Lewin instructed the official party to depart. Many people were beginning to feel that effective power in New Zealand no longer lay with politicians but with trade union leaders. This accounted for much of the hostility to waterside workers when they became involved in a lengthy industrial dispute with the State over wages in 1951.[17]

In 1935, however, all this was in the future. There was an air of anticipation as Savage's Government took office. The *New Zealand Herald* reported that the public seemed disposed to give the new government a chance to demonstrate its abilities.[18] Expectations of heightened state activity were not confined to unionists. Businessmen had been warming to interventionist policies for many years. A leading building contractor, James Fletcher, who already had a string of significant buildings to his credit, told the Auckland Rotary Club in March 1930 that he favoured revitalising industry, using the services of a 'young, virile, non-political' Department of Industries and Commerce and a more adventurous banking sector. In Fletcher's view, professional men and 'thinkers' had roles to play as well.

Are they on the running board, or are they behind the wheels of industry with the levers that their professional status and knowledge give to them? I think not. Do they recognise the opportunity in the value of research to assist our car back on to the road, to get its wheels on the metal and clear of the mud and the bog?

Fletcher was calling for a more adventurous State and an active bureaucracy. In the years to come he forged close personal friendships with Savage, Fraser and Labour's Minister of Finance, Walter Nash.[19]

By 1934 many businessmen were reading the tea leaves. In November 1934 A. M. Seaman, President of the Associated Chambers of Commerce, expressed the view that there was a 'tendency towards State control' and that businessmen 'should themselves participate in it'. Seaman noted there was 'more conscious and concerted planning of certain of our national activities'. He thought the trend would continue for some years. He warned his members against being 'King Canutes', telling them that it would be wiser to 'seek to guide the forces that have been loosed, rather than . . . continuing merely to oppose'. If there was to be paternalistic control then it 'must be exercised by experienced commercial men'.[20] Seaman's advice was endorsed by the *Auckland Star*, which noted that the State would inevitably engage in more regulation, and suggested that businessmen should factor this into their plans. The economist J. B. Condliffe, perhaps the best-known of a quartet of Canterbury University College economic thinkers from the 1920s, returned to New Zealand during the 1935 election campaign. He observed that New Zealand's socialism was divorced from doctrine; it was due instead to what he called 'colonial opportunism'. He added: 'Every group has sought to obtain from the State as much as possible.'[21] Most sectors of the New Zealand economy were now contributing to what Paul Johnson calls the 'political framework' of interventionism that lasted another 40 years.[22]

Support for state activity from businessmen was tinged with wariness because of Labour's earlier 'vestigial Marxism'.[23] Labour's 1918 platform had pledged to extend 'public ownership of national utilities' and promised speedy 'national control of the food supplies of the people', adding that where there was national ownership of any industry 'at least half the board of control in each case shall be appointed by the Union or Unions affected'. That platform had also endorsed higher tax on top incomes and lower tax for families.[24] Over the years the language became less strident, but Labour's policy lost none of its paternalism. 'To build the ideal Social State with the available material is the purpose of the Labour Party,' declared a policy document issued on 17 April 1933. 'The purpose of all production, primary and secondary, is to supply the social and economic requirements of the people, and the duty of the State is to organise productive and distribution agencies in order to utilise the natural resources for this purpose.' The document promised 'guaranteed prices, organised employment in primary and secondary industries', and 'a vigorous public works policy, local and national, at wages and salaries based on national production . . .'. Secondary industries would be fostered 'so as to ensure the production of those commodities which can be economically produced in the Dominion, thus providing employment for our own people, with the resultant increase in the internal demand for our primary and secondary products, with less dependency on the fluctuating and glutted overseas markets'.[25] Paternalism and protectionism moved hand in hand throughout policy documents.

During the 1935 campaign Savage declared that 'social justice must be the guiding principle, and economic organisation must adapt itself to social needs'. He talked constantly of 'intelligent use of the Public Credit'.[26] Commentators detected a more doctrinaire approach to the role of government than had come from the leader of any previous government. Professor Horace Belshaw, who had been a member of Coates's Brains Trust, observed that the new government's policies rested 'on the belief that coordinated economic and social planning by the state is necessary for economic and social development'.[27]

Labour's bold words, however, were usually matched by an equal dose of caution. Aware of some apprehension in the business and commercial sectors that caused holders of New Zealand securities to sell in the days after the 1935 election, Savage tried to cool things with the statement that it was the new government's intention simply 'to begin where Richard John Seddon and his colleagues left off'.[28] In the pre-Christmas period the new Prime Minister visited hospitals and orphanages where he distributed presents and told children that he hoped they would see his government as a friend. The Cabinet made several popular gestures including payment of a Christmas bonus to the unemployed and to recipients of charitable aid. Wellington and Otago Training Colleges would reopen, and five-year-olds who had been kept from schools since 1932 as an economy measure were to be readmitted. Relief rates of pay were increased, Maori being paid the same rates as others. There was a general belief in Labour circles that shorter working hours and higher incomes were necessary if a wide cross-section of people were to share in the benefits of improved machinery and technology.[29] Early in the New Year the flamboyant Minister of Works, Bob Semple – straying somewhat from Savage's earlier assurances about the adequacy of local resources – told an audience in Reefton that the Government intended to encourage overseas investment to help with development, and assured investors that they would not be exploited.[30] From the very beginning, ministers gave mixed messages.

There were still conservatives in the mid 1930s who opposed state intervention. Some expressed their views forcefully. In 1935 a young Canterbury employer, B. H. Riseley, declared, 'If we teach the people to rely on the State they will never be able to fend for themselves. Both employers and employees are leaning on the State. . . . We are teaching our people to rest on the State, and that is wrong.'[31] Professional people, especially lawyers and accountants, also tended to keep their distance from the new government. Writing to Coates after the election, an Auckland lawyer said 'it is surprising how many fellow citizens seem to have discovered that Labour represents just what they have been looking for'. One MP called these people 'fairweather friends'.[32] Yet, with diminishing opposition to state involvement among businessmen and the National Opposition reduced to nineteen seats, there was little option but to engage in constructive dialogue with Savage's Government.

Labour's first year in office was its *annus mirabilis*. Fifty-nine public Acts of Parliament were passed. A further 93 sets of statutory regulations were promulgated, a number that grew to 207 in 1937. The Department of Internal Affairs, which published the *Gazette*, was obliged to reorganise its printing schedules.[33] This new legal framework that emerged set the stage for Labour's next fourteen years and had a profound influence on the following half century.

Over the New Year 1936 the Government contemplated a radical measure. In order to solve the housing shortage, ministers were contemplating making housing a direct function of central government. They toyed with buying Fletcher Construction so that it could build state houses around the country for rent to low income people. James Fletcher refused to sell his company, but cooperated fully with Under-Secretary John A. Lee, Arthur Tyndall, who became Director of the Housing Construction Division, and the Government Architect while they purchased land and drew up plans for state houses. Within months, Fletchers had won contracts to build houses for the Government in Auckland and Wellington. They averaged 1050 square feet, and 40 per cent of them had three bedrooms. The first was completed in Miramar in March 1937. The Government guaranteed Fletcher Residential Construction Company's account to an overdraft limit of £200,000 to ensure that there were no construction delays.[34] Four hundred units were built in the year ending March 1938. By 1942 the Director of Housing Construction had contracts

State houses springing up like mushrooms in Miramar, 1938. ATL F-61277-1/2

with 345 builders. A total of 16,522 homes 'of a modern standard of comfort' had been completed by then and had been let at a variety of rentals to people in the medium and lower income groups.[35] By 1949 one house in every three being built in New Zealand was a state house. The Government had spent £76.2 million in total on rental housing, and more than 6000 workmen were employed by contractors to the Housing Division. Ormond Wilson observed that state housing 'was . . . markedly superior to any group housing that had gone before'.[36]

State housing was not all plain sailing. Political problems bedevilled the allocation process. Initially there were ballots for the subsidised accommodation, but many who won were clearly less needy than those who missed out. Allocation committees were established in the 1940s. But there was a persistent belief that political influence was necessary to get into a state house. An elaborate points system evolved in the 1970s to determine the priority of cases on the waiting list. Some people found this possible to manipulate, too. Moreover, there was a problem with those tenants whose financial situations, for one reason or another, improved after they got into state houses. Poor people on waiting lists – and there were more than 45,000 unsatisfied applicants in 1950 – resented the growing affluence of some tenants. Short of periodically applying a means test to occupants – which successive governments felt it politically unwise to do – there was no easy way of dislodging undeserving tenants. As Gael Ferguson observes, 'the Labour Government created a favoured group of tenants who were not always those most in need'.[37]

Labour's first piece of legislation was the Reserve Bank of New Zealand Amendment Act which became law on 8 April 1936. It cancelled private shareholding in the Reserve Bank, bringing it firmly under the control of the Minister of Finance. Some Labour politicians held high hopes for the legislation. Clyde Carr, MP for Timaru, saw Keynesian overtones in the measure, claiming it would make money 'immediately available' to state departments for restoring depression cuts and lifting salaries, wages and pensions to 'a decent level'. These moves, he believed, would increase spending power and stimulate demand. Other banks would be obliged to 'fall into line or get out'. In practice, the relationship between the Government and the bank changed little, as Gary Hawke has shown. The bank – as it had since 1934 – continued to give effect to the cautious monetary policy of the Government. Early in April 1936 Savage gave a public assurance that it was not the Government's intention 'to sit down and merely turn the handle of the printing press'.[38]

Under Walter Nash, Reserve Bank credit helped fund state housing, and assisted with another piece of Labour policy – 'guaranteed prices' for dairy farmers.[39] The gradual evolution in Labour's thinking that led to passage of the Primary Products Marketing Act 1936 has been told elsewhere.[40] While Labour had promised guaranteed prices to all agricultural exporters, the Bill covered only dairy farmers, since they were deemed to be in the greatest need. Nash had earlier told Parliament that a dairy farmer 'is entitled to a reasonable payment for the work he does'.[41] The Government's intention was to end the market price fluctuations that made dairy farming such an unpredictable occupation. As in Seddon's day, the words 'fair', 'just' and 'reasonable' were bandied about. The Primary Products Marketing Bill used the terms 'usual conditions', 'efficient producer', and 'sufficient net return'. It spoke of the Government's intention to ensure farmers an 'adequate remuneration for the services rendered by them to the community'. Farmers were entitled to a 'reasonable state of comfort'.[42] These were subjective terms capable of many interpretations, but were part of Walter Nash's flexible concept of social equity. Ministers were setting out on a course of social engineering designed to smooth the hills and hollows of life, lifting some groups and spreading wealth more widely, making use of tax revenue where necessary.[43] It became a difficult journey; assistance to one beneficiary often caused envy among others. Under Labour's paternalistic state the 'politics of envy' became a more noticeable feature of political debate. Over time, everyone came to see access to public expenditure as a right; most believed they were not getting as much as someone else.

Intensive negotiations between ministers and the Dairy Board were held during the days before the passage of the Act on 15 May 1936. It was finally agreed that the Government would purchase all dairy farmers' produce at a set price. The Board would then liaise with the newly created

Primary Products Marketing Department to ensure that maximum returns were realised from the on-sale of dairy produce abroad. Money received from sales above the guaranteed price would accumulate in a Dairy Industry Account and be used to subsidise payouts when the overseas market fell. The Government quietened critics of this reduction in the powers of the Dairy Board by ensuring that many Board officials were appointed to the new department. Some Opposition MPs claimed that the Government was 'confiscating' farmers' produce. But this criticism subsided when the guaranteed prices announced for butter (13.5 pence per pound) and cheese (15.1 pence) were higher than could reasonably have been expected from a precise reading of Labour's election promises.[44]

In its first year the Dairy Industry Account paid farmers more than was realised from sales abroad. The Marketing Department ran up a debt of £272,000, which was eventually written off by the Government. When overseas prices improved in 1937 and a surplus built up in the account, farmers agitated for a more generous payout. A pattern whereby dairy farmers expected to socialise their losses and capitalise their gains became well entrenched in the years ahead.

The innovations that began in 1936 had some unintended consequences. For a time, the payment on butter fat made the production of liquid milk less attractive for farmers to produce. By 1944 supplies had dropped to the point where domestic town milk supplies were endangered. In the Milk Act 1944 the Government extended a guaranteed price at a sufficiently attractive level to town milk suppliers to divert milk from butter and cheese production for urban supply. However, a combination of guaranteed prices for milk and subsidies that became part of stabilisation during the war kept the price of milk to consumers so low that some farmers worked out that it was cheaper to buy back subsidised milk for stock feed than to use their own produce.[45]

The Government phased down the central role of the Marketing Department in the post-war years and it was eventually abolished in the early 1950s. Beginning in 1947 its dairying functions were devolved on to the Dairy Products Marketing Commission. In 1952 the National Government won agreement from farmers that the Dairy Industry Account would be self-balancing, thereby ending top-ups from the taxpayer. Price-fixing was transferred to a Dairy Products Prices Authority in 1956, which in 1961 was restructured as the Dairy Production and Marketing Board.[46] By this time other forms of assistance to farmers were in place. They covered imported phosphate, subsidies to rabbit boards, funding for herd-testing, payments to the Veterinary Services Council and the hardy annual from the 1920s, the carriage of fertilisers by rail.[47] In the meantime, there was no doubt that Nash's scheme had done much to ensure stability in the traditionally volatile dairy industry. In 1948 an Apple and Pear Marketing Board was created, and in 1953 eggs, citrus fruit and honey, were each put under the producer board system of marketing. In the 1970s kiwifruit joined the other powerful boards, each with a selling monopoly.

At the outbreak of World War II, meat and wool were also brought under the control of the Marketing Department.[48] A system of bulk purchasing by the British Government returned; it was similar to that which had operated between 1915 and 1920. Government-to-government negotiations determined prices. A number of advisory organisations were established, including a National Council of Primary Production to advise on all aspects of primary production. In 1946 a Wool Disposal Commission took over the marketing of wool. It was restructured as the Wool Commission in 1952 with the intention of smoothing prices for wool producers. It did so by establishing a 'floor price' which saw the Commission topping up farmers' returns if wool auctions produced prices lower than the 'floor'. A surplus was expected to build up in the Commission's accounts in good years. Decisions by the Commission were always made after consultation with ministers.

A Meat Stabilisation Account with a similar purpose was established in 1942. It built up large financial reserves which were used after the war for various forms of assistance to farmers, including research. In 1947 the Meat Board took over most of the Marketing Department's meat-selling functions. In 1955 the National Government agreed to allow surpluses that had been built up to be used on a price-smoothing regime operated by a Meat Export Prices Committee, which, along with other marketing agencies, was indirectly controlled by the Meat Board. Over the years, governments, no matter which party was in power, played a major part in these developments both with legislation and funding. Since products of animal origin still averaged 65 per cent of the total value of New Zealand's exports as late as 1979, governments believed they had a vital interest in continuing to negotiate bulk-selling agreements with the British Government. Farmers had learned from experience that governments could be very useful to them.[49]

After passage of the Primary Products Marketing Act the Labour Government became preoccupied with the concerns of urban workers. Within days of assuming office the Department of Industries and Commerce was requested to report on the likely effects of returning salaries and wages to their 1931 levels. The department generally favoured such a move but pointed out that it would increase the costs of production, and some industries would have difficulty absorbing them. Noting overseas trends, officials told the minister: 'In order . . . to secure local industry and to foster industrial development it would appear that equivalent increased tariff or exchange protection, or other control of importations, would be required to offset probable benefits to overseas producers of such [an] increase in New Zealand costs'.[50] This protectionist message was taken up by the New Zealand Manufacturers' Federation, which requested that any wage rise or a reduction in hours worked should coincide with increased tariff protection.

While Labour MPs had given qualified support for raising the tariff in 1934, as ministers they were uneasy, fearing that higher tariffs could collapse the system of primary product quotas so tortuously negotiated at Ottawa. Savage therefore demurred at the manufacturers' request, but the Government went ahead with the introduction of the 40-hour week. The Prime Minister soon discovered that restoring wage and salary cuts 'was not as easy as it looks'.[51] Those employers who believed they would be unduly affected by the 40-hour week were told to plead hardship to the Arbitration Court in the hope of securing a delay in its application to a particular industry. This proved a vain hope. In June 1938 Judge W. J. Hunter of the Arbitration Court announced that the Court would not be concerned with the ability of an industry to pay increased wages, and that problems with competition from overseas were a matter for the legislature.[52]

On 8 June 1936 the I.C.&A. Amendment Act became law. It restored compulsory arbitration in labour disputes, authorised the Arbitration Court to incorporate the 40-hour week in awards, and gave the Arbitration Court the power to fix the 'basic rate of wages' at a level which in the opinion of the Court would be 'sufficient to enable a man in receipt thereof to maintain a wife and three children in a fair and reasonable standard of comfort'.[53] This 'family wage' was a statement of the Government's social intention which the Court was expected to bear in mind when fixing wages. It bore no relationship to the capacity of an industry to carry any extra costs involved. In the event, the Court's first effort at establishing a 'basic wage' for adult workers announced in November 1936 resulted in a modest increase; the level of £3 16s per week was less than the wage of £4 0s 8d set in 1931 before the cuts. Some Labour supporters were critical of this decision, believing it broke a promise.[54] In due course ministers found it necessary to engage in a variety of other measures to ensure that their declarations of social intent could be fulfilled.

In June 1936 the Factories Amendment Act also became law after a slip-

Dan Sullivan, Minister of Industries and Commerce 1935–47, at the Lipton Tea factory, Wellington.
ATL F-70060-1/2

up on the parliamentary order paper allowed it to go through earlier than Cabinet intended.[55] The Act incorporated the 40-hour week and specified pay rates for overtime. This had major ramifications for employers, and its date of application was delayed until 1 September 1936. Manufacturers' and farmers' costs quickly rose. Government departments also experienced higher-than-anticipated wage bills. Rerostering at hospitals opened up job opportunities for nurses, cleaners and kitchen hands. Inflation was already becoming a concern, and the 40-hour week gave it a further nudge, causing problems for the Government's policy of food price stabilisation. Every government intervention into the marketplace seemed to carry a cost, yet politicians retained a supreme faith that they could regulate or legislate against any unpleasant side-effects of their policies. On 12 August 1936 the Government enacted the Prevention of Profiteering Act in the belief that some prosecutions would deter manufacturers and retailers from making excessive price increases to cover their rising wage bills.[56]

Earlier in the year Labour's Minister of Industries and Commerce, Dan Sullivan, had gazetted new price levels for flour, wheat and bread under the Board of Trade Act 1919. In his press statement he anticipated that workers' wages would soon be raised.[57] Minimum prices for motor spirits, first set in 1933, were raised in the hope that price cutting could be eliminated. A 3d per gallon gross profit was guaranteed to the retailer so as to ensure 'a fair return for his labour'. The *Standard* was enthusiastic about price control: 'Price-cutters are no good in any business', it proclaimed.

Bob Semple (Minister of Works 1935–41, 1942–49), who was responsible for a vast state construction programme. ATL F-115893-1/2

'They are responsible for the payment of low wages and the working of long hours.' Where many saw price-fixing as a device to keep the necessities of life within the reach of the poor, others expected that it would be part of a wider plan that would enable wages and conditions to be set not by the market, but according to some general idea about what was fair and reasonable. Labour's command economy was moving into top gear.[58]

There were problems from the beginning. On 12 August, with new overtime rates and a reduction in working hours only days away, master bakers waited on Sullivan and requested an immediate increase in the price of bread. Five days later Cabinet approved a price rise of a halfpenny per 2 lb standard loaf, taking the price to 5.5 pence, with an extra halfpenny for home delivery. A new set of regulations was telegraphed to all master bakers' associations. Within weeks there were further complications. Grocers argued that the margin of one penny per loaf for retailing was inadequate, given their requirement to adopt the 40-hour week and the Court's wage rise. The stark reality was that bakers were not able to control the costs of their materials, and these were rising. It was all reminiscent of problems encountered with price control during the inflationary days of 1918–20. Like his predecessors, Sullivan was finding that price control, no matter how laudable its intention, guaranteed him a hot seat.[59]

The minister refused grocers' requests for a price increase, but they

L. J. Schmitt, a very active Secretary of Industries and Commerce 1935–45, after his retirement. ATL F-88757-1/2

then launched a press campaign against the Government. Cabinet held out during 1937. In order to gain better control over prices in this politically sensitive market, a Wheat Committee was set up. Sullivan was its deputy chairman, while wheat growers, millers and bakers were represented on it. All wheat for milling was purchased by the committee and resold to flour millers, who in turn sold their flour, bran and pollard through the committee. By this time flour-mill workers wanted higher wages and disputed that this would inevitably push up the price of bread.[60] The reality that labour costs always constituted the bulk of any industry's costs of production was a puzzle that few union leaders understood.

At the beginning of 1938 bakers sent copies of their balance sheets to the Secretary of Industries and Commerce, L. J. Schmitt, with a plea that he intervene with the minister. A deputation waited on Schmitt on 27 January; one baker told him that because of the shorter hours now being worked he was obliged to employ six extra workers; another told the minister that delivery drivers had been paid £3 19s 2d per week at the time of the price increase in August 1936 but had subsequently been awarded £4 7s by the Arbitration Court. Another claimed there had been a drop-off in the rate of work of his delivery staff, while a fourth pointed to a recent increase in the price of motor fuel that his company was having to carry. Collectively they argued for either a reduction in the price of flour or an increase in the price of bread. The Government held out. Some bakers publicly criticised the Government during the 1938 election campaign.[61]

The Government was in a bind. Many votes could be at risk if there was a bread price rise; on the other hand, holding out against bakers' demands when their argument was so compelling inevitably led to accusations of unfairness, a concept that so many aspects of government policy claimed to be against. Savage temporised. After Labour's stunning victory on 15 October 1938 bakers returned to the attack. In a memo to Sullivan on 11 January 1939 Schmitt argued for a bread price rise but floated a new idea with his minister: the Government might care to keep prices stable by paying subsidies on flour. Ministers warmed to the suggestion. Use of government money could get bread price control out of the newspapers. Bureaucrats were soon involved in a major study of bakers' costs. With the threat of a bakers' strike before him, Sullivan announced in February 1939 that the Government would 'grant relief'. A subsidy regime that amounted to a cost-plus system was soon in force. It turned bread prices into a matter of regular, behind scenes negotiations between bakers and bureaucrats, with the taxpayer footing the bills.

Standard loaves of bread were kept at a low price compared with other daily necessities until 1977 as part of a growing system of stabilising food prices. In 1942 subsidies were introduced on butter so that its domestic price to consumers could be kept substantially below the export value. Stabilisation as such was defended on the grounds that cheap food helped the poor. When the National Government freed some food items from price control in 1950 it felt obliged to continue subsidising bread and by 1953 the taxpayer was contributing £5 million each year to wheat and flour and an equal amount to butter.[62] These costs were now part of an elaborate food and gas subsidy regime that cost the taxpayer £17.5 million that year. The only noticeable alteration to the bread regime was the National Government's refusal to continue subsidising bread deliveries. This saw the end of home deliveries and of the assortment of bread tins that adorned many verandahs.[63]

The Government's food subsidy regime occasionally had unintended effects on the market for other products. With the intention of maximising the production of butter for the British market, the Labour Government retained a restriction on the local availability of fresh cream. Ice cream manufacturers resorted to using subsidised butter in large quantities. When cream became available again in 1950 there was no subsidy to keep its price down, so ice-cream manufacturers continued to use subsidised butter. At the end of 1951 the National Government endeavoured to make them pay the full unsubsidised price for butter; but it soon became clear that pastry cooks and biscuit manufacturers were also availing themselves of cheap butter and any effort to oblige them to pay the full price would be impossible to police. The problem persisted until butter subsidies were abolished in the 1970s.[64]

Meantime the Labour Government had been seeking to fund employment for those out of work. In the Government Railways Amendment Act 1936 Semple gave the Railways Board of 1931 'its running shoes', bringing operations back into a Railways Department. Once again a general manager was responsible to the Minister. At public works sites wheelbarrows ('Irishmen's motorcars' Semple called them) were abolished in favour of modern machinery.[65] The Government authorised new rail and road work, and many airports were soon under construction. State agencies were again expected to fulfil the Government's employment objectives while delivering their services. The number of Railway employees increased 72 per cent between 1934 and 1940. Not surprisingly, Railways' net revenue declined sharply until wartime recruitment mopped up many underemployed Railway workers. Public Works employees doubled by the end of 1939; many relief workers who had been on Public Works projects during the depression were transferred to permanent employment and basic rates of pay. The number of Post Office employees also rose by nearly 50 per cent during the same period. While New Zealand's trading departments were expected to operate as employment agencies they were unable to make business decisions on a strictly commercial basis. However, government policy thinned the ranks of the unemployed, although there were still 8000 receiving the dole in the winter of 1938, with another 30,000 in subsidised work.[66]

The view reemerged that to work for the Government was a secure form of employment that carried superannuation rights and involved less arduous workloads than the private sector. Not only were agencies such as Railways expected to employ more people than were needed to provide an efficient service but passenger and freight rates were pegged at low levels in the belief that such action would generally assist business and consumers. The concept that there should be an adequate return on capital simply faded away. Dan Sullivan expressed Labour's view of railways when he said:

> The advance of settlement, the opening up of new country and the increase in its productiveness, the provision of employment for large numbers, the cheapening of the means of transport for both goods and passengers, and many other items must all be reckoned as a value obtained for the expenditure in addition to the mere monetary returns earned by the system.

Implementing this philosophy over time became expensive for the taxpayer, especially when Railways needed to invest in new rolling stock. The Government resorted to tougher regulations against competition from road transport in the carriage of bulk goods. But monopoly status did not return Railways to profit, and produced many anomalous situations for those employed in the private transport industry.[67]

Labour's activist State found it difficult to engineer job creation in the private sector. Ministers wanted more jobs, especially in manufacturing, which was employing 80,000 workers in 1935. In February 1936 Sullivan outlined his views on secondary industry. His statement envisaged an early version of what came to be known as 'import substitution'.

> I consider that while recognising that for some time to come the welfare and prosperity of New Zealand must be to a large extent dependent upon our export markets, the expansion of secondary industries and the building up of a greater internal industrial system will do much towards the mitigation of the harmful effects of the fluctuations in the prices received overseas for our primary products. It is the earnest aim of the Government to secure the employment in industry of 50,000 odd unemployed workers in this country, and the expansion of our internal industrial system is one of the main methods by which this re-employment can be achieved.[68]

Implementation was another matter.

Savage told a deputation of manufacturers on 7 May 1936 that he was a 'visionary', adding that 'we must insulate ourselves from abroad'. He believed that it would be possible to achieve this by higher tariffs, by controlling exchange, or by using import licensing. After a great deal of rhetoric, the Prime Minister assured the deputation that the Government 'realised that as they lifted the standard of life it would require still more protection against the production of lower standard [countries] outside'.[69] However, Nash was about to go to London in the hope of negotiating another bilateral trading agreement for New Zealand's primary produce. He fought strongly against any tariff increases that might anger British exporters, and be seen as contrary to the spirit of the Ottawa agreement. Nash assured the manufacturers that he was prepared to consider other (unspecified) forms of asssistance to industry to enable them to 'get a decent return on the capital invested and to pay those working in it'.[70]

In the event, the Government monitored the effects of increased costs on industry, talked of price controls, but tolerated moderate price adjustments, even when these impacted adversely on some companies, especially in the woollen industry. Manufacturers were kept waiting many months before the nature of any further governmental assistance was revealed. Meantime, retail sales increased because of improved spending power. But production costs rose inexorably, and manufacturers were restless at government delays, especially since officials seemed intent on devising more complex forms of regulation for their industries.[71]

Meantime, Industries and Commerce was developing a system for licensing new as well as existing industries and running an efficiency slide rule over them. Like many ministers, Sullivan had been influenced by Clinkard's submission to Parliament in 1932, even though he did not like the man. Sullivan appears to have believed that the small New Zealand market meant that in many cases only one producer would be needed to satisfy local demand for a product. However, a bureaucratic eagle eye would be necessary to prevent abuses by any company granted monopoly status. Overseas investors wishing to establish new companies in competition with New Zealand-based enterprises were kept waiting while the Government worked out its policies.[72]

The Industrial Efficiency Bill, originally known as the 'Industrial Planning Bill', was enacted in October 1936. Regarded by officials as one of the most important measures of the year, it gave the Government wide powers to regulate industries. The legislation was described in what was now becoming a ritually paternalistic preamble. It was 'an Act to promote the economic welfare of New Zealand by providing for the promotion of new industries in the most economic form and by so regulating the general organisation, development and operation of industries that a greater measure of industrial efficiency will be secured'. The Act incorporated a Bureau of Industry which had been functioning since May. This Bureau existed until 1956. It had powers to license industries, to conduct inquiries, and to make recommendations on how best to assist, either by way of subsidies, grants, loans, tariff concessions, preferences, embargoes 'or otherwise howsoever with a view to the establishment of new industries or the development of existing industries'. The Bureau could prepare plans for any industry and involve itself with the training of skilled people deemed essential to that industry.[73] There was no single instrument to assist any particular industry, but rather an array of measures that bureaucrats could recommend to the minister after receiving submissions.

The Bureau of Industry identified many areas where local production could be stimulated to satisfy the local market. Sardine canning, soap, rennet, flax processing, petrol pumps, asbestos cement, tyres and tubes, lacquers, electric ranges, car batteries, radios, linseed oil, woollen goods and wooden boot lasts were all identified as areas for expansion. They were included in a growing number of industries that required a licence. Efforts were made to encourage greater use of coal for electricity generation. In July 1936 consideration was given to boosting imports of completely knocked down (CKD) cars for local assembly – an industry that had begun in a small way in the Hutt Valley as early as 1926. There was much research into the clothing industry which seemed to have the potential for jobs, and interest was soon being shown in the plans of several Australians who were developing a large timber mill at Whakatane and employing 220 people by the beginning of 1938.[74]

The Bureau's members consisted of senior public servants. L. J. Schmitt, the new Secretary of Industries and Commerce, chaired the body. An Australian by birth, he had worked as an accountant for Broken Hill Proprietary and had served in the New Zealand Board of Trade's price control division at the end of World War I before serving as Trade Commissioner in Sydney. The Bureau usually met in the department's head office in the Government Life Building in Customhouse Quay on Monday afternoons. Initially, members had confidence that tariff protection would afford the necessary level of assistance to developing industries. However, ministers' unease about a British backlash to higher tariffs led them to explore other forms of assistance, such as subsidies.

In July 1936 Cabinet told the Bureau that it was not government policy 'to extend financial assistance to any one unit in an industry where that unit was in competition with other units in the same industry'. Ministers and bureaucrats were cautiously feeling their way towards a new relationship between the State and industry. After months of delay in 1937–38 while Nash laboured over trading arrangements with the British, the Bureau decided to recommend several different forms of assistance to new industries depending on what seemed most likely to work. Common to all their recommendations was that there be a series of campaigns to persuade the general public and local authorities to buy locally made products.[75]

The Bureau set up a specialist committee to handle pharmacy licensing where it was clear that the Government's intended health plans would involve major public expenditure. In January 1937 the New Zealand Official Drug Tariff and Dispensing Price List was issued. It prescribed limits for quantities of drugs that could be dispensed and stipulated the prices at which they could be sold. Complex negotiations took place between departmental officials and drug companies over what constituted a 'fair profit'. Eventually a Pharmacy Council emerged from these discussions. It distributed licences to retail chemists according to population needs, and controlled cooperative buying of drugs.[76]

The Government was no longer acting as umpire between competing business interests; it was becoming a regulating agent, as well as an active defender of those companies deemed likely to provide stability and employment for New Zealanders. The principal agency of State in all this activity was the Department of Industries and Commerce. It serviced producer boards, investigated fruit and vegetable marketing, produced elaborate plans for the tobacco and flax industries, subsidised some industries to keep them competitive, and rationalised and regulated the distribution of a wide range of products. When import licensing was introduced in December 1938 the department became the body that advised the Customs Department on whether to grant a licence and if so, for how much.

A centralised economy on this scale needed expert advice on many matters. In 1937 a Standards Institute was established with Schmitt as its 'permanent head'. Peopled with representatives of professional bodies such as engineers, architects, chemists and the DSIR, it met from time to time and tendered advice on technical matters. The Institute endeavoured to establish standard specifications for a variety of products such as plumbing and electrical materials, as well as paint that was manufactured in New Zealand.[77] The first three years of the Labour Government marked a huge leap in bureaucratic involvement in New Zealand's economy. The Government Life building became the engine room of the new economy. Ministers and their officials, as Paddy Webb had promised in January 1936, were becoming 'builders, thinkers, creators, repairers'.[78]

Registering all existing industries and licensing new ones deemed worthy of government assistance (there were 34 of them by March 1941) was a major bureaucratic undertaking. It involved many application forms and much processing of paper. For a while there was confusion because companies selling motor spirits found they were required to register twice – once under the Explosives and Dangerous Goods Amendment Act 1920 and again under the Industrial Efficiency Act 1936. Meetings of the Bureau often bogged down as bureaucrats struggled over applications for permission to erect or shift pumps at individual service stations. Pharmaceutical licensing was a perpetual nightmare because the Boots Ltd chain was competing very successfully with local pharmacies, which constantly sought protection.[79]

Licences granted to industries occasionally went to overseas interests. Dunlop, Bristol Myers, Colgate-Palmolive, Philips, HMV, Vesta and Exide Batteries, Beatty Brothers, Electrolux, Felt and Textiles, Slazenger, Phillips and Impey, Reckett and Colman, Bushells, and Korma Mills were just some of the overseas firms that established manufacturing industries in New Zealand under licence.[80] However, occasionally the system of licensing produced results which the bureaucrats had not intended. Anticipating that only one licence for a new enterprise would be granted, some entrepreneurs sought and received the licence, then failed to proceed, blocking another who was serious about entering the market. Occasionally bureaucrats got out of their depth. Such was the case with plans to register the Leicester trade.

Leicester goods made from a mixture of wool and silk enjoyed a brief popularity during the 1930s. In September 1936 the Bureau of Industry sought information about the extent to which such goods were being produced in New Zealand. It appeared that some clothing manufacturers made a limited number of items, but bureaucrats formed the impression they could be produced on a much larger scale, with the prospect of many jobs being created. Wearproof Hosiery Ltd of Sydney applied for an exclusive licence and tariff protection and gave a guarantee that they would employ 200 New Zealanders in the production of a range of Leicester socks if they were given a total monopoly of the New Zealand market. Officials, and eventually the Minister of Industries and Commerce, were impressed. Wearproof assured officials that they could retail the Leicester socks at no more than the current landed price of imports. Nash demurred, fearing once more that British manufacturers would deem a ban on sock imports into New Zealand a breach of the Ottawa agreements. Officials at the Bureau of Industry would not take 'no' for an answer and continued negotiations with Wearproof into 1939. Elaborate plans were drawn up for the production of up to 300,000 dozen pairs of socks per annum. The surplus would be exported to Australia. However, in the middle of 1939 news that Sullivan intended to license the Leicester trade and provide a monopoly to Wearproof got out. It was immediately clear that during the two years of discussions between Wearproof and officials, existing manu-facturers in New Zealand had themselves been responding to fashion demands and were producing a growing array of Leicester goods. Officials backed off. Korma Mills of Australia eventually became involved in sock production in New Zealand, building a large factory in Pah Rd, Auckland. Monopoly status on the scale desired by Wearproof was not granted. Bureaucrats had simply underestimated the capacity of private enterprise to respond to fashion demands.[81]

The system of industrial licensing intensified the already close relationship between officialdom and businessmen. Each depended on the other; fraternisation grew. As far as the public was concerned, if manufacturers produced goods under licence, then the Government was responsible for the quality of goods. Files of complaints built up; within the garment industry alone they covered everything from the materials used to the accuracy of labelling. In September 1954 Mabel Howard MP, New Zealand's first woman Cabinet Minister, waved a pair of bloomers in Parliament that she believed were wrongly labelled 'large', and complained of lax labelling supervision by the Department of Industries and Commerce![82] By the 1950s there was scarcely any area of industrial production that was not the subject of licensing or bureaucratic scrutiny, much of it ineffectual. Controls and regulations had proliferated like weeds.

The year 1938 will always be regarded as a landmark in the development of New Zealand's welfare state. Passage of the Social Security Act in September 1938, a few weeks before Labour's re-election, marked the high point of public confidence in the all-provident State. In later years Labour politicians viewed it as Labour's greatest achievement.[83] The Act came into force on 1 April 1939. It consisted of a system of state benefits and what politicians intended to be a universal health service. Subsistence payments to the old, the sick, the unemployed and to widows and orphans, most of which had been increased in 1936, were now included in the omnibus legislation. Treasury officials warned against the proposed levels of pensions, arguing that the whole scheme seemed posited on the continuation of 'a level of comparative prosperity'.[84] Health benefits were progressively brought into force over the next few years – mental hospital treatment on 1 April, maternity benefits in May, and free in-patient general hospital treatment in July 1939. Out-patient, pharmaceutical, X-ray and general medical services benefits came in 1941, physiotherapy benefits in 1942, and district nursing (1944), laboratory diagnostic benefits (1946) and dental benefits for children up to the age of sixteen in 1947. Cash benefits were mostly means-tested, but health care was available to all. A special Social Security Fund was established into which was paid a 5 per cent levy on all salaries, wages and other income. There was a registration fee of 5 shillings per annum payable by males aged from sixteen to twenty and all females, and of £1 per annum by all males over twenty. It was envisaged from the beginning that Parliament would have to top up the fund by the amount that these taxes fell short of payouts.[85]

Various forms of national health insurance had been discussed by politicians and officials for many years. The development of Labour's ideas from the slogans of 1935 into the comprehensive legislation of 1938 has been discussed elsewhere.[86] Many explanations of the need for the Act were given during its germination, none more engaging than the comment of the Prime Minister when dealing with taunts from his political opponents:

I want to know why people should not have decent wages, why they should not have decent pensions in the evening of their days or when they are invalided. What is there more valuable in our Christianity than to be our brother's keepers in reality? . . . . I want to see people have security. . . . I want to see humanity secure against poverty, secure in illness or old age.[87]

Elsewhere Savage described the Social Security Act as 'applied Christianity'.

The comprehensive nature of the Social Security Act impressed overseas observers. Writing in 1954, R. Mendelsohn claimed that the all-embracing nature of New Zealand's legislation influenced Western European policy makers after World War II. The British historian, Asa Briggs, has also noted that New Zealand's social security legislation 'deeply influenced . . . other countries'. By 1940–41 public expenditure on Social Security was more than four times what had been paid out on health and welfare in 1935. By the end of the 1940s New Zealand's expenditure on Social Security amounted to nearly 10 per cent of GNP. This was proportionately higher than the amount spent at that time in most other developed countries.[88]

However, when observers spoke of the 'comprehensive' nature of New Zealand's system, they were referring to the fact that the Social Security Act wrapped pensions and health care together in the one piece of legislation. In reality, the health-care component was not comprehensive. It was cobbled together in a series of agreements made between ministers and interest groups over a nine-year period. Each agreement was the best that could be reached at the time. Taken together, there were inconsistencies amongst these benefits from the very beginning. Because of doctor intransigence, the General Medical Services Benefit never covered the full cost of surgery visits. Moreover, there was no mechanism for increasing the benefit so that it would keep pace with inflation. Over time this meant that patients carried a growing portion of the cost of a visit to the doctor. However, pharmaceutical, X-ray and pathological benefits paid total costs but depended on doctor referral. Evidence built up over the years that the very poor were making less use of general practitioners, and it became clear that they were therefore missing out on the other benefits that could be accessed only through a GP. A health-care scheme designed with universality in mind became a boon to the middle and upper income groups who could afford to pay their doctors' bills and therefore gained access to the other benefits. This was the very antithesis of what Labour politicians originally intended.[89]

Under the direction of Peter Fraser, Savage's deputy who took over as Prime Minister on 1 April 1940, there were significant advances in publicly provided education, principally at the secondary and tertiary levels. In 1936 'free' post-primary education was made available to all children until age nineteen. This quickly encouraged all children to seek some secondary education. In 1944 the minimum school leaving age was set at fifteen. When the number of bursaries was substantially increased, numbers attending technical colleges and universities also leaped. The Government was determined to ensure formal education for all who were willing to avail themselves of it. More money for education, as a later Minister of Education, T. H. McCombs acknowledged, was never a problem with the Labour Cabinet.[90]

While Fraser was largely self-taught, education was his real passion in life. He read widely and developed a talent for tapping the ideas of academically trained minds. Dr C. E. Beeby, who joined the Department of Education in 1938, was a philosopher with research experience at Harvard and a Ph.D from Manchester University. His immediate background was in educational research and he admitted to little administrative experience. One of his first tasks in the department was to write a speech for Fraser. The minister particularly liked several sentences and they have often been quoted:

> The Government's objective, broadly expressed, is that every person, whatever his level of academic ability, whether he be rich or poor, whether he live in town or country, has a right, as a citizen, to a free education of the kind for which he is best fitted and to the fullest extent of his powers. So far is this from being a pious platitude that the full acceptance of the principle will involve the reorientation of the whole education system.

Beeby, who became Director of Education at the beginning of 1940, has spoken of the 'revivalist' feeling in educational circles at the time, adding that 'Fraser spoke what men and women of good will were thinking and groping for'. Fraser's declaration of intent was never openly challenged in his lifetime.[91] Minister, director, educators and most of the wider public accepted 'equality of opportunity' and a full and 'free' education as laudable goals. Departmental policies were adjusted in the confident belief they could be achieved. Curricula were broadened, class sizes reduced, and libraries improved. Pre-schooling was stimulated. A nutritional supplement for school children was provided in the 'free milk' scheme introduced in 1937, at an estimated cost to the taxpayers of £30,000 in its first year. Specialists in speech training were appointed to schools, and there were regular visits by doctors and nurses; they became associated in many children's minds with a variety of vaccination programmes and the distribution of 'free apples', each wrapped carefully in tissue paper.

An instalment of socialism? School milk after 1937. ATL F-1937-1/4

Accrediting of University Entrance was introduced in 1945 and a national School Certificate examination for fifth formers began in 1946. Beeby stressed that it was government policy not to hurt the general interests of a majority of pupils by concentrating on the needs of a few. He added, however, 'The Department is anxious to maintain high academic standards for the scholarly, but . . . this end must not be allowed to interfere with the schools' main function of giving a full and realistic education to fit the bulk of the population, culturally and economically, for the world of today.' Some critics believed that standards were falling in the quest for equality of opportunity; one newspaper called the new trends in education 'Beebyism'. In 1978 Beeby conceded that equal opportunity had been much harder to achieve than he thought it would be in the late 1930s.[92] Social engineering was moving at a fast pace towards goals that were not always attainable.

The huge hike in government expenditure after 1935 – it rose nearly 46 per cent between 1935 and 1939 – when coupled with wage increases, fuelled inflation in the pre-war years. Demand for imports rose steadily and in 1938 there was some capital flight from New Zealand as investors became worried about the magnitude of Labour's election-year spending. Export prices had already dipped and New Zealand's overseas capital reserves slid alarmingly. The welfare state's first election-year foreign exchange crisis – of which there were to be many more – presented Walter Nash with a serious challenge. For months there had been debate among officials about how to respond to shrinking overseas reserves. The conventional response of deflation held no attraction to an expansionary government, while devaluation would have been the reverse of Savage's earlier promises to return the pound to its pre-1933 value.

Because of fears that higher tariffs would lead to British retribution, the only acceptable option seemed to be some form of direct control on foreign exchange. For many months Customs officials had been gathering material for Nash on protective measures taken in 27 other countries, including Denmark, whose system seemed to appeal to officials.[93] On the evening of 6 December 1938 Nash made a major announcement. In order to ensure that New Zealand maintained enough funds to meet its overseas debt commitments, the Government would henceforth license all New Zealand imports and exports; imports would enter the country only under permit. Sterling transfers that drew on New Zealand's external credit would be restricted by the Reserve Bank.[94] In effect the Government now controlled money transfers into and out of New Zealand.

Manufacturers who had been pushing for further tariff protection until the last moment described themselves as being 'more dazed and bewildered than if a national earthquake had convulsed both islands'.[95] They referred to 'a watertight trade barrier that had been erected around New Zealand's coasts' – a comment that echoed the view expressed by a Belgian newspaper a few months earlier when it called New Zealand 'a sealed compartment, with her frontiers practically closed'.[96] Some Labour backbenchers claimed to see import controls as a mechanism that would facilitate construction of a new Jerusalem. W. T. Anderton, MP for Eden and grandfather of the later reforming Minister of Finance, Roger Douglas, told Parliament:

> We now exercise control over imports and sterling, and are thus able to prevent a position ever arising again where millions of pounds may fly from our country willy-nilly or at a whim and fancy of individuals who want to spoil the efforts of the Labour Government. Import control has come, and, as a government, we have to see to it that the control is exercised scientifically, and that the things we import balance our exports. We have to see . . . that the resources we possess within our country are utilized to the maximum for the benefit of this Dominion. There can be nothing wrong with the policy because it involves living within our means and providing a standard of living which, we say, should

at all times be maintained. . . . Within New Zealand we have all the materials and wealth necessary to bring to the people a standard of living far exceeding anything in the world today.[97]

Savage's enthusiasm underpinned Anderton's idealism. At a press conference on 7 December the Prime Minister sang his familiar song about self-sufficiency, telling reporters that 'scientific selection of imports' was 'the practical expression of our insulation plan'. Asked whether luxury imports were likely to be affected, the Prime Minister commented that the luxuries of today were the necessities of tomorrow, and 'there was nothing too good for the people of New Zealand. . . . Our job is to provide a foundation for all starting with first things. The best music, the best means of travel, the best education, the best of everything, is good enough for the people of New Zealand. . . .' Savage concluded with the words: 'Anyone who attempts to build New Zealand and lift the standard of life without taking a reasonable measure of control of our overseas trade will fall down on the job.'[98] To politicians, bureaucrats and social reformers alike, 'insulation' seemed to be a vague philosophy of optimism, autarky and nationalism, wrapped in pseudo-scientific clothing.

The ever-practical Nash, however, was more realistic. To him, import controls were essentially a crisis measure to meet the shortage of foreign exchange. He denied that the new controls were socialistic, noting that similar measures had been introduced in many capitalist countries. He promised 'to provide security and continuity of demand to manufacturers who are entering into the production of commodities at present imported. They will be given a maximum measure of protection so long as they supply commodities at reasonably economic prices'. The minister continued:

> The major Government objective is to utilise the resources of the Dominion in maintaining and extending the standard of living of all our people. To do this we must extend production, primary and secondary, within the Dominion to its fullest extent, while at the same time giving maximum trade preference to our best customer, the United Kingdom.[99]

The Government believed it had found a device that would protect New Zealand industry without pushing up the retail price of British imports, thus jeopardising delicate trade arrangements with London. The quantity of imports would be regulated by 'scientific' controls, not the retail price. In the process, ministers and bureaucrats would take unto themselves the task of balancing domestic demand, production and retail prices, adding that to the battery of planning and other functions they already performed.

Given the fact that New Zealand was, according to the League of Nations, more dependent on external trade than any other nation on earth, autarky was a policy unlikely to succeed in the long term.[100]

Importers vehemently opposed import licensing, especially when a continued shortage of overseas funds during 1939 forced the Government to introduce 'exchange authorities' which spread the availability of funds over specified periods of time. In May 1939 Gainor Jackson of Devonport, who was a supporter of the National Opposition, succeeded in having the regulations struck down in the Supreme Court. This necessitated validating legislation in the Customs Act Amendment Act of September 1939.[101] But, just as most American businessmen adjusted eventually to the New Deal, New Zealand's manufacturers settled down to tolerate, even enjoy the new regime, although few importers ever reconciled themselves to it. In January 1939 the manufacturers' journal, the *New Zealand National Review*, called Nash's reforms 'statesmanlike and constructive'. Using language with military images that could have graced a handbook on National Socialism or Stalinism, the *Review* added a note of warning:

> This new progressive and wealth-producing policy will not be implemented and brought to fruition without bitter opposition and ceaseless attempts to sabotage and paralyse it. We are deliberately and determinedly turning aside from the old road of 'laissez-faire', 'rafferty' rules, and go-as-you-please, and the new one of earning our wealth by the sweat of our brows (instead of borrow-boom-and-burst) is not going to be an easy path to the millennium. Organising our industrial development will demand the best brains and the men most skilled in management and enterprise for the job. They will need cheap capital and credit, willing labour, and fair reward for their work. . . . Those who direct and control industry must no longer be regarded as predatory capitalists, but as captains of the companies and regiments of industrial production, performing the essential function of establishing the most productive contact between labour and materials.[102]

Just as ministers believed they were taming capitalism and turning it into something indistinguishable from socialism, so did many in the private sector believe they had ensnared the Government's apparatus for their own ends.

While there were plenty of conservative critics who protested that the term 'socialist' that Labour's leaders occasionally used was a stage on the road to communism, careful observers were reluctant to dignify Labour's changes with any philosophical label. Echoing André Siegfried's judgement 40 years earlier, Sam Leathem, an Auckland manufacturer and economist wrote early in 1939: 'It is probably true that as a people we distrust, even despise theory; we dislike argument on ultimates; we pride ourselves on being practical'.[103] In a spirit of paternalism New Zealand's leaders were feeling their way towards what they hoped would be a fairer society.

Much of the regulatory legislation which passed between 1936 and 1938 was couched in such general terms that it called for judgements from ministers and their officials that many were scarcely competent to make. Moreover, in exercising their judgements they were politicising a great array of decisions hitherto made by private individuals and companies. In so doing, the Labour Government made the business of government infinitely more complex, and helped turn several generations of politicians into 'Aunt Sallies' to be blamed for every ill in the land. Yet, Labour's experimentation had a worthy purpose: the Government intended to see that everyone was adequately housed, fed, clothed and educated. Sixty years later, with the benefit of hindsight, it is a matter of judgement as to whether some of the political decisions, particularly those in the industrial sector, produced more than temporary benefits for lower income people – those closest to Labour's heart.

In one important respect Labour's efforts to balance competing forces ran into early trouble. Many union leaders became impatient. Some were unhappy that the introduction of the 40-hour week to their industries was delayed, while others grizzled about the Arbitration Court's wages policy and believed they could do better by what they called 'collective bargaining'.[104] During 1937 there was pressure for legislation to improve ventilation and other problems in factories. Some of the better placed unions such as the waterside workers, who regarded themselves as natural leaders, embarked on political strikes and 'go-slows' on a variety of issues.[105] Freezing workers, miners and fertiliser workers happily took direct action on wages and conditions. However, given the economic strategies that ministers had adopted, greater control over rising wage rates was essential. The Government saw itself as the arbiter and adopted what it thought was a policy of fairness for all. Minimum wage rates were increased for both the public and private sectors, but keeping overall control on wage levels was an essential part of Labour's regulated State.[106]

It therefore became a fundamental tenet of Labour policy that workers adhered to the principles of compulsory arbitration. This eventually made a collision with the more militant end of the trade union movement inevitable. Sensing this, the Government armed itself with greater disciplinary powers by pushing through an amendment to the I.C.&A. Act in July 1939. It gave the Minister of Labour the powers to deregister a striking union and to recognise another in its place. In a classic statement of the Government's attitude, H. T. Armstrong told the unions that compulsory unionism carried with it a responsibility: 'If we say to the employers, "You will not be permitted by law to employ other than members of a union", surely it is only reasonable to throw the responsibility on to the union to see that the law is observed so that industry will not be disrupted from time to time. . . .'[107] The corporate state, it seemed, had arrived in New Zealand.

For the moment, however, confidence in what Robert Higgs calls 'pervasive statism', was at its height. Export receipts zigzagged upwards from £46.5 million in 1935 to £73.7 million in 1940,[108] helping to sustain rising private and public expenditure. Factory production rose 36 per cent between 1936 and 1940, while effective wage rates also increased steadily.[109] In 1939, according to the English economist, Colin Clark, New Zealand enjoyed the highest level of real income in the world, although Margaret Galt has more recently questioned whether this was correct. Certainly the economy seemed to be in sound shape after the depression. Building permits were rising steadily, more houses were built and manufacturers expanded production. The country's ports were busier than ever before. Customs and Sales Tax revenue increased. More electric power was being consumed, farmers were mechanising at a rapid rate, and total deposits in savings banks were still rising until war broke out.[110]

The benefits of state activity were not confined as narrowly to males of European descent as they had been during the Liberal era. Women played a more vital role in Labour politics than they had ever done in the Liberals' days. More and more women were joining the work force, especially the public service. Their pay rates, however, still lagged far behind men's. The basic rate of pay fixed by the Arbitration Court on 2 November 1936 was £3 16s for adult men and £1 16s for adult women.[111] Maori benefited from the political alliance with the Labour Party that had been developing since E. T. Tirikatene, MP for Southern Maori, joined the Labour caucus in 1932. Labour tolerated no racial distinction in relief work, nor in eligibility for pensions. The introduction of the Social Security Act saw the growing numbers of older Maori become automatically eligible for the first time since 1901 for the old-age pension. And it was payable at the same rate as for Pakeha. Not surprisingly, Labour received a big electoral benefit from the promised changes, winning three of the four Maori electorates in the 1938 election.

One government stipulation is of particular interest. Although Labour's leaders had cautiously endorsed the Coalition Government's payment of a

Labour stresses the State's generosity in its 1938 election advertisement.
ATL F-126539-1/2

dole in 1934, they never felt comfortable paying people without some work in return. In the period between 1936 and 1939 the Government provided as many jobs as possible for the unemployed, most of them through what was known as Scheme 13. The First Labour Government believed strongly in the work ethic. 'Work', Nash told the Labour Party's Annual Conference in April 1936 'must be the title to wealth.'[112] As numbers on relief diminished, Maori were slower to find work than others. Ministers worried that granting Maori the same benefits as Pakeha seemed to be a factor in rising crime and alcoholism. A more 'protective' policy towards Maori emerged after 1937. A portion of their benefits was sometimes retained and paid by way of orders to storekeepers. Special efforts were made to provide work for Maori. The Native Department received additional funds to enable it to provide jobs of an 'essential and productive' nature.[113]

Poorly devised paternalism undermined Labour's land development policies for Maori, yet they continued in force for another generation. In a series of Acts passed under the guiding hand of Sir Apirana Ngata after 1929 the State took a more prominent role in land development schemes for Maori. The Board of Native Affairs Act 1935 and a companion measure the following year led the Department of Native Affairs to settle Maori families on farms. The goal was to 'assure [Maori farmers] a reasonable standard of living'. However, a system whereby settlers in many cases were granted a weekly wage while the farm's income was paid to the department removed incentives for settlers to improve the productive capability of the properties. Successive governments claimed that their Maori policies were meeting with considerable success. There were considerable achievements in housing Maori and access to hospital care and education improved. But a combination of state paternalism and the fact that the farms' principal asset, the land itself, could not be traded, meant that options for Maori were often closed off. The plentiful gorse and a generally unkempt appearance of some Maori properties had more to do with government policy than any intrinsic inability of Maori to farm.[114]

In 1939 New Zealand was on the eve of spending more than £250,000 celebrating the centennial of European settlement.[114] Both the Government and the public felt they had much to be proud of. But before the festivities began the country was embroiled in another world war. In New Zealand, as in every other country, events between 1939 and 1945 pushed the Government into an even more central role in people's lives. And war, as Robert Skidelsky caustically notes, 'is an excuse for every collectivist to get into business'.[115]

Chapter 8

War and the Omnipotent State

In the mid 1960s the Government Statistician, J. V. T. Baker, reviewed the Labour Government's earlier policy of insulation. He remarked that it 'required either unlimited overseas funds or irksome internal restraints'.[1] New Zealand seldom had enough of the former and within a few years most people believed there were too many of the latter. Moreover, with a high level of government spending on domestic programmes (and Nash spent to the limit each year), more taxes were needed to fund the Government's growing array of social programmes. However, for several decades after the 1930s the public became accustomed to state experimentation, confident that the politicians – first Labour, then after 1949, National – would eventually find the right mix.

There were occasional threats to Labour's programme. In 1937–38 the world economy slowed, causing New Zealand's export prices to slip; many years later, during the First National Government's term of office, there was a slight recession in 1952–53 as the Korean war drew to a close, causing wool prices to drop. Otherwise, the country's overseas earnings rose fairly steadily until 1957–58. Only then, with the British already showing considerable interest in a European Common Market, were the first serious questions asked about the sustainability of New Zealand's insulated, centralised economy. And even then, most people believed that any setbacks would be only temporary.

In 1937 Nash had hoped for a trade agreement with Britain whereby, in return for easy access for British goods to the New Zealand market, Britain would scrap the quantitative restrictions that applied to imports of New Zealand's primary products after the Ottawa conference. In the event, the British refused to move beyond the Ottawa accords. Nonetheless, prices for New Zealand's products on the London market did recover in 1939 and bulk purchasing arrangements operated during and after the war, much as they had between 1915 and 1920. New Zealand's mounting export returns sustained a long period of domestic prosperity which was on a scale unknown since 1895–1920. Governments occasionally required producer boards to retain portions of export income lest its full release added to inflation. While primary producers were seldom content with what they received in the hand and constantly lobbied for full and immediate remuneration, or for government concessions here or subsidies there, the historian can trace a steady upward movement in standards of living, particularly in the rural sector.

Successive governments, however, were constantly confronted with threats to the prosperity they happily laid claim to. As Friedrich Hayek was to note a few years later, societies that were intent on big spending to abolish unemployment found themselves living with the threat of 'a general and considerable inflation'.[2] Inflation became an ever-present danger in New Zealand under the welfare state. Price rises threatened the effectiveness of spending programmes aimed at lower socio-economic groups and put pressure on interest rates; inflation also guaranteed unrest among the unions, especially those that had always been sceptical about the Labour Party or those who believed they could do better by using industrial muscle. Strikes and 'go-slows' intensified when inflationary pressures were strongest. Labour's ministers devoted much energy to price stability. They believed it was essential to their survival in office.

After several years of deflation in the early 1930s, rising prices became noticeable by the middle of 1936. They went up nearly 7 per cent in 1937 following the wage increases of 1936. In all, prices increased 12.5 per cent between the end of 1935 and March 1938. The Department of Industries and Commerce estimated that 'effective wages' rose nearly 24 per cent during the same period, which explains Labour's growing support from the employees and mounting apprehension among employers. By the outbreak of war in September 1939, prices were nearly back to the level of the late 1920s.[3]

We have already seen how concern about bread prices led the Government into an expensive subsidy programme. Private housing rentals were not handled so easily. On 10 May 1936 Savage announced that the Government would prohibit 'excessive rents'.[4] A Fair Rents Act was passed on 11 June. Like Massey's legislation that it replaced, it was to exist for one year only but was constantly renewed. It defined a basic rent as that paid on 1 May 1936. In the event that landlords and tenants could not agree on a 'fair' rent, then a magistrate would hear the parties and set it. The law prescribed that a fair return on the landlord's investment was between 4 and 6 per cent of the capital value of the property, plus rates, repairs and depreciation. Some tenants promptly labelled rents set under these criteria as excessive. Landlords' representatives, on the other hand, argued that more of them would, as they had in earlier years, simply exit the market in search of higher returns. Some did, especially when the provision of state units at subsidised rentals tended to lower private sector rentals. However, the housing shortage in the cities did not go away entirely and demands for 'key money' put upwards pressure on rents. A variety of methods was used to get round the regulations. Officials clearly became uneasy about aspects of the Fair Rents Act. Eventually the Government included private rentals in the wartime Economic Stabilisation Emergency Regulations of December 1942. However, throughout the 1940s there were complaints about inequities in the rental market and endless stories of people evading the rules.[5]

Reflecting the Labour Government's general suspicion that private entrepreneurs, left to their own devices, would profiteer, the Government retained the Coalition's controls over phosphate prices, road services fares and freights (1931), petrol (1933), milk (1933) as well as bread and flour regulations dating back to World War I. Savage's Ministry went further. It imposed controls on butter, cheese, fruit, honey, eggs and onions.[6] The deteriorating international scene led ministers and officials to contemplate more controls. In 1937 the Government established an Organisation for National Security (ONS) consisting of top bureaucrats who met within the Prime Minister's Department under the secretaryship of Lt Colonel W. G. Stephens. Officials prepared sets of controls to be implemented in the event of war breaking out. Most were in draft form by the time of the Munich crisis in September–October 1938. Among them were plans for a price tribunal to administer controls, details of which were approved by Cabinet on 20 September 1938.[7] In the meantime, officials used the Board of Trade Act 1919 and its amendment of 1923, plus the Prevention of Profiteering Act 1936, to underpin their surveillance of price movements. On 2 June 1939, by which time inflation was rising in anticipation of war, the Board of Trade (Price Investigation) Regulations were issued. Henceforth prices of goods and services were to be increased only after prior application to a Price Investigation Tribunal. It comprised a Judge of the Arbitration Court and an officer from Industries and Commerce. The tribunal was given the power to fix the prices of goods, including those not previously on the market.

The next price control move was not so carefully planned. When the budget of 1939 increased the sales tax on beer, and brewers were allowed by the new tribunal to pass increased costs straight through to consumers, there was, according to Mr Justice Hunter of the Arbitration Court, 'hell

GETTING NOWHERE FAST

The cartoonist, Lonsdale, looks at the predicament faced by Paddy Webb, Minister of Labour, 1940. NZ Observer

to pay'.[8] On 1 September 1939 the Government rushed through the Price Stabilisation Emergency Regulations. They were gazetted under the Public Safety Conservation Act 1932. These moves took controls a step further. The regulations defined goods and services widely; they declared 1 September to be the 'fixed day'; and decreed, somewhat cumbrously, that 'no person who on the fixed day was engaged in [the] business of selling any goods shall sell goods of the same nature and quality in the same quantity and on the same terms of payment, delivery, or otherwise at a price which is higher than the lowest price at which he sold or was willing to sell such goods on the said fixed day'. Similar restrictions applied to services. The Minister of Industries and Commerce was given authority to appoint an investigator with the powers of a judicial inquiry to look into suspected breaches of the regulations.[9]

New Zealand declared war just before midnight on 3 September 1939, immediately after Great Britain. For many months Labour ministers had been mulling over their responses in the eventuality of war. For most of them the experience of World War I had been seminal and they were determined to adopt what they called a policy of 'equal sacrifice'. Both Paddy Webb and Peter Fraser had served time in gaol for opposing the Military Service Act 1916 that introduced conscription. At the time, the Labour Party's official newspaper, the *Maoriland Worker*, had fulminated against conscription and Massey's Government. It accused Massey of 'fastening the chains of militarism on the young life of the Dominion' while the Government 'cringed and grovelled before the profiteer and exploiter'.[10] In June 1938 Savage recalled World War I with the comments that 'while the men were dying, other people were getting rich. That is not going to happen again'.[11] Fraser declared in September 1938 that if war broke out 'all the wealth and all the services would be placed at the disposal of the country' and that there 'would be no conscription of human beings without conscription of wealth'.[12] A carefully controlled economy was essential to any Labour-run wartime administration.

Many sets of regulations were cleared by Cabinet on 4 September 1939 and promptly gazetted. Factory Emergency Regulations, Electricity Emergency Regulations, Enemy Trading Regulations, Building Emergency Regulations, Wheat and Flour Emergency Regulations, Supply Control Emergency Regulations, Oil Fuel Emergency Regulations, Foodstuffs Emergency Regulations, Medical Supplies Emergency Regulations, Mining Emergency Regulations, Primary Industries Emergency Regulations and Timber Emergency Regulations were promulgated under the Public Safety Conservation Act 1932. Factory, Food, Electricity, Mining and Timber Controllers were appointed, each with wide powers to regulate, control or prohibit activities deemed injurious to the 'public interest'. More controllers were added as the need arose. Nash made it clear that the war would be financed from a separate War Expenses Account which was to be financed by a combination of borrowing, a national savings scheme and extra charges on stamps, liquor and cigarettes. It was clear from debates in Parliament that there was general agreement that public works spending could be trimmed back for the duration of the war. On 13 September 1939 the Emergency Regulations Bill was given its second reading. Its powers were very wide. Regulations could be issued for many purposes, amongst them 'the taking of possession or control, on behalf of His Majesty, of any property or undertaking' or 'authorising the acquisition, on behalf of His Majesty, of any property'. These moves were justified on the grounds that it was the Government's 'duty' to 'mobilise the entire resources of our country'.[13] They sat neatly with a Government which, in any event, had long decided to command the economy.

The Prime Minister by this time was mortally ill but Savage's ministers, led by his able deputy, Peter Fraser, were as determined as he had been to guard against wartime speculation and the hoarding of goods. Using their new powers, they hoped to safeguard the economic and social policies that had been put in place over the previous four years. So anxious were ministers about equality of sacrifice that Fraser expressed the opinion at one point that it might prove necessary to put everyone on a soldier's rate of pay, which at that time was 7s per day. S. G. Holland of the National Party labelled this 'mischievous humbug and utter rot'; Nash soon conceded that it was scarcely practical.[14]

Whatever the Government's intentions – and Sullivan was adamant that 'fair and reasonable' prices would be maintained[15] – achieving price control in wartime proved extremely difficult. Shipping quickly became chancy, freight costs rose and many raw materials were diverted to war production. Some imported products virtually disappeared. The value of sterling fell on international markets. Moreover, as Schmitt told Sullivan in September 1939, administering the blanket regulations produced 'some really difficult administrative problems', not least because there were many commercial people proffering conflicting advice to ministers and officials.[16] The Tribunal's workload increased rapidly and members felt their way forward, seeking the cooperation of manufacturers, grocers and other retailers. Forms setting out the information required by the Tribunal for price rises were soon made available. H. L. Wise, who was Industries and Commerce's representative on the Tribunal, outlined many of the difficulties in a booklet, *War-Time Price Control in New Zealand*. In order to smooth the impact of rising prices, the Tribunal began averaging the cost of old and new stock, obliging traders to absorb some of the impact of mounting costs.[17]

While there was greater restraint of prices in New Zealand than elsewhere in the British Commonwealth,[18] it was clear by the end of 1939 that the Tribunal had been unable to enforce complete price stability. On 20 December 1939 Cabinet gave the Tribunal greater powers in the Control of Prices Emergency Regulations. In a controversial move, the Price Tribunal, as it was now called, was allowed to hold judicial inquiries in private or public, as it chose. It could hear witnesses on oath and require the production of all relevant books and documents. These documents were pertinent to the issuing of Price Orders by the Tribunal – of which there were to be more than 500 before hostilities ceased. The documents helped determine whether a uniform price was fixed for a particular locality or for the whole country. So great became the work of the Tribunal that two Associate Members were added in July 1941, one with foodstuffs experience, the other with knowledge of clothing and footwear. Many male and female price inspectors were appointed. By 1942 there had been 430 convictions for breaches of the regulations.[19]

One particularly difficult application to the Price Tribunal came from Whakatane Paper Mills Ltd. Established with Australian money and the beneficiary of a private act of Parliament in 1936 guaranteeing the company a supply of power,[20] the mills began producing cardboard at the end of 1937 and expanded into hardboard. The number of employees reached 220 by the middle of 1938. H. A. Horrocks, the company's managing director, was a hard businessman, inclined to extravagant public utterances. He constantly sought government assistance, despite earlier assurances to Savage, Sullivan and Nash that the company would be self-sufficient. Like Walmsleys of England and David Henry of New Zealand Forest Products, Horrocks wanted also to expand into the production of pulp and paper but ran up against the State Forest Service's conviction (supported by the Bureau of Industry) that there should be only one pulp and paper producer, the State. Whakatane Paper Mills Ltd ran up freight bills with Railways and was slow to pay them. Late in 1939 the company applied for permission to raise the price of their products. The Price Tribunal refused the application. Early in the New Year, Horrocks issued dismissal notices to 232 workers, blaming the Price Tribunal and the Government. Horrocks told the press that his directors were 'not prepared to allow the mill to be run exclusively by bureaucratic control' and that the Government was attempting to 'substitute dictation for cooperation' and that this was 'strongly resented by Australian interests'.[21]

Such tactics in a Labour electorate held by the slimmest of margins put the Government under extreme pressure. While for a time ministers seem to have contemplated allowing imports of cheaper board from abroad to compete with Whakatane's product, they had little political option but to submit to Horrocks. Sullivan agreed to a full, open inquiry into the mill's accounts before Judge Hunter. On 1 April 1940 a price increase was allowed.[22] However, relations between the Government and Horrocks remained bad.

Officials believed that Whakatane Paper Mills was exploiting its monopoly position and in 1941 Cabinet seriously considered taking over the mill and running it for the duration of the war, but delayed a decision, fearing a public reaction. Both Horrocks and David Henry, managing director of another Australian-backed company, New Zealand Forest Products Ltd, kept pestering the Government to allow them to expand into the production of pulp and paper using timber from the State's forests. In 1941 there were discussions, driven initially by machinery manufacturers, about a state-owned or supported pulp and paper mill. A. R. (Pat) Entrican, Director of State Forests, wanted to ensure that the huge number of exotic trees now ready for milling in the central North Island were processed expeditiously; James Fletcher was more than willing to construct a plant for the purpose. War preoccupations restrained progress but Entrican began gathering information from overseas about what would be required to construct a large, export-oriented pulp and paper mill.[23] From this time onwards there were also talks with overseas interests about their possible involvement with a state mill.

What had occurred between the Government and Whakatane Paper Mills was replicated from time to time with other companies. New Zealand Forest Products Ltd was no easier to deal with. In 1943 David Henry attacked the Government over price control and especially over its refusal to grant his company a licence to produce pulp and paper. 'An industry with immense possibilities is being strangled in a straitjacket of government inertia', he told his shareholders. This belligerent stance by an organisation with many employees in the marginal Rotorua electorate, which was 'supported by a well-orchestrated chorus of demands by Forest Products' shareholders', eventually won the company a licence to produce pulp and paper. The State Forest Service was granted one at the same time but was in no position yet to take it up.[24] What this showed was that large enterprises with many employees strategically located in marginal electorates could bring pressure to bear on any government that was deeply involved in micro-economic management. To counter these pressures, ministers and officials usually resorted either to regulation and/or ownership. This, as will be seen, is what happened with Tasman Pulp and Paper Ltd in the early 1950s. And it became inevitable that the domestic cost structure would rise when either monopoly status or political lobbying, or a combination of both, enabled well-placed manufacturers to bullock their way past normal licensing procedures.

The Labour Government found it difficult keeping abreast of the myriad of regulations, controllers, tribunals and inspectors that they established during the war. Departments were spread over a wide area of central Wellington by 1940. As Savage's health declined, and he spent more and more time either in hospital or at his home at 66 Harbourview Road, Peter Fraser took effective control. He insisted that all departments keep his office informed of developments. Under Fraser's command the Prime Minister's staff expanded rapidly. Fraser came to rely on a group of senior officials, including Joe Heenan, Under-Secretary of Internal Affairs, Bernard Ashwin, Secretary to the Treasury, and Carl Berendsen, Foss Shanahan and Alister McIntosh from the Prime Minister's Department.[25] By December 1940 regulations, some of them drafted by the Law Drafting Office, others by the Crown Law Office and several from departments on their own initiative, were flowing so fast that Ashwin complained to Nash, who requested that henceforth all regulations be prepared in the one

James Fletcher, Commissioner of Defence Construction, 1943. ATL F-606-1/4

office.[26] For a time central control was re-established, but in June 1942 Heenan, whose department was responsible for publishing the *Gazette*, insisted that the Law Drafting Office should now draft all regulations and then submit them to ministers through the Prime Minister's Department.[27] In the superheated wartime atmosphere structures could change daily and the records provide frequent examples of overlapping jurisdictions and administrative snafus.

Fraser himself worked extremely long hours and his routine was chaotic. Surviving on a diet of tea, toast and cream cakes, which he would devour at any time of the day or night, he kept his key officials around him until the small hours of the morning, sometimes insisting that they accompany him home for further discussions. They in turn, with the exception of Berendsen, who loathed him, developed huge respect for the Prime Minister's intellectual abilities and were constantly worried about his, and his wife's, health (she died early in 1945). While Fraser could be petty and sometimes wasted time arguing over trivia, his determination to win through never faltered. In the eyes of his supporters, who included most of the civil servants with whom he dealt, his was one of the most powerful intellects to which they were exposed. Quoting poetry one minute, then revealing an almost photographic memory the next about some small detail buried in a submission to him, the former watersider's views of the role of the State ruled unchallenged for the duration of the war.[28]

The Government's anti-inflation policy came under serious challenge in 1940. The Department of Industries and Commerce acknowledged in its report for the year ended 31 March 1940 that effective wages had fallen nearly 4 per cent.[29] Trade unions lodged claims for substantial wage rises and tried to get confidential information from the Price Tribunal to assist a series of cases before the Arbitration Court.[30] Deputations of workers and employers plagued ministers with bits of special pleading. In May 1940 the Court was authorised to issue blanket general wage orders applying to all workers under its jurisdiction. The first General Wage Order (5 per cent) was issued in August 1940.

Further steps had to be taken. Fraser convened a conference at Parliament on 4 September 1940. It represented most productive sectors of the economy and considered what was now referred to as the policy of 'stabilisation'. Besides Fraser, there were three other ministers present: Nash, Sullivan, and Lee Martin, the Minister of Agriculture. The Prime Minister told the sector representatives that the war was obliging the Government to engage in 'planning on a large scale' and that this required cooperation from all sectors 'in a big and generous way'. He wanted those present to assist with policies that would enable the war to be handled 'in the most fair and equitable manner'. After surveying the economy, delegates were invited to consider 'the possibility of stabilising costs and prices and wages and to discuss expanding production so that the strain of war expenditure may be successfully borne and the standard of living maintained as far as possible'.[31]

When Fraser finished, Nash delivered a homily about the need for the current generation to carry the cost of the war rather than loading it on to posterity. Just as he had indicated a few weeks earlier in his budget, he proposed to use taxation and as little borrowing or Reserve Bank credit as possible, so as to keep the lid on inflation. But further price controls would be necessary. After much posturing, during which farmers and mine-owners criticised the lack of 'high pressure' work by employees and unionists responded in kind, the conference settled down to consider a list of options and alternatives. The stamp of officialdom and the wily interventions of Fraser's trusted lieutenant, F. P. Walsh, can be seen in the list of recommendations drawn up by a committee of the conference. The committee met various sector controllers. Members grilled Wise of the Price Tribunal, then listened at length to L. J. Schmitt of Industries and Commerce. He surveyed his department's activities since 1936, praised the lift which import licensing had given to many industries and painted a picture of his department as the nerve centre of the economy. Schmitt's enthusiasm for the certainties which planning guaranteed to manufacturers would not have been out of place in a Soviet five-year planning exercise.[32] The result was that committee members eventually recommended equal sacrifices, the maintenance of relative living standards and the stabilisation of wages and essential food, rents, clothing, fuel and light. State subsidies, they said, should be resorted to only when they 'cannot be avoided and then only under stringent control'. Finally, the committee supported a national savings scheme and endorsed family allowances, especially for those with large families.[33]

However, the Government did not take all the advice immediately, persisting instead with existing policies. Wages were kept under tight control; the Court was restrained from awarding increases at intervals of less than six months. Sales taxes doubled, customs taxes rose, a new scale of death and gift duties was introduced and income and company taxes increased. The top tax rate payable on earned incomes above £3,700 rose to 77.5 per cent.[34] A list of 38 commodities on which prices were 'stabilised' was put into operation on 1 September 1941.

However, prices continued to rise. Labour Party activists became restless. The language of sacrifice was not enough. Fraser, Nash and Sullivan were peppered with letters of concern from union secretaries. The Wellington Labour Representation Committee told Sullivan in April 1942 that it was firmly of the opinion that the Price Tribunal was proving unable to 'prevent exploitation'.[35] A further 5 per cent wage increase was paid from 7 April 1942 but it was restricted to males earning less than £5 per week and women earning less than £2 10s per week. Price Control officials were now encouraged to tour the country, explaining their methods of operation to interest groups, especially workers.[36] The Government was finding it extremely difficult to fight a war, especially one that was at its most desperate stage, while maintaining its social policies at the same time.

By the end of 1942 Fraser had no option but to go further again. For some months now the Economic Stabilisation Committee had been arguing for more controls.[37] On 15 December the Prime Minister announced what he called a 'Charter of Economic Security'. The Government intended to stabilise the prices of 110 items and individual rates of pay, incomes, and rents. Farm products, many of them already stabilised, were not to increase in price and any returns from exports above that price were to be paid into 'pool accounts'. Land prices were soon controlled and transfers made subject to approval of a Land Sales Court. The Prime Minister conceded that ministers had been aware for some months that existing controls were no longer adequate and that they were worried at the growing evidence of black marketing. In a lengthy statement of the Government's philosophy, Fraser added:

> Seven years ago the Government . . . pledged itself to the ideal of social security, to the ideal of a society in which the fear of poverty should be banished from every home. That ideal is well on the way to being realised. . . . Now social security implies something much more than a system of money benefits for people who have suffered unemployment or some economic misfortune. It implies an order of society in which every citizen – wage earner, trader, professional man, or pensioner – is safeguarded against economic fluctuations. It is my plain duty to say that social security in this wider sense of the term is in danger. . . . It is in danger because the impact of war has let loose forces which, if they are not firmly checked, will throw our economic system into disorder.[38]

To underline the importance which the Government attached to stabilisation, the burly Bernard Ashwin, Secretary to the Treasury, was appointed Director of Stabilisation. He headed a six-man commission made up of politicians and sector representatives which lasted, albeit with changing personnel, until 1950. They included F. P. Walsh, who was soon occupying an office in Treasury House in Stout Street. The group of people with effective control over the wartime economy had narrowed even further.

An understanding was reached with Walsh that there would be no more wage rises for the duration of the war unless the Wartime Price Index showed that prices had increased by more than 5 per cent.[39] To keep the lid on prices, the Government had no option but to resort to more subsidisation of essential commodities. Treasury tried, not always successfully, to maintain a clear distinction between inherited pre-war subsidies and those which could be charged to the War Expenses Account. Costing £500,000 in 1938–39, the amount paid out in subsidies rose to a net £6.6 million in 1945–46, with meat, sugar, tea, clothing and coal all having been added to the pre-war list. By this time subsidies were the equivalent of 2.5 per cent of national income. In the words of J. V. T. Baker, they were now 'a significant component of the New Zealand pattern of financial transactions'.[40] And even with subsidies, as Ashwin pointed out later, prices at times 'did come close to the agreed 5 per cent . . . mark and it was necessary for the Government Statistician to do some juggling'. On one occasion higher onion prices threatened to tip the index over the 5 per cent threshold. Ashwin recalled later: 'I told [the Government Statistician] the country's economy was not going to be upset by the price of onions and so we withdrew the item [from the list] and got below the 5 per cent mark again. The country was saved!'[41] Later in the decade, however, onion prices were subsidised for a time when officials no longer felt so free to tamper with the index.

The advent of stabilisation in December 1942 marked the beginning of a process linking wage increases to movements in the price index rather than to productivity growth. Although the Wartime Price Index was removed in June 1945, indexation of wages continued to be seen as a key element in stabilising New Zealand's economy. Primary producers' pool accounts became an equally vital component of stabilisation. By regulation they retained a percentage of the generous returns which agricultural products were receiving from the British. Between 1942 and 1946 more than £23 million was retained in farmers' stabilisation accounts and by 1951 this had stretched to £116 million. Had the money been paid straight across to farmers as it had been in similar circumstances in 1914–19, it would greatly have fuelled inflation. One economist expressed the opinion to the author that the pool accounts were possibly the most important measure in holding wartime inflation.[42]

Stabilisation rested on several foundations. First was the relatively conservative fiscal policy followed by Nash during the war years. He budgeted for surpluses and this restrained inflation. Secondly, there was a public acceptance that the relative economic standing of various classes at the end of 1942 would be frozen for the rest of the war. There was certainly very little room for changing relativities, although there were several amendments to the Economic Stabilisation Regulations after 1942, to enable some levelling-up of wages for poorly paid workers, who would be unfairly treated were they to be frozen at their December 1942 levels. In 1945 the Arbitration Court began the practice of standard wage pronouncements. Under these, further small alterations to relativities were incorporated into across-the-board wage increases. Overall, however, the system was fairly rigid. Gary Hawke shrewdly observes: 'The whole structure depended on the willingness of groups within the community to subordinate their interests to the perceived need for resources to be mobilised towards the war.'[43] Once the war was over, the willingness to accept a freeze on relativities slowly evaporated. As some appeared to do better than others, the politics of envy became more ingrained in everyday life. What has often been referred to as the New Zealand 'tall poppy syndrome', whereby those with apparent advantages are chopped down by the envious, received a significant boost in the aftermath of war.

While the macro decisions worked well overall, micro efforts were not always successful. One example relates to efforts in 1942 to control clothing prices, which seemed to rise inexorably. The Standards Institute's staff was boosted and it was set to work on cost-saving devices. Reviving something that had been contemplated by Massey's Board of Trade in 1919, Sullivan persuaded Cabinet on 23 October 1942 to direct the Factory Controller to enforce Standards Institute specifications for the production of 'austerity clothing'. Officials were convinced that private enterprise could be directed to get more finished products from the scarce cloth they were using. They spent many hours calculating the annual clothing needs of the population. After discussion with interested parties, the Shirts and Pyjamas Manufacture Control Notice was issued on 29 October under the Factory Emergency Regulations 1939. It provided that no owner or occupier of a factory within the meaning of the 1939 regulations 'could manufacture any men's, youths' or boys' shirts or pyjamas in contravention of the provisions of the said specifications'. Other rules governed the making of men's trousers, while there were also specifications for women's and girls' clothing and knitwear. The production of plus fours and similar trousers was prohibited; limits were placed on the number of pockets in trousers; and the width of the legs was to be standardised. Hem lengths for dresses were prescribed by regulation, as well as the number of buttons. The regulations stipulated limits on the number of pleats in men's and boys' trousers; they specified the size of 'turnups', and even attempted to do away with buttons on boys' knickers and on short trousers! The Standards Institute also turned its attention to the size and quality of hankerchiefs and a control notice was issued later dealing with men's and women's outer clothing. Clothing inspectors began calling on factories to ensure that the regulations were complied with.[44]

There were problems from the start. At the point where the regulations came into force many manufacturers had forward orders for goods that were outside the specifications. The Bespoke Master Tailors Association complained that it had not been represented on the Standards Institute's committee. Kirkcaldie and Stains were told to write to the Factory Controller explaining why they were not complying with the regulations. Some tailors simply refused to fall into line. They were buoyed by the clear signs of public resistance to 'austerity clothing'. Lists of pending prosecutions built up. Worst of all, the intended savings did not eventuate. The notion, so fervently believed by bureaucrats, that private manufacturers were wasteful turned out to be an illusion. The Government pressed on for a time, issuing new regulations covering men's work clothing. However, by October 1944 the Factory Controller's enthusiasm for the experiment was clearly waning.[45]

Walter Nash and Peter Fraser meet over a cup of tea in Washington DC, 1944.

The work of the various wartime control agencies is worthy of brief mention, if only to show the extent to which wartime anxieties bred authoritarianism. The ONS had set up a National Supply Committee. Sullivan became Minister of Supply and Munitions when a War Cabinet consisting of Fraser, Nash, Frederick Jones (Minister of Defence) and two Opposition members, J. G. Coates and Adam Hamilton, was sworn into office on 16 July 1940. A Supply Council under Sullivan's chairmanship with Ashwin as his deputy, met regularly. In 1942 representatives of the Joint Purchasing Board of the American Forces in New Zealand also attended meetings. By now there were thirteen controllers, all with wide powers. At the end of 1942 they were placed under the direction of a triumvirate consisting of G. H. Jackson, who was Director of Production, F. R. Picot, who was Commissioner of Supply, and L. J. Schmitt, who was Wheat and Flour Controller. Schmitt was also responsible for flax production, tobacco supplies, the Bureau of Industry and the Price Tribunal.[46] The Ministry of Supply with a staff that grew to 550 introduced motor fuel rationing in the early days of the war; it lasted until 1 June 1950. Sugar, tea and clothing rationing followed in 1942 and in 1943 butter was also rationed. Ration books were issued and individuals were restricted to 8 oz of butter per week in order to release more for the armed forces and the British. Meat was rationed between March 1944 and September 1948. Some other items such as cheese and eggs remained in short supply. Most rationed items were price-controlled and subsidised. Rationing and subsidisation were seen as ways of ensuring shortages did not drive up prices and that everyone therefore had equal access to a limited supply of goods. However, as J. V. T. Baker points out, shortages, rationing and price control led to black marketing. Several retailers were jailed for illegally selling motor spirits in 1942; but the sale of farm produce was harder to control and by the middle of the year it was common knowledge that there was a large illegal market for eggs in both Auckland and Wellington.[47]

On 14 January 1942 regulations were issued giving the National Service Department powers to direct men and women to fill gaps left in 'essential industries', many of which were struggling to find enough workers to satisfy orders. It was soon clear that officials had underestimated the number of industries wishing to be categorised as 'essential'. A second list had to be issued on 10 February 1942. During the first six months of 1942, 5000 'direction orders' were issued; these rose to 15,000 during the second half of the year. Before the war finished 176,000 orders had been issued.[48]

From September 1939 the Building Controller was given wide powers. He could set rules for the granting of building permits by local authorities. In 1941, to ensure adequate materials for defence construction, he banned the large-scale use of reinforcing steel and corrugated iron in any private construction work. Many private house designs were changed to take account of the shortage of roofing and other materials.[49] On 11 March 1942 James Fletcher was appointed Commissioner of Defence Construction and given the widest powers. 'For the purpose of exercising his functions', said his terms of appointment, 'the Commissioner may give such directions as he thinks fit to any officer of the Public Service in relation to the exercise of any powers possessed by them, whether under any Act or regulations or otherwise, including any powers that may be delegated to them by any Minister or other authority.' The fact that Fletcher drew no government salary and held his position because of his close contacts with ministers, with whom he was on a first-name basis, greatly increased his mana. His methods were unorthodox but the respect in which he was held enabled him to operate effectively between 1942 and 1945.[50]

The dynamic Fletcher was not the only person given wide powers by Cabinet minute. Ashwin was appointed Deputy Chairman of the Supply Council in the same manner and had no statutory authority for the exercise of his powers. His job was to ensure there was enough military equipment for the country's needs. Ashwin coordinated, directed, coerced, cajoled and improvised for several years, using commonsense and the high degree of natural authority that he possessed. At one point, on his own admission, he summarily shifted ammunition production from Mt Eden to the Waikato to ensure greater security of production.[51] Arbitrary rule was not uncommon during the darkest days of the war.

Meantime, in Customhouse Quay the Department of Industries and Commerce and its associated agencies were toiling away on their manufacturing policies. By the end of the war 6300 manufacturing units in 36 branches of business had been registered with the Bureau of Industry. They were employing 122,500 workers, 41 per cent more than were in factory production in 1935. Engineering had been the biggest single area of expansion, although footwear, clothing and the woollen industry all saw their employees increase by more than 50 per cent over the decade.[52] Whether the growth stemmed from bureaucratic intervention or was the product of the highly protected environment in which manufacturers now operated, or whether their wartime contracts were of critical importance, or some mixture of all these, will always be debated. Certainly much industrial activity during the war was the result of contracts secured through the Supply Council to provide for New Zealand's armed forces, the American forces in the South Pacific and the Eastern Group Supply Council. Airline lubricators, boots, chronometers, overcoats, ladders, nails, waterbottles and radio equipment were exported to assist in the wider war effort. Many new small industries using a variety of improvised methods sprang up in 1940–42 to service wartime needs. Metal buttons, typewriter ribbons, inks and stains for footwear, potato-sorting machines, enamel stewpans and casseroles, gas-producing machines for automobiles, can-sealing compounds, plywoods, egg-grading machines and wooden handles were also produced. Several things were manufactured in New Zealand during the war that were never produced again.[53] After an initial burst of licensing new industries in the late 1930s and producing plans for some of them, the Bureau of Industry settled on between 32 and 36 licensed industries for the duration of the war. The Bureau simply lacked the personnel to engage in the full-scale planning necessary to license any more.

Industries securing wartime contracts from the Government almost always found them lucrative. Urgency meant that competitive contracting was replaced with 'cost-plus' contract work, much of it allocated on terms that proved expensive to the Government. Sometimes resources were wasted. Contractors were paid for proven expenditure with an additional

General Freyberg with Prime Minister Fraser in Italy, 1944; winning the war and getting alongside the soldiers was part of Labour's political strategy.

percentage to cover overheads and profit. Some contractors managed to wring an extra percentage from the Government, exploiting 'to the full' their strategic positions, according to the Audit Office. Specially generous contracts applied to private construction of buildings, ship construction and repair work, and for the manufacture of munitions. Normal marketplace risks were replaced by an unprecedented degree of comfort and security for many manufacturers.[54] F. J. Pohlen, who was accountant at the Ministry of Supply and Munitions, told a meeting of manufacturers in 1944 that a 'cost-plus contract' paying a return of 6 per cent on the capital employed in the production of munitions after payment of the standard income tax 'must be regarded as almost a gilt-edged investment. There is little risk of loss under the contract and it gives a better return than, say, a Liberty Bond or an investment in the Victory War Loan.'[55] Even the Excess Profits Tax after 1940 failed to dent many contractors' enthusiasm for 'cost-plus'. Like many before and since, they liked the predictability of doing business with the State.

The case of J. Watties Canneries exemplifies one wartime relationship that developed between a well-placed company and the Government.[56] In December 1941 Treasury guaranteed the company's overdraft to a limit of £8,000 to enable it to install new can-making machinery deemed essential to provision the troops. In March 1943, on the recommendation of the Food and Rationing Controller, the company secured a government building loan of £8,500 at 5.26 per cent to enable it to erect a building and expand into dehydrating vegetables and fruit for the American and New Zealand armed forces. A few months later the Bureau of Industry shut out competition from Thompson and Hills Ltd by refusing its application to enter the canning business in Hawkes Bay, thus guaranteeing monopoly status to Watties. Soon after this, the Government agreed to purchase another 500 tons of Watties' produce for supply to the armed forces. In 1944 Watties was producing a huge quantity of goods on behalf of the Government in a new building paid for by taxpayers. By now the Government was reimbursing most of Watties' expenses, including office and laboratory overheads, as well as depreciation. Moreover, if the Government wished to dispose of its assets, Watties had obtained the option to purchase at valuation – which, given that competition had been shut out – was bound to be a difficult calculation. The War Cabinet advanced another £10,000 to Watties in 1944 and paid a loss of £7,100 on the production of canned apples. That year, not surprisingly, Watties enjoyed record overall profits. James Wattie told shareholders that the war had brought about a demand for canned goods 'not previously known'.[57]

The first indication that the Crown might wish to dispose of its Watties assets came in October 1944. The Government decided to sell the building it had paid for, and the figure of £9,000 was initially suggested by Treasury. Watties was in no hurry to respond; it had use of the building and was working on its own expansion plans. In August 1946 the company was obliged by its contract to exercise its option to buy the government plant. Treasury believed the building and machinery were now worth £12,000 and estimated that they would cost £15,000 to replace. The Ministry of Works thought the real value nearer to £40,000. Watties played hard to get. They paid off their remaining government loans, continued to use the State's building, but refused to reach a settlement, although their production and profits were expanding at a fast clip. For a time Watties argued that they were not much interested in the plant, then made an offer of £7,000. Finally agreement was reached that they would pay £17,000 in cash, with interest payable from August 1946. Cabinet blessed the deal on 4 March 1948. Watties then pleaded a shortage of cash and persuaded

Nash to grant them a State Advances loan. Treasury reluctantly agreed, suggesting an interest rate of 4.5 per cent per annum for prompt payment. Nash generously reduced this to 4.25 per cent. Nothing, it seemed, could be too good for wartime comrades.

Watties enjoyed their close relationship with the Government and came up with other ideas for concessions or direct help in the years ahead.[58] Looking back, it is clear that officials and ministers played a significant part in developing this new, privately owned industry at a time when the market for canned goods could never have been better. Investors' desires for profits, wartime requirements and the Government's general ambition to stimulate an industry which employed many, especially in the marginally held seat of Hastings, happily coincided in an arrangement that was satisfactory to all. The taxpayer footed much of the bill.

No matter how lucrative the arrangements with the Government, many established manufacturers became wary of bureaucratic controls, preferring looser forms of cooperation within their various sector groups of the Manufacturers' Federation. The National Party in opposition often complained about the growing mass of regulations. In October 1939 S. G. Holland, who was a loud backbencher and soon to be the party's leader, called the Labour Government a 'reckless crew of political "experimenters"'.[59] For a long time the gravity of the war deafened people to such complaints. However, in 1943 Labour's *dirigiste* economy began to overreach itself. The growing criticism was partly because a general election was on the horizon. But complaints to ministers about aspects of stabilisation were rising. The *New Zealand Truth* began a campaign against some of the regulations. On 11 August 1943 it stated forcefully that many were 'bewildering to those who had to abide by them' and required 'an army of inspectors to enforce them'. *Truth* blamed the Government 'for issuing regulations which reveal so blatantly that wishful thinking is the dominant note instead of commonsense'.[60] Other complaints were on the increase; many manufacturers, for instance, were becoming restless about what they saw as an erosion of their margins compared with those of retailers.[61] Envy and suspicion became constant handmaidens of bureaucratic intervention.

Labour narrowly survived the election on 25 September 1943. The Government lost eight seats – all of them in the North Island – and won only one new one, when Sir Apirana Ngata was defeated by an obscure Labour candidate in Eastern Maori. At 9.30 pm on election day, some of Fraser's closest confidants thought 'the ship was sunk'.[62] But the arrival of the servicemen's votes a few days later rescued several members, including the Minister of Health, A. H. Nordmeyer, and backbencher W. T. Anderton. The election result began turning ministers' minds towards the postwar period and normalisation of the economy. What, however, was 'normality'? Clearly it was not to be a world where the State pulled back from its active role in economic policy. Both politicians and bureaucrats intended to play a big part, using the experience gained in wartime. We can see the thinking of the men in Customhouse Quay from the draft of a speech they sent up to Sullivan for delivery to the Manufacturers' Federation's annual conference in October 1943. It argued for a policy of 'planned and controlled trade and industry' to sustain a 'planned social system'.

> The economic stability and progress upon which depends all future progress in social reform cannot be left to the chances of unaided individual enterprise in a world of promiscuous international competition. National policy must step in to secure for our producers a reasonable prospect of success, whether in supplying the needs of a balanced economic life at home, or in developing our export trade.
>
> We are no longer what we once were, the overwhelmingly greatest and consequently cheapest producers in the world. That place is now occupied by the United States. On the other hand our standard of living and costs of production are far higher than those of many others who today are as fully equipped technically as we are. It is for the nation to use its powers of direction and guidance, of direct assistance, of the bargaining power of our rich home market, to secure favourable conditions from those who for economic and political reasons are most willing to cooperate with us and most need our cooperation.

Full of hubris, the draft speech looked forward to a world of plans and planners protecting New Zealanders from adverse overseas developments and guiding local business towards socially desirable ends.

It is conceivable that had Sullivan been a stronger minister, both intellectually and physically (he was often ill and had less than four years to live), the shape of the postwar economy might have been slightly different. However, while he could be irritable and moody, he happily complied with officials who were keen on planning, pointing out that he had first advocated this himself as far back as 1918. Years later, a journalist noted that Sullivan could have an audience believe 'that every shirt or pair of shoes made in New Zealand was of tremendous quality even if it wasn't'.[63] In October 1943 Sullivan delivered his officials' speech with gusto, noting that while there had been a 'high degree of regimentation' during the war, the Government had not socialised industry 'nor does it intend to'. Assuring businessmen that it was not his intention 'to irritate unnecessarily or to restrict wilfully', he added: 'Planning and control will be necessary after the war – planning to ensure continuity of production, and control to ensure equitable distribution. . .'[64]

Wartime experience and the unquestioning support of their minister gave officials at Industries and Commerce confidence that they knew what was best for the country. An experimental planning authority called the Organisation for National Development was established in 1944.[65] It gave way to an Industrial Development Committee chaired by Sullivan but it did not survive as a stand-alone agency. It included representatives of manufacturers as well as the trade union movement, with officials from Industries and Commerce doing most of the work. The committee set out to cultivate industries that used New Zealand raw materials. Rope, twine, textiles, carpets, woollen goods, pulp and paper, dried milk products, chemicals and the canning of fruit and vegetables all caught the eyes of officialdom. 'It is most desirable that efforts to develop New Zealand's industrial economy should be directed first to those lines of production which are allied to our national resources and to our primary products', said the department's annual report. Sub-committees were already in place for the footwear, radio and electric ranges in addition to the still operational plans for flax, tobacco and the pharmacy industry.[66] Yet, when Industries and Commerce was restructured, the Industrial Development Committee melded back into it. After November 1945 the department had two distinct units, one dealing with industry where planning was now located, the other with commerce. By this time Industries and Commerce which had employed 160 permanent officers in 1936 had 584 on its payroll – a growth trend that was shared by many other parts of the public service.[67]

Industries and Commerce was without a permanent head for several months in 1946. Like that of so many top officials, Schmitt's health was causing trouble by the end of the war. He lessened his workload by moving sideways into the newly created position of Secretary of the Tourist and Publicity Department. His old job at Industries and Commerce was advertised. The top candidate was the former secretary, G. W. Clinkard, who had been with the Ministry of Supply in London for much of the war. Sullivan's long-time distrust of Clinkard and his family connections led the minister to veto his appointment. After an interlude, P. B. Marshall, who had a background in the primary sector, was appointed secretary. However, Clinkard appealed to the Public Service Appeal Board and became Secretary of Industries and Commerce once more towards the end of 1946. A job had to be found for Marshall. He moved sideways into what soon became the lame duck position of Commissioner of Supply.[68]

Those with big ambitions for industry were firmly in control once more. Clinkard was soon busily at work establishing eleven commodity sections within the department, each with a controlling officer who was to exercise suzerainty over a huge list of manufactured items. A most ambitious Industries and Commerce Bill was drafted for introduction. It planned to give the department virtually complete power to control industrial development in New Zealand in any manner that the minister or bureaucrats believed to be in the public interest.[69] Fortuitously, perhaps, Dan Sullivan died on 8 April 1947. Some weeks later, on 29 May, the able 46-year-old Arnold Nordmeyer, who had been Minister of Health since 1941, took the portfolio of Industries and Commerce. Shrewder than Sullivan, sharing none of his antipathies and less prone to being swept along by his officials' ideas (he did not proceed with Clinkard's bill), Nordmeyer nonetheless found himself enmeshed in the web of controls and schemes that had been spun during twelve years of continuing governmental experimentation.

While officials were nurturing plans and juggling jobs, Walter Nash realised as early as the middle of 1944 that some wartime controls were becoming a needless irritant. In July Nash commissioned a review of all 243 sets of regulations that had been gazetted since the beginning of the war. A short list of those deemed unnecessary was produced, but officials also tendered several more pages of regulations that would be needed after the war, and a further 54 that ought to be converted into permanent legislation.[70] The rules covering the Arbitration Court were relaxed slightly, and early in 1945 rigid wage stabilisation was slightly modified. In March there was a small wage rise. Concerns were growing about the application of import licensing. Early in 1945 the Factory Controller, G. A. Pascoe, told Nash that the Industries Committee deciding import licensing priorities was 'exercising an influence over manufacturing units far beyond what could have been contemplated'. The 'insidious' influence of officials was interfering 'most unusually' in the internal distribution of limited raw materials. According to Pascoe, officials were simply too busy to do the work expected of them, and some businessmen were suffering adversely from arbitrary decisions. He recommended that the committee be reconstituted with new terms of reference. The Manufacturers' Federation wanted a Trade Control Commission to handle import licensing and tariffs, and was urging the introduction of flexible policies as well as lower taxes.[71]

It is not clear how much notice was taken of these pieces of advice. The role of the advisory group now known as the Industries Committee was constantly under scrutiny, with its own members unhappy about its precise interface with the Customs Department that issued import licences. In 1946 the committee was renamed the Executive Advisory Committee to the Commissioner of Supply. Various pressures kept impinging on its work. No strict procedure was adhered to for awarding import licences; ministers themselves often intervened when constituents or interest groups sought to bypass what were said to be proper channels. Moreover, it was clear that import licences were being sold by those lucky enough to have secured them, a practice which inevitably added to a manufacturer's costs. There were constant crosscurrents within Industries and Commerce. Pascoe thought the proliferation of 'backyard' industries was costly to the economy, noting in a memorandum to Nordmeyer that they often made goods 'which normally could be much more economically imported without jeopardising full employment'.[72]

Some experiments, such as 'austerity clothing', obviously had to be dealt with. On 20 April 1945 the *Dominion* reported a retailer as saying that the 'the public is sick and tired of austerity goods'.[73] In May the Factory Controller was instructed to cancel the rules as soon as possible. They were withdrawn later that month and pending prosecutions against manufacturers who had failed to comply were abandoned.[74] A slow, general process of deregulation was soon under way after VE Day on 8 May 1945. Manpower controls were gradually lifted. They had mostly gone by November. By the end of the year 133 sets of Emergency Regulations had also been lifted.

However, in line with officials' earlier recommendations, 362 sets of regulations were retained, and an Emergency Regulations Amendment Bill was passed in December 1945 to keep those deemed essential to post-war planning in place for one more year. The Act was then extended in 1946 and again in 1947, despite mounting criticism from Holland, the National Party's leader, who described the re-enactments as having 'all the elements of a communist system, of totalitarianism and dictatorship' because they enabled regulations to be enforced without parliamentary consent.[75] Eventually the Government passed the Economic Stabilisation Act in November 1948. It placed many of the wide powers that ministers had been using for some years into statutory form.[76] A select committee chaired by Clyde Carr, MP for Timaru, worked steadily through remaining regulations and cautiously approved occasional further revocations. The Standards Institute remained and issued recommendations about standards for garment manufacturing and other industries for many years to come.

*

As in 1914–19, wartime authoritarianism spilled over into domestic issues like education, broadcasting and liquor. In a tone of disappointment, the former Labour MP Ormond Wilson observed later that 'one of the inherent tendencies of bureaucracies is the enforcement of conformity'.[77] In a manner reminiscent of World War I, school curricula were carefully monitored and uniforms enforced at all state secondary schools. The internal struggle within the Labour Party that resulted in the expulsion of John A. Lee, the flamboyant MP for Grey Lynn, was part of the Government's striving for conformity. Refused a position in Cabinet in 1935, Lee increasingly marginalised himself within the Labour caucus with policy criticisms that took on a more personal tone as Savage's health deteriorated. Worried by the inflationary implications of Lee's constant advocacy of more Reserve Bank credit, and discomfited by the occasional inference that foreign loans could be dishonoured, ministers came to detest Lee, seeing him both as a threat to their concept of insulation as well as their hegemony within caucus. Playing on wartime fears, and holding Savage's illness in part against Lee, the combined forces of the parliamentary Labour Party and the union-dominated Central Executive of the Labour Party succeeded in expelling him from the party at its annual conference in March 1940. Only the Speaker, W. E. Barnard, and a few party officials went with Lee, although, as several historians have shown, Lee's departure had more serious consequences at the party's grassroots. However, Lee's efforts to launch a new party, the Democratic Labour (later Soldier Labour) Party, came to little. He faded from the scene, his name becoming a synonym for disloyalty and maverick economics. His expulsion was a victory of sorts for the leadership of the Labour Party and for their narrower, less experimental vision of the country's future.[78]

Developments within broadcasting are another pointer to Labour's desire for tight social control. State interest in this medium had been growing since 1921 when the first provisional permits were issued by the Post and Telegraph Department for transmission and reception. After 1925 private broadcasting was in the hands of a state-sanctioned monopoly run by William Goodfellow and Ambrose Harris. This monopoly came to an end in 1931. It was not ideological consideration so much as public discontent at the limited array of programmes and pressure from some university educators wanting a higher level of educational content, that led Forbes's Government to set up a National Broadcasting Service to be run by a ministerially appointed board.[79] A 'raggle-taggle army of local outfits' broadcast privately owned, regionally sponsored commercial programmes under fairly strict state regulations administered by the NBS.[80]

Labour leaders were uneasy about a state-run broadcasting system so long as they did not hold the reins of power. Their discomfort was heightened by ministerial interference with a pro-Labour 'Friendly Road' broadcast by a charismatic radio parson, Colin Scrimgeour, on the eve of the 1935 election.[81] Once in office, Labour's opposition to a state system faded. The Broadcasting Act which passed on 11 June 1936 required all broadcasting to be in public hands. It abolished the Broadcasting Board and commissioned the Minister of Broadcasting (the Prime Minister) to produce a national service.[82] On 8 June 1936 the Prime Minister declared that the Government was 'going to be master of publicity. We are not going to wait for the newspapers or the Opposition to tell the people what we are doing. We are going right ahead. That is plain, is it not?' He added that the deliberations of Parliament would be broadcast direct to the people.[83] It was axiomatic to the reformer's mind that, once apprised of the details of what Labour had in store for them, the wider public would be bound to approve.

Newspapers and Opposition politicians howled at the prospect of a state-run broadcasting service falling into the clutches of Labour ministers, especially when Clyde Carr MP attacked 'the biased press' during the debates, and declared that the Government intended to 'cut the claws of this monster'.[84] However, with broadcasting, as in so many things, cautious action followed bold words. Savage told the *Standard* that he wanted to see broadcasting conducted 'on proper lines' and was seeking a 'topnotcher' to head it.[85] On 1 December 1936 Professor James Shelley of Canterbury University College, whose W.E.A. courses in the 1920s had always appealed to Holland, Fraser and Nash, became Director of the National Broadcasting Service. By the end of 1936 a large new building was being constructed for 2YA. A giant radio mast rose above Titahi Bay.

Shelley wove his way skilfully through the petty jealousies within the new medium. He set basic standards for regional stations, while allowing them considerable autonomy. He and Heenan played a major role in stimulating the arts. From 1947 until 1988 annual broadcasting fees subsidised a symphony orchestra. However, like the *New Zealand Listener*, which began in June 1939 with Oliver Duff as its editor, the National Broadcasting Service in its early days was a fairly conservative institution, not too highbrow, cautious of its political masters, and reluctant ever to shock the public. Some thought it reliably dull and run by a killjoy.[86]

Commercial broadcasting was a bird of different feather. Here the Government had a more overtly political goal, as Savage explained. 'This modern medium of communication has become one of the outstanding features of economic and social life', he told a *Standard* reporter in November 1936. 'Its social value has, as yet, hardly been realised. . . . Radio has proved to be the most powerful force for propaganda devised. . . .' Savage promised not to misuse radio, but stressed its value to businessmen who needed the 'latest medium of publicity' to advertise their New Zealand-made goods. As Prime Minister, he wanted to see 'truthful and reliable advertising of good products', a role which Daisy Basham, better known as 'Aunt Daisy', performed with gusto on commercial radio for a quarter of a century.[87] Constant advertising of New Zealand-made goods was an essential ingredient of Savage's self-dependent, insulated society.

However, 'Uncle Scrim', as he was widely known, was much more difficult to deal with than Shelley. The parson was as flashy as the professor was grey. Scrimgeour drove a hard bargain with ministers when the new Act obliged the Government to purchase his small, failing Auckland commercial station. He emerged as Controller of Commercial Broadcasting, while many of his former staff operated initially from the station's headquarters in Queen's Arcade, Auckland.[88] Scrimgeour was less prepared to tolerate political interference with programming and when Kenneth Melvin's 'History Behind the Headlines' day-to-day account of international events from Europe was suppressed in 1939, he let irate listeners know who was responsible.[89] When Savage, who was Scrimgeour's sole ministerial patron, died, government antagonism became more obvious. Scrim's radio eulogies of John A. Lee after his expulsion from the Labour Party angered Fraser. After a number of further transgressions, Scrim was called up for military service in an obvious move to silence him. In 1943 he was sacked. He stood against Fraser in the 1943 election where he scored 15 per cent of the vote in Wellington Central and cut a large hole in the Prime Minister's majority.[90] But it was Shelley's caution that prevailed in Broadcasting House when the National and Commercial arms were eventually combined. The Labour Government preferred it that way.

Expressions of dissent in films and magazines also worried the ministry. On the outbreak of war Heenan recalled a number of anti-war films. *All Quiet on the Western Front*, *The Road Back*, *They Gave Him a Gun*, *Three Comrades*, *Dawn Patrol*, *The First World War* and *Shopworn Angel* were all believed to depict the horrors of war sufficiently realistically to impede recruiting campaigns.[91] An old Labour stalwart, J. T. Paul, was appointed Director of Publicity a few weeks later. He was responsible to the Prime Minister. Between them they ran 'a formidable system of censorship and of control over public expression of opinion'.[92] *Tomorrow* magazine soon ran into trouble. After the 1938 election it continued to espouse the declared goals of the Labour Government but was critical of aspects of economic policy and opposed the move toward conscription, which was eventually introduced in the middle of 1940. It criticised the so-called 'phoney war' in Europe and carried an article by Lee that was critical of Savage. In the tense days surrounding the fall of France and the surrender of Belgium this was too much. Paul complained to Fraser; the Attorney General, Rex Mason, labelled some of the articles 'subversive'. The Superintendent of Police called on the printer of *Tomorrow* and its last issue appeared on 29 May 1940. Everywhere social engineers, particularly those striving to safeguard their domestic achievements in a time of war, found it necessary to be authoritarian.

The concept of trust control of liquor which developed in 1943–44, and which has survived for half a century, was rooted in the notion that there was a need for public authorities to tighten control over the distribution of alcohol. Throughout Labour's history, liquor had always been an issue dividing friends. Savage had worked for a brewery; Fraser drank little or nothing; Nash, when he drank, did so privately. Labour MP's always insisted that issues concerning alcohol were conscience issues in Parliament and not subject to the whip. When more than 60 per cent of the voters in the Invercargill Licensing District voted at the 1943 election to restore liquor sales to their area, the issue of what form this should take landed on Cabinet's plate. Nash sought advice from his officials on whether the State or the local municipality should run the new liquor outlets in Invercargill. Ashwin was not enthusiastic about municipal control. He tended to favour state control because uniform standards would be easier to maintain. Others supported this view, arguing that a state monopoly would remove competition from the liquor trade. Competition was seen to be the cause of so much that was bad about the sale and consumption of alcohol.[93]

However, locals in Invercargill preferred that key decisions remain with the locals. They set up an Invercargill Municipal Control and Ownership of Licensed Hotels Committee.[94] Invercargill was a marginal seat and Cabinet agreed to the concept of a locally elected committee to establish and run hotels. The community would benefit from the distribution of any profits. The Invercargill Licensing Trust Act passed on 29 March 1944 and the Government soon lent the trust £50,000 to establish outlets in the area. A Treasury official assured the minister that the advance would be secure: 'With the trust exercising a monopoly and not having to pay anything for goodwill, it would only be through the most careless mismanagement that the trust would encounter financial difficulties'.[95]

In June 1944 Cabinet agreed to guarantee further trust borrowing from the Bank of New Zealand to a limit of £200,000. The trust was required to pay tax at a rate of 70 per cent on its profits, which left little for capital development, let alone distribution to the community. Nonetheless, the Trust Board pushed ahead with an ambitious building programme and by April 1947 had a total overdraft with the BNZ of £267,579. The Justice Department was now responsible for overseeing the trust and was not happy with the quality of decision-making. One of its officials told Ashwin that he doubted whether private enterprise would have constructed so many outlets, noting that the potential bar business at two hotels 'is insufficient to justify the capitalisation involved'. He continued: 'It must not be overlooked . . . that none of the members of the Trust has any experience of hotel management or the liquor trade, indeed, few have any business experience.'[96]

This lack of business and financial skills remained a problem for the growing number of trusts – there were 14 in existence by the middle 1970s. When licence restoration carried at a general election the public until the mid 1990s opted to support a trust at the ensuing poll. People believed that the local community, rather than the 'liquor interests', would benefit from profits. However, some trust boards made careless decisions and several have been able to survive only because of the monopoly status they enjoy in their area. The profits distributed locally were, for the most part, small.[97]

Once wartime powers were assumed, they were seldom surrendered lightly anywhere in the world. In New Zealand they became entangled in postwar policy formation to such an extent that the transition was virtually seamless. In their determination to ensure there was no repeat of the economic upheaval at the end of World War I, Peter Fraser's ministers developed an elaborate programme for rehabilitation for the 224,000 people who served during the war. If it was to be successful, rehabilitation required a continuation of the legislative and regulatory underpinning found so useful during the war. It was to be a repeat, this time on a grander scale, of the State's contractual obligations to early settlers who had been led to believe they would be looked after.

Demobilisation was handled cautiously; the peak months were from June 1945 to May 1946.[98] At the point of discharge, service personnel received a gratuity of 2s 6d for every day spent overseas and 8d per day for service in New Zealand. The money was paid into a Post Office Savings Bank account and received a 5 per cent bonus each 31 March on the sum

Expanding health services; a district nurse checks a Maori baby's progress on the Waihara gumfields, late 1940s. ATL F-46725-1/2

remaining in the account. Nearly £23 million was paid out in gratuities. A National Employment Service assisted service personnel in finding civilian employment. This was no onerous task because of the buoyant state of the labour market. A Rehabilitation Department had been set up in November 1943 under the Rehabilitation Act passed two years earlier. Through a variety of assistance schemes involving trade-training (11,000 returnees received assistance), university bursaries and general educational assistance (27,000 beneficiaries), land settlement schemes (12,500 were settled), business (11,500 were granted loans) and housing and furniture loans (a total of 64,000 were granted, while another 18,000 returnees were allocated state houses), service personnel were eased back into normal lives. In all, a total of £264 million was advanced to them, much of it (£192 million) in loans. The cost of administration was barely 2 per cent of the total paid out.[99] It is generally agreed that rehabilitation went much more smoothly in 1945 than it had in 1919, due to the foresight of officials and the skilled administration of the minister, C. F.(Gerry) Skinner MC, himself a recently returned war hero. But there can be no doubt that the absence of unemployment during the next twenty years did more than anything else to ensure success.

244

However, in the postwar world Fraser's Government left little to chance. Public Works projects, especially hydro-electrical construction, were given high priority as the Ministry of Works struggled to satisfy escalating demand for electricity. By March 1949 there were 5000 more workers employed on state projects than there had been in 1944. Treasury warned the Minister of Finance about overheating the economy.[100] The Government pushed ahead, although it realised that continuing controls would be necessary if it was to survive at the ballot box.

The twin goals of maintaining full employment and spending more on welfare at a time when so many service personnel were coming back into the community with pent-up ambitions to spend their record savings-bank deposits,[101] threatened a huge increase in demand for imports. Shortages of raw materials and finished products compounded the problem. Faced with runaway inflation or tight controls, Labour passed a Control of Prices Act in November 1947. It put the Price Tribunal into statute for the first time, and outlined its regulatory powers.[102] More subsidies were introduced to restrain retail prices. Sugar, wheat, bread, butter, cheese, milk, eggs, oatmeal, phosphates, cornsacks, many fertilisers, fertiliser bags, cow covers, and the transport by road and sea of timber and fertilisers were now subsidised. Various payments were made for the eradication of noxious weeds and rabbits and for the testing of cows. When Ashwin reported to his minister in February 1947 that subsidies were running at £800,000 above budget, and were certain to cost an extra £4 million for the year 1947–48, Nash asked Leicester Webb, the Director of Stabilisation, to conduct a study of the likely costs of removing subsidies altogether.[103] The reply made dismal reading; they were now economic woof and warp. The Government tentatively removed some farming subsidies as well as those on tea and sugar. Rail and shipping charges were allowed to rise. The following year, with an election on the horizon Nash increased subsidies once more. Their cost reached £14.6 million for the financial year 1949–50.[104]

Government subsidies and special grants became such an integral part of postwar stabilisation that most people came to believe they had a right to them. In 1947 Fraser received a request from the Canterbury Cricket Association for subsidies on their purchases of bats, balls and clothing,[105] while a group of Motueka tobacco growers testily informed the Tobacco Board in November that they took 'strong exception on principle' to the notion that they might contribute to the cost of flood protection work in their area. Local authorities 'have an obligation' to do the work, 'and the Government has a greater obligation to supply the finance'.[106] The incoming

Minister of Finance, S. G. Holland, observed in his budget in August 1950 that 'many people have a fallacious idea that what the State provides does not cost them anything'.[107]

Fraser retained office against all odds at the general election on 27 November 1946. Some ministers were astonished by the Government's victory, albeit by the narrow margin of four seats.[108] The reasons for success were not hard to find. First, Labour's vision of a carefully stabilised postwar world sat squarely with developments elsewhere. In most countries, as Skidelsky notes, 'war was lauded as a model for peace in its planning of national life, control of credit, direction of major national industries and investment'.[109] Sporting a similar array of subsidies, controls and licences to New Zealand's, Ben Chifley's Australian Labor Government won re-election in September 1946.[110] Clement Attlee's Labour Government was unveiling its plans for a welfare state in the United Kingdom, and in June 1945 Mackenzie King enjoyed yet another victory at the polls in Canada with promises of expanding welfare;[111] Truman was soldiering on against strong Republican Party opposition with his version of the New Deal, soon to be called the Fair Deal. Socialists in Europe enjoyed what in some cases turned out to be a brief hold on office. Collectivism was at full tide. Everywhere the public seemed ready to support Keynesian spending policies and Fabian social goals.

Secondly, Fraser handled election year skilfully. The soldier votes had been vital to his survival in 1943, which was why he set such store by making a success of rehabilitation. In addition, from 1 April 1946 the means test on family benefits was abolished and the payment per child was set at ten shillings. The total number of family benefit payments immediately jumped from 42,637 to 230,021. Payable usually to a mother, family benefits became a significant factor in most family budgets. Universal superannuation payments were to increase steadily over the next few years. Laboratory diagnostic benefits came into force on 1 April 1946 and dental benefits for adolescent children were scheduled for the following year. The Excess Profits Tax that had been siphoning off a significant proportion of the windfall wartime profits of some businesses was abolished. Nash told Parliament: 'The economic machine must run smoothly, incentives must be given both to labour and to capital, there must be an equitable distribution of the national income, and the tax system must be so adjusted as to contribute to the maximum in attaining our objectives.'[112]

Fraser enticed Major General Kippenberger, a man of extraordinary talents, who had suffered severe injury in the penultimate stage of the war, to head up a generously funded war history programme. The appointment caught the imaginations of many returned servicemen. But the Prime Minister went further, reaching out to a wider community with several developments of cultural significance. The New Zealand Literary Fund was established. A Cultural and Recreational Trust Account using profits from lotteries was also created at Heenan's suggestion, with decisions on allocations to recreational and arts groups being kept in ministers' hands or those of their appointees. A Community Arts Service soon appeared, offering jobs for performing artists, many of whom secured contracts to visit schools.[113] Labour enjoyed considerable support after the war from New Zealand's developing intelligentsia. They endorsed many of the party's social goals and liked its efforts to boost culture.

Thirdly, as many newspapers noted, trade unions behaved themselves during the election campaign of 1946. From the time it came to office, union militancy was Labour's Achilles heel. Leaders of strategically placed unions were happy to avail themselves of Labour's social reforms but their leaders were irked by what they saw as frozen income relativities. F. P. Walsh's strong support in March 1946 for stabilising wages was not shared by militants.[114] Postwar stabilisation and the control of wages which was an essential component of it seemed to indicate that life under a Labour Government was now as good as it was ever going to get. Some believed they could win better conditions outside the rigidly controlled economy. Others wanted more controls on capital and fewer on labour. Whenever they argued for a wage rise before the Arbitration Court, Federation of Labour officials minutely scrutinised farmers' returns and the level of guaranteed prices lest they succeeded in altering their relativities with workers. Not willing to risk a rupture with people whom he regarded as kith and kin, Fraser gave several unions their own specialist tribunals where they could air their grievances. But whatever the tribunal, Labour insisted on maintaining the principle of compulsory arbitration. Wage increases for one group had a habit of spreading quickly into other sectors, with inflationary results.[115]

During the war several unions, particularly the watersiders and the miners, had caused constant trouble. One outside observer was not impressed with the attitudes of many New Zealand unionists. An official at the American Embassy in January 1942 reported to his seniors in Washington that 'on average, the New Zealand workman and union member gives the appearance of doing as little work as he can get away with and of having only secondary interest in doing well what little he does'.[116] Even in government circles there was a perception that workers were taking things rather too easily. Each year Nash's postwar budgets contained homilies about the need to increase productivity. He believed that economic growth was inadequate to sustain the growing weight of expenditure which the Government now carried. In fact, as we shall see, trying to ensure stability as well as growth required much more than better work habits within the labour force. Nevertheless, the miners' activities during the war illustrate the way in which an attitudinal problem developed among many workers once they realised that a labour shortage guaranteed them jobs no matter how little effort they made.

Between 1935 and 1945 New Zealand went from having a surplus of coal to a drastic shortage. This was partly due to a rising demand for coal to produce electricity. With Public Works construction of dams declining after the outbreak of war, more use had to be made of other sources of energy. However, a major contributor to the crisis that developed was the deteriorating relationships between the miners' unions, the private owners and the Government. In earlier times, Labour's leaders had advocated state ownership of all mines; Harry Holland introduced a Bill in 1924 to nationalise them, and place them under a board of control on which there would be workers' representatives. Many union leaders hoped that the governments of Savage and Fraser would follow this course. However, Labour ministers became uneasy at what they perceived to be a pressure campaign from the miners' leaders.[117] Miners' political campaigns irritated mine owners, and as one historian has remarked, workers and management 'confidently expected bad faith from [each] other'. A situation of 'fundamental ill will' existed in most mines by the time war broke out.[118]

In the long run the policy adopted by the Labour Government only made matters worse. Desperate to increase the output of coal, yet not ready to capitulate to the unions' political agendas, the Government cajoled, berated and bribed mine owners and workers. Ministers hoped that union leaders could be divided from the rank and file and that a sense of patriotism would assert itself. Generous incentives were provided. Subsidies to mine owners began in April 1940 so that they could increase wages yet restrain the retail cost of coal. The standard 5 per cent wage rise was paid to miners later in the year, followed by a further 13.8 per cent from 1 May 1942. This required more subsidies: they reached £370,000 for the financial year 1942–43. In 1943 the mines were declared to be an 'essential service' so that miners could be held back from war service. But employer–employee relationships deteriorated and production lagged.[119]

Meantime, the Government had purchased two abandoned mines in Taranaki in 1938 and when the private owners of the Blackball Mine moved to close it in 1941, Cabinet decided to purchase it for £30,000. When the

Government responded to miners' strikes in the Waikato in September 1942 by agreeing to take over the affected mines and run them for the duration of the war while paying the owners generously, workers concluded that it might be possible to persuade the Government to purchase all mines. In the end, this is what happened.

Absenteeism became a chronic condition at many mines in 1941–42. There was no material improvement after the Government promulgated the Industrial Absenteeism Emergency Regulations on 20 May 1942. The *Greymouth Evening Star* ran an article in March 1943 about 'wilful absenteeism' at some mines, commenting that it seemed to be part of a political agenda. The Minister of Mines, Paddy Webb, who had been voicing strong disapproval behind the scenes, noted publicly that younger miners in particular were showing 'some measure of irresponsibility'.[120] By this time miners were well paid compared with other sectors of the workforce. Yet the practice of knocking off early, refusing to work Friday and/or Monday, while turning up to work on Saturday, when the pay was at overtime rates, became a common practice.[121]

Before long, other private owners of West Coast mines began to sense that either having the State run their mines for the rest of the war or, better still, selling them to the Government made economic sense. Over the next few years most mines were sold to the Government while the payment of subsidies soared to £1.15 million for the financial year 1946–47. Industrial unrest continued.[122] Meanwhile, there was considerable criticism of the Government for engaging in what some saw as 'socialism

Bob Semple opens the 30,000th state house, 1949. ATL F-29926-1/2

249

by stealth'. But Nash responded with the comment that coal resources were not something 'which should be left to the profit-earning motives of private enterprise'.[123] With no apparent enthusiasm, the Government passed the Coal Act 1948. It brought all remaining mines under state control with 'reasonable compensation'.

In effect the Government's misguided generosity to employers and workers helped the miners' leaders to achieve peacefully the socialisation of a strategic asset. Once the Government had paid acceptable prices for some mines, they established a benchmark for others. The owners quickly cashed up. However, there was no noticeable improvement in coal output. In fact, production actually deteriorated at the Waikato mines after the Government took over their administration in 1942.[124] By the end of the decade the State possessed assets and a workforce that would cost the taxpayers dearly in years to come.

After the election in 1946 industrial relations deteriorated further. Early in 1947 seamen, carpenters and freezing workers tried to pressure the Arbitration Court to issue a generous wage rise; when their tactics failed, they began a campaign against the principle of compulsory arbitration. The carpenters announced that they were contemplating de-registering from the I.C.&A. Act in the hope that they could regain the right to strike.[125] Meantime the New Zealand Waterside Workers' Union started a campaign to get a workers' majority on their wage-fixing tribunal, the Waterfront Industry Authority.[126] In effect, at a time of over-full employment the more strategically placed workers wanted to exploit their status. Relationships with the Government and employers went from bad to worse. Fraser and Semple hit back at union critics, the Prime Minister telling the annual conference of the Federation of Labour in June 1947 that 'the people of New Zealand did not help to fight and defeat Hitler to allow a large part of his dictatorship ideas to be planted here'.[127]

In the belief that union discontent was confined to a few leaders, the Government passed an amendment to the I.C.&A. Act in 1947. It required the holding of a membership ballot before any strike action was undertaken. This had little effect, and throughout 1948 and 1949 there were constant industrial skirmishes, while stories of 'spelling' and 'featherbedding' on the waterfront frequently reached the news media. A significant minority of Labour's kith and kin were now in revolt against the Government's policy of stabilisation, at least that part relating to wages.[128] Events came to a head in February 1949, when Auckland carpenters decided on a go-slow following a small pay increase awarded by the Arbitration Court. The Minister of Labour, Angus McLagan, deregistered the Auckland Carpenters'

This National Party campaign advertisement in 1949 implies big changes if National is elected. ATL F-106471-1/2

Union from the I.C.&A. Act and recognised a new union in its place. All carpenters wishing to work within a 56-mile radius of Auckland city were obliged to join the new union. The strike fizzled out, but considerable hostility to Fraser's Government was evident during the run up to the election and manifested itself in opposition to the Prime Minister's August 1949 referendum on the introduction of compulsory military training. By this time union militants had completely lost confidence in the Labour Government. The National President of the New Zealand Waterside Workers' Union, 'Jock' Barnes, conspicuously worked for the election of the National Party during the election campaign, hoping that a change of government would lead to some freeing up of the controls over organised labour.[129]

The Labour Government limped through 1949 towards the election held on 30 November. Nash seemed to be losing his sure economic touch as he allowed the Government's spending to race ahead, incurring dire warnings from Ashwin at Treasury.[130] Fraser's close confidants were dispirited. Heenan wrote to a friend in the middle of the year expressing his opinion that 'the industrial boys' and the manufacturers were abusing their positions and 'not playing the game'. Strikes in an election year by those who professed to be Labour supporters spoke for themselves but many manufacturers were 'getting very careless of the quality of their products'.[131]

The National Party took advantage of the tired mood within the Labour Party. National candidates spoke generally about lower taxes and freedom from controls which had clearly become a heavy albatross around Labour's neck. However, their leaders were not specific about which ones they intended to lift. Their dominant campaign slogan was 'Make the pound go further'. Keith Holyoake, deputy leader of the National Party, expressed the view that the election would be 'fought in the kitchen. It is a cost-of-living, a shortages, and a restrictions election, and womenfolk will play the biggest part in it.'[132] His prediction was probably right. The Labour Party's portion of the vote slipped to 46.5 per cent and it lost eight seats, including those of two Cabinet ministers, E. L. Cullen (Agriculture) and Arnold Nordmeyer (Industries and Commerce) as well as three of its more promising backbenchers, Ormond Wilson, Martyn Finlay and Tom Skinner. Fourteen years of mostly cautious, yet occasionally bold, economic experimentation, a war, reconstruction, endless pragmatism and considerable social activism seemed as though it might have come to an end. A year later, Fraser was dead. Yet Labour's political and economic legacy lived on for a great deal longer.

Chapter 9

Freedom or Controls? National Deals with Labour's Legacy

New Zealanders spent the years from 1949 to 1984 trying to keep Labour's welfare state operational. By 1950 the State was spending nearly 30 per cent of the country's Gross Domestic Product each year. In a country of 2 million people, the public service employed 30,000, and another 85,000 were directly or indirectly being paid by the State.[1] The State's payroll, its ambitious capital works programme, and the policies of various state trading enterprises enabled it to play a major role in the economy.[2] The private sector was dominated by the processing and marketing of agricultural production; yet only 20 per cent of the total workforce was now involved in farming and related activities which produced approximately 85 per cent of New Zealand's overseas earnings. The major export lines – meat, wool and dairy products – were handled by a variety of public agencies, and most went to one market, the United Kingdom.

Manufacturing had developed rapidly since 1935. It now employed 25 per cent of the work force, a high proportion of them in small production units that thrived behind the protective fences of import controls and tariffs. More than 62 per cent of New Zealand's factories had ten or fewer workers.[3] Their output was almost entirely for domestic consumption. Small production runs inflated costs. The State registered all industries. It lent money to many, subsidised some items that featured on the Consumer Price Index (CPI) and through a variety of mechanisms influenced most aspects of the marketplace in which they traded.

The application of price control to most goods in the CPI, and to others not in it, operated on a 'cost-plus' basis. Manufacturers provided the Price Tribunal with figures detailing their costs and on top of these an allowance was made for 'reasonable profit'. Since there was a constant shortage of workers (Holland estimated there were 33,000 vacant jobs in October 1951), labour costs rose steadily. The gap between the Arbitration Court's average award wages and the actual sum paid to workers widened. More work was done at overtime rates too. These costs were passed on to the consumer. Work habits, as the 1952 report of the Royal Commission into the Waterfront Industry showed, were deteriorating in some areas. A booklet published by the Department of Internal Affairs in July 1952 noted that New Zealand life moved at a slower pace than in many European countries, and that 'there is not quite the same struggle for existence. . . .' Ten years later the Monetary and Economic Council referred to 'an attitude of relaxed ease' among the workforce. Theft from workplaces was not uncommon, the price of such 'perks' being added to overheads and ultimately passed on to the consumer. Since there was little domestic competition in the production of many items, and import licensing prevented similar goods entering the New Zealand market from abroad, 'cost plus' was virtually a licence to make money at the consumer's expense.[4]

New Zealand had developed an economy where there was no unemployment, but the cost structure rose steadily. And so did tax rates. As the Government's advisers often pointed out, escalating taxes were a disincentive to private investment and enterprise. A ministerial committee on taxation reform headed by a Christchurch accountant, T. N. Gibbs, was established in 1950. It was the first such inquiry since 1924. Gibbs's review of developments during the intervening period noted that the tax take, which constituted 14 per cent of national income in 1925–26, had doubled to 28 per cent by 1949–50. The top marginal tax rate in 1950 remained at 77.5 per cent, the same as it had been at the end of the war. Whereas the percentage of tax revenue spent on social services amounted to 5.9 per cent in 1925–26, it was now 15.3 per cent. Health, education and monetary transfers to those deemed deserving had risen ninefold in the intervening 25 years. In a cautionary note that was similar to warnings that Ashwin had been giving to Nash, Gibbs concluded:

> There has been established by the welfare programme a series of commitments that appear rigid and difficult to modify. These commitments can be supported only by a continuous expansion of the national economy, which must come from a real increase in volume of production and not merely from increases in values . . . through continuing inflation. If the economy does not expand, the welfare programme will be endangered both from yields from taxation and the probable increase in claims on the fund.

Under the combined burdens of high protection, rising labour costs, poorer standards of work and high taxation by world standards, it was not long before the country's economic growth rate subsided; in 1962 a report from the Monetary and Economic Council noted that between 1949 and 1961 the New Zealand economy 'has earned the unfortunate distinction of having one of the slowest annual rates of growth of productivity among all the advanced countries of the world'.[5] The viability of Savage's insulated economy was under threat.

Gibbs's warning about the vulnerability of New Zealand's welfare state went virtually unnoticed at the time. Generations came to believe that governments could allocate resources more successfully than the market and that centrally driven economic intervention was for the wider public good. Grandparents who had lived through two world wars and a depression welcomed the security of pensions and health care in their twilight years; parents expected that the State would help with housing, educate their children from birth to tertiary level, provide them with low-cost health care and, through a network of tariffs and other regulatory mechanisms, ensure that full employment continued. Children grew up in what Savage once called a 'cradle to grave' system, something that more sceptical Americans labelled 'womb to tomb socialism'.

It was an intimate society, where staff appointments to schools and university exam results were reported in the newspapers, along with traffic fines and art union winners. It was also a world of strict social controls. The tight restrictions of the Shops and Offices Act 1936, which was amended in 1955 (it changed little in practice), limited shop trading hours. Shops were closed over long weekends. Sunday shopping was prohibited and considerable controversy surrounded any application by retailers' associations to trade on Saturdays. Late opening on Fridays was common. Dairies could sell 'exempted goods' over a weekend but everything else had to be locked away out of view. From the late 1940s until the Shop Trading Hours Amendment Act of 1980, Saturday trading was prohibited in most awards. Broadcasting remained firmly in the State's hands and this monopoly was unchallenged until a pirate radio station began broadcasting from a ship in the Hauraki Gulf in December 1966. The state-owned *Listener* followed a cautiously conservative line on most things. Cinema prices were regulated by the Government, while the films themselves were censored by a branch of the Department of Internal Affairs. Its head, Gordon Mirams, strove to exclude, or at least to cut severely, those depicting violence and sex. When offered the option of 10 o'clock hotel closing or a continuation of the '6 o'clock swill' in a referendum on 9 March 1949, the public stuck with the status quo. Only with betting on horses was there any willingness to strike out in a new direction; voters supported the introduction of off-course totalisator betting by a wide margin.[6] For the most part the insulated economy operated in a tightly controlled social environment, one with floors, ceilings and heavy curtains.

At mid-century the centralising forces within New Zealand were at their peak. The powers of Cabinet government increased steadily. While the upper house known as the Legislative Council had never been a robust institution, it faded in public esteem after the failure of bills to reform it at the time of World War I. As the years passed, the upper house became little more than a rubber stamp for decisions of the House of Representatives. The new National Government in 1950 fulfilled its promise to abolish the council and met with little opposition. Henceforth, the legislative process became even swifter, the Governor-General's assent to bills often being given within hours of their passage through the now unicameral parliament. A later prime minister was to label New Zealand 'the fastest lawmaker in the west' and to title a book on the subject *Unbridled Power*. Government by regulation was commonplace; few bills were without regulatory powers and each year several volumes of regulations were promulgated by the Executive Council, which usually met after Cabinet each week with the Governor-General presiding.[7]

Governments performed balancing acts, endeavouring always to deliver as much as possible in the least intrusive manner because they realised that the public appetite for wartime regimentation was abating. Some freeing up of the economy was both wanted by interest groups and promised by the National Party in 1949. However, many anomalies resulted from tentative moves in the 1950s and 1960s to ease back on economic and social controls. Continuing high taxes, escalating government expenditure, declining national economic performance and an increasingly difficult world trade scene eventually exhausted Labour's legacy.

The National Government led by Sidney George Holland took office on 13 December 1949. Aged 57, with a face that was 'all hills and hollows', the new prime minister appointed himself Minister of Finance. He held this position until after the election of 1954. Holland had a Christchurch background in small business and accounting. He had been the only new face on the Coalition benches after the 1935 election and rose rapidly to leadership of the Opposition in November 1940. John Marshall, who was a junior minister in the new Government, later described Holland as a 'vigorous, buoyant, positive personality . . . . an ordinary man with . . . . an air of confidence'. He had a powerful voice and great stamina. But Holland was not an ideas man; his political philosophy could, according to Marshall, 'be written on the back of an envelope'.[8]

Like the Labour Government of 1935, neither the new prime minister nor any of his ministers had held office before. Only one of the departmental

Changing the guard on 13 December 1949: Peter Fraser hands over to Sidney George Holland. ATL F-75156-1/2

heads with whom the new ministry was dealing had experience as a permanent head under anything other than a Labour Government. In the opinion of one senior Treasury official at the time of the change, most public servants felt comfortable with the command economy.[9] What made Holland's position more difficult than Savage's was that the intellectual climate in which National was operating was much less congenial to change than Savage had experienced. In 1936 collectivism was well on the way to its zenith worldwide; it still commanded a wide following in the 1950s. There were regular press comments lauding developments in Russia,[10] and the counter-attack against collectivism led initially by Friedrich Hayek and later by the Chicago School of Economics was only in its infancy. Jack Marshall had read Hayek's *Road to Serfdom* and espoused 'liberalism' in his maiden speech.[11] The Minister of Education, Ronald Algie, had been Professor of Law at Auckland University College after which he edited the National Party's periodical, *Freedom*. Clifton Webb, the Attorney General, W. J. Broadfoot (Postmaster-General) and W. A. Bodkin (Internal Affairs) were small-town solicitors, while Frederick Doidge (External Affairs) had some knowledge of the wider world, having been a Fleet Street journalist. The new Minister of Health and, from December 1950, Industries and Commerce as well, was Jack Watts. He was a Christchurch lawyer who had done well at university. Few others seem to have read much, although Keith Holyoake, the Deputy Prime Minister, endeavoured to keep up with books about New Zealand's politics and history.[12] Most ministers had farming or small-town backgrounds and were instinctively suspicious of big government, especially when, to their minds, it had been overly concerned with promoting full employment in the cities by methods that pushed up farmers' costs.

At first, Holland's ministers and their officials circled each other uneasily. Some Treasury officials hoped for more disciplined expenditure, but other bureaucrats simply criticised the intellectual capabilities of their new masters. Requests that officials reduce the length of complex memoranda raised eyebrows.[13] While the declared policies of the governing party changed after December 1949, putting them into practice proved more difficult and over the next few years the new Government was largely deflected from its purpose, settling instead for the rhetoric of freedom while it administered most of the regulations and controls inherited from Labour.

With encouragement from Ashwin, Holland set out early in 1950 to wind back the State. Land sales were freed from control in February, which led to an immediate increase in the number of rural properties on the market. Many building controls were removed, which caused an upsurge in construction. Early in March the Government lifted some exchange controls.[14] Ashwin had told Nash that Labour's decision to pump £32.6 million of Reserve Bank credit into the economy in 1949, mainly to promote a huge capital works programme, was inflationary.[15] He repeated this message to the new Prime Minister in December 1949 and again in March 1950, telling him that inflation was being 'fed and perpetuated' by 'too high a level of State expenditure'. The Government's subsidy regime was exceeding budget, while the revenue side of the next financial statement would be £15 million less than necessary unless remedial action was taken. By this time wheat flour and bread subsidies were costing nearly £4 million per annum, butter and milk £2.4 million each, coal £2.3 million, tea £1.4 million, wool £1.4 million and railway losses another £1.5 million. Ashwin recommended reducing subsidies by a total of £12 million, and allowing the State's trading enterprises to charge more for their services:

> In my opinion the Government would be unwise to attempt to scramble out of immediate difficulties by tinkering with the problem which in that case would still be facing them next year, perhaps more aggravated. . . . While the action proposed is drastic . . . it is a necessary step in achieving financial stability, and it is better to get it all over in one operation than to have to chip at it in successive years.[16]

258

The changes would come at a cost; Ashwin pointed out that saving £12 million in subsidies was likely to result in an increase of more than 6 per cent in the CPI.[17]

Holland took the risk. On 5 May 1950 he broadcast to the nation that he was cutting subsidies by £12 million. Butter, bread, flour, eggs, gas, milk, telephones and railway fares would all increase in price; butter rationing would cease and subsidies on tea, coal and wool were to be removed altogether. In a highly political statement which accused the former Labour Government of hugely increasing its use of Reserve Bank credit in its last year of office, Holland described inflation as the biggest problem facing New Zealand. He described it as 'remorseless and relentless', 'the cruellest enemy of the working man's pay envelope', something which 'worked day and night' and 'underground'. Despite Ashwin's estimate, Holland claimed that the changes he was announcing would add only 4 per cent to the CPI.[18] In order to minimise the impact of these price rises on the most vulnerable sections of society, many social security benefits were increased from 8 May.

Cabinet went further. While vigorously reaffirming their intention to maintain full employment and stabilisation, ministers nonetheless abolished Labour's Economic Stabilisation Commission. Members received letters thanking them for their services on 22 May 1950.[19] In his budget speech in August, Holland spoke of selling some state assets and nominated the National Airways Corporation as a likely contender. A royal commission was soon empanelled to look into the growing debts of the New Zealand Government Railways and there was talk of closing some branch lines that were not paying their way.[20] Holland promised less development work by the Ministry of Works, suggesting that local authorities should shoulder more responsibility.[21]

National had campaigned with the slogan 'Own Your Own' and candidates talked of 'a property-owning democracy'. The new Government set about encouraging more private house construction and scaled down the number of state houses being built. Tenants of state houses were given the option to buy. Holland gave a ringing declaration of National's philosophy in his 1951 budget:

> The Government believes that New Zealanders are at their best when they are freed from direction and interference of the State; that they work hardest when incentives are provided; that private ownership of the means of production, distribution, and exchange is best for people; that most people have an inherent desire to own things, especially the homes in which they live and raise their families; that an abundant supply of goods is the best system of price control

259

yet devised; that the average New Zealander is inherently honest and trustworthy, and that black marketing and such like devices only arise when normal liberties and freedoms are interfered with.[22]

However, it was not long before the National Government, its sails billowing with talk of private enterprise, was virtually becalmed. While many newspapers praised Holland's announcements and the Wellington Chamber of Commerce saw the subsidy reductions as 'a real step forward', the price increases they caused were soon exacerbated by inflationary pressures flowing in from abroad as a result of the West's general rearmament programme and the outbreak of war in Korea. Earlier in the year Peter Fraser had described Labour's subsidy regime as 'sound and socially just' and in the interests of 'the family man'; Holland's speech of 5 May he labelled 'a depression utterance'. Other Labour spokesmen portrayed subsidy reductions as a return to 'an uncaring world'.[23] An angry deputation of union leaders met Holland on 23 June 1950, claiming that the Arbitration Court's recent interim wage order would not fully restore workers' standards of living. A few weeks earlier, several of the more militant unions had walked out of the FOL and set up a rival body, the Trades Union Congress. There followed many months of intense rivalry between the two groups, as the TUC, in particular, tried to impress unionists

Members of the new waterfront union being trucked on to the Auckland waterfront by the army, May 1951. Auckland Star

everywhere with the gains it intended to make from the use of militant tactics. There were skirmishes on the waterfront between May and September 1950; Jock Barnes and the New Zealand Waterfront Workers' Union sought more freedom from tight wage restraints. Barnes's quest proved to be a lonely, and ultimately disastrous, mission.[24]

The Government quickly came under pressure from employers and the National Party's own ranks to take a tough line with union militants. Many harboured a visceral detestation of 'wharfies'. The Korean War produced calls once more for wartime sacrifices and the Government toned down its talk of 'economic freedom'. Inflation was running at 10 per cent by the end of 1950, and it rose to 12 per cent in 1951.[25] Receipts for wool reached such an all-time high that the Government moved to dampen the inflationary impact by retaining a total of £51 million in two Wool Retention Accounts.[26] Nor would it release all goods and services listed in the CPI from price control. At the end of 1950 at least two thirds of them were still controlled.[27] Given the rapid rate of inflation and the immediate political threats it posed to standards of living, National's ministers were starting to warm to the regulated economy.

What finally converted Holland's Government to controls was the waterfront dispute that lasted for 151 days between February and July 1951. A complex dispute over wages in February led the union to apply pressure to employers by refusing to work overtime at all ports. When Barnes insisted on direct bargaining with port employers and would not accept the findings of an independent arbitrator, the wages system that had existed for many years was imperilled. On 16 February the Acting Prime Minister, Keith Holyoake, gave the watersiders an ultimatum to return to full work and submit their case to arbitration, or face removal of their conditions of employment. To reinforce this ultimatum, Holland on his way back to Wellington observed with inflammatory rhetoric: 'Any individual or group of individuals who stands in the way of the country's preparations for defence to ensure peace . . . by limiting the handling of goods is a traitor, and should be treated accordingly.'[28] This was a very strong hint that the Government intended to get tough with any workers who attempted to break out from the controlled economy. Barnes did not heed the warning. Over the next ten days, commission control was removed from the waterfront, a State of Emergency was declared under the Public Safety Conservation Act 1932, drastic Emergency Regulations giving the Government wide powers were gazetted and the New Zealand Waterside Workers' Union was deregistered. Troops began working ships on 27 February. The *Auckland Star*'s editor smugly wrote: 'The Government now has an opportunity to teach the leaders of the waterside workers' union and all who follow them so submissively a lesson that is more than overdue.'[29]

Holland and his forceful Minister of Labour, William Sullivan, used every power they had inherited from the wartime government, including press censorship and the opening of mail, and a great deal of red-blooded rhetoric, to smash the watersiders' national union and nip in the bud any union efforts to operate outside the confines of compulsory arbitration. The watersiders and their dwindling allies responded with several acts of sabotage and a good deal of victimisation of those who disliked Barnes's quest for martyrdom and wanted to return to work. As tempers frayed, the Government also backed the Labour Opposition into a difficult corner, extracting from its new leader, Walter Nash, the comment that 'we are not for the watersiders, nor are we against them'.[30] Riding high with the public, and with the Federation of Labour and every newspaper in the country behind his efforts to humble the 'wharfies', Holland could not resist the temptation to cash in politically. The five-month crisis had been a welcome diversion from inflation and the perceptions that had been building up that government policy was feeding it. On 1 September 1951 the National Party secured another three years in office, winning four more seats (all of them port electorates) from Labour.[31] In the weeks that followed, the Government tightened up the I.C.&A. Act and inserted several draconian clauses into the Police Offences Act, including one establishing a crime of 'seditious intention'. The Government sought to make all forms of direct action illegal. The National Party was indulging itself.

The TUC collapsed and there was a marked fall-off in union militancy for the next few years. But most political victories have their costs. The Government triumphed over a section of the trade union movement that National supporters most detested at the price of virtually ceasing its attempts at macroeconomic reform. Having preached the need for retaining controls over wages during the dispute, the ministry was soon being badgered by workers, whose incomes were under tight restraint, to return to rigid price control. Holland agreed during the 1951 election campaign to an increase in subsidy payments on butter, bread, flour and gas. In October that year Cabinet further extended subsidies to soap makers. Hides, pelts and bobby calf skins were soon added to the subsidy list because of the flow-on effect of high world prices on domestically made shoes. Some of the money for the subsidies came from the Meat Pool Account.[32] These payments were in addition to the taxpayer-funded subsidies on other items. Collectively, subsidies were soon costing £14 million per annum.

Fiddling with subsidies in order to restrain retail prices became a regular feature of Holland's administration. But the constant changes met resistance from some. A large and grumpy deputation from farmers' organisations complained to the Prime Minister on 31 May 1951 that using some of the surplus from the Meat Pool Account to hold down the domestic price of hides, pelts and bobby calf skins was unfair and represented a transfer of money from the producing sector to consumers. Holland responded that farmers were doing very well economically, that the unions felt they should be sharing the benefits of high overseas prices and that the current industrial unrest was in part a manifestation of the envy that many felt about rural prosperity. By raiding the Meat Pool Account the Government in effect expected farmers to make a contribution towards overall economic stability.[33] However, when overseas prices eased back in 1952, producers asked for help. As a means of keeping prices down they suggested reducing sales taxes. This was a request for subsidies by another name. Treasury, Industries and Commerce and Board of Trade officials all had different views on what to recommend to their ministers. In the end the status quo prevailed for a time.[34]

The cost of subsidies mounted. When those paid on some forms of transport were included, the total estimate for 1952–53 was £17.5 million. The list of subsidised goods included wool, butter, eggs, milk, calfskins, wheat and flour, gas, tallow for soap, and tallow for margarine. Bread, milk and butter subsidies were further raised in December 1953.[35] Holland made it clear in his budget on 27 August 1953 that he was unhappy with the high level of subsidies. However, they were paid because, as a Treasury file noted, not to do so would 'almost certainly' justify an Arbitration Court wage rise, leading to further price rises.[36] This was the same reasoning that had been used ten years earlier in the darkest days of the war.

Price controls were another source of tension within the Government. For many years they had been regarded as an essential concomitant to subsidies; if controls did not exist, then subsidies to producers were likely to escalate rapidly. But by 1950 price controls were also being applied to many unsubsidised items in the CPI. A total of 188 people, or 42 per cent of the entire staff of Industries and Commerce in 1951, was employed in the Price Control Division. Early in 1951, Professor Colin Simkin, a regular commentator on the state of the economy, detected a change in the atmosphere around Parliament; ministers were clearly showing signs of bowing to pressure to reintroduce price controls that they had earlier begun dismantling.[37] Yet the National Government continued to talk of pruning unsubsidised items from the list of price controlled items. Clearly

Bernard Ashwin (left), Secretary to the Treasury 1939–55, with his successor, E. L. Greensmith, and Minister of Finance, Jack Watts, June 1955. ATL F-27633-1/2

dissatisfied with the strong advocacy of controls from H. L.Wise, who was director of the division, Watts amended the Control of Prices Act during the 1953 session.[38] In December he declared that the National Government believed that an 'abundant supply of goods and free competition' would 'achieve better results and act as a more natural control of prices than any administrative system of price control'. He then added equivocally that price control was 'an arm of economic policy' which was necessary 'only because of inflationary pressures, shortages, import restrictions, and other impediments preventing the operation of free competition'.[39]

With an election coming up and Labour's stocks rising, Watts reconstituted the Price Tribunal under the chairmanship of Judge D. J. Dalglish. A study of profit margins and returns on capital was commissioned from a Wellington accountant, J. Haisman, while Dalglish conducted a lengthy inquiry into price control in March and April 1954. During the hearings there were disagreements between officials. The Associated Chambers of Commerce criticised Industries and Commerce views, suggesting they ran counter to the Government's declared policy. Treasury produced a document in April 1954 entitled 'Background to Price Control Policy'. It reviewed the effectiveness of price control over recent years and concluded that export and import prices, as well as supply and demand, played the major part in the domestic price structure and that price controls had had little impact. Treasury argued that it was 'almost impracticable' to control meat, fruit and vegetable prices, adding 'if price control had not been in operation during the last few years it is questionable whether prices of the items now controlled would have risen much more than they did'. Arguments continued over the efficacy of price controls, but the inquiry of the Price Tribunal came down on the side of their retention in specified circumstances. Since inflation had begun to rise again, Cabinet accepted this advice. Ministers wanted the Government to be seen to be trying to bring prices under control in the run-up to an election. Show rather than substance was dictating policy. On 13 November 1954 the National Party held on to power, albeit with a reduced majority.[40]

In effect, National's ministers were grappling with a tar baby; they did not like Labour's economy but they could not figure out how to escape from it. Bureaucratic debate intensified. There was endless crossfire both within Cabinet and among officials. Those favouring continued controls kept the upper hand. Holland stated in January 1955 that the Government would 'crack down' on traders making 'exorbitant profits'.[41]

The following month both the Manufacturers' Federation and the Retailers' Federation tried to argue that freedom from controls was not necessarily inconsistent with price stability. Watts, who became Minister of Finance after the 1954 election, bent in the direction of freedom; when opening the Retailers' Federation conference in March 1955 he announced that the Government was prepared to release some goods from price control. A Control of Prices Amendment Bill in 1956 kindled hope amongst deregulators that the Government intended to shrug off price controls altogether, especially when Eric Halstead, who became Minister of Industries and Commerce in March 1956, talked of abolishing the Price Tribunal.[42] Between 1955 and 1957 there was a slow but steady reduction in the number of bureaucrats within the prices section of Industries and Commerce. However, ministers remained edgy about the possible political repercussions of decontrol and the Tribunal survived. By now the wider community was having difficulty reading the National Government. In August 1955 Federated Farmers told Watts that their members were finding it 'increasingly difficult to follow the Government's policy on the questions of competition and price control'.[43] This perception was damaging to the National Party, yet it lingered for many years. At no time before 1984 did the party manage to reconcile the conflicts between their philosophical goals and what was deemed necessary to retain office.

Establishing acceptable principles to govern imports was equally bewildering to Holland's Government and bedevilled its relationships with the manufacturing sector. National's first Minister of Customs, C. M. Bowden, who for the first year in office was also Minister of Industries and Commerce, issued a statement about the future of import licensing on 1 November 1950. He talked of the 'urgent need to reform the import licensing system' and declared that the National Government wanted to 'abolish import control when possible'. He added, 'To the extent that import control is retained, the purpose will be to conserve overseas funds and assist local manufacturers, at least until the adequacy or otherwise of present Tariff duties as a means of protecting local industries can be properly examined.'[44] The new Board of Trade Act 1950 required the Board to advise the Minister of Customs about customs duties.[45] Meantime in May 1950 an Import Advisory Committee had been set up under the Board. It was chaired by retired Supreme Court judge, Sir David Smith. It began a laborious examination of all tariffs. Ashwin supported the move away from import controls, favouring reliance on tariff protection. He told Smith that entry to New Zealand of as many as 300 items was currently prohibited for no other reason than to protect local producers from competition. This, Ashwin believed, was 'a most unhealthy state of affairs'; such protection would eventually have to be done away with, and 'the sooner the job is tackled the better'. He added that while 'individual hardship' might occur, an end to protection 'would assist in reducing excessive demand and be in the general interest'. Referring to New Zealand's obligations to GATT, which both Labour and National were slow to acknowledge, Ashwin told Smith that 'we cannot afford to try isolationism in trade matters' – a view that he also expressed regularly to ministers until his retirement from Treasury on 1 July 1955.[46]

The work of the Import Advisory Committee moved slowly. Watts was anxious not to cause any disruption to local industries nor to threaten full employment. Some officials kept arguing that existing policies froze manufacturing on what, in some cases, was an 'uneconomic basis'. One warned that 'full employment to be secure cannot . . . be based merely on a policy of retaining existing labour and other resources in their present uses at all costs. . . . . The objective should rather be full employment on a sound and lasting basis in which resources are given enough free play to find their most effective use.'[47] This observation went to the crux of the Government's difficulties; maintaining full employment by tight controls always seemed in practice to involve overshooting the mark. This resulted in huge numbers of job vacancies, despite an increase in the rate of immigration between 1951 and 1953. A high rate of job vacancies em-powered unions who succeeded in winning settlements above award rates. A high level of domestic liquidity kept pushing up demand for imports. Meantime, tight controls reduced manufacturers' flexibility. Some were permitted to move their factories into the suburbs or into small towns in search of workers. This had a beneficial by-product: more often than not it was women who answered the call and the percentage of women within the factory workforce rose from 23 per cent in 1948 to 25 per cent in 1962. But the incentives of the 1950s all conspired to keep investment locked into current production methods and product ranges. Governments viewed most changes as a threat. If manufacturers were allowed freedom to shift their resources about at will, then that would almost certainly result in pools of unemployment from time to time. Such a prospect terrified ministers.

The Government kept hoping it could gradually become more flexible. About 750 items had been removed from import control by 1951, although more than 300 items covering most of the main products manufactured in New Zealand continued to be produced in what the World Bank later called New Zealand's 'hothouse for local industries'. The pace of removal slowed; only twenty more items, most of them relatively minor, were delisted over the next three years.[48] When the number of notified employment vacancies fell in 1953, ministers worried that the protective barriers around manufacturing might now be inadequate. Decontrolling the stabilised economy proved much harder than they first anticipated.

In his 1954 report Sir David Smith discussed the problems he had encountered with import controls, but concluded on an upbeat note:

> Though some manufacturers did not object to the removal of import licensing, most of them have claimed that they could not survive without it. However, most industries which have been decontrolled are surviving very well. My own view is that the efficient New Zealand manufacturer who makes articles of good quality and who has been keeping his brand before the public, does not know how strong his position really is. He tends to overlook the fact that since the war wages actually paid overseas have increased and that freight and landing charges have all risen. . . . The local manufacturer also tends to overlook the fact that pride in New Zealand and in being a New Zealander has grown in recent years, and that with it, has grown . . . the desire to support New Zealand manufactures of good quality.[49]

Smith had put his finger on something important. Quick to grasp the State's helping hand in the 1930s, many businessmen now needed much cajoling before they ventured forth on their own. As soon as Smith dropped back to a half-time role at the end of 1954, the Government's enthusiasm for decontrolling imports and revising tariffs – which by now was little more than lukewarm – evaporated. In April 1955 the Auckland Manufacturers' Association suggested abolishing the Board of Trade and its committees.[50] Cabinet kept it, saying it wanted to decontrol more New Zealand-made goods 'when general economic conditions are appropriate',[51] but the time never seemed to be right. In 1955 and 1956 when overseas prices sagged, some items were actually brought back under import controls again.

While the social engineers were arguing about how the Government's social goals could be achieved within a more flexible environment, ministers were obliged from time to time to take short-term action to deal with reverses in the financial situation. When overseas prices were high in 1950–51, the Government failed to heed the advice from Smith and from Ashwin[52] and was so generous with import licences that when the price of wool fell sharply over the summer of 1951–52, imports flowed into the country at an unsustainable rate. Ministers took fright and introduced a system of what was called 'exchange allocation'. Officials were told not to use the word 'control', since it was contrary to the overall message which the National Party was trying to promote.[53] Bank sales of exchange to importers were limited to 80 per cent of their purchases in 1950. Wherever an importer sought foreign exchange in excess of this basic allocation, a special application to the Reserve Bank was required. Such applications were decided on their merits after consultation with committees at Industries and Commerce. When import payments continued to exceed the Government's target into 1953, exchange allocations were further reduced to 40 per cent of the 1950 figure. Exchange allocations were relaxed again in the run-up to the 1954 election.[54] Many observed that National's way of handling foreign exchange had become Labour's by another name.[55]

In spite of large returns from primary produce in 1950–51, New Zealand's overseas reserves ebbed and flowed for the rest of the decade.[56] A constant shortage of overseas exchange was the single greatest threat to the full-employment economy. It became the centrepiece of a conference on economic stability held in Wellington in May 1953 under the auspices of the New Zealand Institute of Public Administration. Bureaucrats and academics who attended agreed that full employment, which in practice seemed to be 'over-full employment', inevitably resulted in demands for imports on a scale that outstripped New Zealand's overseas earnings. This made import and price controls essential. There were a few dissenters. Leicester Webb, the former Director of Economic Stabilisation, implied in his speech that the era of rigid controls necessary to ensure that stabilisation worked was no longer feasible eight years after the war. He went further, asserting that the National Government's creation of semi-autonomous marketing boards for primary produce, which had the capacity to fix farmers' levels of remuneration in consultation with a Marketing Advisory Council of bureaucrats, had already made price stability unlikely.[57] Others at the conference, most notably a Treasury official, G. J. Schmitt, son of the former Secretary of Industries and Commerce and a personal assistant to Ashwin, seemed more optimistic. Schmitt wrestled with various options available to the Government. He said:

> I believe that it should be possible so to arrange the relationship between local prices and imports that demands for imports could generally be fully satisfied and yet that full employment could be maintained. Such a situation would be one in which local costs of production and prices were kept far below imported costs (by means of suitable exchange rate and tariff policies and by price control). Then any labour discharged from one employment would be immediately absorbed by another employer faced with a demand that he could not supply because of lack of labour, but which he certainly could win from his overseas competitor. The difficulty about such a system is that it would employ two price levels for similar goods or else an opportunity for businessmen to make considerable profits, which would be objectionable to some classes in the community. These profits would, however, be reduced by taxation. This alternative as a long term policy deserves closer attention. . . .[58]

Schmitt's speech was quoted widely and not always accurately.[59] There was criticism. The *New Zealand Herald* headed an editorial 'Economics of Socialism in the Treasury'.[60] The *Auckland Star* was more judgmental about the goal of full employment, noting that the term had to it 'a satisfying, complacent, fatly prosperous sound to it'.[61] The *Hawkes Bay Herald Tribune* adopted a more lofty overview to which hindsight gives some credence. The editor thought that New Zealand's current prosperity had nothing to do with planning and was based instead on 'bounteous and expanding production and high overseas prices'. If prices were to fall, then 'the airy theories of the planners would provide no real solutions'. He concluded with the words: 'In the long run our living standards depend on work and production. An economy based on planned scarcities is a mockery.'[62]

Schmitt's speech caught the eye of the *Herald*'s Saturday satirist, Whim Wham. On 16 May 1953 he wrote:

If you want the Enjoyment
Of Full Employment
And the full-fed Flaccidity that
That can provide,
You'll just eat your Plateful
And try to look grateful,
For it's Godzone Country
Where you reside.

The conference in May 1953 pointed up one of the fundamental problems of planners everywhere. Where their interventions did not at first succeed, most were prepared to try again. Wellington's bureaucrats were searching to find the right balance between State and individual responsibility. In the spirit of paternalism that had become a central feature of New Zealand welfarism, they believed that they, rather than the market, could find the answer to problems. Besides, regulations and controls produced an ever-growing public service from which officials could not fail to benefit. M. J. Moriarty, a later Secretary of Industries and Commerce, pointedly asked the conference to consider 'whether we are retaining a sufficient central direction of economic affairs to create the conditions in which stability may be obtained'.[63] For most who were present, the question was rhetorical.

There was no obvious diminution of the role of planners within Industries and Commerce during the 1950s. Clinkard retired in 1950 and P. B. Marshall returned to head the department until he, in turn, retired in 1957. Some departmental committees were abolished and many aspects of the Government's assistance to manufacturing were reassessed during 1952–53. The number of permanent officials in the department subsided, standing at 316 on 31 March 1956.[64] Yet, having dislodged Dr W. B. Sutch from his position at the United Nations because they did not trust his politics, National ministers seemed powerless to prevent the arch proponent of protection and planning from returning to a senior research position within Industries and Commerce. In 1956 he was promoted to head the division dealing with manufacturing protection and development, as well as import controls.[65]

By the middle of the decade departmental officials were keeping tabs on most aspects of the economy and were strongly encouraging any industry deemed to have export potential. Officials were building up files on every imaginable economic activity in New Zealand. Among the department's thousands of files are ones on buttons, clothing, stout, wine, deer, tobacco,

Dr W. B. Sutch, the controversial Secretary of Industries and Commerce (1958–65), who never doubted the desirability of state activity.
ATL C-23147

seaweed, split peas, fruit cases, stationery, toys, stock feed, dog food, pig bristles, cattle horns, creosote, soap, sports goods, wallboard, bicycles, nuts and bolts, plastics, space heaters, wire, anchors, tyres, nylons and full length hosiery. Boarding houses, funeral charges and tailors' prices came under bureaucratic scrutiny. Permission was needed for constructing a flour mill in Oamaru, expanding a plant making insulating material in Otahuhu, or the purchase of new cranes for the Tauranga waterfront. The Land Settlement Promotion Act 1952 set out to prevent undue aggregation of land. A Land Valuation Committee was charged with deciding whether a farm already owned was sufficient to support the would-be purchaser of land in a 'reasonable manner and in a reasonable standard of comfort'. Additional purchases were authorised where they were likely to raise a farmer's standard of living 'to a level more in keeping with that of the majority of the farming community or where the public interest favours the expansion of his farm'.[66] Nothing, it seemed, escaped the eye of officialdom.

For many years the National Government was unable to decide whether to retain Labour's Industrial Efficiency Act 1936, the Bureau of Industry with its licensing regime, as well as the restructured Board of Trade. The concept of licensing appealed to some businessmen but offended others. Watts, who was liked by officials (one recalls him as 'efficient, well balanced and capable of quick decisions'),[67] could vacillate on some issues like his colleagues. He was never happy with industry licensing, yet a deteriorating balance of payments situation by 1956 seemed no time to surrender any control mechanisms. A new Industries and Commerce Act came into force on 1 April 1957. A pale imitation of the draft bill that had circulated a decade earlier, it nonetheless provided the department with very wide powers to promote and encourage industry and exports, and to assist with the location of industries 'in those localities most economically suitable'. The Act repealed the Industrial Efficiency Act 1936, but the powers of the Board of Trade 1919 were retained and continued licensing of industry was provided for in the Licensed Industries Regulations 1957. The number of industries requiring a licence was now less, but the manufacture of pulp, paper and board, paua shells for sale, and tyres and tubes remained on the list.[68]

While there were frequent bursts of rhetoric about the virtues of self-help, using the State's powers to assist farmers was something that came naturally to the National Government. In his budget of 1950 Holland extended grants to wheat growers. Robbed of market prices under rigid stabilisation, they found Labour's subsidies did not produce a return that was as good as could be obtained from alternative uses of the land. In the late 1940s wheat had to be imported once more. Tax exemptions for farmers had initially been introduced by Nash. Holland extended them to include drains, fences, dams, erosion, landing strips and clearing weeds. Generous depreciation allowances were allowed on farm equipment, accommodation and farm buildings. The importation of agricultural machinery in the early 1950s reached all-time records. By 1955 few farms were without tractors and many possessed other expensive and often rarely used implements as well.[69] New subsidies were introduced to keep down the cost of imported phosphates, while farmers were able to claim back the sales tax on petrol used in farm machinery.[70] Assistance in the form of tax breaks for primary industries became a regular feature of budgets from the 1950s until the early 1980s.

Unknown to most people was the level of state assistance enjoyed by primary produce marketing boards in the 1950s. For many years governments tolerated a system where boards were allowed to finance their seasonal overdrafts with Reserve Bank credit at 1 per cent interest. The Meat, Apple and Pear, Citrus, Honey, Milk and Poultry boards were all treated in the same way but the Dairy Board usually ran the largest overdraft which frequently peaked at £30 million. When surpluses built up in the Dairy Board's accounts it was allowed to invest in government stock at between 3 per cent and 3.75 per cent. Treasury officers constantly opposed the continuation of what amounted to backdoor subsidies to boards and

Watts admitted in 1955 that 'they have no real entitlement to the preferential treatment they now receive'.[71] However, the time was never opportune to end the privilege. When export prices turned down in 1957 and the Dairy Board sought to increase its overdraft at 1 per cent interest in order to tide farmers over low prices, the Labour Government tried to force the board to accept market rates of interest. When this was stoutly resisted, the Government decided to be more open about its assistance. A direct subsidy of £5 million was included in the 1958 budget. There then followed many months of behind-scenes warfare as the Dairy Board not only sought to have the loan treated as a gift but requested further 1 per cent finance to use on plant, vehicles, advertising and administrative costs. Ultimately Holyoake's National Government wrote off the £5 million. Boards returned to their 1 per cent interest rates, with National MPs always defending them from any criticism. In 1973 Brian Talboys, a former Minister of Agriculture, claimed 'there is no more imaginative, businesslike, and energetic marketing organisation in this country than the New Zealand Dairy Board'. He failed to acknowledge that much of it was being done with 'cheap' money.[72]

Whenever one sector's efforts were seen to be rewarded, others argued for similar largesse. National, like Labour before it, developed its hierarchy of the deserving and assiduously looked after its supporters. But as the raft of tax breaks and subsidies to the agricultural and business sectors expanded, the Government's revenue base slowly contracted. It became noticeable that ordinary wage and salary earners, in whose interests the welfare state had been devised, enjoyed few opportunities to write off expenses. They shouldered a growing portion of the country's taxation. This became one of the biggest inequities of the centrally directed welfare era.

In a burst of entrepreneurial zeal worthy of Vogel or a later prime minister, Robert Muldoon, Holland's Government became directly involved in the construction of the biggest industrial project in New Zealand's history until that time. The story of the origin of the Tasman Pulp and Paper Company has been told in part by Morris Guest.[73] By the time of the change of government in 1949, the only thing holding back development of a major pulp and paper plant to process the State's quarter million acres of exotic forests in the central North Island was a shortage of development capital. Pat Entrican of State Forests had long been urging a state-funded project, arguing at one point that having the Government involved in forestry was 'as essential . . . as the maintenance of law and order'.[74] In the meantime he succeeded in blocking the granting of a licence to Forest

*A. R. Entrican, Director of the New Zealand
Forest Service, who had visions of a huge state
forestry enterprise, with him running it.*
National Archives

Products and Whakatane Paper Mills for production of newsprint.[75] Entrican
convinced his minister, C. F. Skinner, of the need for state involvement in
the production of pulp and paper. In April 1949 the Labour Cabinet
approved 'in principle' the construction of a mill. Ministers believed that
there was a net gain to be made in foreign exchange and that the State
'could do certain jobs just as well as private enterprise'.[76] Meanwhile,
Fletcher Construction's interest in building such a mill was growing.

Ashwin, however, kept warning Nash that a development estimated to
cost at least £10 million would overstrain the Government's resources at a
time when there was already huge state investment taking place in hydro-
electricity construction. Citing the example of British Petroleum, which
had carried most of the costs of its entry into the New Zealand marketplace
in 1946–47, Ashwin argued that overseas interests should be encouraged
to put up the capital to develop the increasingly valuable forest asset.[77]

The National Party at first seemed to oppose what was known as the
'Murupara project'. Keith Holyoake described it as a 'senseless scheme',
although he later claimed to be have been opposed to it only if the
Government had to finance the mill. In August 1950 Holland and his
Minister of Forests, E. B. Corbett,[78] took Ashwin's advice and decided to
test world interest in developing a mill to process trees from the Kaingaroa
Forest. The Prime Minister made it clear he preferred not to invest state
capital in the scheme. Enticing overseas investment, however, proved much
harder than either politicians or their officials anticipated. On 1 April 1951

State money created a town at Kawerau, helped build Tasman Pulp and Paper (foreground), a railway line to the port at Tauranga and new berthing facilities.
National Archives

Corbett issued proposals for the right to purchase for a period of 75 years an annual quantity of 23 million cubic feet of exotic softwoods and to cooperate with the New Zealand Forest Service in developing an integrated plant consisting of a sawmill, a pulp mill and a newsprint mill. The Government reserved the right to subscribe 15 per cent of the share capital. It declared a willingness to provide power for the plant, said it would construct a 'modern overseas port' at Tauranga, provide a railway connection to the port, build 400 rental houses at the plant for employees, and assist with immigration for 'any skilled workmen' the purchaser might wish to bring to New Zealand. The document invited proposals by 1 November 1951 for constructing an 'integrated plant'.[79] Big government was getting even bigger.

In spite of efforts by Fletchers to round up British and American investors, none was forthcoming. Those Americans who had been identified as possible investors in the mill were involved heavily at the time in their own North American ventures. When tenders closed, a hastily cobbled-together scheme from a newly formed, and as yet unregistered company, Tasman Pulp and Paper, was the only bid received. Fletcher Holdings Ltd was prepared to put £700,000 (44 per cent of the value of Fletcher Holdings at the time) towards the anticipated cost of building the mill. The rest of Tasman Pulp and Paper's money would come from borrowings, debentures and the Government's 15 per cent contribution.[80] An officials' committee was set up to examine the proposal, and to review market possibilities for newsprint. Eventually it was concluded that 46,000 tons of an anticipated annual production of 75,000 tons of newsprint could probably be exported to Australia.

By now Ashwin was worried that the Government seemed to be the underwriter of the mill's construction and would be carrying all the costs of the infrastructure as well. The infrastructure was estimated to cost approximately £15 million. On 7 December 1951 the committee recommended that the scheme go ahead only if an overseas loan for a substantial part of the total cost of the mill and its infrastructure could be raised – which it eventually was. After a long wait, a loan of £10 million at 4.75 per cent, raised by the New Zealand Government from the American Export-Import Bank, was confirmed in November 1953. Meantime, in the expectation of finding the money, the budget of 1952 had announced that some of that year's surplus due to the previous year's wool boom would also be put into the total Tasman development. Treasury arranged overdraft facilities for the mill's construction. Plans for a public float were put into operation in 1954. While Sir James Fletcher chaired the new Tasman Pulp and Paper Co. Ltd that was registered on 2 July 1952 and his son, J. C. Fletcher, and an Auckland solicitor, L. J. Stevens, represented the private sector, three top public servants, Ashwin, Entrican and E. R. McKillop, Commissioner of Works, were also on the initial board. Its first secretary, who was appointed in August 1953, was G. J. Schmitt, whose father had played such an important role in encouraging manufacturing under the Labour Government.[81]

As a series of intense discussions and knife-edge negotiations proceeded, the National Government warmed to the vast project. On 21 July 1954 Holland adjourned the House in order to discuss the Government's involvement. In some pre-election hyperbole he claimed that as a result of the Tasman scheme the country was 'just leaping ahead'. More than £2 million of state money had already been spent and he anticipated that another £13 million would be needed for the railway line, 450 houses at Kawerau where the plant was being built and another 300 at Murupara in the centre of the forest. Labour supported the project, seeing it as a forerunner of further joint enterprises, a sentiment that was endorsed by the National MP for New Plymouth, who hoped that the Government would assist with the development of oil, iron and steel projects in Taranaki.[82] By the time the newsprint machine started up on 29 October 1955 the State had contributed £2 million of the £6 million share capital in Tasman and it owned half of Kaingaroa Logging Co. Ltd, which acted as a link between the Forest Service and the mill by supplying it with logs. The Government had also, as promised, financed all of Tasman's infrastructure.[83]

Tasman expanded its share capital on 1 January 1960 by bringing in the English newsprint producers, Bowaters, who had mills in Canada and the United States. Bowaters' willingness to transfer some large newsprint contracts to Tasman was instrumental in further expansion at Murupara. Government overdraft guarantees were forthcoming in 1960 and a second newsprint machine opened in December 1962. By this time, after some years of well-intentioned if inexperienced management, Tasman had moved into black figures. However, according to Geoff Schmitt, who became Managing Director in 1963, the Government's taxation regime, and particularly its depreciation allowances, delayed, rather than assisted, the company's struggle to profitability.

At the point where the State sold its shares in 1979, taxpayers had not yet reaped the dividends they deserved. However, a major addition to New Zealand's industrial infrastructure had been made. Kaingaroa forest was now being managed in a sustainable manner and, true to the spirit of import substitution, New Zealand publishers were receiving paper from local mills. The balance of payments was benefiting from exports of the mill's surplus. Moreover, the port facilities at Mt Maunganui were soon also being used for pastoral and horticultural exports. There can be no doubt that much of the stimulus to growth in the Bay of Plenty region resulted initially from the forestry industry. And the precedent of joint state–private sector involvement in major industrial projects had been established, something which Walter Nash's Government built on with plans to develop a steel mill and Robert Muldoon carried to excess with his 'Think Big' projects of the early 1980s.

Tasman eventually played a significant part in reducing the deficit in New Zealand's trans-Tasman trade. It was a largely unprotected, international company that was expected to operate competitively on the world market. This was not easy. Tasman's first few years were difficult and losses piled up. It was the backing of the Government, its continued confidence in Sir James Fletcher, his son (J.C., as he was known) and Geoff Schmitt that helped the company to survive its early years. When the company got into serious strife in 1977 and faced bankruptcy, it was the Government that backed it. By this time there were new people in charge; the Government insisted on some further changes at the management level as the quid pro quo to further support.[84]

Comfortable personal relationships developed between private sector leaders, bureaucrats and politicians. Lunches, drinks or 'cold calls', as J. C. Fletcher called them, where businessmen visiting Wellington would call unannounced on senior Industries and Commerce officials, bankers and politicians, were common. Occasional access to company holiday homes or boats for officials, union leaders and politicians kept the world of the controlled economy ticking along.[85] In an era of generous tax allowances and cost-plus pricing, the costs were easily passed on to consumers. Surprisingly, perhaps, it was not a world where corruption thrived, although in other countries regulations and controls were often exploited by officials. In the life of New Zealand's centralised economy there were very few prosecutions and only occasional rumours of kickbacks, many of which turned out to be without foundation when subjected to scrutiny.[86]

While Tasman Pulp and Paper involved the biggest outlay of government funds on any single enterprise to date, it was by no means the State's only new business venture in the first postwar decade. The New Zealand and Australian governments were the sole (and equal) partners in Tasman Empire Airways Ltd, which flew to Sydney, Nandi, Aitutaki and Papeete. TEAL had a capital of £2 million. By 1956 it had also received an advance from the New Zealand State Advances Corporation of a further £550,000. Cabinet appointed the company's directors. The Sydney and Nandi routes, which connected with international flights further afield, posted profits but the 'Coral Route' to the Pacific islands continually ran at a loss.[87]

National Airways Corporation was founded in 1946 when the Government took over several small aviation companies after having controlled most of their planes under emergency regulations for much of the war. The corporation's capital of £1 million was entirely provided by the New Zealand Government which, as with TEAL, was directly involved in the purchase of new aircraft and the building and modification of airports and hangars. Holland's 1950 proposal to sell NAC came to nothing. The airline was advertised both in Australia and the United Kingdom but in the end no applications considered acceptable to the Government were received. A file note in 1957 observes that private capital had been scared away because so many factors influencing the profitability of NAC were under the control of the Government, especially charges for airways facilities which were owned, operated and maintained by the Crown. Government also set airport dues for the use of runways and facilities. A statement by the

A National Airways Corporation's workhorse, the DC3, at Paraparaumu, 1951.
ATL F-40512-1/2

Labour Party that if NAC were to be privatised, a Labour Government would repurchase it at the first opportunity, also acted as a disincentive to any would-be purchaser.

In 1953 the National Government decided instead to restructure the corporation's board of directors and to retain the airline in public hands. While NAC's passengers, freight and profits continually grew during the 1950s, considerable advances of government money were needed to finance the purchase of Vickers Viscount and Fokker Friendship aircraft between 1957 and 1961. Moreover, smaller centres that were anxious for air services usually took their case first to the Government rather than NAC. The corporation was never free from political interference.[88]

Before his death in 1947, D. G. Sullivan involved the Government in a joint venture with Skellerup Industries Ltd and Cerebos Salt to develop the natural salt deposits at Lake Grassmere. It was called the Dominion Salt Co. Ltd. The State's input to the faltering company increased in 1949 and by 1956 £150,000 in 4 per cent preference shares had been taken up by the State. This amounted to 25 per cent of the company's total capital. A report to ministers in 1965 suggested that the company was trading on its monopoly status, and that its management 'leaves much to be desired'. The Government was discovering that monopolies had to be carefully monitored. Yet, when the company was restructured in 1965 the Government invested another £150,000 in it. Once involved with ventures, the State found it extraordinarily difficult to resile from them.[89]

In 1953 the Government also set up the New Zealand Packing Corporation to begin vegetable and fruit processing factories and related trading in quick frozen and dehydrated products in Pukekohe and Motueka. The corporation spent £294,000 on the two plants which posted a net profit of £42,000 in the year to 31 October 1956. The whole venture was conceived as a seeding operation; it remained in the Government's hands for barely five years, at which point it was sold.[90]

While it tolerated public control in some areas and experimented itself, the National Government tried to reduce the cost of the bureaucracy. In January 1952 a Committee on the Machinery of Government was established with the Acting Prime Minister, Keith Holyoake, in the chair. Holyoake informed the Treasury and PSC representatives who were present that he wanted to ensure 'proper organisation of the machinery of government'. Over the next two years ministers rearranged several government departments. By restructuring the Public Service Commission in 1951 and removing the PSA's nominee, ministers were trying to halt the inexorable rise in the number of public servants that had been such a feature of Labour's administration. In April 1952, with numbers totalling 53,437 (52,046 on 1 April 1950), the Machinery of Government Committee turned its attention to retirement rules for state employees with a view to ceasing the practice whereby many stayed on after age 60.[91] The rate of growth in the number of state employees slowed. The committee also recommended abolishing the Town Planning Board. In 1953 the Town and Country Planning Act amended the original legislation of 1926 by devolving more power to local authorities whose decisions could be appealed to a Town and Country Planning Appeal Board. However, National's desire for efficiency in central government did not stretch to concern about wastage at the local level. Holland's Government pulled back from Labour's plans to reform local government. The political preserve of many National Party functionaries, local councils escaped restructuring until a Labour Government undertook the task between 1985 and 1989.[92]

National's record with railways provides further evidence of expediency. Conscious that the number of railway employees had grown steadily under Labour, a Royal Commission recommended in 1952 that a Railways Commission be established to administer the service. The goal was to remove railways from political control once more and to oblige management to run 'efficient and economical passenger and goods services'.[93] After passage of the Government Railways Amendment Act 1952 five directors were duly appointed on 12 January 1953. By restructuring services and applying a policy of user-pays, the Commission quickly turned Railways from a loss of £1.4 million in 1952 to a profit of £1.46 million in 1955. In the process, however, the sensitivities of many locals were trampled. Major protests developed in Nelson when the long-promised, but only partly constructed line to Inangahua was scrapped and the rails lifted. Further trouble erupted in 1956 in the Hutt Valley, where the electric train service was losing more than £230,000 pa and the feeder bus service another £75,000 pa. The Commission sought to remedy costly duplication in Railway Road Service and train timetables and questioned whether the bus service might be sold. While in theory the work of the Commission was at arm's length from the Government, Labour MPs blamed the Minister of Railways for every tough decision made by the Commission. With a difficult election coming up, ministers were sensitive; National held the Nelson seat by a narrow margin and both the seats of Onslow and Wellington Central were barely Labour's way. The following parliamentary exchange in October 1956 provides some of the flavour of the debate:

> Mr Michael Moohan (Lab. Petone): 'The buses are public property, and are owned by the Railways Department. It is the job of the Railways Department to provide an internal service throughout the Hutt Valley, in addition to the electric train service. Everyone does not live on a railway line. We want a positive, progressive policy.'
> Mr J. J. Maher (Govt. Otaki): 'Even if the service shows a substantial loss to the taxpayers generally?'
> Mr Moohan: 'The Government is showing bigger, better and brighter losses for every activity it handles. . . . The people in the Hutt Valley are entitled to the best passenger service possible.'

A few minutes later Philip Holloway, the new MP for Heretaunga, reminded the minister that regulations prohibited private sector competition with railways, so the Government had no option but to provide a bus service. 'Unless a change is made by legislation, the Government has undertaken for all time the responsibility of giving a good and efficient bus and rail service.'[94]

To Labour's astonishment, the Government crumpled. During the committee stages of a minor Railways Amendment Bill a few days later, the minister tabled a Supplementary Order Paper abolishing the Commission and returning Railways to ministerial control, where both Labour and the public clearly felt effective power should reside. National's brief experiment

Sonja Davies (on the rail track facing the camera) leads a group in protest at plans to close the uneconomic Glenhope railway line, 1954. Nelson Provincial Museum

with efficiency in railways had come to an abrupt halt. Railways posted a small loss in 1957 and the following year was in red figures to the tune of more than £1 million.[95] But there was no gratitude from the voters; National lost Nelson in the 1957 election and Labour's majorities in both Onslow and Wellington Central increased.

As big government grew more expensive, so did the cost of maintaining Labour's social programmes. In the years after the war, expenditure on Social Security, Health and Education consistently grew at a faster rate than the economy as a whole.[96] Most social security benefits were boosted in 1950–51, and allowable extra incomes were raised. The level of payment of Universal Superannuation to 65-year-olds doubled in October 1951 and the rules covering Widows' Benefits were made more generous in 1954.[97] Health costs marched steadily ahead. Decision-making had been largely centralised by 1950. Departmental files show that most items of expenditure went to Wellington for authorisation; the purchase of flannelette for hospital boards went to Treasury for authorisation in October 1951, Cabinet approval was needed before £6,677 was spent on sealing the road to Tokanui Hospital the following year. When Hastings needed

Ministers Watts (left), Holland (centre) and Doidge (right) lobbied by hospital nurses at Parliament Buildings, May 1951. ATL F-27630-1/2

£3,136 to fund a pilot project to fluoridate the water supply in 1952, Cabinet had to approve. Even an ex gratia payment of £14 to a St Helen's Hospital patient whose coat had been accidentally damaged had first to be cleared with the Director General of Health.[98]

Despite tight control over incidental expenditure, the cost of public hospitals kept exceeding budget and officials proved unable to stop it. Some local authorities complained about being expected to contribute towards hospitals when there seemed to be so little control over their escalating expenditure. In 1950 the Director of the Hospital Division within the Department of Health admitted he was concerned at rapidly mounting costs. Available beds had grown by 33 per cent during the previous decade, the number of outpatients by 212 per cent, and staff at public hospitals now numbered 15,468 or 86 per cent more than in 1940. Big salary adjustments had recently been made to assist boards to find enough qualified staff.[99] In February 1952 the department warned the Secretary of the Treasury that hospital boards were likely to spend £862,000 more than the £7.2 million allocated to them in the budget – a cost overrun of more than 12 per cent. Ashwin, in turn, told Holland that in his opinion, the Department of Health 'should take active steps to induce boards to exercise

283

economy in expenditure and also for the Department to achieve savings in other items of its vote'. Of the 37 hospital boards then in existence, 24 had overspent during the year. Proper expenditure control should, in Ashwin's view, 'be a condition of next year's grant'.[100] This refrain was sung every year in the decades that followed.

Marshall was Minister of Health by this time. He told the Prime Minister that the overruns 'demonstrate the lack of effective control on the expenditure of Hospital Boards and the tendency for independent boards who are responsible for expenditure, but not for raising the money, to be less careful than they might be in controlling expenditure'.[101] Marshall had identified the principal problem with boards. Having found it, however, he compounded the problem by relieving boards of their remaining obligations to raise revenue through local property rates, which in 1950 contributed 21.7 per cent of public hospital expenditure. From 1952 there was a progressive reduction in the local rate levy to support public hospitals and, in the Hospitals Act 1957, central government took over sole responsibility for funding all public hospital services.[102] Locally elected boards, however, continued to exercise power over hospitals and their services. A departmental analysis of health services prepared in 1974 noted that once boards no longer had to provide part of the finance themselves, 'their expenditure escalated'.[103]

The school dental service, 1954. ATL F-30256-1/2

Holland's Government sought to restructure the hospital system in order to bring ballooning expenditure under control. A Consultative Committee on Hospital Reform was established under the chairmanship of Harold Barrowclough, who was shortly to become Chief Justice. The committee's report of February 1954 suggested amalgamating many of the smaller boards, decentralising the Department of Health into five regional authorities, and assisting private hospitals to take some of the surgical load off public hospitals. The same considerations that led National to tread softly with local government reform now caused them to shy away from forced hospital board amalgamations, although several boards voluntarily joined with their neighbours over the next decade.[104] Nor did a government which was centralist in practice, if not at heart, agree with regionalisation. Loan facilities, including suspensory loans, were extended to private hospitals after 1952 and in 1957 a wage and salary subsidy for private hospitals was also made available. Meanwhile, the patient/day subsidy for private hospitals that had been paid by the Government since 1939 was increased from time to time. In 1969 a consultation subsidy for visits to specialists was also introduced.[105]

A dual system of health care developed steadily from the 1950s and in 1961 several Auckland surgeons formed the Southern Cross Medical Care Society which provided an insurance scheme to cover private health care. Some years later the Government was persuaded to make contributions to private health insurance tax deductible to encourage self-help. By 1984 more than 35 per cent of New Zealanders were enrolled in the supplementary private health care system.[106] There is no indication that subsidising the private sector restrained the rate of increase in public hospital costs, although a leaner private sector that could be selective in the medical interventions it chose to perform was often held out to be more efficient than the swelling public sector.

The short-lived Labour Government between 1957 and 1960 endeavoured to bring public hospital building programmes under control, perceiving that the on-going running costs soon exceeded the initial price of any building or new piece of equipment. However, the introduction of equal pay for state employees in three stages in 1961–64 had a big impact in the hospital sector with its predominantly female workforce.[107] In June 1966 the Minister of Health, Donald McKay, advised boards that they must keep within their budget allocation of £88.7 million for that year. They took little notice. Boards overspent by £2 million and the Health Department now began a much more systematic scrutiny of their budgets. This too had little effect.

By the late 1960s rising inflation and costly relativity disputes between groups of health workers, all of them ultimately solved at the Cabinet table on an ad hoc basis, pushed costs along. Political expediency can again be observed behind both the pay agreements and a willingness to approve large numbers of additional staff in election years.[108] In 1971 mental health workers bypassed their salary-fixing procedures, went straight to the Prime Minister and got what they wanted. The same happened with dental nurses in March 1974 when they invaded Parliament Buildings en masse. On that occasion Labour's Prime Minister, Norman Kirk, ordered his minister, R. J. Tizard, to 'get those nurses out of this building'. They departed with a better pay settlement than they had been able to negotiate so far.[109] Remuneration within the public sector was meant to be settled by established mechanisms. Health and education workers were learning that carefully placed media publicity, and threats of direct action, usually resulted in ministerial intervention. The results of such unbudgeted wage settlements were simply sent on to the taxpayer.

Tizard, who became the Minister of Health in 1972, was shocked at the state of hospital board accounts and their apparent waste and extravagance.[110] In 1973 he legislated to make members of hospital boards personally liable for over-expenditure incurred 'without due regard' for the need to live within fixed allocations.[111] Tizard's legislation presupposed that board members elected as community advocates would be able to undertake directors' responsibilities and control boards' expenditure and, further, that governments would be firm, no matter what the consequences. In fact, the electoral process threw up few members with administrative or financial skills. Most boards were at the mercy of powerful staff pressure groups, and entrenched and often strong-willed executives.

In spite of warnings about over-expenditure, the Auckland Hospital Board's staff numbers rose rapidly in 1972–75. Having given an assurance in August 1974 that there would be no further staff appointments during the rest of the financial year, board officials appointed another 703 staff before the end of the financial year. The Health Department was critical of the Auckland Board, noting that while its catchment area was experiencing steady population growth, the board seemed constantly to overspend the rapidly increasing funds provided to it.[112]

The Minister of Health met Auckland Hospital Board members on 30 July 1975 to remonstrate with them but all they had to offer by way of savings was some cut-backs to the 'meals on wheels' service! It was clear that if the minister was to insist on the Board balancing its budget he would be saddled with the responsibility for staff layoffs a few weeks before

Free medicine? Produced barely seven years after the Pharmaceutical Benefit went into operation, this Minhinnick cartoon illustrates the ever-present problem of wastage. Part charges were introduced in later years but the first flat fee for drugs did not come until 1 February 1985. NZH

a general election. When Auckland was seen to get away with its overspending, the Otago Hospital Board began complaining that the Government was preventing it from expanding its services. This refrain was soon being sung by the Wellington Hospital Board as well.[113] Newspaper editors fell in behind the pressure groups, making it even more difficult for the Government to hold the line.[114] Yet by this time it was facing a budget deficit of more than $1 billion. There was worse to come as the economy deteriorated.

In reality, governments had long since lost control of hospital expenditure. By 1975 it constituted about 74 per cent of the total money allocated annually for public health. So muddled was the system of hospital funding and management that no one seemed able to devise a strategy for bringing the juggernaut under control. The Cabinet Policy and Priorities Committee was informed on 3 September 1975 that over-expenditure in the Health budget had reached $30.84 million for the year. Like so many ministries before and since, the Cabinet succumbed to the pressure and simply paid up.[115] Moreover, a controversial December 1974 White Paper with the Government's plans for a better integrated health service was attacked vigorously by interest groups. It was quietly buried after the 1975 election. But the problems identified by the White Paper did not go away so quietly; some are still with us, largely because governments have failed to grapple with them. If there is any message to be learned from the lengthy health-care saga, it is that the combined pressures from patients and providers will always overwhelm any public health budget.

The escalation in educational expenditure was nearly as rapid. Referring to the postwar baby boom, Holland's Minister of Education, R. M. Algie, observed in 1952 that 'the tide which has flooded through the post-primary schools . . . is now lapping at the doors of the University.'[116] Costs rose steadily, particularly at the secondary and tertiary levels, as higher percentages of students stayed at secondary schools and then went on to universities.[117] The President of the New Zealand Educational Institute (NZEI) told his members in October 1956 that if they lobbied for public support they could force the politicians to give them more generous salary increases.[118] Such tactics resulted in costly wage settlements at all levels of the educational system.

As with health sector groups, the Government tried, but could not devise, a satisfactory arms-length method of determining pay rates. Most decisions went to Cabinet surrounded by a cacophony of special pleading. And each increase granted to one sector would be followed by arguments about shifting relativities from another.[119] The result was that spending on Education, as on Health, consistently grew at a faster rate than the country's GDP in the two decades after the war. Treasury warned the Minister of Finance that this state of affairs was not sustainable.[120] Yet there was a new issue developing that carried a high potential price tag. In 1956 W. S. Otto of the Holy Name Society petitioned Parliament with the full support of the Catholic hierarchy for state aid to private schools.[121] The plea was rejected but the National Government 'agreed in principle' to subsidise some teaching in the run-up to the 1957 election; and the Labour Party matched the offer.[122] Not until the eve of the 1969 election did Labour offer substantial aid to private schools and the Private Schools Conditional Integration Act was not passed until October 1975, by which time governments had been steadily increasing their subsidies to private schools.

Adding to expenses was the way in which local pressure groups increasingly obliged the Government to take over complete funding of some school facilities that had previously received no more than top-up subsidies. Assembly halls, gymnasia, swimming pools and school hostels, which in earlier years had been part-funded by alumni and local authorities, were accepted by Holland's Government as a wholly state-funded responsibility. Treasury officials struggled to define criteria for assistance but exceptions kept being approved by ministers and restraint mechanisms were overturned. By the 1970s some secondary schools were gaining approval for a second fully funded gymnasium, as well as improvements to swimming facilities.[123] The State in many social areas had become the plaything of lobby groups whose ability to manipulate the press made it impossible for ministers to resist.

Meanwhile, by 1957 National's prospects at the coming election were not looking good. World commodity prices declined in 1955, rallied slightly at the time of the Suez crisis in 1956, then slipped badly in the second half of 1957.[124] Government spending remained high. Watts complained to his Cabinet colleagues in November 1955 that many of them did not seem to appreciate how necessary it was to restrain expenditure.[125] High spending increased demand for goods and put growing pressure on the country's diminishing London reserves. Wholesalers and retailers became grumpy about the Government's credit squeeze, but the Reserve Bank announced in April 1957 that the ratios of deposits which banks and insurance companies had increasingly been obliged to invest with the Government would be further tightened. Colin Simkin observed in May that unless private imports were checked by tighter bank credit, 'we are heading either for another balance of payments crisis, or for the restoration of exchange control'. All New Zealand's economic problems, he said, 'come back to the Government. . . . There is much talk, but no great mystery about inflation. There are well tested methods for bringing [inflation] under control', he continued. 'The only mystery is why they are not applied in New Zealand. They have been applied in other countries, and we are amongst the few which have not achieved stable prices in the last few years.'[126] There was a growing perception that the National Government was paralysed by the possibility of electoral defeat and had simply decided to let things run, in the hope of getting past election day.

Morale within National was low and several ministers decided to retire. The party did poorly in two byelections, one in Riccarton in October 1956, the other in Bay of Plenty the following April. Holland had suffered a heart attack or stroke in 1956 from which he never fully recovered. For many months Keith Holyoake did much of the Prime Minister's work. Finally, after pressure from several senior ministers, Holland informed the National Party conference on 12 August 1957 that he needed a rest and was going to retire.[127] However, he seemed oblivious of the coming election and took another five weeks to leave office.[128] Keith Holyoake was not sworn as Prime Minister until 20 September 1957. By this time the election was only 71 days away.

While there was some talk of a 'revitalised' Labour opposition,[129] the Labour Party made fairly heavy weather of the 1957 session. The victim of poor candidate selections over many years, it contained few stars and was led by the veteran Walter Nash, nearly 76 years old. Yet, such was his competition within the Labour caucus that the historian J. C. Beaglehole observed that Nash 'looked like the only young man among them'.[130] After a campaign described by Beaglehole as marking the nadir of the democratic process, in which the two major parties outbid one another with promises about what to do with 'surplus' tax revenue that would be generated in 1958 by the switch from annual payment of taxation to a 'pay as you earn' (PAYE) regime, Labour scraped into power with a majority of two, or more accurately, one, after providing the Speaker.[131] Having effectively set the political agenda since the war, Labour itself now had to grapple with the first sudden, serious threat to the insulated economy.

Chapter 10

Labour and National Struggle with the Economy, 1957–72

O nce the National Party had tempered its free market rhetoric in the early 1950s and adjusted to the regulated economy, arguing in effect that its ministers were better able than Labour to administer the welfare state, the scope of political debate in New Zealand narrowed. Labour candidates occasionally spoke of 'socialism', although it was now an ill-defined creed, meaning little more than a general willingness to keep on using the State's powers. Between 1957 and 1984 both main parties accepted price controls, subsidies, tariffs, import and credit controls; only a few differences in emphasis lay between the two. Labour enjoyed only six years out of the 27 in office; its ministers were cautious fiscally, but more likely than their opponents to increase funding for social services. National, on the other hand, always preached freedom, extolling the virtues of a world with fewer controls, but moved cautiously. The ratchet upwards of state involvement in the economy was difficult to reverse. As a result many voters perceived that elections had become a choice between Tweedledum and Tweedledee, where the rhetoric was out of all proportion to the likely consequences of one or other of them being elected.[1]

Not surprisingly, a gap opened up for a third political party. Building on a hankering after monetary reform that dated back to dairy farmer angst in 1934–35, and the 'wild money men' who wanted free use of Reserve Bank credit[2] during the early days of the First Labour Government, the Social Credit Political League fielded a full list of candidates for the 1954 election. It won 8.62 per cent of the total vote on that occasion, but no seats. One commentator likened the new party to the French Poujadist movement of the 1950s – 'the one-man businessman's detestation of the taxes which fuel the contemporary state, his resentment of the controlling paperwork which overwhelms him and his suspicion of the unionists whose highest ranks rival him in status while their lower ranks assert standards for paid help which he cannot meet'.[3] Holland's Government established a Royal Commission of Inquiry into the Monetary, Banking and Credit Systems in

Elections had become auctions by the 1950s.
Labour's newspaper billboard puts the question
bluntly in November 1957.

March 1955. It placed Social Credit's nostrums on trial, took copious evidence, and politely conveyed the verdict that they were muddle-headed.[4] Since the major parties had become – to use Harold Innes's phrase – 'as attractive politically as yesterday's cold rice pudding', Social Credit retained a capacity to act as a spoiler between the two main parties for the next 30 years. Its popularity waxed and waned according to the degree of irritation voters felt with National and Labour. Social Credit won an occasional seat, redefined its messages but succumbed eventually to the collapse of the corporate state in the 1980s and the emergence once more of significant philosophical differences between the two main parties in the 1990s.[5]

Both Labour and National felt it politic to resort to extravagant promises at election time in the hope of gaining support – and then to accuse each other of using 'bribes'. Labour's carelessly expressed promise to reduce income tax to coincide with the introduction of PAYE in April 1958 led their weekly, the *Standard*, to publish a billboard on the eve of the 1957 election reading 'Do You Want £100 or Not?'[6] There were many more electoral 'bribes' over the years ahead, culminating in what historian Keith Sinclair regarded as the biggest of them all,[7] when Robert Muldoon promised in 1975 – and delivered fifteen months later – National Superannuation at the rate of 80 per cent of the average ordinary time wage to a married couple over 60, without raising taxes.

*

When they took office on 12 December 1957 Walter Nash and his Minister of Finance, Arnold Nordmeyer, found themselves facing a substantial foreign exchange crisis. For the year to March 1958 imports exceeded exports by nearly £40 million. By 1 January 1958 the net overseas assets of New Zealand's banking system had fallen to less than £45 million, the lowest level since the war. Butter, lamb and wool prices continued to fall for most of 1958.[8] Between the last quarter of 1958 and the last quarter of 1959 world trading conditions improved and export prices rose, but they sagged again in 1960. The New Zealand economy was entering a much less stable trading environment, one that placed Savage's insulated economy under greater strain.

By this time New Zealand was beginning a long fight to retain access to the British market. Slowly after the war Britain became immersed in the negotiations taking place within Europe over the formation of a common market. Discussions culminated in six continental countries signing the Treaty of Rome in March 1957. In spite of soothing visits from British ministers, including Prime Minister Harold Macmillan in January 1958, New Zealand's fears mounted. By 1960 the six were formulating a common agricultural policy and the following year Britain announced that it would apply to join what was becoming known as the European Economic Community (EEC). Some of the strongly protectionist attitudes of EEC members clearly threatened New Zealand's trade. Eventually Britain joined the common market on 1 January 1973 and the issue of continuing membership was put beyond doubt in a referendum in 1975. Despite prolonged efforts and a few successes in the fight to preserve access to Europe for its former colonies, such as the Ten Point Plan for New Zealand announced in Luxembourg in June 1971, Britain accepted the rules of the common market, thus turning its face against its imperial past. The impact on trading relations with Commonwealth countries was immense. New Zealand could no longer regard itself as Britain's outlying farm. The search for new markets for old products stepped up.[9]

Faced with the exchange crisis of 1957, Nash and Nordmeyer acted as though it was a repeat of the predicament faced by the First Labour Government in 1938. This time, however, Labour ministers were able to blame their opponents. In a radio broadcast on New Year's Day the Prime Minister claimed that the National Government had allowed 'the most rapid slide in the history of New Zealand trade' to occur.[10] He ruled out devaluation, overseas borrowing and a sudden reduction in purchasing power. Reflecting the current attitude that general prosperity rested on the welfare of farmers, Nash announced that priority would be given to

Walter Nash, Prime Minister 1957–60, back at his desk at 10.40 pm after a dinner party, December 1959. Auckland Star

dairy farmers, who would be paid their guaranteed price even though it was higher than current export receipts. Of particular significance was Nash's announcement that the Government would return to comprehensive import licensing to safeguard overseas reserves. A new schedule for import licences was issued; all previous licences were revoked. Credit would be carefully controlled to restrain demand. Over the next two years it also became necessary, despite Nash's better judgement, to borrow in Australia, New York and London.

All this sounded ominously like a return to wartime austerity. Keith Sinclair caught some of the flavour of the moment when he described Nash as sounding like Father Christmas one minute and Scrooge the next. The National Party dismissed Nash's 'crisis', claiming that reserves were greater than the Prime Minister admitted and that Labour's real intention was 'to slip a straitjacket' of controls and regulations on the economy once more.[11] While it seems clear in retrospect – although it was much debated at the time – that the National Government had let the economy run in 1957, it was also true that Labour ministers felt more at home in a controlled environment; more than two thirds of Nash's Cabinet had been in Parliament during the Savage-Fraser era, several of them in senior positions. As if to underline their faith in controls, early in 1958 Cabinet approved the appointment of 50-year-old Dr Sutch to fill the position of Secretary of Industries and Commerce, which had been vacant for many months following the retirement of P. B. Marshall.[12] Ever since his days in Coates's office, Sutch had been an evangelist for big government and the notion that it would always produce better social results than the marketplace. He was an economic nationalist who believed passionately in the effectiveness of import controls. The minister with whom he worked after 1960 was to praise Sutch's intelligence, his imagination and enthusiasm but called him 'a strange, frustrated, arrogant, secretive man with a brilliant quicksilver mind, facile, ingenious, crafty, devious, deceitful'.[13]

With the encouragement of the young, energetic Philip Holloway, who was his minister between 1957 and 1960, Sutch began boosting departmental numbers once more, actively recruiting university graduates to his cause.[14] The tone of departmental reports became urgent. Sutch painted a grim future for New Zealand unless there were comprehensive plans to improve the country's sluggish economic growth. The 1958 report made it clear that a paternalistic government would pick winners by selecting those industries it deemed to have the best potential for contributing to the New Zealand economy. The chosen would receive financial assistance.[15] Over the next twelve months an Industrial Development Fund was established with £11 million in foreign exchange held at the Reserve Bank for allocation to promising projects.[16] This was the forerunner of the Development Finance Corporation established in 1964, which in turn spawned the Small Business Agency in 1976. In a world where credit was so rigidly controlled because of the dangers of over importing, the Government had to find a way to assist those believed most likely to boost export receipts. Complexity seemed always to beget further layers of complexity.

Holloway and Sutch worked closely together. In a speech in January 1958 entitled 'The Part to be Played by New Zealand Industries', Holloway talked of the need to develop New Zealand's raw materials. He used Labour's familiar calls for more work, for sacrifices and for buying New Zealand-made goods. Woollen mills, footwear, furniture, and leather-producing industries were singled out, while engineering industries were told to make better use of their machinery. Holloway hinted at coming reductions in the importation of food items, signalling that New Zealand food producers should be prepared to take up the slack.[17] Meantime, Sutch urged industries to make better use of his department's expertise. He noted that many industrial units that had developed since 1936 had been unduly dependent on imported raw materials. As a consequence, the local 'added value' component of industrial production had remained steady as a percentage of GDP.

The kind of manufacturing that developed in the past has in some ways made New Zealand even more vulnerable to external fluctuations. . . . The need is for development of a sort that can reduce excessive dependence on fluctuating exchange receipts; that can earn overseas exchange; or that can make substantial exchange savings possible. The need is not only for a defence against threats to the standard of living. There is need for a positive approach which will lead to even higher living standards, for these standards are themselves continuously in jeopardy.[18]

Sutch's opposition to the earlier policy of fostering import substitution industries was acceptable to Labour, as was his new policy called 'manufacturing in depth'. The new theme song was sung lustily to the 100 delegations attending the Industrial Development Conference in June 1960. On that occasion Sutch restated the problem that had been at the heart of the conference on Economic Stabilisation in 1953. It was the same one that had worried Gibbs in 1951, for which Gibbs had a more market solution. Sutch declared that 'while the social security and full employment policies are stabilising elements for internal economic life, their very constancy ensures a high level of demand whatever the balance of payments. The more generalised the living standard and the more constant the availability of jobs for all, the more difficult it is to do without exchange control and import selection.'

The problem, as Sutch saw it, was that 'rigidity' had been introduced into a most vulnerable and 'precariously based economy'. The solution, in Sutch's view, lay in more government intervention, not less. No believer in the 'global village', Sutch told delegates that free access to markets and the free flow of capital based on competitive private enterprise 'will be a concept for the history books'. He had no confidence in the GATT. While private enterprise would play its part in the late twentieth century, international competition would 'increasingly have behind it the power of the State'. New industries would be based on the most up-to-date developments. Central direction was vital to this future. Developing new markets, ensuring greater skills within the workforce, initiating major industrial projects, and channelling investment into them were all vital elements of his command-style economy.[19] This vision was acceptable to many on New Zealand's political left. The Christchurch-based *New Zealand Monthly Review*, which was launched in 1960 by several survivors of *Tomorrow*, became a mouthpiece for the Sutch doctrine.

Neither Sutch nor the political left in New Zealand was acting in a vacuum. What Robert Skidelsky calls 'collectivist creep' was gathering worldwide momentum once more.[20] Confidence in the capacity of planners to produce beneficial outcomes received a boost throughout the world from the achievements of Soviet scientists with Sputnik in 1957, from John F. Kennedy's victory in the 1960 American elections and from the momentum which took Harold Wilson's Labour Government to Downing Street in October 1964. Sutch was no more than collectivism's evangelist within the New Zealand bureaucracy and Wolfgang Rosenberg at the University of Canterbury was its high priest in academic circles.[21]

Meanwhile, Holloway was showing himself to be an activist minister. The Cabinet Economic Committee in 1958 decided he should explore the potential of the Japanese market for New Zealand coal exports; three trial shipments left for Japan in September. The following January the Government assured Parliament that it would do 'everything possible' to establish a long-term coal business with Japan.[22] Investigations were undertaken into the economic advantages of laying an electricity cable between the South and North Islands to transfer the South's abundant supplies to the North where more than 70 per cent of the population now lived. In April 1960 the officials' committee recommended that the costly exercise proceed.[23] However, most other schemes, and there were 240 new or expanded projects with a capital investment of £74 million, were shrouded in some degree of secrecy for commercial reasons. Holloway conceded in Parliament in April 1960 that the Government was actively pursuing 'about 12' of them.[24]

Plans to build a cotton mill in Nelson were debated publicly. In July 1959 the chairman of Smith and Nephew Ltd, a British cotton-producing firm, visited New Zealand. After discussions with government officials and then with Holloway on 8 February 1960, Nash announced on 1 March, while opening construction on a revived railway connection between Nelson and the South Island Main Trunk, that a large cotton mill costing £4 million would be erected in Nelson. It would initially produce meat wraps, denim, drills and sheeting, and employ 300 workers. After several anxious months, during which Smith and Nephew had second thoughts, an agreement was signed on 12 August 1960, three months before the general election. The Commonwealth Fabric Corporation, as it was now called, was eventually to allow New Zealand financial participation in the project. The Government guaranteed that it would use import licences to ensure the corporation 80 per cent of the New Zealand market for its initial products until 1964, with a longer period for later products. Prices to be charged for goods were not to exceed 'the fair average price . . . for such products at the time of the company's first commitment'. Construction of the plant was the responsibility of private enterprise, but without the

*Arnold Nordmeyer, Minister of Industries
and Commerce (1947–49) in the First
Labour Government and author of the 'black
budget' when he was Minister of Finance
(1957–60).* ATL C-23149

Government's generous guarantees the scheme would not have reached this stage.[25]

Another substantial industrial project was an aluminium smelter at Tiwai Point in Southland. On 19 January 1960 the Minister of Works, Hugh Watt, signed an agreement with Consolidated Zinc Pty enabling the company to construct a plant that would process bauxite imported from Australia. Part of the deal was that the company would construct a large hydroelectricity project at Lakes Manapouri and Te Anau. In October 1960 the agreement was given legislative endorsement.[26] Plans for an iron and steel industry, which had been the goal of the First Labour Government, were also being dusted off.[27] Instead of developing the limonite deposits in Golden Bay, which turned out to be much smaller than initially thought, Cabinet on 13 October 1958 approved the establishment of a merchant bar mill to produce between 40,000 and 50,000 tons of steel annually from scrap. This led to Fletcher Holdings beginning work on the £3.85 million Pacific Steel venture at Otahuhu in 1960 with the assistance of loans from the Development Finance Corporation.[28]

Meanwhile, an interdepartmental committee of officials, which had been set up in October 1958, was looking into the longer-term development of the North Island's ironsands deposits. In February 1959 it recommended a joint government and private company to undertake the ironsands research, although forces within the Ministry of Works, probably with Sutch's backing, preferred 'complete control' to remain in the Government's hands.[29] Fletchers was also interested in this project and had invested much time and money in negotiations with West Coast Maori and in its own research. Both Sutch and Holloway, however, concluded that Fletchers, with its stake in Tasman and Pacific Steel, was overreaching itself. Although it was not announced policy, officials, and particularly Sutch, seem to have determined that no one concern should be able to become a dominant player within New Zealand industry. At a meeting on 30 March 1960 to announce the Government's chosen partner in the ironsands investigations, it was revealed that 51 per cent of the private sector involvement was to be in the hands of Australian interests controlled by Kormans who had no background in steel. Fletchers and a South Island rival consortium attacked the plans vigorously, and according to George Fraser 'the meeting ended in chaos, with Sutch alternating between screams and speechlessness'. Stories soon leaked out about the Government's preference for overseas bidders.[30] The plans had to be shelved and in June 1960 Holloway announced that the Government would entrust the necessary ironsands research to a wholly government-owned company, New Zealand Steel Investigating Co. Ltd, under the watchful eye of a board chaired by Auckland industrialist Woolf Fisher. The company was asked to make recommendations on structure, location, capitalisation, ownership and a programme for development of an ironsands steel industry.

While the Labour Government gained little kudos from its behaviour over steel, a considerable degree of momentum towards industrialisation was building up. The Industrial Development Conference in June received a great deal of publicity. On 24 April 1960 Nordmeyer had told a Dunedin audience that industry was to be brought under government control to an even greater extent.[31] A few days later Holloway announced that the Government was prepared to build factories and lease them to private enterprise, especially in regions where employment opportunities were needed.[32]

All these developments were watched avidly by interested parties, the National Opposition, the press and traditional opponents of state control. The Christchurch *Press* vociferously attacked the cotton mill proposal, believing that it appeared likely to become a dangerous monopoly producing high-priced goods at a time when competition from Asian products was reducing world cotton prices. The Textile and Garment Manufacturers' Federation, its members all themselves benefiting from import controls, set up a fighting committee to oppose the mill, fearing that its monopoly status would inevitably force up the price of locally made garments.[33] The *Evening Post* complained that the Government's plans for building factories meant more bureaucratic control, less freedom for entrepreneurs, and probably less choice for consumers.[34] The Hastings Chamber of Commerce argued that high tax rates were stifling initiative. If they were reduced and the raft of controls that had built up over the years were dismantled, private enterprise itself could build factories and expand output where appropriate.[35] While the National Opposition generally suspended judgement on the Government's schemes, the party's paper, *Freedom*, sniffed that Holloway's factories would no doubt be built in marginal electorates.[36] Notwithstanding this criticism that had more than a grain of truth to it, the Government pressed ahead and acquired land; by October 1960, 50 applications to rent state factories had been received.[37]

Meantime the fresh crop of Labour politicians who entered Parliament in 1957 were as enthusiastic as their ministers about expanding the role of government and protecting the economy. The new MP for Roskill, Arthur Faulkner, declared in his maiden speech that 'social experiments are regarded as part and parcel of the New Zealand way of life, and that gives our people a passport everywhere'. His constituents wanted 'a Government that will do something to develop this nation, and provide it with the opportunity of getting as close as it can to self-sufficiency'. Faulkner denied that the average person wanted 'mollycoddling from the cradle to the grave' but went on to assert:

> He wants orderliness in his family life; he wants security for the farmers, the workers, the manufacturers, and, yes, for the importers as well. He wants some sense of assurance that when he is aged . . . a kindly State will provide for him a reasonable standard of living. The same can be said of the infirm, and of youth.[38]

Another new MP, Norman Kirk, declared his support for a social programme 'which will promote the housing of our people, protect their health, and ensure full employment and equal opportunity for all'.[39] R. J. Tizard acknowledged the changing trade environment in which New Zealand was now operating and sought to use the good offices of the Government to promote trade in new markets. On an issue closer to his constituents' pockets, he argued that the Government should control interest rates on hire purchase agreements.[40] Michael Joseph Savage's activist philosophy was still very much alive and in Kirk's talk about 'equal opportunities' there was a hint of the later enthusiasm for complex social engineering that came to dominate the thinking of some within the Labour movement.

The Labour Government used old policy mechanisms in an effort to bring the 1957 exchange crisis under control. However, the promises from the campaign trail soon haunted members. Tax refunds and more government spending did not sit well with the economic realities of 1958. The income tax rebate to compensate for the movement to PAYE cost £21 million and the introduction of 3 per cent loans for housing (supplemented on 1 April 1959 by a new provision enabling the Family Benefit to be capitalised in advance) caused house construction to speed up.[41] Labour's Minister of Housing, Bill Fox, increased the rate of state housing once more, often in marginal electorates; critics called the products 'Fox's boxes'. With all this activity came bigger demand for imported components. Early in 1958 Nordmeyer sought to increase the ratios which trading banks had to invest with the Reserve Bank and in his budget on 26 June 1958 he felt it prudent to take, as well as give. While many welfare benefits as well as universal superannuation were increased, Labour emphasised its support for families by lifting tax rates for working couples without families and for single people. The level at which people began to pay income tax was reduced from £375 to £338 for the 1958–59 year, and to £300 in subsequent years. The top marginal income tax rate, which had been reduced by National in 1954, remained at 60 per cent, and for companies 67.5 per cent. Duties on beer, cigarettes, petrol and cars nearly doubled and Estate and Gift Duties increased.[42]

Nordmeyer's 'Black Budget' removed any remaining sheen from Labour's election promises. The fiscal crisis saw unemployment top 1000 early in 1959, in spite of the Government's special work programmes in Forestry, Post and Telegraph and Railways and a cut back to immigration. It was the highest level of unemployment since the war, although there were still more than 6000 notified job vacancies. Nordmeyer loosened the purse strings when export prices improved at the end of 1958. In the last half of 1960, both government spending and bank lending reached high levels despite another slump in export prices. This produced a trade deficit in the year to June 1961 of £58 million.[43] Public Service Commission employees, including temporaries and casuals, reached 62,000 in Labour's last year.[44]

However, the boomlet was too late; Nordmeyer never lived down his 'Black Budget'. John Marshall later called it 'white hope' for the National Party.[45] The impression had become deep rooted that Labour was led by puritans who stood for austerity and a return to wartime regulations and controls. Since the parties differed so little in their goals and methods, politics had become a battle of perceptions as much as realities. With television beginning its first broadcasts in June 1960, the run-up to the general election on 26 November 1960 was the first in which New Zealand's leaders had to project themselves on screen. None found the medium easy, but Labour fared worst. Nash by this time was nearly 79 years old. His opponents had a bigger war chest and were much better organised. Labour lost seven seats to National. Keith Holyoake's rejuvenated National Party was back in office for what was to be a twelve-year reign.[46]

Once more Labour ministers had stepped up the level of government involvement in the economy and once more their National successors had to come to terms with their inheritance. Harry Lake, the new Minister of Finance, regarded by his colleagues as solid and conservative and by his opponents as dull and uninspiring, was immediately faced with the now familiar run on foreign exchange. Trading bank advances were tightened, an internal loan of £10 million was raised and Nordmeyer's extra import licences of 1960 were suspended. Money for overseas travel which had long required permission from the Reserve Bank became even harder to get. State housing was wound back and the rules governing State Advances housing loans tightened. In his budget on 20 July 1961 Lake told Parliament that 'we are attempting to do more than we can achieve with the resources available'.[47] The 'start-stop' routine was becoming such a regular feature of New Zealand's political economy that the Monetary and Economic Council and its chairman, Frank Holmes, began arguing for extending the term of Parliament from three to four or even five years to enable 'longer term planning' and a higher rate of growth. The Council believed that faster growth was essential given the expectations that New Zealanders had of their government.[48]

A signal that Holyoake's Government intended to continue with 'steady expansion of industry by private competitive enterprise', as National's manifesto had promised, came with Lake's announcement on 17 April 1961 that New Zealand was to lodge a formal application to join the International Monetary Fund, the World Bank and the International Finance Corporation. By this time New Zealand was the only Commonwealth country that was not a member. Treasury had tried to convince National's ministers in the early 1950s to join the fund and in 1956 told Watts that with the London loan market contracting, World Bank loans looked to be the only prospect for development capital at competitive rates for large schemes such as Tasman Pulp and Paper.[49] Watts vacillated, and the Labour Government, despite Nash having favoured membership at the time the fund was established in 1944, opposed joining on vaguely anti-American grounds. Newspapers were divided on the issue.[50]

Keith Holyoake, Prime Minister 1957 and 1960–72, opens the Bowen Street State Building with his Minister of Works, W. S. Goosman, 1961. Evening Post

Lake set out the implications of IMF membership in a white paper.[51] Few can have read it, for the decision produced a storm. As Keith Sinclair describes it, 'anti-American leftists, anti-American funny-money men, Social Creditites and economic troglodytes in general' petitioned Parliament against the National Government's decision.[52] Rosenberg produced a tract opposing membership, arguing that New Zealand's full employment stemmed from its capacity to insulate itself against sinister world forces that would seek to interfere in the New Zealand economy, force it to abolish import controls, and accept a level of unemployment. He followed this up a few years later with a vitriolic attack on the growing levels of foreign investment in New Zealand, arguing instead for a greatly expanded role for the Development Finance Corporation as a laundering agent for the overseas investment needed for industrial expansion.[53] The devotees of insulation were becoming worried that New Zealand's faltering economy was being used as an excuse to internationalise it. This opposition to government policy was all posited on the assumption that it was possible to prevent internationalism.

The Government marched on. Having joined the fund to avail itself of the necessary credit, National's ministers did not accept uncritically every recommendation by the World Bank. Nor did the Government stick with every expansionary scheme inherited from Labour. Towards the end of 1961 the cotton mill came under intense attack, led principally by Samuel

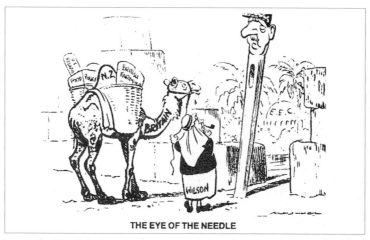

THE EYE OF THE NEEDLE

Cartoonist Lonsdale features the EEC wake-up call for New Zealanders, 1961.
Auckland Star

Leathem, President of the New Zealand Textile and Garment Manufacturers' Federation. Leathem told an Auckland meeting that the cotton mill agreement gave the mill monopoly status protected by import control and customs duties in those types of fabrics it chose to make. 'We can understand the granting of temporary monopoly privileges to enable an infant industry to get on its feet. We . . . are utterly opposed to the granting of permanent monopoly to anyone.' At a time when New Zealand manufacturers were selecting more than 500 different designs from overseas samples of cotton each year, Leathem argued that the range of 100 new designs which the mill would produce would lead to a 'kind of austerity' that would incite New Zealand women to march on Wellington 'with rolling pins in their hands'.[54] Nash disputed some of these claims about his cotton mill agreement,[55] but Jack Marshall, the new Minister of Industries and Commerce, after initially indicating an intention to proceed with the mill, had second thoughts. He announced in January 1962 that the company's offer to withdraw from the agreement would be accepted. However, there was to be compensation from the Government for the company's expenses to date. This eventually cost the taxpayers £1.4 million.[56]

Other major development schemes met with happier outcomes. The Cook Strait Cable was built and the aluminium smelter at Tiwai Point went ahead. However, in 1961 Consolidated Zinc found that the cost of constructing the necessary electricity generating capacity was beyond it. Holyoake's Government was convinced that the smelter was economically sound so it accepted responsibility for constructing the largest power plant

F. P. Walsh (President of the Federation of Labour) on the right, talking tough,
accompanied by K. M. Baxter (Secretary) in the hat, May 1961.
ATL, *Dominion* Collection, F-456741-1/2

in New Zealand.[57] The first aluminium was produced in April 1971. The pricing agreement for electricity has been in and out of the news ever since because of a perception that the initial agreement was too generous to the company, soon known as Comalco. Threats were made by the Muldoon Government in 1977 to impose higher prices on Comalco by legislation. Many years later Marshall, who was Minister of Industries and Commerce at the time of the 1963 amended agreement, claimed the Bluff smelter was 'a jewel in the crown of New Zealand industry' because of the earnings of overseas exchange from the plant.[58]

Progress towards erecting a steel mill using New Zealand's iron sands was steady, if not spectacular. After gaining much help from American consultants, Fisher's investigating team reported favourably in December 1962. Further investigations resulted in a recommendation to Marshall in December 1964 that the Government become a 'substantial shareholder' in a mill. To be sited on the north side of the Waikato River mouth, the mill would process west coast iron sands using New Zealand coal. The report suggested that the steel could 'make an important contribution to the balance of payments by saving exchange'. It would be marketed at a

Minhinnick pictures Walsh of the FOL, Holyoake and the New Zealand worker negotiating a wage round in 1963. NZ Herald

price 'matching the average of prices for steel products from the United Kingdom, Australia and Japan'.[59] In March 1965 plans were approved by Cabinet for the erection of a steel mill at a different site to the north – Glenbrook, on an arm of the Manukau Harbour. The Government purchased the land and took responsibility for railway connections and housing, just as it had at Tasman. New Zealand Steel Ltd was incorporated on 26 July. The Government agreed to subscribe up to 25 per cent of the shares in the company, and D. W. A. Barker, now Secretary to the Treasury, and M. J. Moriarty, now Secretary of Industries and Commerce, joined four private sector directors in the new company chaired by Sir Woolf Fisher.[60] By this time the Government through its departmental involvement with the project had contributed a large, unquantifiable share of the investment.

As with Tasman, the Government hoped that private investors would flock to take up shares in the company. They did not. This was partly because the Government decided to restrict foreign ownership to 20 per cent of the shares. This decision reflected the growing public paranoia about foreign participation at a time when many felt that further insulation of the New Zealand economy was both necessary and feasible. Another

Onekaka's private steel mill, Golden Bay, producing pig iron in the 1920s.

factor counting against the project was continuing doubt about whether New Zealand Steel could ever be a financial success. In 1968 the World Bank report on the New Zealand economy praised Pacific Steel but suggested that production runs were unlikely ever to be on a sufficiently large scale to be economic.[61] These developments eventually led the Government to take up 46 per cent of the shares in the new company. The following year the Minister of Finance guaranteed $4 million worth of unsecured bonds, the money being used to fund a mill to produce steel pipes. New Zealand Steel made its first galvanised steel from imported black coils in November 1968 and its first billets of steel from iron sands the next year. The iron-making process was not perfected until 1973; production expanded steadily after that. Doubts about the mill's viability continued to plague it. However, the Muldoon Government during the years of 'Think Big' ignored much contrary advice from officials and lifted the State's investment in New Zealand Steel, in effect throwing good money after bad. After the Labour Government was obliged to accept responsibility for debts in a complex restructuring of the mill in December 1985 the enterprise was readied for sale. It was sold to the tottering Equiticorp empire in October 1987 for $328 million. By that time more than $1 billion of taxpayers' money had been wasted on the enterprise.[62]

From earliest times the steel mill was plagued with bad industrial relationships stemming largely from the fact that there were too many unions engaged in a war for coverage of workers. Marshall claimed that the mill contributed much to New Zealand's infrastructural developments.[63]

The mostly state-funded New Zealand Steel mill at Glenbrook, 1987.

Yet the persistent talk in 1997 about the possibility that its latest owners, BHP, might be obliged to close it raises doubts about whether such an ambitious piece of technology in a small country like New Zealand would ever have begun, let alone survived, had it not been for huge state support.

Of more significance than any of these developments was the visit paid to the Prime Minister by J. B. Price, Chairman of Shell-BP-Todd Oil Services Ltd in October 1961 to tell him that the company had found natural gas in commercial quantities in Taranaki. A few days later on 18 October, Price told an officials' meeting that while they had not yet discovered much oil, the Kapuni gas field near Eltham and Hawera was 'most encouraging'. It contained both gas and condensate and at a rate of usage of 100 million cubic feet per day could have a life of 30 years.[64] Private exploration, which had already cost £5 million, was continuing at a cost of £30,000 per week. Politicians and officials were immediately seized of the magnitude of this news; in time it was to transform Taranaki and the port of New Plymouth and to impact on every aspect of New Zealand's energy use. There was soon talk of reticulating gas to many cities in the North Island.

While a private consortium had done the initial investigations, ministers were soon directly involved. At the very least the Government intended to regulate the industry and it was generally expected that it would become an investor in some parts of the infrastructure. Representatives of Taranaki local authorities saw Holyoake on 11 June 1962 to request protection for locals from 'the exploiting oil companies' and also to seek concessional gas prices for the region so as to attract downstream industry or a 5 per cent royalty for the region from all gas produced. The Government demurred.[65] On 28 August 1962 Holyoake informed the consortium that the Government intended to provide 'any reasonable assistance' to the industry. If the gas could not be used in a petro-chemical industry then the Government would negotiate to purchase it for electricity generation which would be needed when existing hydro generating capacity reached peak demand. Holyoake added cautiously that it all depended on price: 'I am sure you will appreciate that no government could commit the country to such an undertaking unless satisfied that the price is fair and that the return to your own company is not more than is reasonable having regard to all relevant circumstances'.[66] In December 1962 the Petroleum Amendment Act was passed which dealt with refinery licences, gas pipelines and the need for ministerial authorisation for them. The Act set up a Commission of Inquiry to consider applications and it granted rights of entry to land for exploration.[67] Consultants were soon appointed to advise the Government and feasibility studies on pipelines were undertaken. Marshall was probably right when he wrote 25 years later of 'a quiet industrial revolution'.[68] The National Government drove much of it.

National's boldness on the industrial front continued to be matched by a willingness gradually to expose New Zealand's economy to the wider world. The driving force seems to have been the realisation that industrial promotion required overseas capital and expertise – often Australian and American – plus Australian raw materials for the smelter, and Australian markets for newsprint. Growing unease – Lake called it 'apprehension' in his 1962 budget – at Britain's determination to join the EEC drew Australia and New Zealand closer. While there had been tariff agreements with individual Australian states in the 1890s and a number of tariff reductions in 1922, followed by a further agreement in 1944, it was Nash's Government in August 1960 that agreed to the establishment of the Australian-New Zealand Consultative Committee on Trade.[69] Marshall stepped up the pace of bilateral discussions.[70] Sutch and the political left in New Zealand saw a closer relationship with Australia as a breach in New Zealand's perimeter fence against the world. 'Australian industries can at all times oust most New Zealand industries in their present stage', declared Rosenberg, as he argued for tighter, not looser protection.[71] Frank Holmes, however, who soon took employment with Tasman Pulp and Paper, and similar minds within Treasury argued strongly for closer ties with Australia, especially in forest products. Both governments realised that cooperation was in their mutual interest. Eventually in July 1965 the New Zealand–Australia Free Trade Agreement (NAFTA) was signed and it took effect from 1 January 1966. It was a partial agreement, limiting free trade to some raw materials, manufactured goods and a few agricultural products. However, New Zealand's manufacturers wailed about potential threats to their viability. When the heat evaporated, Marshall told them that their 'unreasonable, pig headed and obstructive opposition' had enabled him to negotiate rather more safeguards for them than would otherwise have been possible.[72] New Zealand was slowly being drawn towards the wider world.

Holyoake's National Government seldom rushed things. Political scientist Robert Chapman observed that between 1960 and 1972 the Prime Minister's greatest feat 'was the slowing down of every process which, if speedily dealt with, might have represented change and political harm'. Holyoake himself liked to use the expression 'Steady does it'.[73] As in other countries, when it came to dealing with the regulated domestic economy, little changed. Tariff reform, which had been moving along at glacial speed in the 1950s, finally resulted in a new tariff regime and a Tariff and Development Board to monitor the schedule from 1 July 1962. Although ministers kept saying they preferred tariffs to import controls, they kept both after the new schedule came into force. Licences were traded from time to time and in 1965 there was an unseemly political row in Parliament when accusations were levelled that J. S. Meadowcroft, President of the National Party, was trading in import licences. Critics of import controls hammered away at them; Frank Holmes stated in July 1968 that 'New Zealand [has] erected over the years many barriers to expansion by efficient enterprises and many props for the support of the relatively inefficient. Almost certainly the most important of these is our system of import licensing and exchange control.' The Tariff and Development Board engaged in costly hearings to review the level of protection enjoyed by thousands of small and large industries. They usually resulted in decisions to retain the status quo.[74] The system kept being defended by Industries and Commerce as essential to guarantee new industries a sufficient share of the New Zealand market. Having said this, officials acknowledged that protection introduced 'commercial rigidities inconsistent with the

310

attainment of the fullest efficiencies in production'.[75] In 1963 an Export Incentive Licensing scheme whereby exporters had their existing import licences topped up with bonus import licences was introduced. This measure was part of the focus on exports that culminated in the Export Development Conference of that year.[76] The Prime Minister believed that there was political kudos to be gained from licensing and asked Marshall for details about licences before visiting marginal electorates in the run-up to the 1963 election. National Party members, however, disliked price controls, although Sutch championed them. The system retained some political usefulness; when sugar prices rose in 1963 Holyoake asked Marshall to consider price control.[77] Manipulating controls for political effect, as with so many other aspects of policy, was part of New Zealand's woof and warp.

The National Government's trade policy consisted of what Paul Wooding calls 'a system of layers put down at intervals over time without consideration for its overall structure'. At the bottom was a set of tariffs on which was built an import licensing system which, in turn, had another layer of export incentives added to it in 1963. Then came the limited free trade arrangements with Australia from 1966. The result, says Wooding, was 'a highly uneven pattern of effective subsidy to economic activities, an average level of protection high by comparison with OECD countries and a high degree of dependence on import licensing which made estimating the levels of protection very difficult'. Like many aspects of social policy, each addition to trade policy was a creation of the moment and was laid down with little thought to its impact on the existing mosaic. The policy was expensive: some parts depended on subsidies, while little revenue was gleaned from tariffs.[78] Put together with other controls, Holyoake's trade policy continued to drive up New Zealand's cost structure and impeded the growth of internationally competitive industries, as the World Bank noted in 1968. Every time costs rose, prices increased, and wages were dragged with them.[79]

Not surprisingly, tax levels remained high throughout the 1960s. In 1968 the top marginal income tax rate was still 60 per cent but it was payable on income earned over $7,200 pa, which was a high income for the time. Lake decided in 1966 on another review of taxation and a six person committee chaired by L. N. (later Sir Lewis) Ross produced a detailed report in October 1967 which noted that New Zealand collected a high proportion of its tax revenue from direct taxation and that its rates of corporate taxation were extremely high by world standards. Ross recommended a flattening of income tax rates to provide incentives for work and a partial shift to wholesale taxes, with improvements to welfare benefits to compensate low income people who could find themselves initially disadvantaged. Rather than a blanket tax on goods and services, the Ross Committee suggested a wholesale tax on luxury items such as motor vehicles and alcohol at between 20 and 40 per cent, exempting ambulances, fire engines, buses and earth-moving equipment altogether. It recommended an 8 per cent tax on all consumer goods, as well as on a selected range of services such as overseas travel, drycleaning, hairdressing, motels and restaurant expenditure.[80] It was both a far-sighted and judgemental review, reflecting the social attitudes of its time. As with so many reports over the years, the Government adopted some recommendations and ignored others. Taxes in New Zealand remained high and there was little willingness to shift towards sales taxes, mainly because at the time the report was released inflation was increasing.

Labour market developments during the 1960s tended to lock the Government and employers into higher costs. National had talked in 1957 of establishing an inquiry into what many supporters believed to be waste in the public service. Nash's Government rejected the suggestion but on returning to office in 1960 the National Government established a Royal Commission under the chairmanship of Justice Thaddeus McCarthy. The report presented in June 1962 did not produce the sort of findings that many Government supporters hoped for. It studiously avoided making any judgements about the efficiency or otherwise of the service or its staff and was criticised for its inability to penetrate beyond the facade of many departments. One commentator called it 'an exercise in culture-bound model-building' and expressed disappointment that the report, which recommended the establishment of a State Services Commission (SSC) to replace the old PSC, did not also suggest a form of open, direct instruction about government policy to the SSC. Moreover, instead of reducing the 41 government departments now in existence, McCarthy suggested another two be established. Nor did the report recommend the flexibility in staffing arrangements that some observers thought essential to a modern service.[81]

An Advisory Committee on Higher Salaries soon began trying to establish 'fair relativities' with private sector positions, awarding significant increases to top public service salaries as it progressed.[82] But since there was no slide rule run over departments in any systematic way to see whether payrolls could be pruned, the exercise simply added to mounting costs. Meantime, Labour's moves to introduce equal pay for women employees in the public service, which came in three steps after 1961, also added to the ballooning costs of government. A further Royal Commission report in August 1968 on salary and wage fixing in the State Services, again headed by McCarthy, was no more robust in its analysis.[83] New Zealand had developed a rapidly expanding bureaucracy equipped with rules for remuneration that guaranteed escalating costs. The Government was in no mood to chance radical reform. Cabinet decisions in 1968 to trim departmental functions deemed superfluous were easily reversed.[84]

Employment within the private sector experienced the same rigidities. In his discussion of industrial relations between 1946 and 1967 John Martin refers to the 'corporatism' that had developed during and after the war that 'locked in the existing system'; vested interests on both sides saw little need for change.[85] Election promises by the National Party to abolish compulsory unionism came to a climax in 1961 with the introduction of an I.C.&A. Amendment Bill. There was considerable opposition to abolition from the *New Zealand Herald*. While compulsory unionism seemed to many to be a denial of freedom of association, it had proved its worth by assisting the Government to crush striking unions in 1951. In the end the 1961 Act was a compromise which enabled compulsory unionism to continue where it was negotiated as part of an award.[86] Union membership continued to grow.[87]

During the 1960s the Arbitration Court was increasingly reduced to its wage-order function; issues that threatened to become troublesome were taken directly to the Secretary of Labour or to the Minister. Tom Shand, Holyoake's Minister of Labour in 1960–69 was a big, tough, independent individual. 'Our object is to have peace – a fair peace, not peace at any price', he told his first press conference in December 1960. 'I hope they didn't choose me just because I could be tough.'[88] His bluntness and honesty appealed to the unions; Tom Skinner, later President of the Federation of Labour, described him as 'an outstanding Minister of Labour', which meant in practice that Shand was pragmatic and usually came to see things from the unions' point of view. Yet employers also respected Shand and he seems to have been the only one who occasionally had reservations about what was happening under his stewardship. In reality, industrial relations were being centralised to a greater degree than ever before.[89] It seemed politically easier to step in whenever there was trouble and to try to defuse a crisis before it developed. This practice resulted in many more threats of strikes than a decade earlier and generally softer settlements. The Government did not have the same incentives as private sector employers to hold out against union threats. Employers, depending as they did on the Government for so many things, usually accepted settlements that were beyond what they had planned for. In the protected environment that still existed in the 1960s, costs were simply passed on to consumers. As John Martin observes, 'the fundamental problems in New

Zealand's system of industrial relations remained untouched'.[90]

A good example of what Muldoon called 'the unholy alliance' between unions and employers occurred in June 1968. The Arbitration Court responded to an application from the union movement for a 7.5 per cent wage rise with what came to be known as the 'nil general wage order'. Nationwide confrontation threatened. The Government supported the employers' and unions' decision to take the issue back to the court. Both sides now agreed to a 5 per cent rise, with only the judge dissenting from the majority decision. While the outcome maintained industrial peace the court's reputation, in Marshall's view, had been lowered still further. Tom Skinner, President of the Federation of Labour from 1963 to 1979, agreed with this analysis.[91] Unions realised that by direct pressure on employers, wage rates could be obtained above any award. The Government was soon witnessing an escalation in wages that added fuel to imported inflation.

Opinions in favour of freeing the economy from controls, and any government moves in that direction, were always controversial. Holloway spoke of the frustration felt by all politicians with a concern for the future when he told a 1963 conference on manufacturing that 'there can be no co-ordinated efficient development without the tacit consent of the public as a whole. This is necessary before politicians will lead, or those who would work to stop progress can be restrained. . . . Can we really say that most people are interested in the future, or have they been soothed with the syrup of complacency?' The previous three decades, he suggested, would come to be known as the 'thirty easy years'. No politician, it seemed, was prepared to act, before first seeking a consensus.[92]

The subsidence of the New Zealand economy from the middle of the 1960s froze rather than liberated initiative. Fear was in the air. Sectional interests became more strident in their demands. Problems were things for governments, with whom voters still felt something akin to a contract, to wrestle with. This thinking dominated the wider world of commercial relations as Harold Wilson in Britain and Lyndon Johnson in the United States encountered mounting difficulties. Paul Johnson notes that state intervention grew in all parts of the globe when world trade began to subside.[93] Interventionism had become locked into the national psyche. Politicians had designed the system that was in trouble; they accepted that it was their responsibility to try to fix it.

New Zealand's eternally vulnerable economy was one of the first to suffer. There was a pre-election spend-up in 1963, and another in 1966.[94] Net overseas assets of the banking system trended downwards after reaching

314

R. D. Muldoon (Minister of Finance 1967–72, 1975–84), seated second left, and Jack Marshall (Minister of Industries and Commerce 1960–69), seated centre, surrounded by senior civil servants and interest groups at the first meeting of the National Development Council, March 1968. Evening Post

a peak in the middle of 1964. This reflected a slide in export prices that became serious when the bottom fell out of the wool market at the end of 1966. Lake restrained credit sufficiently so as not to harm National's re-election chances in November. By this time, however, there was considerable public discontent; it did not switch to Labour, which had adopted an unpopular stand against New Zealand's involvement in the Vietnam War. Instead dissatisfaction with National made its way across to Social Credit. They won 14.5 per cent of the total vote and their first seat in Parliament (Hobson) but National retained office. Holyoake pronounced the economy to be 'in good heart' but export prices for meat, butter and fruit sagged. On 10 February 1967 Lake's credit squeeze was intensified. Subsidies on wheat, flour and butter were abolished, reducing the outlay on food subsidies from $37 million in 1966 to $17.8 million in 1968.[95] The milk-in-schools programme that had existed since 1937 was abolished to squeals of outrage from Labour. State house rentals increased and Post Office and rail charges rose. State Advances lending on new houses was curtailed and hire purchase regulations tightened. The family benefit increased as part compensation.[96]

Harry Lake died suddenly on 21 February 1967. Two weeks later Holyoake appointed the 46-year-old Robert Muldoon to the Finance portfolio. He was a pugnacious, able cost accountant, whom university students soon nicknamed 'Piggy'. In May Muldoon further restrained bank credit. Sales taxes on motor vehicles increased to 40 per cent and petrol prices rose. Roading construction slowed once Muldoon diverted much of the petrol tax to the Consolidated Fund. Alcohol and tobacco taxes were raised. Muldoon began what became his familiar trademark of selecting winners when he bestowed further incentives on the tourist and fishing industries and boosted tax deductions for manufactured exports. The result from these measures was a $90 million drop in import payments in the year to March 1968.[97] In November 1967, several months after the introduction of decimal currency that had become identified with Muldoon, the Government took the opportunity of a 14.2 per cent British devaluation of the pound sterling to devalue the New Zealand dollar by 19.45 per cent. This gave a small boost to farm incomes and further deterred imports.

The employment scene changed rapidly. A shortage of labour in 1965 switched to unemployment of 6556 by 31 March 1968. Manufacturing production fell for the first time in more than 30 years. It was much the most serious economic reversal since the war. Despite more than a generation of encouragement to manufacturing, exports from that sector were uncompetitive in price because of the hothouse environment in which they were produced, and they contributed little to foreign exchange earnings. The World Bank pointed out that New Zealand was still largely dependent on the same narrow range of agricultural exports as in the 1930s. And farmers' profits, as their organisations claimed, were slipping because domestic inflation kept rising at a faster rate than export receipts. In May 1969 one farming leader argued for another devaluation of the currency to boost farm incomes. Like Britain, the New Zealand economy seemed to be on a permanent downward trajectory.[98]

In this uneasy environment calls for a National Development Conference gained an audience. The goal was to arrive at some kind of consensus on how to accelerate growth. An Agricultural Development Conference had met in 1964.[99] Throughout that year Sutch, who was regarded as an advocate of centrally driven, or 'imperative planning', had been pushing for a 'National Efficiency Conference' to discuss the quality of management, technical training requirements and the need for better labour relations in industry. Marshall demurred.[100] In January 1965 the State Services Commission announced that Sutch would take early retirement from his position as Secretary of Industries and Commerce. It was widely believed that the Government had forced the SSC to act, although this was denied by the chairman, L. A. Atkinson.[101] M. J. Moriarty took over as secretary but the thrust within the department towards more comprehensive planning continued. While staff numbers were back to 500, the prevailing international mood meant that departmental officers with plans had to be heard.[102]

Interest in planning and targets for growth went well beyond the bureaucracy. The Labour Opposition, several National Party branches, as well as the Manufacturers' Federation, were discussing it. In 1968 the guru of American planning, John Kenneth Galbraith, visited New Zealand and gave a series of well-attended lectures celebrating the end of the market and the arrival of an age of planned industrial expansion.[103] The Minister of Finance had already sought Treasury advice about the desirability of establishing a New Zealand planning organisation. Henry Lang, who took over as Secretary to the Treasury in 1968, replied with some details about the British experiments that began in 1962 with a National Economic Development Council, better known as NEDDY. Lang doubted whether New Zealand's statistics were generally of a sufficient standard to undertake a similar planning exercise in New Zealand but added that in the agricultural area, where they were of a better quality, the Agricultural Development Council and the Agricultural Production Council had been able to set 'indicative' plans. These aimed at a growth rate of 4 per cent pa. When New Zealand's statistical base had improved, Lang thought it would 'be desirable to extend planning to other sections of the economy'.[104]

Industries and Commerce agitated while Treasury placated. Progress was slow. Treasury established an Economic Planning Section which met regularly while the department gradually built up its knowledge of experiments overseas. Officers concentrated on French planners who had developed the concept of 'indicative' planning which was taken up by Harold Wilson's Government after 1964. Treasury favoured plans that would provide targets and statistics rather than engage in 'imperative' planning that conjured up images of the Soviet Union's economy. Sutch and Rosenberg were seen to favour 'imperative' planning and were therefore marginalised from this intellectual process. Frank Holmes, then at Tasman Pulp and Paper, and Bryan Philpott from Lincoln College, both of them soon to be professors at Victoria University, as well as Jim Rowe of the New Zealand Institute of Economic Research, were in close touch with Treasury's unit. After 1970 Philpott's department at Victoria University experimented with several elaborate models.[105]

The new version of 'scientific' planning slowly captured the imagination of ministers and top officials. If it were to be successful, planning could not be confined to industry leaders. All interested groups needed to identify consciously with any plan, its targets and efforts to influence the public.

Wide consultation was soon being discussed. This process became an opportunity for many groups to advance gender issues and peddle a variety of other causes. Ministers started to realise that some of their freedom to act would, of necessity, be circumscribed; extra spending here or a soft wage settlement there could impact adversely on any plan.[106] Yet, throughout it all, officials maintained a sense of humour. One parodied Henry V's speech before Harfleur:

> Once more into the breach, dear friends, once more;
> Or close up – but first must we our objectives define. . . .
> Nor must we try to do too much too quickly.
> But simulate the action of the tiger;
> Coordinate the sinews, integrate the blood
> With broad total expenditure programme levels. . .
> Cry 'God for the Target, the Planners – and the Plan!'[107]

Frank Holmes talked up the virtues of planning in speeches around the country and convinced the Chambers of Commerce in May 1967 to call for a 'National Economic Council' which would recommend a raft of further incentives for selected economic activities.[108] Treasury, however, was beginning to feel that it was being stampeded into something that officials could not control. In April 1967 Noel Lough observed that the department had 'neither the machinery nor the present intention to undertake such an exercise'.[109] Yet Treasury was reluctantly obliged to inform Muldoon in June 1967 that 'the tide was washing' in the direction of planning and that 'some form of an overall national planning advisory body is more or less inevitable in the long run'. Treasury doubted whether the exercise would be of much use but something good might come from allowing various sectors in the economy to air their views. Officials cautioned the minister, noting that under current conditions, where the Government's measures to restrain the economy were beginning to bite, any national gathering 'will be used as a means of pushing the claims of individual sectors and consequently putting pressure on Government'. This piece of foresight convinced ministers of the need to have all interests represented, so that no single group could dominate proceedings.[110]

Treasury was struggling to keep ahead of the play. Officials persuaded Holyoake to make soothing noises to the Chambers of Commerce, to defer any immediate action on planning but to signal that a National Development Council could well be established in due course.[111] Early in 1968 the Government finally announced a National Development Council. A preliminary gathering was to take place in August which would be the forerunner to a plenary National Development Conference a few months before the General Election in 1969. Muldoon and Marshall made it clear to officials that they would be controlling the process. They would keep parliamentarians away from proceedings and possibly chair sessions themselves. On 3 March 1969 Cabinet duly endorsed this. It was decided that the National Development Council would be permanent. Six sector advisory councils (Manufacturing, Forestry, Fisheries, Minerals, Tourism and Fuel and Power) as well as the existing Agricultural Production Council, the Building Advisory Council and the Transport Commission would be represented on the NDC. Each sector was to maintain a direct line of communication with the relevant minister. The secretariat for the whole planning exercise would be located in Treasury, a piece of news that led a rather sour Dr Sutch to warn that the whole exercise was being designed to soften New Zealanders for a world of unemployment.[112]

Ministers had clearly decided that if interest groups were to have the conference they wanted, then they would manage proceedings, particularly if there were political benefits to be obtained. They cautiously let Lang, as Secretary to the Treasury, chair the early advisory council meetings and then when it became clear that the whole process was not going to be a disaster, Marshall decided to take over the plenary sessions of the conference.[113]

Meantime a great many academic papers about targets were produced, although debate continued amongst officials about whether the exercise was likely to produce useful results in the longer term. Professor John Roberts of Victoria University was sceptical from the start. Harbouring similar doubts to Treasury's, he warned that unless a clear, authoritative central strategy could be agreed upon, each sector 'may simply elaborate its demands for support to the point where the economy, far from being rationalised by the process . . . is led into a morass of competing demands'. He added that in his view, there were 'substantial perils' in institutionalising pressure groups. While means existed to prevent this happening, they required political will.[114] Behind Roberts's comments lurked a doubt that Holyoake's Government, renowned for its reluctance to be decisive about anything, could muster the necessary elan to extract much from the planning process.

The National Development Conference met at Parliament in May 1969 with as much fanfare as the Government could orchestrate. Eddie Isbey, a leading trade union figure, called the exercise a Cecil B. de Mille extravaganza with a star-studded cast. Jack Marshall was awarded Oscars by the press for his competent chairmanship. The huge talkfest involved 600 people in sector committees and working parties. They passed 632 resolutions and agreed on a number of recommendations put before them by the targets committee.[115] It was argued that a long-term growth target of 4.5 per cent pa required restraint on consumption, higher levels of savings, an increase in capital investment in the private sector and careful research and identification of new investment projects likely to produce a high rate of return. While some resolutions talked of the desirability of opening up the economy, almost every plea was for more state intervention.

Participants heard what they wanted to hear. Muldoon incorporated those recommendations he liked into his budget on 26 June 1969. The document contained new export, forestry and tourism incentives, further assistance to the Fishing Industry Board, more generous tax breaks for dairy, wool and industrial research and there were new depreciation allowances for meat processors. Further transport subsidies were provided for fertilisers. Successful farmers would be helped by State Advances loans to expand the size of their farms. Several significant changes to the finance industry were announced. National Development Bonds were launched, as well as an incentive savings bond scheme. Capital issues controls over finance companies were abolished, although the government stock ratio system, whereby financial institutions were required to hold a percentage of their borrowings in the form of government securities, took its place. However, merchant banks specialising in commercial financing were allowed to operate for the first time.[116]

In the aftermath of the conference an elaborate planning structure emerged. Sector councils serviced by various departments met from time to time, reviewed their targets and the progress made towards goals. They reported in September or October each year to a meeting of the National Development Council. Some groups complained at being left out of the consultation process; trade unions were irritated at having to operate through the existing Manpower Planning Unit within the Labour Department, while the universities seemed not to fit neatly into any sector council. Treasury's planning division attempted to keep some form of control over the exercise. Confidence lasted for some time. In May 1970 the *Listener* published a full-page spread on the NDC explaining how the system was meant to work.

However, while a handful of academics praised the planning exercise, there were doubters even among them.[117] It proved impossible to maintain the momentum of 1969,[118] and rapidly rising inflation (it reached 10 per cent in 1970) and a flagging economy meant that the growth target of 4.5 per cent pa could not be achieved in the early years of the plan. Between 1970 and 1974 growth averaged less than 2.8 per cent annually. Frank

Holmes tried to argue that the targets themselves were 'artificial', that 4.5 per cent should never have been agreed to and that the failure to achieve it did not necessarily mean that planning itself was a waste of time. But he could not stem the rising scepticism about the NDC, which was turning into an expensive exercise. Constant complaints from planners and bureaucrats about the inadequacy of New Zealand's statistics forced Cabinet to approve another 33 officers for the Statistics Department.[119]

In the election of 1969 the Muldoon phenomenon was a force to be reckoned with. He was an aggressive, confident, self-proclaimed 'counter-puncher', who appeared always to know what he was talking about. He had learned to stare at his television audience straight down the barrel of the camera. Coupled with the NDC planning exercise, Muldoon's confidence was enough to carry Holyoake's Government to its last victory over a slowly rejuvenating Labour Party. What looked like defeat for National early on the evening of 29 November became a win by six seats, soon to slip to four when Tom Shand died two weeks later and his seat of Marlborough was won by Labour in a by-election. But National suffered the fate of many a government that has overstayed its time; Gordon Coates, George Bush, Paul Keating and John Major are just some of the other twentieth-century leaders who were elected when their parties had really run out of steam and who eventually paid a severe penalty. By the end of 1970 National was tired. The Prime Minister was in hospital and Muldoon's bubble was bursting. There was talk of ministerial retirements, inflation ballooned and industrial unrest rose rapidly.[120]

Nevertheless, the public hoped that the omnipotent State could restore equilibrium. Farmers suffering from rising inflation but uncertain export returns sought and received a further raft of subsidies. On top of help to dairy farmers willing to switch to beef came drought relief in May 1970, further fertiliser subsidies, and the establishment of a Special Assistance Fund for farmers. Then came a Federated Farmers' request in February 1971 for a 'cost adjustment scheme' involving as much as $100 million annually. It drew some tart remarks from Professor Ken Cumberland of Auckland University, who felt such a scheme would not provide farmers with the necessary incentives to diversify or to improve their marketing techniques. He labelled it a 'degrading, shameless disaster' designed to provide agriculture with 'an artificially low cost structure so that it could stay where it had been for decades'.[121] The Government did not fully accept the proposal but granted an extra $16 million to the Wool Board during 1971–72. A Stock Retention Incentive Scheme was also introduced.

Norman Kirk, Labour's leader, called it 'a family benefit for sheep'. The scheme assisted 30,000 farmers and cost nearly $50 million in its first year. In the view of one Southland farmer it caused many farmers to over-estimate their sheep numbers.[122] Many farmers were uneasy and spoke of self reliance but in reality big subsidies had become part of their lives.

Lurking behind most problems in 1970 was inflation. In an attempt to curb it the National Government announced a price freeze on 17 November. It lasted until a complex price-justification system took effect on 15 February 1971. Parliament was now summoned to pass a Stabilisation of Remuneration Act which set up a Remuneration Authority. Marshall, now Minister of Labour, sought to enforce existing wage agreements and to ensure that when they were renegotiated, increases did not exceed 7 per cent unless the newly created authority had given its consent. The FOL opposed the move and, as Tom Skinner later pointed out, the experiment did not work because employers fell in behind the unions and the 7 per cent maximum became a starting point for negotiations. Quite often it acted as a springboard for higher agreements. In May 1971 the Monetary and Economic Council warned against the 'wage-price spiral' that was developing and argued strongly that restraints were unlikely to remove the pressures that gave rise to them. Arch-regulators like Sutch wanted tighter controls and one professor advanced a case for taking wages out of the hands of employers and unions and placing them under the rigid control of an Incomes Board. In Conrad Blyth's view, inflation and regulations had produced a situation where behind the scenes 'a massive shift in the distribution of real wealth' was taking place, 'with the wide boys and smart cookies making money, and the suckers – and there are a lot of business suckers about – losing money, after you make allowance for inflation'.[123] The Government picked and chose between competing bits of advice, preferring in the end to use old-fashioned controls with which it was familiar. Another price freeze was introduced in March 1972 and further regulations were gazetted under the Economic Stabilisation Act 1948. They were no more successful than the previous set, especially when Muldoon spent up generously in his budget of June 1972.[124] Local authority rate demands rose by between 20 and 35 per cent in many parts of the country, threatening people on fixed incomes. The country was getting its first taste of sustained inflation. Soon there was an air of crisis, and of a government living from week to week.

Industrial unrest reached a level in 1971–72 that had not been seen since 1951. Many unions that had distanced themselves from the Labour Opposition during the 1960s, preferring to go it alone, began mending

The Governor-General, Sir Arthur Porritt, swears Jack Marshall into office as Prime Minister, February 1972. Evening Post

bridges. Norman Kirk, who had led the Labour Party since December 1965, gained pledges of support from trades councils in the run-up to the election of 1972. There was only one opinion poll between 1969 and the election of 1972 that did not show Labour in front.

On 7 February 1972 Sir Keith Holyoake, as he became in 1970, resigned the prime-ministership. He was the third longest serving prime minister in New Zealand history, not far behind Seddon and Massey. His pompous demeanour masked a tough centre which enabled him to rule his sometimes disputatious ministers with seeming ease and good will. His Government, however, will be remembered more for the opportunities lost than for those it seized. His deputy, Jack Marshall, beat Holyoake's preferred choice, Muldoon, in the ensuing National caucus ballot for the prime-ministership. But Marshall could not survive the mood for change which showed every sign of increasing, even as commodity prices rose throughout 1972. Using the slogan 'It's Time for a Change', Norman Kirk's Labour Party swept to office on 25 November 1972 with nearly 49 per cent of the vote and a majority of 23 seats in the 87-member Parliament. Once more the public had elected Labour to try to wring improvements from a highly regulated, centrally driven economy. But New Zealand was now operating within an increasingly volatile world environment.

Chapter 11

Big Government Begins to Overreach Itself, 1972–79

By 1972 world trade had recovered from depression and war, and during the previous quarter century had grown at the remarkable average annual rate of over 7 per cent. Industrial production had rocketed up and standards of living had moved in the slipstream. During the late 1960s came signs that all was not well. The American stockmarket slowed and share values ceased growing altogether in 1968. Productivity figures subsided and inflation became a more serious international problem, driven in part by American intervention in Vietnam. In the years after World War II more and more Middle Eastern oil had poured on to the world market keeping energy prices low. Western economies as well as Japan became dependent on cheap oil. However, beginning in the early 1970s, Middle Eastern exporters moved to restrict the flow of oil in the hope of increasing profits from their greatest asset. Oil prices rose, and money began flowing away from the developed countries in what Paul Johnson notes was 'by far the most destructive economic event [for the West] since 1945'.[1] Developed economies entered upon a period of 'stagflation'. From a quarter century of record growth, they slowed down to nil or, in some cases, negative growth by 1974–75. Unemployment rose steadily. By the early 1980s it reached levels that were unparalleled since the Great Depression. Because governments continued to spend big, inflation moved upwards.

Since few countries in the world were more dependent for their livelihood on world trade than New Zealand, not even its highly insulated economy could fail to be affected by these trends. In fact, New Zealand anticipated the world downturn. Its economic growth lagged behind the best world performers after the war, and slumped in 1965; over the next quarter century New Zealand's average growth rate of 0.8 per cent per annum was almost the lowest of all its regular trading partners. Its inflation, however, was at the top end.[2] The impact of slow growth and inflation on New Zealand's welfare state was debilitating. The severity of the downturn, especially after the first oil shock in 1973, gave the collective anxiety that was observable everywhere within the western world a particularly sharp edge in New Zealand. This explains in large measure why citizens began rethinking the relationship between the people and the State earlier, and in a more sustained manner, than in many richer countries. Most experienced a changing tide; New Zealand suffered a tsunami.

Many New Zealanders were reluctant to accept an end to the golden weather. With the improvements in medical science the numbers of elderly grew; they formed pressure groups aimed at redistributing state spending away from younger people to themselves, on the grounds that their payment of taxes over the years amounted to a contract which had to be fulfilled. Politicians became more solicitous of the growing legions of older voters. However, there was increasing resistance to high levels of personal income tax being channelled toward those whose own resources, in many cases, meant they did not need state assistance. The rough and ready national consensus that viewed government as an instrument for the collective will and which had underpinned 30 years of welfare state and steadily rising expenditure began to crack and eventually to crumble. At the end of the 1970s political parties began to rethink their approach to the State's responsibilities.

A wind-down in the welfare state could not have been further from Norman Kirk's mind when he took office as Prime Minister on 8 December 1972. Born in Waimate in 1923, Kirk's family had suffered the ravages of depression, unemployment and war. As an early biographer, John Dunmore, observes, poverty set limits on everything the young Kirk did.[3] Leaving school at twelve, he taught himself several manual skills in a variety of jobs. He built his own house in Kaiapoi from bricks he made; he also read eclectically. After several years as Mayor of Kaiapoi, he narrowly won the seat of Lyttelton in 1957. He quickly made an impact in the House, where Walter Nash picked him as a future leader.[4] Five years later Kirk was both president and leader of the Parliamentary Labour Party. Forceful in debate and occasionally intimidating, Kirk was head and shoulders above his colleagues by the time he became Prime Minister. He came to be revered like no other Labour leader since Savage. What influenced everything his Government touched was his premonition that he would not make old bones. Urgency to leave his mark can be read in every page of Labour's extravagant 1972 Manifesto. The Prime Minister took it with him to Cabinet, caucus, the House, or briefings of officials, and would thump it vigorously while explaining his government's intentions.[5]

The manifesto was probably the most paternalistic document in New Zealand's history.[6] Its authors showed complete confidence in the capacity

'Taking up where Savage left off': Norman Kirk, leader of the Labour Party 1965–74, photographed in 1966.

of governments to intervene effectively in social and economic affairs and little appreciation of how the difficulties currently affecting New Zealand's economy might limit its capacity to carry extra spending. In this regard there was a harmony of views between older and younger generations of New Zealand's political left. Most of the seventeen new Labour MPs in Kirk's caucus were between their mid twenties and early forties; they were self-confident products of a big spending era and inclined to think well of it. Many held tertiary qualifications. Some had been part of the revival of the left on campuses during the 1950s and 1960s and were stirred by foreign policy debates, the Vietnam war, a romantic search for an egalitarian society and a more carefully defined sense of New Zealand's independent national identity.[7] Frank O'Flynn QC was one of the older, and certainly the most illustrious, of the new intake of Labour MPs. He spoke for all of them when he said:

> The aim of the Government is to give the people . . . the leadership that is necessary to rebuild [the] social system, to provide equality for all . . . citizens, an education system, and other assistance that will enable every citizen to develop his abilities to the full and play a proper part in society – to provide a social system that will take proper care of the young, the old, the handicapped, and the sick as a matter of right and justice, not as a matter of charity. The Government also intends to ensure that the nation once again plays a worthy

Norman Kirk after assuming office, December 1972. Huge expectations of a successful revival of state activism rested on him until his death on 31 August 1974. Press

part in world affairs and becomes a champion of the rights of small nations and of moral attitudes in international affairs.[8]

The whole campaign of 1972 centred on the need to increase growth in order to improve standards of living. Kirk, who was Keynesian to the core, exuded confidence that a big-spending Labour Government would retrieve prosperity. To him, all problems resulted from a poverty of vision and imagination. Bold use of the Development Finance Corporation and the funds of a compulsory New Zealand Superannuation scheme which the party intended to introduce, would provide the necessary investment capital. This would be aided by a generous expansion of tax incentives and interest-free loans of up to 70 per cent of the value of new plant and machinery for selected industries. There would also be a raft of tax breaks for wage and salary earners.[9] It was Sutch's doctrine in neon lights.[10]

A detailed account of the Third Labour Government, as well as assessments of its effectiveness, has been published elsewhere.[11] Higher export prices during 1972, especially for wool, created an air of anticipation that Kirk's Government would be able to live up to its extravagant promises. In spite of a cautious Treasury briefing to the incoming government that warned against letting the belt out too far, Kirk announced that a special Christmas payment would be made to most beneficiaries. This kindled

327

memories of 1935 and seemed a good omen. One Auckland sharebroking firm advised its clients in December 1972 that it looked forward to 'a stable and expanding economy'.[12] However, the rules applying to overseas investment were tightened in line with Labour's suspicious approach to foreign investment that was not tied specifically to industrial projects. In January 1973 the new Minister of Finance, Bill Rowling, announced criteria to govern each application in order to ensure that it was 'not excessive in relation to the benefits which New Zealand receives from this investment and that no overseas company is able to operate against the national interest'. Labour's belief that it could insulate the country against the machinations of the wider world was still alive and well. This time, however, the Government would rely less heavily on import controls (although a great many continued to be used), and more on various forms of direct assistance 'applied selectively' to industry.[13] In this, Labour foreshadowed the approach adopted by Robert Muldoon in the late 1970s and early 1980s.

When Parliament assembled in February 1973 it moved quickly to enact several spending measures. In order to provide better security for low-income people being threatened by rising property rates, a Rates Rebate Bill was introduced. The brainchild of Henry May, Minister of Local Government, it provided a set of rebates payable by central government. It was estimated to cost $5 million in its first year. In 1978 the scheme cost taxpayers nearly $9 million. Since the measure lifted some of the rates burden from the more vulnerable sections of the community, it had the side effect of freeing local councils from the need to be so careful with their spending. Local authorities had been benefiting from increasing subsidies since the 1870s. They received further help in 1973 with the creation of a Ministry of Recreation and Sport. It introduced a subsidy regime which councillors could direct towards community groups. There was talk of restructuring territorial local authorities to make them more efficient but in the end little more was achieved than the imposition of a regional tier of government. Since Joe Heenan's efforts in 1946–47, governments had also been lifting their contributions to the arts; the Kirk and Rowling Governments between 1972 and 1975 more than doubled the total paid from the Consolidated Fund and the Lottery Board to the Queen Elizabeth II Arts Council.[14]

On 14 June 1973 before a packed House and a gallery largely made up of young people, Rowling delivered his first budget in the knowledge that overseas reserves stood at a record $1 billion.[15] He spoke of the need for 'faster progress' towards Labour's goals and of the Government's intention to restrain inflation during that process. He indicated that Labour accepted indicative planning but was sceptical about the NDC planning structure and was reviewing it. Government assistance would be channelled through a wholly government-owned Development Finance Corporation towards industries that already were, or showed the potential to become, internationally competitive. Repeating a phrase often used by Kirk, Rowling added that economic growth would 'be regarded as the servant of our social needs and not as the master of our environment'.[16] He took comfort from the fact that domestic consumption was up, that unemployment was falling and that there had been a big jump in the amount of overtime and shiftwork. This would now be subject to lower tax rates to encourage even more effort. Rowling intended to provide incentives for faster growth to underpin full employment and ensure a 'fairer distribution of income'. Earlier in the year he had sought to dampen inflation by introducing a retention scheme for a portion of wool producers' incomes. As part of the inflation control programme the Government intended to stabilise the cost of services directly under its control, such as Post Office, rail, and bulk power charges. This had been promised in Labour's manifesto. Bigger subsidies would also be paid to hold down the domestic prices of sheepmeats, milk, woollen goods and sugar;[17] fish prices were frozen; and a system of maximum retail prices was to be be introduced on a wide range of retail products. A Property Speculation Tax was signalled to curb land speculation that had begun in anticipation of a hike in centrally driven house building. There would also be a further range of subsidies – including concessionary rail charges for transport to and from the South Island, and more encouragement to industrial development outside the main centres.[18]

There was more to come as Labour sought to rush growth for social purposes. Rowling announced that new efforts would be made to promote tourism through the Tourist Hotel Corporation, which had been costing the taxpayer dearly for several generations. State spending on housing and electricity capital works would increase. Fourteen per cent more would be spent on education and 19 per cent extra on health. Most welfare benefits went up. A system whereby pensioners paid only half their telephone accounts began on 1 October 1973. This principle was extended on 1 January 1975 to television licence fees for income-tested beneficiaries. In a major announcement with consequences for the longer term that the minister cannot have imagined, Rowling promised a Social Security Amendment Bill that would add a Domestic Purposes Benefit to the large array of existing welfare benefits. A New Zealand Superannuation Scheme would also soon be the subject of legislation. An indication of the optimistic climate existing at the time came with the announcement that Rowling would continue the personal income tax rebate first introduced by Muldoon the previous (election) year.[19]

Kirk smiled paternally throughout Rowling's long speech. The Prime Minister was clearly delighted with the magnitude of what his Government was doing in its first year. Rowling's first Budget was a giant further step in social engineering, building on measures found useful in wartime. Labour's belief that governments could successfully order the world in which people lived, worked and traded was at high tide. And it came at a time when the world trading scene was just beginning a high dive.

Kirk's plans quickly lost their gloss. Wage pressures were now so high that Cabinet, then the Government caucus, were obliged to act on 9 August 1973. On the recommendation of the Minister of Labour, Hugh Watt, a wage stabilisation order of 8.5 per cent was announced. This figure was to be reduced by any increases negotiated since 1 February. However, there would be a further rise for public servants in October because of a complex 'ruling rates' analysis that gave them periodical top-ups. All pay increases were expected to hold for at least six months. As during the war, they would increase only if the CPI had risen by more than a set amount – in this case 4 per cent. Kirk promptly declared that an increase of 45 per cent in MPs salaries recommended by a Royal Commission would be put on hold,[20] hoping thereby to lower popular expectations of further wage increases. He failed to calm industrial unrest. It raged spectacularly at the Tasman Pulp and Paper plant in Kawerau for some weeks and broke out in other places as well. The combination of a big spending budget, a large wage order and rapidly increasing import costs was pushing inflation along at breakneck speed, and well-positioned unions used their industrial muscle.

There was worse to come. Kirk received a jolt when he attended a Commonwealth Heads of Government meeting in Ottawa in August 1973. Besides establishing close relations with several leaders from Third World nations, he realised from general discussions the full extent to which world trade was slowing down and stock markets faltering, while inflation galloped ahead. Like Savage a generation earlier, he concluded that New Zealand could take further steps to insulate itself. 'The overseas situation must be shut out as much as possible', he told caucus on his return.[21]

Inflation showed no signs of abating. The public became anxious.[22] So Cabinet decided to revalue the New Zealand dollar by 10 per cent on 9 September 1973 to lessen the impact on the economy from imported inflation. At the same time, the export of hogget and mutton was stopped in the hope that more supplies for domestic markets would reduce pressure

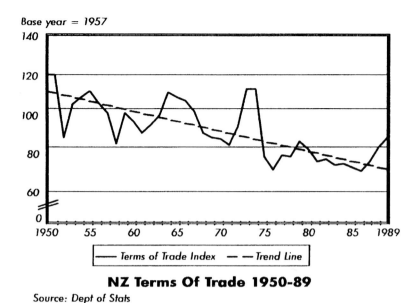

NZ Terms Of Trade 1950-89

Source: Dept of Stats

The downwards trajectory for New Zealand's terms of trade 1950–89. From Graham T. Crocombe, Michael J. Enright and Michael E. Porter, Upgrading New Zealand's Competitive Advantage, *Oxford University Press, 1991.*

on local prices. In case these moves did not succeed in restraining meat prices, a complex system of 'reference prices' for export meat was imposed from 1 November; overseas receipts above the reference price level would be diverted into a stabilisation fund to be used to ensure that meat prices were kept at an acceptable domestic level. Some fish destined for export was diverted to the domestic market and meatmeal and tallow exports were controlled to ensure that domestic prices did not force up consumer items such as eggs, poultry, pigmeats, cooking margarine and soap. Again there was talk about a system of Maximum Retail Prices (MRP). Since there was still adequate overseas exchange, some extra import licences were issued for consumer goods, including cars. Housing shortages would be tackled more enthusiastically with a mixture of state and private house building; those experiencing escalating private sector rents were urged to make more use of rent appeal authorities.[23] It was a set of measures on a similar scale to the announcements by Fraser's Government in December 1942. However, there were no quick solutions for rising oil prices. They shot up after the Yom Kippur war in October 1973. Arab producers decided to use oil supplies as a diplomatic weapon against Western countries that had, for the most part, supported Israel. Kirk urged New Zealanders to make more use of public transport.

The most difficult measure to implement was the price justification scheme being worked on by Warren Freer, the Minister of Trade and Industry (as the old Industries and Commerce portfolio was now called). With the cooperation of the Price Tribunal, Freer had been seeking to produce a system of public notification of 'fair and reasonable prices' since March 1973.[24] What he hoped would take a few weeks to devise took another sixteen months. Complex discussions with officials, the Price Tribunal and manufacturers' representatives centred on methods for determining 'maximum distributive margins' for use in calculating the final Maximum Retail Price.[25] There were lengthy debates in Cabinet and caucus before MRP finally went into force on 1 July 1974. The process had taken so long to implement that many manufacturers had had to calculate, then recalculate, their costings for the figure to be placed on the indelible MRP shield printed on all regulated merchandise. Confusion surrounded the scheme from the start; many officials doubted whether it could ever be made to work. The Campaign Against Rising Prices, whose support Freer had anticipated, attacked it and sections of the union movement were becoming very unhappy with continuing high inflation, believing the answer lay in better wages, which they could win through direct action. The National Opposition ridiculed MRP and some manufacturers, as they always had, made money out of this latest effort at price control. The Government attempted to recalculate fair levels of pre-tax profit in the Stabilisation of Prices Regulations 1974, Amendment No. 2, promulgated in June 1975,[26] but the cumbersome MRP scheme lingered and the Government looked inept.

Meantime ministers had been debating a growth strategy aimed at lifting the country's performance above the average level of achievement since the war. Treasury argued for fewer controls in the belief that deregulation was more likely to produce the right environment for better growth; Trade and Industry, now led by the headstrong Jack Lewin, was adamant that with targets and planning better results were certain to emerge. Each department advanced its own viewpoint fiercely and eventually the Cabinet Policy and Priority Committee told them to reconcile their differences. On 8 May 1974 ministers expressed a general preference for assistance to the manufacturing sector but were vague on the specifics as to how this assistance should be extended. The minute of the meeting is wordy and ministers seemed genuinely baffled by the conflicting advice they were receiving.[27]

Labour's unsuccessful efforts to control prices were partly overtaken by a substantial piece of legislation introduced in August 1975. The Commerce Bill's long title gives a clue to its all-embracing intentions. It was to 'assist in the orderly development of industry and commerce and to promote its efficiency, and the welfare of consumers, through the regulation, where desirable in the public interest, of trade practices, of monopolies, mergers, and takeovers, and of the price of goods and services'. Freer saw it as a vital part of the Government's growth strategy. It would help to ensure fair competition in the marketplace and produce better outcomes for consumers. A Commerce Commission replaced the Price Tribunal. The commission had both inquiry and judicial functions, especially where mergers or takeovers were proposed. The National Opposition opposed the Bill vigorously, especially its wide regulatory powers. National argued that the legislation gave too many powers to the Department of Trade and Industry and was a 'bureaucratic nightmare'.[28] Nevertheless, the Bill passed on 8 October 1975. It provided the regulatory framework for commercial activity in the following years and sustained only a few amendments, most notably those in 1976 and 1983.

What really undermined Labour's efforts at price control was the fact that government spending continued at a high level. The financial situation in 1973 allowed for such expenditure but when ongoing costs had to be factored into the budget of 30 May 1974, the climate was much less congenial. After a long summer drought and sliding export prices, especially for meat, revenue projections looked much less rosy. Rowling found himself saddled with a ballooning liability for subsidies which were being pumped up by inflation. And there were costs associated with the newly established government-owned New Zealand Shipping Corporation that Kirk had been urging since the mid-1960s in the hope that it would revitalise coastal shipping. After several delays, Cabinet finally approved the project on 2 July 1973. The Shipping Corporation proved to be a white elephant, losing nearly $5 million in the year to 31 August 1979 and more than $7 million the following year.[29] There were costs, too, with the New Zealand Export-Import Corporation, which was a new government body aimed at boosting the country's trade. It was the same with the newly created Rural Banking and Finance Corporation that was separated out from the old State Advances Corporation, now named the Housing Corporation. Increased benefit payments, new training, export and production incentives, and further money for regional development, culture and recreation, housing, education and health pushed expenditure up by 19 per cent for 1974–75. A huge extra weight was being added to the ship of state at a time when the economic tide was ebbing rapidly. Optimistic growth strategies and expensive social programmes meant that Labour was using up its good will at an alarming rate. The bumper year of 1972–73 was now a distant memory.

The Accident Compensation Commission, which opened its doors on 1 April 1974, was one of the new, and ultimately costly, schemes. It had its genesis in Justice Woodhouse's 1967 Royal Commission report on compensation for personal injury. Further studies resulted in 'landmark' legislation by Marshall's Government.[30] Previous employers' liability arrangements dated back to British law in the 1840s which had been brought up to date in the New Zealand Employers' Liability Act 1882 and refined in a number of Workers' Compensation Acts between 1908 and 1956. Woodhouse expressed the opinion that 'just as modern society benefits from the productive work of its citizens, so should society accept responsibility for those willing to work but prevented from doing so by physical incapacity'.[31] The new scheme was funded by levies on employers, the self-employed and motorists and paid according to a 'no fault' principle. It paid full medical costs and 80 per cent of an accident victim's lost earning capacity up to a set sum, until the age of 65. There were several lump sum benefits as well. Kirk's Government added to the cost of the scheme by extending coverage to non-earning victims of accidents, with the extra burden carried by the Consolidated Fund.[32]

The Commission became a Corporation in 1981. Neither was free from controversy. Problems of defining accidents, the scope of medical reimbursements and constant claims of malingering clouded Woodhouse's vision of a fairer society. The very existence of such a comprehensive system for accident victims threw into stark relief the less generous benefits available to victims of illness or physical deterioration. An industry developed where large numbers of patients with the connivance of their doctors chose to define illnesses as accidents, thus pushing up ACC costs and the money required to fund the system. For some employers, ACC levies became substantial burdens, while many ordinary people who were ill were left grumbling about the inequities of life. Seated in the middle of a haphazardly constructed welfare state, ACC had its benefits trimmed by successive governments that lacked both the money and the willingness to eliminate anomalies or to pay for the abuses to which ACC was being subjected. While a great many people have benefited from its services, ACC has been costly both for taxpayers and employers. Consumers have carried the costs of ACC in the prices they pay for goods and services and the imposition has been greatest on those with the lowest incomes.

The Third Labour Government also inherited the Royal Commission on Social Security which had been set up under Justice Thaddeus McCarthy in September 1969 in response to a request from the National Development Conference for an 'independent and penetrating examination' of social security. Like McCarthy's other inquiries, his report on Social Security in March 1972 gave a full summary of developments to date, questioned few fundamentals, made recommendations that carried a huge price tag and could scarcely be described as a 'penetrating' inquiry. 'We have not been persuaded that our social security system should be radically changed at this time', said the report.[33] Some increases, such as a doubling of the Family Benefit to $3 per child, per week, had been incorporated into Muldoon's 1972 budget, while the General Medical Services Benefit,which increased in 1969 for some categories of patients, was further increased for all categories in 1972 and then again in December 1974. Other recommendations of the McCarthy Royal Commission such as the Domestic Purposes Benefit were left to Labour to implement. Meantime, rapid inflation was calling into question the adequacy of some of the increases made as recently as 1972. The Government's commitment to welfare was rising steeply at a time when New Zealand's economic capacity to carry extra burdens was being seriously challenged. The warnings of the Gibbs taxation committee of 1951 look prophetic in retrospect.

There was a prescient quality to Norman Kirk's illness which followed an operation for varicose veins on 10 April 1974. The ups and downs in his health over the next few months both reflected and affected the declining state of the economy and sagging public confidence in his government. Kirk's death in the Wellington Home of Compassion on 31 August removed from New Zealand life at one blow Labour's last credible enthusiast for big government. In retrospect it seems that the tears in the days that followed were for more than the passing of an unusually talented man. An era was ebbing away.[34]

There was a flicker of hope that Rowling, who took over as Prime Minister on 6 September 1974, might be able to rescue both the economy and the Labour Government. The new Prime Minister differed fundamentally in style from his predecessor. 'I wouldn't pretend for a moment to be a Norman Kirk' were his first words as Prime Minister. Smaller and softly spoken, he liked the description – 'a decent sort of chap' – that the media bestowed upon him. 'Throw me into a crowd and I'd disappear. . . . I'm not an effervescent person, I'm not belligerent, I'm not a great orator. I like reasoned and quiet judgements, and I suppose I'm not spectacular', he told a journalist early in 1975.[35] Some Labour MPs began talking privately a few weeks after Kirk's death about holding an early election, in order to seek a fresh start. Rowling demurred. Time, however, was not on Labour's side. The collapse in economic growth around the world that caused commodity prices to sag in 1974, coupled with rising oil prices, gave no ground for optimism. Once more it looked as though Labour's leaders were being forced to switch from playing Santa Claus to Scrooge. Meantime, the unceremonious dumping of Jack Marshall from the leadership of the National Party by Robert Muldoon in July 1974 gave inspiration to the Opposition and heightened tensions within Parliament.[36]

By the end of 1974 public opinion polls were running against the Rowling Government. Bob Tizard, the new Minister of Finance, was every bit as much a Keynesian as Kirk and Rowling. But he was forced to concede that while full employment remained Labour's top priority, the deteriorating balance of payments would reduce growth rates and make new spending difficult. On 24 September 1974 Tizard devalued the New Zealand dollar by 6.2 per cent. He told a meeting on Auckland's North Shore a few weeks later that the Government hoped to 'ward off recession and unemployment'.[37] But the turnaround in New Zealand's current account had swung from a surplus of $250 million to a deficit approaching $600 million. He expected real growth to be less than 1 per cent in the year to June 1975.[38] Even this dismal assessment of the severity of the economic turnaround was too sanguine; in April 1975 Tizard conceded that the prospects of a quick recovery in the world economy looked even bleaker.[39] In the year to June 1975 there was a balance of payments deficit of $1.43 billion.[40] The Government had borrowed nearly $1 billion abroad by the middle of 1975.

Tizard's problem was that Labour's increased spending had been predicated on a better revenue flow and lower inflation. By budget day on 22 May 1975 subsidies alone were costing $162 million and topped $182 million in the year to March 1976. They had been the subject of intense debate within Cabinet and the Labour caucus. Against the better judgement of many senior ministers, MPs decided that the 1972 promise to stabilise those costs over which Government exercised control should be honoured. However, with milk held at 4 cents a pint in the belief that it would help low income families, farmers were now receiving the equivalent of 6.36 cents per pint when they sold their milk. Those who bought milk back at the subsidised rate to feed to pigs, calves and lambs were able to enjoy a considerable financial advantage. The milk subsidy had become one of the dearest and least effectively targeted forms of family assistance in the chequered history of the welfare state.[41]

The Government's willingness to let public service numbers rise, as a means of mopping up growing unemployment, helped drive Tizard's budgeted increase in expenditure to 28 per cent. This came on top of Rowling's 26 per cent actual increase the previous year.[42] Yet the Labour Government felt there was still room for new spending. A standard tertiary bursary and additional house lending found their way into the 1975 budget. On top of a general wage increase that was included in the budget, these threatened to strain it severely. In a complex juggling act Tizard reduced tax rates for many on lower incomes, while returning the top marginal rate to 60 per cent and boosting sales taxes on several consumer items. The price of petroleum products rose once more as vaulting world prices bore in upon a small economy which, like so many others, had geared itself to oil consumption.

Tizard estimated his budget deficit would be about $500 million. By December 1975 inflation had reached 15.7 per cent. Coupled with the effects of a further 15 per cent devaluation on 14 August 1975, the actual deficit for the year reached more than $1.1 billion.[43] At the time of his budget, however, Tizard believed that the worst was over and that a policy which he admitted was one of 'both risk and sacrifice in the pursuit of social and economic justice' was a worthy goal.[44] He was voicing the thoughts of his caucus and many within the wider public; there was nothing in New Zealand's recent past to prepare them for another generation of low world commodity prices.

The economic turnaround between 1973 and 1975 was so sudden, and so drastic, that it provided an unparalleled opportunity for a political opportunist. Muldoon attracted a personal following which he called 'Rob's Mob'. It was a collection of the disaffected, numbering among them pensioners terrified by inflation and nostalgic for better times, anti-abortion crusaders caught up by a morals issue of the moment and many from the rural sector that was now suffering acutely from stagflation. The National Party's election spending in 1975 was the largest in its history to date.[45] The campaign was unparalleled for its ferocity; claims and counter claims, character assassinations and carefully planted insinuations wafted through the press and danced across television screens.[46] Rowling's Government paid a price for its profligacy and went down to heavy defeat on 29 November 1975. Muldoon's mix of nostalgia, extravagance and belligerence comforted voters in their state of unease. Labour's parliamentary majority of 23 turned into the same margin for National.

*

Rowling's Cabinet had not been strong; nor was the new Muldoon Ministry which took office on 12 December 1975. While his deputy, Brian Talboys, J. B. ('Peter') Gordon, Duncan McIntyre, George Gair, Les Gandar and Hugh Templeton all had experience, there was a long tail to it. When the new Prime Minister, like Sid Holland before him, appointed himself Minister of Finance, he became New Zealand's economic supremo. As Templeton later revealed, standing up to Muldoon in Cabinet was not easy during his eight and a half years at the helm. Derek Quigley, one who did, was summarily fired in 1982.[47] Most senior ministers, including Muldoon's deputies in the Finance portfolios, were often not shown key Treasury briefing papers. The Prime Minister's Department, which had been planned during Rowling's time, became a separate entity from Foreign Affairs. It was headed by a senior Treasury official, Bernard Galvin, between 1975 and 1980. The office grew in power. Little of significance was announced by any minister without its sanction.[48]

The stark reality, however, was that neither party in 1975 had any remedy for the economic setback which the Institute of Economic Research called 'the deepest and most prolonged post-war recession amongst the industrial capitalist countries'.[49] In Great Britain, the United States and Australia, similar policies of managing economic demand and selective stimulation were faltering. Yet no other policies looked palatable to the welfare generation. The basic problem was that big spending in a small economy like New Zealand's at a time of rampant inflation only increased demand for scarce foreign exchange and necessitated further borrowing both overseas and domestically and/or further devaluation. Retrenchment, on the other hand, would rapidly increase unemployment, which was rising steadily in New Zealand in any event, reaching 14,000 by census day in April 1976.[50] Muldoon ridiculed Labour's policy cake as 'borrow and hope' but cooked from the same recipe book. The inherited political wisdom of 40 years still prevailed and as yet there were no signs of rethinking within either party's caucus.

On the day he took office Muldoon released some briefings he had received on the state of the economy. They were gloomy. He told reporters that 'a small cut in the standard of living is necessary, but it need not be very painful for the average citizen. There is not about to be a great depression, but a few things have to be tidied up.'[51] These words summarised Muldoon's overall approach to economic management. He would constantly use the words 'fine tuning'. Despite his penchant for sweeping statements and a reputation for ruthlessness, he moved cautiously, adjusting this and tinkering with that in a manner that some businessmen found

Prime Minister Robert Muldoon and B. V. Galvin, Permanent Head, Prime Minister's Department, 1978.
Evening Post

disconcerting. When it seemed not to be working he would divert public attention from his economic management. Nuclear ship visits, Pacific Island 'overstayers', a Maori land occupation at Bastion Point in Auckland and sporting contacts with South Africa leading up to a Springbok rugby tour of New Zealand in 1981 in the run-up to his third general election, provided continuing sideshows from which the Prime Minister was a master at extracting the maximum political capital.[52]

For the first two years Muldoon accepted some advice from his Treasury officers. Within ten days of taking office the new ministry pruned immigration numbers, cut many subsidies and allowed rail, electricity and postal charges to rise. The price of milk doubled to 8 cents, although a subsidy of 3 cents a pint remained. Bread rose 1 cent for a standard loaf on 12 January 1976. Applications for new house loans were temporarily suspended in order to take some heat out of the building sector.[53] The Federation of Labour was told that the expected wage increase in January 1976 would be lower than expected. The press noted a mood of 'dour realism' settling over ministerial offices. Meetings of Cabinet and its committees often ran into the evening.[54] The incoming ministry told officials that it wanted to see resources shift back to the private sector.

The Government targeted the public service for restraint, since more than 20 per cent of New Zealand's total labour force was now directly on the State's payroll, considerably above the historical average of the last decade of 18.8 per cent. What some called a public service culture in Wellington had reigned largely unchallenged for years. A journalist working in the city at the time recalls the scene:

> anything approaching the definition of real work was regarded, particularly in government departments, as a form of perversion; turning up for an eight-hour day . . . was all that was required; the *Dominion* crossword would see an army of grey-cardiganed clerks through nicely until morning tea time, and the first edition of the *Evening Post*, to help while away the afternoon, was on the streets at 1 pm; the Public Service Association ruled the city. . . .[55]

National ministers were not so daring as to challenge this head on but they did cap public service numbers. On 8 March 1976 Cabinet applied a staff ceiling to all departments except Education and Health. The universities were also exempted. Several major construction projects were also placed on hold. However, no guidelines were issued to explain the principles behind the restraints and a strong suspicion developed that decisions were being made on the basis of whether the outcomes were likely to injure the National Party's electoral coalition. On 8 April 1976 the Cabinet Committee on Expenditure decided not to remove the remaining milk subsidy. Even in his bold first few months, caution was Muldoon's watchword.[56]

Some of the Government's supporters in the wider community thought a level of unemployment would provide 'the necessary incentive for the average person to become more interested in his job', but ministers were not prepared to go so far.[57] While saluting the traditional goal of full employment,[58] Muldoon's Government did risk removing parts of the insulation in which the economy had been so tightly wrapped for many years. In a major statement on 2 March 1976 the Cabinet revoked the Interest on Deposit Regulations in the hope that flexible interest rates would enable trading banks to compete more easily for funds and play a bigger role in house lending. Controls on overdraft rates would also be removed.[59]

Yet, having removed one layer of protection, Muldoon became uneasy about shifting others. He seemed happier using import and price controls than any National predecessor and in March 1979 both he and Lance Adams-Schneider, his Minister of Trade and Industry, strongly defended import controls against their critics. Like Holland in 1951, Muldoon also argued for price controls, telling the Council of Building Industries in March 1976 that they were an essential accompaniment to wage restraint: 'It would be inequitable to single out a particular industry or group for

Evans summarises the mad rush on budget day in anticipation of higher prices, July 1976.
NZ Herald

exemption from either set of controls'. Not all agreed. Professor Allan Catt of Waikato University supported him; but the *New Zealand Financial Times* called price controls 'one of New Zealand's more disastrous social and bureaucratic experiments', arguing that they fostered inefficient industries by applying cost-plus and were really a political device for 'redistributing income from the efficient firm to the consumer by way of manipulation of prices'.[60]

Muldoon was cautious with subsidies. Having railed against them in Opposition, he slashed them on taking office, then let them mount again until after the 1978 election by which time they were costing $120 million p.a. In 1979 Muldoon trimmed subsidies a little, only to see them rise to $158 million in 1980. As with Labour, price controls were part of his armoury to keep prices, and hence wages, in check at a time when the Government continued to spend freely. When people questioned their worth, Muldoon would agree with them. Subsidies, he told one correspondent, 'conceal the real costs of items involved and can therefore result in a misallocation of resources within the economy. It is important that prices should reflect the real costs of production.'[61] Having said this, Muldoon never found an appropriate time to get rid of them all.

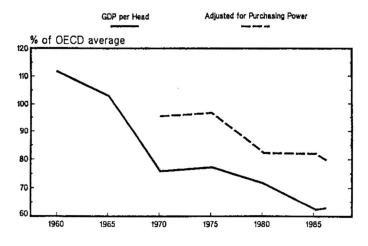

New Zealand's Income Per Head Relative to the OECD Average
1960 – 1986

GDP per Head   Adjusted for Purchasing Power

Source: OECD National Accounts 1960–1985 vol.1

PRODUCTIVITY GROWTH
business sector: average % change at annual rates

Total Factor Productivity	average	New Zealand	US	Japan	Germany	Australia
1960s to 1973*	2.8	0.6	1.5	6.1	2.8	2.1
1973-79	0.7	-2.5	-0.1	1.8	1.8	0.6
1979-86	0.6	0.6	0.0	1.7	0.8	0.5

Source: OECD Economic Studies, No.10, Spring 1988
*Note: Starting year: New Zealand 1963, U.S. 1960, Japan 1967, Germany 1961, Australia 1961

These graphs and figures speak for themselves. From the New Zealand Planning Council report, The Economy in Transition to 1989, *Wellington, 1989.*

Not content with the existing battery of controls, Muldoon armed himself with new weapons. In the Economic Stabilisation (Cost of Living) Regulations 1980 the Arbitration Court was asked to take changes in the rates of personal taxation into its calculations before deciding on wage increases. In 1981 Treasury officials were also put to work on a complex investigation into taxation and the extent to which any cuts could be factored into the CPI. Officials advised against tampering with the basic structure of the index. Muldoon eventually desisted.[62]

Like Kirk, Muldoon admired what he labelled New Zealand's 'egalitarian tradition'. He declared he would use his powers to ensure 'equal opportunity for all New Zealanders'. He intended to see that the burden of adjusting to a lower standard of living would be shared equitably, 'with those on the lowest incomes suffering the least hardship'.[63] Muldoon claimed that his various controls were to help 'the ordinary bloke'. His solicitude never sat easily with the National Party establishment. As debate grew in financial and business circles, with more and more people questioning whether his controls could work or whether they simply retarded growth and efficiency, unease turned to criticism. Some younger National MPs were questioning whether the public any longer received value for money from increased government expenditure.[64] There were still a few, however, who seemed enthusiastic about government intervention in the economy and liked plans, rules and regulations as much as the Labour MPs they had defeated in 1975.[65]

Eventually Muldoon tired of Treasury criticisms of controls and regulations. Such advice conflicted with his own inclination to manage the economy. Above all he admired Lee Kuan Yew of Singapore, who presided over a highly centralised State. When the cutbacks of 1976 overshot the mark, exacerbated the recession in 1977 and produced a fall in the growth rate of -1.8 per cent for the year, the Prime Minister decided to become more interventionist.[66] His budgets reverted to the pattern of a decade earlier and were peppered with livestock incentive suspensory loans, new fertiliser subsidies, noxious plant control subsidies, livestock TB detection programmes, lucerne establishment grants, tax rebates on pesticides used by pipfruit growers, investment incentives for industrial machinery, regional investment allowances, new export incentives, government guarantees for loans raised for new tourist accommodation, forestry encouragement loans, fishing industry subsidies and rebates, grants to encourage the use of natural gas and a great many other forms of targeted assistance.[67] Like the Third Labour Government that he regularly criticised, the Third National Government was equally convinced that New Zealand's growth rate could be stimulated by selective interventions. In April 1976, at the urging of Talboys, who was Minister of National Development, the old planning structure was rejigged. Sir Frank Holmes was appointed to head a task force on the future of economic and social planning. A Planning Council and a Commission for the Future, which had been promised in National's manifesto, were subsequently established. Treasury officials were sceptical about the usefulness of these bodies but ministers were hoping to widen their sources of advice. However, they liked little of what they received from the Planning Council.[68]

There is little evidence that Muldoon's interventionism had beneficial results in counteracting adverse movements in overseas prices. Export receipts gave only a flicker of recovery in 1977 and declined later in the year. In his budget on 21 July 1977 Muldoon estimated that New Zealand's terms of trade had slipped by between 35 per cent and 40 per cent since 1973. Inflation, which reached nearly 18 per cent in the middle of 1976, fell back to 12 per cent a year later. It then rose again, pushed along by a steady increase in government spending, which rose 10.2 per cent in real terms between 1975 and 1978.[69] Industrial unrest became more intense. There were several threats of union deregistration and lengthy troubles at Ocean Beach freezing works in Southland. Muldoon experimented for some months with a price freeze. Some idealists hoped that worker participation in management might improve employee morale. Early in 1978 Deputy Prime Minister Brian Talboys made an impassioned plea for workers and employers to change their attitudes to work, and to accept that more effort was required.[70] Words had little effect.

Studies of individual industries that had begun with ceramics in 1975 continued. The Government sought to align those who were prepared to cooperate with the Department of Trade and Industry's advisors to the modern trading environment. According to Muldoon, the goal was to encourage resources 'to move into industries which are, or have a good prospect of becoming, internationally competitive'.[71] Like a generation of ministers before him, Muldoon hoped to pick winners. However, none of his panaceas could be more than a Bandaid to an economy in such deep trouble. While weekly earnings rose nearly 16 per cent in the year to October 1978, the total number of private sector jobs contracted. Public sector job creation programmes tried to take up the slack. But there was a net outflow of people from the country of more than 63,000, many of them skilled people, between 1976 and 1979.

In spite of Muldoon's efforts, unemployment continued to increase. It reached 50,000 in August 1978.[72] There was renewed talk of the need for an 'active labour market' where the Government accepted responsibility for retraining and transferring workers from an area of redundancies to another with growth prospects. By now economic growth was virtually static and budget deficits increased each year. As an economic stimulant, Keynesian tax and spend was dead but neither political party seemed willing

After attacking Labour's 'borrow and hope', Muldoon followed the same policy.
Auckland Star

to acknowledge it. In a depressing prediction in August 1977, the OECD warned that on a moderate growth prediction New Zealand was likely to be obliged to borrow $9.5 billion before 1985 if it was to keep travelling the same course.[73]

While the National Government had pruned expenditure in 1976, the introduction of National Superannuation added a huge extra burden to the Consolidated Fund. Labour's New Zealand Superannuation, which had begun on 1 April 1975, was a contributory scheme. By the time of the election $79 million had been invested in it. Without changing the law, Muldoon informed employers on 15 December 1975 that they could cease collecting the levies for Labour's funded scheme; their actions would be validated legislatively at a later date.[74] The Prime Minister now introduced an unfunded system called National Superannuation to be paid for from existing taxation. From 9 February 1977 the new scheme paid 70 per cent of the average ordinary-time weekly wage for a married couple over 60 years of age, rising to 80 per cent from 30 August 1978. The single rate was 60 per cent of the married rate. Payments were adjusted every six months in line with surveys carried out by the Department of Labour. The payments were subject to a ten-year residence test. There was no means test unless a spouse for whom the benefit was claimed was under 60. However, 'National Super' payments were taxable.

Undoubtedly the most generous benefit ever to have been introduced in New Zealand's history, National Superannuation quickly doubled in dollar terms the annual cost of the former old-age pension and super-annuation combined.[75] Muldoon insisted that no increase in taxation would be necessary, an assurance that led some to label it 'Piggy Super'. But such assurances were posited on the assumption that economic growth would move along at an average rate of 3 per cent per annum, which showed no signs of becoming a reality. As a result, 'National Super' contributed to the ballooning deficit which Muldoon financed by borrowing, thus saddling future generations with the responsibility of paying a generous pension to the current legions of elderly.[76] During the twenty years the scheme has been in operation it has remained the most costly, and hence the most controversial, welfare benefit. Less expensive, but steadily increasing in cost, was Labour's Domestic Purposes Benefit. It was claimed by 17,231 people in 1975, by nearly 50,000 in 1983, and by 108,709 people in 1996.[77] With more than 50,000 unemployment benefits being paid by 1983,[78] the escalating expenses attached to New Zealand's welfare system were precisely what the 1951 Gibbs Committee had warned against.[79]

Governments which hold out false hopes quickly lose popularity. Muldoon only narrowly held on to power at the election on 25 November 1978. The National Party received fewer votes across the country than Labour but managed to keep a parliamentary majority. As the economy fluctuated in 1977–78 and inflation rose again, it became cystal clear that Muldoon had no magic wand. In 1979 he faced another crisis, this one partly of his own making. Having allowed government expenditure to rise by nearly 21 per cent in election year, he was now staring at a deficit of more than $2.3 billion unless there were economies. 'Our plight', wrote the editor of the *New Zealand Herald* early in January 1979, 'is one of sustained excessive pressures on overseas funds, internal inflation which remains too high, a huge budget deficit, and unemployment which would be worse if tens of thousands had not fled to greener fields. . . . Some sort of correction seems virtually inevitable before much longer.'[80]

As Muldoon floundered, advice poured in from many quarters. Several Auckland business leaders made a plea for more flexibility; the taxation specialist, L. N. Ross, declared that New Zealand had become 'a soft and flabby society, lulled into a false sense of wellbeing by a social welfare system that yet may prove too costly to maintain'. He added that in his opinion people had become too dependent on the Government and on bureaucratic direction and protection 'to the detriment of personal initiative, enterprise and work'.[81] The Auckland Harbour Board blamed its lack of profitability on overmanning, high waterfront levies and the central wage-fixing policies of the Waterfront Industry Commission. Some farming leaders talked of the need for restructuring to encourage 'efficient export industries', something that Ian McLean, one of Muldoon's new MPs, supported in a well-written booklet that he had produced for the Planning Council.[82] The Chairman of Progressive Enterprises Ltd, Brian Picot, sought a change in New Zealanders' attitudes and thought the Government needed to become the principal educator. Len Bayliss, chief economist at the Bank of New Zealand, who had previously served in the Prime Minister's Department, argued for an end to Muldoon's 'usual array of ad hoc policies'. Bayliss argued that subsidies, incentives, new committees and advisory boards were no more than short-term reactions to pressure group demands.[83]

Interest groups that had welcomed big government more than a generation before were losing their faith. The Grocery Manufacturers Association had gone along with price controls in earlier years. At its annual conference in October 1978 the association discussed a world without controls and regulations and grilled Harry Clark, Secretary of Trade and Industry, when he addressed members. Clark found the Auckland Manufacturers decidedly apprehensive when he met them early in April 1979. On the one hand they accepted that there needed to be some restructuring; on the other hand they could not work out how to jettison the whole protective apparatus. Clark later told Talboys that manufacturers

Cartoonist Bromhead comments on Muldoon's credit squeezes, 1979. Auckland Star

seemed constantly to be looking for 'scapegoats' which they believed were contributing to their sector's poor export performance.[84] Meantime the New Zealand Chambers of Commerce, which had never been enthusiastic about big government, although they had, for a time, held high hopes of centralised planning, published and circulated a paper by Sven Rydenfelt of Sweden. It pointed out that the Swedish economy and welfare system, which New Zealand advocates of big government often quoted as models for reform, were nearing collapse.[85] Interest groups seemed ready to change, but in what direction?

Dr Donald Brash had some ideas. He was general manager of Broadbank Corporation and convenor of the Planning Council's Economic Monitoring Group that had taken over from the Monetary and Economic Council. He told an audience in February 1979 that he hoped the Prime Minister would grasp the challenge of the hour and tell the nation the cause of its difficulties. He described these as 'a combination of external factors and policies followed by governments of both political parties over many years'. What was needed, he said, was 'a package of measures' to rectify the situation. He suggested devaluation accompanied by the phasing out of all export incentives. Import controls as a major means of protecting New Zealand's industry should be abolished, along with price controls and barriers to foreign investment. Brash suggested a progressive switch to indirect taxation and a 'vigorous attempt' to cut government spending, including some trimming of National Superannuation.

Brash's advice angered some, was debated by others and ultimately bore a similarity to decisions that were taken after the election of July 1984. He represented a growing number of reformers who seemed prepared to think the unthinkable – a world with fewer controls. The President of the Chambers of Commerce, J. R. Greenfield, backed him with a call for people with the political 'courage, determination and skill' to lead New Zealanders through the process of change. Talk was reviving in business circles about the desirability of a four-year parliamentary term that would give politicians more room to manoeuvre.[86]

However, the political willpower to embark on substantial change was missing. Both major parties were led by traditionalists. In 1978 several young free-marketeers augmented those already in the National caucus. More were to follow in 1981.[87] But Muldoon's paternalistic style of economy still held majority support, although the margin was becoming fine. As Hugh Templeton describes it, the Prime Minister's 'old comrades in arms were fading by his side'. In October 1980 a group of younger National MPs tried to topple Muldoon from the prime-ministership after

Leader of the Opposition, W. E. Rowling, visiting New Zealand Steel's construction site, 1977. NZH

he failed to give whole-hearted support to Brash, who was National's candidate in the East Coast Bays by-election in September 1980. A determined Muldoon soon humbled the 'colonels', as they were labelled. His eventual success was more a tribute to his guile than to any strong belief in his policies.[88]

Neither was the Labour caucus happy with its economic direction. The late 1970s was a defining era for left wing parties in many countries, especially in Australia and New Zealand, where they were out of power and regrouping their forces.[89] Rowling straddled the New Zealand Labour caucus uneasily between 1975 and 1978. A team of new, younger MPs elected in 1978 supported him for a time,[90] but their opinions became more diverse. Some were uneasy about increasing centralisation and endless economic tinkering. Others were social engineers and keen to involve central government in a variety of causes, especially those relating to women's affairs. The strength of this latter group was augmented in 1981 and they were to argue vociferously for equal pay, access to abortion, advancement for nurses, midwives, social workers and teachers, the use of schools for peace studies and a downgrading of those things believed to advantage boys. These issues, involving as they did a high degree of central direction, interested them more than the state of the economy. A division was opening within the Labour caucus between those who wanted to promote state intervention on the grounds that they knew best and those who felt that big government had passed its 'sell-by date' and that it was imperative to get the economy right before there would be any new money to spend on social agendas.

Among the latter group, Rowling set teeth on edge when he dismissed Brash's arguments for freeing up the economy in February 1979. 'The experts should stop making sweeping statements about the need for change and sacrifice. This only scares people and makes them reject the advice,' he told a leadership course at Lincoln College. Rowling's homily sounded rather like Muldoon's instruction to his officials not to bring him advice that might threaten his Government's hold on office.[91] Rowling's solution to New Zealand's problems was more manpower planning which accepted full employment as a goal and an active state sector in housing and community care. New Zealanders should acknowledge that 'the quality of life is not measured in terms of dollars and efficiency alone,' he added.[92] To those in the Labour caucus who shared the party's traditional ambition to assist people, but who wanted new ways of doing it, Rowling and his senior spokespeople seemed to be stuck in a well-worn groove that was taking neither the country, nor the party, anywhere.

On 1 November 1979 Bob Tizard was replaced as Deputy Leader of

The 'Fish and Chips Brigade' after trying to topple Rowling from the leadership of the Labour Party, 12 December 1980: from left, David Lange, Michael Bassett, Roger Douglas, Mike Moore. NZH

the Labour Party by David Lange.[93] However, Tizard's continuing influence over economic policy led the MP for Manurewa, Roger Douglas, who was the only one of the younger Labour MPs with ministerial experience, to produce an 'alternative budget' to Muldoon's in 1980. He followed it up in November with a booklet *There's Got to be a Better Way! A Practical ABC to Solving New Zealand's Major Problems.*[94] For some years now Douglas had been an advocate for tax reform and had successfully made it Labour's issue at the 1978 election. He was involved in the business world, having taken over his family's drug company, and was in the process of turning it into a significant exporter to Australia. Douglas thought Labour's official commitment to further tinkering with a high spending economy was an expensive waste of time. He argued for a fundamental rethink. In the middle of 1980 he resigned as Labour's spokesman for Trade and Industry so as to preserve his freedom to produce further policy initiatives. As he roamed the caucus propounding new ideas, the numbers of disaffected Labour MPs grew. In December 1980 pressure was applied to Rowling to step aside. But he retained his leadership in a caucus confidence motion by one vote – his own.[95] Since it was now clear that central direction of New Zealand's economy was not producing the intended results, its defenders were everywhere under attack. However, the old world, like King Charles II, was an unconscionable time a-dying.

Chapter 12

Big Government's Last Hurrah, 1979–84

Treasury's post-election economic report was delivered to Muldoon in December 1978. It struck a cautionary note.[1] He withdrew from public view for a time, seemingly shocked by the size of the swing against his Government and the limitations which the economy continued to impose upon him. He restructured his Cabinet with more confident, competent, younger ministers. However, the second round of oil price hikes early in 1979 sobered them all. A task force of officials scrutinised departmental spending in the hope that savings could be made.[2] Hugh Templeton, who was Associate Minister of Finance at the time, notes that far from heeding those who were now openly arguing for a more market economy, Muldoon began spinning endless further interventions through his mind.[3]

Muldoon became what Gary Hawke calls 'an inveterate meddler, an overconfident, self-proclaimed economic manager with a demagogic streak. He was clever, but undisciplined; he thought of the balance of payments today, the fiscal deficit tomorrow, but never seemed capable of balancing all the relevant factors at the same time. He had the misfortune to be in office at a time when this mattered.'[4] Muldoon applied tighter credit restrictions in March 1979 and there were more farm, tourist, export and forest incentives in his budget on 21 June 1979. A very expensive Supplementary Minimum Price scheme for farm produce had been first introduced in the 1978 budget in the hope that SMPs would provide greater stability to farmers' incomes, thus enabling them to plan and invest to increase their production. The SMP scheme was extended in 1979. By 1984–85 it was costing nearly $1.5 billion each year.

Muldoon was now pushing, pulling, squeezing and hammering the economy into what he hoped would become a desirable shape. However, there were usually unintended results from his efforts; the bigger the intervention, the bigger the distortion to the economy. SMPs were paid at rates that were sufficiently far above likely market returns to pass signals to farmers that were unreal. Not only did SMPs pad out the budget deficit but incentives to farmers to adapt to changing market demands were replaced by incentives to produce more of what they always had produced. Moreover, because farmers were paid for their produce no matter what it fetched on the market, the Meat Board noticed that they lost interest in processing and marketing, something which in the past they had always kept under careful scrutiny.[5] By 1984 the board was obliged to take the sheep meat, store it, and accept total responsibility for marketing it – which was becoming increasingly difficult. By the middle of 1984 there was little cool-store capacity left in the country and ultimately some of the meat on which SMPs had been paid was rendered down to fertiliser.

There were similar unintended consequences from the Government's continued willingness to extend credit to the Dairy Board at 1 per cent interest. By March 1980 the overdraft of the board stood at $500 million. Ministers did not like the policy, Treasury was adamantly opposed to it but the time to change never seemed 'opportune'. Instead of having to pay a commercial rate of interest, which at that time would have cost in the region of $60 million pa, the board paid only $5 million interest while the taxpayers paid the other $55 million. Ministers suspected that the board was still receiving interest on some of its subsidised money and there is no doubt that the board could afford to hold on to stock longer than it would have done in normal market conditions. Assistance of this kind brought increasing complaints from Australian producers, who felt that New Zealand's farmers were unduly advantaged in the world's marketplace and that this was outside the spirit of NAFTA. And subsidies of this sort certainly added to Muldoon's budgetary woes.[6]

There was another unintended by-product of SMPs. Since the state payments provided old-style security for production, land prices rose and young farmers found it increasingly difficult to buy farms. Those who did manage to jump the price and interest hurdles (the latter having risen steadily after interest rate controls were lifted in 1976) found themselves carrying high costs. Many farmers struggled to bring marginal land into production in response to homilies from the Government to produce more. Parts of the agricultural industry were entering the world of make-believe. The gap between market realities and everyday farm experience kept widening. Those farmers who followed the Government's advice, borrowed more and invested in developing marginal land became the ones who found adjustment to reality so much more painful in the years after 1984 when controls and regulations were lifted.[7]

Farmers were never united in support of Muldoon's price subsidies. Self-reliance was always close to the surface. Some, like Don Middleton and Brian Chamberlin, who were Auckland provincial presidents of Federated Farmers in the late 1970s, pushed for more investment in agriculture, but like other exporters they were principally concerned about the country's rate of inflation and argued it should be no more than the average of New Zealand's trading partners if there was to be a future for agriculture. Trimming government expenditure and reducing farmers' costs was their way forward.[8] Price subsidies were no long-term answer. Chamberlin believed they masked the declining profitability of farming, were unsustainable over time and risked the ire of the General Agreement on Tariffs and Trade (GATT), to which New Zealand subscribed. When SMPs and subsidies were abolished between 1984 and 1987, many farming leaders welcomed the arrival of a more market-oriented approach to agriculture and the determination of successive governments to conquer inflation.

Meantime, import controls remained part of Muldoon's industrial protective network. However, he accepted advice from the IMF and decided in 1979 to let some of them out to tender. He also claimed to have discovered a more flexible system that would 'deal with those few instances where import licensing protection has allowed manifestly excessive costs to emerge in our raw material, componentry, and capital equipment industries'. Licences for competing imports would be issued where it could be shown that a current beneficiary of a licence was charging excessive prices.[9] Wages were now largely set by the Government and usually announced in the budget after discussions with the Federation of Labour, whose president until 1979, Tom Skinner, kept in close touch with the Prime Minister.[10] An increasingly expensive array of employment promotion schemes was also put in place, including subsidies to employers who were willing to take on extra staff for a period of not less than six months. Predictably, some of the less scrupulous put off existing staff and availed themselves of the cheaper labour. Later analysis showed that the beneficiaries of much industry assistance at the time were not those engaged in in-depth manufacturing; rather were they companies losing their ability to compete with imports, which employed a low skill work force and which were located in Auckland and Wellington. Government assistance was not going to those for whom it had originally been intended.[11]

By the end of the 1970s debate was growing within National's ranks about the desirability of taxation reform. When Brash argued in 1979 for a shift towards sales taxes, he was only advocating something that was National Party policy. Yet implementing it was another matter. Because Muldoon lacked a comprehensive strategy to reform all parts of the tax

Muldoon and National Party colleagues engaged in a tug of war (with the economy?).
Auckland Star

system at once, Hugh Templeton's proposals in 1979 to increase sales taxes on boats, caravans and pottery invited outrage from those who believed they were being singled out. When the Government came under pressure from boat builders, Muldoon decided to exempt young people from the boat tax,[12] then backed off selective sales taxes for a time. In 1982 he suggested another raft of goods, including books, as likely targets. Again an uproar, and again the same result. However, a group of officials from the Department of Statistics and Treasury was soon working with a task force on taxation reform headed by Malcolm McCaw. Picking up the earlier arguments of the Gibbs and Ross committees to the effect that New Zealand placed too much emphasis on taxing income and not enough on taxing spending, they continued to develop a comprehensive sales tax proposal during 1983–84. Their studies were ultimately put to good use when decisions were made in 1984 to proceed with a Goods and Services Tax to come into effect in 1986.[13]

Seasoned political observers were often surprised that Muldoon, who liked to present himself as streetwise, could create such problems for himself. His suggestion of a 'fiscal regulator' in the 1979 budget that would allow the Government to alter personal tax rates from time to time without reference to Parliament, suffered the same fate as his early sorties into sales tax. While the idea of automatically adjusting taxes made economic sense and was promoted by Sir Frank Holmes, the idea had to be dropped because

Rising Unemployment

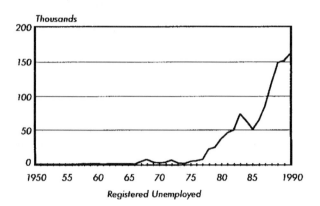

Thousands

Registered Unemployed

Source: Monthly Abstract of Stats 1954-90
(latest = October 1990)

High state spending failed to provide answers; unemployment crept upwards at first, then rose rapidly after 1976. From Crocombe, Enright and Porter, Upgrading New Zealand's Competitive Advantage

of a full frontal assault from constitutional experts and from some within the National caucus. When Muldoon contemplated cutting the Government's subsidy to the Family Planning Association in 1982 and introducing charges for pharmaceuticals, interest groups again scuttled the proposals. Muldoon's Government had become a ministry of advances and retreats. The Prime Minister once described himself as a 'preserver' rather than a 'reformer', which possibly explains the cautious, often self-defeating, aspect to those changes he sought to make under budgetary pressure.[14]

The Third National Government took tentative steps to free New Zealand from some of the social restraints inherited from earlier times. At the end of 1980 the Shop Trading Hours Amendment Act introduced Saturday trading. Jim Bolger, the minister in charge of the Bill, told the House that the Government believed New Zealanders 'now have the maturity to work with less Government direction, and with less guidance by regulation'.[15] A timid Racing Amendment Act gave off-course betting facilities to greyhound-racing enthusiasts as well, but the Government kept control over the number of racing days in the annual calendar, despite urgings from some quarters to give the Racing Authority greater autonomy. Talk of establishing casinos to attract tourists to New Zealand got a frosty reception from Muldoon, as did suggestions from Allan Highet, his Minister of Internal Affairs, who sought the green light to set up Lotto. Muldoon liked to present himself as a friend of the horse-racing industry and painted alternative forms of gambling as unfair competition with racing for the public's discretionary spending. In the process he was defending a historical privilege for one sport, while minimising choices for the wider public.

Liquor legislation had been edging in a more liberal direction since 1960, when the Sale of Liquor Act was amended to allow the consumption of wine in restaurants.[16] Ten o'clock closing in 1967, a reduction in the drinking age to 20 in 1969 and permission in 1980 for eighteen-year-olds to be on licensed premises if accompanied by a 'parent or guardian' were part of a slow but steady relaxation of the laws. However, careful censorship of films was maintained. A classification system handled by the Cinematograph Films Censorship Board was established in 1969 but in 1978 Highet indicated an intention to tighten censorship. In the event this was not what happened; in the Cinematograph Films Amendment Act 1980 Highet concentrated on abolishing the requirement for exhibitors and renters of films to be licensed – something which had protected the two main cinema chains from competition for many years.[17] When the broadcasting system was reformed in 1976, Muldoon insisted that the Government retain control of television and ensured that it was obliged by legislation to 'have regard to government policy'. The Government refused to grant requests for the introduction of FM radio. Had it not been for the *Listener*'s growing propensity to criticise the Ministry, its monopoly on programme advertising material would almost certainly have remained.[18]

A referral system for women seeking an abortion was set up in the Contraception, Sterilisation and Abortion Act 1977 but an earlier indication in 1974 that National members would vote to decriminalise homosexuality came to nothing once the party was in office. Not until 1986, by which time New Zealand was nearly the last country in the Commonwealth with restrictive legislation, were private homosexual acts between consenting partners over the age of sixteen legalised. Nor did the women's movement find Muldoon's Government congenial. There were few women MPs in the National caucus and no women ministers between 1975 and 1984.[19] However, after 1982 an able, urban liberal, Sue Wood, chaired the National Party's organisation and was able to counter some of the unease felt in party ranks at the Prime Minister's occasional gratuitous chauvinism.

While Muldoon liked to spend many weeks overseas at a time and annually visited the OECD in Paris,[20] he was in no rush to open New

Persistent Inflation

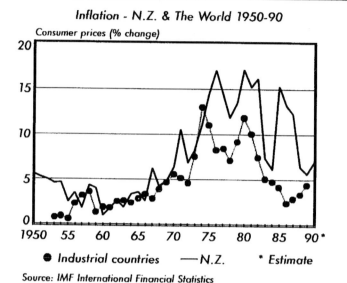

Inflation - N.Z. & The World 1950-90

Consumer prices (% change)

● **Industrial countries** ——**N.Z.** * **Estimate**

Source: IMF International Financial Statistics

New Zealand's inflation rate pulls ahead of other countries' after 1965. From Crocombe, Enright and Porter, Upgrading New Zealand's Competitive Advantage

Zealand's economy to the wider world. The introduction of international credit cards in the 1970s made it more difficult to control the outflow of foreign exchange for travel purposes but remittances for other purposes still required Reserve Bank permission. The Prime Minister was cool to suggestions from Talboys and Templeton that efforts be made to upgrade the NAFTA trade agreement between Australia and New Zealand. Talboys and his opposite number in Canberra, Doug Anthony, were both farmers, who saw a need to work together against agricultural protectionism which restricted markets for antipodean producers. There was a growing realisation, especially in Australia, that the world was dividing into trading blocks that would necessitate greater trans-Tasman cooperation. In any event, by the late 1970s Australia was well on the way to becoming New Zealand's biggest trading partner.[21]

Discussions about Closer Economic Relations (CER) began in earnest in March 1980. They moved ahead only slowly; Muldoon was listening both to his Minister of Trade and Industry, Lance Adams-Schneider, and to local manufacturers, who talked change but were reluctant to face any wholesale destruction of protective fences. Negotiations were put on hold about six months before the 1981 election, then revived early in 1982. A draft agreement was approved by the Australian Cabinet on 15 March. According to Hugh Templeton, Muldoon delayed New Zealand's response for many months, even after there were indications of support for CER from the reformers within the Labour Opposition. In December 1982 Muldoon eventually agreed to the wide-ranging but phased tariff reductions involved in CER. But the agreement then had to wait until the following March for final approval by the new Hawke Labor Government in Australia. An unprecedented degree of exposure to the wider world was slowly being opened up for New Zealand's traders. Muldoon gradually warmed to CER. In the budget of 1982 he acknowledged that it was likely to reduce some of New Zealand's protective barriers. One can deduce from his comments that he was becoming disenchanted with some of the special pleading by manufacturers who continued their love affair with import controls and/ or tariffs. Never slow to claim credit even when his enthusiasm had been lukewarm, Muldoon asserted in January 1983 that CER would come to be seen as one of his government's greatest achievements.[22]

The need for alternative sources of energy absorbed much of Cabinet's time from early 1979. Warren Freer's 1973 'take or pay' agreement with the Maui gas consortium obliged the Government to make decisions about using the gas, which was scheduled to come on stream in June 1979. A Liquid Fuels Trust Board was established under the chairmanship of Dr Colin Maiden in November 1978. Its job was to promote the use of natural gas with a view to reducing New Zealand's dependence on imported fuels. The board's work assumed a degree of urgency after the revolution in Iran at the beginning of 1979, which quickly led to a rise in world oil prices. Crude oil became hard to procure. In March 1979 New Zealand's stocks of gasoline fell below twenty days' supply, which had always been regarded as the safe level. Bill Birch, a Muldoon loyalist who was his new Minister of Energy, introduced a system of 'carless days' or, as the Minister of Maori Affairs, Ben Couch, with his talent for malapropisms called them, 'careless days'. Motor racing was banned. Fuel-saving experiments had only limited results; the planners soon discovered that much more fuel was consumed by spectators who went to horse racing than was saved by banning motor racing. 'Carless days' lasted six months and resulted in savings of 3 to 4 per cent in petrol demand.[23] The experiment served a more important purpose; it convinced the public that the country faced an energy crisis.

Making full use of Maui gas in order to reduce New Zealand's dependence on imported fuel became a Muldoon Government crusade. The Maui partners were working on the production of Liquid Petroleum Gas

(LPG), which was aimed principally at the South Island to which natural gas could not be reticulated. A series of grants and tax write-offs to encourage gas installations was incorporated into the 1979 budget[24] and more were announced in November 1980. Exploration for new oil and gas deposits stepped up. Amendments to the Petroleum Act dealing with prospecting licences and rights of entry to land were pushed through Parliament in 1980. The goal was to make New Zealand 50 per cent self-sufficient in petroleum products instead of its current 10 per cent.

Meantime schemes were emerging for saving electricity while expanding its availability. Interest-free loans were made available to encourage the installation of solar water-heating systems. A large power station at Huntly was given the go-ahead. When it had first been proposed in 1972–73, it was to use coal; now there was talk of gas. Eventually, after much delay, the planners decided on a mixture of coal and gas. Ambitious plans were hatched for additional South Island hydro-electricity production on the Clutha River. One estimate put a price tag of nearly $3.5 billion on what was under discussion.[25] A second smelter to be built by Alusuisse, Fletchers and CSR at Aramoana near Dunedin would absorb the spare electricity capacity. There were plans for another North Island power station, to be built at Marsden Point by the Electricity Department. The earlier mentioned expansion of New Zealand Steel at Glenbrook, which used local coal and electricity, became part of the self-sufficiency crusade.

A government-owned corporation, Petrocorp, was established to advise the Government on prospecting. It was also charged with constructing an ammonia-urea plant at Kapuni at a cost estimate of $84 million (it eventually cost $112 million). The plant would produce 35,000 tonnes of urea for New Zealand farmers and another 115,000 tonnes for export. Despite considerable misgivings in Cabinet about its usefulness, Petrocorp also constructed a methanol plant at Waitara. The Government also aimed to have 150,000 cars converted to Compressed Natural Gas (CNG) by December 1985. By now there were hopes that besides reducing dependence on imported fuel, these schemes might produce a surplus that could be exported, thereby benefiting New Zealand's balance of trade.[26]

Annual energy plans were developed in the hope that public and private sector bodies involved with production, distribution and sale of energy could devise mechanisms for coordinating their activities.[27] The Liquid Fuels Trust Board studied alternative fuels, including synthetic products.[28] This led to the setting up in September 1980 of the New Zealand Synthetic Fuels Corporation. It was finally agreed by the Government and Mobil on 12 February 1982 to press ahead with construction of a synthetic fuel

Falling Relative Living Standards

**New Zealand's GDP per Capita
Relative to Other Countries**

Source : BERL

Falling living standards and productivity. From Crocombe, Enright and Porter,
Upgrading New Zealand's Competitive Advantage

plant at Motunui, near Waitara. Synfuels, as it became known, was initially budgeted to cost $1 billion. It was planned to open at the end of 1985 and eventually to supply 30 per cent of New Zealand's liquid fuel needs. Once produced, the fuel would be shipped to Marsden Point for blending with refinery-produced petrol. Synfuels used state-of-the-art technology to produce additional methanol from natural gas. Meantime, in April 1979, the Government and the oil industry had agreed to expand the Marsden Point refinery, although the go-ahead for construction was not finally given until the end of 1981. Eventually Marsden Point would be linked with Wiri in South Auckland by a 163-kilometre pipeline costing nearly $100 million to construct. It would carry petroleum products to the region where approximately 30 per cent of New Zealand's total is consumed.

This huge increase in activity involved bureaucrats, scientists, academics and industry in an interlocking series of committees and quangos. The economy became more centralised by the day. The Ministry of Energy, which was established in 1977, had 8000 employees by 1980. Ministers anticipated that the various projects would soon be employing another 10,000 people, whose efforts would enable the proportion of GDP being spent on imported petroleum products to drop from 5 per cent to 3 per cent.[29] The public sector investment in these projects was enormous. While the private sector was involved in Maui gas production, Marsden Point and Synfuels, the Government took the lion's share of the risks involved.

Trade unions soon realised the urgency which ministers attached to the schemes and used their bargaining power to force up wages. Costs kept being revised upwards. Marsden Point, in particular, experienced endless industrial trouble and cost overruns at every stage.

The Labour Party meantime continued to preach the need for industrialisation. During the 1978 election campaign Roger Douglas produced plans for more intensive domestic processing of wool by building a number of carpet manufacturing plants. Jack Ridley, a former Rhodes Scholar who was also a Labour MP, was working on a number of public works projects aimed at generating employment. However, Muldoon's decision to lift people's horizons by asking them to 'Think Big' effectively trumped the Labour Opposition. The public responded with some enthusiasm. The Prime Minister made inflated claims about the benefits of the energy schemes during the November 1981 election campaign. It followed two months of distracting violence during a Springbok Rugby tour, which was then mollified to some extent by a visit from the Queen. National Party leaflets claimed that one of the downstream benefits of 'Think Big' would be the creation of 410,000 new jobs during the 1980s. Like Sir Joseph Ward's £70 million loan in 1928, this had considerable appeal at a time of unemployment. Those on the dole or on subsidised work programmes now numbered 72,000; economic growth in the year to October 1981 was minus 0.8 per cent.[30] Despite doubts being expressed publicly about the costings and likely benefits of several projects, 'Think Big' helped the National Party retain power on 28 November 1981.[31] But it was a narrower victory than in 1978; again National polled fewer votes than Labour but this time the overall majority was only two seats, the margin having been provided by a court ruling on an election petition in the Taupo electorate.[32]

In reality, as the London *Financial Times* had pointed out early in 1980, New Zealand was going through a period of 'rapid and unchecked economic decline'. Per capita income had fallen 11 per cent in real terms since 1974. This stemmed principally from low commodity prices on the world market, high domestic inflation and negligible growth. Inflation was being propelled along by ever higher government spending and by the protected nature of the New Zealand economy.[33] Treasury officers were becoming alarmed and a tough post-election analysis of the economy was sent to Muldoon at the end of 1981 in a plea for substantial economic reform. Treasury's briefing was called 'Economic Strategy: Overview'. The result of a team effort, it was an indictment of several generations of economic intervention. After expressing the opinion that New Zealand's economic performance in recent years 'left much to be desired', it noted the dissatisfaction in the community over inflation (currently 16 per cent) and a growth rate which was now barely 30 per cent of the average within the OECD countries. Despite many years spent promoting export industries, New Zealand's export growth rate between 1961 and 1979 was the lowest in the OECD. The biggest problem, according to Treasury, stemmed from the fact that achieving full employment by any available expedients remained the principal goal of economic policy. The regulations and controls that had been put in place in the vain hope of maintaining it had reduced New Zealand's capacity to adapt to a changing world trading environment. Noting the ineffectiveness of Keynesian pump-priming in current conditions, the report noted that 'any attempt to stimulate growth by pumping up aggregate demand internally still produces unacceptable deficits well before resources in the economy are fully employed'. It continued:

An overriding reason for our inability to secure higher growth in incomes from the use of our productive resources has been our reluctance to rely on market prices throughout the economy to allocate resources to the best use. In essence we have not allowed the price system to reflect sufficiently the true worth to the country of the resources employed in many areas. In the areas where government policy influences these prices, they have often not been set in a manner consistent with efficient resource allocation and economic stability. This includes the major prices in the economy which are the prices of foreign exchange, labour, capital, energy and other natural resources.

Treasury went on to argue that the New Zealand dollar was over-valued, that real wage growth greatly exceeded what was warranted by improving productivity and changes to the terms of trade and that for this reason employers had been dispensing with workers as rapidly as possible, thus pushing up unemployment. High personal tax levels discouraged workers entering the labour market and gave little or no incentive to those in the workforce to work overtime. The report argued that many regulations and controls had the effect of locking investment into areas where the returns to the economy were 'far below what those resources could yield elsewhere'. The high level of protection for New Zealand's industries 'imposes unnecessary costs on exporters and undermines economic management by promoting inflation through cost-plus pricing and general inefficiency'. While acknowledging that the studies of individual industries had produced some useful results, the report argued that there was no point in looking at any sector of the economy in isolation. A comprehensive approach to economic change was required.

The most telling part of the Treasury report related to the privileges that various sector groups had built up over the years. 'Virtually every regulation or misallocation of public sector resources has a client group that is benefiting from it and will resist reform.' Yet the Government needed to recognise that regulations rarely benefited the less advantaged. 'Import controls do not on balance promote employment but merely preserve jobs in some places. Price controls do not often lead to cheaper goods. Transport regulations do not lead to an efficient and cheap transport system. Losses by Air New Zealand benefit its staff rather than travellers. For reform . . . to be effective requires the government to have the will to face the entrenched beneficiaries of these situations.'[34] Officials were arguing that the system that had been built up over the years had bestowed privileges on people, many of them undeserving. Something approaching a revolutionary change to the State's functions was required.

Treasury was arguing that state interventionism, once an important factor in economic advancement, was now holding the economy back. Each intervention, undertaken for the best of motives, had resulted in a degree of economic inflexibility that was now making the growth needed to fund the Government's social policies impossible to achieve. Officials were pleading for a system where resources could be moved about more easily in order to maximise efficiency. This they believed was a necessary pre-condition before there would be a steady increase in growth.

Bernard Galvin had shifted from the Prime Minister's Department to become Secretary to the Treasury in 1980. He had problems with his health. Perhaps because of his time at Muldoon's elbow he was more sympathetic to government interventionism than many of his officers. However, he signed off the Treasury report on the economy to his minister, who took bags of summer reading with him when he repaired to a small holiday home at Hatfield's Beach north of Auckland.[35] Whether the Prime Minister read Treasury's criticism of economic management, let alone took heed of its message, will always be in doubt. Such a full frontal attack on decades of economic management probably had little appeal to someone who thought only about segments of the economy at a time and as Gary Hawke noted, had difficulty balancing all relevant factors simultaneously. Muldoon seldom shared critical documents with his Associate Ministers of Finance or with other senior ministers. Others in the Cabinet seem not to have appreciated the high level of concern that was building up within New Zealand's premier department.[36]

Once more Muldoon placed faith in several indications that the corner might have been turned. He was receiving reports about growth in consumption, investment, exports and manufacturing. In reality it was all the result of his election year spend-up and, as had always happened in the past, the balance of payments deficit widened after the election.[37] Muldoon chose those figures that suited him in his first major speech of 1982. In spite of the fact that inflation was nudging 16 per cent, he told the Orewa Rotary Club on 12 January in his annual address that the economy was 'in remarkably good shape'. There was no reason why the 'Think Big' projects, which were accelerating in pace, should not lead to steady economic improvement. Having allowed the dollar to devalue slowly for several years, he now decided to hold it steady, arguing that this was not the right time to increase the cost of imports.[38] 'Think Big' just might be the ultimate elixir for growth.

However, 'Think Big' turned into a giant albatross. Speed was necessary if there was to be progress enough to please the voters before the next election. But cranking up the pace proved difficult. Already Muldoon had run into trouble with the National Development Bill in October 1979. It was designed to enable major development proposals to be declared works of national importance so they could use a shortened planning consent procedure. Fiercely fought in Parliament, the Bill was regarded as evidence of arrogance in high places. This perception dogged the Clutha Development (Clyde Dam) Empowering Bill introduced on 24 August 1982. It sought to set aside a Planning Tribunal decision on water rights that threatened to delay the construction of the largest hydro dam in New Zealand. Some now saw in 'Think Big' a threat to established legal processes. Keeping building on schedule was a nightmare; the Clyde Dam and the Huntly power station fell years behind forecasts and the second smelter at Aramoana collapsed when Alusuisse pulled out, complaining that the price agreement for power that had been made with the Government in September 1981 rendered the project uneconomical. Converting cars to CNG did not catch on with the public; the equipment was bulky and expensive and the goal of 150,000 cars using this fuel by 1985 soon seemed illusory.[39]

Worse for Muldoon was the cost of his grand schemes. By the early months of 1982 the Prime Minister was struggling with a mounting deficit. Annual borrowing by the Government climbed steadily from $1 billion in 1976 to $1.445 billion in 1979 to $1.524 billion in 1981 to $2.158 billion in 1983 and to $3.1 billion in 1984.[40] The overseas component of New Zealand's accumulated debt increased; it had been $1.4 billion at 31 March 1976 and stood at $12.4 billion by March 1985. It was later estimated that the Government's real net debt (total debt less offsetting government financial assets and inflation) tripled between 1975 and 1979, and tripled again between 1979 and 1985.[41] Meanwhile, servicing debt cost 6.5 per cent of the Government's budget in 1975; it had risen to 17 per cent by 1985. Government expenditure as a percentage of GDP stood at 30.5 per cent in 1975. By 1984 it exceeded 41 per cent.[42]

The key assumption behind the biggest of the 'Think Big' projects was that the world price of oil would inexorably rise and that the energy projects would enable New Zealand to cut back on its bill for oil imports, which were now $1 billion more than in 1978.[43] However, international oil prices flattened out in the early 1980s and declined a little in the middle of the decade. This soon made the calculations behind some projects look dubious. At the end of 1982 Cabinet decided that it would be prudent to sell some of the State's 75 per cent share in the Motunui synthetic petrol plant, billed as 'New Zealand's biggest single venture to date'. Birch indicated that the Government was prepared to sell up to 49 per cent of Petrocorp's shares in the ammonia-urea plant at Kapuni and some of the Government's share in Synfuels as well. However, the oil companies did not want to buy, saying that they expected financial returns to be inadequate.[44] It began to seem as though the speculative Muldoon had out-Vogeled Sir Julius himself.

Few of the 410,000 downstream jobs that 'Think Big' was meant to generate were apparent five years after the projects were launched. The Fourth Labour Government elected in 1984 decided to rid itself of several projects, since there was every prospect that they would keep losing money for many years to come. Synfuels at Motunui, which was 75 per cent state-owned, eventually cost $1.85 billion to build. Mobil was guaranteed a 16 per cent return on its 25 per cent investment but the taxpayer carried all the risks of the joint venture and faced a trading loss of $460 million in 1986, when the plant opened. In 1990 the Government sold its interest in Maui gas and transferred its 75 per cent share in Synfuels to Fletcher Challenge, having sustained a huge loss; the taxpayers' investment in Petrocorp was worth $800 million and it, too, went to Fletchers. The Marsden Point Oil Refinery extensions eventually cost $2.3 billion, some of it financed by a special petrol tax. The scheme was mothballed before commissioning, then sold to the oil companies for $30 million. Having recently invested more than $1 billion in New Zealand Steel, the Crown sold its share in 1987 to Equiticorp for $328 million. The total expenditure of $5.64 billion on four projects[45] was really a speculative venture, the debts from which have restricted the country's growth potential ever since. Roger Douglas said in his 1986 budget that 'Think Big' illustrated that politicians were not good at picking winners. He added that in this case 'political calculation was allowed to get the better of commercial judgement'. Few could disagree.[46]

Inflation continued to mount in 1982 as the Government pushed ahead with its expensive projects. With double digit rates throughout the period 1975–82, New Zealand was experiencing inflation at a level that was much higher than the average of its trading partners. In the year to June 1982 New Zealand's inflation was 17 per cent, while the rate in Britain, the United States, Japan and Germany hovered around 5 per cent.[47] This in turn made New Zealand's exports less competitive on world markets. 'New Zealand's international competitiveness cannot fall much further', Garry Tait of the Employers Federation warned.[48] An economist, Kerry McDonald, estimated that between 1971 and 1980 New Zealand's labour cost per unit of output increased by 177 per cent, while in Australia the figure was 114 per cent and for New Zealand's other main trading partners, 94 per cent. Without change, and with the dollar held at its current value, New Zealand, he claimed, would sink.[49]

All these developments contributed to the slowing of New Zealand's economic growth to negligible proportions. The standard of living rose by only 0.3 per cent between 1975 and 1984. In the quarter century to 1989, New Zealanders grew their economy by 20 per cent, while the Japanese increased theirs by 175 per cent.[50] Muldoon kept trying to disguise these realities with his battery of export incentives and other spurs to production. When first contrived in the 1960s, incentives succeeded in inducing behaviour which governments believed desirable. By the 1980s, however, they seemed merely to be redistributing income. This was a system that worked well for some. In October 1981 Fletcher Challenge, New Zealand's largest company, revealed that in the past year it had received $30.65 million in export incentives from the Government. When this was offset against a tax bill of $32.04 million, the company contributed little to the Government's coffers.[51] It was Harold Wilson who had quipped some years before that the welfare state, whatever the intentions behind it, seemed to have become a public assistance board for mendicant capitalists.[52]

Muldoon had fought desperately to hang on to office. But by the middle of 1982 he was faced with high wage demands, huge capital requirements for the 'Think Big' projects and the prospect of runaway inflation.[53] The Prime Minister did not know where to turn for inspiration. While on a trip to the OECD in May, this time without a Treasury official at his side, he was advised by an American economist to impose a wage–price freeze. To an interventionist like Muldoon the idea had appeal. When he returned home and discussed a freeze with his officials, he ran into a wall of opposition; a memo was sent to him jointly signed by the Secretaries to the Treasury and of Trade and Industry, as well as by the Governor of the Reserve Bank. This rare display of unity among the Government's economic advisers failed to dissuade the Prime Minister. In an act described by Hugh Templeton as 'bold, indeed desperate, generalship', Muldoon went ahead. He raised the issue of a wage–price freeze at Cabinet as an oral item without any supporting paper; the ministers, many of them uneasy, agreed to passage of the necessary regulations. On 22 June 1982 it was gazetted under the Economic Stabilisation Act 1948, which had been kept on the statute books after the Commerce Act came into force.[54] In the end it was not a Labour Government that finally slipped a straitjacket on the economy but the leader of a party which had once claimed to oppose central economic direction.

Introducing the wage–price freeze enabled the Prime Minister to assert personal control over virtually every aspect of the economy. But this man 'of quicksilver moods and temperaments' was unable to give any indication to his caucus or to the general public about how or when the freeze would end.[55] Since the Government's spending did not decline, the budget deficit grew. Even stronger inflationary pressures built up within this rigidly controlled economy. When the freeze was finally abolished at the end of 1984, inflation burst out and high interest rates rose even further. It took another six years to bring them under control.

The slight bubble in economic figures in early 1982 quickly turned into an illusion. There was a wage–tax trade off in the budget on 5 August but confidence was ebbing. Price rises stabilised after the freeze but unemployment rose. Including those on the Government's special work schemes, there were 100,000 unemployed in December 1982.[56] On 11 January 1983 the Sage of Orewa felt obliged to tell the Rotarians that he expected 1983 to be a 'dull' year, with a big government deficit and depressed export returns.[57] The largest net outflow of people from New Zealand since the late 1880s was draining skills away from the country. In all there was a net departure of nearly 150,000 between March 1976 and November 1983.

What growing numbers of people, if not the Prime Minister, were beginning to realise was that no amount of economic intervention could possibly shield New Zealanders from the effects of many years of low commodity prices and the destructive efforts of governments to lessen their impact on living standards. Many of the controls and regulations, introduced for the best of motives since the time of Savage, Nash and

Sullivan, only made things worse. Price support mechanisms could tide farmers over a year or two of downturns; import controls could help industries in their infancy; price and wage controls could work in wartime, when the public was prepared to submit to centralised control; subsidies could help smooth fluctuating prices for a while. But over an extended period, such interventions produced their own sets of anomalies. Collectively they made the adjustment process for New Zealanders to long-term market instability more difficult. Governments gave producers the wrong incentives and they failed to change their products; others refrained from investing their money where it was likely to get the best long-term returns for the country, preferring instead something that enjoyed protection. When Muldoon erected several further storeys on the jerry-built structure he had inherited from past governments, he simply delayed the inevitable and made the dénouement more painful. As time passed, New Zealand continued to fall further behind the countries with whom it traded. Having enjoyed a standard of living in the early 1950s that was third in the world, it had slipped to twenty-first by the middle of the 1980s.[58]

Muldoon failed to acknowledge the gravity of the situation. His most immediate problem in 1982 came from within his own party. The sacking from the Cabinet of Derek Quigley for a mild speech that questioned aspects of the Government's financial policy was followed by the imposition of the wage–price freeze and in October the introduction of a very complex Income Tax Amendment Bill (No.2). These events caused much unrest within the National Party's organisation.[59] In July an official of the Canterbury–Westland division of the party called for the Prime Minister's resignation, saying that he was 'no longer the man for the job'. Further party criticism followed.[60] Morale among National MPs was low. National's whips had had to call on the Speaker's vote to save them in a parliamentary division and in 1983 two National MPs crossed the floor on aspects of the Income Tax Amendment Bill (No.2).[61] On 15 March 1984 Jim McLay was elected to be Muldoon's deputy. His youth and polish, however, seemed only to highlight the shopworn appearance of his Prime Minister and Cabinet, several of whom were unwell by this time.

Much more serious for the National Party was the declared intention by Wellington property magnate Robert Jones, previously a close friend of Muldoon's, to form a new party in opposition to National at the next election. Angered by the freeze and the tax legislation, Jones gathered around himself a group of National malcontents from the party's heartland and was soon running at 10 per cent in the polls. Templeton believes Jones was seen by these people as 'an antagonist who could get rid of

Muldoon and press the case for radical economic reform rather than a messiah who would lead them to the promised land of easy money'. When old friends fall out, relationships often turn rancid quickly. By the early part of 1984 Jones was calling Muldoon a 'dictator'; Muldoon replied that Jones was 'hysterical'. Libel writs began flying.[62]

Meantime the Labour Party was also rent by division. By the end of 1982 it was clear that Rowling lacked the numbers to survive as leader. On 17 December 1982 he announced that he was standing down. Over the holiday period he issued several press statements critical of Muldoon; one argued for 'a fundamental change in New Zealand's economic direction' but ended up with his by now familiar list of further interventions.[63] However, the era of Tweedledum/Tweedledee politics was passing. By now there was a clear majority within the Labour caucus for a change in economic direction, although specifics had yet to be finalised. The reformers sided with Auckland lawyer David Lange.[64] He took over as leader on 3 February 1983 with Geoffrey Palmer, a former law professor, as his deputy. The new finance spokesman was Roger Douglas, who by now was Labour's most articulate advocate of a new economic approach, and had gathered around him a team of young thinkers led by Dr James Holt, Associate Professor of History at the University of Auckland, Doug Andrew, from Treasury, and Geoff Swier.[65] Lange was soon softening the public for some major changes, telling one audience that all sections of the community had to accept that there would be 'winners, losers, costs and benefits' as a result of the changes Labour wished to see made.[66] A small number of social engineers within the Labour caucus was unhappy. They centred their loyalties on the president of the party, Jim Anderton, who tried to keep the cause of the paternalistic state alive within the Labour Party. Anderton tried to block the new policies that were being developed and enunciated by Lange and his caucus spokespeople. Eventually Anderton decided to seek a parliamentary seat himself in the hope that he could take the caucus by storm with a return to old-style interventionism. His chance never came. It was only some years after Anderton left the Labour Party in 1989 that his brand of interventionism began to reappear within Labour. During this period the Labour Party, that had contributed more than any other political organisation to big government, had managed to reduce as well as remodel it.

During 1983–84 National's growing group of reformers had no option but to watch their Labour opponents move on to territory which they felt belonged to them. Since 1975 there had been a growing number within the National caucus favouring restructuring. One success was the merger of Air New Zealand and National Airways Corporation on 1 April 1978 that followed a secret feasibility study. Proponents of the merger argued that at least $10 million could be saved in administrative costs and from better integration of services. Four years later the National Government corporatised Railways once more, in the hope that its growing losses could be turned around. This time the change had little impact. The ordeal of debating change with senior Railways personnel in committee and then reading reports of the discussions next day in the newspapers dampened Muldoon's willingness to press on with structural reforms.[67] In 1982, after a four-year study, a Transport Amendment Bill was introduced following much debate within caucus. It passed in October 1983. The legislation delicensed some parts of the industry and removed the 150-kilometre protection enjoyed by Railways against competition from road transport.[68] In the same year Government Life Insurance was corporatised. Industry studies also continued and ministers talked frequently with manufacturers about the desirability of reducing protection, without achieving much consensus.[69]

It was proving impossible to unravel decades of controls and regulations with ad hoc reforms conducted within no clear philosophical framework except a feeling in the minds of ministers that there was a need for more freedom. Moreover, there seem to have been no plans to reform state trading agencies such as the New Zealand Forest Service, the Mines Division of the Ministry of Energy and the Tourist Hotel Corporation, which had been losing large sums of money for many years. The time had arrived when drastic moves to bring about efficiencies, coupled with policies to arrest the Government's mounting deficits, were urgently needed. The reformers within the National Government were being overtaken by events. As Muldoon failed to respond to the growing unease on a range of issues, disarray within National's ranks became more obvious. Anger with Muldoon grew. By the time Parliament met in May 1984 several members of the National caucus were, to quote Templeton, 'openly hunting the tiger'.[70]

As the world's economy moved out of recession during 1983–84 New Zealand's lagged behind. When the new Labor Government in Australia devalued by 10 per cent early in March 1983, Muldoon cautiously followed with a 6 per cent devaluation of the New Zealand dollar, hoping to minimise the impact on the price of imports. Unemployment fell slightly at the beginning of 1984. However, many smaller businesses were finding trading conditions difficult and the number of bankruptcies grew. Trade unions complained that the economy was 'dangerously brittle', although they continued to push for higher wages.[71] There were constant strikes and go-slows. The Government removed barriers to companies wishing to enter the freezing industry. By now the country had too many killing facilities but no one seemed able to resolve how to deal with the excess capacity. For 30 years the National Party had talked about making membership of trade unions voluntary. The Minister of Labour, Jim Bolger, finally pushed through the Industrial Law Reform Bill, which resulted in a considerable drop in union membership. In March 1984 a union employee was killed when a bomb exploded at Wellington's Trades Hall. Police later asserted that the incident was unrelated to the current industrial unrest. However, there was no denying that unions were angry that their power was diminishing. Industrial relations were tinder dry.

Meantime, Muldoon's relations with the media deteriorated steadily as the press refused to see things his way. Prime Minister and journalists seemed at daggers drawn after Keith Allen, the Minister of Customs, claimed to have been assaulted by three men when walking home from his office in mid-March 1984. Muldoon sought to protect his minister with stories that the press and public found unbelievable.[72] In April 1984 the *Auckland Star* speculated that Muldoon's attacks on the media were becoming part of a strategy to divert attention from the brittle state of the economy.[73] The National Government seemed to be in danger of imploding.

There will probably always be debate about why Muldoon on the night of 14 June 1984 took the highly unusual step of announcing an early election. He said that the decision by two of his backbenchers to withdraw support from the Government in a vote on an Opposition private member's bill had rendered his government's position impossible. Hugh Templeton argues that the Prime Minister's diabetic state caught up with him and that his fateful decision was probably instantly regretted.[74] The Labour Party was certain that the Prime Minister was simply 'throwing in the towel', as Lange described it, because from every vantage point his budget figures could not be conjured into an election winner and going to the polls early was the lesser of two horrors.[75]

Whatever the truth about Muldoon's health, there is some evidence to support Lange's view. Treasury officials told outsiders that they had difficulty getting Muldoon to concentrate on the forthcoming budget.[76] The Labour Government that took office on 26 July 1984 soon discovered why. There was every possibility that if things had carried on the way they were, the budget deficit would have been nearly $5 billion for the year to March 1985. Not only were costs increasing at an unsustainable rate in Health, Education and Welfare but there were huge bills for 'Think Big' coming to book. Moreover, underlying inflation was certain to break into

David Lange being sworn into office as Prime Minister by Governor-General,
Sir David Beattie, 26 July 1984.

hyperinflation as soon as the freeze was lifted. Most of the State's trading departments had become a dead weight on the exchequer. The Railways Corporation was staring at a deficit of $105 million; the Tourist Hotel Corporation, which had been overseeing substantial taxbreaks to the hotel industry since 1969, was losing $27.5 million;[77] the State's coal mining, now a branch of the Ministry of Energy, was going to cost the taxpayer nearly $155 million; there was every possibility that the Shipping Corporation would lose $11 million; and the New Zealand Forest Service with all its trading potential would need an injection of nearly $250 million. The Post Office, which, besides its core activity, had a savings bank and a booming business in telecommunications, was likely to make a profit of no more than $300 million because of several areas of cross subsidisation within the organisation. Subsidies on milk consumed $30 million each year; grants, subsidies and SMPs to farmers would require about $1.5 billion, while the Meat and Dairy boards were still availing themselves of Reserve Bank credit at 1 per cent interest.[78] On top of all these debts, the Government's Estimates carried many hundreds of grants and subsidies to organisations and services that had come to rely on state help, some dating back to before World War I. The general public had come to think of the

New Zealand Government as a milch cow with endless teats. Government departments employed nearly 86,000 people in March 1984 and, according to Hugh Templeton, more than another 100,000 were paid indirectly from the Consolidated Fund. State subsidies on superannuation payments to retired public servants ran to nearly $130 million for the year to March 1985 and were increasing at a rapid rate.[79] The load of many generations was topped off with Muldoon's National Superannuation. After decades of poor commodity prices the combined weight had brought the country to its knees.

New Zealand had seen its Government become increasingly involved in all aspects of the economy since earliest times. It had centralised its decision-making on Wellington and finally allowed the critical economic decisions to fall into the hands of one man. What resembled a command economy could not continue without radical change. There were elements of a Greek tragedy to it all. Derek Quigley observed some years later that the National Party had been in office too long. 'It was arrogant, tired, out of touch with reality, divided by internal conflict and frightened to move against the myriad [of] special interest groups it had itself created.'[80] The major character in the drama, Robert Muldoon, was isolated, unwell, convinced that New Zealand was 'too small to let market forces loose' and boxed in by his own past decisions. Once labelled by a journalist as the Rocky Marciano of New Zealand politics, Muldoon was punch drunk.[81] The ageing pugilist refused advice from the Acting Governor of the Reserve Bank, Roderick Deane, to devalue the currency when a run on the New Zealand dollar began in the early stages of the election campaign.[82] While some of the severity of the situation was conveyed by Treasury officials to McLay when he was Acting Prime Minister in May 1984, Muldoon kept the rest of his Cabinet in the dark about the advice he was receiving and refused to discuss problems in any detail with his deputy.[83]

Muldoon's old political tricks no longer worked in 1984. The halls were often half empty and the election rhetoric flat. Each day, the opinion polls, which had been pointing to a Labour victory for many months, suggested that a change of government was more likely. Since Roger Douglas had talked openly about possible devaluation in 1983, this only increased the pressure on New Zealand's overvalued exchange rate. In the four weeks after 14 June 1984 the Reserve Bank was obliged to borrow $1.7 billion to prop up the currency.[84]

On 14 July 1984, a day when it teemed with rain, a record 95 per cent of eligible voters went to polling places. They voted for change, although no one was sure what to expect. David Lange's Labour Party won 43 per cent of the popular vote in a four-way split with National (36 per cent), Jones's New Zealand Party (12.25 per cent) and Social Credit (7.6 per cent).[85] The new government had a majority of seventeen seats and the youngest set of ministers since the 1850s. They quickly showed a determination to restructure New Zealand from top to toe. Over the next decade the Labour Government, and the National Government that followed in 1990, fundamentally altered the nature of political life. New Zealand moved from an idealistic collectivism that was still a part of New Zealand's political mindset 144 years after the Treaty of Waitangi, to a more thoughtful balance between individualism and collective action. The only matter still in doubt is whether the Labour and National governments after 1984 have convinced the public that they are more likely to benefit in the long run from governments that are modest regulators rather than enthusiastic doers.

Notes

Introduction

1. Carole Seymour-Jones, *Beatrice Webb: Woman of Conflict*, London, 1993, p.240; Beatrice and Sidney Webb, *Visit to New Zealand in 1898; Beatrice Webb's Diary with Entries by Sidney Webb*, Wellington, 1959, pp.8, 14, 38.
2. Michael Holroyd, *Bernard Shaw* (One Volume Definitive Edition), London, 1997, p.670. See also Desmond Stone (ed), *Verdict on New Zealand*, Wellington, 1959, pp.127-37. Shaw's trip to New Zealand was recalled in the *Press*, 14 April 1990, p.26 and the *Dominion Sunday Times*, 17 November 1991, p.9. See also *Australian Financial Review*, 5 January 1994.
3. H. D. Lloyd quoted in Desmond Stone (ed), p.64. See also Peter J. Coleman, *Progressivism and the World of Reform: New Zealand and the Origins of the American Welfare State*, Lawrence, Kansas, 1987, p.52. Lloyd is quoted at length on New Zealand in Caro Lloyd, *Henry Demarest Lloyd*, New York, 1912, pp.104ff.
4. Coleman, *Progressivism*, p.54. See also Peter J. Coleman, 'New Zealand Liberalism and the Origins of the American Welfare State' in *Journal of American History*, Vol. 69, No.2, September 1982, p.372. Parsons wrote *The Story of New Zealand*, which was edited by C. F. Taylor and published in Philadelphia in 1904.
5. Coleman, *Progressivism*, p.62. The author wrote his Ph.D thesis at Duke University in 1963 on the Socialist Party of America, 1912–1919, and was struck by the number of references to New Zealand in American socialist publications.
6. Coleman, *Progressivism*, p.76.
7. James Bryce, quoted in Desmond Stone (ed), p.89.
8. André Siegfried in Desmond Stone (ed), p.81. See also André Siegfried (ed. David Hamer), *Democracy in New Zealand*, Wellington, 1982.
9. Siegfried, *Democracy in New Zealand*, pp.89-90.
10. André Métin published *Le Socialisme Sans Doctrines* in 1901.
11. These issues are discussed in Donald Denoon, *Settler Capitalism: The Dynamics of Dependent Development in the Southern Hemisphere*, Oxford, 1983.
12. J.B. Condliffe, *New Zealand in the Making*, 2nd ed, London, 1959, p.183.
13. Keith Sinclair, *A History of New Zealand*, London, 1959, pp.173, 161.
14. J.C. Beaglehole, *New Zealand: A Short History*, London, 1936, pp.59-60.
15. A recent discussion of Wakefield's ideas is to be found in Erik Olssen, 'Mr Wakefield and New Zealand as an Experiment in Post-Enlightenment Experimental Practice', *NZJH*, Vol. 31, October 1997, p.198.
16. David Hamer, *The New Zealand Liberals: The Years of Power, 1891–1912*, Auckland, 1988, p.45.
17. Sinclair, *History*, p.184. Reeves described the influences affecting his legislation in his memoirs quoted in Sinclair, *William Pember Reeves: New Zealand Fabian*, Oxford, 1965, p.210.
18. Erik Olssen, *Building the New World: Work, Politics and Society in Caversham 1880s–1920s*, Auckland, 1995, pp.222-3.
19. Ormond Wilson, *An Outsider Looks Back*, Wellington, 1982, p.63. The author has viewed Peter Fraser's personal collection of books held in the Alexander Turnbull Library and noted that two volumes of Marx's *Capital* were among the 1300 books. They did not appear to have been much used. The third and fourth volumes were nowhere to be seen.
20. Head Office files of the Labour Party, especially those xeroxed by P. J. O'Farrell, provide much evidence of fights against communists. See MS Papers 1501, files 2, 3 and 7, ATL.

21. Bruce Brown, *The Rise of New Zealand Labour: A History of the New Zealand Labour Party*, Wellington, 1962, pp.171-2.
22. Baxter offered this as a likely explanation for his nickname when the author interviewed him in May 1965.
23. The author owns a collection of the pamphlets that Holland wrote, plus Holland's personal copy of Edward Bellamy's *Looking Backwards*.
24. *Grey River Argus*, 30 November 1935, p.5.
25. See two pages of biographical material about Savage that was distributed to the press (date unspecified) in Nash, 1177/0319/0430, NA.
26. Barry Gustafson, *From the Cradle to the Grave: A Biography of Michael Joseph Savage*, Auckland, 1986, p.118.
27. Sinclair, *History*, p.258.
28. Fraser is quoted by James Thorn, *Peter Fraser: New Zealand's Wartime Prime Minister*, London, 1952, p.143. See also Derek A. Dow, *Safeguarding the Public Health: A History of the New Zealand Department of Health*, Wellington, 1995, pp.141-2. In Fraser's message to the electors of Wellington Central before he won the seat in a by-election in October 1918 he did not use the word 'socialism'. He asserted that the Labour Party 'stands for the peaceful and legal transformation of society from private to public ownership, and the increasing democratic control of land and industry'. See MS Papers 1900/08, ATL.
29. Keith Sinclair, *Walter Nash*, Auckland 1976, p.20.
30. W.B. Sutch, *The Quest for Security in New Zealand, 1840 to 1966*, Wellington, 1966, p.176.
31. Quoted by Brian Easton, *In Stormy Seas: The Post-War New Zealand Economy*, Dunedin, 1997, p.63.
32. *Press*, 20 March 1936, p.6.
33. See John Dunmore, *Norman Kirk: A Portrait*, Wellington, 1972. There is much detail about Kirk and a copy of *This Man Kirk* in Bert Roth's papers, MS Papers 6164-047, ATL.
34. See Dean Jaensch, *The Australian Politics Guide*, Melbourne, 1996, p.19. At the NZLP conference in May 1977 Rowling described any effort to return to the policy objective of 'socialism' as 'a bloody great step backwards'. There is a report of O'Flynn's speech to the Mt Eden Branch of the Labour Party in the *Central Leader* (Auckland), 16 August 1977, p.46.
35. The words appear in Barry Gustafson, *The First Fifty Years: A History of the New Zealand National Party*, Auckland, 1986, p.182.
36. Gustafson, *National Party*, pp.9-10.
37. Gustafson, *National Party*, p.183.
38. The term was often used by Muldoon's old friend turned foe, Sir Robert Jones. Richard Prebble, a Labour critic of Muldoon's, wrote years later that Muldoon 'talked like a Tory and spent like a liberal socialist (and delivered New Zealand the worst of both worlds)' Richard Prebble, *What Happens Next*, [Auckland] 1997, p.24.
39. The figures are from the report of the Gibbs Committee on Taxation, *AJHR*, 1951, B-8, p.4. See also R.O. Douglas, 'Statement on Government Expenditure Reform', 19 May 1986.
40. See, for instance, Brian Easton (ed), *The Making of Rogernomics*, Auckland, 1989; Francis G. Castles, Rolf Gerritsen and Jack Vowles (eds), *The Great Experiment: Labour Parties and Public Policy Transformation in Australia and New Zealand*, Auckland, 1996; Jane Kelsey, *The New Zealand Experiment*, Auckland, 1995; Chris Rudd and Brian Roper, *The Political Economy of New Zealand*, Auckland, 1997. There is a revealing article about the nostalgic thinking of one Auckland University economist in the *New Zealand Listener*, 29 November 1997, pp.30-32.
41. Tom Brooking, 'Use it or Lose it: Unravelling the Land Debate in Late Nineteenth-Century New Zealand', *NZJH*, Vol. 30, October 1996, pp.141-62.
42. J.E. Le Rossignol and W.D. Stewart, *State Socialism in New Zealand*, New York, 1910. John A. Lee's skimpy catalogue of state intervention entitled *Socialism in New Zealand*, London, 1938, also runs to 300 pages.

43. Melanie Phillips, 'Fallacies and Illusions about the Welfare State', *Times Literary Supplement* (*TLS*), 14 March 1997, p.13.

44. John E. Martin, *Holding the Balance: A History of New Zealand's Department of Labour 1891–1995*, Christchurch, 1997, pp.226-8. In 1968, when the Arbitration Court considered the economy too weak to warrant a wage increase, the politicians stepped in and ensured that there was a 5 per cent increase. In August 1973 an 8.5 per cent increase issued under the 1948 Economic Stabilisation Act was decided politically, as were budget announcements about wage increases at the end of the decade. The quote about post-1968 trends comes from Brian Easton, *Stormy Seas*, p.106.

45. For most of the time until 1910, wool was New Zealand's largest revenue earner and was worth more than meat, butter, cheese, wheat and oats combined. At the height of the Korean War, receipts from wool constituted 51 per cent of the country's total export value, *NZH*, 7 January 1998, p.A-11. It has been claimed that in 1955 New Zealand was sending proportionately more exports to the countries in the European Community (most to the United Kingdom) than any of the twelve members are exporting to each other, Brian Easton, *In Stormy Seas*, p.8.

46. The same thing happened in the United Kingdom. See David Howell's review of Edmund Dell, *The Chancellors: A History of the Chancellors of the Exchequer*, London, 1996, *TLS*, 29 November 1996, p.10.

47. 'Report of the Department of Trade and Industry, *AJHR*, 1979, G-14, p.5.

48. See Derek Quigley, 'Economic Reform: New Zealand in an International Perspective', *Round Table*, Vol. 339, 1996, p.312. Quigley notes that over a 20-year period from the early 1960s to the early 1980s per capita income growth in New Zealand averaged 1.4 per cent pa, compared with the OECD average of 2.9 per cent pa. During these years the Government's tax take was rising steadily and workers' actual take-home pay was negative when the tax increases are taken into account. Donald Brash in 'New Zealand's Remarkable Reforms', Institute of Economic Affairs, London, June 1996, p.3, asserts that New Zealand's economic growth was only half the OECD average between 1950 and 1984.

49. Public opinion polling of attitudes to specific professional groups began in New Zealand in August 1975. Opinions of politicians and of the political process were worse by 1990. See Hyam Gold and Alan Webster, *New Zealand Values Today*, Palmerston North, 1990. See also *Sunday Times*, 24 October 1993, p.A4. The *NBR* 'Respect List' is to be found in the issue of 30 January 1998, p.16. Collapsing confidence in politicians and the Government clearly became a factor in the growing interest in alternative political systems that resulted in the referendum vote in favour of MMP in November 1993.

50. See Stephen Britton, 'Recent Trends in the Internationalisation of the New Zealand Economy', *Australian Geographical Studies*, Vol. 29, April 1991, pp.3-25.

51. The term which was in vogue in Europe was applied to the New Zealand economy by C. Weststrate in his *Portrait of a Modern Mixed Economy: New Zealand*, Wellington, 1959.

52. *NZH*, 17 April 1998, A-15.

53. Hugh Templeton, *All Honourable Men: Inside the Muldoon Cabinet 1975–1984*, Auckland, 1995, p.184.

54. Donald T. Brash, 'New Zealand's Remarkable Reforms', p.5.

55. Brent Wheeler, 'Reforming Regulatory Regimes – the New Zealand Experience', *Economic Papers: Economic Society of Australia*, Vol. 14, No.3, September 1995, p.41.

56. Sutton first used the term in 1986 in a caucus debate with maverick Labour MP, Jim Anderton. The phrase was often used later by David Lange and Richard Prebble, and businessman Alan Gibbs used it in a speech to the New Zealand Society of Accountants in April 1989. See Deborah Coddington, *Turning Pain into Gain; the Plain Person's Guide to the Transformation of New Zealand 1984–1993*, Auckland, 1993, p.51.

57. Lewis Evans, Arthur Grimes, Bryce Wilkinson with David Teece, 'Economic Reform in New Zealand 1984-95: The Pursuit of Efficiency', *Journal of Economic Literature*, Vol. 34, December 1996, p.1857.

58. Many of the state's early activities to assist agriculture are dealt with by Alan Grey, *Aotearoa*

and New Zealand: A Historical Geography, Christchurch, 1994, Chapt. 7.

59. Quinquennial spending on railways in 1885–1935 is outlined by Alan Grey, p.323. In March 1981, the year before the New Zealand Railways Corporation was formed, railways employed 21,244 people. *NZOYB*, 1982, p.329. A decade later more freight and passengers were being carried by rail but its number of employees stood at less than 5000.

60. R.O. Douglas, memo, 'Bahrain Coolstore', to Labour Cabinet Ministers, 13 December 1984, in the author's possession.

61. At a Cabinet Meeting on 15 June 1949 unease was expressed by ministers about this development, AAFD, 811/1a/1/1/1, NA.

62. A combination of high tariffs on new vehicles and the requirement to include up to 40 per cent of domestically made componentry made cars very expensive by world standards, *NZH*, 30 January 1969.

63. See David Thomson, 'Friendly Societies in New Zealand', unpublished manuscript, 1995. The author possesses a copy.

64. In response to concern about rising hospital costs, Peter Fraser's Cabinet on 9 February 1949 agreed to establish a single Hospital Commissioner to 'control and allocate' hospital board funds, AAFD 811/1a/1/1/1. The position was not created before the party lost power.

65. Referring to the changes in lifestyle choices that followed the introduction of the Domestic Purposes Benefit in 1973, Dr Gareth Morgan has observed: 'Whether desirable or not, it is unlikely that the original designers of the policy anticipated that this would be the result', *NZH*, 2 December 1997, p.A-13. The same could be said of Accident Compensation. Little has been published in New Zealand on a breakdown of the recipients of welfare, but a recent study in the United Kingdom reports that 25 per cent of British households with the highest incomes receive welfare, and that another 15 per cent of sickness and disability payments go to homes on or above the median income. *Weekly Telegraph*, Issue 336, 31 December 1997-6 January 1998, p.12.

66. See New Zealand Planning Council, *The Economy in Transition: Restructuring to 1989*, Wellington, 1989, p.7. For GDP per capita rankings see the tables in Paul Kennedy, *Preparing for the Twenty-First Century*, Toronto, 1993, pp.351-2. If Luxembourg were added to Kennedy's table New Zealand's ranking would be twenty-second. The Planning Council (p.7) says that New Zealand's income per capita stood at nineteenth among OECD nations by 1985. This OECD rating is used by Brian Easton, *In Stormy Seas*, p.27. Neither the OECD nor the Easton tables includes Kuwait, Singapore and the United Arab Emirates, all of which had a higher standing than New Zealand in Kennedy's tables. The 1993 OECD Economic Survey of the New Zealand economy (p.11) notes that the years 1950–85 were years of high productivity worldwide, but that in New Zealand productivity gains were 'subdued'. The comment about the British economy comes from Dell, *The Chancellors*, p.369.

67. Between 1967 and 1973 New Zealand's inflation rate averaged 6.8 per cent pa, well above the OECD average of 4.7 per cent pa. See OECD Economic Surveys, *New Zealand*, Paris, 1975. The problems New Zealand encountered with inflation during the 1970s are discussed in Conrad Blyth, *Inflation in New Zealand*, Auckland, 1977.

68. Quigley, 'Economic Reform', p.311.

69. Dr Roderick Deane quoted in Marcia Russell, *Revolution*, Auckland, 1996, p.56.

70. Robert Skidelsky, *The World After Communism*, London, 1995, p.141.

71. Dell, *The Chancellors*, p.10.

Chapter 1 Establishing Order in Colonial New Zealand

1. A.H. McLintock, *Crown Colony Government in New Zealand*, Wellington, 1958, p.56.

2. Ranginui Walker, *Ka Whawhai Tonu Matou: Struggle Without End*, Auckland, 1990, p.98.

3. Harrison M. Wright, *New Zealand 1769–1840: Early Years of Western Contact*, Cambridge,

Massachusetts, 1959, p.87.

4. Lindsay Cox, *Kotahitanga: The Search for Maori Political Unity*, Auckland, 1993, pp.39-43. A readable general discussion of the interaction between Maori and Pakeha before 1840 is to be found in Alan Ward, *A Show of Justice: Racial 'Amalgamation' in Nineteenth Century New Zealand*, Auckland, 1995, pp.3-40.

5. Quoted by Alan Ward, p.43. Claudia Orange in her book *The Treaty of Waitangi*, Wellington, 1987, pp.17-18, is inclined to dismiss the claims of anarchy in the north in the 1830s. I am indebted to the young researcher Ned Fletcher for his contrary comments entitled 'Living Without the Law' contained in a letter to Judith Bassett dated July 1997.

6. See J. Rutherford, *The Founding of New Zealand*, Dunedin, 1940, p.26. J.C. Beaglehole, *New Zealand: A Short History*, London, 1936, p.18. There is an attempt to analyse Kororareka in Ormond Wilson, *Kororareka and Other Essays*, Dunedin, 1990, pp.109-120. For comments on early Maori efforts to regulate trade see R.P. Hargreaves, *From Beads to Banknotes*, p.16.

7. The population estimates are contained in Judith Binney, Judith Bassett and Erik Olssen, *The People and the Land*, Wellington, 1990, p.33. There is an interesting graph of Maori and non-Maori population growth in New Zealand in G.R. Hawke, *The Making of New Zealand: An Economic History*, Cambridge, 1985, p.10.

8. The memorandum of 3 February 1840, Shortland's report to Hobson of 20 June and details of the bank draft are in IA/1/1 and 2, 1840, CSIC, National Archives (NA).

9. J.D. Salmond, *New Zealand Labour's Pioneering Days*, Auckland, 1950, p.1.

10. Wakefield's 'A Letter from Sydney' (1829) and his 'The Art of Colonisation' (1849) are reprinted in M.F. Lloyd Prichard, *The Collected Works of Edward Gibbon Wakefield*, Auckland, 1969. See especially pp.115, 169 and 763.

11. John Miller, *Early Victorian New Zealand*, London, 1958, p.43.

12. John Martin, 'A "small nation on the move": Wakefield's theory of colonisation and the relationship between state and labour in the mid-nineteenth century', unpublished manuscript, 1996. I am indebted to John Martin for showing me a copy of this manuscript.

13. Beaglehole, Chapt. 2. There is a good description of the relationship between early governors and the New Zealand Company in Patricia Burns, *Fatal Success: A History of the New Zealand Company*, Auckland, 1989. See especially Chapt. 27.

14. Keith Sinclair, *A History of New Zealand*, Harmondsworth, 1959, p.72.

15. Alan Ward, pp.45-46. Keith Sorrenson in 'Maori and Pakeha' in Geoffrey Rice (ed), *The Oxford History of New Zealand*, 2nd ed, Auckland, 1992, pp.149-50, argues that there was some recognition of Maori law over a number of years.

16. Ranginui Walker, p.99.

17. Acting Postmaster, Kaipara, to Governor, 14 April 1841, IA/1/6, CSIC.

18. Details about what people expected of the Government, and the protest memorandum are to be found in IA/1/1, 2 and 3 1840, CSIC, NA. The provision of education tended in most settlements to be regarded as the responsibility of the New Zealand Company, or the churches. Requests for help can be found in IA/1/103, 1852, 52/643, CSIC.

19. Lady Martin, wife of New Zealand's first Chief Justice, helped run a hospital for Maori for many years. See Raewyn Dalziel, 'The Colonial Helpmeet: Women's Role and the Vote in Nineteenth-Century New Zealand', *NZJH*, Vol.11, October 1977, p.177. For details about the low level of charity among the wealthy see Jim McAloon, 'Colonial Wealth: The Rich in Canterbury and Otago 1890-1914', Ph.D thesis, University of Otago, 1993, pp.267ff.

20. See J.F. Churton to Governor, 5 July 1841 and W. Hobson in reply, 6 July 1841, IA/1/7, CSIC. W. Halse to Police Magistrate, New Plymouth, 16 January 1846, IA/1/49, CSIC. For a list of indigents in the early 1850s see IA/1/84, 1850, 50/171, 50/349; 1852, IA/1/101, 52/54; IA/1/102, 52/276; CSIC. For admission to hospital see P. Dunn to Colonial Secretary, 5 January 1850, IA/1/84, CSIC. The report to the Governor from the Colonial Surgeon, 1 January 1852, IA/1/101, 1852, 52/198 makes especially interesting reading. Details about the psychiatric hospital are given in Colonial Secretary to John Finlay, 23 January 1852, IA/4/7, and Colonial Secretary to William Hay,

11 June 1852, CSOC. The contract price for the hospital was £528. Alan Ward notes that under Grey between 1845 and 1853 Maori access to social and welfare services, such as they were, was common. See *A Show of Justice*, pp.86-87.

21. For details about pensions, see IA/1/84, 1850; IA/1/101, 1852, 52/98, CSIC.

22. See H.R. Jackson, *Churches and People in Australia and New Zealand, 1860-1930*, Wellington, 1987, pp.23-24.

23. Margaret Tennant, *Paupers and Providers: Charitable Aid in New Zealand*, Wellington, 1989, pp.11-12, and p.1. Also Burns, Chapt. 27.

24. See Erik Olssen, *A History of Otago*, 1984, Chapt. 5; Tom Brooking, *And Captain of their Souls; An Interpretive Essay on the Life and Times of Captain William Cargill*, Dunedin, 1984, Chapts 4 and 5; also W.P. Morrell, *The Provincial System in New Zealand*, 2nd ed, Christchurch, 1964, Chapt. 1. See also W. Cargill to Lt. Governor, 29 April 1851, IA/1/ 126, 51/676, CSIC. The New Zealand Company by this time was heavily in debt and unable to help much with any of the settlements which it had initiated.

25. W.J. Gardner, 'A Colonial Economy' in *The Oxford History of New Zealand*, p.62. See also L.C. Webb in J. Hight and C.R. Straubel, *A History of Canterbury*, Vol. 1, Christchurch, 1957, pp.206-7.

26. H. Williams to W. Hobson, 19 June 1840, IA/1/1, CSIC.

27. G.R. Hawke, *Government in the New Zealand Economy*, Wellington, 1982, p.5. See also Paul Wooding in Alan Bollard & Robert Buckle (eds), *Economic Liberalisation in New Zealand*, Wellington, 1987, p.86.

28. *The Oxford History*, p.59.

29. Eight days after New Zealand received recognition as a separate colony on 16 November 1840, Hobson became known as Governor and Commander-in-Chief over the Colony of New Zealand. McLintock, p.99.

30. Marion E. McEwing, 'The Protection of Manufacturing Industries in New Zealand: From the Nineteenth Century Protectionist Movement to the Syntec Report', MA thesis, University of Otago, 1985, p.6. Customs dues are itemised in the *NZ Government Gazette*, No.2, 14 July 1841, IA/1/10, 1842, CSIC. For the month of December 1841 customs dues collected in Auckland produced a revenue to Government of £666, of which £534 came from imported spirits. Wellington produced £1441, and Russell another £493. As the economy slumped in 1842 there was a steep drop in customs revenue. In the financial year 1856-57 customs dues represented 95 per cent of central government's revenue. See 'Estimates', IA/1/173, 1856, 56/2763, CSIC.

31. David Nathan and Israel Joseph applied on 7 December 1840 and William Brown early the next year. See IA/1/4, 1840, CSIC; IA/4/1, 1840-43; IA/4/7, 1852, CSOC, NA.

32. See J. Henry to Colonial Secretary, 23 and 27 April 1846, IA/1/48, NA.

33. See Colonial Secretary to J. Norman, 16 November 1852, letters 379 and 389. Also Colonial Secretary to W.R. Finlayson, 11 November 1852, all IA/4/7, CSOC. See also W. Spain to Governor 7 March 1842, IA/1/11, CSIC. There is a list of licence fees paid in 1852 in IA/1/102, CSIC. Licences for the sale of ammunition are referred to in IA/4/ 10, CSOC and IA/1/182, 57/802, CSIC.

34. Colonial Secretary to E. Constable, 12 January 1853, letter no. 12, IA/4/7, CSOC.

35. R.C.J. Stone, *Makers of Fortune: A Colonial Business Community and its Fall*, Auckland, 1973, p.6. Jim McAloon, *Nelson: A Regional History*, Queen Charlotte Sound, 1997, p.16, argues that most of Nelson's early settlers were poor. Some of the hopes and realities surrounding early migration are discussed in W.D. Borrie, *Immigration to New Zealand, 1854-1938*, Canberra, 1991, Chapt. 1.

36. The difficulty in persuading younger women to emigrate is dealt with by Charlotte Macdonald, *A Woman of Good Character*, Wellington, 1990, pp.2-3.

37. Russell Stone, *James Dilworth*, Auckland 1995, p.87, notes that the Auckland Savings Bank waited for several weeks before it got its first deposit of £10. For comments about the 1860s see p.118.

38. Hawke, *The Making of New Zealand*, p.60. Banking returns showing the assets and liabili-

ties of the New Zealand Banking Company and the Union Bank of Australia in 1841 are to be found in IA/1/9, CSIC.

39. Olssen, *A History of Otago*, p.66.
40. McAloon, thesis, p.108.
41. W.K. Hancock, *Australia*, reprint ed, Melbourne 1961, p.52.
42. Paul Kennedy, *The Rise and Fall of the Great Powers*, London, 1989, p.193. The term 'railway mania' is used by E.G. Pilcher in his early history of New Zealand's railways in *NZOYB*, 1894, p.377, although the term was more usually used to describe railway company amalgamations, and carried a hint of questionable business practice. I am indebted to Gary Hawke for several observations about railways in the nineteenth century.
43. See submission from the Surveyor General to Felton Mathew, 19 August 1840, IA/1/3, CSIC.
44. W. Shortland to W. Wakefield, 13 October 1842, IA/4/1, CSOC.
45. See J. Churton to Governor, 27 July 1841, IA/1/8; William Hughes to Colonial Secretary, 23 March 1846, IA/1/48. See also IA/1/101, 1852, CSIC.
46. I am indebted to Paul Goldsmith who discovered material about the Rimutaka Road when researching for the Waitangi Tribunal's Rangahaua Whanui report on the Wairarapa.
47. See Edmund Bohan, *Edward Stafford: New Zealand's First Statesman*, Christchurch, 1994, pp.37-38. In this respect Stafford was the first of a long line of Nelson politicians.
48. See E.W. Stafford to H. Sewell, 18 December 1856, IA/4/10, 56/3848, CSOC. Stafford's letters to Sewell (IA/4/11) over the next two years provide further details. There is a fairly full account of the moves to arrange subsidised mail services in Howard Robinson, *A History of the Post Office of New Zealand*, Wellington, 1964, Chapt. 10.
49. There is a description of the issues involved with shipping subsidies in Raewyn Dalziel, *Julius Vogel: Business Politician*, Auckland, 1986, pp.100-3. For a later debate over the San Francisco mail service see Michael Bassett, *Sir Joseph Ward*, Auckland, 1993, pp.25-26. See also 'Ocean Mail Services', *AJHR*, F-6, 1904. There are regular reports in the *AJHR* tabling correspondence on the issue.
50. Hawke, *Government in the New Zealand Economy*, pp.9-10. Donald Denoon, *Settler Capitalism: The Dynamics of Dependent Development in the Southern Hemisphere*, Oxford, 1983, pp.71ff, notes the importance of governmental borrowing to all southern settler societies in the nineteenth century. 'Governments were generally judged by their ability to float loans, and their skill at disbursing those funds in capital work projects throughout the country', p.73.
51. Burns, pp.271-81.
52. A clear outline of the provisions of the 1852 Constitution is to be found in W.P. Morrell, *The Provincial System*, p.58.
53. See Michael Bassett, *The Mother of All Departments: A History of the Department of Internal Affairs*, Auckland, 1997, p.31.
54. *The Oxford History*, pp.61-64. See also J.B. Condliffe, *New Zealand in the Making: A Study of Economic and Social Development*, London, 1959, pp.141-2.
55. Alexander Brady, *Democracy in the Dominions: A Comparative Study in Institutions*, Toronto, 1952, p.263.
56. Geoffrey Blainey, *A Shorter History of Australia*, Melbourne, 1995, p.53.
57. Rollo Arnold, *The Farthest Promised Land: English Villagers, New Zealand Immigrants of the 1870s*, Wellington, 1981, contains much material about the settlers of the 1870s. But one of the central arguments in this chapter is that expectations of the State were well set before the time of the Vogel settlers.
58. Erik Olssen, 'Wakefield and the Scottish Enlightenment', in *Edward Gibbon Wakefield and the Colonial Dream: A Reconsideration*, Friends of the Turnbull Library, Wellington, 1997, p.48. The comment about 'ample government' comes from Hancock, p.52.
59. W.H. Oliver, *The Story of New Zealand*, London, 1960, pp.57-60.
60. Miles Fairburn, *The Ideal Society and its Enemies: The Foundation of Modern New Zealand Society, 1850–1900*, Auckland, 1989, p.25, and pp.240-1.

61. Hancock, *Australia*, p.55.
62. Quoted in Sinclair, *A History of New Zealand*, p.157.
63. P.W. Barlow, *Kaipara: Experiences of a Settler in North New Zealand*, London, 1888, pp.176-81.
64. André Siegfried, *Democracy in New Zealand*, Wellington, reprint, 1982, pp.54-55. See also David Hamer's introduction, p.ix.
65. Hawke, *Government in the New Zealand Economy*, p.7.

Chapter 2 Settlers Search for Prosperity

1. Hawke, *The Making of New Zealand*, pp.10-11.
2. Erik Olssen and Marcia Stenson, *A Century of Change: New Zealand 1800–1900*, Auckland, 1989, p.148.
3. Sinclair, *A History of New Zealand*, p.97.
4. R.C.J. Stone, *Young Logan Campbell*, Auckland, 1982, p.204.
5. Stone, *Young Logan Campbell*, p.186, quotes Campbell in 1853 saying that he was exporting lumber, cheese, butter, oats, potatoes and hay to the Australian goldfields.
6. Hawke, *The Making of New Zealand*, p.32. Colin Simkin in *The Instability of a Dependent Economy*, Oxford, 1951, p.25, says that wool peaked at 76 per cent of all exports in 1860. The number of sheep reached 20 million by 1900. A.H. Reed says in *The Gumdiggers: The Story of Kauri Gum*, Dunedin 1972, p.108, that 800 tons of gum was exported in 1853 with an export value of £1,600. According to the *NZ Listener*, 27 August 1965, p.3, the average annual value of flax exports 1853–60 was nearly £2,500.
7. Stone, *Makers of Fortune*, p.8.
8. Judith Bassett, *Sir Harry Atkinson, 1831–1892*, Auckland, 1975, pp.10-12.
9. McAloon, *Nelson*, p.45; Edmund Bohan, *Edward Stafford: New Zealand's First Statesman*, Christchurch, 1994, p.81.
10. Olssen, *A History of Otago*, pp.42-49.
11. See W.P. Morrell, *The Provincial System in New Zealand, 1852-76*, 2nd ed., Christchurch, 1964, p.60. For disputes, see IA/4/175, 1853, p.190, and IA/4/184, 1862, pp.137, 154, 155, 218, CSOC.
12. W. David McIntyre (ed), *The Journal of Henry Sewell, 1853-7*, Vol. 2, Christchurch, 1980, p.311.
13. See particularly E.W. Stafford to H. Sewell, 17 October 1857, IA/4/11, pp.15-23. For a discussion of shipping subsidies, see Howard Robinson, *A History of the Post Office in New Zealand*, Wellington, 1964, pp.102-113, 130-141. Also the annual reports and correspondence regarding negotiations each year in the *AJHR*, F-6. By 1881 a parliamentary select committee was considering the need to construct ships specially for the New Zealand-London trade. See *AJHR*, 1881, I-9.
14. W. Gisborne to J.W. Watt, 6 January 1857, IA/4/10, 57/105, p.5, CSOC. The *Gazette* notice was backed by a resolution of Parliament on 16 August 1858. In a later debate in Parliament, William Fox asserted that the sum offered was £5,000. See *NZPD*, 11 August 1869, p.421. There is a brief reference to early conjecture about a flax industry in Charles Hursthouse, *An Account of the Settlement of New Plymouth*, London, 1849, p.105.
15. W. Gisborne to Baron de Thierry, 26 September 1856, IA/4/10, p.131; 10 December 1858, IA/4/12.
16. Expressions of interest in the reward are to be found in IA/4/10, p.31 and p.33. See 'A King Dethroned', *NZ Listener*, 27 August 1965, p.3.
17. *NZPD*, 5 August 1869, pp.282-4; 415-25. See also IA/1/280, 69/2564; 69/2582; 69/2401, CSIC. Much detail about public efforts on behalf of the flax industry is to be found in *AJHR*, 1870, D-14.
18. W. Gisborne to Flax Commissioners, 21 September 1869, IA/4/25, p.376.
19. There is some information about flax subsidies in IA/4/72, p.29. *NZOYB*, 1913, pp.657-

8. For agitation from the 1880s, see *NZPD*, 18 July 1883, p.642; 10 June and 11 August 1886, p.396; 17 May 1887, p.286-8; 9 and 14 July 1891 and 15 July 1891, p.55 and p.135 and p.194; 25 August 1893, p.343; 31 July 1895, p.319. There is detail about hopes for the industry during the Great Depression in IC/1/4/89, part 2, and IC/1/2/7, W709. A set of regulations under the Industrial Efficiency Act 1936 was gazetted on 20 January 1938. See IC/1/2, part 4. There are some vivid descriptions of working in flax mills around Foxton in the late nineteenth century in Miles Fairburn, *Nearly Out of Heart and Hope*, Auckland, 1995, pp.40ff. There is a brief summary of the flax industry's history in *The Encyclopaedia of New Zealand*, Vol. 1, Wellington, 1966, pp.703-5. There is a little information about flax production at the bottom of the South Island in Margaret Trotter, *The Forgotten Flax Fields: Linen Flax in the South*, Invercargill, n.d. For details of flax production after World War II, see annual reports of the Linen Flax Corporation, *AJHR*, H44 and H-44B.

20. See IA/4/10, p.5. For background to the industry see Lanna Coughlan, 'The Growth of State Forestry in New Zealand – a Brief Review', *NZJPA*, Vol. 26, 1964, pp.66-79. Also A.L. Poole, *Forestry in New Zealand: The Shaping of Policy*, Auckland, 1969, pp.7ff.

21. See *AJHR*, 1906, B-6, p.4. Also report on state nurseries, *AJHR*, 1912, C-1B, p.2. There is a brief historical introduction on the State Forests Department in the Forestry files at National Archives.

22. The text of Seddon's speech is to be found in *AJHR*, 1896, H-24, p.7.

23. *AJHR*, 1904, H-33, and 1920, B-6, p.xiv.

24. *AJHR*, 1909, H-24. For the expansion of powers see the War Legislation and Statute Law Amendment Act, 1918, in Statutes, 1918, p.89.

25. *AJHR*, 1870, F-1.

26. John H. Angus, *Papermaking Pioneers: A History of New Zealand Paper Mills Ltd.*, Mataura, 1976, pp.24-26.

27. *AJHR*, 1870, F-1.

28. See *NZG*, 19 February 1874. See IA/1/321 (74/429); IA/4/40, p.112.

29. See Edwin Oakley to Colonial Secretary, 19 October 1858, (58/1807) IA/4/12, p.349; also IA/4/15, p.231, p.254, p.265.

30. *AJHR*, 1873, I-4. Also IA/4/65, p.125.

31. There is some information about the silk industry in two letters IA/4/27, p.187, and p.589. The quotation comes from the report of G. A. Schoch who investigated the silk industry in 1886. *AJHR*, 1887, Session 2, H-1.

32. *AJHR*, 1871, G-36 and G-14.

33. *AJHR*, 1870, F-1.

34. *The Year Book of New Zealand, 1885-86*, p.108.

35. See correspondence to the Governor, March-April 1860, IA/1/213, CSIC. For a discussion on the origins of the war see Alan Ward, 'The Origins of the Anglo-Maori Wars: A Reconsideration', *NZJH*, Vol.1, 1967, p.148. There is a good summary of the origins of the wars and the issues involved in M.P.K. Sorrenson, 'Maori and Pakeha', *The Oxford History*, pp.141-57. See also James Belich, 'The Governors and the Maori', in Keith Sinclair (ed), *The Oxford Illustrated History of New Zealand*, Auckland, 2nd ed., 1996, pp.75-98.

36. James Belich, *Making Peoples: A History of the New Zealanders*, Auckland, 1996, p.236.

37. The Colonial Secretary's outwards letter books, IA/4/14,15 and 16 provide much evidence about the domestic problems and the nature of claims made on the Government during the war. The Government also became involved in the settlement of soldiers after the war. Ministers selected and officials surveyed land for farms. Their size in the Tauranga area depended on rank: a field officer got 400 acres, a sergeant 80 acres and a private 50 acres. Once taking possession, settlers were struck off the Government's payroll, although they received free rations for 12 months. See Evelyn Stokes, 'Te Raupatu O Tauranga Moana: The Confiscation of Tauranga Lands, A Report for the Waitangi Tribunal', Hamilton, 1990, p.46.

38. See *NZG*, No.17, 26 June 1857. A copy of a licence to import/sell/repair guns is to be found in IA/4/12, p.225.
39. See Colonial Secretary to A. M. Smith, 25 November 1875, IA/4/35.
40. *NZPD*, 13 September 1878, p.170.
41. *LT*, 6 April 1861. I am indebted to John E. Martin for this reference.
42. In W. Gisborne to J. Martin, 1 April 1864, the Whitaker-Fox Ministry outlined the rules that were to underpin immigration. IA/4/15. J.B. Condliffe in his *New Zealand in the Making*, 2nd ed., London, 1959, p.163, dated the notion of a contract between settlers and the Government ten years later, during the Vogel era.
43. W.P. Morrell, *The Gold Rushes*, 2nd ed., London, 1968, pp.260ff.
44. The census returns for 1881 are to be found in *AJHR*, 1881, H-21A. After Otago, Canterbury was the next biggest provincial area with 112,115. Auckland had 99,216, and Wellington 61,354. Nelson had 26,297, Hawkes Bay 17,354, Taranaki 14,852, Westland 14,782 and Marlborough 9,304.
45. Olssen and Stenson, p.171. An assessment of the economic impact of gold is to be found in Hawke, *The Making of New Zealand*, pp.39-41.
46. W.D. Borrie, 'The Peopling of Australasia, 1788–1988,' in Keith Sinclair (ed), *Tasman Relations*, Auckland, 1988, p.205.
47. Stone, *Makers of Fortune*, p.8.
48. Of those miners who came in 1861, one estimate is that there was only one woman for every 100 men, and on the West Coast it was 25 women for every 100 men. Olssen and Stenson, p.170.
49. *AJHR*, 1866, B-8.
50. The full text of the commission's findings is to be found in IA/92/1, NA. See also *AJHR*, 1866, D-7A. A full list of employees is to be found in *AJHR*, 1869, D-21.
51. See J.E. Le Rossignol and W.D. Stewart, *State Socialism in New Zealand*, New York, 1910, Chapt. 9. Gary Hawke in *The Making of New Zealand*, pp.110-12 discusses central government's motivation for these measures.
52. The 1870 debates are to be found in *NZPD*, 18, 30 August 1870, pp.107-401; the 1872 debates begin in *NZPD*, 23 July 1872, pp.32ff.
53. See 'Report of Public Trust Office', *AJHR*, 1977, B-9, p.11.
54. Fox is quoted in J.A. Dowie, 'Business Politicians in Action: The New Zealand Railway Boom of the 1870s', *Business Archives and History*, Vol. 5, February 1965, p.36. Gisborne, *NZPD*, Vol. 9, 23 August 1870, p.184.
55. *ODT*, 30 June 1870, editorial.
56. *NZH*, 6 July 1870, editorial.
57. Ibid, p.226; *EP*, 12 July 1870, editorial.
58. Quoted by Dalziel, *Julius Vogel*, p.126.
59. Keith Sinclair, *A History of New Zealand*, p.151.
60. See W. Gisborne to J. Knowles, 1 December 1869, IA/4/25, p.656; Gisborne to F.D. Bell and I. Featherston, 23 December 1869, *AJHR*, 1870, D-4. John Morrison to Colonial Secretary, 2 December 1869, IA/1/280,(70/288) sets out Morrison's views on immigration.
61. Raewyn Dalziel, *The Origins of New Zealand Diplomacy*, Wellington, 1975, Chapt. 3. See also Rollo Arnold, *The Farthest Promised Land: English Villagers, New Zealand Immigrants of the 1870s*, Wellington, 1981, pp.41-47.
62. Quoted in Olssen and Stenson, p.235.
63. Arnold, op.cit. See Vogel's correspondence with the Agent-General, *AJHR*, 1875, D-1.
64. Quoted from an 1885 article by J.A. Dowie, p.33.
65. See G.S. Cooper to Ross, Hotson, Peyman and Walker, 19 July 1870, 70/1748, IA/4/26, p.664, and IA/4/27, p.32. Also IA/4/26, p.574.
66. There were two major debates on railways: the first in September 1870, *NZPD*, 6,7,9, 10, 12 September, pp.534ff, the second in November 1871, *NZPD*, 10 November 1871, pp.992ff. J.E. Le Rossignol and W.D. Stewart, *State Socialism in New Zealand*, pp.56-59

discuss some of the battles surrounding early construction. Legal ructions over the contracts with Brogdens lasted many years. See William Downie Stewart, *The Life and Times of the Rt Hon Sir Francis H.D. Bell*, Wellington, 1937, p.55. There is also detail in 'History of Railways 1863–1963', *NZOYB*, 1963, pp.1175-93.

67. N.H.M. Dalston, *NZOYB*, 1894, p.386. Details about the arbitration process are to be found in *AJHR*, 1896, D-4; *NZOYB*, 1902, pp.428-9.

68. E.G. Pilcher, *NZOYB*, 1894, p.385. There is an historical summary of railways in *An Encyclopaedia of New Zealand*, Wellington, 1966, pp.31-43.

69. Rossignol and Stewart, Chapt. 4, has additional statistical detail about the construction of railways and other public works.

70. *NZOYB*, 1895, pp.167-8. The Auckland–Drury line built by Brogdens in the 1860s cost between £3,500 and £4,000 per mile. See *AJHR*, 1870, D-30. See J.G. Ward, 'Government Ownership of Railways' in *The Red Funnel*, Vol.11, No.4, 1 May 1906, (Dunedin), p.291.

71. See Secretary to the Treasury to the Prime Minister, 17 May 1929, T/1/52/584.

72. *NZOYB*, 1894, pp.380ff; *NZOYB*, 1902, p.428.

73. See IA/4/27, p.117. Le Rossignol and Stewart, p.53.

74. See Howard Robinson, *A History of the Post Office in New Zealand*, Wellington, 1964, pp.143-7.

75. A.C. Wilson, *Wire and Wireless: A History of Telecommunications in New Zealand, 1890-1987*, Palmerston North, 1994, p.35.

76. See IA/1/321, (74/507); also Wilson p.50, and p.61. Also *NZOYB*, 1902, p.433.

77. Hawke, *The Making of New Zealand*, pp.81-82.

78. Roger Douglas, 'Julius Vogel: A Battler and a Gambler', *New Outlook*, May/June 1986, p.57.

79. The main debate on the abolition of the provinces is to be found in *NZPD*, Vol.17, beginning 6 August 1875, pp.218ff. See also *NZPD*, Vol. 23, 9 October 1876, pp.121ff. Vogel agreed with Atkinson that an end to provincialism would save money. See J.Vogel to J Macandrew, 13 April 1876, *AJHR*, 1876, A-4.

Chapter 3 The Search for Security

1. See IA/4/36, p.492. A list of provincial staff laid off is in *AJHR*, 1877, Vol. 1, A-9a. Local government is dealt with in Bassett, *The Mother of All Departments*, pp. 59-60. See also Michael Bassett, 'The Context of Local Government Reform' in P. McDermott, V. Forgie & R. Howell, *An Agenda for Local Government*, Palmerston North, 1996, pp.29-37. Also Graham Bush, *Local Government in New Zealand*, Auckland, 1995, p.10. Details about subsidies are to be found in *AJHR*, 1906, B-6. Later secretaries of Internal Affairs argued that the availability of subsidies from central government was a major factor in the multiplication of local authorities. See A.G. Harper to B.C. Ashwin, 29 April 1940, T/1/40/70. Sir Patrick O'Dea expressed similar sentiments to the author in 1995. There are other memos in this Treasury file on the subject of local authority subsidies dated 8 September 1927 and 1 June 1936.

2. Webb, Hight and Straubel, p.179, pp.217-8.

3. Terence Hodgson, *Colonial Capital: Wellington, 1865–1910*, Auckland, 1990, p.30.

4. Olssen, *A History of Otago*, p.87; W.P. Morrell, *The University of Otago: A Centennial History*, Dunedin, 1969, pp.5-7.

5. *NZPD*, Vol. 25, 3 September 1877, p.241. See also the contribution of Dr Pollen, *NZPD*, Vol. 26, 2 October 1877, pp.119ff. There is a detailed study of the Education Act 1877 in Roger Openshaw, Greg Lee and Howard Lee, *Challenging the Myths: Rethinking New Zealand's Educational History*, Palmerston North, 1993, Chapt. 5.

6. *AJHR*, 1880, H-1a. Initially the per capita grant per student to primary schools was £3 15s per pupil.

7. See Keith Sinclair, *A History of the University of Auckland, 1883–1983*, Auckland, 1983, pp.14-31.
8. *NZPD*, Vol. 24, 3 August 1877, p.241.
9. Derek A. Dow, *Safeguarding the Public Health: A History of the New Zealand Department of Health*, Wellington, 1995, p.17; G.W.A. Bush, *Decently and in Order; The Government of the City of Auckland, 1840–1971*, Auckland, 1971, pp.40-41.
10. Laurie Barber and Roy Towers, *Wellington Hospital, 1847–1976*, Wellington, 1976, pp.3-5.
11. Olssen, *A History of Otago*, p.83.
12. See Dow, p.34. The payment regimes in 1878 are set out in IA/4/40, pp.541, 566.
13. The Colonial Secretary set out the basis for funding in a letter to the Chairman of the Waimate County Council, 23 July 1877, IA/4/211, pp.257-9. See also IA/4/40, pp.176, 317. See also Colonial Secretary to C. Nedwill, 3 January 1878, IA/4/40, p.154.
14. See G.S. Cooper to Mayor of Christchurch, 26 March 1878, p.440, IA/4/221. See also IA/4/50, pp.270, 317, 128.
15. See IA/4/55, p.737; also IA/4/45, p.295. Until 1885 the Colonial Secretary's outwards correspondence is a mine of information about hospital grants and the difficulties that Government experienced with claims.
16. By 1983 there were huge discrepancies in the numbers of hospital beds per population in various parts of the country. Dunedin, with its medical school, and Wellington, with its proximity to the seat of government, had succeeded in lifting their ratio of beds to much higher levels than Auckland and other areas of population growth.
17. See Bassett, *Ward*, pp.119-20.
18. See debates on the Charitable Institutions Bill, *NZPD*, Vol. 24, 27 July 1877, pp.73ff.
19. See IA/4/36, pp.683, 685, 730; IA/4/40, p.641; IA/4/50, p.588; IA/4/55, pp.57, 716, 723; IA/4/45, pp.25, 44; IA/4/50, p.80. There is a file on charitable aid cases in IA/1/348 (77/732). See also letters about orphanages, IA/4/46(79/4783).
20. For examples of special pleading, see IA/1/338, (76/756); IA/1/322, (74/868); IA/1/338, (76/936); IA/1/509, (88/436). See also *AJHR*, 1876, H-23.
21. Judith Bassett, *Atkinson*, pp.40-42.
22. For a table of public indebtedness 1879–1906, see *AJHR*, 1906, B-18A, p.2. For the antics of Grey's Government, see David Hamer, 'The Agricultural Company and New Zealand Politics, 1877–1886', *Historical Studies*, Vol. 10, no.38, 1962.
23. Judith Bassett, *Atkinson*, p.71. The lead-up to, and tenure of, Hall's Ministry is dealt with by Jean Garner, *By His Own Merits: Sir John Hall – Pioneer, Pastoralist and Premier*, Christchurch, 1995, Chapt. 8.
24. See Ian McGibbon, 'Alfred Saunders', *DNZB*, Vol. 1, Wellington, 1990, pp.383-5.
25. *AJHR*, 1880, H-2. See comments by Alfred Saunders, quoted in R.J. Polaschek, *Government Administration in New Zealand*, Wellington, 1958, p.33.
26. The report of the commission is to be found in *AJHR*, 1880, H-22. Papers relating to the commission are in IA/100/1. See also *AJHR*, 1883, Vol. 3, H-30. Also IA/1/401, (80/2765).
27. John E. Martin, 'Unemployment, Government and the Labour Market in New Zealand, 1860–1890', *NZJH*, Vol. 29, October 1995, p.176.
28. For comments on the 'land jobbers', see Stone, *Young Logan Campbell*, p.94.
29. J. Barr, *The City of Auckland 1840–1920: A History*, Auckland, 1922, pp.120-4, lists many of the fires that ravaged early Auckland.
30. Heather Shepherd, 'The Nature and Role of Friendly Societies in Later Nineteenth Century New Zealand', BA Hons paper, Massey University, 1976, p.46, asserts that a friendly society was established in New Plymouth in the very earliest days of settlement. See also Tennant, p.14. See David Thomson, *A World Without Welfare: New Zealand's Colonial Experiment*, Auckland, 1998.
31. *NZPD*, Vol. 20, 29 June 1876, pp.235ff.
32. Ibid, Vol. 24, 25 July and 7 August 1877, pp.59, 245.

33. See *AJHR*, 1878, H-14; 1879, H-12, Session 2. Of the original societies 70 were branches of the Independent Order of Odd Fellows or Manchester Unity; 38 were branches of the Ancient Order of Foresters; one was a branch of the Ancient Order of Shepherds; three were branches of the Independent Order of Rechabites; three were Sons and Daughters of Temperance; six were members of the Hibernian Australasian Catholic Benevolent Society and there were several others. For further detail about friendly societies at this time, see David Thomson, op.cit.
34. *NZPD*, Vol. 42, 10 July 1882, pp.183ff; Judith Bassett, *Atkinson*, p.111.
35. See Downie Stewart, *Bell*, p.63.
36. *NZPD*, Vol. 42, 10 July 1882, pp.183-90.
37. Ibid, p.185.
38. Ibid, p.189.
39. Ibid, p.194. Grey's place in Liberal folklore is discussed by David Hamer, *The New Zealand Liberals, The Years of Power, 1891–1912*, Auckland, 1988, pp.16-19. For the contribution to the statue, see IA/4/89, p.160.
40. Few hospitals kept accurate records of those in receipt of assistance. The *NZOYB* 1902 reports that of the 19 Charitable Aid Boards distributing outdoor relief in 1901, three kept records of such assistance, and from these a total of 1861 people, including 1096 children, were receiving assistance. The number receiving indoor relief stood at 1167 at the end of 1901. *NZOYB*, 1902, p.373.
41. *AJHR*, 1906, B-18A, p.2.
42. Tables relating to immigration and emigration in the period 1877–1891 are to be found in R.J. Campbell, '"The Black Eighties" – Unemployment in New Zealand in the 1880s', *Australian Economic History Review*, Vol. 16, March 1976, pp. 70-82.
43. William Downie Stewart, *William Rolleston*, Christchurch, 1940, pp.140-1.
44. Judith Bassett, *Atkinson*, pp.143-4. See also P.S. O'Connor, 'Keeping New Zealand White, 1908–20', *NZJH*, Vol. 2, April 1968, pp.41-65; Bassett, *Ward*, pp.151-2.
45. W. P. Reeves explained these beliefs in 'Protective Tariffs in Australia and New Zealand', *Economic Journal: The Journal of the British Economic Association*, London, Vol. 9, 1899, pp.36-44. The politics of the tariff are discussed in Keith Sinclair, 'The Significance of the "Scarecrow Ministry", 1887–1891', in R. Chapman and K. Sinclair (eds), *Studies of a Small Democracy*, Auckland, 1963, pp.102-26.
46. For comments on the development of New Zealand's tariff, see Paul Wooding 'Liberalising the International Trade Regime', in Alan Bollard and Robert Buckle (eds), *Economic Liberalisation in New Zealand*, Wellington, 1987, p.86. An account of the various protection leagues in the years before 1888, and an assessment of the effects of the tariff, is to be found in Marion E. McEwing, MA thesis, University of Otago, 1985, pp.10-47.
47. For Reeves's comments, *NZPD*, Vol. 60, 1888, p.497. This comment was drawn to my attention by John E. Martin and is contained in his unpublished manuscript, 'Labour in a new world: Labour origins and the state in nineteenth century New Zealand'. See also W.P. Reeves, *The Long White Cloud*, London, 5th impression, 1956, pp.258-9. A list of items exempted under the Customs Duties Act Amendment Act 1900 is to be found in *AJHR*, 1901, H-49. For comments, see Siegfried, p.158.
48. See the debates over the 1890 no-confidence motion in Atkinson's Government, *NZPD*, Vol. 67, 1 July 1890, pp.191ff. These are dealt with by Timothy McIvor, *The Rainmaker: A Biography of John Ballance*, Auckland, 1989, pp.165-7. See also David Hamer, *The New Zealand Liberals*, Chapt. 1. In his pre-sessional address in June 1890 Joseph Ward laid great stress on the need to settle the land because it would bring prosperity to the towns. See *ST*, 10 and 14 June 1890.
49. Of the eight ministers who served in Ballance's Cabinet, four (William Pember Reeves, Joseph Ward, Alfred J. Cadman and James Carroll) had either been born in New Zealand or grown to maturity in it. Ballance (1866), Patrick Buckley (1865) and Richard John Seddon (1866) had each come to New Zealand after the New Zealand Government had first promised to guarantee jobs to migrants. John McKenzie (1860) was the only mature

immigrant in the ministry with more than 30 years' experience of New Zealand. See also Bassett, *Ward*, pp38-39.

50. Bassett, *Ward*, p.114.

51. J.G. Ward, 'Government Ownership of Railways' in *The Red Funnel*, Vol. 11, no. 4, 1 May 1906, p.294.

52. Between the census of 1891 and 1901, Wellington's population rose by 44.32 per cent compared with Auckland's 31 per cent, Christchurch's 19.22 per cent and Dunedin's 14.22 per cent. By 1916 Wellington's population (95,235) had surpassed that of Christchurch (92,733), but Auckland (133,712) was now way out in front as the biggest city in New Zealand. See *NZOYB*, 1896, p.88; 1902, p.214; 1916, p.62.

53. *AJHR*, 1890 and 1912-13, F-1.

54. *AJHR*, 1891, D-5a, and 1912 D-2.

55. See the 1881 appeal to the Colonial Secretary and his reply, IA/4/50, p.551.

56. A discussion of rising numbers during these years is to be found in Ian S. Ewing, 'Public Service Reform in New Zealand, 1866–1912', MA thesis, University of Auckland, 1979. For statistics see *AJHR*, 1891 and 1912, H-28. Also *NZOYB*, 1895, p.81 and 1913, pp.97, 865. The figures for 1904 are contained in *AJHR*, 1905, H-5b. This set of figures does not include teachers, who numbered more than 5000 in 1905. See also Le Rossignol and Stewart, p.197.

57. There is a speech of Ward's where he sets out his beliefs in *NZPD*, Vol. 120, 4 July 1902, pp.93-98. A description of the 1908 scheme is contained in *NZOYB*, 1911, p.72.

58. See for instance *AJHR*, 1900, H-36. Railways had 1687 on its books, the Post Office 1001, and Defence 169.

59. Hamer discusses this point, *The New Zealand Liberals*, p.15.

60. *Press*, 25 July 1892. For background to McKenzie, see T.H.W. Brooking, 'Sir John McKenzie and the Origins and Growth of the Department of Agriculture, 1891-1900', MA thesis, Massey University, 1972. Also Brooking, '"Busting Up" the Greatest Estate of All: Liberal Maori Land Policy, 1891-1911', *NZJH*, Vol. 26, April 1992, pp.78-98, and W.J. Gardner, *A Pastoral Kingdom Divided, Cheviot 1889–94*, Wellington, 1992, Chapt. 7.

61. Of note about the Land and Income Tax Act 1891 was that besides exempting the first £300 of income, which meant that few people paid any income tax, another £50 was exempted for the payment of life insurance premiums, indicating the Liberals' strong belief in self-help. See *NZOYB*, 1895, p.279.

62. See the comments of William Rolleston, *NZPD*, Vol. 78, 13 September 1892, p.61. A good summary of McKenzie's land reforms is made by S. Percy Smith in *NZOYB*, 1894, pp.201ff. See also Keith Sinclair, *The Liberal Government 1891–1912*, Auckland, 1967, pp.17-20.

63. Hamer, *The New Zealand Liberals*, p.143. See *SDN*, 15 August 1894; 18 August 1894. See Jim McAloon, thesis, pp.176, 234.

64. Le Rossignol and Stewart, p.26.

65. See *Auckland Savings Bank Centenary*, Auckland, 1947, pp.62-68; Gordon McLauchlan, *The ASB: A Bank and its Community*, Auckland, 1991, pp.52-55. Also Keith Sinclair and W.F. Mandle, *Open Account: A History of the Bank of New South Wales in New Zealand*, Wellington, 1961, pp.123ff.

66. Stone, *Makers of Fortune*, pp.193-5.

67. Bassett, *Ward*, p.51; N.M. Chappell, *New Zealand Bankers Hundred: A History of the Bank of New Zealand, 1861–1961*, Wellington 1961, Chapt. 10. There is an account of negotiations between the bank's representatives and ministers in James Drummond, *The Life and Work of Richard John Seddon*, Christchurch, 1906, pp.207-8.

68. *NZH*, 2 July 1894. A full account of the debates is given in the *NZH*, 30 June 1894.

69. The complex story surrounding Ward's collapse is told in Bassett, *Ward*, Chapts 5-7.

70. G.R. Hawke, *Between Governments and Banks*, Wellington, 1973, p.13.

71. Neil C. Quigley, 'The Mortgage Market in New Zealand, and the Origins of the Government Advances to Settlers Act 1894', *NZ Economic Papers*, Vol. 23, 1989, pp.51ff.

72. Bassett, *Ward*, pp.51-53, 56-59. Ward's speech when introducing the Bill sets out clearly what his intentions were. See *NZPD*, Vol. 85, 14 September 1894, pp.684ff.
73. Peter Coleman, 'The New Zealand Welfare State: Origins and Reflections', *Continuity*, no. 2, 1983.
74. *NZOYB*, 1913, pp.695-9.
75. *NZH*, 16 October 1894, editorial. See also earlier editorial comments by the *SDN*, 8 August 1894.
76. Quoted in Bassett, *Ward*, p.97. There is a succinct account of labour relations before 1894 in James Holt, *Compulsory Arbitration: in New Zealand: The First Forty Years*, Auckland, 1986.
77. *Press*, 20 July 1892. See Keith Sinclair, *William Pember Reeves: New Zealand Fabian*, London, 1965.
78. Sinclair, *Reeves*, p.111. Reeves gives his own version of his labour legislation in *The Long White Cloud*, pp.314-21.
79. Quoted in Holt, p.25.
80. The term 'social engineering' is used by K.R. Howe in *Singer in a Songless Land: A Life of Edward Tregear, 1846–1931*, Auckland, 1991.
81. *NZOYB*, 1902, p.425; Howe, pp.76-80. R.J. Campbell, 'Unemployment in New Zealand, 1875–1914', M.Phil thesis, Massey University, 1976, deals with unemployment and has a number of graphs and sets of statistics. There is an article on the state farms experiment in *NZOYB*, 1894, p.243.
82. Howe, pp.83-84. Tregear summarises the labour legislation in *NZOYB*, 1894, pp.362ff. See John Martin, *Holding the Balance: A History of New Zealand's Department of Labour, 1891–1995*, Christchurch, 1996, pp.39-60.
83. Sinclair, *Reeves*, p.17. See also Holt, p.17, and Howe, pp.85-86. Reeves's comment is quoted in G.W. Clinkard, 'Wages and Working Hours in New Zealand 1897–1919', *NZOYB*, 1919, p.862.
84. Holt, p.34, cautions against accepting that the main purpose of the Act was the fostering of trade unions.
85. Holt outlines the evolution of rules relating to strikes, pp.72-85.
86. Holt, p.25.
87. See G.W. Clinkard, p.908.
88. *AJHR*, 1912, Session 2, H-18, pp.lxxxiv, cv.
89. G.T. Booth at the annual general meeting of the Canterbury Employers' Association, 1902; see Annual Report, p.11. Gilbert Anderson, address, 6 December 1904, Canterbury Employers' Annual Report, 1905, p.21. Also comments of J.A. Frostick, Canterbury Employers' Association report 1911, p.17. The Secretary of the Canterbury Employers' Association, Henry Broadhead, deals with employers' views in *State Regulation of Labour and Labour Disputes in New Zealand*, Christchurch, 1908.
90. Holt, pp.57, 106.
91. Holt, p.37. Broadhead, Chapt. 7, discusses the development of minimum wages. Deakin's ideas about 'fair' wages are discussed in J.A. La Nauze, *Alfred Deakin: A Biography*, Melbourne, 1979 ed., pp.410ff.
92. Bassett, *Ward*, p.138. Ten years earlier when Ward was in London talking up New Zealand to investors considering advancing money to facilitate his Advances to Settlers scheme, he told the Royal Colonial Institute that New Zealand's per capita wealth was £232 compared with the United Kingdom's £247. See extract from *Journal of the Royal Colonial Institute*, Vol. 26, London, June 1895. Also *SDN*, 2 May 1895. In 1911 J.A. Frostick of the Canterbury Employers' Association claimed that at £335 per head, New Zealand was ahead of Great Britain on £291 and the USA on £263. See Annual Report, 1911, p.17. For an analysis of New Zealand wealth see Margaret N. Galt, 'Wealth and Income in New Zealand c1870-c1939', Ph.D thesis, VUW, 1985.

Chapter 4 The Essential Goodness of State Action

1. Gilbert Anderson acknowledged in December 1904 at a meeting of the Canterbury employers that many of them were Liberals, but were 'worried' by aspects of government policy. Canterbury Employers' Association, Annual Report, 1905, p.20.
2. See Peter J. Coleman, *Progressivism and the World of Reform: New Zealand and the Origins of the American Welfare State,* Kansas, 1987, p.16, p.41. See André Métin, *Socialism Without Doctrines,* Sydney, reprint of 1901 publication, 1977.
3. *Visit to New Zealand in 1898; Beatrice Webb's Diaries with entries by Sidney Webb,* Wellington, 1959, p.55. Quoted also in Carole Seymour-Jones, *Beatrice Webb: Woman of Conflict,* London, 1992, p.240. Sidney's comments are quoted in Francis Castles, *The Working Class and Welfare: Reflections on the Political Development of the Welfare State in Australia and New Zealand, 1890-1980,* Wellington, 1985, p.12.
4. Coleman, p.49.
5. Hamer (ed), *Siegfried's Democracy in New Zealand,* p.xxxiv.
6. Coleman, p.25. For a discussion of Bellamy, see Joseph Schiffman (ed), *Edward Bellamy: Selected Writings on Religion and Society,* New York, 1955.
7. Quoted by David J. Rothman, 'The State as Parent', in Allen F. Davis and Harold D. Woodman (eds), *Conflict and Consensus in Modern American History,* Lexington, Massachusetts, 1988, p.262.
8. Miles Fairburn, *Nearly out of Heart and Hope,* pp.237-9.
9. Judith Bassett, 'Sir Harry Atkinson', MA thesis, University of Auckland, 1966, p.147; McIvor, *The Rainmaker,* Chapt. 6; Sinclair, *Reeves,* p.46; Howe, *Tregear,* p.75. J. B. Condliffe in his *New Zealand in the Making,* London, 1959, p.181, carries an unidentified comment by Reeves about his views on the interchange of ideas in New Zealand at the time of his reforms.
10. McIvor, p.117. David Hamer devotes Chapt. 2 of *The New Zealand Liberals* to a discussion of the intellectual underpinning to liberalism.
11. Race Mathews, *Australia's First Fabians: Middle Class Radicals, Labour Activists and the Early Labour Movement,* Cambridge, 1993, studies the Australian Fabian movement. He concludes that it was somewhat ephemeral until after World War II. There appears to be no similar study of Fabianism in New Zealand, although Sinclair and Howe refer to the impact that the *Fabian Essays in Socialism* of 1889 had on Reeves and Tregear. According to Margaret Lovell-Smith, Kate Sheppard and the Lovell-Smiths in Canterbury participated in discussions about the ideas of the Fabians in the 1880s and 1890s and adopted the slogan 'plain living and high thinking', *Plain Living High Thinking,* Christchurch, 1994, p.40, pp.53-54. There are a few papers about the Auckland Fabian Club from 1928 till the 1960s in the University of Auckland MSS and Archives, A-63. The quotes of Shaw are in G.B. Shaw, *The Fabian Society,* London, 1892, pp.3, 25-27. There are several books about the British Fabians. See Anne Fremantle, *This Little Band of Prophets: The Story of the Gentle Fabians,* London, 1960. Also Norman and Jeanne MacKenzie, *The Fabians,* New York, 1977, and Ian Britain, *Fabianism and Culture,* Cambridge, 1982.
12. Keith Hancock, *Australia,* Brisbane reprint, 1961, pp.71-82, discusses the tariff in Australia. See also J.A. La Nauze, *Alfred Deakin: A Biography,* Melbourne 1979, pp.411ff. Hancock, p.76, quotes a 1929 report which estimated that Australia's tariff had raised Australia's prices about 10 per cent higher than they would otherwise have been under a purely revenue tariff. No similar assessment seems to have been made of the cost of New Zealand's post-1888 tariff. Ward spent time with Deakin. See Bassett, *Ward,* pp.140, 151, 152-5. For a discussion of Jensen and others in Australia, see Frank Farrell, 'Australia: A Laboratory of Social Reform' in Farrell (ed), *Traditions for Reform,* p.4.
13. There are some rough minute books for Christchurch and Wellington Fabian groups, 1908–1915 in MS 314, ATL. They convey few names or useful information about the subjects under discussion.
14. David Thomson, 'Welfare Before the Welfare State', unpublished MS, p.146.

15. Hawke, *The Making of New Zealand*, pp.113-6. There is a short debate about what moti-vated the Liberals in W.H. Oliver, 'Social Policy in the Liberal Period', *NZJH*, Vol.13, April 1979, pp.25-42. Ward's views on the role of the State were probably best expressed at the time of the passage of the Wages Protection Bill in 1898 when he said that all classes in New Zealand were entitled to protection by the State. Bassett, *Ward*, p.97. Richard Newman at one point likens Ward to a judge of the Arbitration Court imposing a solution on policy disputes, and 'steering a middle course'. See R.K. Newman, 'Liberal Policy and the Left Wing, 1908-1911', MA thesis, University of Auckland, 1965, p.389.
16. Newman's thesis is a major study of the left-wing Liberals, many of them middle-class radicals.
17. Quoted in Sinclair, *Reeves*, p.210.
18. Sinclair, *History*, p.184. Hamer quotes Reeves as having said that colonists needed to learn how to 'make shifts, invent devices, confront the unexpected' and that politicians learned to be 'handy in emergencies'. Hamer, *The New Zealand Liberals*, p.37. J.C. Beaglehole, *New Zealand: A Short History*, p.59. Simon Upton, 'When "liberal and progressive" was OK', *New Zealand Books*, Vol. 5, Number 4, October 1995, p.19.
19. I am grateful to Simon Upton for an opportunity to discuss this distinction within catego-ries of conservatives.
20. See Downie Stewart, *Rolleston*, p.128; *Bell*, pp.74-78, and *NZPD*, Vol. 83, 29 June 1994, p.152. McAloon, p.183.
21. Coleman, p.40, argues that the experimental phase concluded in 1894 and both Sinclair, *History*, and R.T. Shannon, 'The Fall of Reeves, 1893–1896' in Chapman and Sinclair, *Studies*, pp.127-52, see Reeves's departure in 1896 as a sorry blow to the Government's reforming zeal.
22. *NZOYB*, 1895, pp.173ff, discusses these issues. Life insurance is discussed by David Thomson in 'Welfare before the Welfare State', unpublished manuscript 1995, pp.79ff.
23. Le Rossignol and Stewart, pp.190-1. A departmental account of the background to old age pensions is contained in *The Growth and Development of Social Security in New Zea-land: A Survey of Social Security in New Zealand from 1898 to 1949*, Wellington, 1950. In 1896 a total of 199 people received pensions from the Government, 135 of them civil servants, who were paid under the State Service Act, 1866. The rest received small pay-ments, mostly per diem allowances, for wounds received during the wars of the 1860s. See *AJHR*, 1896, H-26.
24. See Tennant, p.100. Elderly Maori could be granted 'rations' by the Native Department. When Maori were paid pensions prior to 1938 they were usually below the levels paid to Pakeha.
25. The backbencher quoted is Ward, *NZPD*, Vol. 104, 1898, pp.577-8. One Liberal who opposed the non-contributory pensions, J. W. Kelly of Invercargill, discussed his opposi-tion in *ST*, 22 March 1898. He lost his seat in 1899 because Seddon endorsed another candidate, J. A. Hanan. For other pension detail, see *NZOYB*, 1902, pp.519-24; 1913, 704-10. Le Rossignol and Stewart, pp.184-5, explain how the income test applied, as does the departmental survey, pp.23-24. The Thomson quote comes from 'Society and Social Welfare', in Colin Davis and Peter Lineham (eds), *The Future of the Past: Themes in New Zealand History*, Palmerston North, 1991, p.100. The barrier to resident Asians receiving pensions was removed by the Pensions Amendment Act 1936. Unnaturalised aliens, how-ever, were still barred.
26. Ward's estimate of 3000 widows likely to qualify for the pension (*AJHR*, 1911, B-6, p.xxviii) was somewhat wide of the mark. By 1916 1890 were drawing the benefit and they were costing the taxpayer only £37,000 instead of the £55,000 he had estimated in 1911. See *NZOYB*, 1916, p.525.
27. *NZOYB*, 1911, p.639. The Oddfellows (Manchester Unity), Druids and Foresters were the three biggest societies, sharing more than 55,000 of these members. For Ward's com-ments, see the budget of 1911, *AJHR*, B-6, pp.xviii-xxviii.
28. The scheme is set out in detail in *NZOYB*, 1913, pp.719-21. The comment about it being

a 'Government friendly society' is quoted by Elizabeth Hanson, *The Politics of Social Security: The 1938 Act and some later Developments,* Auckland, 1980, p.25.

29. *NZOYB*, 1928, p.640.
30. The report of the Department of Health, *AJHR*, 1902, H-31, contains a lot of information about Auckland city health problems, sanitary needs and Maori health.
31. *AJHR*, 1913, H-31, pp.2-3. By 1917 six doctors and seven school nurses had examined more than 100,000 schoolchildren and given lectures to teacher trainees. See *AJHR*, 1917, E-11.
32. *NZOYB*, 1913, pp.172-5. See also Dow, pp.48-57. The quote comes from *AJHR*, 1913, H-31, p.3.
33. Devonport is described as 'the healthiest portion of [the Auckland] district' in the Health Department's Annual Report, *AJHR*, 1909, H-31, p.44. The dentists' appeal to the Government is to be found in *AJHR*, 1905, H-31A.
34. St Helen's hospitals, named after Seddon's Lancashire birthplace, opened in Wellington in June 1905, Dunedin in October 1905, Auckland in June 1906 and Christchurch in April 1907. There is some interesting information about the Auckland St Helen's Hospital in the report of a Commission of Inquiry, *AJHR*, 1913, H-31B.
35. Charlotte Parkes discusses the 'medicalisation' of maternity services in Linda Bryder (ed), *A Healthy Country,* Wellington, 1991, pp.165-80. P.M. Smith, *Maternity in Dispute: New Zealand 1920–1939,* Wellington, 1986, p.1. A discussion of mortality figures and sanitation is to be found in Geoffrey W. Rice, 'Public Health in Christchurch, 1875–1910: Mortality and Sanitation', in Bryder, pp.85-108.
36. *Evening Star* (Dunedin), 5 August 1893.
37. There were 4743 teachers in 2214 public primary schools by 1912. They taught 162,536 children. See *NZOYB*, 1913, pp.204-5.
38. *NZOYB*, 1913, p.239.
39. Ibid, pp.199, 217. The literacy figure in 1874 had been 68 per cent, and in 1894 77.25 per cent. See *NZOYB*, 1894, p.64.
40. There is information about industrial schools in *AJHR*, 1901, E-3 and E-3A.
41. *AJHR*, 1906, E-1, pp.xxvii-xxxii. By 1920 the Government was also providing £3,000 pa in subsidies for the purchase of books in rural public libraries. The money was paid to libraries in places with fewer than 1500 people. It was for books 'of a high standard of merit'. See *AJHR*, 1921, E-10; *NZOYB*, 1913, pp.218-47.
42. Elected for Wellington East on 24 November 1908, McLaren won the seat with Liberal support as a result of Ward's 'second ballot' legislation.
43. *NZOYB*, 1913, pp.697-9.
44. See Barbara Fill, *Seddon's State Houses: The Workers' Dwelling Act 1905 & the Heretaunga Settlement,* Wellington, 1984. A badly written booklet, it nevertheless contains some useful information. There is other material in Barbara Fill, 'Dwellings for Workers', *Historic Places in New Zealand,* No.6, September 1984, pp.15-16. A fuller, more careful study of early government housing measures is Gael Ferguson, *Building the New Zealand Dream,* Palmerston North, 1994. See especially Chapt. 2.
45. *NZOYB*, 1921-22, pp.453-4. There are regular reports to the Minister of Labour about Workers' Dwellings. See especially *AJHR*, 1908, H-11B, p.2.
46. *AJHR*, 1901, C-4, p.26. A brief history of State Mines is given in *NZOYB*, 1913, pp.593-6. See Drummond, p.277.
47. See *AJHR*, 1901, C-6; 1912, C-3 and C-3A, p.2. See also P.R. May, *Miners and Militants: Politics in Westland,* Christchurch, 1975, p.102.
48. The words were used by Ward in his 1909 budget, *AJHR*, B-6, p.11.
49. *AJHR*, 1917, C-2A, p.3. There is a file on coal prices in IC/1/9/26. For comments on State Mines' accounting practices see L.H. Eillers to Under-Secretary, Mines Department, 19 December 1919, T/1/200. Detail about industrial unrest is in *AJHR*, 1920, C-2A. The write-down in asset values is mentioned in the 1913 budget, *AJHR*, 1913, B-6.
50. Le Rossignol and Stewart, p.286. See the Treasury file on State Mines after 1918, T/1/

200. *NZOYB*, 1939, pp.405-6.

51. For workers' compensation see 'Labour Legislation' in *NZOYB*, 1902, pp.421-4. Also John A. Lee, *Socialism in New Zealand*, London, 1938, pp.199ff. The best background to the introduction of State Insurance is Arthur Manning, *Cover Story: The History of the State Insurance Office, 1905-1980*, Wellington, 1980, pp.13ff.

52. There is a copy of the instructions in Alan Henderson, *Competition and Co-Operation: The Insurance Council and the General Insurance Industry in New Zealand, 1895–1995*, Wellington, 1995, p.21. Henderson's booklet provides a succinct analysis of State Fire and its sometimes uneasy relationship with its competitors.

53. Le Rossignol and Stewart, pp.167-78. Manning deals with reinsurance, p.18.

54. Henderson, p.23. For profits and assets of State Insurance in 1979, see *AJHR*, 1980, B-21, pp.2-3.

55. *NZOYB*, 1902, pp.557-60. The story of Hanmer is told by Ian Rockell, *Taking the Waters: Early Spas in New Zealand*, Wellington, 1986, Chapt. 10. There is information about the early development of the department in the introduction to the collection (TO) in National Archives.

56. Bassett, *Ward*, p.118, p.121. In his last term as Prime Minister (1928–30), when he was dying, Ward spent many months at Princes Gate Hotel in Rotorua. For a description of Rotorua baths in 1902, see A. Wohlmann to T. E. Donne, 3 October 1902. Other details about the building of the Aix baths are to be found in TO/1/1901/5/3. There were problems with the doctor's subsidy. See *AJHR*, 1902, H-2, p.7.

57. The second volume of D. M. Stafford's history of Rotorua entitled *The New Century in Rotorua*, Rotorua, 1988, Chapt. 2, tells the story of early tourism.

58. See *AJHR*, 1906 and 1908, H-2 . Rockell provides much information about the early department and its spa bath activities.

59. For Allen's budget of 1914, see *AJHR*, 1914, B-6. For reports of the department, see *AJHR*, 1914, H-2; 1915, H-2; 1916, H-2; 1918, H-2, p.3; 1925, H-2, p.2; 1931, H-2; 1934, H-2, p.6; 1960, H-2, p.4. In their earliest days the baths at Rotorua charged one shilling for use of a private bath and threepence to swim in the public pools. To stay at the Rotorua Sanitorium in 1902 cost ordinary patients £1 10s per week, which covered accommodation, food, medicine, medical attention and full access to the thermal pools. See *AJHR*, 1902, H-2A. The story of the Blue Baths is told by Philip Andrews, 'Rotorua's Blue Baths', *NZ Historic Places*, No. 59, July 1996, pp.25-26.

60. See for instance *NZPD*, Vol.132, July 1905, pp.246-7. See J.C. Beaglehole, p.58.

61. Quoted by Le Rossignol and Stewart, p.17.

62. Hamer, *The New Zealand Liberals*, p.46.

63. Ward's farmers' association was not as well based as he hoped. It became the principal victim of the merger between the Colonial Bank and the Bank of New Zealand in 1895, and in July 1897 Ward went bankrupt. He revived his fortunes quickly, and by 1900 J.G. Ward and Co was making good profits again.

64. *ST*, 8 August 1893.

65. *AJHR*, 1902, H-17. There is material about the development of the department in the introductory notes to the files (IC) in National Archives.

66. There is a file on the St Louis Exposition and the Christchurch exhibition in IA/25/11. See also *AJHR*, 1905, H-17, p.1. Some of the Crystal Palace prizes are shown in *AJHR*, 1906, H-17, pp.29ff. For a discussion of the exhibition, see Jean Sharfe, 'The New Zealand International Exhibition at Christchurch in 1906-07,' *History Now*, Vol. 1, No. 2, October 1995, pp.27-31.

67. IA/4/76, pp.515, 699. For fish, see *AJHR*, 1901, H-37. For flax, see *AJHR*, 1890, H-45, and IA/4/72, p.29. Later developments with the distribution of trout ova and fry are dealt with in *AJHR*, 1926, H-22, p.3.

68. See Seddon to Agent General, 31 July 1899, *AJHR*, 1900, H-47. For poultry see *AJHR*, 1905, H-17, p.20.

69. See H. Pollen to W.R. Morris, 26 September 1899, IA/4/88, p.194. See request for

assistance with a fish hatchery, IA/4/107, p.420.

70. *NZOYB*, 1913, p.547. There were eight of them by 1912. See *AJHR*, 1912, H-21A and H-21B. Good records for the farms seem only to have been kept from 1904 onwards.

71. *AJHR*, 1909, H-17, p.7.

72. As a result of resolutions passed at the Imperial Conference in 1907, New Zealand adopted the title of Dominion rather than Colony in September 1907. Henceforth Colonial conferences became Imperial conferences. The Colonial Secretariat became the Department of Internal Affairs and the Colonial Secretary became the Minister of Internal Affairs.

73. See IA/1/348 (77/1030).

74. An initial approach to Government to help with funding of fire services had been made as early as 1874. See IA/1/322. See also G.S. Cooper to W. Lightfoot, 1 March 1878, IA/4/40.

75. See Michael Bassett, *Mother of all Departments*, Chapt. 3. Also the New Zealand Business Roundtable publication, *The Provision and Funding of Fire Services*, Wellington, 1995, pp.3-8.

76. *NZH*, 11 May 1896, p.3. See also editorial quotes on the conference in *NZH*, 17 May 1996.

77. The parliamentary report is to be found in *AJHR*, 1871, H-5. O'Connor, pp.42-44; Manying Ip, *Home Away From Home*, Auckland, 1990, pp.12-13. The changing attitudes of ministers can be traced through IA/4/88, pp.55,178. IA/4/89, pp.589-98,130. IA/4/107, pp.37-41. See also R.F. Lynch to J.W. Card, 16 January 1912, and Minister of Internal Affairs to S.A.R. Guinness, 26 January 1912, IA/4/126. Also *NZOYB*, 1916, p.56.

78. See Ward's comments in Australia in 1907, quoted in Bassett, *Ward*, p.152.

79. M.P.K. Sorrenson, 'Maori and Pakeha', in G.W. Rice (ed), *The Oxford History of New Zealand*, Auckland, 1992, pp.141-66.

80. Ibid, p.165. See also Michael King in Rice (ed), *The Oxford History*, pp.285-307. Also Michael Bassett, *Coates of Kaipara*, Auckland, 1995, p.28.

81. King, *The Oxford History* pp.286-8.

82. John A. Williams, *Politics of the New Zealand Maori: Protest and Cooperation, 1891–1909*, Auckland, 1977, pp.126-7.

83. Michael King, *Te Puea: A Biography*, Auckland, 1977, p.54; Michael Bassett, *Coates of Kaipara*, pp.132-4.

84. Gill Gatfield, *Without Prejudice: Women in the Law*, Wellington, 1996, pp.34-44.

85. *AJHR*, 1908, H-11, p.vii. Kerry Howe discusses Tregear's confused thinking about the role of women, pp.35-36, 89-91.

86. Raewyn Dalziel, 'The Colonial Helpmeet: Women's Role and the Vote in Nineteenth-Century New Zealand', *NZJH*, Vol. 11, October 1977, pp.112-23.

87. The figures are derived from Keith Rankin, 'National Product Estimates for New Zealand, 1859-1939,' *Long-Run Perspectives on the New Zealand Economy, Proceedings of the Sesquicentennial Conference of the New Zealand Association of Economists*, Vol. 2, Wellington, 1990, pp.352-3.

88. James Allen released the figures on 6 August 1912, *AJHR*, 1912, B6B. They tally with Ward's figure of £64 million released in February 1912 (*AJHR*, 1912, B-6), a figure that did not include State Advances lending.

89. See *Statutes*, 1910, p.86.

90. *AJHR*, 1912, Session 2, H-18. This question about wages and prices had been raised tentatively by Henry Broadhead four years before. He noted that in some cases employers had been forced out of business because cheaper imports were available. Broadhead, p.215.

91. *NZOYB*, 1913, pp.796-7.

92. Coleman, 'The New Zealand Welfare State', p.54. Hugh H. Lusk, *Social Welfare in New Zealand*, London, 1913.

93. Le Rossignol and Stewart, pp.287-8.

94. Robert H. Hutchinson, *The Socialism of New Zealand*, New York, 1916, p.v.

95. Ibid, pp.23, 32.

Chapter 5 World War Winds Up the State

1. A. J. P. Taylor, *English History 1914–1945*, Oxford 1965, p.1.
2. Robert Skidelsky, *The World After Communism: A Polemic for our Times*, London, 1995, p.27.
3. Bassett, *Ward*, Chapt. 14; Barry Gustafson, 'William Ferguson Massey', *DNZB*, Vol. 2, pp.316-9; Ian McGibbon, 'James Allen', *DNZB*, Vol. 3, pp.10-11; Susan Butterworth, 'Alexander Lawrence Herdman', *DNZB*, Vol. 3, pp.211-2.
4. The kauri gum industry reached its exporting peak in the 1890s. As supplies began to diminish, the Liberal Government reserved the digging of gum on Crown land to New Zealand citizens and required from 1899 that prospectors possessed a licence to dig. The outbreak of war effectively closed European markets to gum. The predicament of diggers was raised in Parliament on 7 August 1914. The Kauri Gum Industry Amendment Act passed on 26 October. See *NZPD*, Vol.171, pp.388-92. Reed (Bay of Islands), Coates (Kaipara) and Rhodes (Thames), all of whom had voted with Reform on 6 July 1912, eventually joined the Reform Party caucus. There is a report on the Kauri Gum Industry in *AJHR*, 1917, C-12.
5. W. Downie Stewart, *The Life and Times of the Rt Hon Sir Francis Bell*, Wellington, 1937, p.231.
6. J.H. Bradney, *NZPD*, Vol. 157, 29 February 1912, p.389; J.H. Escott, pp.400ff.
7. *AJHR*, 1912, B-6.
8. A.J. Everton, 'Government Intervention in the New Zealand Economy, 1914–18: Its Aims and Effectiveness', MA thesis, Victoria University of Wellington, 1995, p.xxxi. This is the fullest study of interventionism but it fails to make use of the rich documentation in departmental archives which generally supports Everton's conclusions.
9. For details about the Board of Agriculture, see *AJHR*, 1917, H-29A. For details of the Iron and Steel Industries Act, see *Statutes*, 1914, p.249. Also the budget, *AJHR*, 1913, B-6. See also *AJHR*, 1914, B-6; 1917, C-8 and C-11. For fruit-preserving subsidies, see *AJHR*, 1915, B-19. For details regarding the oil subsidies, see T/1/12/102/1.
10. Robert Higgs, *Crisis and Leviathan: Critical Episodes in the Growth of American Government*, New York, 1987, p.123. See also David M. Kennedy, *Over Here: The First World War and American Society*, Oxford, 1980, pp.93-143.
11. The Regulation of Trade and Commerce Act is in *Statutes*, 1914, p.12. The War Regulations Act and its amendments are to be found in *Statutes*, 1914, pp.128-9; 1915, p.359; 1916, p.103. The use of regulatory powers without reference to Parliament is dealt with by Alex Frame, *Salmond: Southern Jurist*, Wellington, 1995, pp.166-7.
12. Paul Baker, *King and Country Call: New Zealanders, Conscription and the Great War*, Auckland, 1988, pp.15-18.
13. See Jock Phillips, *A Man's Country? The Image of the Pakeha Male*, Auckland, 1997, p.159. Figures in the official year books are somewhat lower. See *NZOYB*, 1921-22, p.182. According to Phillips, about 38 per cent of those who served were volunteers. There is a file on the cost of World War I, T/1/23/144.
14. The electoral difficulties that beset the Government after the election on 10 December 1914 are dealt with in Michael Bassett, *Three Party Politics in New Zealand, 1911–1931*, Auckland, 1982, pp.15-20.
15. Further detail is given about Ward's wartime loans policy in Bassett, *Ward*, pp.225ff. The £68.5 million figure comes from M.F. Lloyd Prichard, *An Economic History of New Zealand*, Auckland, 1970, p.235. See also Massey's budget of 1920, *AJHR*, B-6.
16. *AJHR*, 1915, B-6, pp.xxviff. There is a brief summary of Treasury's activities during the war in a five-page undated, unsigned memo in T/1/23/144. A particularly interesting summary of New Zealand's participation in the war is Sir James Allen's. Massey's Minister of Defence contributed a 17-page account to J.H. Rose, A.P. Newton, E.A. Benians and J. Hight, *The Cambridge History of the British Empire, Vol.7, New Zealand*, Cambridge, 1933, pp.224-41.

17. On 1 September 1914 concern was expressed in Parliament about the rise of rents in Auckland. *NZPD*, Vol. 169, p.668.
18. Ibid, p.xxxi.
19. The Act is to be found in *Statutes*, 1915, p.444. The debate in the Legislative Council is to be found in *NZPD*, Vol. 174, 7 October 1915, pp.805ff.
20. Notes of J. Christie, IC/1/3/1/2, W.709. There is other material about the Board of Trade in IC/1/2/5. See also Everton, p.31.
21. Everton, Chapt. 5, pp.39-134, deals at length with bread prices, where the Government made its 'first and only attempt' at a comprehensive price-fixing regime.
22. See Ward's comments in his 1916 Budget, *AJHR*, 1916, B-6, pp.xx ff. Also Ward's comments, *AJHR*, 1918, B-6. There is a file on the Board of Trade, IC/1/2/2, part 1. See also IC/1/2/5. Bread price regulations are to be found in the *Gazette*, 19 March 1918, p.849, 14 March 1921, p.690. Problems with clothing prices are dealt with in IC/1/10/1/3, part 1.
23. G.W. Clinkard, op cit., p.908, deals with the relative movement in wages compared with prices. Many of the difficulties experienced by the Board of Trade in its attempts to control prices are outlined in its annual report, *AJHR*, 1918, H-44.
24. The debate on the Board of Trade Bill is in *NZPD*, Vol. 184, 12 September 1919, pp.489ff. For details about the emergence of the separate department, see IC/1/2/3, part 1, W709.
25. See IC/1/2/3, part 1, W709.
26. *DOM*, 11 September 1919, p.4; *EP*, 10 September 1919, p.4; *NZH*, 11 September 1919, p.6; *Press*, 11 September 1919, editorial; *ODT*, 11 September 1919, p.4.
27. W.F. Massey to Board of Trade, 24 November 1919, and press statement of 28 November 1919, IC/1/2/3, part 1, W709.
28. Report to Prime Minister, 25 May 1920, IC/1/2/3, part 1, W709. For the departmental comments on the work of the Board of Trade, see *AJHR*, 1921, H-44, especially p.2 and pp.19ff.
29. The file on coal pricing is IC/1/9/26. Everton deals with coal pricing in Chapt. 12.
30. See *AJHR*, 1921, H-44, pp.2-3.
31. A.M. Endres, 'The Political Economy of W.B. Sutch: Toward a Critical Appreciation', in *New Zealand Economic Papers*, Vol. 20, 1986, pp.17-40.
32. See IC/1/2/3, part 1, W709. There is also information relevant to the personnel of the Board in IC/1/2/2, part 1, W709.
33. See report of Dr C.J. Reakes, 31 January 1919, IC/1/2/3, part 1, W709.
34. J.D. Atkinson, *DSIR's First Fifty Years*, Wellington, 1976, pp.14-18. There is more detail in T.W.H. Brooking, *Massey Its Early Years: A History of the Development of Massey Agricultural College to 1943*, Palmerston North, 1977, pp.23ff.
35. See IC/1/2/3, part 1, W709. See *Statutes*, 1923, p.205.
36. Everton, p.406.
37. IC/1/31/140, part 1. See also the report of the visit of L.M.S. Amery, *NZH*, 23 November 1927.
38. See *Statutes*, 1914, p.19.
39. *AJHR*, 1916, H-17 and H-17a. The 1919 report, *AJHR*, 17b, reports that £13,812 had been paid to the NPF by the Government by the end of 1918.
40. *AJHR*, 1917, H-1, p.2.
41. *AJHR*, 1919, H-1. The report anticipated that more would have to be paid in due course.
42. The categories of recipients are set out in *NZOYB*, 1921–22, p.457.
43. *NZPD*, Vol. 174, 1 October 1915, pp.446-7. An outline of the history of miners' pensions is contained in the official publication, *The Growth and Development of Social Security in New Zealand*, Wellington, 1950, pp.27-28.
44. See *AJHR*, 1919, H-30.
45. I am indebted to Dr Ashley Gould for this information.
46. Ashley Gould, 'Soldier Settlement in New Zealand after World War 1: A Reappraisal', in Judith Smart and Tony Wood, *An Anzac Muster: War and Society in Australia and New*

Zealand, 1914–18 and 1939–45, Melbourne, 1992, p.117. The unemployment allowances and training schemes are mentioned in Massey's 1922 budget. See *AJHR,* 1922, B-6.

47. Ibid, pp.123-9. The reports of the Repatriation Department, *AJHR,* H-30 in the years 1919–21 give much detail about the work of the boards and their committees.

48. Geoffrey Rice, *Black November: The 1918 Influenza Epidemic in New Zealand,* Wellington, 1988, p.1, and pp.142-3. Massey's comments are in the 1920 budget, *AJHR,* B-6, p.vii. According to Rice the Health Department later calculated the cost of the epidemic as £220,000. Rice, p.189.

49. *NZOYB,* 1921–22, pp.456-7. There were 474 miners receiving pensions in March 1921. See *NZOYB,* 1924, p.558. The Government informed Parliament at the tail end of the 1918 session that it intended to assist children 'and others who have suffered as a result of the epidemic'. *NZPD,* Vol. 183, 1918, p.1125. See also *DOM,* 13 January 1919, p.4. Further details of the Epidemic Allowances are contained in the official publication, *The Growth and Development of Social Security in New Zealand,* Wellington, 1950, p.28.

50. *NZPD,* Vol. 174, 8 October 1915, pp.817-24.

51. *DOM,* 13 January 1919, p.4.

52. *DOM,* 19 March 1919, p.8. The background to Makgill's comments and the minister's retort to them is dealt with in Geoffrey W. Rice, 'The Making of New Zealand's 1920 Health Act', *NZJH,* Vol. 22, April 1988, pp.3-22.

53. Derek Dow, pp.91-93.

54. C.A. Ralston to Controller and Auditor-General, 18 December 1920, T/1/52/84.

55. See T/1/52/84.

56. B.C. Ashwin to Assistant Secretary, Treasury, 12 September 1927, T/1/52/84.

57. Paul Baker, p.10.

58. Erik Olssen, 'Truby King and the Plunket Society. An Analysis of a Prescriptive Ideology', *NZJH,* Vol. 15, April 1981, pp.3-23.

59. Richard Newman, 'New Zealand's Vote for Prohibition in 1911', *NZJH,* Vol. 9, April 1975, pp.52-71. See also A.R. Grigg, 'Prohibition, the Church and Labour: A Programme for Social Reform, 1890–1914', *NZJH,* Vol. 15, October 1981, pp.135-54. The voting figures for 1919 are to be found in *AJHR,* 1919, H-39. They show that Auckland and Wellington's inner city electorates as well as mining areas populated by single men and the working class were less likely to support prohibition than the more affluent suburbs and well established farming areas such as Taranaki. For a racy general commentary on the liquor laws in New Zealand see Conrad Bollinger, *Grog's Own Country,* Auckland, 1959. There is an article on liquor licensing polls by John D. Prince, 'Look Back in Amber, The General Licensing Poll in New Zealand, 1919–87', *Political Science,* Vol. 48, July 1996, p.48. On prostitution, Bronwyn Dalley has shown that middle-class advocates of propriety were behind Massey's use of the War Regulations to close a lot of one-woman brothels in urban areas in 1915 and 1916. See Bronwyn Dalley, 'Lolly Shops "of the red-light kind" and "soldiers of the King": Suppressing One-woman Brothels in New Zealand, 1908–1916', *NZJH,* Vol. 30, April 1996, pp.3-23.

60. Jock Phillips, *A Man's Country?,* p.74.

61. See *Statutes,* 1915, p.323; 1917, p.122. Jock Phillips, *A Man's Country?,* p.72.

62. See *Statutes,* 1916, p.108.

63. Report of the National Efficiency Board, *AJHR,* 1917, H-34. Ward's budget is to be found in B-6.

64. *DOM,* 30 May 1919, p.5.

65. Erik Olssen discusses the cohesion – or lack of it – that was a feature of the working class in 'The "Working Class" in New Zealand', *NZJH,* Vol. 8, April 1974, pp.44-60. There is an interesting article about the development of a labour culture in Christchurch before 1919 by Libby Plumridge, 'The Necessary but not Sufficient Condition: Christchurch Labour and Working-Class Culture', *NZJH,* Vol. 19, October 1985, pp.130-50. See also Jim McAloon, 'A Political Struggle: Christchurch Labour Politics 1905–1913', *NZJH,* Vol. 28, April 1994, pp.22-40.

66. Introduced in 1908 by Ward's Government, with the object of minimising the chances of the Liberals' losing seats to Massey because of a split between Liberal and Labour on the first ballot, the Second Ballot Act, which required the winning candidate to secure 50 per cent of the total vote, lasted only through the 1908 and 1911 elections before being abolished by Massey's Government in 1913. See David Hamer, 'The Second Ballot: A New Zealand Electoral Experiment', *NZJH*, Vol. 21, April 1987, p.97. See also Bassett, *Ward*, p.165.

67. For the rise of the Labour Party, see Barry Gustafson, *Labour's Path to Political Independence*, Auckland, 1980. Also P.J. O'Farrell, *Harry Holland: Militant Socialist*, Canberra, 1964.

68. There is a discussion of the various attitudes of the early Labour leaders in Jack Vowles, 'Ideology and the Formation of the New Zealand Labour Party: Some New Evidence', *NZJH*, Vol. 16, April 1982, pp.39-55.

69. Webb held the seat of Grey 1913–18 until it was declared vacant because he was unable to attend Parliament owing to his imprisonment. He had refused to be conscripted for war service.

70. The 'Red Feds' are dealt with by Erik Olssen, *The Red Feds: Revolutionary Industrial Unionism and the New Zealand Federation of Labour, 1908-1914*, Auckland, 1988.

71. *NZPD*, Vol. 157, 22 February 1912, p.167.

72. Ibid, Vol. 183, 2 December 1918, p.612.

73. Ibid, 30 October 1918, p.92.

74. *NZPD*, 7 July 1920, p.213.

75. See Robert Chapman, *The Political Scene, 1919–1931*, Auckland, 1969, pp.5-6.

76. The manifesto is discussed in detail in Bassett, *Ward*, p.245.

77. Coates's early days as Minister of Public Works are discussed in Michael Bassett, *Coates of Kaipara*, Auckland, 1995, Chapt. 4.

78. Massey's 1920 budget is in *AJHR*, 1920, B-6.

79. See T. Mark to Permanent Heads, 15 April 1921, T/1/12/358, W.266. Lists of public service salaries for each department 1913–19 are to be found in T/1/12/64/1.

80. According to Alan Henderson, p.397 there were 5312 public servants in 1914, and by 1919 numbers had risen to 6448 permanents with another 2089 temporary staff. The file on minimum salaries is T/1/9/33. The minimum salary for a married man in the public service was initially set in 1914 at £140. By 1921 this stood at £234 15s. With the reduction in public service salaries it fell to £209 15s, and at the end of the depression after further reductions stood in July 1936 at £202 10s.

81. See Bassett, *The Mother of All Departments*, Auckland, 1997, Chapt. 4.

82. There is detail about departmental responses to the Commission in T/1/12/158. See also the reports of the Public Service Commission, *AJHR*, 1923 and 1924, H-14. Massey's budget has useful details, *AJHR*, 1923 B-6, pp.iii-ix.

83. Notes of a deputation to Massey on 12 January 1921 are in T/1/12/360.

84. Bassett, *Coates*, pp.73-74.

85. *Statutes*, 1921-2, pp.648ff.

86. *NZPD*, Vol. 194, 8 February 1922, pp.314, 332.

87. See A.J. Beck, 'The Origins of Dairy Produce Marketing-Control in New Zealand', *NZJPA*, Vol. 24, March 1962, pp.64-83. See also R.W. Dalton, 'Report on the Trade of the Dominion of New Zealand', *Imperial Accounts and Papers*, Vol. 33, London, July 1920, p.6.

88. The story of efforts to influence market prices in 1921 and early 1922 is contained in AG/40/1922/5c.

89. E. Maynell to W.F. Massey, 11 May 1922, AG/40/1922/5c.

90. There is a file of material relating to the pre-election scene, AG/40/1922/6a. The final Act as passed is in *Statutes*, 1923, p.168.

91. The results are to be found in AG/40/1928/9B. See also Beck, p.82.

Chapter 6 The State Under Challenge: the 1920s and the Depression

1. See, for instance, John H. Angus, *Donald Reid Otago Farmers Limited*, Dunedin, 1978, p.68; G.J. McLean, *Spinning Yarns: A Centennial History of Alliance Textiles Limited and its Predecessors*, Dunedin, 1981, p.42. For a comment on the general economic conditions, see Sinclair and Mandle, *Open Account*, Chapt. x. See also Margaret N. Galt, 'Wealth and Income in New Zealand c1870 to c1939', pp.11-12.

2. 'Report of Royal Commission to Inquire into the Land and Income Tax Act', *AJHR*, 1924, B-5. In what seems largely to have been a government public relations exercise the commission argued that tax levels in New Zealand were not excessive. However, it did suggest some changes. In particular the commission argued for shifting the tax burden from land taxes towards income taxes.

3. The best source of information on the politics of railways is D.B. Waterson, 'Railways and Politics, 1908–1928', MA thesis, University of Auckland, 1959. There is information about the building of the North Auckland Main Trunk line in John Prince, 'Northland Politics, 1899–1929', MA thesis, University of Auckland, 1966.

4. *Statutes*, 1914, p.77; *NZOYB*, 1921–22, p.282.

5. Coates's comments about private contractors testing the efficiency of PWD construction gangs are in *NZPD*, Vol. 201, 30 July 1923, p.396.

6. *AS*, 2 June 1927, p.10.

7. Bassett, *Coates*, pp.63-68. See also Public Works statements, *AJHR*, 1921 and 1922, D-1.

8. *NZPD*, Vol. 204, 25 September 1924, pp.1168-9.

9. For numbers of employees, see Railways Reports throughout the 1920s, *AJHR*, D-2. The figure 70 per cent and the average construction costs per mile come from the Memo, H. Valentine and B.C. Ashwin to Minister of Railways, 11 March 1930, T/1/52/584.

10. Coates's statement appears in *NZPD*, Vol. 204, 25 September 1924, p.1168. See also *AJHR*, 1923, D-2, p.1. According to the Secretary to the Treasury, who wrote to Coates on 17 May 1929, the decision not to treat railways as a profit-making concern was originally taken in 1896, T/1/52/584. A precise criticism of Railways' lack of management skills occurred in *NZ National Review*, 15 March 1928, p.13.

11. *AJHR*, 1927, D-2.

12. Bassett, *Coates*, p.136.

13. Memo F.W. Furkert to J.G. Coates, 29 May 1928, T/1/52/584.

14. *DOM*, 13 July 1928, editorial.

15. See Memo H. Valentine and B.C. Ashwin to Minister of Railways, 11 March 1930, T/1/52/584.

16. *ODT*, 18 November 1931.

17. The Report of the Royal Commission into Railways is to be found in *AJHR*, 1930, D-4. See especially pp.60-61. The Transport Licensing Act is in Statutes, 1931, p.414. See Easton, *In Stormy Seas*, pp.182-3, for further details. A later speech of relevance by the then Minister of Transport, George Gair, appears in *NZPD*, Vol. 453, 30 September 1983, pp.2772-6.

18. See Railways Inquiry Report, 17 September 1930, *AJHR*, 1930, D-4. See the figures contained in Memo H. Valentine and B.C. Ashwin to Minister of Railways, 11 March 1930, T/1/52/584. In the financial year 1979–80, every part of Railways' operations was losing money, the total loss for the year amounting to almost $90 million. See *AJHR*, 1980, F-7, p.20. There is detail about the road service purchases in 'History of Railways 1863–1963' in *NZOYB*, 1963, pp.1175-93.

19. *NZOYB*, 1939, p.234.

20. Memo Secretary to the Treasury to Acting Minister of Railways, 11 November 1930, T/1/52/584.

21. *EP*, 13 November 1930.

22. R.M. Burdon, *The New Dominion: A Social and Political History of New Zealand Between the Wars*, Wellington, 1965, Chapt. 8. See also Rosslyn J. Noonan, *By Design: A Brief*

History of the Public Works Department Ministry of Works, 1870–1970, Wellington, 1975, Chapt. 5. Bassett, *Coates*, pp.67-69.

23. *Statutes*, 1903, p.54. There is information about the background to this Act in *NZPD*, Vol. 153, 28 October 1910, pp.134ff.

24. *Statutes*, 1910, p.70. There is detail about the Government's plans in the 1910 budget and the Public Works Statement, *NZPD*, Vol. 153, 15 November 1910, p.677. See also Cynthia Hasman, 'Hydro Development on the Waikato', MA thesis, University of Auckland, 1965.

25. See *NZPD*, Vol. 153, 28 October 1910, pp.134ff. Luke's statement is on pp.196-7 and Rigg's on p.196.

26. See the details surrounding the gazetting on 13 May 1920 of a licence to use water in part of Cook County, Gisborne, ED/1/2/0/38.

27. Bassett, *Coates*, p.66.

28. *AS*, 30 July 1921, p.6.

29. See ED/1/2/0/22/3. The thinking of the Hydro-electric Branch about thermal electricity is discussed in a long article, *DOM*, 28 April 1934.

30. In 1945 a separate State Hydro-electric Department was established, and this eventually changed its name to the New Zealand Electricity Department, and then in the 1980s to the Electricity Corporation of New Zealand (Electricorp).

31. See ED/1/2/0/38.

32. *NZOYB*, 1986–87, p.563.

33. The decisions by electricity supply authorities to charge lower rates for domestic consumers than for industrial users, in the mistaken belief that the policy assisted lower income users, is dealt with by Gary Hawke, 'Economic Decisions and Political Ossification', in Peter Munz (ed), *The Feel of Truth*, Wellington, 1969, pp.221-33.

34. Memo L.H. Eillers to Under-Secretary, Mines Department, 19 December 1919, T/1/200.

35. See *AJHR*, 1934 and 1935, C-2 and C-2A. The State Forest Service's reports are in *AJHR*, 1934 and 1935, C-3.

36. See summary of regulations, IC/1/3/5/2, part 2.

37. See *New Zealand Times (NZT)*, 26 July 1924.

38. Budget 1923, *AJHR*, 1923, B-6, p.15.

39. There is material on house rents in *NZOYB*, 1924, pp.634-6. The efficacy of rent controls during World War I is dealt with by Everton, Chapt. 11.

40. *Statutes*, 1924, p.7. There is some discussion of the housing market in *DOM*, 26 July 1924. Magistrates' Courts decisions for the period contain numerous cases dealing with rent controls and their application.

41. *NZPD*, Vol. 211, 31 August 1926, p.35.

42. A variety of educational statistics is contained in the *NZOYB*. See 1928, pp.219-35.

43. *Statutes*, 1924, p.371, and 1925, p.16. In 1925 nurses and midwives were also required to register.

44. *Statutes*, 1925, pp.109ff.

45. The rules are outlined in the official publication, *The Growth and Development of Social Security in New Zealand*, p.29.

46. *Statutes*, 1924, p.108.

47. *Statutes*, 1924, p.53.

48. *Statutes*, 1926, p.447.

49. See the comments of J.T. Hogan MP, *EP*, 2 November 1931; *SDN*, 10 November 1931, editorial. See also IC/1/3/25, part 1.

50. Bassett, *Coates*, p.68. The comment was made by John A. Lee.

51. Family Allowances are outlined in the official publication, *The Growth and Development of Social Security*, p.29. The initial payment was of two shillings per week for each child in excess of two and was payable until the child turned 15.

52. Bassett, *Coates*, p.105.

53. In May 1914 some architects supported by the Municipal Electors' Association persuaded

Massey's Ministry to contribute £350 towards a national tour of public lantern lectures on town planning. *DOM*, 23 May 1914, p.3.

54. See Bassett, *Coates*, p.107; *Statutes*, 1926, p.562. A collection of plans lodged with the Department of Internal Affairs is located in W/39 and 40.

55. The issue is discussed in Bassett, *Coates*, pp. 108-9.

56. Ibid, pp.117-21; J.H. Gaudin, 'The Coates Government: 1925–1928', MA thesis, University of Auckland,1971, pp.41-87.

57. See Memo, Secretary of the Treasury to Acting Minister of Finance, 26 February 1919, T/1/12/16/1.

58. See *AJHR*, 1926, B-5.

59. *NZOYB*, 1930, p.661.

60. Ibid, 1930, pp.662-3. The list of subsidies is itemised in Memo of F. Campbell (President of the NZ Manufacturers' Federation) to J.G. Cobbe, 25 June 1929, IC/1/2/7, W709. See also *EP* and *DOM*, 26 June 1929.

61. W.P. Reeves, *State Experiments*, p.333.

62. Gary Hawke, *The Making of New Zealand*, p.116.

63. There are interesting papers relating to the 1928 Industrial Conference in T/57/4/8, W. 1926.

64. The story of the 1928 election is told in Bassett, *Coates*, pp.137-45. See also Michael Pugh, 'The New Zealand Legion and Conservative Protest in the Great Depression', MA thesis, University of Auckland, 1969, and J.H. Gaudin, op.cit. Michael Pugh deals with the ideology of right-wing protest in 'Doctrinaires on the Right: The Democrats and Anti-Socialism, 1933–36', *NZJH*, Vol. 17, October 1983, p.103.

65. Bassett, *Ward*, p.277. There is detail about the various departmental efforts to mop up unemployment in IC/1/4/89, part 1. See also R.T. Robertson, 'Government Responses to Unemployment in New Zealand, 1929–35', *NZJH*, Vol.16, April 1982, pp.21-23.

66. D.E. Moggridge, *Maynard Keynes: An Economist's Biography*, London, 1992, p.483.

67. Robert Higgs, *Crisis and Leviathan*, pp.159, 193.

68. Keith Sinclair, *A History of New Zealand*, p.247.

69. See Memo, Secretary of IC to T.S. Weston, 5 October 1928, IC/1/4//89, part 1.

70. 'Unemployment in New Zealand', *AJHR*, 1929, H-11B.

71. See *Poverty Bay Herald*, 2 November 1929, editorial; *ODT*, 24 January 1930, editorial; *AS*, 23 January 1930, editorial.

72. See, for instance, F. Norris to J.G. Ward, 22 February 1930. Answering on behalf of the ailing Prime Minister, J.B. Donald told Norris that ministers took his ideas 'seriously', IC/1/4/89, part 1. See also Moggridge, *Keynes,* Chapt. 19.

73. *NZ National Review*, 15 January 1929, pp.29, 30.

74. See the file of letters to the Department of Industries and Commerce, IC/1/4/89, part 1. Also the submission by F. Campbell (President of the NZ Manufacturers' Federation) to J.G. Cobbe, Minister of Industries and Commerce, 25 June 1929, IC/1/2/7, W709.

75. *Sun*, 28 February 1929, editorial.

76. See *Evening Star*, 7 June 1929, editorial. Also *Wanganui Chronicle*, 10 July 1929, editorial.

77. *NZOYB*, 1930, p.543.

78. *ODT*, 16 February 1932, editorial.

79. Minister of Industries and Commerce to Cabinet, 28 August 1929, IC/1/2/7, W 709.

80. See Memo G.W. Clinkard to Minister of Industries and Commerce, 21 December 1931, IC/1/2/7, W709. Some historians may notice similarities with the monopolies and patents of seventeenth-century England.

81. *AS*, 8 November 1932, p.9.

82. Memo G.W. Clinkard to Industries and Commerce Committee of Parliament, 23 November 1932, IC/1/2/7, W709.

83. *AJHR*, 1934, H-28A, p.8.

84. See the debates on the 1927 tariff, *NZPD,* 13 September and 13-14 October 1927, espe-

cially p.36 and p.43.

85. A file with much material about the complexities of the tariff in the period after 1927 is IC/1/4/128/3.
86. Report of the Tariff Customs Commission, *AJHR*,1934, H-28. See also typescript, 'Industry After the War', IC/1/31/140, part 2. The pages of the *New Zealand National Review*, especially 15 January 1933, pp.35-36; 2 February 1933, p.12; 15 May 1934, p.39; and 15 June 1934, pp.19-21, contain strident arguments for a higher tariff.
87. A.G. Kenwood, *Australian Economic Institutions since Federation*, Melbourne,1995, pp.68-73, deals with Australia's higher tariff policy after Federation in 1901.
88. G.R. Hawke, *The Making of New Zealand*, pp.127-8. See also G.R. Hawke, 'Depression and Recovery in New Zealand', in R.G. Gregory and N.G. Butlin (eds), *Recovery from the Depression*, Cambridge, 1988, pp.113ff.
89. *AJHR*, 1934, D-9, p.1. Hawke, 'Recovery', p.126.
90. Ibid, p.149.
91. There were a number of subcategories of schemes where the rules were slightly different so as to cater for some special need. See *NZOYB*, 1936, pp.648ff. There is information about subsidies for, and regulations affecting, various kinds of work in IC/1/3/5/2, part 2. A full outline of the schemes is to be found in R.T. Robertson, 'Government Responses to Unemployment, 1929–35', loc.cit. See also R.T. Robertson, 'Isolation, Ideology and Impotence: Organisations for the Unemployed During the Great Depression, 1930-1935', *NZJH*, Vol. 13, October 1979, p.149.
92. Memo Unemployment Board to G.W. Forbes, 19 March 1931, IC/1/4/89, part 2.
93. See *Auckland Sun*, 6 September 1930; *NZH*, 20 November 1930.
94. *Sun*, 8 May 1931, editorial. See also *NZH*, 26 May 1931, editorial. See also *DOM*, 16 May 1931. I am indebted to Jill Holt for drawing this reference to my attention.
95. Details about the campaign are to be found in IC/1/4/169/3, part 1. See especially G.W. Clinkard to Minister of Industries and Commerce, 2 December 1931.
96. A. Brittain to G.W. Forbes, 12 May 1931, IC/1/4/89, part 2.
97. Details about the work of the Economy Committee are to be found in T/1/52/663.
98. All figures relating to Railways employees are from *AJHRs*, D-2.
99. John E. Martin, 'The Removal of Compulsory Arbitration and the Depression of the 1930s', *NZJH*, Vol. 28, October 1994, p.133.
100. Details of these efforts are provided in Bassett, *Coates*, Chaps 10–11. Devaluation is discussed by Grant Fleming, 'Keynes, Purchasing Power, Parity and Exchange Rate Policy in New Zealand During the 1930s Depression', *NZ Economic Papers*, Vol. 31, 1997, pp.1-14. The members of the Brains Trust were Dr R.M. (Dick) Campbell, Professor Horace Belshaw and Dr W.B. Sutch. The *Auckland Star* on 26 October 1934, p.6 noted that the 'authoritarian' powers given to the Dairy Commission were part of a general world-wide trend. The *Press* on 26 October 1934, p.16, worried because such organisations 'tend to err on the side of over-zealousness'.
101. See Bassett, *Coates*, pp. 226-7.
102. G.R. Hawke, *Between Government and Banks: A History of the Reserve Bank of New Zealand*, Wellington, 1973, p.13.
103. The circumstances surrounding introduction of the Bill are in Bassett, *Coates*, pp.203-4.
104. J.G. Coates, *The Reserve Bank of New Zealand and the Gold Question*, Wellington, 1933, p.3.
105. *Statutes*, 1989, p.2547.
106. Shaw arrived in New Zealand on 15 March 1934 and spent several weeks touring the country. His visit is recalled by Christopher Moore, *Press*, 14 April 1990, p.26. The description of Shaw is Moore's. See also *Dominion Sunday Times*, 17 November 1991, p.9. Also (Australian) *Financial Review*, 5 January 1994. James Thorn in *Peter Fraser: New Zealand's Wartime Prime Minister*, London, 1952, says on p.159 that Shaw met many Labour people while in New Zealand, and that on the party's election in 1935 he sent a long message of congratulations.

107. See Barrie Macdonald and David Thomson, 'Mortgage Relief, Farm Finance, and Rural Depression in New Zealand in the 1930s', *NZJH*, Vol. 21, October 1987, pp.228-50. The story of the Democrat Party is told in Michael Bassett, 'The 1935 Election and the 'Kelly Gang': An American Observation', *NZJH*, Vol. 28, April 1994, pp.80-85. See also Michael Pugh, 'The New Zealand Legion and Conservative Protest in the Great Depression', MA thesis, University of Auckland, 1969, Chapt. 6, and Bassett, *Coates*, pp.210-11, 222 , 228. The 'national State socialism' criticism came from T.C.A. Hislop, *Press*, 5 November 1935, p.12.

108. Bassett, *Coates*, p.202. New Zealand newspapers had been quoting Keynes's views from time to time. See *ODT*, 20 January and 30 January 1931; *NZH*, 7 June 1933, p.10.

Chapter 7 Labour, Social Security and 'Insulation'

1. The story about the editor was given to the author many years ago by a *Press* reporter. Other information, including Williams's comments, is to be found in the *Press*, 28 November 1935. The description of Williams is in Ormond Wilson, *An Outsider Looks Back*, Wellington, 1982, p.70; Bassett, *Coates*, p.229; *Press*, 9 December 1935, p.12. Savage's plea is in the *Standard*, 26 February 1936, p.6. *Economist*, 28 December 1935, quoted in *Tomorrow*, 26 February 1936, p.6.

2. Miles Fairburn, 'Why Did the New Zealand Labour Party Fail to Win Office until 1935?', *Political Science*, Vol. 37, December 1985, pp.101-24. See also Robin Clifton, 'Douglas Credit and Labour', *Comment*, No.12, July 1962, pp.23-29.

3. Holland asked Nash to buy him books on these subjects while Nash was abroad in 1933. See H.E. Holland to W. Nash, 15 January 1933, Nash Papers, N2416, National Archives. There is material about Fraser, Nash and the WEA in Michael King's interview of Dr C.E. Beeby, 4 July 1978, Fraser/King Papers. Cole's *The Simple Case for Socialism* was reviewed in the *Standard*, 4 November 1936, p.6. The quote from Cole comes from Skidelsky, p.65.

4. Andrew J. Cutler, 'Intellectual Sprouts: *Tomorrow* Magazine 1934–1940: A Cultural, Intellectual and Political History', MA thesis, University of Canterbury, 1989, pp.28-35. See also Rachel Barrowman, *A Popular Vision: The Arts and the Left in New Zealand, 1930–1950*, Wellington, 1991. I am indebted to my friend and former colleague, Rt Hon Frank O'Flynn for a discussion about the books that were in vogue among the left-wingers that he knew in the 1930s. Savage's comment about 'national planning' appears in the *Press*, 1 May 1936, p.14. See Ormond Wilson, p.63. For articles about Russia see the *Standard*, 23 September 1936, p.16; 4 November 1936, p.3, and 26 November 1936, p.6. The Stakhanovite movement began in 1935. The coalminer who was patronised by Stalin allegedly increased his daily output sevenfold by organising a more efficient division of labour.

5. Scholefield's comments are to be found in the *Press*, 14 February 1936, p.7. The same paper had reported on 24 December 1935, p.14 that the Canterbury Public Library had been doing record business. Morgan Williams MP admitted to being influenced by Edward Bellamy. See Ormond Wilson, p.70. The 45-page report by civil servants, 'The Problems of Industrial Planning', April 1937, is located in qMS 1477, ATL. There is information about Stephens in Bassett, *The Mother of All Departments*, Chapt. 7.

6. Skidelsky, p.55.

7. Keith Sinclair, *A History of New Zealand*, p.258.

8. Savage's statement is in the *Poverty Bay Herald*, 31 July 1935, p.4. See R.T. Robertson, 'Government Responses to Unemployment', *NZJH*, Vol. 16, April 1982, p.38.

9. *NZOYB*, 1936, p.638. See Erik Olssen, '100 Years of the Union Movement' in J. Phillips (ed), *Towards 1990*, Wellington, 1989, p.71.

10. *NZYOB*, 1943, p.585. The comments are those of J.A. McCullough, *NZPD*, Vol. 245, 1936, pp.195-6.

11. There is much detail about union activity within the Labour Party in Barry Gustafson, *From the Cradle to the Grave: A Biography of Michael Joseph Savage*, Auckland, 1986. See especially pp.160-2. The views of Jim Roberts were given prominence in the *Standard*, 25 March 1936, p.7. He looked forward to the greater influence that unions would have in decision-making.

12. Fraser received reports from Walsh about union attitudes to the Government. See Walsh to Fraser, 21 January 1936. On 16 March 1940 Walsh sent him a summary of a speech that had been delivered in Dunedin by Dr D.G. McMillan, MP for Dunedin West. See MS Papers, 0274/336, ATL. There is a brief summary of the life of F.P. Walsh (1896–1963) by George McDonald in MS Papers 0274/710, ATL. See also obituaries, *EP*, 16 May 1963; *DOM*, 17 May 1963.

13. Olssen, '100 Years of the Union Movement', p.78. Some sense of the extent to which Walsh dominated in Wellington union and party circles in pre-war years can be gained from his papers MS Papers, 0274/337.

14. See notes of deputation to the Minister of Marine, 30 January 1937, MS Papers, 0274/336. While Fraser promised to study these requests, there is no evidence that he acceded to either of them.

15. The story of the Stewart Island Ferry is to be found in T/1/52/409. With improvements to manning levels and salary increases the service was making losses of approximately £5,000 pa by the mid 1950s which the Government paid for. The story of subsidies to the Chatham Islands, where a considerable portion went to shipping, is told in Bassett, *The Mother of All Departments*, pp.190-4. There are many other examples of increasingly costly subsidised services. In his unpublished memoirs, Morgan Williams MP claims that the unreasonable attitudes of unionists 'wore out' H.T. Armstrong, who was Minister of Labour 1935–38, and implies that the unions prospered when the 'playboy' Paddy Webb took over as minister between 1938 and 1946. See 'Views on Labour Leaders', MS Papers 998, ATL.

16. Bert Roth, *Remedy for Past Evils: A History of the New Zealand Public Service Association from 1890*, Wellington, 1987, Chapt. 7.

17. Frank O'Flynn reminded me of these nicknames. O'Flynn recalls several leading unionists in Wellington buying large new cars in the late 1930s. For Lewin's conduct, see Bert Roth, *Remedy*, p.119.

18. *NZH*, 29 November 1935, p.13.

19. Neil Robinson, *James Fletcher: Builder*, London, 1970, pp.88-91.

20. *AS*, 2 November 1934, p.5. See also *Press*, 29 November 1935, p.12.

21. *AS*, 6 November 1935, p.6. See also A.M. Endres, 'J.B. Condliffe and the Early Canterbury Tradition in Economics', *NZ Economic Papers*, Vol. 25, 1991, pp.171-97.

22. Paul Johnson, *Intellectuals*, New York, 1988, p.285.

23. *NZ Listener*, 15 March 1963, p.18. The term was used by the historian, R.M. Burdon.

24. 'Platform of the New Zealand Labour Party' as amended by the 1918 Conference.

25. 'Labour Has a Plan', republished, Christchurch, 1980.

26. Quoted by Keith Sinclair, *A History of New Zealand*, pp.255-7.

27. Horace Belshaw (ed), *New Zealand*, Berkeley, 1947, p.123.

28. *Standard*, 4 December 1935.

29. Gustafson, *From the Cradle to the Grave*, p.184. The Christmas bonus of £1 for single and £2 for married relief workers was paid each year against the advice of Treasury officials through Christmas 1939. See T/1/40/544/6.

30. *Press*, 24 December 1935, p.14; 14 January 1936, p.10.

31. *Press*, 12 November 1935, p.12.

32. Bassett, *Coates*, p.229; *Press*, 9 December 1935, p.10. Sullivan told a deputation of businessmen on 10 March 1936 that their request for less government interference in business was not the consensus view amongst those he had spoken with, and that he had received many requests for 'interference'. *Press*, 11 March 1936, p.10.

33. See J.W. Heenan to Permanent Heads, 27 October 1936, IC/1/3/1/2, W709. This file has much material about the use of regulations from 1915 onwards.

34. Robinson, Chapt. 9. Interview of Sir James C. Fletcher, Auckland, 27 November 1996. There is a full-page spread of the design of some of the early houses in *Standard*, 18 November 1936, p.7. There is much material about the first state houses in HD/1/5/1, W1353.

35. *NZOYB*, 1943, pp.336-7. Roly Metge, 'The House that Jack Built', MA thesis, University of Auckland, 1972, has much material about state housing. There is much publicity material about the first state houses in HD 1/5/1, W.1353. See also Gael Ferguson, Chapt. 3.

36. For material about state housing at the time of the change of government in 1949, see HD/1/29/0. See also *NZOYB*, 1951-52, pp.534-5. Ormond Wilson, pp.66-67.

37. Gael Ferguson, p.158. She argues, p.157, that state house rentals were subsidised only in the years 1945–62, but J.V.T. Baker, the Government Statistician, points out that rentals were uneconomic from the beginning, and only became more so with the passage of time. See *The New Zealand People at War: War Economy*, Wellington, 1965, p.9. Keith Sinclair discusses political influence in housing allocations in *Walter Nash*, p.157.

38. Carr's views are in the *Standard*, 25 March 1936, p.10; Hawke, *Between Governments and Banks*, pp.65-66. For Savage's comments, see *Press*, 6 April 1936, p.10. In 1945 after considerable pressure from 'credit-men' in the Labour caucus, the Government also bought out the private shareholders in New Zealand's largest trading bank, the Bank of New Zealand. While they thought their compensation was too little and petitioned for more, their anger faded. The Bank of New Zealand continued to function as a trading bank with a state-appointed board of directors, and followed orthodox policies until privatised in 1993. The 1945 nationalisation – disapproved of by many ministers who saw it as unnecessarily alarming to the business community – was the second and last of Labour's bank nationalisations, although a great many controls and regulations were introduced over the years that affected the ready availability of credit. See N.M. Chappell, *New Zealand Banker's Hundred: A History of the Bank of New Zealand, 1861–1961*, Wellington, 1961, pp.363-4. Also Keith Sinclair, *Walter Nash*, p.243. There is a brief summary of amendments to the original Act by Paul Dalziel in Brian Roper and Chris Rudd (eds), *State and Economy in New Zealand*, Auckland, 1993, pp.74ff.

39. According to the Reserve Bank publication, *Overseas Trade and Finance with Particular Reference to New Zealand*, 2nd ed, 1966, p.203, a total of £12.2 million worth of credit (£5.6 million of it for housing) was issued by the Reserve Bank for government programmes between 1936 and March 1939.

40. See particularly the scholarly thesis by R.J.M. Hill, 'The Quest for Control: The New Zealand Dairy Industry and the Guaranteed Price, 1921–36', MA thesis, University of Auckland, 1974, especially Chapt. 4.

41. *NZPD*, Vol. 244, 1936, p.145-6.

42. *Statutes*, 1936, p.60.

43. Hill, p.366.

44. Hill, p.323. Some government supporters firmly believed that the new system of marketing would eliminate speculators. See Harold Innes in the *Standard*, 30 September 1936, p.2; 7 October 1936, p.2; 14 October 1936, p.2.

45. I am indebted to Professor Gary Hawke for providing examples of this practice.

46. Hill shows, pp.393-4, that a surplus in the account of £437,800 in 1937–38 turned into a deficit of £1.9 million at the end of the 1938–39 season. Eventually guaranteed prices were integrated into the Labour Government's general stabilisation policy that operated during and after World War II. Hill gives details about subsequent changes to price-fixing arrangements, pp.396ff.

47. See *NZOYB*, 1947–49, p.877 and *NZOYB*, 1951–52, p.385. The fertiliser subsidies were angled particularly for the benefit of farmers farthest from a lime works. John A. Lee, *Socialism in New Zealand*, London, 1938, p.8, comments about farmers' attitudes towards state activity.

48. There is an excellent 21-page history of the way in which meat and dairy products were handled in 1938–48 in T/40/648/5.

49. There is much detail about marketing in B.L. Evans, *A History of Production and Marketing in New Zealand,* Palmerston North, 1969. See especially p.132. See also C. Weststrate, *Portrait of a Modern Mixed Economy,* 2nd ed, Wellington, 1966, Chapt. 4. The figure about New Zealand's exports is to be found in *NZOYB*, 1979, p.498.

50. D. Woodward to Secretary of Industries and Commerce, 6 January 1936, IC/1/31/171, part 1.

51. Labour's 1934 views on the tariff are to be found in *NZPD,* Vol. 239, 22 August 1934, pp.338-54. For views in office see *Press,* 3 June 1936, p.12.

52. *DOM,* 18 June and 15 July 1938.

53. *Statutes,* 1936, p.74, clause 5. There is a major file dealing with introduction of the 40-hour week, IC/1/31/171, part 1.

54. *Standard,* 28 October 1936, pp.7-8; 4 November 1936, p.8, editorial.

55. J. Heenan to Dr R.M. Campbell, 12 September 1936, MS 1132/30, ATL.

56. *Statutes,* 1936, p.211.

57. *Press,* 10 February 1936, p.12.

58. *Standard,* 19 February 1936, editorial, p.6. There are comments about petrol prices in the Department of Industries and Commerce annual report, *AJHR,* 1937, p.30. See also Manual for Junior Officers in Industries and Commerce, IC/1/2, part 4, p.6. In 1936 fertiliser prices were also fixed with different margins of profit allowed in the South Island from the North Island.

59. Some of the difficulties are discussed in R.M. Barker, 'Price Fixation', *NZ Financial Review,* December 1936.

60. See W. Johnson to M.J. Savage, 11 January 1937, IC/1/28/9/1. There is material relating to the flour mill workers in IC/1/28/9/7.

61. *ODT,* 29 September 1938. See also *NZH,* 12 October 1938.

62. There is a file on butter subsidies in T/1/27/6/1. See also *NZOYB,* 1956, p.491. Over the years, bakers increasingly got round price control by producing different varieties of bread that were never subject to control.

63. This story about bread price control was gleaned from IC/1/28/9/1. There is a careful analysis of subsidies in D. Barker to C. Weststrate. 6 December 1954, T/53/67.

64. See Secretary of Treasury to Minister of Finance, 14 March 1957, T/1/27/6/1.

65. Semple used the term 'running shoes' in January 1936. See *Press,* 10 January 1936, p.10. His reference to wheelbarrows is in the *Press,* 4 January 1936, p.12.

66. Most figures are from the *NZOYBs,* 1936, 1939 and 1943. See also Baker, *War Economy,* pp.6-7.

67. Quoted in 'History of Railways 1863-1963', *NZOYB,* 1963, pp.1188-92. Details about the increasing cost of rolling stock are to be found in E. Alington to Secretary to the Treasury, 26 July 1951, T/1/62/40/1. There is much material of interest about Railways in the late 1940s in this file.

68. *Press,* 21 February 1936, p.12.

69. Notes of a deputation of manufacturers, 7 May 1936, p.21, IC/1/31/171, part 1. Comments in support of protection had recently been made by an up-and-coming National MP, S.G. Holland. See *Press,* 22 April 1936, p.12.

70. Notes of deputation, 7 May 1936, IC/1/31/171, part 1, p.11.

71. The Dunedin District Officer of the Department of Industries and Commerce reported on 18 August that Mosgiel Woollen Co. was no longer able to compete with English competitors. See IC/1/31/171, part 1. There is criticism of government delays in the *New Zealand National Review,* 15 January 1937, p.9 and p.43; 15 July 1937, p.9; 15 August 1937, p.43; 15 December 1937, pp.35-39.

72. Sullivan's distrust of Clinkard seems to have stemmed from the fact that he was the son of the Coalition MP, C. H. Clinkard. Bad relations between the two men caused Clinkard to resign as Secretary of Industries and Commerce in 1935. He took the position of Trade Commissioner in Brussels. I am indebted to Professor G. J. Schmitt, whose father succeeded Clinkard as Secretary, for this observation in an interview, 20 March 1997. For

details about registering companies see IC/1/3/5/2, part 2. There had been discussions about registration as far back as 1917. See IC/57/1/9, W1926.

73. *Statutes*, 1936, p.406. See also *NZOYB*, 1939, pp.806-8. The Bureau of Industry's Minute Books beginning with the first meeting in the minister's office on 18 May 1936 are to be found in IC/44/1, W2268. There is considerable material about the workings of the Bureau in the Industries and Commerce annual reports, *AJHR*, H-44, from 1937 onwards.

74. There is much information about Whakatane Paper Mills in T/1/52/539.

75. Initial members of the Bureau were L. J. Schmitt (Secretary of Industries and Commerce, who was chairman), A. H. Cockayne (Agriculture), G. H. Mackley (Railways), Aickin (Railways), E. T. L. Spidy (Railways), J. S. Hunter (Labour), E. D. Good (Customs), J. H. Forrester (Customs), G. C. Rodda (Treasury), T. H. Sherwood (Mines), Dr E. Marsden (DSIR), A. D. McGavock (Forestry), A. R. Entrican (Forestry), G. A. Pascoe (I&C), D. W. Woodward (I&C), R. V. Jackson (I&C). Arthur Tyndall of the Mines Department served on the Bureau for a time. A secretariat, consisting of Industries and Commerce personnel, made many decisions on the advice of standing committees of the Bureau, and these were confirmed at regular meetings of the full board. The Cabinet ruling on monetary assistance is to be found in minutes of the Bureau's meeting of 13 July 1936. See Minute Books, IC/44/1, W2268, pp.23-24. The author wishes to thank Professor G. J. Schmitt for much information given about his father.

76. Files covering the licensing of the pharmacy industry are IC/1/49/1, 2 &3. L.J. Schmitt to D.G. Sullivan, 24 May 1938 gives a four-page history of pharmacy licensing, IC/1/49, part 4. One Labour backbencher, Dr D.G. McMillan, wanted the Government to establish its own drug importing business. See McMillan to M.J. Savage, 13 December 1936. There is press comment about the new scheme in the *Taranaki Daily News*, 14 September 1937 and the *DOM*, 13 October 1937.

77. Reports of the Standards Institute are to be found in *AJHR*, H-44a, from 1938 onwards.

78. *Press*, 14 January 1936, p.10.

79. The Bureau's Minute Book from page 71 onwards deals regularly with petrol selling and pharmaceutical licensing. See IC/44/1, W2268.

80. See 13-page typescript, 'Industry After the War', in IC/1/31/140.

81. The file with the story of the Leicester trade is IC/1/9/5/1, part 1.

82. There are many complaints to be found in the file IC/1/9/5/1. Material about the debate on the Merchandise Marks Bill 1954 and Mabel Howard is to be found in IC/1/10/1/3, part 1.

83. Arnold Nordmeyer described it in this manner, Interview with Keith Sinclair, 26 May 1970, p.8, transcript in the author's possession.

84. Secretary of Treasury to W. Nash, 28 March 1938, T/1/52/479. On 27 May 1938 Bernard Ashwin, the Assistant Secretary, strongly urged Nash to reconsider the financial aspects of the proposed bill before it was passed, and when Nash refused, Ashwin argued for setting the Social Security tax at 7.5 per cent to 'relieve' the Consolidated Fund. This was the tax level that Fraser's Government had to adopt in 1946 as costs escalated. In its first eight years of operation, Social Security required top-ups from the Consolidated Fund totalling £61.8 million. *NZOYB*, 1947–49, p.416.

85. The best summary of Social Security benefits as enacted in 1938 is to be found in the official pamphlet, *Social Security*, Wellington, 1938. See also the official publication, *The Growth and Development of Social Security in New Zealand*, Wellington, 1950.

86. See *The Growth and Development of Social Security*, pp.21-48; Elizabeth Hanson, *The Politics of Social Security: The 1938 Act and some later Developments*, Auckland, 1980; J.B. Lovell Smith, *The New Zealand Doctor and the Welfare State*, Auckland, 1966; D.G. Bolitho, 'The Introduction of Social Security, *NZJH*, Vol. 18, April, 1984, pp.34-49; Dean E. McHenry, 'The New Zealand System of Social Security', *Social Science Review*, Vol. 25, March 1951, pp.48-59. There is an interesting file on government discussions about health and pension schemes in T/1/52/479.

87. *NZPD*, Vol. 51, 1938, p.649. Labour backbencher Dr D.G. McMillan had expressed the common Labour viewpoint when he said that health insurance was necessary because of the widespread hardship that could result from sudden illness, and the inability of people to insure adequately against emergency costs. See *Standard*, 26 August 1936, p.15.

88. These quotes are from Francis G. Castles, *The Working Class and Welfare: Reflections on the Political Development of the Welfare State in Australia and New Zealand, 1890–1980*, Wellington, 1985, pp.27-28. Baker, *War Economy*, has some useful statistics on pp.6-7.

89. The author deals with these issues in 'Health Care History: Costly Health Care: A Lesson from New Zealand', *Health Care Analysis*, Vol. 1, November 1993, pp.189-96.

90. *NZOYB*, 1943, pp.106-7; pp.115-7. McCombs, who was Minister of Education 1947–49, made these comments in an interview with Michael King, 17 February 1980, transcript p.21, King/Fraser Papers. There is a summary of developments within Education, 1935–45, in Nancy M. Taylor, *The Home Front*, Vol. 2, pp.1116-82.

91. C.E. Beeby, *The Biography of an Idea: Beeby on Education*, Wellington, 1992, pp. xvi-xvii. There is an account of Beeby's appointment in the transcript of Michael King's interview of him, 4 July 1978, King/Fraser Papers.

92. Ibid, Chapt. 7. The author has clear memories of the school health service at Owairaka School between 1943-48. Beeby's quote about standards is from his book, p.167. His 1978 concession is contained in his interview with Michael King.

93. See, for instance, attachments to E.D. Good to W. Nash, 14 November 1938, Nash Papers (NASH), 2308/0404. There is further information in NASH 2313. Hawke, *The Making of New Zealand*, pp.164-6, discusses the Government's options.

94. Nash's announcement and the *Gazette* notice are printed in the *DOM*, 7 December 1938. See also *Statutory Regulations*, 1938/160 and 161. There is a history of import licensing during its first twenty years of operation in an official publication by the Reserve Bank, *Overseas Trade and Finance*, 2nd ed, 1966, part 5. See also A.A. Smith & J. Burney, 'Import Licensing' in R.S. Deane et al. (eds), *External Economic Structure and Policy*, Wellington, 1981, pp.427-55.

95. *New Zealand National Review*, 15 December 1938, p.9. Manufacturers had been pushing throughout 1938 for a permanent tariff review. Sullivan warmed to their advocacy, especially since the review process might stop manufacturers 'voicing their complaints through the newspapers'. See memo, D.G. Sullivan to fellow ministers, 6 September 1938, IC/1/31/171/2.

96. *La Gazette* (Brussels), 1 August 1938, to be found in file IC/1/31/171, part 1.

97. *NZPD*, Vol. 254, 26 and 27 July 1939, p.793. See also Hawke, *The Making of New Zealand*, p.164.

98. *EP*, 7 December 1938 and *DOM*, 8 December 1938. Other reports of the speeches are in NASH 2308/0209/0404.

99. Quoted in *New Zealand National Review*, 15 January 1939, pp.9-10. Nash's Private Secretary, W.B. Sutch, outlined this argument in a pamphlet 'The Policy of Import Selection', Wellington, 1939, copy in NASH 2313.

100. *NZOYB*, 1943, p.145.

101. Bassett, *Coates*, pp.246-7. See also *Statutes*, 1939, p.407. W.B. Sutch told Nash in a memo dated 25 January 1939 that he believed that among importers only 30 were adamantly opposed to import controls, NASH 2308/0209/0404.

102. *New Zealand National Review*, 15 January 1939, pp.9-10. See also N.F. Crimp (Secretary, Auckland Manufacturers' Association) to W. Nash, 23 January 1939, NASH 2313. For information about American businessmen and the New Deal, see Higgs, p.214.

103. S. Leathem, 'Policies and Trends in New Zealand', *Economic Record*, June 1939, p.40.

104. *NZH*, 1 May 1936, p.10; *Press*, 5 May 1936, p.10. See also editorial in the waterside workers' newspaper, the *New Zealand Transport Worker*, 2 February 1940.

105. See *NZPD*, Vol. 249, 1937, p.1125. Also *New Zealand Transport Worker*, 14 April 1938.

106. There is a file on minimum salaries for public servants, T/1/9/33. They were first introduced in 1914. Not until the level was set at £243 pa in 1942 did the minimum salary for

civil servants pass the level of 1921.

107. *NZPD*, Vol. 254, 1939, p.473. There is critical comment on the legislation in *Tomorrow*, Vol. 5, 2 August 1939.

108. Higgs, p. 211. For statistics see *NZOYB*, 1943, p.145.

109. Clark is quoted in Keith Sinclair, *A History of New Zealand*, Auckland, 4th revised ed, p.278; Margaret Galt, Chapt. 1; *NZOYB*, 1943, p.145.

110. A 'Report on the State of Industry', 24 November 1936, gives interesting statistics on the first year of Labour's rule. See IC/1/2, part 4. See also *NZH*, 1 May 1936. See also Baker, *War Economy*, pp.12-14.

111. *NZOYB*, 1939, p.704.

112. *Press*, 14 April 1936, p.8

113. The file on unemployed Maori is T/1/40/544/9. Scheme 13 involved the unemployed in full-time subsidised work with local authorities, school committees and sports bodies. For a discussion of Labour's policies toward Maori, see Claudia Orange, 'A Kind of Equality: Labour and the Maori People, 1935–1949', MA thesis, University of Auckland, 1977, Chapt. 3.

114. See *NZOYB*, 1959, pp.460. Evidence about the heavy-handed restrictions imposed on Maori farmers is to be found in Maurice Alemann's submission to the Waitangi Tribunal, WAI 674/229, 10 November 1997.

115. See Bassett, *The Mother of All Departments*, Chapt. 5, for details about the Government's involvement in the centenary celebrations.

116. Skidelsky, p.73.

Chapter 8 War and the Omnipotent State

1. Baker, *War Economy*, p.16.

2. F. Hayek, *The Road to Serfdom*, Chicago, 1944, pp.207-8. The socialist economist Gunnar Myrdal seems to have shared this view. See quote in R.S. Parker (ed), *Economic Stability in New Zealand*, Wellington, 1953, p.116.

3. Baker, *War Economy*, p.22. See also *AJHR*, 1938, H-44, p.20.

4. *Press*, 11 May 1936, p.12.

5. There is a general description of the working of the Fair Rents Act in 'Proceedings of the Stabilisation Committee', 1940, T/70/1, pp.188ff. There is some information on competition with state house rentals in Gael Ferguson, pp.153-4. The original Bill is outlined in the *Press*, 3 June 1936, p.10.

6. There is a brief summary of pre-war price control in H.L. Wise, *War-time Price Control in New Zealand*, Christchurch, no date [1942], Chapt. 4.

7. Some files covering the work of the ONS are in IC/1/3/21, parts 1 & 2. Details about discussions regarding price control, especially the meeting of the Price Control Committee on 16 September 1938, are in IC/1/54/2. Sir George Laking in an interview with Michael King on 14 August 1986 recalled many aspects of the work of the ONS.

8. In September 1944 Hunter was reflecting on the history of price control in an address to Auckland manufacturers. The text of his comments is in IC/4/59/11.

9. *Statutory Regulations*, 1939/122. There are details about Cabinet's actions in IC/1/54/2.

10. *Maoriland Worker*, 13 February 1918. For other quotes see WAII, 21, 64B (CN116), NA.

11. *DOM*, 3 June 1938.

12. *EP*, 21 September 1938.

13. See *Statutory Regulations*, 1939/143, 145, 146, 147,148. The measures are listed in IC/1/3/21, part 2. To these were added the Sugar Emergency Regulations, which established a Sugar Controller who was to ensure the continuity of supply of sugar, its storage and distribution. See Secretary of Supply to W.B. Sutch, 28 February 1940, IC/1/3/21,

part 2. For a discussion of the Emergency Regulations Bill, see WA II, 21, 64B (CN116), part 2, p.3. The justification was given by Fraser, *NZPD*, Vol. 256, 13 September 1939, p.102.

14. *NZPD*, Vol. 256, September 1939, p.232 and p.384.
15. *NZPD*, Vol. 256, September 1939, p.225.
16. Memo L.J. Schmitt to D.G. Sullivan, 26 September 1939, IC/1/54/2. There is a discussion of early difficulties with price control in *AJHR*, 1940, H-44, pp.4-8.
17. H.L. Wise to R.M. Barker, 30 October 1939, IC/1/54/2. There is a tentative outline of departmental thinking on price stabilisation in this file, dated 8 September 1939. See Wise, p.19. There are letters to Nash commenting on, or complaining about price controls in NASH 2313.
18. There are comparative figures with other countries in *AJHR*, 1940, H-44, p.17.
19. Wise, pp.20-22. Minute Books of the Price Tribunal are to be found in IC/44/5399, W2268.
20. The Whakatane Paper Mills Water Supply Empowering Bill.
21. The story of the Government's dealings with the mill is to be found in T/1/52/539. See also IC/1/21/1/1, part 1. The press statement is in *DOM*, 10 January 1940.
22. There is a full account of the finding in *DOM*, 2 April 1940.
23. There is a Treasury memo dated 25 March 1941 about the possibility of a state pulp and paper mill costing an estimated £1.6 million. Treasury was not opposed, even if the mill initially ran at a loss. See T/1/52/539. Early discussions about a pulp and paper mill are referred to in Neil Robinson, *James Fletcher: Builder*, p.135, and Selwyn Parker, *Made in New Zealand: The Story of Jim Fletcher*, Auckland, 1994, Chapt. 3. There are comments about the Whakatane case in *AJHR*, 1940, H-44, pp.7-8. Early developments in what became the Tasman Pulp and Paper Company are dealt with by Morris William Guest, 'The Murupara Project: The Tasman Pulp and Paper Company Ltd and Industrial Development in New Zealand 1945–1963', MA thesis, VUW, 1997, pp.36ff.
24. See H. Landon Smith to P. Fraser, 11 November 1942, T/1/52/539. This file has a lot of material about the Government's relationships with the various forest interests. See also Brian Healy, *A Hundred Million Trees: The Story of N.Z. Forest Products*, Auckland, 1982, pp.108-9, and John H. Angus, *Papermaking Pioneers: A History of New Zealand Paper Mills Limited and its Predecessors*, Mataura, 1976, p.132.
25. See P. Fraser memo to all ministers, 8 February 1940, IC/1/3/21, part 2. There is useful material about Fraser's wartime methods in Alister McIntosh, 'Working with Peter Fraser in Wartime: Personal Reminiscences', *NZJH*, Vol.10, April 1976, pp.3-20. The series of interviews of friends of Fraser conducted by Michael King in 1977–82 is very enlightening.
26. B. Ashwin to W. Nash, 19 December 1940, T/53/88.
27. J. Heenan memo to all Permanent Heads, 26 June 1942, T/53/88.
28. There are assessments of Fraser by several of his closest wartime officials. See John Henderson interview of Sir Bernard Ashwin, March 1970. I am indebted to Barry Ashwin for his assistance in seeing the text of this interview. See also Keith Sinclair interview of Sir Carl Berendsen, 8 January 1971, Fraser-King Papers, and McIntosh, 'Working with Peter Fraser', pp.3-20. There are other interviews of McIntosh by Michael King in the Fraser-King Papers. The correspondence between J.W. Heenan and Dr R.M. Campbell from 1936–45 contains snippets about Fraser's working habits. MS Papers 1132, Folder 30, ATL. See also Ormond Wilson, *An Outsider Looks Back*, Chapt. 10.
29. *AJHR*, 1940, H-44, p.8.
30. See H.L. Wise and Judge Hunter to D.G. Sullivan, 16 July 1940, IC/4/59/11.
31. 'Report of the Proceedings of the Economic Stabilisation Conference, 1940', bound volume, T/52/835.
32. Schmitt's comments are in the volume of the 'Proceedings', pp150ff, T/70/1.
33. 'Proceedings', pp.96ff, T/52/835.
34. Budget of 1940, *AJHR*, 1940, B-6. The taxation figure comes from *NZOYB*, 1943, p.368.

35. See M. Moohan to D.G. Sullivan, 20 April 1942, IC/4/59/11. See also files of correspondence, MS Papers 4100/18/18/1, ATL. The Economic Stabilisation Committee
tried to persuade the Government to introduce an interim order fixing all internal prices,
wholesale and retail, from 11 December 1941. See 'Economic Stabilisation Committee',
no date, T/72/1.
36. *NZOYB*, 1943, p.561. There are details about the touring by Price Control officers in
IC/4/59/11.
37. See Secretary ESC to D.G. Sullivan, 7 December 1942, T/72/1.
38. The full text of Fraser's statement is in the *DOM*, 16 December 1942, p.6. There is comment in Thorn, p.213.
39. Wise outlines precisely how this system worked in *Wartime Price Control*, pp.36-37.
40. The subsidy figures come from Baker, *War Economy*, pp.306-7. Baker discusses the workings of the Wartime Price Index, pp.309-14. Treasury's attempt to distinguish between
categories of subsidy is outlined in B. Ashwin to A. Hamilton, 27 May 1942, T/53/167.
There is an itemised list of all subsidies paid by the Government from the Consolidated
Fund as of 31 March 1942, and another listing those charged to the War Expenses Account and dated 28 July 1942, in T/53/167.
41. Henderson interview with Sir Bernard Ashwin, March 1970. In fact there was to be no
across-the-board wage increase until 17 March 1945 when standard rates of pay were
raised by 3.5 pence an hour. A Minimum Wage Act passed in December 1945 and came
into effect on 1 April 1946. See Baker, *War Economy*, pp.322-3.
42. For the figures about the pool accounts, see *AJHR*, 1951, B-5, p.69. Sir Frank Holmes in
an interview with the author on 12 March 1997 accorded the retention of surpluses in the
pool accounts as a key factor in the success of wartime stabilisation.
43. For detail about the changes to the regulations see L.C. Webb in R.S. Parker (ed), *Economic Stability in New Zealand*, Wellington, 1953. John Martin, *Holding the Balance*,
pp.224-8, has detail about changes to wage fixing. Hawke's comment is in *The Making of
New Zealand*, p.172.
44. There is a lot of detail about these clothing experiments in IC/1/10/1/3, part 1.
45. See the file of submissions on the subject, IC/1/10/1/3, part 1. There are more details
about these experiments in T/1/72/2/1. See also 'Notes for Mr Pascoe re Deputation to
Wait Upon the Minister', undated, IC/1/10/1/3, part 1.
46. Memo D.G. Sullivan to all controllers, 21 December 1942, IC/1/2/22, W709.
47. Baker, *War Economy*, pp.465-74.
48. Baker, *War Economy*, pp.100-101. There is a file about 'essential industries' in IC/1/55/
11/2, part 1. John Martin, *Holding the Balance*, pp.218-25, deals with manpower directions.
49. Baker, *War Economy*, pp.225-6.
50. Baker comments on Fletcher's powers and his exercise of them in *War Economy*, pp.227-9.
There is a detailed account of Fletcher's conduct, much of it from Fletcher's own memory,
in Neil Robinson, *James Fletcher: Builder*, Chapt. 10.
51. Henderson interview of Ashwin.
52. *NZOYB*, 1947-8, p.361. See also 'Industry After the War', 13-page typescript, IC/1/31/
140, part 2.
53. Samuel Leathem, 'Industry and Industrial Policy', in Horace Belshaw (ed), *New Zealand*,
Berkeley, 1947, p.169. See also *AJHR*, 1942, H-44, p.2.
54. Baker, *War Economy*, Chapt. 13.
55. Quoted in C.H. Blaikie, 'Cost-Plus Contracts', WAII, 21, 57c, NA.
56. There is a neat background account to the establishment of Watties Canneries in M.B.
Boyd, *City of the Plains: A History of Hastings*, Wellington 1984, pp.240-1.The story in
this chapter is drawn from Treasury files, T/1/47/390.
57. *Hawkes Bay Herald-Tribune*, 22 September 1944.
58. See *DOM*, 7 January 1949.
59. *NZPD*, Vol. 256, 6 October 1939, p.772.

60. See IC/1/31/140, part 2.
61. See Secretary of the Manufacturers' Federation to D.G. Sullivan, 8 October 1943, IC/1/31/140, part 2.
62. J.W. Heenan to Dr R.M. Campbell, 21 October 1943, MS Papers 1132, Folder 30, ATL.
63. Leslie Hobbs, *The Thirty Year Wonders*, Christchurch, 1976, pp.96-97.
64. See typescript 'Industry after the War' as well as the minister's speech, IC/1/31/140, part 2.
65. Baker, *War Economy*, p.530. The OND, however, met several times a week in the evening and war-weary officials soon tired of the effort involved. Comments of Professor G. J. Schmitt, 20 March 1997. Schmitt was personal clerk to Ashwin at the time.
66. *AJHR*, 1946, H-44, pp.5-18.
67. *AJHR*, 1947, H-44, p.4. The total number of permanent and temporary employees of the Public Service Commission stood at 10,800 in 1936; it rose to 17,246 in 1939, and by April 1946 reached 28,484. See *AJHR*, 1937-8, H-14; 1939, H-14; 1947, H-14, p.10
68. There is some information about these appointments in IC/1/2, part 4. The story about the Marshall-Clinkard appointments comes from Professor G. J. Schmitt, interview, 20 March 1997.
69. The planned reorganisation is set out in D.W. Woodward to Section heads, 15 March 1948, IC/1/2, part 4. The draft bill is to be found in IC/1/3/5/2, W709. Among the functions of the department were the following clauses: 'To investigate the financial structure and costs of existing or proposed new industries so as to determine whether the arrangements or operations are to the benefit of the economy of New Zealand'; 'To encourage, in relation to any industry, the adoption of uniform methods of accounting, costing and the preparation of statistics'; 'In respect to industries which are receiving protection, by way of import restriction, tariff, subsidy, registration or in any other form, to maintain a close scrutiny of the financial accounts and records, products and methods of the industries to ensure that the benefits of any such protection are accruing to the public in terms of quality and price'.
70. See the initial directive and the 'Survey of War-time Controls', 1 December 1944, IC/1/3/21, part 3.
71. See Factory Controller to W. Nash and A.H. Nordmeyer, 23 February 1945, IC/1/2/7, part 2, W709. Also Secretary NZ Manufacturers' Federation to P. Fraser, 21 December 1945, IC/1/31/140, part 2. *Press*, 17 November 1944.
72. G.W. Pascoe to A.H. Nordmeyer, 15 July 1947, IC/1/2/7, W709. Pascoe's influence was removed from the department in the middle of 1948, when he retired. There is general information relevant to the Industries Committee in IC/1/2/7, part 2, W709.
73. *DOM*, 20 April 1945.
74. D.G. Sullivan to G.A. Pascoe, 4 May 1945, IC/1/3/21, part 3.
75. A full list of those Emergency Regulations lifted in 1945 and of the 362 retained is to be found in *AJHR*, 1945, H-46. Holland's reaction is in *NZPD*, Vol. 279, 1947, p.979.
76. *Statutes*, 1948, Vol. 1, p.347.
77. Ormond Wilson, *An Outsider Looks Back*, p.96.
78. Much has been written about John A. Lee, his expulsion and its effects on the Labour Party. See particularly Erik Olssen, *John A. Lee*, Dunedin, 1977, and Olssen, 'The Impact of John A. Lee's Expulsion upon the Labour Party', *NZJH*, Vol. 12, April 1978, pp.34-49. Also Keith Sinclair, 'The Lee-Sutch Syndrome', *NZJH*, Vol. 8, October 1974, pp.95-117, and Bruce Taylor, 'The Expulsion of J.A. Lee and the Effects on the Development of the New Zealand Labour Party', MA thesis, University of Canterbury, 1970.
79. There is much useful detail about the background to broadcasting in Ian Carter, *Gadfly: The Life and Times of James Shelley*, Auckland 1993, Chapt. 8. There is specific detail about the nature of the contract with Goodfellow and Harris, and later developments, in T/1/52/682.
80. Carter, p.202.
81. This event is mentioned in greater detail in Bassett, *Coates of Kaipara*, p.227. See also

Carter, p.203, who calls the incident a 'Ruritanian fiasco'; *Standard,* 15 January 1936, p.1; and *NZH,* 18 July 1992.

82. *Statutes,* 1936, p.167.

83. *Press,* 9 June 1936, p.10. There are comments about the practical difficulties surrounding the broadcasting of Parliament in Carter, p.232.

84. *Press,* 10 June 1936, p.12.

85. Quoted by Carter, p.204.

86. Carter notes that in 1937 Shelley forbade a public debate on IYA on the topic of socialism and later also prevented Ormond Burton talking about pacifism. Carter, pp.237-8.

87. *Standard,* 4 November 1936.

88. Details of the negotiations with 'Scrim' are in T/1/52/682/1.

89. Bassett interview with Samuel Leathem, 20 March 1977, in the author's possession. Leathem was a member of a deputation to Savage on the subject.

90. For a general, and not always reliable, discussion of Scrim, see Les Edwards, *Scrim: Radio Rebel in Retrospect,* Auckland, 1971.

91. Bassett, *Mother of All Departments,* Chapt. 5.

92. There is a succinct summary of the issues surrounding the closure of *Tomorrow* in Andrew J. Cutler, 'Intellectual Sprouts'. The quote is from F.L.W. Wood, *The New Zealand People at War,* Wellington, 1958, p.124. A more general discussion of censorship is to be found in Nancy M. Taylor, *The Home Front,* Chapt. 19.

93. Much information for this section comes from T/1/40/704/1. See also Report of the Royal Commission into the sale of liquor, *AJHR,* 1974, H-5, part 12.

94. J.F. McArthur, *Licensing Trust Development in New Zealand: A History of Licensing Trusts,* Wellington, 1967, p.13.

95. E.L. Greensmith to W. Nash, 15 June 1944, T/1/40/704/1.

96. [B.L. Dallard?] to B. Ashwin, 15 April 1947, T/1/40/704/1.

97. Recent changes to the licensing legislation have, among other things, permitted liquor sales from supermarkets. This has proved popular, and public enthusiasm for trusts decreased rapidly when it became clear that this convenience would not be available if residents in an area supported trust control. Only a true believer in the trust concept could conclude that the experiment has stood the test of time.

98. Baker has a graph of demobilisation numbers, *War Economy,* p.503. There are quarterly figures given on p.631.

99. Baker, *War Economy,* pp.518-9. See also W.H. Oliver, 'The Origins and Growth of the Welfare State', in A.D. Trlin (ed), *Social Welfare and New Zealand Society,* Wellington, 1977, p.24.

100. Figures are drawn from *New Zealand Official YearBooks.* There were electricity blackouts in the winters of 1946 and 1947, with problems in the latter year exacerbated by a very dry summer 1946–47, which reduced the water flow on the Waikato River to a record low level. The Treasury warning to Nash came in August 1949. See Morris Guest, 'The Murupara Project', p.40.

101. *NZOYB,* 1947–49, p.523.

102. *Statutes,* 1947, p.445.

103. B.C. Ashwin to W. Nash, 12 February 1947, T/53/167. The anticipated subsidies for 1946–47 were £14.54 million, and for 1947–48 were £18.405 million. In the white paper 'The New Zealand Economy 1939-51', *AJHR,* 1951, B-5, p.37, it is estimated that without the 1947 changes, subsidies would have reached the sum of £20 million at a time when the Government was budgeting for total expenditure of £105 million.

104. Acting Director of Stabilisation to W. Nash, 5 August 1947, T/53/167.

105. See A.H. Nordmeyer to Canterbury Cricket Association, 8 May 1947, T/53/167.

106. N.J. Lewis to Secretary, Tobacco Board, 14 November 1947, T/1/47/277. Set up in 1936 under the Tobacco Growing Industry Act 1935 which was pushed through Parliament at the urging of the young Keith Holyoake, MP for Motueka at the time, the Board aimed to prevent over-production of leaf which would result in uneconomic prices for

growers. See Memo for Junior Officers, 1948, p.7, IC/1/2, part 4.

107. *AJHR*, 1950, B-6, pp.13-14.

108. Author's interview of Sir Arnold Nordmeyer, 9 December 1977, p.21. Text in the author's possession.

109. Skidelsky, p.68. Ormond Wilson recalls that he based his arguments for state intervention in economic and social affairs when he returned to Parliament in 1946 'on the trend of the world at the time', *An Outsider Looks Back*, p.145.

110. For a discussion of Australia's postwar economic policies, see L.F. Crisp, *Ben Chifley: A Biography*, Melbourne, 1961, Chapt. 19.

111. Ramsay Cook, 'The Triumph and Trials of Materialism' in Craig Brown (ed), *The Illustrated History of Canada*, Toronto, 1987, pp.463-4.

112. *The Growth and Development of Social Security*, p.115. See also *AJHR*, 1946, B-6.

113. The story of cultural developments in 1946 is told in Bassett, *The Mother of All Departments*, Chapt. 6.

114. There is a file on stabilisation among F.P. Walsh's papers, MS Papers 0274/171, ATL. For press reaction to Walsh's views, see *AS*, 13 June 1946, editorial.

115. See R.S. Parker, 'New Industrial Tribunals in New Zealand', *Economic Record*, Vol. 26, December 1950, p.254. Parker identifies the Waterfront Industry Commission and the Waterfront Industry Authority, the Government Railways Industrial Tribunal, the Post and Telegraph Staff Tribunal, and the Government Service Tribunal. The comments about the FOL's practice before the Arbitration Court and the rapidity with which every wage rise spread are made by Leicester Webb, in R.S. Parker (ed), *Economic Stability*, pp.18-19.

116. Cox to US Secretary of State, 28 January 1942, RG84/800/10, US Archives, Washington, DC.

117. There were stoppages at West Coast mines within weeks of Labour coming to power. See *Press*, 27 February 1936, p.12.

118. C.H. Blaikie, 'Wartime History of Mining', pp.9-33, MD/1/15/300, Vol. 1.

119. *NZOYB*, 1943, pp.304.

120. *Greymouth Evening Star*, 19 March 1943; *Westport News*, 22 March 1943; *Press*, 20 March 1943.

121. See file on absenteeism in the mines, MDIC/4/4/29, Vol. 1. C.H. Benney of the Mines Department told the Secretary of the Stabilisation Committee on 20 March 1943 that miners were well paid, providing comparative figures to illustrate his case. MS Papers 0274/171, ATL.

122. Blaikie, pp.58-76. He provides details about sale negotiations. There was a miners' strike at Easter 1947 that affected train timetables and interrupted holiday travel.

123. *AJHR*, 1947, B-6, p.21.

124. Blaikie, pp.40-46.

125. *ODT*, 20, 21 February, and 6 March 1947.

126. *ODT*, 2 May 1947.

127. *ODT*, 9 June 1947.

128. For a wider discussion of deteriorating industrial relations in the late 1940s, see Michael Bassett, *Confrontation '51: The 1951 Waterfront Dispute*, Wellington, 1972, Chapt. 1.

129. Bassett, *Confrontation*, p.32.

130. See especially B. Ashwin to W. Nash, 13 April 1949, T/1/52/835/5.

131. J. Heenan to Sir E. Davis, 20 May and 16 June 1949, MS 1132/51, ATL.

132. *ODT*, 17 November 1949. The election has been analysed by Sylvia E. Fraser, 'The 1949 General Election', MA thesis, University of Otago, 1967.

Chapter 9 Freedom or Controls? National Deals with Labour's Legacy

1. B.C. Ashwin to S.G. Holland, 22 March 1950, p.8, T/53/167.

2. Leicester Webb in R.S. Parker, *Economic Stability*, p.21.

3. *NZOYB*, 1951–52, p.499.
4. The number of vacant jobs appeared in Holland's second budget presented on 18 October 1951, *AJHR*, 1951, B-6, p.4. The figures for the gap between award and actual wages are to be found in the National Party's 1954 election material, PM/21/18/1. The quotation from the citizenship booklet comes from Bassett, *The Mother of All Departments*, p.151. The quote from the Monetary and Economic Council comes from Report No. 2, May 1962, p.87. C.A. Blyth notes New Zealand's low rate of growth during the 1950s in 'Economic Growth 1950–60', Research Paper, Wellington, 1961. The comments in the report of the waterfront Royal Commission are to be found in *AJHR*, 1952, H-50, pp.21-27. During university holidays the author worked for five years as a driver in the soft drink industry, where there was a great deal of pilfering but only a few successful prosecutions. The freezing industry suffered badly from the stealing of meat by employees and police raids on men's locker rooms were common. The problem lasted into the 1970s and was frequently discussed at meetings of Federated Farmers. See *Northern Farming World*, July 1976, p.4.
5. The tax figure is to be found in *NZOYB*, 1951–52, p.579. The report by T. N. Gibbs's committee is to be found in draft form in T/1/40/106/2/1. The final version is in *AJHR*, 1951, B-8. The quote is on p.50. Ashwin's similar advice to Nash is in Ashwin to Nash, 13 April 1949, T/1/52/835/5. In his first budget in August 1950 Holland also made some of these points strongly. *AJHR*, 1950, B-6, p.23. The comment about New Zealand's growth is to be found in Monetary and Economic Council, *Economic Growth in New Zealand*, No.2, Wellington, May 1962, p.5. Growth figures for later years are provided by Roger Douglas, *Unfinished Business*, Auckland, 1993, p.24. See also Paul Dalziel and Ralph Lattimore, *A Briefing on the New Zealand Macroeconomy 1960–1990*, Auckland, 1991, p.2.
6. One example of controversy about the flexibility of shop trading hours came in 1960 with an application by the East Coast Bays Association for longer hours. See *NZH*, 2 April 1960, p.20. There is a newspaper story about the first serious challenge to the broadcasting monopoly in *Sunday Star-Times*, 1 December 1996, p.A11. For discussion about film censorship, see Bassett, *The Mother of All Departments*, Chapt. 8. Also Redmer Yska, *All Shook Up: The Flash Bodgie and the Rise of the New Zealand Teenager in the Fifties*, Wellington, Chapt. 5. The referendum on TAB betting was on the same day in 1949 as the liquor referendum. Results are given in J.O. Wilson, *New Zealand Parliamentary Record, 1840–1984*, Wellington, 1985, p.301.
7. W.K. Jackson, *The New Zealand Legislative Council: A Study of the Establishment, Failure and Abolition of an Upper House*, Dunedin, 1972, pp.166ff. See also Geoffrey Palmer, *Unbridled Power*, Auckland, 1979.
8. There is an entry on S. G. Holland (1893–1961) in *An Encyclopaedia of New Zealand*, Wellington, 1966, Vol. 2, pp.107-8. See also John Marshall, *Memoirs*, Vol. 1, Auckland, 1983, pp.140, 254. The description of Holland's face came from the author's mother.
9. R.S. Parker, *Economic Stability*, p.25. The comment came from Ian Lythgoe, who was Private Secretary to the Minister of Finance in 1949. Interview 11 December 1995.
10. In the newspapers during the month of October 1956 the author noted two pieces of praise from New Zealanders recently in Russia. See the comments of P.G. Stevens, *NZH*, 26 October 1956, p.12, and Sir David Smith, *EP*, 31 October 1956, p.12.
11. Marshall, *Memoirs*, Vol. 1, pp.304-9.
12. Barry Gustafson, *The First Fifty Years: A History of the New Zealand National Party*, Auckland, 1986, p.56, describes Clifton Webb as an 'intellectual', although the biography written by his daughter, Sheila M. Belshaw, *Man of Integrity: A Biography of Sir Clifton Webb*, Palmerston North, 1979, provides no evidence of wide reading. The author was told by Sir Keith Holyoake in 1974 that he endeavoured to keep abreast of books about New Zealand.
13. See Bassett, *Mother of All Departments*, Chapt. 7. J. O. Wilson, who later became Parliamentary Librarian, told the author on 6 September 1995 that Holland very rarely used the

library. It is clear from the letters between Alister McIntosh and Carl Berendsen in the early 1950s that McIntosh had little respect for the abilities of some ministers. See Ian McGibbon (ed), *Undiplomatic Dialogue*, Auckland, 1993, pp.186ff. Heenan, who had just retired, but retained an office in the Government Buildings, expressed reservations about the new order in his correspondence with Dr J. C. Beaglehole and Sir Ernest Davis. See J. C. Beaglehole to J. W. Heenan, 12 May 1950, MS Papers 1132/16; Heenan to Sir E. Davis, 25 October 1950, MS Papers 1132/52, ATL. Dr W. B. Sutch, whom the new Minister of External Affairs, F. W. Doidge, worked hard to dislodge from his position at the United Nations on political grounds, only to have him return to Wellington to a senior position in Industries and Commerce, wrote some years later about Holland's lack of experience and small contribution to the War Administration in 1942. See W.B. Sutch, *The Quest for Security in New Zealand, 1840–1966*, Wellington, 1966, p.310. Sutch expressed his criticism of Holland's Cabinet to the author on several occasions in the 1960s and early 1970s.

14. Details of the changes to exchange controls were published in the *Gazette* on 9 March 1950. They are also set out in T/53/88.

15. B.C. Ashwin to W. Nash, 24 August 1949, quoted by Guest, 'The Murupara Project', p.40. Ashwin expressed his disquiet at Labour's spending promises during the 1949 campaign. See Ashwin to W. Nash, 12 October 1949, T/53/167. See also Ashwin to Nash, 13 April 1949, T/1/52/835/5.

16. See Memo 'Works Programme and Inflation', 21 December 1949, T/1/25/23. Also B.C. Ashwin to S.G. Holland, 22 March 1950, T/53/167. This substantial memo contained a lot of disquieting news about the state of the economy.

17. B.C. Ashwin to S.G. Holland, 27 April 1950. There is another memo from Ashwin to Holland on the likely effect of subsidy removals dated 24 April 1950, T/53/167.

18. *DOM*, and *EP*, 6 May 1950.

19. C.M. Bowden to members of the ESC, 22 May 1950, T/72/1.

20. Statements about the future of NAC were in the 1950 budget statement and in the *New Zealand Government Bulletin*, 2 November 1950. B.C. Ashwin to S.G. Holland, 19 December 1950, T/1/62/40/1, contains useful information. Headed by Sir John Allum, the railways royal commission reported in 1952. It recommended charging economic fares on lines, suggested many economies, and called for turning the department into the New Zealand Railways Corporation. See 'Report of Royal Commission to Inquire into and Report upon the New Zealand Government Railways', *AJHR*, 1952, D-3 and *NZOYB*, 1959, p.377.

21. *AJHR*, 1950, B-6, pp.10-13.

22. *AJHR*, 1951, B-6, p.18. Harry Dudfield, a one-term MP from Gisborne, expressed the same philosophy succinctly: 'This Government is a private enterprise government. . . . We on this side of the House want to see everybody in the country a small capitalist, owning his own home, his car, and all the amenities that go to make a modern home. If a man is a farmer or farm worker we want to see him owning his own farm, because we want to encourage a nation of small capitalists. We believe . . . that the people can spend their money far better than the State can. . . .' *NZPD*, Vol. 303, 29 July 1954, p.800. There is much detail about National's housing policy in HD/1/29/0, and some further details in PM/21/18/1. See also Gael Ferguson, pp.179-95, and Marshall, *Memoirs*, Vol. 1, pp.144-53.

23. Fraser's statement of 21 February 1950 is to be found in MS Papers 0274/172, ATL. See also *EP*, 13 May 1950, p.10; *EP*, 6 May 1950, p.8 and editorial; *Southern Cross*, 8 June 1950.

24. The story is told in full in Bassett, *Confrontation '51*, Chapt. 2. There is a 52-page pamphlet written by a research officer of the National Party, John Gordon, *Crisis on the Waterfront: The Story of the 1951 Strike*, Wellington [1952], that contains useful material.

25. 'The New Zealand Economy 1939–51', *AJHR*, 1951, B-5, pp.69-70.

26. Ibid, p.69.

27. Ibid, p.34.
28. *NZH*, 17 February 1951. See Bassett, *Confrontation '51*, Chapt. 3.
29. *AS*, 22 February 1951, editorial.
30. *NZH*, 14 May 1951.
31. The four extra seats won by National were Gisborne, Napier, Lyttelton and St Kilda.
32. See Memo B.C. Ashwin to S.G. Holland, 9 October 1950, and CM(50)70, 11 October 1950, T/53/67. See also 'The New Zealand Economy 1939–51', p.37. There is a file dealing with the administration of subsidies in the early 1950s, T/1/52/835/1.
33. Minutes of the deputation to the Prime Minister, 31 May 1951, in T/53/67.
34. See file note, 'Soaps and Synthetic Detergents', T/53/67.
35. See file note, 'Stabilisation Subsidies', dated 23 May 1952, T/53/67.
36. The budget comments are in *AJHR*, 1953, B-6, p. 21. The two-page file note on subsidies in 1954 is to be found in T/53/67.
37. *Press*, 24 February 1951.
38. *AJHR*, 1951, H-44, p.32; Wise's regular memos on price control are in IC/1/9, W2268.
39. Watts's declaration is to be found in IC/1/10, W2268.
40. The Treasury memo of 1 April 1954 is to be found in IC/1/10, W2268. The decision of the Price Tribunal on 21 June 1954 is to be found in T/1/52/835/5. National's margin at the 1954 election was 45:35 seats over Labour. This was the first election at which Social Credit stood a full slate of candidates; they won 11 per cent of the total vote, but no seats. There was a major redistribution of seats before the 1954 election and it is difficult to make clear comparisons with 1951. However, Labour won back Gisborne, Napier, Hastings, Palmerston North and Rotorua from National.
41. *Freedom*, 12 January 1955.
42. *NZH*, 23 October 1956, p.14. There is press comment on the Control of Prices Amendment Bill in *NZH*, 25 October 1956, p.12.
43. J.C. Adams, to J.T. Watts, 19 August 1955, IC/1/10, W2268. The Chambers of Commerce, like the retailers and manufacturers, sounded off against controls. See T/1/52/655.
44. 'Ministerial Statement', *AJHR*, 1950, J-4, pp.1-3.
45. Sir David Smith produced a summary of the work of the Board of Trade on 25 March 1954, IC/1/2/2, part 1.
46. B.C. Ashwin to Sir D. Smith, 17 July 1950, T/1/61/2/2, part 1. See also Ashwin to S.G. Holland, 6 March 1951, and submission to Cabinet Committee on Economic Policy, 23 June 1954, T/1/52/835/5. Ashwin's personal file is to be found in T/1/90 PF, W2220.
47. Background paper, 'Board of Trade Future Policy', 1952, IC/1/2/2, part 1.
48. 'The World Bank Report on the New Zealand Economy, 1968', *AJHR*, B-4, p.32. See also *AJHR*, 1953, H-44, p.13. Also Smith's report on the work of the Board of Trade, 25 March 1954, IC/1/2/2, part 1.
49. Smith's report, 25 March 1954, IC/1/2/2, part 1.
50. *EP*, 28 April 1955.
51. See CP (55) 912, 7 October 1955, in IC/1/2/2, part 1.
52. See advice of Import Advisory Committee to Minister of Customs, 14 July 1950, T/1/61/2/2. Ashwin's advice to the Prime Minister on 6 March 1951 is in T/1/52/835/5.
53. I am obliged to Professor G. J. Schmitt for pointing out this nicety to me.
54. Details are from *NZOYB*, 1956, p.293. See also Cabinet reminder to the Board of Trade, CM(53) 205, where the Board was told that there 'may be circumstances' where import licensing was 'the only satisfactory means of protecting some local industries'. There is much information about the operation of exchange allocation (the Reserve Bank usually called it 'exchange control') in T/1/61/2/2.
55. Import licensing and tariffs in this period are discussed by G.R. Hawke, *The Making of New Zealand*, pp.260-1.
56. 'Economic Survey 1956', *AJHR*, 1956, B-5, pp.4-5; 'Economic Survey 1958', *AJHR*, 1958, B-5, pp.21-23.

57. R.S. Parker, *Economic Stability*, pp.10-32.
58. Ibid, p.109.
59. *DOM*, 13 May 1953; *EP*, 13 May 1953, p.13.
60. *NZH*, 14 May 1953, editorial. The comments in the editorial resulted in a letter from several academics present at the conference, pointing out that the paper had misrepresented what Schmitt had said. *NZH*, 16 May 1953, p.16.
61. *AS*, 14 May 1953, editorial. The financial editor of the *Star* published a more thoughtful piece on 23 May 1953, p.4.
62. *Hawkes Bay Herald Tribune*, 18 May 1953, editorial.
63. Parker, *Economic Stability*, p.73.
64. See IC/1/2/7, part 2, W709. See also *AJHR*, 1957, H-44.
65. Soon after he was appointed, Sutch's research activities within the department caused conflicts with staff and it seems that the Secretary, P. B. Marshall, suspected that Sutch's abrasive personality was the problem. See Minutes of Staff Meeting, 9 June 1952, IC/1/2/7, W709, part 2. There is a good outline of Sutch's mid-1950s views on manufacturing in *Here and Now*, No 57, February 1957, pp.13-14.
66. See T/1/52/761. Also IC/1/10/1/3, part 1. There is a memo from P.B. Marshall on the working of the Land Settlement Promotion Act 1952, dated 1 February 1957, in IC/1/3/41, W709.
67. The comment about Watts comes from Professor G. J. Schmitt.
68. See IC/1/21/1/1, part 1, which contains, among other things, a paper outlining the workings of industrial licensing within the pulp and paper industry. Also *NZOYB*, 1956, p.588. The Industries and Commerce Act is in *Statutes*, 1956, Vol. 1, p.369.
69. *AJHR*, 1950, B-6, pp.25-27. The number of farm tractors increased by 116 per cent in 1950–59, and there was a huge increase in other implements. See 'Economic Survey 1960', p.23. The author worked regularly on a farm in the Waikato between 1950 and 1957. When he began there was no tractor, only draught horses. By 1955 the farm had a tractor, a truck, a large hay-baling machine, a mower and a hay-rake, all of them imported. Others in the district were equipping in similar fashion, taking full advantage of Holland's generous depreciation allowances.
70. Many farmers in the district where the author worked thought nothing of using their cheap motor spirits in their cars, thus avoiding paying road taxes.
71. J.T. Watts to Secretary to the Treasury, 31 August 1955, T/40/648/8.
72. The rest of the information is drawn from this file and from T/82/4/17, Box 664, W4446. Talboys's quote comes from *NZPD*, Vol. 382, 22 February 1973, p.140. I am indebted to Paul Goldsmith for assistance with these files.
73. Guest, 'The Murupara Project'. There is much detail about the role of the Fletchers in Selwyn Parker, *Made in New Zealand*, Chapt. 3.
74. Guest, p.35. There is some information about the background to Tasman Pulp and Paper in George Fraser, *Both Eyes Open: A Memoir*, Dunedin, 1990, pp.108ff.
75. There is information about dealings between Entrican, forest interests and ministers in the 1940s in T/1/52/539. I am indebted to Professor G. J. Schmitt for information about the 1940s licences in a letter to me dated 10 June 1997. NZFP was awarded a licence to produce kraft paper about 1950.
76. The comment was from Walter Nash, *NZPD*, Vol. 293, 3 November 1950, p.3985. Skinner gave a good outline of Labour's attitudes to the whole project in a wide-ranging debate on 'the Murupara Project' in *NZPD*, Vol. 303, 21 July 1954, pp.602-5.
77. Quoted by Guest, pp.40-45.
78. Holyoake's comments were debated in Parliament, *NZPD*, Vol. 293, 3 November 1950, pp.3982-4. Until 31 December 1949 the minister was known as the Commissioner of Forests.
79. E.B. Corbett, *Kaingaroa State Forest: Proposals for the Sale of Logs from Kaingaroa State Forest, New Zealand*, Wellington, 1951.
80. Holland outlined the development of the National Government's involvement in *NZPD*,

Vol. 303, 21 July 1954, pp.596-616.

81. The Tasman Pulp and Paper Company Ltd's share prospectus issued on 18 August 1954, which was kindly lent to me by Professor G. J. Schmitt, contains much information about the background to the company.

82. *NZPD*, Vol. 303, 21 July 1954, pp.602-5. Also the comments of E. P. Aderman MP, p.197.

83. As of 13 September 1955, the Government had extended £4.5 million to Tasman. See E.L. Greensmith to J.T. Watts, 13 September 1956, T/1/4/1, pp.2-4. By 1967 the Government owned about 20 per cent of Tasman. Bowaters (UK), Reeds (UK) Australian Newsprint Mills, Fletcher Holdings and the general public (who held about $2 million of the $21.4 million equity) were the other shareholders. By this time 85 per cent of Tasman's exports were of newsprint and 10 per cent chemical pulp. See 'The World Bank Report on the New Zealand Economy 1968', *AJHR*, B-4, p.43.

84. There is information about Tasman's problems in 1977 in Hugh Templeton, *All Honourable Men: Inside the Muldoon Cabinet, 1975–1984*, Auckland, 1995, pp.78-80.

85. George Fraser in *Both Eyes Open*, p.114, refers to lunches with Dr W.B. Sutch. Jack Marshall in his *Memoirs*, Vol. 2, p.42, refers to 'shared family holidays' with industrialist Sir Woolf Fisher. Ian Lythgoe, Chairman of the State Services Commission 1971–75, when interviewed on 11 December 1995, noted the happy arrangements that developed in the cost-plus environment between businessmen, bureaucrats and politicians. The author remembers that for approximately 20 years, Todd Motors in Wellington sold Rootes Group cars (Chryslers and Hillmans as well as Chrysler outboards) to politicians of both parties at a discount and at interest rates below normal market rates. Politicians and bureaucrats were regularly entertained by private sector interests and on occasions non-monetary favours were extended. Small presents of liquor at Christmas were common.

86. The author was told by a manufacturer of carbon brushes in Auckland of one example of low-level corruption. A Customs Department official in Wellington was said to leave the room after hearing a plea for extra import licences. Applicants usually found that a £10 note left in the open top drawer of the desk brought a satisfactory result.

87. See E.L. Greensmith to J.T. Watts, 13 September 1956, 14 March 1957, and 26 November 1957, T/1/4/1. A report by Treasury on TEAL's accounts in 1951 is to be found in T/1/47/349.

88. Details about relationships between the Government and several private airways from 1936–47 are to be found in T/1/52/312, W2591. See especially A.R.F. Mackay to W.B. Sutch, 26 June 1940. There is a lot of material dealing with efforts to sell NAC in CA/1/98/9/19. Agitation for regional services is reported in *NZH*, 10 December 1958.

89. The file on the Dominion Salt Co. is T/39/11, part 1, W2446. See also *Press*, 28 February 1966, editorial.

90. See E.L. Greensmith to J.T. Watts, 13 September 1956, T/1/4/1.

91. The Treasury file relating to the committee is T/1/50/293. In the file is a 1952 Cabinet summary entitled 'Retirement of State Employees'. It has an historical appendix tracing the State's changing retirement policies in relation to railways since 1902. By 1 April 1956 public service numbers reached 55,102. See Henderson, p.398. The numbers of Railways, Post Office and Public Works employees were fairly static between 1950 and 1956. There are some details about National's campaign for efficiency in the public service in PM/21/18/1. Administration of the Town and Country Planning Act was transferred from Internal Affairs to the Ministry of Works in 1953.

92. The story of National's changes to local government legislation is told in Bassett, *The Mother of All Departments*, Chapt. 7.

93. The words were used by the Minister of Railways, W. S. Goosman, in *AJHR*, 1953, D-2, p.1.

94. Debates on the situation in Nelson are to be found in *NZPD*, Vol. 309, 23 August 1956, p.1330. The spat over buses and trains in the Hutt Valley is in *NZPD*, Vol. 310, 19 October 1956, pp.2627-8. See also *EP*, 19 October 1956, p.12, and *NZH*, 20 October 1956, p.14.

95. The trading profits and losses of Railways are to be found in the annual reports, *AJHR*, D-2.

96. Henry Lang, former Secretary of the Treasury, assessed Health expenditure as a percentage of GDP at 3.8 per cent in 1935, 4.5 per cent in 1948–49, 4.7 per cent in 1960–61, 5.6 per cent in 1973–74 and 6.6 per cent by 1981–82. See H.G. Lang, 'Health Policy Formulation in New Zealand', *International Journal of Health Planning and Management*, Vol. 2, April 1987, p.144. The Gibbs taskforce in its 1988 report 'Unshackling the Hospitals', Wellington, 1988, p.46, estimated total health funding as a proportion of GDP as of 31 March 1987 at 6.94 per cent. The 1987 OECD report on the New Zealand economy noted that health spending between 1963 and 1984 rose at a faster rate overall than economic growth.

97. See briefing note, 9 July 1965, T/1/73/1, W2907. Also J.T. Watts, 'New Zealand Economic Survey 1956', *AJHR*, 1956, B-5, pp.34ff. In 'The Helping Hand' in the file entitled 'A National Record' there is a full list of the upgrades to health and welfare, 1949–54. See PM/21/18, part 1.

98. See File T/1/62/15.

99. *AJHR*, 1950, H-31, pp.37-41. R.L. Macalister of the Wellington City Council complained about 'astronomical' rises in hospital costs in *EP*, 11 May 1950, p.8.

100. J.E. Engel to B.C. Ashwin, 25 February 1952; B.C. Ashwin to S.G. Holland, 28 February 1952, T/1/62/15.

101. J.R. Marshall to S.G. Holland, 21 March 1952, T/1/62/15.

102. 'A Health Service for New Zealand', better known as the white paper, *AJHR*, 1974, H-23, pp.60-61. See also Marshall, *Memoirs*, Vol. 1, pp.181ff.

103. *AJHR*, 1974, H-23, p.65.

104. Marshall in his *Memoirs*, Vol. 1, pp.182 and 185, acknowledges that political considerations caused the Government to resile from election policy promises to amalgamate smaller boards.

105. Department of Health publication, 'A Review of Hospital and Related Services in New Zealand', Wellington, 1969, p.20. Cabinet documents about assistance to private hospitals 1959–60 are to be found in T/26/25.

106. Michael Bassett, 'Costly Health Care: A Lesson from New Zealand', *Health Care Analysis*, Vol. 1, November 1993, pp.189-96. A very perceptive analysis of developments after passage of the Social Security Act is G.M. Fougere, 'From Market to Welfare State? State Interventions and Medical Care Delivery in New Zealand', in C. Wilkes and I. Shirley, *In the Public Interest: Health, Work and Housing in New Zealand*, Auckland, 1984, pp.76-89.

107. There is a file about hospital finances 1958–60 in T/26/25. The impact of equal pay is dealt with in T/1/40/738.

108. There is a file about pay negotiations for various hospital groups of employees, T/1/79/75. The same file gives full details about requests for more staff in 1969, Treasury's responses and Cabinet's final agreements.

109. Details of negotiations in 1971 and 1974 were handled by Ian Lythgoe, Chairman of the State Services Commission at the time. In an interview on 11 December 1995 he reminded the author that Roy McKenzie, who conducted most of the face-to-face negotiations with the dental nurses in 1974, went home in a state of shock on the day of Kirk's intervention and died that night. There was to be further ministerial intervention over nurses' and junior doctors' pay in 1986, involving the author as Minister of Health. As a general rule, whenever politicians became involved, health workers succeeded in getting better pay than they could negotiate with their statutory salary-fixing authorities.

110. See R.J. Tizard to Cabinet, no date [early 1973], T/1/40/56, part 10, W2591.

111. 'A Health Service for New Zealand', better known as the White Paper, *AJHR*, 1974, H-23, p.67. There is a Treasury file on the background to this legislation, T/1/40/56, W2591. The author was a member of the Statutes Revision Committee of Parliament that heard submissions on the legislation.

112. R. Dickie to T.M. McGuigan, 23 July 1975, T/1/40/56, W2591.

113. Jonathan Hunt MP, who was chairman of Parliament's Public Expenditure Committee for part of the 1972–5 Labour Government's term, told the author he had received a similar comment about the high cost of meals on wheels when interviewing the Auckland Hospital Board. Interview, 20 December 1996. For Wellington's comments about spending restraints see *EP*, 12 and 13 August 1975.

114. Besides the comments of the *Evening Post*, see *ODT,* 16 September 1975. There are other examples in T/1/40/56, W2591.

115. See PP(75)M37, part vi, 3 September 1975, T/1/40/56, W2591.

116. *AJHR*, 1952, E-1, p.3. See also 'Economic Survey 1956'. In 1971 the Education Department published a 31-page summary of educational developments entitled 'Education Costs and Performance, 1945–1970'. It pointed to the fact that educational spending was growing as a proportion of the budget and expected the trend to continue.

117. *AJHR*, 1956, B-5, p.109. See also *NZOYB*, 1956, pp.162-3.

118. The comments of C.B. Lewis are in *EP*, 27 October 1956, p.14. A previous official of the NZEI had argued similarly in 1950. *EP*, 8 May 1950, p.6.

119. There is Cabinet material relating to teachers' salary claims in 1958 in T/26/4, and a history of the stages of ministerial involvement in the primary teachers' pay claim of 1970 in T/79/74, W2733, part 1. There are comments about 'discrepancies' between educational groups' remuneration in *NZH*, 2 April 1960, p.20.

120. A Treasury brief outlining these points to the Minister of Finance on 9 July 1965 was couched in terms that were similar to those expressed in the Gibbs Committee's report of 1951. See T/1/73/1, W2907.

121. The issue of state aid to private schools was debated in October 1956. See *NZPD*, Vol. 310, 24 October 1956, pp.2724ff. See also *NZH*, 25 October 1956, p.14; *EP*, 17 October 1956, p.15.

122. There is information about the issue of assistance to private schools during the 1957 campaign in T/26/4.

123. There is a file on capital expenditure on school projects 1950–57, T/1/62/9. The author as MP for the area intervened on behalf of Rutherford High School in Te Atatu in 1974 and won approval for a second gymnasium.

124. 'Economic Survey 1958', *AJHR*, 1958, B-5, pp.21-23.

125. J.T. Watts, Memo to Cabinet, 23 November 1955, T/1/61/1/9.

126. C.G.F. Simkin, 'Economic Survey', 17 May 1955, T/1/61/1/9. There were critical comments about the credit squeeze from the past president of the Wellington Chamber of Commerce in *EP*, 26 October 1956, p.13. Keith Sinclair in *Walter Nash*, p.305, has details about the warnings reaching the Government by the later part of 1957.

127. Gustafson, *The First Fifty Years*, pp.71-72. Marshall tells of Holland's last year in office in his *Memoirs*, Vol. 1, pp.252-6.

128. Alex McKenzie, president of the National Party, plus several of Holland's Cabinet colleagues visited him and finally persuaded him to resign. Information supplied to the author by a member of the family of E. H. Halstead, Minister of Industries and Commerce 1956–57. The story is partly confirmed by Colin James, whose information came from Holyoake. See *NBR*, 16 May 1997, p.19.

129. The comments are to be found in *EP*, 27 October 1956, p.14 and *NZH*, 29 October 1956, p.8.

130. J.C. Beaglehole, 'New Zealand Since the War', *Landfall*, No. 58, June 1961, p.143.

131. Labour won five city seats, Roskill and Tamaki in Auckland, Lyttelton and St Albans in Christchurch, and St Kilda in Dunedin. The sixth seat was the provincial city of Nelson.

Chapter 10 Labour and National Struggle with the Economy, 1957–72

1. The author was an active member of the Labour Party after 1959 and a candidate at every general election from 1966 to 1987, and regularly heard observations of this kind. Robert

Chapman in his 'New Zealand Politics Since the War', *Landfall*, No. 63, September 1962, p.252, says 'the most obvious feature of New Zealand's postwar politics' is 'the similarity of the two main parties'. Alan Robinson noted in 1969 that 'ideological discussion has virtually disappeared from party competition [and] election programmes contain a great amount of common material'. See Alan Robinson, 'Political Trends in the 60's', *Pacific Viewpoint*, Vol. 10, May 1969, p.99. Also Nigel S. Roberts, 'Consensus and Confusion: Politics in the 1950s', *New Zealand's Heritage*, p.2583.

2. The phrase is Keith Sinclair's, *Walter Nash*, p.305. It refers to those who wanted to make use of Reserve Bank credit at no interest.
3. Robert Chapman, 'New Zealand Since the War', p.253.
4. The Report of the Royal Commission is to be found in *AJHR*, 1956, B-3. The analysis of Social Credit's submissions is to be found on pp.345-99. There are Treasury files on the Royal Commission in AALR T52/970, W3226.
5. Social Credit's first victory was in the far north electorate of Hobson in 1966, a seat that it held for one term. It won Rangitikei in a byelection in 1978, holding it until 1984, and the seat of East Coast Bays in another by-election in 1980, retaining it until 1987. In the 1984 election Social Credit also won the Auckland seat of Pakuranga on a complex four-way split. Harold Innes comments pungently on the politics of the time in *The Status Quo Seekers*, Wellington, 1963.
6. There is a photo of the *Standard*'s billboard in Hector MacNeill, *God Defend New Zealand*, Wellington, 1960, back endpaper.
7. Keith Sinclair in a written comment to the author, 1992.
8. 'Economic Survey 1958', *AJHR*, 1958, B-5, pp.23-24. The situation facing the new Government is described by Keith Sinclair in *Walter Nash*, pp.305-7. I am grateful to Rt Hon R. J. Tizard for discussing with me the Second Labour Government, in which he was a backbench MP. Interview, 10 June 1997.
9. There is an 85-page white paper tracing the history of the EEC and its impact on New Zealand thinking in *AJHR*, 1961, A-21. A Treasury file, T/1/61/5/2, contains much material about the early years of the EEC. John Marshall, *Memoirs*, Vol. 2, Auckland, 1989, Chapt. 6, describes the negotiations he conducted with the British. The Ten Point Plan for New Zealand is to be found in *NZH*, 24 June 1971, p.1.
10. Quoted in R.M. Chapman, W.K. Jackson and A.V. Mitchell, *New Zealand Politics in Action: The 1960 General Election*, London, 1962, p.34.
11. Chapman, Jackson and Mitchell, pp.37-47. See also *AJHR*, 1958, H-44, pp.9ff. Sinclair, *Walter Nash*, p.307.
12. The National Government allowed the department to be administered by L. A. Atkinson in an acting capacity during 1957 rather than approve Sutch, their old *bête noire*. Sinclair describes the controversy in *Walter Nash*, pp.341-2. Jack Marshall assesses the life of Sutch in his *Memoirs*, Vol. 2, pp.142-9. To date there has been no satisfactory answer to the criticisms Marshall makes.
13. Marshall, *Memoirs*, Vol. 2, p.143.
14. Standing at 296 on 31 March 1958, they rose to 330 in 1960 and to 433, including those in overseas posts, by 1962. *AJHR*, 1959, H-44; 1961, H-44; 1962, H-44, pp.66-70.
15. *AJHR*, 1958, H-44, pp.12-19.
16. *AJHR*, 1959, H-44, pp.20-21. Since the mid 1950s several groups had been calling for some form of industrial financial assistance, among them the Associated Chambers of Commerce. See T/1/52/655.
17. The text of the speech is in T/1/61/2/2.
18. *AJHR*, 1960, H-44, p.11. Sutch's thinking is analysed by A.M. Andres, 'The Political Economy of W.B. Sutch: Toward a Critical Appreciation', *New Zealand Economic Papers*, Vol. 20, 1986. There is further material about W.B. Sutch in 93/319/1/18, ATL. See also *NBR*, 15 March 1982 and *NZ Times*, 27 November 1983, p.9.
19. W.B. Sutch, 'Programme for Growth', speech to Industrial Development Conference, June 1960. There is a discussion of Sutch's views in W.D. Rose, 'Manufacturing Develop-

ment Policy in New Zealand, 1958–1968', *Pacific Viewpoint*, May 1969, pp.57-75.

20. Skidelsky, p.83.

21. Rosenberg was Senior Lecturer, then Reader in Economics at the University of Canterbury. A German refugee, who was educated both in Berlin and Wellington, he was secretary of the NZ Monthly Review Society and author of several pamphlets about full employment and industrialisation in New Zealand.

22. See *NZPD*, Vol. 322, 22 July 1960, p.840. Progress was very slow on coal. It was not until late in 1979 that significant amounts of coal began to be exported to Japan. In the financial year 1980–81 140,000 tonnes of coal were exported. See *AJHR*, 1981, D-11, p.3.

23. *NZH*, 2 April 1960, p.13.

24. Austin Mitchell, *Politics and People in New Zealand*, Christchurch, 1969, p.73. See also Holloway's remarks, *NZH*, 1 April 1960, p.12. In a briefing for National backbenchers on 21 March 1972, the Minister of Finance, Robert Muldoon, released details of many of the schemes under active consideration by the Labour Government between 1958 and 1960. They included Alcan Industries in Auckland, an oil refinery at Marsden Point, a gin distillery in Auckland, projects for making screws, steel wire, telephone cables and sheet glass. Many of these schemes ultimately went ahead with government assistance. See Marshall Papers, MS Papers 1403/88/3, ATL.

25. The story of the origins of the cotton mill was outlined by Stanley Whitehead MP after the scheme was scrapped at the end of 1961. See *NZPD*, Vol. 330, 22 June 1962, pp.381ff. Sinclair gives many details in *Walter Nash*, p.344-5. There is a more detailed outline in Mitchell, *Politics and People*, pp.75-80. See also Holloway's comments, *NZH*, 1 April 1960, p.12. There is other material about this controversy in T/1/52/761/9. For a brief summary of the issues with the mill, see Jim McAloon, *Nelson: A Regional History*, Queen Charlotte Sound, 1997, pp.202-5.

26. There is some detail about the smelter in Sinclair, *Walter Nash*, pp.343-4.

27. The development of an iron and steel industry in New Zealand has a long history dating back to government promises of 'bonuses' for the development of iron from sands in the Taranaki region in the 1870s and then again in 1914. The Otago Rolling Mill Co. operated as a family concern from 1886 to 1953. It is believed to have produced the first steel in New Zealand, mostly from scrap metal. In 1921 the Onekaka Iron and Steel Co.Ltd. began mining ilmenite deposits in Golden Bay, producing quality iron. Despite some government assistance in securing supplies of coal, the company struggled during the Great Depression and closed in May 1935. On the eve of the 1935 election there was talk of reviving the foundry (*DOM*, 20 November 1935, p.11.) The First Labour Government passed the Iron and Steel Industry Act 1937, which gave the Government power to establish a state industry for the production of iron, steel and steel products.(*NZOYB*, 1939, p.402.) During the war the Government attempted to evaluate the precise size of the ilmenite deposits at Onekaka and invested considerable sums in the plant. But little was produced. Eventually in April 1947 Mr Justice Blair awarded the Onekaka Iron and Steel Co Ltd.(in liquidation) £85,000 with interest at 5 per cent from the Government backdated to 15 March 1938 and Golden Bay Proprietary Ltd £41,796 with back interest, because of their claim that the Government had not fulfilled an agreement.(*EP*, 3 April 1947) Clearly the reason why Onekaka was never fully developed was that the deposits of ore turned out to be much less than had originally been thought. There is information about Onekaka in T/1/47/303. See also Frank W. Fahy, 'Onekaka Ironworks – A Part of New Zealand's Heritage', *Transactions*, Vol. 19, November 1992, pp.17-21. Also J.N.W. Newport, 'Some Industries of Golden Bay', *Journal of the Nelson Historical Society*, Vol. 13, No. 5, 1975, pp.5-26. I am greatly indebted to David Bold, a Ph.D student at the University of Auckland, for information about the history of New Zealand's steel industry. I also benefited from a discussion with J. W. Ridley, Chief Engineer at New Zealand Steel 1965–70, on 16 June 1997.

28. There is information about the complex negotiations over steel in Selwyn Parker, *Made in New Zealand: The Story of Jim Fletcher*, Auckland, 1994, Chapt. 6, and in George Fraser,

Both Eyes Open, Dunedin, 1990, pp.112-5. There are further files on New Zealand Steel in AALR, T/39/7, Box 73, W4446, NA. Also AALR, T39/7/8, W4446, and AALR, T39/7/8/3, W4446. 'Think Big' expansion files relating to steel are to be found at AALR, T/6/43 W3993. Pacific Steel's prices were to be fixed at lower than average prices for imported products. Sales would be price controlled. The Government would use controls to protect the company from 'unfair' competition. If the company did not fulfil its promises then the Government reserved the right to permit imports. See R.D. Muldoon to All Government Members, 21 March 1972, Marshall Papers, MS Papers, 1404/88/3, ATL.

29. Commissioner of Works to W.B. Sutch, 12 February 1959, T/1/39/7/2. The minutes of the officials' committees are to be found in this file.

30. *NZH*, 2 April 1960, p.13. George Fraser, *Both Eyes Open*, pp.114-5, asks questions about how the economic nationalist, Sutch, managed to come up with a consortium of Australians as the preferred partners of the Government. Historian David Bold is currently investigating Sutch's behaviour, which seemed so out of character with his repeated declarations of New Zealand nationalism.

31. *EP*, 27 April 1960.

32. *DOM*, 28 April 1960.

33. Mitchell, *Politics and People*, pp.81-83.

34. *EP*, 27 April 1960, editorial.

35. *Hawkes Bay Herald Tribune*, 29 April 1960. Federated Farmers also opposed aspects of industrialisation. See Mitchell, *Politics and People*, p.81.

36. *Freedom*, 3 May 1960. Some National MPs criticised aspects of the Government's development plans. D.J. Eyre, MP for North Shore, called them plans for 'complete socialisation'. See *NZPD*, Vol. 323, 2 August 1960, p.54.

37. *EP*, 14 October 1960. There is more information about state factories in T/1/52/761/9.

38. *NZPD*, 22 January 1958, p.23.

39. *NZPD*, 17 June 1958, p.93.

40. *NZPD*, 11 June 1958, pp.17-19.

41. The Family Benefits (Home Ownership) Act passed into law on 2 October 1958 and came into force on 1 April 1959. In its first two years of operation more than £12 million was capitalised on a total of nearly 20,000 benefits. See *NZOYB*, 1962, p.918. In the year to March 1960 a record 21,600 houses were constructed. See 'Economic Survey 1960', p.22.

42. The text of the budget is in *AJHR*, 1958, B-6. See also *NZOYB*, 1959, p.789. The top marginal tax rate had been reduced by the National Government during the early 1950s and now stood at 60 per cent.

43. 'Economic Survey 1961', p.26. See also budget 1961, *AJHR*, 1961, B-6.

44. 'Economic Survey 1961', pp.40-41. See *AJHR*, 1961, H-14, pp.26-30 and 1962, H-14.

45. Marshall, *Memoirs*, Vol. 2, Auckland, 1989, p.1.

46. National won three city seats, Tamaki, Wellington Central and St Albans, and four regional centres, Gisborne, Hastings, Rotorua and Palmerston North.

47. *AJHR*, 1961, B-6, p.6.

48. Monetary and Economic Council, *Economic Growth in New Zealand*, No.2, Wellington, May 1962, Chapt. 1. A referendum was held on the term of Parliament on 23 September 1967. The three-year status quo defeated a four-year term by more than 2:1. See J.O. Wilson, *New Zealand Parliamentary Record*, p.301.

49. See B.C. Ashwin to S.G. Holland, 14 March 1952, and E.L. Greensmith to J.T. Watts, 20 April 1956, T/1/52/880/2/2.

50. Sinclair, *Walter Nash*, pp.242-245, and p.351. Several newspaper editorials in 1958 are to be found in T/1/52/880/2/2.

51. 'International Monetary Fund and World Bank', *AJHR*, 1961, A-12.

52. Sinclair, *Walter Nash*, p.351.

53. W. Rosenberg, *What Every New Zealander Should Know about the International Monetary*

Fund, Christchurch, 1961; *What Every New Zealander Should Know about Foreign Investment in New Zealand*, Christchurch, 1966.

54. Samuel Leathem, address to Auckland Manufacturers Association, January 1962, text in author's hands.

55. *NZPD*, Vol. 29, 10 November 1961, pp.3508ff.

56. See S. Greenburg to H. Lake, 25 June 1964, T/1/52/761/10. Marshall gives the story of the cotton mill from the time National took office again until its scrapping in his *Memoirs*, Vol. 2, pp.15-18. See McAloon, *Nelson*, p.204.

57. A new agreement was given legislative endorsement in October 1963. Raising the level of Lake Manapouri to facilitate the production of electricity caused considerable political embarrassment to the National Government between 1970 and 1972, culminating in a parliamentary petition with 250,000 signatures opposing raising the lake. For discussion of the smelter see Marshall, *Memoirs*, Vol. 2, pp.43-44. See also *NZ Gazette*, 13 April 1961, p.544; *Statutes*, 1963, Vol. 1, p.244. Much detail about the 1963 agreement is contained in the Act's schedule. Hugh Templeton, *All Honourable Men: Inside the Muldoon Cabinet, 1975–1984*, Auckland, 1995, Chapt. 8, has some details about the smelter.

58. Marshall, *Memoirs*, Vol. 2, p.45.

59. 'Report of the Provisional Board of the New Zealand Steel Company', 9 December 1964, Wellington, 1965, p.37. A more technical report, 'The Ironsands Project', produced by W.S. Atkins and McLellan & Partners to the Investigating Company in November 1964, is in the possession of David Bold. There is an 81-page history of New Zealand Steel from early times until 1981 prepared for Treasury by P. Lissington, and a briefer history of the early years in the prospectus of New Zealand Steel Ltd, 1966, both of them lent to me by David Bold.

60. The National Government consistently argued that the mill should be privately owned, but that the Government would contribute seeding capital. See *NZPD*, 23 August 1963, a summary of which was provided by David Bold. There is information about the plant in *AJHR*, 1966, H-44, pp.5ff.

61. 'The World Bank Report on the New Zealand Economy, 1968', p.41.

62. Lissington deals with the debates at the Cabinet level, in 1981, pp.70-73. Roger Douglas discusses the restructuring debate of 1985 in *Toward Prosperity*, Auckland, 1987, Chapt. 15. Court cases in 1996 and 1997 resulted in rulings that the Crown had an obligation to repay $267.5 million to the receivers of Equiticorp, meaning, in effect, that the Crown's investment in the mill had completely evaporated.

63. Marshall, *Memoirs*, Vol. 2, pp.42-43. There is information about New Zealand Steel's later years in *AS*, 12 September 1981, p.1 and *NBR*, 23 May 1997, p.7.

64. Minutes of Officials' meeting, 18 October 1961, T/39/16, part 1, W2446. There was an announcement in the *DOM*, 21 October 1961, which claimed that the field of gas could be worth £23.75 million.

65. The deputation's presentation is in T/39/16, part 1, W2446.

66. K.J. Holyoake to J.B. Price, 28 August 1963, T/39/16, part 1, W2446.

67. *Statutes*, 1962, Vol. 1, p.764.

68. Marshall, *Memoirs*, Vol. 2, p.46.

69. P.J. Lloyd, 'Australia–New Zealand Trade Relations: NAFTA to CER', in Keith Sinclair (ed),*Tasman Relations*, Auckland, 1987, pp.142-63; A.E. Bollard and M.A. Thompson, *Trans-Tasman Trade and Investment*, Wellington, 1987, p.1.

70. Marshall, *Memoirs*, Vol. 2, Chapt. 3.

71. See Wolfgang Rosenberg, *A Guidebook to New Zealand's Future: Winds of Change over New Zealand*, Christchurch, 1968, p.181.

72. Ibid, p.28. See also Paul Wooding, 'Liberalising the International Trade Regime', in Alan Bollard and Robert Buckle (eds), *Economic Liberalisation in New Zealand*, Wellington, 1987, pp.86-101. I am indebted to Sir Frank Holmes for a long interview on 12 March 1997 in which he discussed his role in the NAFTA process. For official documents see 'New Zealand's Trade with Australia' and 'New Zealand–Australia Free Trade Agreement',

including exchange of letters, *AJHR*, 1965, A-19 and A-17.

73. Robert Chapman, 'From Labour to National', in W.H. Oliver (ed), *The Oxford History of New Zealand*, Wellington, 1981, p.365. See also John Gould, *The Rake's Progress? The New Zealand Economy Since 1945*, Auckland, 1982, p.90.

74. The allegations by Dr A.M. Finlay MP against Meadowcroft were not proven. In any event, trading in import licences had become common enough by this time. The comments of Frank Holmes are to be found in *NZH*, 27 July 1968. An example of a fairly typical Tariff and Development Board investigation is the inquiry conducted in 1972 into the tariff and import protection received by Donald Brown and Co Ltd, Newton, Auckland. A small family company employing a staff of 18, which had produced carbon brushes for electric motors and dynamos since 1938, the company wanted to retain its protection. Several sets of submissions were required, legal fees incurred, a visit to the factory made by the Board, and a lengthy hearing in Wellington. Six months after the inquiry began the company was informed that it would be able to retain all its protective mechanisms. See IC/4/1/168, W2357. Interview with Donald Brown, 16 May 1997.

75. See Hawke, *The Making of New Zealand*, p.261. See *AJHR*, 1965, H-44, p.6.

76. There is detail about the 1963 conference in IC/57/1/20, W1926.

77. There is material indicating National Party doubts and Sutch's strong advocacy of controls in IC/1/10, W2268. See also Holyoake request, MS Papers 1814/214/3, ATL. Stabilisation subsidies on the price of sugar were introduced in June 1963, then eased in 1964. It was noted that when the price of sugar fell after the introduction of subsidies, most manufacturers did not pass on the benefit they received in lower prices. *AJHR*, 1965, H-44, p.19.

78. Paul Wooding, 'Liberalising the International Trade Regime', p.90.

79. 'The World Bank Report on the New Zealand Economy 1968', p.14.

80. See 'Taxation in New Zealand', *AJHR*, 1967, B-18. Ross gives a short account of his life in Ann and Laurie Gluckman (eds), *Identity and Involvement: Auckland Jewry, Past and Present*, Vol. 2, Palmerston North, 1993, pp.70-84.

81. There is some background to the Royal Commission in G.E. Caiden, 'The State Services in New Zealand', *NZJPA*, Vol. 25, March 1963, pp.11-21. For criticism of the findings, see especially pp.12-14. The report itself is to be found in *AJHR*, 1962, H-41.

82. Alan Henderson, *The Quest for Efficiency*, p.314.

83. See *Royal Commission into Salary and Wage Fixing Procedures in the New Zealand State Services*, Wellington, August 1968.

84. See, for instance, the ease with which changes proposed to Internal Affairs were reversed. Bassett, *The Mother of All Departments*, pp.200-01.

85. John Martin, *Holding the Balance*, p.279.

86. See Michael Bassett, 'The National Party and Compulsory Unions', typescript, 1983; this was distributed widely. Copy in the author's possession. See also *NZH*, 17 June 1961, editorial. Overwhelmingly union members voted to retain what was called 'the unqualified preference clause' in their agreements. See *Parliamentary Order Paper*, 5 August 1983, p.483.

87. There were 332,362 members in 1960 and 394,748 in 1972.

88. *AS*, 16 December 1960.

89. John Martin, *Holding the Balance*, pp.287-91. See Tom Skinner, *Man to Man*, Christchurch, 1980, p.119.

90. Martin, *Holding the Balance*, p.291.

91. Marshall, *Memoirs*, Vol. 2, p.117. Tom Skinner gives a summary of events surrounding the 'nil general wage order' in *Man to Man*, Chapt. 6. Gary Hawke, *Government in the New Zealand Economy*, pp.45-47, picks out some of the trends in wages and pricing policy 1950-70. See also A. Williams, 'Industrial Relations' in Peter A. Lane and Paul Hamer (eds), *Decade of Change: Economic Growth and Prospects in New Zealand, 1960–1970*, Wellington, 1973, pp.109-26.

92. P.N. Holloway, 'Government Policies and Assistance in Manufacturing Development', in

C.A. Blyth (ed), *The Future of Manufacturing in New Zealand*, Wellington, 1964, pp.195-215.

93. Paul Johnson, *Modern Times*, Chapt. 19.

94. 'The Current Economic Situation and Outlook', Report of the Monetary and Economic Council, No. 7, June 1964, p.5, notes that expenditure grew by 3.2 per cent in 1961–62, by 4.9 per cent in 1962–63 and by 12 per cent in 1963–64. 'Economic Review 1968', *AJHR*, B-5, p.8, shows how gross domestic expenditure and imports moved upwards in tandem between 1963–66. The Monetary and Economic Council Report, No.17, September 1969, stated 'It is now clear that effective action to remedy the 1965–67 balance of payments crisis was not taken early enough'.

95. Holyoake's statement appears in *AS*, 4 February 1967. For details about reduced subsidies see *NZOYB*, 1968, p.706. New Zealand switched to decimal currency on 10 July 1967 when $2 became the equivalent of £1.

96. Details are provided in 'Economic Review 1967', *AJHR*, B-5, p.9.

97. Ibid, p.11. See also *NZH*, 3 May 1968, p.12.

98. 'The World Bank Report on the New Zealand Economy 1968', pp.13-14. Farmers' complaints about rising costs appear in *NZH*, 1 April 1969. See also the call for a 20 per cent devaluation, *AS*, 15 May 1969. Edmund Dell, *The Chancellors*, Chaps 11 and 12, deal with the constant pressures on sterling.

99. See I.B. Johns, 'Agricultural Sector Planning in New Zealand', *Political Science*, Vol. 24, April 1972, pp.2-14.

100. See Cabinet papers on the subject, IC/57/1/20, W1926.

101. The Public Service Association in a pamphlet 'What the Newspapers Wouldn't Print about the Sutch Case', Wellington, 1965, argued that the SSC had succumbed to ministerial pressure and that some members of the SSC were interested in Sutch's vacant post. The PSA brought a private prosecution against Marshall arguing that he had breached the State Services Act. It was dismissed. See Marshall, *Memoirs*, Vol. 2, p.142.

102. *AJHR*, 1965, H-44, p.53.

103. See J.K. Galbraith, *The New Industrial State*, Boston, 1967, on which Galbraith's New Zealand lectures were based. For Treasury's views, see H. Lang memorandum, 29 November 1965, T/1/73/1, part 1, W2907.

104. H. Lang to H. Lake, 21 September 1965, T/1/73/1, part 1, W2907. There is much detail about the British NEDC in Edmund Dell, *The Chancellors*, pp.269ff.

105. I am indebted to Professor Gary Hawke and Roger Kerr, who discussed this emerging planning process with me. Sir Frank Holmes, as he became in 1975, had been Macarthy Professor of Economics at Victoria University in 1959–67, was then Economics and Planning Manager at Tasman Pulp and Paper in 1967–70, before returning to Victoria as Professor of Money and Finance 1970–77. He was Chairman of the New Zealand Planning Council 1977–82.

106. File T/1/73/1, part 1, W2907 contains many indications of anxiety in high places at the ramifications of planning.

107. The typescript is to be found in T/1/73/1, part 1, W2907.

108. See E.V. Adams to K.J. Holyoake, 1 June 1967, T/1/73/1, part 1, W2907. There is other information about Treasury's role in T/1/73/30/1, part 1, W2907. See also T/1/73/18, W2907.

109. T/1/73/1, part 1, W2907.

110. Treasury memo to R.D. Muldoon, 8 June 1967, T/1/73/1, part 1, W2907.

111. K.J. Holyoake to E.V. Adams, 9 August 1967, T/1/73/1, part 1, W2907.

112. A debate about the conference's intentions between Sutch and Henry Lang is to be found in *NZH*, 22 April 1969; 24 April 1969.

113. See file notes about ministerial briefings, especially 26 November 1968. Also 'Summary of Sector Committee Views', 15 January 1969, and CM69/7/17, in T/1/73/1, part 2, W2907. I am obliged to Professor Hawke, who discussed some of the detail surrounding the conference in a letter to the author, 15 June 1997.

114. The comments of Roberts and others are to be found in T/1/73/1, part 2, W2907.
115. The recommendations of the targets committee appear in *NZH*, 29 April 1969, p.14.
116. *AJHR*, 1969, B-6.
117. *Listener*, 25 May 1970, p.8. There is other material about the aftermath of the 1969 conference in T/1/73/1, part 2, W2907.
118. Interview with Sir Frank Holmes, 12 March 1997.
119. In A.R. Low to R.D. Muldoon, 2 May 1972 and R.D. Muldoon to A.R. Low, 11 May 1972, the problem with statistics was discussed. See AALR, T73/2, Box 549, W4446. After 1972 the Third Labour Government expressed reservations about aspects of indicative planning. More *dirigiste* than their opponents, they restructured the Targets Advisory Group and outlined a set of assistance policies for industry. A series of 'Industry Studies' began in a search to identify what assistance was needed to produce faster growth. There is much material about planning 1972–75 in AALR, T73/2, Box 549, and T73/1/6, Box 548, W4446.
120. See comments in *Trans Tasman*, 26 November 1970.
121. See *NZH*, 24 February 1971; 2 March 1971.
122. *AJHR*, 1972, B-6, pp.11-12. See the maiden speech of Aubrey Begg MP, *NZPD*, Vol. 382, 27 February 1973, p.282.
123. Skinner, *Man to Man*, pp.120-1. See also Monetary and Economic Council Report, No.21, 'Economic Trends and Policies', May 1971, p.45, and the report in *AS*, 27 May 1971, p.3. The council made a number of specific recommendations in its report (No.22) entitled 'Inflation and the Labour Market' in December 1971. Sutch's arguments were outlined in a YC programme broadcast on 8 December 1971 and printed in the *Listener*, 17 January 1972, p.13. Professor Conrad Blyth advanced his argument for an Incomes Board in *AS*, 30 September 1972, p.19.
124. Newspapers were quick to condemn the extra spending in the 1972 budget, pointing out that it would only push inflation to higher levels. See *NZH*, 23 June 1972, editorial; *AS*, 23 June 1972, editorial; *Press*, 23 June 1972, editorial; *DOM*, 23 June 1972, editorial; *ODT*, 23 June 1972, editorial. The *Herald* observed on 27 June 1972 that Muldoon's budget 'will be judged over the next six months less by what has been handed out to the taxpayer, the mother or the beneficiary, than by what the concessions mean in buying power. If the spiral [of inflation] cannot be restrained, no one is better off.' A 'Review of the Current Economic Situation – December 1972' prepared for Muldoon summarises the strengths and weaknesses of the economy. It was distributed to all new MPs. It pointed on p.11 to rapidly rising wage levels and to 'considerable' increases in food prices but the outgoing government accepted no responsibility for the trends.

Chapter 11 Big Government Begins to Overreach Itself, 1972–79

1. Johnson, *Modern Times*, p.669.
2. Douglas, *Unfinished Business*, p.25. See C.A. Blyth, 'New Zealand and the International Economy in 1974', address to the Export Institute of New Zealand, 24 April 1974. Also London *Financial Times*, 18 January 1980.
3. John Dunmore, *Norman Kirk*, Palmerston North, 1972, p.25.
4. Entry in the diary of the Chief Labour Whip, Henry May, 10 September 1959.
5. An enlarged heart since childhood had occasionally given Kirk trouble, especially when he was very overweight during his first twelve years in Parliament. It was his varicose veins and his determination to have both legs fixed at once in 1974 that led on to the blood clot that eventually killed him on 31 August 1974. In an interview on 10 June 1997 Rt Hon R. J. Tizard, who was Kirk's Minister of Health 1972–74 and Minister of Finance 1974–75, suggested that Kirk's determination to have policy specifics in such detail stemmed from his perception that victory in the 1969 election had eluded him because of vagueness. Clearly there were other factors causing Labour's loss in 1969 but the author, who was a

candidate, recalls the lack of policy specifics that an ill-chosen slogan 'Make Things Happen' managed to highlight.

6. Released on 31 October 1972 by the New Zealand Labour Party in Wellington, the red-covered document was entitled '1972 Election Manifesto: New Zealand Labour Party'.

7. A pamphlet produced by the Princes Street Branch of the Labour Party in 1966, 'Opportunities for the Sixties', which the author helped to write, was an elaborate wish list seeking government intervention and funding for a vast array of educational initiatives. Equally instructive is the 1973 publication by the Labour Party Youth Advisory Council, D. Butcher (ed), 'Labour Party Young Socialist Positions'. See also H. Keith (ed), 'New Zealand in the Nineteen Seventies: Economic Development', Auckland, 1968. Kirk was fond of using the word 'nationhood' and titled a booklet during the 1969 campaign *Towards Nationhood*, Palmerston North, 1969, and another in 1972 containing speeches by his leading spokespersons called *Target Nationhood*. Kirk had a precise view of New Zealand's national identity. It consisted, among other things, of having a distinctive passport, distinctive New Zealand honours and designating the sovereign as Queen of New Zealand.

8. *NZPD*, Vol. 382, 1 March 1973, p.414.

9. Perhaps the clearest statement of Labour's concerns and the economic changes they intended to introduce came from W. E. Rowling in Norman Kirk (ed), *Target Nationhood*, Wellington, 1972, pp.93-103.

10. Sutch sought to influence Kirk's thinking, but his only preferment was the chair of the Queen Elizabeth II Arts Council 1973–75. He tried to increase the protective environment for textile and woollen goods in 1974. See W.B. Sutch to J.P.Lewin, 24 January 1974, AATJ, 7428/2/1/32, W3566. Sutch was charged with a breach of the Official Secrets Act in 1975, tried and acquitted, but died in September 1975.

11. For an account of the period 1972–75, see Michael Bassett, *The Third Labour Government: A Personal History*, Palmerston North, 1976; also Ray Goldstein with Rod Alley, *Labour in Power: Promise and Performance*, Wellington, 1975. The Treasury's briefing note dated 8 December 1972 to the incoming government is in AALR, T52/822/6, W4446.

12. 'The Election and the Market', December 1972, from Buttle, Wilson, Rutherfurd & Co. The stock market rose steadily for a time. On 13 June 1973 the index stood at 1803 compared with 1478 at the same time in 1972. W.E. Rowling to All Government Members, 26 June 1973, p.3, in Michael Bassett Papers.

13. Press statement 'Overseas Investment in New Zealand', by Minister of Finance, 12 January 1973. Minutes of meetings of the Cabinet Committee on Policy and Priorities beginning with the meeting on 26 March 1973, in which it was decided that emphasis would be placed on achieving a faster rate of economic growth by use of 'incentives applied selectively to encourage the required changes to the economy'. Emphasis would be placed on manufacturing. Import licensing would be retained but the tariff review would continue. See CM 73/14/29. Further papers dealing with changing priorities are to be found in PP(74) M25, part 2.

14. More detail is given about the Rates Rebate scheme and other early spending in Bassett, *The Mother of All Departments*, Chapt. 9.

15. The author has drawn on some of his notes written at the time. See also Bassett, *The Third Labour Government*, Chapt. 5. There is useful information about funding of the original Queen Elizabeth II Arts Council, established in 1964, in AANY W3208, NA.

16. *AJHR*, 1973, B-6, p.3. Rowling's March 1973 Cabinet submissions about economic growth and his further refinements in October and November are to be found in T/1/73/28, W2907.

17. Bassett, *The Third Labour Government,* pp.131-2. Subsidies rose to $107.4 million in 1973–74.

18. The Property Speculation Tax was eventually repealed in 1979. A model 'new town' was to be established at Rolleston in Canterbury, and much work was put into the scheme. Work ceased after the election of 1975, although town planners and some local body

politicians continued to argue for the establishment of new towns to take pressure off metropolitan areas. See *NZH*, 5 December 1975, p.1; 9 December 1975. The Rolleston project is discussed in the *Listener*, 28 February 1976. There are files in AALR, T52/764/20, W3266 on Rolleston, at National Archives. Warren Freer outlined the Government's approach to regional development on 5 July 1973 in a speech entitled 'Industrial and Regional Development in New Zealand', published in Auckland by the New Zealand Geographical Society.

19. Rowling followed up his speech by circulating to all Government MPs an eight-page letter dated 26 June 1973 setting out his futher plans, Bassett Papers.

20. The decision to hold MPs pay increases gave rise a few weeks later to the introduction of overseas travel concessions for members and ex-members.

21 Kirk's speech to caucus on 16 August 1973 is summarised in the author's caucus notes, and dealt with briefly in *The Third Labour Government*, p.70.

22. A National Research Bureau poll in November 1973 found that the public regarded inflation as the most important problem facing the country.

23. Prime Minister's telegram to all Labour MPs, 9 September 1973, and the large file of 'Background Notes' sent to them the following day, Bassett Papers.

24. W. Freer to A.G. Rodda, Price Tribunal, 12 March 1973, IC/1/10, W2268. Rodda in his reply of 20 March suggested a scheme and raised no difficulty about timing. There is much material about the intricacies involved in implementing MRP in IC/52/4, W2268.

25. See Secretary Trade and Industry to President Price Tribunal, 20 June 1973; Barry Purdy, Retailers' Federation, to Secretary, T&I, 11 July 1973; C.E. Beard to President Price Tribunal, 20 and 25 July 1973; H.E.J. Martin to President Price Tribunal, 25 July 1973, IC/52/4, W2268.

26. See Bassett, *Third Labour Government*, pp.144-5. Peter Shirtcliffe of Molenburg Breads told the author in December 1996 that he quickly realised that estimates as to a fair retail price for bread were always calculated on averages and that a smart businessman knew that trimming overheads would guarantee substantial profits under price control. There is material about calculations of pre-tax profits in AALR, T61/1/22/2, Box 278, W4446.

27. There is a file T/1/73/28 W2907 which deals with the Government's growth strategy. See especially the files on Cabinet Policy and Priorities Committee, 8 May 1974, PP(74)M 25 part 2, and the papers attached.

28. The second reading of the Bill is to be found in *NZPD*, Vol. 401, 24 September 1975, pp.4742ff.

29. There is an interesting file on the Shipping Corporation, T/1/39/27, W2446. See also *AS*, 30 June 1973, 'Weekender'. Reports of the corporation are to be found in *AJHR*, F-13.

30. The adjective was used by Marshall at the third reading of the legislation, *NZPD*, Vol. 381, 18 October 1972, p.3445. The best historical treatment of ACC is Ian Campbell, *Compensation for Personal Injury in New Zealand: Its Rise and Fall*, Auckland, 1996.

31. Campbell, pp.44-45. The Royal Commission report entitled 'Compensation for Personal Injury in New Zealand' was published in Wellington, December 1967.

32. There is a handbook by J.L. Fahy, *Accident Compensation Coverage*, Wellington, 1980, which gives detail about the ACC and its various benefits.

33. The Royal Commission report 'Social Security in New Zealand' was published in Wellington, March 1972, p.32. The report is analysed by Elizabeth Hanson, *The Politics of Social Security*, Auckland, 1980, pp.133-9.

34. Kirk's illness, death and funeral are dealt with in Bassett, *Third Labour Government*, Chapts 11 and 14. The observation that Kirk's years marked the 'end of the golden weather' was made by David McLoughlin in *North and South*, October 1996, p.69.

35. *AS*, 1 March 1975; *Christchurch Star*, 4 March 1975, editorial; *Listener*, 1 March 1975, p.11, and 8 March 1975, p.18.

36. The *Auckland Star* carried an article on 13 July 1974 under the headline 'House Explodes into Open Warfare in the Wake of "Gentleman Jack's" Departure from Leadership'. Robert

Muldoon, *The Rise and Fall of a Young Turk*, Wellington, 1974, gives his view on the Third Labour Government, and his *Muldoon*, Wellington, 1977 gives the Muldoon version of Marshall's toppling in Chapt. 7. *Muldoon* ends in 1977; Muldoon's *My Way*, Wellington, 1981, carries his story to 1981.

37. R.J. Tizard, 'The Economic Situation', Wellington, October 1974.
38. *North Shore Times-Advertiser*, 7 November 1974, p.14.
39. R.J. Tizard, 'The Economic Outlook', Wellington, April 1975, p.5.
40. New Zealand Institute of Economic Research, 'Quarterly Predictions', September 1975, p.3.
41. By December 1975 inflation was running at 15.7 per cent and had carried the cost of subsidies above $180 million. See *DOM*, 23 December 1975. I am indebted to Professor Gary Hawke, who saw farmers buying back the subsidised milk and had the economic advantages of doing so explained to him. Gary Hawke to author, 3 July 1997. Tizard reminded the author that most dairy farmers at the time admitted to selling their milk in bulk, while putting out milk bottles to receive subsidised milk for their domestic use. The subsidy figure for the year to March 1976 appears in the 1977 Budget, Table 7, *AJHR*, B-6, p.52. See also AALR, T/61/1/9/24, Box 269, W4446.
42. See H. Lang to R.D. Muldoon, 2 December 1975, p.7, AALR, T/52/822/6, W4446.
43. Muldoon's onslaught on the budget is to be found in *NZPD*, Vol. 397, 27 May 1975, pp.1382-96. For his later statements about the deficit, see *NZH*, 13 December 1975, p.1.
44. *AJHR*, 1975, B-6. Tizard was confident that the economic downturn would last no longer than the middle of 1976. See his comments to a Panmure audience, *Courier*, 19 February 1975, p.3.
45. Party president, G. A.Chapman confirmed this in *AS*, 11 December 1975.
46. See Bassett, *Third Labour Government*, Chapt. 22. See also text of interviews with defeated Labour MPs on 4 December 1975, Bassett Papers.
47. Hugh Templeton, *All Honourable Men: Inside the Muldoon Cabinet, 1975-1984*, Auckland, 1995. Jim McLay, when interviewed on 7 July 1997, told the author that there were six or seven ministers who would argue with Muldoon but the others adopted what McLay called a 'Trust Rob' approach.
48. Jim McLay, who became Deputy Prime Minister in 1984, told the author on 18 June 1987 that after the 1981 election he had not been shown the Treasury briefing that raised many hard questions about the economy. The Prime Minister's Department is discussed in *EP*, 15 December 1975. There are files on expenditure within the Prime Minister's Department 1977–80 in AALR, T62/35, Box 448, W4446.
49. New Zealand Institute of Economic Research, 'Quarterly Predictions', September 1975, p.3.
50. *NZOYB*, 1979, p.768.
51. *NZH*, 13 December 1975, p.1. The full Treasury report to the Minister of Finance is dated 19 December 1975 and is to be found in AALR, T52/822/6, and T52/822/6/1, W4446.
52. One of the first journals to comment on Muldoon's talent for sideshows was the *New Zealand Company Director and Executive*, May 1977, in its regular column, 'Round the Lobbies'. It noted that Cabinet reshuffles, a royal tour, and by-elections in Pahiatua and Mangere had stopped electors thinking about price rises.
53. The Government claimed it was saving $252 million ($84 million on electricity subsidies, $83 million on Post Office charges, $57 million on railways, and $28 million on milk). See *DOM*, 23 December 1975. Subsidies quickly rose again. See *AS*, 7 November 1978, p.6.
54. *AS*, 17 January 1976. Jim McLay in an interview on 7 July 1997 recalled many late meetings of Cabinet and its committees.
55. Public Service figures are to be found in Treasury to G.F. Gair, 1 March 1976, T/1/3/23, part 2, W2591. The quote is from David McLoughlin, *North and South*, July 1997, p.42.
56. The deliberations of the Cabinet Committee on Expenditure are to be found in T/1/3/

23, part 2, W2591. Hugh Templeton describes some aspects of Muldoon's financial management in *All Honourable Men*, Chapt. 7.

57. These views were expressed by J.G. Russell to a meeting of the Otago Chamber of Commerce. *EP*, 4 December 1975, p.22.
58. See Speech from the Throne, *NZPD*, Vol. 403, 23 June 1976, p.18.
59. Muldoon's 15-page press release on 2 March 1976 sets out his interest rate policy in relation to housing, Bassett Papers. On 6 September 1977 Muldoon explained that interest rates had to rise in a time of inflation or it simply did not pay to save. *EP*, 7 September 1977.
60. *Press*, 15 March 1979. Muldoon's comments about price and wage controls are to be found in R.D. Muldoon to G.F. Knowles, 16 March 1976, AALR, T/61/1/22/3, Box 278, Vol.3, W4446. See Allan Catt, 'Why Businessmen Should Support a Price Control Policy', *NZ Economist*, June 1976, pp.5-8. Also *NZ Financial Times*, 10 May 1977. The Stabilisation of Prices Regulations 1974 were replaced on 6 April 1979 by the Price Surveillance Regulations. These required every trader to retain records of price increases and to allow the Secretary of Trade and Industry to investigate the prices of any goods and services. In some circumstances the Secretary could recommend that prices be referred for a public inquiry before the Commerce Commission.
61. See Muldoon's correspondence, AALR, T/61/1/9/24, Box 269, W4446.
62. For subsidy levels see the budget tables each year, Table 7. There is detail about negotiations over tax levels and the CPI in AALR, T/61/9/1/6, W4446.
63. See Muldoon's budget comments, *AJHR*, 1976, B-6, pp.2-3. Also his press statement of 2 March 1976, p.3.
64. See the comments by J.K. McLay MP, *NZPD*, Vol. 403, 29 June 1976, p.102; by A.P.D. Friedlander, MP for New Plymouth, p.206; and W.E. Cooper, MP for Otago Central, p.299.
65. See the comments of Barry Brill, MP for Kapiti, *EP*, 15 December 1975; M.J. Minogue, MP for Hamilton West, *NZPD*, Vol. 403, 9 July 1976, p.454; and H.N. Austin, MP for Hobson, *NZPD*, Vol. 403, 8 July 1976, p.424.
66. I am indebted to Jim McLay for this observation about Muldoon and Lee Kuan Yew. The growth figure is from *AJHR*, 1979, G-14, p.5.
67. Muldoon's budgets are to be found in *AJHR*, 1976-83, B-6. Both the tax consultant Arthur Valabh and Sir Roger Douglas agree that Muldoon's approach to the economy changed in 1977, when he perceived that deregulation was politically dangerous. Discussion with both Valabh and Douglas, 14 February 1997.
68. There is a lot of information about the new planning structures 1976–80 in AALR, T/73/1, Vols 6, 7, and 8, Box 548, W4446. Reports of the Commission for the Future are to be found in *AJHR* from 1979, D-10. Early in 1978 the Planning Council published *Planning Perspectives 1978-83*, which preached the necessity for changing attitudes and argued for efficiency.
69. *AJHR*, 1977, B-6, p.3. *AS*, 7 November 1978, p.6.
70. Worker participation was given much publicity in 1977–78. See especially the *Listener*, 23 July 1977, pp.20-22. Talboys' comments are in the *AS*, 25 February 1978, p.1.
71. There are files relating to a number of industry studies in AALR, T/73/28/1, Box 562, W4446. The quote comes from the 1976 budget, *AJHR*, B-6, p.17. Some Treasury officials were sceptical about the likely success of industry studies. See speech notes of N.V. Lough, 12 April 1978, AALR, T/73/28/1, Box 562, W4446.
72. See *EP*, 31 January 1979, p.1; *Sunday Star*, 9 August 1992, p.A-9. See also Bank of New South Wales 'Review', No. 27, October 1978, p.1.
73. The 1985 budget tables show that interest on New Zealand's public debt consumed 2.5 per cent of total taxation revenue in 1976 and 12.7 per cent in 1985. See *AJHR*,1985, B-6a, p.42. The OECD report is in *NZH*, 24 August 1977.
74. Muldoon was taken to court over this unilateral act and was criticised by the Chief Justice. See Palmer, *Unbridled Power*, pp.187-90.

75. *NZOYB*, 1979, p.146. The principal extra cost came from extending a state pension to people between 60 and 65 with means. Only some of the extra expenditure was regained in taxation. In dollar terms the outlay on Social Welfare was $784 million in 1975–76 and $1.932 billion in 1979–80. See *NZOYB*, 1981, p.151. See also *AS*, 7 November 1978, p.6.

76. The historian David Thomson has written about what is sometimes labelled 'inter-generational theft'. See *NZH*, 31 October 1987, Section 2, p.2. Also David Thomson, *Selfish Generations? The Ageing of New Zealand's Welfare State*, Wellington, 1991.

77. *NZOYB*, 1975, p.147; *NZH*, 14 June 1997, p.G3.

78. *NZOYB*, 1987–88, graph, p.339. See also 1986–87, p.335.

79. See Chapt. 9, page 2.

80. *NZH*, 2 January 1979, editorial. See also *AS*, 7 November 1978, p.6.

81. *AS*, 22 August 1978.

82. *AS*, 29 December 1979, p.4. *NZH*, 23 March 1979. See Ian McLean, *The Future for New Zealand Agriculture: Economic Strategies for the 1980s*, Wellington, 1978. McLean re-stated his arguments in *NZH*, 19 January 1979, p.6.

83. *NZH*, 26 March 1979. Bayliss's comments are in *AS*, 29 November 1978, p.3.

84. See B.W. Dunlop to J.W.H. Clark, 5 October 1978. Also J.W.H. Clark to B.E. Talboys, 23 April 1979, AATJ, (IC) 7428, 2/1/32, W3566. There are other complaints in this file from pressure groups and trade associations about controls and regulations. There is a jargon-riddled article that contains a number of interesting details by Brian S. Roper, 'Business Political Activism and the Emergence of the New Right in New Zealand, 1975 to 1987' in *Political Science*, Vol. 44, December 1992, pp.1-23.

85. Sven Rydenfelt, 'The Rise and Decline of a Welfare State', reprinted by NZ Chambers of Commerce, Wellington, February 1979.

86. *AS*, 9 February 1979. Brash stressed the need for tax reform in a further speech, *AS*, 24 February 1979. Brash and the Planning Council had been preaching tax reform since May 1978. See *EP*, 20 May 1978, p.40. The only parts of Brash's 'package' that were not part of the reforms after 1984 were the suggestions that death duties be abolished and that a capital gains tax should be introduced. Greenfield's comments are in the *EP*, 15 March 1979. The four-year term was advocated by taxation specialist L.N. Ross, *AS*, 22 August 1978.

87. National's intake in 1978 consisted of Michael Cox (Manawatu), Douglas Kidd (Marlborough), Ian McLean (Tarawera), Geoff Thompson (Horowhenua), Don McKinnon (Albany), Robin Gray (Clutha), Winston Peters (Hunua), Bruce Townshend (Kaimai), Pat Hunt (Pakuranga), and Paul East (Rotorua). Not all were 'free marketeers' but those who were joined forces with like minds from the 1975 intake, such as Jim McLay (Birkenhead), Warren Cooper (Otago) and Derek Quigley (Rangiora), to form a consid-erable group within the National caucus who favoured freeing up the economy. They were joined in 1981 by Simon Upton (Waikato), Ruth Richardson (Selwyn) and John Banks (Whangarei).

88. Hugh Templeton, pp.139-52. Muldoon makes a few comments about the coup attempt in his *My Way*, pp.162-7. I am grateful to Jim McLay for his account of the plotting against Muldoon, which began, he says, from an evening of 'whisky and wickedness' among cau-cus colleagues.

89. There is information about the same process of change within the Australian Labor Party in Peter Walsh, *Confessions of a Failed Finance Minister*, Sydney 1995, Chapt. 5.

90. The new Labour intake after 1975 consisted of David Lange, who won a by-election in Mangere in March 1977, while the new Labour MPs in 1978 consisted of David Butcher (Hastings), John Terris (Western Hutt), David Caygill (St Albans), Ann Hercus (Lyttelton), Stan Rodger (Dunedin North) and Ralph Maxwell (Waitakere). Rejoining the caucus were Mike Moore (Papanui), Michael Bassett (Te Atatu), Kerry Burke (West Coast), Joe Walding (Palmerston North), Frank O'Flynn (Island Bay) and Jack Ridley (Taupo). By-elections in 1979–80 produced Geoffrey Palmer (Christchurch Central), Bruce Gregory (Northern

Maori) and Fred Gerbic (Onehunga), while the 1981 election brought in Fran Wilde (Wellington Central), Margaret Shields (Kapiti), Helen Clark (Mt Albert), Philip Woollaston (Nelson), Michael Cullen (St Kilda), Bill Jeffries (Heretaunga), Phil Goff (Roskill), Peter Neilson (Miramar), Geoff Braybrooke (Napier). Colin Moyle (Hunua) rejoined the caucus in 1981, defeating Winston Peters in Otara.

91. See Ian Templeton, *Sunday Star*, 9 September 1992, p.A-9.
92. *EP*, 15 February 1979. Rowling outlined what was labelled 'A Five-Year Plan for New Zealand's Economic Health' in the run-up to the 1981 election. See *AS*, 12 October 1981, p.6.
93. Vernon Wright, *David Lange: Prime Minister*, Wellington, 1984, Chapt. 14.
94. Roger Douglas, *There's Got to be a Better Way! A Practical ABC to Solving New Zealand's Major Problems*, Wellington, 1980. The book begins with the comments: 'As at no other time in its history, New Zealand stands a divided, confused, dispirited Nation. It lacks a sense of clear direction for the future. Its loyalties are torn between conflicting interests, each determined to extract the maximum for itself with no regard to others. Its standard of living has dropped and continues to drop visibly. It stands on the brink of economic ruin. It has stifled innovation for mediocrity.'(p.9) There is a brief chapter on Roger Douglas in Simon Collins and Tony Keesing, *Rogernomics: Is there a Better Way?* Wellington, 1987, pp.2-17.
95. Bassett caucus notes, 12 December 1980, Bassett Papers.

Chapter 12 Big Government's Last Hurrah, 1979–84

1. 'Current Economic Situation', 1 December 1978, AALR, T/61/1/9/24, Box 269, Vol. 9, W4446.
2. Files of the task force are to be found in AALR, T/33/18/5, Box 28, W4446.
3. Hugh Templeton, *All Honourable Men*, p.117.
4. Gary Hawke to the author, 3 July 1997.
5. See file note following Treasury officials' discussion with the Meat Board on 18 March 1982, AALR, T/82/2/5, Box 659, W4446. There are other papers about SMPs in AALR, T/83/1, Box 675, W4446.
6. See Dairy Board file, T/82/4/17, Box 664. There are similar stories about the Meat and Wool boards in T/82/2/17, and T/82/3, Box 661, W4446. For the earlier story of 1 per cent financing of boards, see Chapt. 9.
7. The era of increasing farm subsidies and the problems they caused for farmers are discussed in Brian Chamberlin, *Farming and Subsidies: Debunking the Myth*, Wellington, 1996. The figures relating to farm subsidies are included in *AJHR*, 1986, B-6, p.25. The story of one farming couple who in 1979 made an application for assistance to the Marginal Lands Board (set up in 1951 to award concessional loans to deserving applicants) is told in a commission of inquiry report entitled 'The Marginal Lands Board Loan Affair', *AJHR*, 1980, H-5. There is information about rising farm prices in T.M. Berthold to J.H. Falloon, 7 April 1983, AALR, T/83/1, Box 675, W4446. I am indebted to Professor Gary Hawke for comments on the predicament faced by many farmers in the 1980s.
8. See Chamberlin's comments, *Northern Farming World*, April 1978, pp.1-2; also Provincial President's Address, 1 May 1979. Auckland Federated Farmers resolved at their conference in June 1976 that they were 'not in favour of any price smoothing scheme . . . unless the Government agrees to some satisfactory form of restriction on internal inflation'. The same conference argued that Federated Farmers should 'take the strongest possible action to curb the declining profitability of farming and our decreasing relativity with other sections of the community'. See *Northern Farming World*, July 1976, p.4. I am indebted to Brian Chamberlin for his interview in April 1997.
9. *AJHR*, 1979, B-6. Changes to import licensing in the 1970s, and criticism of the whole experiment since 1938, are discussed in A.A. Smith and J. Burney, 'Import Licensing', in

R.S. Deane, P.W.E. Nicholl and M.J. Walsh (eds), *External Economic Structure and Policy*, Wellington, 1981, pp.432-5.

10. A cost-of-living increase was incorporated in the budget on 3 July 1980. *AJHR*, 1980, B-6, p.11. Muldoon and Skinner had neighbouring houses on Auckland's eastern seafront and Sunday meetings between the two were regular occurrences. Skinner retired as President of the FOL in May 1979 and was succeeded by W. J. Knox, who had been Secretary.

11. Details of these schemes are set out in *AJHR*, 1980, B-6, pp.20-22. There is an analysis of the beneficiaries of industry assistance in J. Gibson and R. Lattimore, 'Causes of the Pattern of Manufacturing Industry Assistance in New Zealand, 1981-82', *NZ Economic Papers*, Vol. 25(1), 1991, pp.100-22.

12. Hugh Templeton, p.120.

13. There is material about Treasury's work on taxes in AALR, T/61/9/1/6, W4446.

14. See Muldoon's comments quoted by Ian Templeton, *Sunday Star*, 9 August 1992, p.A-9.

15. *NZPD*, Vol. 434, 4 November 1980, p.4685.

16. In 1961 the commission granted licences to 11 restaurants in New Zealand. John Gould observes that until the licensing changes in the early 1960s, if one wanted to celebrate, one 'had a choice between a meal in a brewery hotel, where one was rushed through four predictable if wholesome set courses in sixty minutes flat (so as to save on penal overtime rates); or, in one or two of the larger cities, a very rare "quality" restaurant where, if one was prepared to risk the quite high probability of a visit by the police, the management would turn a blind eye to an introduced bottle of wine, preferably disguised as lemonade; or a meal in a superior fish-and-chip saloon, probably with tiled walls and a linoleum floor', *The Rake's Progress?*, p.67. There is more detailed historical information on changes to the law in the report of the Royal Commission into the Sale of Liquor, 1974.

17. *AS*, 7 November 1978.

18. Hugh Templeton, Chapt. 6.

19. Muldoon's caucus between 1975 and 1978 contained two women out of 55 members (Labour two out of 32); between 1978 and 1981 one out of 51 members (Labour three out of 40); and between 1981 and 1984 two out of 47 members (Labour six out of 43). National's failure to promote women was the subject of a long article by Judith Aitken, subsequently Chief Executive of the Ministry of Women's Affairs, in *NBR*, 14 December 1981, p.7.

20. Hugh Templeton, p.142. Fearing that Muldoon would take advice while overseas that could impact adversely on the New Zealand economy, Treasury usually sent a senior official with him to keep tabs on the information the Prime Minister was receiving. The only trip on which Treasury failed to send an official was the one immediately preceding the imposition of the wage–price freeze in June 1982. Discussion with B.V. Galvin, Secretary to the Treasury 1980–86, on 23 June 1997.

21. *NZOYB*, 1981, p.607; p.592; 1986-87, p.651.

22. Hugh Templeton, Chapts 13, 17 and 18, deal with CER and his difficulties with Muldoon. Some of the background to CER is also dealt with in a speech by Jim McLay, 'CER and the Shifting Winds of Politics to the Year 2000', 1994, of which the author has a copy. See also P.J. Lloyd, 'Australia-New Zealand Trade Relations: NAFTA to CER' in Sinclair (ed), *Tasman Relations*, Chapt. 8. The official documents associated with CER were printed in *AJHR*, 1983, A-20. An interesting booklet on the background to CER is Colin James, *The Tasman Connection: A New Path*, Wellington, 1982. See the 1982 budget, *NZPD*, Vol. 445, 5 August 1982, p.1756, for comments about CER. Muldoon's later claim about CER is to be found in *NZH*, 12 January 1983, p.3. A review of the trading relationship between New Zealand and Australia following CER by Sir Frank Holmes entitled 'The Trans Tasman Relationship' was published by the Institute of Policy Studies, Wellington, in 1995. Another view was expressed by Greg Ansley, *NZH*, 1 May 1997, p.D2.

23. The savings from carless days are mentioned in the Energy Plan, 1980, D-6a, p.30.

24. An outline of the measures is contained in *AJHR*, 1980, D-6, p.9. I am indebted to Hon. Jim McLay, who discussed with me on 7 July 1997 the air of crisis that surrounded many of the 1979 Cabinet energy decisions.

25. There are four files about the Huntly power station up to 1978 in AALR, T/40/196/35, Box 192, W4446. The cost estimate comes from *NZH*, 11 September 1981, p.16. The station ran into competition from private and local authority producers of power once the industry was deregulated. By 1997 a station that employed 450 staff was down to 175. See *NZH*, 24 July 1997, p.3.

26. Muldoon set out his arguments for 'Think Big' in the last chapter of *My Way*, p.159. Jim McLay told the author on 7 July 1997 that Muldoon was 'nearly rolled' in Cabinet on the go-ahead for the methanol plant at Waitara.

27. The annual energy plans are to be found in *AJHR*, D-6a, starting in 1980.

28. Reports of the Liquid Fuels Trust Board began in 1979 and are to be found in *AJHR*, D-8. The production of methanol was an expensive process in which half the energy value of the gas was lost in the conversion. See *NZH*, 4 January 1982, Review '81, p.32.

29. *AJHR*, 1980, D-6, p.5. The figure for anticipated employees appears in the '1982 Energy Plan', *AJHR*, D-6a, p.4. I am grateful to Bob Tizard, who was Minister of Energy 1984–87, for discussing details of the 'Think Big' schemes.

30. *NZH*, 8 September 1981, p.2; *AS*, 10 October 1981.

31. A major and unfriendly analysis of 'Think Big' appeared in the *AS*, 9 October 1981. See also *NBR*, 14 September 1981, pp.10-11.

32. The final result in Taupo was a majority of 36 for the National candidate. Several other seats were retained by the Government with majorities of under 200. There is an analysis of the 1981 election results by Robert Chapman in *Comment*, August 1982, pp.11-18.

33. *Financial Times* (London), 18 January 1980. There is discussion about this article in AALR, T/61/1/9/24, Box 269, Vol. 9, W4446.

34. The report to Muldoon is in AALR, T52/822/6, W4446 in the form of a signed submission from B.V.Galvin to R.D. Muldoon, undated [December 1981]. Galvin confirmed to the author that he eventually approved the report.

35. On 15 April and 1 July 1997 the author discussed Treasury views with Roger Kerr and Dr Bryce Wilkinson, who were senior Treasury officials at the time. The author also discussed issues with Bernard Galvin on 23 June 1997.

36. Jim McLay, who became Muldoon's Deputy Prime Minister in 1984, told the author that he had never seen Treasury's post-election briefing to Muldoon in 1981 and had reason to believe that the Associate Ministers of Finance had not been shown it either.

37. See briefing papers in AALR, T/61/9/1/6, two volumes, W4446.

38. *NZH*, 13 January 1982, p.3. There is a reflective review on the economy in 1982 by P.J. Scherer in *NZH*, 6 January 1983, 'Review '82', p.22.

39. *NZH*, 4 January 1982, 'Review '81', p.32.

40. The figures for borrowing are drawn each year from the budget documents, *AJHR*, B-6, tables on financing the budget.

41. Douglas, *Unfinished Business*, p.23.

42. See Ian Templeton's figures, *Sunday Star*, 9 August 1992, p.A-9. More complete figures are to be found in Table No.6 of the budget 1985, *AJHR*, B-6a, p.40. Government's domestic borrowing stood at $4.1 billion in 1976 and $15.8 billion in 1985, for a total public debt of $28.2 billion. The percentage figures for expenditure on servicing the Government debt appear in the 1985 budget, *NZPD*, Vol. 463, 13 June 1985, p.4841.

43. This point is argued by Paul Dalziel and Ralph Lattimore in *A Briefing on the New Zealand Macroeconomy, 1960–1990*, Auckland, 1991, p.46.

44. *NZH*, 5 January 1983, p.1.

45. The costs of 'Think Big' are listed in *AJHR*, 1986, B-6, p.27. They do not include losses on several state trading organisations like the Coal Division of the Ministry of Energy whose affairs were affected by the major energy projects. The budget speech on 31 July 1986, *NZPD*, Vol. 473, pp.3294-316, contains further information and commentary about 'Think Big'. There are many Treasury files dealing with the financing of 'Think Big' in AALR, W3993.

46. *NZPD*, Vol. 473, 31 July 1986, p.3301.

47. Douglas, *Unfinished Business*, p.24. See the figures in Peter Scherer's article, *NZH*, 6 January 1983, 'Review '82', p.22.
48. *NZH*, 3 January 1983, p.2.
49. Kerry McDonald, 'New Zealand Sinks with the Weight of Dead Economic Albatross', *AS*, 19 September 1981.
50. Douglas, *Unfinished Business*, p.25. Also John Gould, *The Rake's Progress?* pp.24-26. See also Roger Douglas press statement on 29 March 1984 outlining the real growth figures in GDP since 1975. Bassett Papers.
51. *AS*, 17 October 1981.
52. Quoted in an obituary of Wilson, *Independent* (London), 25 May 1995, p.22.
53. Inflation for the quarter to the end of June 1982 was running at an annual rate of 21.6 per cent. See *AS*, 9 July 1982.
54. Hugh Templeton, p.170. Jim McLay told the author on 7 July 1997 that the issue of the wage–price freeze was raised by Muldoon with his Cabinet as an oral item after discussions with the Cabinet Economic Committee. Those ministers not on CEC saw no papers about the issue and had no opportunity to discuss it with officials. I am indebted to Bernard Galvin, who discussed the circumstances surrounding the imposition of the freeze on 23 June 1997. Professor Gary Hawke also gave details of the background in a letter to the author on 3 July 1997. Both Roger Kerr and Bryce Wilkinson recalled the event in a discussion with the author on 1 July 1997. The courts subsequently declared some parts of the freeze invalid and the Government was obliged to rush through the Economic Stabilisation Amendment Act in December 1982 to validate the Order in Council of June 1982. See *NZPD*, Vol. 449, 16 December 1982, pp.5711ff. The Economic Stabilisation Act 1948 was eventually repealed in 1987.
55. The comment about Muldoon's moods comes from an early biographer, Spiro Zavos, *The Real Muldoon*, Wellington, 1978, p.139.
56. *NZH*, 13 January 1983, p.1.
57. *NZH*, 12 January 1983, p.3.
58. The figures come from Paul Kennedy, *Preparing for the Twenty-First Century*, Toronto, 1993, pp.351-2.
59. Introduced on 12 October 1982, the Bill contained a complex regime to deal with tax shelters that enabled income to be converted into non-taxable capital gains by investment in property and subsequent sales. The Bill also widened some concessions, introduced a new tax regime for film making and provided for the taxation of some lump-sum superannuation schemes. *NZPD*, Vol. 447, 12 October 1982, pp.3919-24.
60. *AS*, 9 July 1982.
61. *NZH*, 17 April 1982, p.1. See Hugh Templeton, p.213.
62. Hugh Templeton, p.207. See *DOM*, 10 February 1984, and editorial, p.6. See also Jones's comments, *NZH*, 26 June 1997, p.A4. See also Bob Jones, *Memories of Muldoon*, Christchurch, 1997. This book is a kind of retrospective apology to Jones's old friend which nonetheless indicates considerable disagreement with the thrust of Muldoon's policies in 1981–84.
63. *NZH*, 11 January 1983, p.4.
64. Lange tipped the scales at 27 stone (370 pounds) when he first entered Parliament in a by-election on 26 March 1977. A stomach operation in 1982 was discussed with a reporter from the *New Zealand Woman's Weekly*, 10 May 1982, pp.4-5. The operation enabled Lange to buy new suits and gave him more energy and mobility. Lange's life until he became Prime Minister is dealt with by Vernon Wright, *David Lange: Prime Minister*, Wellington, 1984. See also *Listener*, 5-11 February 1983, pp.14-17.
65. Holt shifted to Wellington in May 1983 to the position of Chief Historian within the Department of Internal Affairs. A personal friend of Auckland businessman Alan Gibbs, son of the author of the 1951 Taxation Review, Holt wrote several speeches for Lange and Douglas in 1982 and early 1983. Holt died suddenly on 24 July 1983. His paper 'Ideas for the Eighties' written in July 1979 had been published by the Labour Party's Education

Office in 1980. Holt's paper analysing Labour's 1981 election defeat, 'The 1981 Election and the Future for Labour', was circulated to all members of the Labour caucus early in 1982. Doug Andrew was a Treasury officer seconded to Lange's office, and Geoff Swier was a commerce graduate who worked in Labour's Research Bureau and then Douglas's office when he was minister. Labour's economic policy formation between 1981 and 1984 is analysed with the help of Douglas's files, but with no sign of interviewing the participants, by W. Hugh Oliver in Brian Easton (ed), *The Making of Rogernomics*, Auckland, 1989.

66. *NZH*, 17 January 1984, p.1.
67. I am indebted to Hon. Jim McLay for his observations on 7 July 1997 about the debate over the corporatisation of Railways.
68. Announced in the 1978 budget, the review of transport was established in November. The review eventually led to the passage of the Transport Amendment Bill No.5, passed in October 1983. There are four boxes of material relating to the Transport Review in AALR, T/78/13/1, W4446.
69. Industry reform papers 1981–85 are to be found in AALR, T/61/1/9/5, Box 270, W4446.
70. Hugh Templeton, p.210. There is detail about internal opposition to Muldoon in *NZH*, 17 December 1983, p.5.
71. *NZH*, 8 January 1983, p.1. There is some information about the economy in 1983–84 in Treasury's briefing paper to the new Minister of Finance in July 1984, pp.55-63 . It was published on 27 August 1984 under the title *Economic Management*.
72. *AS*, 10 April 1984, editorial, p.A6; *EP*, 12 April 1984, p.4.
73. *AS*, 23 April 1984.
74. There is some discussion about the snap election decision in Marcia Russell, *Revolution*, Auckland, 1996, pp.49ff. See also Hugh Templeton, p.219. Diabetes caused another fatal (for his opponent) mistake when Sir Joseph Ward misread his speech notes during the 1928 election campaign.
75. Lange expressed this opinion to Labour's key spokespeople on the evening of 14 June 1984, when it became known that Muldoon had been to see the Governor-General and had been granted a dissolution. Bassett Papers.
76. Galvin told Gary Hawke some time later that he experienced difficulty getting Muldoon to concentrate on the budget and other Treasury officials at the time conveyed this information to both Douglas and Lange. See also Gary Hawke to the author, 3 July 1997, p.5.
77. Several files dealing with hotel depreciation allowances are to be found in AALR, T/52/991/2/1, Box 258, W4446.
78. Details about Dairy Board borrowing are to be found in AALR, T/82/4/17, Boxes 661 and 664, W4446. Meat Board details are to be found in AALR, T/82/2/5, Box 659, W4446. Stephen Britton, 'Recent Trends in the Internationalisation of the New Zealand Economy', *Australian Geographical Studies*, Vol. 29, April 1991, pp.3-25, estimates that the broad range of producer subsidies came to $2 billion, or 6 per cent of GDP in 1984.
79. All figures are drawn from 'Estimates of Expenditure', 1983–84, and 1984–85, *AJHR*, B-7, part 1. See also the budgets, tables, commentaries and annexes, 1985–86, B-6 and B-6a. Templeton's figure comes from *NZPD*, Vol. 449, 16 December 1982, p.5711. His total figure for employees on the government payroll in 1982 was 187,000. The $11 billion figure was often quoted in the late 1980s, when the Labour Government moved to reduce superannuation rights for public servants.
80. Derek Quigley, 'Economic Reform: New Zealand in an International Perspective', *Round Table*, Vol. 339, 1996, p.311.
81. The phrase about Marciano was used by TV reporter Barry Shaw, *NZH*, 7 August 1992.
82. Brian Easton explores the relationship between ministers and officials over the exchange rate in 'From Run to Float: The Making of the Rogernomics Exchange Rate Policy', in Easton (ed), *The Making of Rogernomics*, pp.92-113.
83. The quotes come from Hugh Templeton, p.211. Jim McLay told the author on 7 July 1997 of his briefings by Treasury during Muldoon's absence from New Zealand, and of

his discussion with the Prime Minister on his return from overseas. McLay's recommendations to the Prime Minister were greeted with dismissive grunts.

84. Roderick Deane, the then Deputy Governor of the Reserve Bank, quoted in Marcia Russell, *Revolution*, p.56.

85. The results of the election in detail are to be found in *AJHR*, 1984, E-9.

Index

Note: Page numbers in *italic* refer to illustrations.

abortion law reform, 357
accident compensation, 334
accident insurance, 107–8
acclimatisation societies, 114
agricultural research, 114
airlines, 259, 278–9, 370
aluminium smelters, 298, 304–5, 365
Atkinson, Harry, 66, 72, 74, 75–7, 78
Australia, free trade agreements with, 309–10, 358–9

Ballance, John, 77–8, 79–82
banking, 85–6, 176–7, 189–90, 301, 340
Barnes, Jock, 251, 261
Beeby, C. E., 205–6
Bell, Francis Dillon, 97
'big government'. *See* state activism
Brash, Donald, 348–9, 350
broadcasting, 239–41, 255
bus services, 155, 162–3
'Buy New Zealand' campaign, 174

capital, shortage of, in colonial NZ, 36–7
civil emergencies, 115
Clinkard, G. W., 170–1, 236–7, 270
clothing manufactures, 227–8
coal mines, 105–7, 150, 157–8, 248–50, 371, 373
Coates, Gordon, 13, 118, 146–7, 150–5, 161–6
commerce, government assistance to, in colonial NZ, 30, 36
Community Arts Service, 247
compulsory military training, 142
Constitution (1852), 44–5
Cook Strait cable, 297, 304
cost of living, 120, 129, 130
'cost plus' method of price fixing, 231–2, 253–4

cotton mill, 134–5, 297–8, 299–300, 303–4
Crown leases (of farm land), 82–5

dairy produce exports, 149, 163–4, 190–1
defence construction, 230
Depression (1930s), 167–78
devaluations: (1933), 176; (1984), 374
Domestic Purposes Benefit, 329, 335, 346
Douglas, Roger, 351, 362, 370

Economic Stabilisation measures (World War II), 224–38, 259
economic stability, conference on, 268–70
education: in colonial NZ, 31; Atkinson's Government's measures, 67–8; Liberal Government's measures, 103–4; Reform Government's measures, 159–60; First Labour Government's measures, 205–7; Holland Government's measures, 288–9
electricity generation and distribution, 155–7
Epidemic Allowances, 139–40
equal pay, 285, 312
European Economic Community, 293, *304*
exchange controls, 208–10, 268, 302. *See also* import licensing
exchange rate, 176, 374
export prices, 147, 167, 173, 177, 215–16, 293, 315, 327, 333
exports: dairy produce, 149, 163–4, 190–1; flax, 44, 46–8; kauri gum, 44, 125; meat, 77, 148–9, 177, 192; wool, 44, 192, 261
exports, state marketing of, 148–9, 192, 272–3

Family Allowances, 162
farmers, government assistance to, 52–3, 54, 114, 164, 169, 175–6, 190–2, 272, 321–2, 352–4

film censorship, 143, 161, 241, 255, 357
fire brigades, 115
fire insurance, 107–8
fishing licences, 114
FitzRoy, Robert, 29, 30
flax industry, 44, 46–8, 170
food price stabilisation, 194–8
food subsidy regime, 197–8, 262, 315, 329, 336–7, 339
Forbes, George, 167
Forbes–Coates Coalition Government (1931–35), 168–78
forestry, 48–50, 52, 273–8, 371, 373
40-hour week, 193–4
Fox, William, 58, *59*
Fraser, Peter, 12, 145–6, 180, 183, 205, 206, 218–19, 222–3
friendly societies, 74–5, 100, 137–8
fruit canning industry, 126, 135, 223–4

gambling, 255, 356–7
General Agreement on Tariffs and Trade (the GATT), 266, 296, 354
Gibbs, T. N., 254–5
goldmining, 51, 55–6
government borrowing: overseas, 38, 46, 59, 72, 120, 336, 338, 365–6; domestic, 129, 365–6
government intervention. *See* state activism
government subsidies. *See* subsidies
Grey, Sir George, 30, 39, 40, 72, 76–7
'guaranteed prices' (for dairy farmers), 190–1

health services: in colonial NZ, 31, 32, 33, 54, 68–71; Liberal Government's measures, 100–103; Reform Government's measures, 126, 140–2; First Labour Government's measures, 204–5; Holland Government's measures, 282–8
Hobson, William, 26–38 *passim*
Holland, H. E., 12, 145–6
Holland, Sidney, 13, 19, 256, 289
Holloway, Philip, 295–7, 299
Holyoake, Keith, 13, 16–17, 258, 289, *303*, 323
homosexual law reform, 357
hospitals. *See* health services
housing: Liberal Government's measures,

86–7, 104–5; Reform Government's measures, 158–9; First Labour Government's measures, 188–9, 216–17, 230; Holland Government's measures, 259–60; Second Labour Government's measures, 301; Holyoake Government's measures, 302, 315; Third Labour Government's measures, 329; Muldoon Government's measures, 339

immigration, 54–5, 58, 60–1, 71–2, 78, 117, 173, 267, 339
import licensing: First Labour Government's measures, 208–10, 238; Holland Government's measures, 266–8; Second Labour Government's measures, 294; Holyoake Government's measures, 302, 310–11; Muldoon Government's measures, 340, 354
import substitution industries, 51, 134–5, 199
Industrial Conciliation and Arbitration Act, 88–91; amendments to, 193, 211–12, 250–1, 262, 313
industrial relations, 87–91, 182–5, 193, 211–12, 247–51, 260–1, 307, 312–14, 322–3, 330, 344, 372
industries: Bain Commission (1880), 73; essential, 230; licensing of, 170–1, 200–4, 271–2; subsidies for, 73, 114, 136–7, 201
Industries and Commerce Department (later Trade and Industry), 113–15, 134–7, 200–4, 231, 236–7, 270–1, 294–7, 299, 332
influenza epidemic, 139
insurance, 57, 100, 107–8, 285, 371
International Finance Corporation, 302
International Monetary Fund (IMF), 302–3
iron and steel production, 51–2, 114, 126, 171, 298–9, 305–8

kauri gum, 44, 124–5
Kirk, Norman, 13, 286, 300, 325, *326*, *327*, 335

Labour Governments: (1935–49), 12–13, 179–214; (1957–60), 290–302; (1972–75), 13, 323–37; (1984–90), 22–3

labour market regulation, 87–91, 182–5, 193, 211–12, 250–1, 312–14
Labour Party, 145–6, 171–2
land drainage, 126
land sales, 29–30, 35, 40, 82–5, 84–5
land taxes, 83
Lange, David, 351, 370
Lee, John A., 239
Legislative Council, 256
Liberal Government (1891–1912), 79–84, 85–92, 93–122
licensing: in colonial NZ, 35–6; of auctioneers, 116; of bus services, 162–3; of fishing, 114; of industries, 170–1, 200–4, 271–2; of liquor, 242–3, 357; of pharmacies, 201; of private electricity generation, 156; of shooting, 114; of transport, 154–5
life insurance, 57, 100, 371
liquor licensing, 242–3, 357
local government reform, 66–7, 280, 328

McCarthy, Justice Thaddeus, 312, 335
McKenzie, Jock, 15, 82–5, *92*
manufacturing industries, 50, 169, 231–4, 253, 316
Maori: declining population, 117–18; health of, 118; First Labour Government's measures, 212–14
Maori land, purchase of, 29–30, 35, 58, 82, 118
Marshall, Jack, 257, *313*, 323, 336
Massey, W. F., 13, 123, *124*, 146–7, 161
meat exports, 77, 148–9, 177, 192
medical insurance, 285
Muldoon, Robert, 13, 14, 17–18, *313*, 315–16, 321, 336, 338–9, 374
Myers, Arthur, 125

Nash, Walter, 12, 180, 224, 237, 262, 290, 293, *294*
National Development Conference/ Council, 318–21
National Efficiency Board (1917), 143–4
National Governments: (1949–57), 19, 256–90; (1960–72), 16–17, 302–23; (1975–84), 17–18, 338–46, 352–75
national insurance, 75–7
National Ministry (1915–19), 125, 128–31

National Provident Fund, 100, 136
natural gas, 308–9, 359–60
New Zealand Company. *See* Wakefield settlements
New Zealand Labour Party, 145–6, 171–2
New Zealand Literary Fund, 247
Ngata, Apirana, 118, 213
Nordmeyer, Arnold, 237, 293, *298*, 299; 'Black Budget', 301

O'Flynn, F. D., 13, 326–7
overseas borrowing. *See* government borrowing

packing (of vegetables and fruit), 280
pensions: increasingly dependent on the State, 21; for servicemen, 54, 138; for widows, 54, 138; Liberal Government's schemes, 98–100; for miners incapacitated by phthisis, 138; Epidemic Allowances, 139–40; Reform Government's measures, 160; First Labour Government's measures, 204–5; New Zealand Superannuation, 329, 345; National Superannuation, 345–6
pharmacies, 201
planning, 316–21, 329, 343–4
Plunket, 142–3
Police, 81
Pomare, Maui, 118
poor relief, 31–2, 34, 71. *See also* unemployment relief
Post Office, 80, 81, 198, 373
Post Office Savings Bank, 57, 373
press censorship, 241–2, 262
price controls: World War I, 127, 129–34, 136; Reform Government's measures, 158; First Labour Government's measures, 194–8, 217–18, 245; World War II, 136, 220; Holland Government's measures, 253–4, 262, 263–5; Third Labour Government's measures, 331–4; Muldoon Government's measures, 340–1
price freezes: (1970–72), 322; (1977), 344; (1982–84), 367–8
primary produce marketing boards, 148–9, 192, 272–3
provincial governments: establishment of, 39–40; abolition of, 20, 43, 65, 66;

provincial governments *(continued)*:
responsibilities under 1852 Constitution, 44–5; active in the economy, 52
public service: growth of, 81, 253, 280,
337; retrenchment, 56–7, 147, 175,
339–40; Saunders Commission (1880),
72–3; review of (1962), 312–13
Public Trust Office, 57–8
Public Works Department, 81
public works programmes, 37–8, 58, 61–
4, 73, 198, 245–6, 329
pulp and paper production, 220–2, 273–8

Queen Elizabeth II Arts Council, 328
Quigley, Derek, 338, 369

railways, 19, 58, 61–3, 80–1, 150–5, 175,
198–9, 259, 280–2, 371, 373
rationing, 229–30
reconstruction (post-1945), 243–52
Reeves, William Pember, 11, 78–9, 87–
91, *92*
Reform Governments: (1912–15), 84–5,
123–6; (1919–25), 131–49, 150–61;
(1925–28), 161–6
rehabilitation (after World War II), 243–4,
246
Reserve Bank, 176–7, 189–90
responsible government, introduction of,
39–40
retirement benefits. *See* pensions
Returned Servicemen's Association, 144
roading, 64, 151–2
Roberts, Jim, 182, *184*
Rolleston, William, 77–8, 97
Rosenberg, Wolfgang, 297, 303
Rowling, Bill, 13, 328, 335–6, 350, 370;
Budget (1973), 328–30

salt production, 279–80
Savage, Michael Joseph, 12, 145, 146,
180, 181, 182
scientific and industrial research, 135
Scrimgeour, Colin, 240, 241
Seddon, Richard John, 11, 49–50, 66, 82,
85, 93, 112
Semple, Bob, 145, 187–8, *195*
settlement schemes, 54, 138–9
sexually transmitted diseases, 128, 143
Shand, Tom, 313, 321

Shelley, James, 240, 241
shipping, 19, 333, 373
shop trading hours, 255, 356
silk industry, attempts to establish, 51, 52
social control, 160–1, 255
Social Credit Political League, 291–2, 315
social security: First Labour Government's
measures, 204–5; Third Labour
Government's measures, 329; Royal
Commission on, 335
'socialism without doctrines', 9–15, 93, 97
Stafford, Edward, 44–58, *45*
Standards Institute, 202
state activism: reasons for, in colonial NZ,
41–2; Vogelism, 58–65; encouraged by
literature from abroad, 94–5; difficulties
with and loss of faith in, 15–23, 346–51
state houses. *See* housing
State Life Insurance Office, 57
'State Socialism', 121–2
steel mill, 305–8
subsidies, cost of, 245–6, 258, 373–4
subsidies, policies on: Holland Government, 258–9, 262–3; Third Labour
Government, 329, 336–7; Muldoon
Government, 339, 341–3
subsidies, provision of: for industries, 73,
114, 136–7, 201, 253; for local
authorities, 328; for private enterprises,
46, 51; for public service superannuation, 374; on food, 197–8, 262,
315, 329, 336–7; on gas, 262; on
hides, pelts, etc., 262–3. *See also*
farmers, government assistance to
Sullivan, Dan, *194*, 200, 224, 237
superannuation (for public servants), 81–
2, 100, 374
Sutch, W. B., 134, 270, 294–7, 299, 311,
316, 319, 327

tariffs, 35, 52, 73, 78–9, 136, 168–73,
266, 309–11, 358–9
taxation: Liberal Government's measures,
83; National Ministry's measures, 129;
Royal Commission (1924), 150; First
Labour Government's measures, 225;
Second Labour Government's measures,
301; Holyoake Government's measures,
311–12; Muldoon Government's
measures, 341–3, 354–6

telegraph lines, erection of, 64
temperance movement, 143
'Think Big' projects, 307, 359–67
timber industry. *See* forestry
Tizard, R. J., 286, 300, 336, 350–1
tobacco growing, 135
totalisator betting, 255
tourism, 108–12, 329, 371, 373
town planning, 30–1, 162
Trade and Industry Department. *See* Industries and Commerce Department (later Trade and Industry)
trade unions, 87–91, 182–5, 193, 211–12, 247–51, 260–1
transport infrastructure, in colonial NZ, 37–8, 58, 61–4
transport licensing, 154–5
Treasury, post-election report on the economy (1981), 362–4
Treaty of Waitangi, 26–7, 30
trust control of liquor, 242–3

unemployment relief, 77–8, 139, 173–4.

See also poor relief
unions. *See* trade unions
United Government (1928–31), 166–8

Vogel, Sir Julius, 58–65, *59*

wage cuts, 175
wage fixing: Muldoon Government's measures, 354
wage-price freeze (1982–84), 367–8
Wakefield, Edward Gibbon, 11, 27, *28*
Wakefield settlements, 27–9, 32–4, 43
Walsh, Fintan Patrick, 183, 184–5, 224, 226, *305*
Ward, Sir Joseph, 11, 80, 85, 112–13, 123, 125, 146, 166–7
water supply, 69
waterfront dispute, 261–2
Watties, 223–4
women in the work force, 212, 267, 285
women's rights, 118–19
wool exports, 44, 192, 261
World Bank, 302